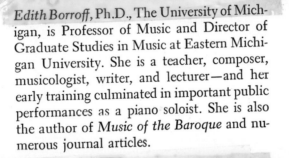

Edith Borroff, Ph.D., The University of Michigan, is Professor of Music and Director of Graduate Studies in Music at Eastern Michigan University. She is a teacher, composer, musicologist, writer, and lecturer—and her early training culminated in important public performances as a piano soloist. She is also the author of *Music of the Baroque* and numerous journal articles.

Music in Europe and the United States: A History

Music in Europe and

Edith Borroff

Eastern Michigan University

the United States   A HISTORY

Prentice-Hall, Inc., Englewood Cliffs, New Jersey

To my sister Marie

in the hope that her gifts

for language and music,

harmonious bending,

may be reflected here

Music in Europe and the United States: A History

EDITH BORROFF

Design by John J. Dunleavy

Prentice-Hall International, Inc., London
Prentice-Hall of Australia, Pty., Ltd., Sydney
Prentice-Hall of Canada, Ltd., Toronto
Prentice-Hall of India Pvt. Ltd., New Delhi
Prentice-Hall of Japan, Inc., Tokyo

Current printing (last digit):

10   9   8   7   6   5   4   3   2   1

13–608083–9

Preface

All music is contemporary and modern; whatever its era, music was originally written in its own present. A composer may think of yesterday or tomorrow, but he can lift his pen only today. And music is unique among the arts. It exists as air waves, and in order to remain alive, it must be created anew in each performance, the past becoming present. Thus history is of special importance in music.

The past can be examined in a number of ways. It can, of course, be seen as a strand or chain leading through time, a chronological series of events, with or without the assumption that what happened at one particular time resulted from what preceded it and, in turn, caused that which followed it. Some historians look for cyclic movements in which certain processes are repeated, seeming to relate many separate events—some of which appear inevitable, once the cycle has been set in motion. Still other historians seek to find alternations between extremes; they think of history as a pendulum, swinging between exploration and exploitation, between innovation and conservatism, between domination and recession, or, in the arts, between formalism and emotionalism (*ethos* and *pathos*).

Such views are superimposed on the basically untidy past, and each reveals part of its meaning. The views are not contradictory but contrapuntal, seeking underlying rhythms of the motion of events through time. We must never forget that the multiview is there and that the examination of the past is, in fact, inexhaustible.

This book aims to present a preliminary view of music of Europe and the United States, based on the six eras that are generally acknowledged to provide a natural frame for such a study. Within each era, I have concentrated on representative forms and stylistic definitions. Quotations are used liberally, so that the era can speak for its own ideals and can be seen, in its own terms, as modern. Every quotation is from the period it discusses.

Only a few composers from each period are discussed, and they are meant to be seen as representative of many other composers. They have been chosen for their importance to historical continuity.

Musical examples have been selected on the same basis. Of the ninety-one examples, eighty are complete works that may be studied and performed from the book. The process of historical (rather than theoretical) analysis can only be suggested, but detailed examinations of a few works—notably the Josquin Mass (Example 31) and the Mozart Symphony (Example 59)—are offered as models for the analysis of many other works equally deserving of study in depth.

Although the problems of notation and editing are not part of a preliminary study, facsimiles of music of the era accompany several of the Medieval and Renaissance examples. These are included to intimate the existence of the problems and pique the curiosity of adventuresome minds, as well as to present the page of music as a changing esthetic experience in itself. To continue this through the history, facsimiles of early editions stand alone in later examples. All other illustrative materials, like the quotations, are from the period they illuminate.

The book was not conceived as a replacement for other avenues of study, but as a basis of cooperation with them, leaving as many options as possible to the complementary approaches. The subject of music history is so immense that a single book can only provide a frame, open a few windows, and suggest further directions. The study of composers or the deeper concentration on a particular style or type of music is a matter of personal predilection or professional interest, best served by additional study and listening to the music itself, with supplementary reading or the guidance of a teacher.

In presenting the central definitions of style, I have not discussed culminative, eccentric, and transitional works. The book is a chronological survey of music, presenting the norm rather than the exception, centrality rather than transition. No matter how great an exceptional work, its greatness cannot be appreciated until it can be recognized as exceptional—after the norm has been mastered. And since the full thrust of a transitional work can be recognized only through recognizing its Janus-like character—its past and its future—significant discussion of it must await the knowledge of both; and this is impossible when the first is known and the second is not.

I think of learning as a spiral and this book as a first round leading, through further study, to a broadening and deepening understanding. For the general reader, I have tried to suggest new directions in listening and reading. For the student, I have tried to consider him first as a general reader who should not give up his love of music but rather expand it as he becomes a professional. For the teacher, I have tried to provide a frame, in cooperation with which he can use his own materials of listening, discussion, analysis, and professional direction, as suggested by the interests of his students and his own musical commitment.

Most terms in the book are used in the traditional sense, but a few have been broadened to make them more useful and to show the more universal applications of certain techniques.

Polyphony denotes the simultaneous use of more than one musical element in a complex fabric. The difference between such a concept and the more limited Western definition is that the elements are not viewed as necessarily melodic.

Triad is used to mean a group of three notes considered as a harmonic entity, whatever their structure.

Cambiata figure is used to refer to the trichord comprising a second plus a third, spanning a fourth. This pattern is close to a universal melodic element and provides the basic unit of the pentatonic scale. I have taken the term from the figure in harmonic context from Fux's *Gradus ad parnassum.*

Isorhythm indicates any rhythmic pattern conceived as independent of pitch factors and used as a structural element. The term was first used by the musicologist Friedrich Ludwig (1872–1930) to apply to certain fourteenth-century structures, but the concept is universal.

Pitches are designated by the international letter system; the designation of each *C* applies to all notes from that pitch up to the *B* a seventh above.

Knowledge of partials is not assumed, but for those who are intrigued by the mathematics of music, the natural division of any sounding body into partial vibrations provides an unending source of fascination. The partial vibrations of a C string, for example, are the following:

The octave is 1:2 (2:4, 3:6, etc.), the perfect fifth 2:3 (4:6, 6:9, etc.)— the whole series is duplicated proportionately from any fundamental tone. Partials are used as natural tones by wind and string players and are recognized as musical and mathematical phenomena the world over. The seventh partial is low by modern Western standards but has evidently served in the cambiata figure.

Nobody writes a book without owing a great deal to many people. But a book such as this, which includes so many areas, is essentially a personal synthesis of work by a number of predecessors and specialists, and my debt to them is enormous. The footnotes can be read as an unfolding gratitude, though they by no means document the complete record.

Those from whom I have sought help in preparing the book have given with the spirit as well as the letter. It is hard to single out individuals for special mention, but I would especially like to thank the British Museum and the University of Michigan Libraries. For musical examples, I thank Janet Knapp, Hans Tischler, Edward L. Kottick, and Louise Cuyler; for translations, Christiane Cooper and Jon Rinka; and for reading in their areas of specialization and for many helpful suggestions, Archabbot Rembert Weakland, O.S.B., Edward R. Reilly, Marjory Irvin, Alan Stout, Hans Tischler, Edward L. Kottick, Marie Borroff, Leon and Sylvia Holman, Ruth D. Wilson, Helen I. Henry, and Evelyn McHugh. I would like to give special thanks to those who tested the charts and summaries in their classes. And I would like to thank *Musart* magazine for permission to use portions of the material in Chapter 30, which originally appeared in that magazine.

The Project Planning Department of Prentice-Hall has made the process of publication interesting and pleasurable. John J. Dunleavy designed the book as both esthetic and practical, Ronni Schulbaum applied just the right amount of blue pencil, and Karen Palochik provided tireless picture research and production work. Alan B. Lesure, the editor, maintained an ideal stance, keeping a long project moving but never crowding the creative process.

It is a marvelous time to write a history of music, with a new esthetic beginning to achieve focus and American music coming into its own. In spite of the inevitable frustrations, it has proved a particular joy, and I can still say amen to Thomas Moore's remark in his *Diary*, on November 7, 1819, "Music issuing out of light is as good an idea as we can have of heaven."

Edith Borroff

Ypsilanti, Michigan

Contents

Preface, v   *Musical Examples, xv*

Part One   **THROUGH THE MEDIEVAL ERA**

1. *Music in the Ancient World*   3

Before Written History. Musical Universals. Medieval Europe.

2. *Minstrelsy*   17

Early Medieval Song. The Goliards. The Troubadours. The Trouvères.
The Minnesinger. Medieval Song in England, Spain, and Italy. Medieval
Dance Music. Composite Forms. Monophonic Performance—Minstrelsy.
Some Composers of Minstrelsy.

3. *Sacred Song*   49

Plainchant.   Plainchant Composition.   Plainchant Style.   Performance of
Sacred Song.   Some Composers of Sacred Song.

4. *Philosophy and Theory*   69

The Hexachord System.   Rhythm.   The Ideals of Medieval Monophony.

5. *Gothic Polyphony*   81

Early Polyphony.   The School of Notre Dame.   Performance.

6. *Popular Polyphony*   105

Polyphonic Dances.   Polyphonic Song.   Performance.

7. *Ars Nova*   113

France.   The New Art in Italy.   The Avignon School.   England.   The
Burgundians. The Fifteenth Century. Some Composers of the Fourteenth and Fifteenth Centuries.

Part Two   THE RENAISSANCE

8. *At the Height of the Renaissance*   147

The Polyphonic Mass. The Motet. Polyphonic Song. Folk Song. Theory.
Performance.   Some Composers at the Height of the Renaissance.

9. *At the End of the Renaissance*   205

Continuing Polyphonic Forms. Monody. Dramma per Musica. Some
Composers of the Late Renaissance.

10. *America*   247

The Toltecs, the Incas, and the Aztecs.   The Spaniards and the Indians.

Part Three   **THE BAROQUE ERA**

11. *The New Style in Italy*   257

The New Ideal of Music.   Italian Leadership.   Some Composers of the Italian Baroque.

12. *The New Style in Europe*   287

French Music in the Seventeenth Century.   English Music in the Seventeenth Century.   German Music in the Seventeenth Century.   Theory. Performance.   Some Composers of the Seventeenth and Early Eighteenth Centuries.

13. *At the End of the Baroque*   321

Vocal Forms.   Instrumental Forms.   Some Important Composers of the Late Baroque.

14. *The New World*   349

Church Music in the Colonies.   Secular Music in the Colonies.

Part Four   **MUSICAL CLASSICISM**

15. *The Modernist Generation*   361

The Classical Style.   Instrumental Forms.   Theory.   Performance.   Some Composers Active in the Modernist Generation.

16. *The Classical Generation*   *381*

Instrumental Forms.   Musical Theater.   England.   Some Important Composers of the Classical Generation.

17. *America and Africa*   *415*

America.   Music in Black Africa.   Black Music in the New World.   Some American Composers of the Eighteenth Century.

18. *Music in the 1780s*   *442*

Dance and Song.   The Piano Sonata.

Part Five   **ROMANTICISM**

19. *The Romantic Classicists*   *453*

Piano Music.   Song.   Some Important Romantic Composers.

20. *A New Republic*   *478*

Formal Music.   Music in the Parlor.   Folk Music.   Some American Composers of the Romantic-Classicist Generation.

21. *The Romantic Generation*   *487*

Centers of Musical Romanticism. Instrumental Music. Vocal Music. Some Composers of the Romantic Generation.

22. *Philosophy and Theory*   *506*

The Philosophy of Music.   Theory.   Performance.   National Attitudes.

23. *The Later Romantics* 519

Musical Factionalism. Song. Operetta. Popular Music. Some Later Romantic Composers.

24. *An Expanding Nation* 542

The Piano. The Gala Performance. The Minstrel Show. Music of the Negro. The American Indian. Popular Music. Religious Music.

Part Six   THE NEW MUSIC

25. *Traditionalists and Iconoclasts* 567

Divided Musical Traditions. The Dance. Musicology. The United States. Some Composers in the Beginning of the Twentieth Century.

26. *Between Two Wars* 590

Seeds of Change. A Period of Transition. Roaring Twenties and Depression Thirties. Some Composers Active between the Wars.

27. *A New Sound* 618

A New Humanism. A New Notation. The New Music. Some Composers Active after World War II.

28. *Philosophy and Theory* 658

Time. Sound. Composition. The Composer.

29. *The United States* 666

A New Mandate. Popular Music. At the End of the Sixties.

Part Seven **HISTORY AND MUSIC**

30. *The Practicality of History* 685

Time. Sound. Embellishment and Improvisation. Western Theories of Music. Idioms. History and the Musical Experience.

Glossary, 717 *Index, 731*

Musical Examples

Chapter 1: 1. *Va loin*, Anonymous.

Chapter 2: 2. *Reis glorios*, Giraut de Bornelh. 3. *Kalenda maya*, Raimbaut de Vaqueiras. 4. *De moi dolereus vos chant*, Gillebert de Berneville. 5. *E, dame jolie*, Anonymous. 6. *Robins m'aime*, Adam de la Halle. 7. *Prendès i garde*, Guillaume d'Amiens. 8. *In' gesach*, Neidhart von Reuenthal. 9. *Nova, Nova*, Anonymous. 10. *La Quinta Estampie Réal*, Anonymous.

Chapter 3: 11. *Exsulta satis*, Anonymous. 12. *Alleluia, Pascha Nostrum*, Anonymous. 13. *Ut Queant Laxis*, John the Deacon. 14. *Kyrie, Orbis Factor*, Anonymous.

Chapter 5: 15. *Alleluia*, plainsong and organum from Santiago de Compostela (excerpts), Anonymous. 16. *Alleluia, Vocavit Iesus*, Anonymous. 17 and 18. *Pascha nostrum* (excerpts), Leoninus. 19. *Haec Dies* (excerpt), Anonymous. 20. *Nove Geniture*, Anonymous. 21. *O Maria virgo Davitica/O Maria Maris stella/VERITATEM* (excerpt), Anonymous. 22. *Balaam/BALAAM*, Anonymous. 23. *Hare, Hare/Balaam!/BALAAM*, Anonymous.

Chapter 6: 24. *Sumer is icumen in*, Anonymous.

Chapter 7: 25. *Je puis trop bien*, Guillaume de Machaut. 26. *Amor con Fede*, Francesco Landini. 27. *De plus en plus*, Gilles Binchois. 28. *L'homme armé*, Anonymous. 29. *A the Syghes*, Anonymous. 30. *Amor con l'arco tesso*, Anonymous.

Chapter 8: 31. *Missa l'homme armé*, Kyrie, Sanctus, and Agnus Dei, Josquin des Prez. 32. *Exaudi Deus*, Heinrich Isaac. 33. *Beatus vir*, Heinrich Isaac. 34. *Bergerette savoyene*, Josquin des Prez. 35. *Isbruck, ich muss dich lassen*, Heinrich Isaac. 36. *Je n'ose être content*, Pierre Certon. 37. *Death and the Lady*, Anonymous. 38. *Brimbledon Fair*, Anonymous. 39. *Rambling Sailor*, Anonymous.

Chapter 9: 40. Agnus, *Missa l'homme armé* (excerpts), Josquin des Prez. 41. *Sanctus and Agnus*, Tomás Luis de Victoria. 42. *O Welt, ich muss dich lassen*. 43. *O Bread of Life*. 44. *Laura gentile*, Cesare Negri. 45. *Flow my teares*, John Dowland. 46. *Amarilli*, Giulio Caccini.

Chapter 11: 47. *Bei Prati, fresci riui*, Alessandro Scarlatti. 48. *Trio Sonata*, Op. 3, VIII, Arcangelo Corelli. 49. *Concerto in C for Two Oboes, Two Clarinets, and Concerto Grosso*, First Movement, Antonio Vivaldi.

Chapter 12: 50. *Acis et Galatée*, Act I (excerpt), Jean-Baptiste Lully. 51. Prelude and Courante, from *Pièces de Clavecin*, Jean-Henri d'Anglebert. 52. *Pavane and Galliard*, William Byrd.

Chapter 13: 53. *The Puzzle*, John Hilton. 54. *Critique*, Anonymous. 55. *Essercizo in a minor*, Domenico Scarlatti. 56. *Prelude and Fugue in C major*, Johann Sebastian Bach.

Chapter 15: 57. *The Stammering Lover*, Thomas Augustine Arne. 58. *Tell Me Then the Reason Why*, Luffman Atterbury.

Chapter 16: 59. *Symphony in B♭ major*, Wolfgang Amadeus Mozart.

Chapter 17: 60. *Chester*, William Billings. 61. *Kedron*, Anonymous. 62. *When Jesus Wept*, William Billings. 63. *The Toast to Washington*, Francis Hopkinson. 64. *Bakwesi song*, elements, Anonymous. 65. *Basuku song*, elements, Anonymous.

Chapter 18. 66. *Sherburne*, Daniel Read. 67. *Sonata in C major*, Hans Leo Hassler.

Chapter 19: 68. *Sonate Pathétique*, Op. 13, First Movement, Ludwig van Beethoven. 69. *Der Lindenbaum*, Franz Schubert. 70. *Der Freischütz* (excerpt), Carl Maria von Weber. 71. *The Ridicule* and *The Madrid Waltz*, Anonymous.

Chapter 21: 72. *Träumerei*, Robert Schumann. 73. *Pleasures of the Town* and *The Devil among the Tailors*, Anonymous.

Chapter 23: 74. *Intermezzo*, Op. 116, No. 6, Johannes Brahms. 75. Scene from *La Traviata*, Giuseppi Verdi. 76. *Tristan und Isolde*, *Vorspiel* (excerpt), Richard Wagner.

Chapter 24: 77. *I'm Troubled in Mind*, Anonymous. 78. *Roll, Jordan, Roll*, Anonymous. 79. *Mary and Marthy*, Anonymous.

Chapter 25: 80. *The "Jelly Roll" Blues*, Ferdinand Morton.

Chapter 26: 81. *Fünf Sätze für Streichquartett*, Op. 5 (excerpt), Anton Webern. 82. *Pierrot Lunaire* (excerpt), Arnold Schoenberg. 83. *Field Holler*, Anonymous. 84. *Depot Blues*, Son House. 85. *Improvisation*, Louis Armstrong.

Chapter 27: 86. *Klavierstücke* III, No. 2, Karlheinz Stockhausen. 87. *Threnody: To the Victims of Hiroshima*, Krzysztof Penderecki.

Chapter 29: 88. *Improvisation*, Charlie Parker.

Chapter 30: 89. Table of Divisions, Silvestro Ganassi. 90. Improvised cadenza from *Merope*, Carlo Broschi (Farinelli). 91. Adagio, *Sonata* V, Op. 5, Arcangelo Corelli.

Part One

THROUGH THE MEDIEVAL ERA

Once, in an unknown time,
A mad and mirthful wight
Whispered some words to slip
Dull meaning's tether,
Which done, they from the lip
Fled frolicsome and light
And fell in merry rhyme
Straightway together.

O might his praise resound
Who speech to song first fired,
Graces, of sounds untaught,
So sweetly winning;
His sons, by him inspired,
Concord in language found,
Nor is the end yet wrought
Of that beginning.

For now, as sweet winds teach
Leaf against leaf to chime,
Boughs, branches, each to each
Harmonious bending,
So words from meaning bend
Each other to befriend,
And of that ring and rhyme
There is no ending.

MARIE BORROFF *

Music in the Ancient World

BEFORE WRITTEN HISTORY

1

Speculation on the beginnings of music is endlessly fascinating, but no certainty is ever likely to come of it. Scholars have propounded a splendid array of theories about the first musical utterances of prehistoric man. They were imitations of bird songs or other natural noises; they were formalized signals of love, battle, or the hunt; they were rhythmic poundings on a hollow log or vocalization more song than speech and possibly preceding both. We know of no people so primitive that they had not developed a musical art, and even the neolithic bone flute found in Central Europe and dated at 28,000 B.C. is far from primitive.

* "The Birth of Song," unpublished poem.

Military musicians. Two plucked string instruments and two sizes of cymbals are shown in this detail from a relief on a wall of the Palace of Ashurbanipal, Assyria, seventh century B.C. (Courtesy of the Musée du Louvre, Cliché des Musées Nationaux.)

All ancient peoples of whom we have knowledge gave music a place of honor; they considered it a potent religious and moral force, intimately related to the most formal, as well as the most informal, aspects of life. But our knowledge of music in ancient civilizations, including European music of the first millenium, is fragmentary. It consists of a collection of peripheral facts that never touch the central core of actual sound. These facts prove the importance and sophistication of music before written history but do not delineate the music itself; they come from a variety of sources.

Works of Art

Many works of sculpture and painting represent musical instruments and often convey as much information about the nature and social context of performance as about the instruments themselves. One of the cave paintings of southwest France (c. 15,000 B.C.) shows a musical bow. A harp is shown in a Mesopotamian painting from the fourth millenium B.C.; a tomb painting at El-Amarna in Egypt, dated at about 2500 B.C., shows a nobleman and his wife listening to two singers accompanied by harps, flutes, and clappers. Most banquet scenes show instrumentalists and dancers.

From a collection of surviving works of art, a view of the scope of musical instruments can be determined. A catalog would include all types in modern usage, except bowed and keyboard strings, plus many types of instruments not used in the West in modern times.

Etymology

The history of words and their usage often contains clues to instrumental construction, usage, or association. The word *music* itself comes from Greek and, even earlier, from Egyptian. The Greek *kithara* has given its name to

4

the zither and the guitar and probably to the fiddle as well. Many Greek and Latin technical terms, transformed but still with a thread of recognition to their original meaning, have become part of European musical usage. Most early words for *flute* were the same as the words for *shinbone,* up through the Latin *tibia;* the word *jubilee* derives from the Hebrew *yobhel,* a ceremonial instrument made of a ram's horn; and the Egyptian hieroglyph SAIBIT (flute or shinbone) was used also to denote *precision, regularity, truth.*

Written records are comparatively late; they show that the use of musical instruments was already venerable when writing was invented. Mythology reveals attitudes and beliefs that may be as old as civilization. Egyptian texts tell of the god Thoth ("three times very, very great") who had created the world by the power of his voice and of the four gods and four goddesses who sang hymns morning and evening to keep the sun on course. Through song, Thoth invented the Egyptian sciences, which included arithmetic, geometry and surveying, astronomy, medicine, surgery, magic, wind and string music, drawing, and writing. (The voice and percussion instruments had long since been properties of the gods.) The sistrum, a metal rattle, was the symbol of protection and was sacred to the goddesses Hathor (associated with the Greek Aphrodite and the Hebrew Astarte) and Bast (associated with Demeter). Bast's festival was one of the greatest of the Egyptian calendar. As late as the fifth century B.C., the Greek historian Herodotus, in describing the festival, noted that 100,000 people arrived to the sound of flutes and finger cymbals and took part in a magnificent procession. *Literature*

The works of Herodotus represent another form of literature, the descriptive social history. Homer's epics were also histories but were couched in poetic terms, separated in time, and suffused with myth and legend. Several books of the Old Testament were histories as well. All these works mentioned musical instruments, songs, and hymns.

Legal documents furnish bits of information. For example, special laws for musicians (in Egypt they were licensed and had to pay a special tax) reveal certain details that can add to the total picture. In Wales, under King Howell Dda (reigned A.D. 904–948), the legal code detailed the treatment of minstrels, specifying their ranks, titles, and pay and including procedures for hiring and an outline of their duties. The code contains over fifteen articles pertaining to musicians at the royal court. They include the following: the royal bard was to receive new clothes three times a year and to be allowed his own horse; instruments were to be provided according to rank—harp, crwth (a bowed string), and bagpipe; the master musician carried his title and held a diploma.[1] *Legal Documents*

[1] Antoine Vidal, *St-Julien-des-Ménestriers et les ménestrels à Paris,* Paris: Quantin, 1878, pp. 8ff.

Many hymns and lyrics survive, from Sumer and Egypt to Greece, Rome, *Hymns and Lyrics*
and the country of the northern barbarians, but only a few fragments of the
music were written down. (Moreover, of these fragments—about a dozen in
all—most were not scores, but were excerpts that were included in theoretical
writings.) Hymnody, the art of the love lyric, and songs of spring and war
seem to be as old as civilization itself and as universal as man. A Sumerian
hymn of c. 2100 B.C. addresses the god Ishtar, "I will speak to thee with the
lyre whose sound is sweet." [2]

Perhaps the most tantalizing source of knowledge of ancient music is sur- *Surviving*
viving instruments. Conditions of temperature and humidity seldom permit
instruments to be preserved intact, but the tombs of Egypt and the peat *Instruments*
bogs of Denmark provided two nearly perfect sites, along with occasional
areas on other continents. In addition to the neolithic bone flute, Sumerian
clappers from about 3200 B.C. survive, and in the Hunan province of China,
archeologists have found stone drums and earthenware pipes dating from

[2] Sir Leonard Woolley, *History of Mankind, Cultural and Scientific Development*, vol.
I, part II, *The Beginnings of Civilization*, New York: Mentor Books, New American Library of World Literature, Inc., 1963, p. 556.

A bronze *lur* (trumpet) excavated from a Danish peat bog. The
trumpet was buried about 1000 B.C., but the metalwork indicates that the Danes were far from primitive. (Courtesy of
the Danish Information Office.)

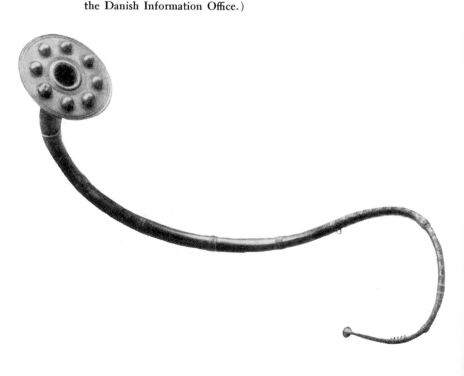

about 1500 B.C. Similar finds in America have led scholars to believe that in neolithic times instruments were brought from China to Mexico. A silver trumpet from the tomb of the Pharaoh Tutankhamon (1320 B.C.) and a group of earlier bronze trumpets found in the Danish peat bogs testify to consummate craftsmanship in the making of instruments, as do the clay figurine flutes of Bolivia and the clay drums of Bohemia.

Most of these instruments cannot be played, and even if they could, the music and the social scene would still elude us, for the playing of an instrument is a matter of tradition and the technique of one culture is not the same as that of another. For example, an orchestral musician who examined a flute found in an Egyptian excavation pronounced it unplayable without a reed, but that same flute had been played without difficulty by one of the Egyptian workers at the excavation. In the same way, a skilled player of the Egyptian flute might declare a modern Western flute unplayable.

Very few fragments of notation survive from the pre-Christian era. The oldest yet discovered is a Sumerian clay tablet, in cuneiform, from about 2000 B.C.; it is a scale, evidently notated for teaching, and not a piece of music. The teaching of hymns and songs by rote in a largely illiterate culture made notated music rare, but more important may have been the preference for the arts of improvisation and variation, which still comprise the musical art of most of the world. The most famous surviving notated song is doubtless the carved gravestone of Seikolos, found in Turkey and probably from the first century of the Christian era. The song appears as a four-line Greek poem in a form typical of the Greek drinking song, with letters to indicate pitches and, above these, symbols for duration.

Surviving Notated Music

Of the many theorists of whose work we have knowledge, the most famous was Pythagoras (c. 582–c. 500 B.C.).[3] He studied in Egypt for twenty-two years and his work with musical proportions must suggest Egyptian theories of the art, for in his day the Royal Academy of Music at Thebes had already been an institution of importance for well over a thousand years.

Music was both rhetoric and mathematics, and as the Greeks defined their pitch system, it was difficult science as well. The vocabulary of Greek theory is extensive, intimidating, and, without the living music, frustrating. Many Greek terms—including scale types, such as *diatonic, chromatic,* and *enharmonic,* and names for modes—have remained in use, though they are now used for concepts the Greeks would not recognize.

Like any lively art, Greek music inspired different reactions. Plato (c. 427–347 B.C.) said of the Phrygian mode that it expressed prudence and

Surviving Discussions of the Theory of Music

[3] Although none of the works of Pythagoras are known to have survived to the present day, they were invoked for authority by virtually every early writer on music in the Western tradition. See Oliver Strunk, *Source Readings in Music History,* New York: Norton, 1950, Chaps. 1–5.

An Irish harp from prehistoric times. The Irish bards were singing to the harp long before written history; their harps were highly prized and often richly worked. (Courtesy of the Trinity College Library, Dublin.)

was ideal for men of peace,[4] but Aristotle (384–322 B.C.) said of the same mode that it was ideal for inspiring enthusiasm.[5] To the Dorian mode, Plato ascribed energy and strength; Aristotle, moderation and settled temper. Such disagreements tell us that the Greeks expected to react to particular modes but tell us little, if anything, about the music.

The Orientals also had a long tradition of music and musical theory. The statements, a century before Plato, by the Chinese philosopher Confucius (551–478 B.C.) that music is "born of emotion," that tone is its substance, and that the musical goal is not mere virtuosity but "spiritual power inherent in nature" can be considered representative of the ancient peoples as a whole.[6] Confucius described over one hundred musical instruments, and

[4] *Ibid.*, p. 5.
[5] *Ibid.*, p. 19.
[6] Chou Wen-Chung, "Toward a Re-Merger in Music," in E. Schwartz and B. Childs (eds.), *Contemporary Composers on Contemporary Music*, New York: Holt, 1967, pp. 309ff.

a theoretical text of the fifth century B.C., the *Go Yuy*, derived scales from a theoretical concept of twelve semitones to the octave.[7]

In general, discussions of music tended toward either its mathematical properties or its effects. The former dealt with intervals and pitch systems and the latter with the moral, physiological, therapeutic, and social values that most cultures have imputed to music.

Traditional Music

Where musical practice remains relatively unchanged, clues to ancient music may be found in later times. The cultures of the Orient have provided glimpses of unchanging ideals, and specialists in Chinese and Indian music indicate that many techniques, even certain pieces, are part of a continuity of four or more millenniums.

Some Hebrew and Christian chants, along with certain hymn tunes, may antedate the Christian era; in other churches, practice may be even older. The sistrum is still reserved for church services in Ethiopia, so the sacred symbol of Hathor and Bast has survived in the Coptic church.

Doubtless some folk music is very old, and certainly many folk instruments, from bagpipes to the jew's harp, date from before written history. "Va loin," a shepherd song still heard in the Auvergne, is said to have been played by Cæsar's Roman legions during the capture of Gaul.

Many scholars have sought clues to the beginnings of music in the musical arts of today's "primitive" peoples, documenting the music of such

[7] Alexander Buchner, *Musical Instruments through the Ages*, London: Spring Books, *n.d.*, p. 7.

Va loin

Example 1

ANONYMOUS

The text says that the songs of our forefathers send themselves forth to realms even beyond the sun. Shepherds still sing this song, believing it to date from Roman times, when Caesar's legions were marching through Gaul. The text is mystical and difficult to translate. (Courtesy of Constance Bergersen.)

groups as the Murung,[8] who are found between Burma and East Pakistan. Music and dancing are vital in Murung community activities, and their chief instruments are double-headed drums and bamboo flutes with an astounding scope of size—from about 6 inches to over 18 feet—fitted to gourd resonators. Such instruments cannot be classed as primitive. Even the Australian aborigines and groups in the jungles of the Amazon and in central New Guinea, all classified as stone-age cultures, have well-developed literatures of legends, songs, and hymns. And they all have a musical tradition that includes vocal music, instruments, and dance.

Understanding the context in which musical practices flourish is vital to the total picture of a musical art. Such understanding may come from a general view of a culture or a specific detail or passing reference, frequently from a nonmusical source. A passing reference in an Egyptian letter of about 300 B.C., for example, relates that the author found a flute and that it was of "the type that plays in the enharmonic genus."[9] This tells us that flutes were of more than one type and that a nonmusician knew one from the other. Again, a condemnation of the teen-age mobbing of a popular kithara player in Athens in the fifth century B.C.—they stole his plectra and tore his tunic—enlivens our knowledge of Greek musical life.[10] And a Portuguese who served from 1513 to 1520 as a secretary to the governor of colonial Goa, in India, wrote of music incidentally in his account of his service.

Social Context

> The Governor always ate to the music of trumpets and kettledrums. In front of the building where he lodged there was a great court where the *naiques*, captains of the native people, assembled. Every Sunday they came to be reviewed by the Governor with their musical instruments and their little trumpets which are very martial. In front of the ranked soldiers stood a man who played on a great double-barreled copper instrument which was heard above all the others and made a startling warlike sound. . . . Dancing women came to the great court with their instruments, because this is how they make their living, dancing and singing at mealtimes.[11]

A general view might seek to illuminate probable Egyptian musical practice of four thousand years ago by discussing the generally high level of culture and the high level of skills in architecture, medicine (including brain and eye surgery), dentistry, astronomy, mathematics, and so on, and arguing from these premises a commensurate skill and appreciation in the art of music. With such a frame of reference and bolstered by the knowledge—however fragmentary—from Egyptian works of art, literature, surviving instruments, and other sources, it would be difficult to make a case for anything less than a deep and powerful musical art.

[8] Roy Pinney, *Vanishing Tribes*, New York: Crowell, 1968, pp. 63–66.
[9] "The Egyptian Flutes," *Musical Times*, vol. 31, no. 574, p. 713ff., December, 1890.
[10] James H. Hall, *Lectures on the History of Music*, unpublished, Oberlin, Ohio, 1944.
[11] Gaspar Correa, quoted in John Dos Passos, "Lendas da India," *New York Times Book Review*, Feb. 9, 1969, p. 2.

MUSICAL UNIVERSALS

Music is essentially various, as languages are various. Yet in the broad sweep of time and place, the music of many cultures has evinced certain characteristics found in widely separated areas. Moreover, the different musical arts incorporated a few concerns that were held to be important in so many cultures that they could be called universals.

The basic stuff of music is sound given impetus through time or, conversely, time given shape by the energy of sound. Living sound (including structured silence), motivation in time, and the intent to be music seem common to virtually all known musical arts. Beyond that, a fascination with the means of sound, both vocal and instrumental, and an intellectual interest in the mathematical aspects of pitch relations seem to be characteristic of various musical arts the world over. The ratios 12:9:8:6, proportions held to be perfect in the ancient world and represented in music by the pitches d^1–a–g–d, (as twelfth, ninth, eighth, and sixth partials), provided a basis of musical theory in widely separated groups. This tetrad incorporates a number of musical interactions of lasting interest to many peoples in many times. It is versatile both melodically and harmonically. It can stand alone or, used as a frame, can be filled in or extended in a number of ways—as in fact it has been.

The concept of music as a harmony mirroring man's ideals is also found over the world. That musical performance does not merely enhance important functions but serves to increase the essential harmony of man in life is an idea held by the Indians of both North and South America and by cultures in Asia, Africa, and Europe. Many instruments are associated with particular occasions or played by certain kinds of people—men only, women only, or members of a certain rank or caste. Many pieces of music are to be sung only at a birth or a death, a coronation, or a specified time of the day or year. The *raga*, a pattern of pitch materials in India, is both a musical and a social designation. The "sankarabhana," for example, is a raga for singers, associated with peace and performed in the morning.

The essential symbolism was intimately related to the peculiar ability of music to combine seemingly opposing elements in a reconciliation called *harmony*, a word whose musical meaning was the quintessence of its applications in all fields of knowledge and experience. "Music is the measure for heaven and earth," wrote Confucius, "the principle of balance and harmony." [12] The *yang* and *yin* represented such opposing elements brought together harmoniously in the ideal man. In Greece the same view was propounded and was the basis of European thought, not only in music, but in the whole realm of knowledge—knowledge of the cosmos, of God, and of

[12] Buchner, *op. cit.*, p. 7.

A South American Indian playing a flute. Such natural music may hold a clue to universal elements in music. (Courtesy of Popular Photography and Ziff-Davis Publishing Company.)

man. A fourteenth-century English translation of a Latin general science text described the human physiology in such terms: "The veins and sinews of the body and pulse thereof, and so all the limbs of the body, are joined together by virtue of harmony. . . . Turn and consider this in your mind, that Music and Harmony unite and accord divers things and contrary." The writer reminded the reader that "Pythagoras called the soul Harmony, accord of melody" and concluded that "perfect music comprehends all things." [13]

The healing capacity of music was based on the same reasoning. The biblical account of David's playing for the troubled King Solomon was parallel in its rationale to the universal view. A summary of the therapeutic power of music was stated in the later Platonic statement that "rhythm and harmony find their way into the inward places of the soul, on which they mightily fasten." [14] Music as entertainment or recreation was part of this same function.

Music's embodiment of the larger cosmic harmonies was considered to deal with words and tones, with voices and instruments, and with high and low pitches, primarily in melodic succession. It could deal with short and

[13] Bartholomaeus Anglicus, quoted in H. H. Carter (ed.), "Armonie, III," *A Dictionary of Middle English Musical Terms,* Bloomington, Ind.: Indiana University Press, 1961, p. 17.
[14] Quoted in Julius Portnoy, *The Philosopher and Music,* New York: The Humanities Press, 1954, p. 22.

long time elements, with movement and quiescence (which Confucius called *yang* and *yin*), with consonance and dissonance.

It is difficult to find universal materials if one looks for an entire language or grammar, but certain idioms and predilections pervade music on a worldwide basis. All cultures have cultivated the lyric song, and many cultures throughout the world put the voice to work as an improvising instrument as well as a lyrical one. In Africa and pre-Columbian America, as well as in Northern Europe, ornate variations were improvised on nonverbal syllables, chosen sometimes for verbal associations but usually for their suitability in producing a fast, supple, and clear line. Such improvisation was called *diddling* in ancient and Medieval Scotland. Rhythms to fit a text (poetry or prose) or to formalize body rhythms (as in work songs and songs of exuberance) also seem universal. Associating percussion sounds with syllables and teaching patterns by rote seem to be related to such practices as diddling. In cultures where drumming is complex, ten or twelve pitches or qualities can be attained on one drum and ten or twelve syllables are needed to recite a rhythmic pattern using them. Some isorhythms are several dozen syllables long; the Africans call them "drum tunes" and give them names.

Many peoples use more than one pitch system. The simplest and perhaps the most universal systems are those based on the ratios 6:8:9:12 as two fourths. For example, *d–g* (6:8) could be used to create a three-note group (a trichord) or a four-note group (tetrachord). Filling the fourth with a single tone a whole step below the upper tone (*d–f–g*) creates a trichord that appears in music of all continents. Making up a scale by combining two such trichords, either *d–f–g* + *a–c–d¹* or *d–f–g* + [g] b♭ c¹ (with the *d¹* added to complete the octave), creates pentatonic scales that are often called universal. In Europe this trichord was used as a basic pattern and is found in surviving song, both secular and sacred. Its increasingly specialized usage culminated in its use in an idiom within the style of sixteenth-century polyphony called the *cambiata*, but the *cambiata figure* is ageless.

Oriental music included similar trichords similarly formed, but with the fourth filled in with a tone a half step from the upper note. The Chinese treatise *Go Yuy*, of the fifth century B.C., derived both types of trichord (along with other figures) from a scale of twelve half steps to the octave. The Greeks wrote of their scales as based on the two fourths; they spelled them downward from *e¹* using two fourths, either *e¹–b*, *a–e* or *e¹–b–f♯* with *e* added to complete the octave. The fourths were filled by two tones, either whole and half steps (which they called the *diatonic genus*), half steps with a minor third (*chromatic*), or two quarter steps with a major third (*enharmonic*). These intervals were used in any order within the tetrachord, but two similar tetrachords were combined to make one scale. Although the theory books that explain the Greek pitch system make it obvious that Greek theory was complex and highly ramified, they reveal little of the musical reality. Of the three genera, the diatonic genus was the heritage of European music, but in Egypt (where the enharmonic flute was found), the Orient, India, Africa, and doubtless elsewhere, diatonic music was practiced along with chromatic and enharmonic types. And even in Europe, chromatic and enharmonic characteristics did not die.

Pitch systems, no matter how theoretically neat, are not music, but they do give us frames of reference, reveal contemporary observation, and demonstrate the scope of choices available to the musician. The Seikolos song and the traditional "Va loin" might suggest that the diatonic genus was basic for lyric music and that the other genera were used chiefly in the elaborate melodic parabolas characteristic of improvised variation. It may be that the Oriental practice, along with that of India, can reveal much about the music of the ancient world.

MEDIEVAL EUROPE

In Western music, the heritage of the Sumerian, Egyptian, and Greek traditions remained strong. The men of Medieval Europe maintained this heritage in their concept of harmony, their love of instrumental color, their practice of dance and song along with a solemn cultivation of sacred music, and their consciousness of remaining mainly within the Greek diatonic genus. Their continuing contact with Oriental and African music emphasized the universal element in their art, an art that takes on renewed importance through its close relationship with much of the current world's music. Yet for most musicians today, the Medieval era, the first great era of modern Western music, is the farthest removed from musical experience, distant because of misunderstanding as well as time. This is regrettable, for the brilliant colors and intricate textures of much Medieval music would delight the tastes of many people today.

The vocabulary of Medieval music is not difficult. Misunderstandings often occur because of our modern ideas about performance, which have changed strikingly since Medieval days. For the traditionally trained musician, the creative role of the performer in earlier eras is difficult to appreciate. In Medieval practice, it was hard to draw a clear line between the roles of performer and composer. In many cases, one man was both. In the thirteenth century, the historian Salimbene wrote of such a man.

> Brother Henry of Pisa was a handsome man, of medium height, generous, amiable, charitable, and merry, . . . beloved by both the clergy and the laity. He knew how to write beautifully and to paint, which some call illuminate, to write songs, both in harmony and in plain song. He himself was an excellent singer, and had a strong and sonorous voice, so that it filled the whole choir. And his treble sounded light, very high and clear, but sweet, lovely, and pleasing beyond measure.[15]

[15] Salimbene, quoted in J. B. Ross and M. M. McLaughlin (eds.), *The Portable Medieval Reader*, New York: The Viking Press, Inc., 1949, p. 556f.

This description suggests the recognition given a monk outside the monastery; the delight, characteristic through many centuries, in the high male voice; and the overriding importance of performance, with its direct and immediate appeal.

Perhaps no technical term in the musical dictionary is more misleading than the word *monophony*. It seems to mean a single kind of sound, but in reality indicates a single written line. In actual practice, Medieval musicians invested this single line with vibrant diversity; they glorified it in contrasts of timbre and register—and theirs was an era rich in instruments and in vocal techniques. Seventy-two different instruments were depicted in the illuminations accompanying the thirteenth-century Spanish songs of Alfonso el Sabio (Alfred the Wise). In addition, the singers introduced *garibles* (embellishments). Highly colored effects were achieved by alternating groups of singers or instrumentalists and by adding percussion parts. And dynamic contrasts resulted through varying the makeup of alternating groups. These effects, which were the province of the producer, were not notated.

Medieval music centered in the forms most societies have devised: songs and lays, to preserve legends and folk wisdom; dances and popular tunes, to provide recreation and to express the sorrows and exuberances of everyday life; and a more austere sacred music, to serve the religious life and add appropriate solemnity to occasions of symbolic significance. It is the nature of the first type of music to be passed along by rote or to be written down in text only; of the second, to change rapidly, reflecting transient joys and sorrows, and to need no documentation, either because of extreme popularity (when everyone already knows the music) or extreme evanescence (when there is no call for a notated form); but of the third, to acquire status lacking to the others, to be preserved and disseminated carefully, to be the province of the learned, and thus to be written down more often than any other kind of music.

It is not surprising, then, that surviving documents give us a preponderant knowledge of the sacred music of the Medieval era. But we must not be led to believe that the documents reflect the importance of musical types in Medieval life. All we know of the Medieval era supports the assumption that a lively secular art was widely practiced and much loved. And there is as much reason to believe that secular music influenced the music of the Church as vice versa. Salimbene, in his discussion of Henry of Pisa, continued:

A Medieval figure with a horn. This is the type of instrument sounded by the hero of the *Song of Roland*. (Courtesy of Photographie Giraudon.)

Brother Henry composed many [melodies] and many sequences, for example, the words and melody of the following song:

O Christ, my God,
O Christ, my Refuge,
O Christ, King and Lord,

after the song of a maid who was going through the cathedral church of Pisa, singing in the popular tongue:

If thou carest not for me,
I'll no longer care for thee.[16]

In any case, it is evident that monks entered the monastery from secular life, well acquainted with the popular music that flourished in their youth; and it is demonstrable that the clergy provided a central core of secular poetry and song. Many of the older lyrics were penned by monks, and as late as the twelfth century, Gertrude, the wife of Duke Henry the Proud, wanting to hear the epic "Song of Roland," requested a performance, not of a minstrel, but of a priest.[17]

[16] *Ibid.*, p. 558.
[17] Philip Schuyler Allen, *Medieval Latin Lyrics*, Chicago: The University of Chicago Press, 1931, p. 248.

The sweet harmony of music not only affords us pleasures, but renders us important services. It greatly cheers the drooping spirit, clears the face from clouds, smooths the wrinkled brow, checks moroseness, promotes hilarity; of all the most pleasant things in the world, nothing more delights and enlivens the human heart.

GIRALDUS CAMBRENSIS *

Minstrelsy

EARLY MEDIEVAL SONG

2

It is clear that the art of song never ceased in Europe. The period from the sixth through the tenth centuries knew a continuing and thriving poetic-musical art, even when few men were literate. There is a great deal of difference between writing a song and writing it down.

The Roman historian Tacitus (c. 55–c. 120) spoke of Germanic tribal lore sung to the harp in the second century,[1] and others told of heroic poetry

* c. 1200. Quoted in J. B. Ross and M. M. McLaughlin (eds.), *The Portable Medieval Reader*, New York: The Viking Press, Inc., 1949, p. 554f.
[1] Quoted in P. S. Allen (ed.), *Medieval Latin Lyrics*, Chicago: The University of Chicago Press, 1931, p. 6.

and song flourishing among the Goths in the fourth, fifth, and sixth centuries. This was the era of the Eddas and the Nibelungen songs that the nineteenth century was to romanticize.

The impact of the confrontation between formal Roman and brusque pagan customs was strong and far-reaching—it created European civilization. The classical meters in pagan hands gave new and robust life to the expression of human feelings in poetry and created an early humanistic art. Of the music for these songs we know little save that the singer accompanied himself with a small harp or other instrument. The only musical form about which information survives is that of the long narrative *lay* (or *lai*; not to be confused with the general term *lay*, meaning any song), which was couched in classical poetic couplets and set in pairs of musical phrases, each performed twice to reflect the *aabbccdd* form of the poem. But it seems doubtful that each couplet would have had a separate musical phrase in a long narrative; more likely the poet drew from a store of interchangeable phrases, which he used freely as he recited.

Irish Minstrels

In the eighth and ninth centuries, the revitalization of European song was furthered by the appearance on the Continent of Irish immigrants; they came as missionaries but among them were minstrels. They founded many of the great monasteries in Europe and developed the music that was the most compelling adornment of these monasteries. But they also entered with zest into the art of secular song.

The golden age of Irish minstrelsy, from about 500 to about 750, had preceded the migration, and the missionaries brought with them their own poetic forms, including the *cantefable*, a narrative poem containing lyric songs. They also brought their Irish wit, but their chief gift was a new concept of verse, which would be the basis for a vibrant musical art.

Whereas classical verse was written as a series of lines, all with the same syllable count and accent plan, the Irish poets introduced *isochronous* verse, in which the accents and time span of the lines were equal but the syllable count could vary.

> Ding, dong, bell,
> Pussy's in the well!

Each of these lines has three stresses and each consumes the same time in recitation, but the second line contains almost twice as many syllables as the first—and it could be expanded even further, to "The pussy fell into the well!" Isochronous verse carried with it a twofold potential—the use of lines of differing syllable counts and the creation of stanza forms with variable elements. Perhaps the most famous form of this type of verse is the limerick.

Both potentials were to prove definitive in their musical ramifications. Two lines of the same syllable count and accent pattern can be served by a single melodic phrase, but "Ding, dong, bell" and "Pussy's in the well!" must have separate musical phrases. The new stanza forms required new musical forms as well, forms in which the musical phrases were not interchangeable but were composed for specific texts.

From A.D. 800 to 1000 an abundant and surpassing poetic-musical art centered in the monasteries. But these were not merely cloisters designed for resignation from the world and contemplation of the hereafter. The monastery was the marketplace for an interchange of ideas. The inception and dissemination of ideas were accomplished by the ever-changing visitors and by the regulars, who were occasionally used as tutors, traveling secretaries, and ambassadors. By the ninth century, there were many well-known poet-composers, among whom were Hrabanus Maurus and Notker (called Balbulus, the Stammerer).   *Monasteries*

What were the popular poems like? They dealt with the subjects such poems always have—love, springtime, wine. But they were songs of the literate, for they were still in Latin, though we know that vernacular songs were flourishing as well. Those that have come down to us are of many types.

> *conflictus,* a dialogue debate, often almost a playlet.
> *eclogue,* a pastoral poem, often telling of an encounter with a shepherdess or milkmaid who was either compliant or adamant.
> *mimus,* an action poem (later, as with Notker, the fable, often Æsopian).
> *canzona,* a love song to a particular lady, in contrast to a general song in praise of love.
> *planctus,* a lament at the death of a lord.
> *carole,* a popular dance song.
> *parody,* often a secular parody of a sacred text, such as the tenth-century drinking parody of the *Ave.*
> *lay,* a general word for song; usually with a lyrical text.

Parallel with the development of the Latin lyric, poets began to incorporate the vernacular tongues. As the vernacular entered the lyrics, specific styles naturally became associated with geographical areas.

THE GOLIARDS

The earliest sign of the trend away from Latin was the incorporation of vernacular into Latin texts. This practice is associated with the Goliards, followers of the legendary Irish "bishop" Golias. (An Irish bishop was the Medieval equivalent of a Kentucky "colonel." [2]) The early Goliards were Irish, but the later ones (tenth to twelfth centuries) represented a variety

[2] *Ibid.,* p. 103.

of areas—from Provence to Britain, from France to the Slavic East. A tenth-century Latin love poem, for example, has a Provençal refrain.

Bilingual poems represent a halfway house between Latin and vernacular lyrics, and the Goliards are of great interest to us because of this. But this interest to musicians is even greater, for they were the first to write down a substantial number of their melodies. Unfortunately, however, their notation was of a simple directional nature, characterizing the melodic gesture without indicating the specific pitches we are familiar with.

In an age when Latin was dying out in common speech, its use was associated with the student; thus it was as student poets, particularly as wandering student poets, that the Goliards were most widely known. Most of them were German, and their Gothic heritage shows in the pagan, even erotic, quality of their poetry, the love songs of which are often short and poignant, sharply different from the courtly love poems of chivalry.

THE TROUBADOURS

In Provence, now southern France, a great art of vernacular song arose toward the end of the eleventh century. This was the lyric of the *langue d'oc*, the language of *oc* (meaning "yes" in the Provençal dialect—as distinguished from *oïl*, "yes" in the northern tongue). Latin lyrics incorporating Provençal (vernacular) lines had appeared a century earlier, and vernacular dance songs had always been popular. Conversely, the new Latin verse forms had been making their way into the vernacular; the langue d'oc was stabilized enough to be the vehicle of a poetic art, and the Provençal way of life could furnish both the subject matter and the means of performance and dissemination necessary to any great poetic flowering.

The feudal system consisted of many small political units, each centering in a stronghold or castle, which competed with the monastery as the seat of cultural exchange, the hospice, and the center of communication and interchange. A single traveler, being virtually helpless, was not feared; he could be welcomed, as indeed he was. Thus, the poet-musicians were amazingly itinerant: of Cercamon (early twelfth century), it was said that "he sought out the whole world wherever he could go"; his student Marcabru, a native Gascon, traveled to Spain, Northern France, and probably England; many went on crusades.

The poet-musician who composed in the langue d'oc called himself a *trobador* (from *trobar*, to find, to invent in verse; a woman was a *trobairitz*). He might be a nobleman, composing as an amateur; or he might be a professional performer—a minstrel or a jongleur.

Jongleurs were more complete entertainers than minstrels (instrumentalists attached to feudal menages), for they were expected not only to

A troubadour with his harp. Singing to the harp was the oldest and, in Europe, the archetypal form of minstrelsy. (Courtesy of Photographie Giraudon.)

play the fidel, pipe, drum, and other instruments but also to sing, juggle, and do acrobatics. Their kind had always existed—they were the mimes who had entertained at the Roman games and pageants through the sixth century. After that, known as *joculatores* (players), they sought what living they could in a culture that had no ready place for them until, at the rise of the troubadour movement, they again attained respectable acceptance. Their role in Medieval life is not clearly understood; like the minstrels, jongleurs were professionally employed, and it may be that payment for their art was the crucial distinction between them and the troubadours. The word *troubadour* implies nothing about payment. But some troubadours seem to have used jongleurs as companions—perhaps as secretaries, accompanists, or simply as side acts, offering additional entertainment in troubadour presentations.

Outside the Christian communities, in the Jewish ghettos of Germany, Spain, and Italy, were musicians known as the *letz* (plural: *letzim*). Because of the nature of ghetto life, the letzim became organizers of entertainment, dance teachers, and dance callers, and even played string instruments in the tradition of the square dance fiddler. Many Renaissance dance masters came from the ranks of the letzim.

Songs of the Medieval tradition dealt with the basic conditions of life, particularly court and feudal life.

A jongleur. Although he might be a skilled musician, the jongleur was often an acrobat as well. (Courtesy of Photographie Giraudon.)

Troubadour Song Types

sirventes, political or moral song, often satirical or vituperative, generally long.

tenso, debate, often improvised, often dealing with the body politic.

ley or *lay,* often a short narrative, often devotional and to the Virgin.

canzo, most often a love song, the early ones personal or erotic, the later ones often courtly.

planh or *planc,* lament, generally at a noble's death.

serena, an evening song, often in persuasion of a lady.

alba, a dawn song, very popular, generally of an unwanted dawn bringing an end to a night of love, often involving a friend who stands guard for the lovers.

carole, a dance song.

pastorela (also called *serrana* or *serranilla*), a pastoral song, often of a compliant or adamant shepherdess.

These song types were clearly defined by subject matter; they were related to verse forms only indirectly, in the sense that certain subjects seemed innately suited to certain kinds of verse. More than 2,650 texts have survived in manuscript collections called *chansonniers* (from the French *chanson,* meaning "song"), and these came from about four hundred different poets.

Perhaps the most famous troubadour was Giraut de Bornelh, who, although of humble blood, was known as the master of the troubadours. He appeared in a tenso with Raimbaut d'Aurenga, Count of Orange, demonstrating that

Alba

the humble and the wellborn could compete as equals in their art. His alba "Reis glorios" is one of the finest lyrics of the era.

The poem is based on a five-line stanza (there was no norm), four lines in iambic meter with five accents and a final short line of two anapests

Reis glorios　　　　　　　　　　　　　　　　　　　　　　Example 2

GIRAUT DE BORNELH

Reis glorios, verais lums e clartatz,	a	Heavenly King, glorious God of light,
Deus poderos, Senher, si a vos platz,	a	Look down with kindly favor, if you will,
Al meu companh siatz fizels ajuda;	b	Upon my friend who, with his lady, still
Qu'eu no lo vi, pos la nochs fo venguda,	b	Reposes. There has he been all the night,
Et adés sera l'alba.	c	*And soon it will be dawn.*

Bel companho, so dormetz o veillatz?　　　Good friend, if you are sleeping or awake,
Non dormatz plus, suau vos ressidatz,　　　Gently arise and sleep no more. Afar,
Qu'en orien vei l'estela creguda　　　　　The East is brightened by the morning-
Qu'amena-l jorn, qu'eu l'ai ben coneguda;　　　star,
　Et adés sera l'alba.　　　　　　　Bringing the day, unless I much mistake;
　　　　　　　　　　　　　　　　　And soon it will be dawn.

Bel companho, en chantan vos apel:　　　Good friend, I sing to you this eager
Non dormatz plus, qu'eu aug chantar　　　　warning;
　l'auzel,　　　　　　　　　　　　I fear your lady's lord will soon appear.
Que vai queren la jorn per lo boscatge;　　Already in the forest I can hear
Et ai paor que-l gilos vos assatge;　　　　A song-bird's love-call to his mistress
　Et adés sera l'alba.　　　　　　　morning.
　　　　　　　　　　　　　　　　　And soon it will be dawn.

TRANS. BY NORMAN SHAPIRO

A troubadour alba from c. 1200. (Music, courtesy of Arno Volk Verlag, Cologne, Germany; lyrics, courtesy of Angel Flores.)

which serves as a refrain or *tornada*. Unity is attained by employing, in addition to the refrain, a rhyme scheme (*aabb*) in iambic lines and by beginning several stanzas (including the four omitted here) with *Bel companho*. In its sentiment, its use of the tornada, and its rhyming stanza form, the alba of Giraut de Bornelh is typical.

Relatively little troubadour melody has come down to us. About 225 of the surviving lyrics are accompanied by their tunes, but they are notated in square *neumes* (noteheads) without rhythmic indications. Because the poems were rhythmic, this is not surprising. Performance meant presenting the poem in song. Medieval rhythm was conceived within a triply divided beat, which is best represented in modern notation as a dotted quarter note (with a speed of mm. 60–75). On this basis, the alba of Giraut de Bornelh is satisfactorily worked out, with embellishing figures appearing in logical positions and the rhythm falling in a manner true to the text.

Carole

In contrast to the sophistication of Giraut's alba, "Kalenda maya," the May dance of Raimbaut de Vaqueiras, is forthright and rhythmically direct, as dances almost always are. It has a long—twenty-line—stanza form, though the lines are so short that the stanza is not long in performance. The poem

A Medieval battle scene. Minstrels accompanied their masters into battle, where music was important for signals and for rousing courage, as well as for pomp and, during respites, for recreation. (From Cantigas de Santa Maria, written for Alfonso X. Courtesy of Ampliaciones y Reproducciones MAS and Patrimonio Nacional.)

Kalenda maya

RAIMBAUT DE VAQUEIRAS

Example 3

Kalenda maya	a	The first of May	Dona grazida,	Gracious Lady,
Ni fuelhs de faya	a	Neither leaf of beech	Quecx lauz'e crida	All praise and cry
Ni chanz d'auzelh	b	Nor song of bird	Vostra valor,	Your worth,
Ni flors de glaya	a	Nor flower of lily	Qu'es abelhida;	Which so entrances;
Non es que'm playa,	a	Gives me pleasure	E qui'us oblida,	And whoever forgets you
Pros domna guaya,	a	Most noble lady,	Pauc le val vida.	Little prizes his life.
Tro qu'un ysnelh	b	Until a speedy	Per qu'ieus azor,	Thus I worship you,
Messatgier aya	a	Messenger come	Don' eyssernida,	Excellent Lady;
Del vostre belh	b	From your own fair	Quar per gensor	For, being best,
Cors que'm retraya	a	Heart can tell me	Vos ai chauzida,	I have chosen you
Plazer novelh	b	New pleasure	E per melhor	As fulfilled
Qu'amors m'atraya,	a	For love to bring me	De pretz complida,	In perfect merit.
E jaya	a¹	And joy	Blandida	Wooed you,
E'm traya	a¹	To pull me	Servida	Served you,
Vas vos,	c	To you,	Genses	Better
Domna veraya;	a	Who are a true lady;	Qu'Erecx Enida.	Than Eric did Enid.
E chaya	a¹	Let him die	Bastida	And now,
De playa	a¹	Of his wounds	Fenida	Finished,
L' gelos,	c	The jealous (one),	N'Engles,	Lord Engles,
Ans que'm n'estraya.	a	Before I take my leave.	Ai l'ESTAMPIDA.	Is the ESTAMPIDA.

A troubadour May dance song, c. 1200. (Courtesy of Arno Volk Verlag, Cologne, Germany.)

speaks of the *estampida*, a type of dancing with percussive foot beats or stamping. The tune of "Kalenda maya" survives with the lyric and, in mirroring the directness of the text, presents a simple musical diction. The first and last of the five stanzas are included in Example 3.

Although Raimbaut's "Kalenda maya" is the earliest notated carole known, the tradition of such dances was an old one even before the troubadour movement began. It is probable that Raimbaut, being a minstrel or jongleur (or both), was closer to the popular dance, which was associated with a broader instrumental practice.

Musical Structure

The basic musical form of the troubadour art comprised a monophonic setting of the single stanza, so the essential unity of the performance was derived through the repetitions of the entire melody as successive stanzas were sung.

The form within single melodies was a *punctus* or phrase form; the Latin for *phrase* was *punctus* (plural, *puncti* or *punctūs*), in English, *point*. The principle was simple—each line of the lyric was set as one phrase of music. The phrases were well delineated and almost always stopped at the end of a long note, a *melisma* (a pattern of several notes on one syllable), or a rest. Such construction stemmed naturally from the poetic form, which was emphasized by punctuation at the ends of lines and important stops at structural points within the stanza. This was to be expected in an era when the poetic form was primary.

Phrase structure within the melody was basically achieved through repetition, most often following the stanza structure at the start of the melody and paralleling the rhyme scheme. The *aa* of Giraut's alba is *aa* in the music; the opening *aaba/aaba* of Raimbaut's carole is the opening *abcd/abcd* in the music. However, the melody, having taken its initial momentum from the verse form, is taken over by its own momentum for the conclusion. This is necessary not only for the validity of the musical line but also for the artistic necessity of wholeness, because the sense of completion in the music must be achieved by a vastly different means from that in the poem.

The alba (Example 2) continues in a gradually falling line; its five phrase finals produce the musical shape

The melodic language is not complex, but the song uses two common embellishments of the style—the *broderie* and the connecting run or *passage*. The broderie uses neighbor tones—upper, lower, or both. The run connects two notes of a leap, often an interval of a fourth, as at the end of the fourth punctus. The embellishment in the tornada is related to both and was also common.

Formally, Raimbaut's dance song "Kalenda maya" is complex but compensates with a simple musical diction. A summary of punctus finals indicates a strong sectional sense, with each phrase group ending on the same final, a return italicized by the short lines in spite of their strong accents on the notes above.

THE TROUVÈRES

Overlapping the troubadour movement, which had originated in the south, was the art of the lyric of the *langue d'oïl*, the northern vernacular of the courts (later to become modern French). The poet-musician of this tradition called himself a *trouvère*, the northern form of *trobador*. He had at hand not only the heritage of the Latin lyrics and the Goliards' poetry, but also the works of earlier Provençal poets. The two languages flourished side by side for a long while, but as the center of the lyric art moved northward, poets who had written in the langue d'oc began to write in the langue d'oïl, and the troubadour gave way, not to a different art, but to a continuing art in another dialect—the dialect of the courtly, stylish life. The apex of the troubadour art came in the second half of the twelfth century, that of the trouvère art about a century later.

In many cases, the artists replaced Provençal terms with new, northern ones. Of these, the most important was the increasingly general use of the term *chanson*, which came to denote a song in almost any of the troubadour forms. *Chanson* has since been used for any song with a French text.

As time passed, poetic form began to take precedence over subject matter. In general, Provençal labels dealing with subjects were dropped or, if transposed (as *alba* to *aubade*, *serena* to *serenade*, and *planc* to *plaint*), became part of elegant and poetic diction rather than part of the working vocabulary of an art. The word *lay* was retained, becoming a general term for a song.

The *vers* was also retained, as a free form without phrase repetitions, but it was soon to decline in favor of the tighter forms that characterized the trouvère movement at its height. In particular, three forms, known as *formes fixes* (set forms), emerged; they were to remain the most popular musical forms for over two centuries. Beginning as poetic schemes, the formes fixes over the years experienced a gradual expansion, so that the single line became a group of lines and a phrase of music became a group of phrases or a section. At that point, the musical aspect of the formes fixes predominated over the poetic aspects.

The Three Formes Fixes

1.   The **ballade** (from Provençal *balada*, a dance) developed from the common practice of mirroring the poetic form of the first few lines of the stanza, generally *abab*, and then completing the musical setting independently. The ballade stanza was generally seven or eight lines long. The poetic form *ababccc*, for example, might be set in the musical frame *ababcde*; if this is considered as 2+2+3, it can be regarded as three musical sections, simply *aab*. The final section, or part of it, was often a refrain (*envoi*).

2.   The **virelai** (probably from old French *vireli*, a jingling dance refrain, and *lay*, a song) had a shorter stanza with a one-line envoi that both began the poem and formed its concluding element. The simple virelai can be diagramed *AbbaA*.

> The old virelai has a delicate sort of a plan:
>   It pleases the eye and it teases the ear;
>   Each line is a new one, until you can hear
> The last line's the same as the first, when you'll know to a man
> The old virelai has a delicate sort of a plan.[3]

Characteristically, the *a* and *b* lines were of different lengths. In its early, single-line form, the virelai could be extended with one or two additional stanzas, as *Abba AbbaA* or *Abba Abba AbbaA*.

3.   The **rondeau** (from old French *rondel*, a circle) was the most regular of the forms. Each stanza formed a complete circle, because at the end there was a return to the opening by a repetition of the first two lines. The two line types opened the poem as *ab* and were followed by three *a* lines, of which the middle one was a duplication of the opening line; in its new position, however, the line had to be heard as A. The three *a* lines were followed by a *b* line; then the repeated opening pair was heard as AB. The total form was thus *ABaAabAB*.

> The two gentle strains of the charming rondeau
>   Lend it its strength and its graces.
> The opening couplet impels it to grow:
> The two gentle strains of the charming rondeau
> Weave back and forth in an answering flow,
>   So the strand of the two interlaces.
> The two gentle strains of the charming rondeau
>   Lend it its strength and its graces.[4]

Although the three formes fixes were originally associated with the dance, they soon became the vehicles for a formal poetry on the subject of the majority of the vernacular songs, courtly love—courtly love for the lady of the castle and also, by extension, for the Lady of the Church, the Virgin.

[3] Edith Borroff, unpublished.
[4] *Ibid.*

The ballade, virelai, and rondeau were often mentioned together in Medieval literature, not only in France but in England as well. In about 1390, an Englishman wrote,

> And ek he can carolles make,
> Rondeal, balade and virelai.[5]

In this case the forms were all dances. But a half-century later, another author wrote,

> Y made for her loue songges,
> balades, rondelles, virallës.[6]

In this case the forms were all chansons. Another author of the same period described a lady who sang as follows (note that the song title is still in French):

> And she began a roundel lustily,
> That *Sus le foyl de vert moy* men call.[7]

Over 2,000 chansons of the trouvère movement have been preserved, and about 1,900 are notated—in contrast to the slim musical legacy of the troubadour movement. But only half as many poets are known—about 210 trouvères compared to more than 400 troubadours.

The ballade at first was a simple setting of a short stanza. "Meschëans d'Amors," by Gillebert de Berneville (fl. 1255–1280), is a charming example. The six-line poetic form, *aaabCB*, uses a refrain (envoi), in this instance, two lines long. The tune for the ballade, though short, is sophisticated. The opening two lines of the stanza use the same musical phrase, but from there the music builds its own design. Repetition of the opening phrase or two was characteristic of troubadour songs, to the extent that the term "canzo," in addition to meaning song in general, came to imply a punctus structure beginning with such a repetition.

Ballade

The trouvères were more directly interested in musical form than the troubadours had been. In naming the ballade, they referred specifically to a form with two musical elements—the opening phrase or phrases that were to be repeated, which thus had to be notated only once, and the remaining phrase or phrases, which contained the poetic refrain.

---

[5] John Gower, quoted in H. H. Carter (ed.), "Carol, III," *A Dictionary of Middle English Musical Terms*, Bloomington, Ind.: Indiana University Press, 1961, p. 63.
[6] Quoted in "Virelay," *ibid*., p. 453.
[7] Quoted in "Roundel," *ibid*., p. 416.

De moi dolereus vos chant

GILLEBERT DE BERNEVILLE

Example 4

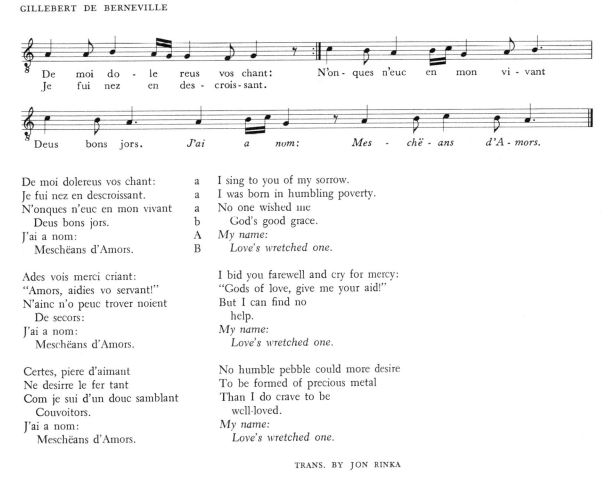

De moi dolereus vos chant:	a	I sing to you of my sorrow.
Je fui nez en descroissant.	a	I was born in humbling poverty.
N'onques n'euc en mon vivant	a	No one wished me
Deus bons jors.	b	God's good grace.
J'ai a nom:	A	*My name:*
Meschëans d'Amors.	B	*Love's wretched one.*

Ades vois merci criant:	I bid you farewell and cry for mercy:
"Amors, aidies vo servant!"	"Gods of love, give me your aid!"
N'ainc n'o peuc trover noient	But I can find no
De secors:	help.
J'ai a nom:	*My name:*
Meschëans d'Amors.	*Love's wretched one.*

Certes, piere d'aimant	No humble pebble could more desire
Ne desirre le fer tant	To be formed of precious metal
Com je sui d'un douc samblant	Than I do crave to be
Couvoitors.	well-loved.
J'ai a nom:	*My name:*
Meschëans d'Amors.	*Love's wretched one.*

TRANS. BY JON RINKA

A trouvère ballade, c. 1270. (Courtesy of Arno Volk Verlag, Cologne, Germany.)

Expansion of the virelai was more striking than that of the ballade. From a five-line stanza, *AbbaA*, the virelai soon grew to a five-unit poem, often of a single long stanza. The anonymous virelai "E, dame jolie" (Example 5), from the thirteenth century, uses eighteen lines to create the form. A, the unit that begins the poem, is a four-line (*abab*) group, whereas *b* is a three-line (*cca*) group. Like the ballade, the virelai can be notated economically with A and *b* written out only once. The singer would know the form, so inclusion of the two musical elements was enough.

Virelai

Example 5

E, dame jolie

ANONYMOUS

A	E, dame jolie,	a	E, lovely lady,
	Mon cuer sans fauceir	b	My heart without falseness
	Met en vostre bailie	a	I put into your keeping,
	Ke ne sai vo peir.	b	Knowing not your peer.
b	Sovant me voix conplaignant	c	Often I lament,
	Et an mon cuer dolosant	c	In my sad heart
	D'une malaidie	a	A malady
b	Dont tous le mous an amant	c	Which moves all lovers
	Doit avoir le cuer joiant	c	Whose hearts should joy
	Cui teilz malz maistrie.	a	In such an ill.
a	Si forment m'agrie	a	So does it please me,
	Li douls malz d'ameir	b	The sweet pain of love,
	Ke par sa signorie	a	That with its signaling
	Me covient chanteir:	b	I agree to sing:
A	E, dame jolie,	a	E, lovely lady,
	Mon cuer sans fauceir	b	My heart without falseness
	Met en vostre bailie	a	I put into your keeping,
	Ke ne sai vo peir.	b	Knowing not your peer.

A trouvère virelai, c. 1275. (Reprinted by permission of the publishers from Archibald T. Davison and Willi Apel, *Historical Anthology of Music*, Volume I. Cambridge, Mass.: Harvard University Press, Copyright, 1946, 1949, by the President and Fellows of Harvard College.)

The rondeau was enlarged beyond the scope of the other forms. A rondeau type (Example 6), with its first two lines repeated at the end but without the repeated A between the central *a* lines (that is, AB*aab*AB), occurs in Adam de la Halle's play *Le Jeu de Robin et Marion*. The roundel intention is complete, but the piece had to be written out in full because it lacks one

Rondeau

Example 6A. Adam de la Halle's *Le Jeu de Robin et Marion*, showing the chanson "Robins m'aime." (Courtesy of the Bibliothèque Nationale, 872 Fr. 25566, folio 39.)

Robins m'aime

ADAM DE LA HALLE

Example 6B

Ro- bins m'ai- me, Ro- bins m'a, Ro- bins m'a de- man- dé- e,

Si m'a- ra. Ro- bins m'a ca- ta co- te- le D'es- car- la- te

bonne et be- le. Sous- ka- nie et chain- tu- rele A- leu- ri- va!

Ro- bins m'ai- me, Ro- bins m'a, Ro- bins m'a de- man- dé- e, Si m'a- ra.

Example 6B (continued)

Robins m'aime, Robins m'a,   *Robin loves me, yes he does,*
Robins m'a demandée, Si m'ara.   *Robin asked me to be his own.*
  Robins m'a cata cotele   Robin gave me scarlet ribbon, fine and lovely,
  D'escarlate bonne et bele.   To twine in my hair
  Souskanie et chainturele   As a ruse to entice me,
Aleuriva!   Tra la la!
Robins m'aime, Robins m'a,   *Robin loves me, yes he does,*
Robins m'a demandée, Si m'ara.   *Robin asked me to be his own.*

TRANS. BY JON RINKA

A trouvère song, c. 1275, of a rondeau type, though not in the forme fixe. (Courtesy of Arno Volk Verlag, Cologne, Germany.)

Prendes i garde   **Example 7A**
GUILLAUME D'AMIENS

Prendes i garde, s'on mi regarde!   *Be on your guard if you gaze on me!*
  S'on mi regarde, dites le moi.   *If you gaze on me, tell me so.*
C'est tout la jus en cel boschaige;   That's all it takes to set me afire;
Prendes i garde, s'on mi regarde,   *Be on your guard if you gaze on me.*
La pastourel' i gardoit vaches: The shepherd girl guards her cattle:
  "Plaisans brunete a vous m'otroi!"   "Lovely brown-haired girl, I pledge myself to
        you!"
Prendes i garde, s'on mi regarde!   *Be on your guard if you gaze on me!*
  S'on mi regarde, dites le moi.   *If you gaze on me, tell me so.*

TRANS. BY JON RINKA

Example 7B

Example 7B (continued)

La   pas-tou - rel' i   gar - doit va - ches. "Plai- sans bru-nete   a   vous   m'o- troi!"

Pren dés   i   gar - de, s'on mi   re - gar - de! S'on mi   re - gar - de, di - tes   le   moi.

A trouvère rondeau c. 1275. A. As notated. B. As sung. (Courtesy of Arno Volk Verlag, Cologne, Germany.)

line, and the omission would keep the singer from assuming the form to be regular and proceeding accordingly.

The rondeau was the most economical of the formes fixes to notate. A work by the fourteenth-century nobleman Guillaume d'Amiens, a later trouvère, provides an excellent example of it (Example 7).

The ballade, virelai, and rondeau share a basic musical concept—they all are expanded forms of unbalanced symmetry derived through the juxtaposition of two contrasting elements. Expansion is heightened by the contrasts, which generally involve differing lengths and melodic designs. This reconciliation of two elements was basic in Medieval thought.

THE MINNESINGER

The Provençal and French lyric composers of the twelfth and thirteenth centuries were constant travelers and spread their art widely. But each of the peoples they influenced already had a well-developed vernacular lyric art, to which the refinements of the new techniques could be joined.

The German-speaking countries provide an excellent illustration of such an area, for even before the Goliards had wandered over the German countryside, a substantial German art song had flourished. German poets were centrally involved with the concept of courtly love, about which a virtual mystique had been developing in Western Europe. In about the year 1200, a monk codified the "Rules of Courtly Love"; there were thirty-one in all, including, for example, "Every lover regularly turns pale in the presence of his beloved." [8] In the introduction, love was defined as "a certain inborn suffering" [9]—a concept of love that was to recur centuries later in German romanticism. The German lyric poet called himself a "love-singer," or *Minnesinger* (the plural has the same spelling). The Minnesinger adopted

[8] Andreas Capellanus, quoted in J. B. Ross and M. M. McLaughlin (eds.), *The Portable Medieval Reader,* New York: The Viking Press, Inc., 1949, p. 116.
[9] *Ibid.,* p. 115.

the canzo of the troubadours and soon had developed the German archetype, the *Barform* (*aab* or *a* :‖ *b*); the Barform was comparable to the trouvère ballade, whose two elements the Germans called the *Stollen* (*a*) and the *Abgesang* (*b*). Other forms were used, but the Barform was the most common.

The two great Minnesinger of the thirteenth century were Walther von der Vogelweide (d. 1230) and Neidhart von Reuenthal (c. 1180–1240). One of Neidhart's May-dance songs is in a free form (Example 8). Its musical phrases do not repeat, so the punctus form is simply *abcdefg*; this is unusual but not unique. Neidhart's work is characterized by a wide range and a high arch at the sixth phrase. The phrase endings reflect both these qualities.

It is clear that Neidhart enjoyed a widely roaming melodic thrust; this was a personal preference, not common among other Minnesinger or among the Provençal and French composers.

In' gesach   Example 8

NEIDHART VON REUENTHAL

In' ge-sach die hei - de Nie baz ge-stalt, In lieh-ter ou-gen-wei - de Den grüe - nen walt. An den bei-den kie - se wir den mei - en. Ir mäg-de, ir sult iuch zwei - en, Gein dir - re lieh-ten su - mer-zit In ho-hem muo - te rei - en.

In' gesach die heide
Nie baz gestalt,
In liehter ougenweide
Den gruenen walt.
An den beiden kiese wir den meien.
Ir mägde, ir sult iuch zweien.
Gein dirre liehten sumerzit
In hohem muote reien.

I never saw the field
In lovelier bloom.
Sunrays the green leaves
Of the wood illume.
With joy, in both we hail the May's advance.
Maidens, now take hands
And merrily haste to meet the summertime
In festive dance.

TRANS. BY MARGARET F. RICHEY

A Minnesinger May dance song, c. 1225. (Courtesy of Arno Volk Verlag, Cologne, Germany.)

The art of the monophonic song remained a separate and defining force in Germany long after other kinds of music were competing for popular favor in the West. The Minnesinger, for the most part, were members of the nobility and lacked the impelling ambition that the presence of professionals gave to the trouvères. As the nobility declined in the new political system and as cities replaced many of the court centers, the lyric art was to defer to middle-class, closed-shop, highly organized guilds. Members called themselves *Meistersinger,* "master singers" (referring to the guild title of *Meister,* for composers of both lyrics and melodies, as distinct from the *Dichter,* who wrote new verses to melodies already in the tradition).

The Meistersinger flourished through the fifteenth and sixteenth centuries, holding Sunday meetings, regulating the competitions of guild members, and adjudicating processes of admission to the guild. Hans Sachs, the most famous of the Meistersinger and immortalized by Richard Wagner in his opera *Die Meistersinger von Nürnberg* (1868), lived from 1494 to 1576.

MEDIEVAL SONG
IN ENGLAND, SPAIN, AND ITALY

England and Spain, which we think of as lying outside Central Europe, were in the thick of political and cultural events in the Medieval and Renaissance eras. Far from being cut off by water and mountain, they were easily accessible by sea in an age when the sea was the surest and safest avenue of travel. In the thirteenth century, the great monarchies in England and Spain rivaled any in the Western world, and the Spanish King Alfonso VIII had an English Queen, Eleanor, daughter of Eleanor of Aquitaine (c. 1122–1204) and Henry II.

Old and Middle English abounded in musical terms. Because learned writers used only Latin, the use of the English vernacular in music indicates the existence of a lively secular art. Many instruments (including the harp, trumpet, fidel, drums, bells, tambourine, and citole), named during the first millennium, retained their names in later centuries. There were many words for singing and many for the kinds of music to be sung—joyful and sad songs, songs of victory and mourning, wedding and work songs. The *glig* (later to become the *glee*) was a song that brought joy.

England

The general word for minstrelsy in England was *gligcraeft,* and before the Norman conquest in 1066, there were two types of people who worked at this art—the *scop,* a permanent member of a household and thus comparable to a court musician, and the *gligman,* an itinerant (the female was called a *gliewméden,* "glee-woman"). After the Norman conquest, the troubadour was imported. Bernart de Ventadorn had served Eleanor of Aquitaine in France and may well have been one of those whom she brought to England when she married Henry II. Eleanor's son, Richard the Lion-Hearted, wrote both in Provençal and in French, the language of the court. But the English lyric persisted and was strengthened by its having to survive outside the court; it never lost its direct human quality to the formal and often empty courtly expressions. Surviving melodies are few; however, the songs of the few monk-poets were notated, and those that survive exhibit the wide range, long line, and interest in melodic thirds noted in Neidhart's May songs.

Because the English lyric developed freely, it was open to advancing ideas in a way that the heavily traditional court music could not be. Whatever the reason, in the British Isles the practice of singing in parts started so early that its beginnings cannot be traced. A historian wrote of the Welsh in the twelfth century.

> The Britons do not sing their tunes in unison, like the inhabitants of other countries, but in different parts: so that when a company of singers meet to sing, as is usual in this country, as many different parts are heard as there are singers, who all finally unite in consonance and organic melody [in the soft hexachord]. . . . This method of singing has taken such deep root among this people, that hardly any melody is accustomed to be uttered simply or otherwise than in many parts. . . . And, what is more astonishing, their children, as soon as they begin to sing, adopt the same manner.[10]

But the monophonic lyric was practiced as well, and the surviving songs attest to their beauty and modernity. The English influence was to assume increasing importance during the thirteenth and fourteenth centuries, and at the beginning of the fifteenth century, it was to become definitive in directing the course of the musical art on the Continent.

In the thirteenth century, Spain may well have been the most cosmopolitan of European countries. Long before Canterbury became the object of visitation from the devout, the Spanish Cathedral of Santiago (Saint James) de Compostela was an important religious and cultural center. This cathedral, which is in Galicia, in northwestern Spain, drew an enormous number of pilgrims from France, England, Italy, Germany, and even the Slavic East. Alfonso X, el Sabio (the Wise), made the Spanish court a brilliant center, not only maintaining contacts with England (musically a progressive nation) by importing musical retinues, but also welcoming the notable Moorish contributions to scientific and artistic thought. The King made the court a cosmopolitan meeting place of Moor and European, scholar and artist; he sponsored work in law, architecture, mathematics, astronomy, illumination, historical studies, and, of course, music. Alfonso lived from 1221 to 1284; his long tenure on the throne, from 1252 to 1284, comprised one of the great reigns in European history.

To musicians, Alfonso el Sabio is best known for the great song collection he had copied and extravagantly illustrated (illuminated). The manuscripts contain 414 *Cantigas de Santa Maria* (Songs of Holy Mary), dedicated

Spain

---

[10] Giraldus Cambrensis, quoted in F. M. Padelford (ed.), *Old English Musical Terms*, Bonn: P. Hanstein's Verlag, 1899, p. 7f.

A troubadour and a group of minstrels. (From Cantigas de Santa Maria, Cantiga 1, Lámina 2, written for Alfonso X. Courtesy of Ampliaciones y Reproducciones MAS and Patrimonio Nacional.)

to the Virgin Mary and patterned on those of Gautier de Coincy, the monk trouvère whose songs had preceded the cantigas by two generations. In many cases, the cantiga presents a little story of some miracle attributed to the Virgin, generally a folk tale; many are homely incidents in which Mary helps pilgrims who have lost their way or her statue smiles at a penitent.

For the most part, the cantigas were virelais or related forms; many were dance songs. The illustrations in the manuscripts are very lovely, and the Prologue speaks knowingly of the art of songwriting. "Since writing songs is an art which entails deep understanding, a troubadour should therefore be endowed with this virtue, and with enough powers of reason to be able to understand what he wishes to say and then to express it well; for it is thus that good songs are made." [11]

Italy

Provençal troubadours were writing in Italy by the end of the twelfth century, and many Italian lyricists began to write in Provençal rather than in their own vernacular. When the troubadour influence met the Italian religious renewal (St. Francis of Assisi died in 1226), the result was that Italian lyrics turned, on the one hand, to the secular hymn and, on the other hand, to courtly love, with its view of ladies as almost sacred inspirations.

Italy was divided: in Sicily, Frederick II (d. 1246) maintained a court of unusual brilliance similar to that of Alfonso el Sabio in Spain; the small city-states created merchant centers; and the famous Italian teaching orders, of which the Franciscans are representative, were founding religious centers

[11] Translation by the author.

throughout the country. It is natural that the lyric art developed severally, to serve each kind of center in its own way. The latter half of the thirteenth century saw the culmination of these developments.

The court was a focus of the troubadour art; both visiting and native poets emulated the Provençal models either in the langue d'oc or their own vernacular. Raimbaut de Vaqueiras was among the troubadours who had visited as far south as Naples by the end of the twelfth century (he went also to Sicily), and about 1285 Adam de la Halle also went to Naples, where his musical play *Le Jeu de Robin et Marion* was produced and where he died. The school of Italian troubadours flourished from about 1190 to 1310 and included Enzo Re (c. 1225–1272), Frederick's illegitimate son. The music has not survived.

The Italian lyricists are among the great poets in history. They centered in Florence and Arezzo and brought the concept of the troubadour stanza to fruition in the short verse form called the *sonnet* (from Provençal *sonet*, a little song).

Italian sonnet writers are represented by such luminaries as Dante Alighieri (1265–1321), a Florentine whose adulation for his "divine Beatrice" immortalized the courtly love ideal of a lady known only from afar, and Francesco Petrarch (1304–1374), born in Arezzo of Florentine parents. Their transcendent verses obscured the music, of which we know virtually nothing, to which their lyrics were sung.

The religious centers, encouraging the lay societies and secular brotherhoods (organizations for less formal worship than monastic life demanded), gave rise to an art of secular hymns called *laude spirituali*, "spiritual songs of praise," that comprised the basis of the new informal devotions. St. Francis was himself the author of some of the most famous of them, including the "Canticle of the Sun" and the "Canticle of the Creatures." These songs, in reality troubadour songs with religious texts, incorporated wholeheartedly the trouvère principles of two contrasting elements (A and B) and a refrain (in Italian, *ripresa* or *ritornello*). Many forms resulted through these principles, and a few exactly duplicated the form of the trouvère virelai, which was called *ballata* in Italian. (The word originally was *balada*, the Provençal for "dance song," testifying to the long-continuing association of secular monophony with the dance.)

MEDIEVAL DANCE MUSIC

Troubadour and trouvère songs were intended to be danced to as well as sung, and the names *ballade*, *virelai*, and *rondeau* all derive from words meaning "dance" or "to dance."

The two major types of dancing in Medieval Europe were the *carole* or *carola*, the group or choral dance, and the *danse* or *danza*, the couple dance. The carole, by far more common, was danced by groups, either in a circle,

Nova, Nova

Example 9

ANONYMOUS

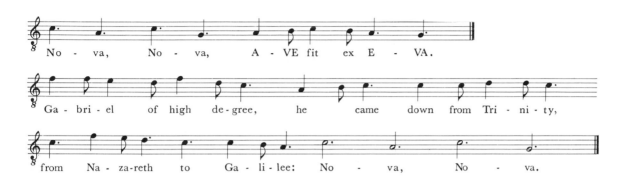

No - va, No - va, A - VE fit ex E - VA.

Ga - bri - el of high de - gree, he came down from Tri - ni - ty,

from Na - za - reth to Ga - li - lee: No - va, No - va.

Gabriel of high degree,	Then said the angel: Dread not thou,
He came down from Trinity,	For ye be conceived with great virtue
From Nazareth to Galilee.	Whose name shall be called Jesu.
I met a maiden in a place;	Then said the maiden: Verily,
I kneeled down afore her face	I am your servant right truly;
And said: Hail Mary, full of grace.	*Ecce, ancilla Domini.*

When the maiden heard tell of this,
She was full sore abashed y-wis,
And weened that she had done amiss.

An English carole from a fifteenth-century manuscript (the carole may be older). "Nova, Nova" is the Latin for "News! News!" a typical injection of Latin and incorporation of Medieval secular custom, in this case the calls of the town crier. The verses present Mary's highly human reaction to the announcement by the angel Gabriel that she would bear the Son of God—"Weened that she had done amiss" means "thought she had done something wrong." The final line is a scriptural quotation from Mary's reply to Gabriel, as it appeared in the Magnificat. It is generally translated, "Behold the handmaiden of the Lord." (Courtesy of Stainer and Bell, London.)

a long line, or two facing lines. One literary source, from the end of the thirteenth century, spoke of men dancing "hand in hand," [12] and Chaucer wrote about a dance of "ladies four-and-twenty, and yet more." [13] The music for such dances was based on a recurring refrain—which was a circular musical form—so the virelai and rondeau, which shared the roundel principle, were admirably suited to it.

[12] Robert Manning, quoted in Carter, "Carolend," *op. cit.*, p. 64.
[13] Quoted in "Daunce," *ibid.*, p. 114.

The English, in addition to dancing to the French formes fixes, developed their own form of the carole, which had been danced in the British Isles in ancient times (it is believed that choral dances were an important part of the ceremonies at Stonehenge, for example). The music of the English carole is actually the simplest form of the refrain or roundel construction—the opening refrain, called the *burden*, was followed by the variable stanza, called the *verse*, after which the burden was repeated. Verses alternated with the burden throughout the length of the dance, and the carole concluded with a final repetition of the burden. Thus the form of the carole was simply *AbAbAbAbA*, etc., always ending with *A*. Many of the English, as well as German, carole texts, particularly those celebrating religious holidays, included snatches of Latin—an interesting reversal of the Goliard habit of incorporating vernacular phrases into their Latin poems.

Dance songs were often played on instruments, but on the Continent, at least one dance form developed as an instrumental—or at least nonverbal —form. It was called the *estampie*, a name that originally had referred to a kind of stamping step but by the end of the thirteenth century seems to have referred to a principle of musical construction. The phrase-verse structure was replaced by a related one of puncti accumulating in pairs, each punctus performed twice in a row and then not reappearing in the dance. Thus each punctus was really a double phrase. To unify a form that might otherwise sound like a list of unrelated double phrases, two endings were used: the first one generally rose and was called the *ouvert*, "open ending"; the second one generally fell and was called the *clos*, "closed ending." If the two endings are labeled *x* and *y* and the phrases to be repeated are *a*, *b*, etc., the form can be clearly perceived as *axay bxby cxcy*, and so on.

Again we find that reconciliation of two opposing elements so congenial to the Medieval mind. The problem of length is solved not by a text but by the requirements of the dance itself. Additional puncti lengthen the work but do not otherwise change its musical relationships.

Example 10A. *La Quinta Estampie Réal.* Eight estampies appear on two pages of a thirteenth-century French manuscript. Each punctus, with its ouvert and clos, has its own line. (Courtesy of the Bibliothèque Nationale, Ms. Fr. 844, folio 104vo.)

La Quinta Estampie Réal

Example 10B

ANONYMOUS

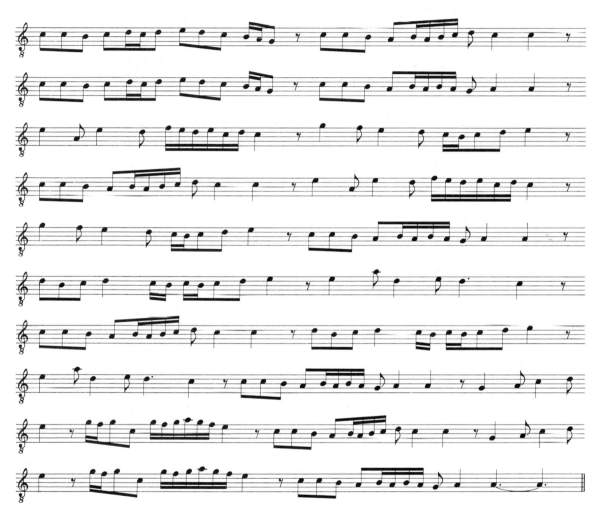

The Fifth Royal Estampie, from a series of dances in a thirteenth-century manuscript.

The estampie was the most important dance form to be conceived for instruments in the Medieval era. It is of special interest for two reasons: first, like the formes fixes, the estampie continued into the polyphonic techniques; also, the earliest known keyboard work, found in an English manuscript of about 1325 (the Robertsbridge Codex), is an estampie of six puncti.

COMPOSITE FORMS

Plays

The extended musical monophonic forms of Medieval secular monophony derived their length from the juxtaposition of songs and dances, overlying a dramatic context rather than defining it. Typical of such an extended work is the *Play of Daniel*, a liturgical drama produced in Beauvais in the thirteenth century. Such dramas were presented in the churches (or at the church doors) but were secular in structure and were often produced by the laity. This was the case with the *Play of Daniel*, which, according to the prologue of the surviving manuscript, was "created by the youth of Beauvais." The play began with a trumpet flourish followed by a procession and was accompanied by a series of songs and choral pieces, all monophonic, which provided the contrast primary to the Medieval concept of a musical work. It was a powerful drama.

Less dramatic but more amusing are the musical plays of the later trouvères, which were based on the same principle of juxtaposed songs and dances. However, being secular in subject, they made use of the trouvère forms and centered in the ideas of the court and the formalized games of courtly love.

Puys

Related to the composite forms was the *puy*—a gathering of minstrels for long presentations, meetings, and contests. Trouvère was pitted against trouvère in the *tenso*, "improvised debate"; a single event involved several pairs of contestants improvising dialogue on the same subject, giving an overall unity to a day of song. Solo improvisation, vocal and instrumental, was also a feature of the puy. Minstrels came in great numbers, and triumph brought them fame.

The most famous puys were at Arras in the thirteenth century (Adam de la Halle's city and time), London in the fourteenth century, and Evreux in the sixteenth and early seventeenth centuries (Lassus was a laureate at Evreux). The rules for the London puy, written in French in 1320, specified that the members of the jury should be knowledgeable "in song and in music" and that the winner was to be crowned and titled king. In France, the puy continued into the eighteenth century, but the only surviving puy may be the Welsh *eisteddfod* ("session"), held yearly. Its current definition clearly shows its twelfth-century origins: "An annual congress of bards, minstrels, and literati of Wales, at which orations and contests in harping, singing, and poetry are conducted with ceremony." [14]

A jongleuresse with clappers. In dance performances, the time was often kept by a woman, generally with clappers or a handbell. (Courtesy of Photographie Giraudon.)

[14] *Webster's New International Dictionary of the English Language*, 2d ed., Springfield, Mass.: Merriam, 1944.

MONOPHONIC PERFORMANCE—MINSTRELSY

Although there are few surviving documents of secular monophony before 1200 and much of what does remain is undeciphered, we know a good deal about the art of minstrelsy, which was certainly the most frequently and widely practiced of the musical arts of the Medieval era. Minstrelsy incorporated both the art of composition of secular poetry and music and the arts of performance, including poetic recitation, singing, instrumental performance (accompanying or autonomous), and those arts that we think of today as vaudevillian—dancing (for an audience), miming, juggling, acrobatics, animal acts, and so on. The troubadour-trouvère, minstrel, and jongleur were roughly comparable to composer, instrumentalist, and entertainer, respectively. There was a good deal of overlap, however, so many musicians fitted two—or even three—of these descriptions.

The overlap of roles was recognized in a set of articles that were drawn up to establish the Corporation of Minstrels of the City of Paris, an organization born of the late trouvère association with city life. This document sheds light

Corporation of Minstrels

Pipe-and-tabor players. The pipe is narrow and overblows a fifth (second to third partials) so that three fingerholes can suffice to provide a scale. The instrument can thus be played with one hand, freeing the other to beat the small drum, or tabor, which was generally attached to the waist. (From Cantigas de Santa Maria, written for Alfonso X. Courtesy of Ampliaciones y Reproducciones MAS and Patrimonio Nacional.)

on several matters and is delightful in itself. It is dated "Monday the day of the feast of the Holy Cross [14th] of September of the year 1321" and, after the usual salutation, declares, "Be it known to all that we, with one accord of Minstrels & Minstrelesses, Jougleurs & Jougleresses, living in the city of Paris, have ordained and do ordain the points and articles here-below contained and defined. . . ." [15] The eleven articles are concerned with regulations for hiring practices, the training of apprentices, and so forth. Minstrels were not to change jobs, even if they received a better offer, once they had accepted an engagement; they were not to send substitutes, except in cases of "necessity" such as illness or imprisonment. Thirty-six members, of which at least eight were women, signed the document. (At that time, Paris had a population of about 275,000.) The head of the Corporation had the title King of the Minstrels, which had been an unofficial title for over four centuries. The Corporation maintained its own chaplain and supported its own church, named after its patron saint, Saint-Julien-le-Pauvre. The group also built a hospital to care for its sick and aged.

It continued to thrive, with branches at Orléans, Amiens, Bordeaux, Abbéville, and Blois, and in the seventeenth century, its membership expanded to include organists, harpsichordists, and dancers. In 1697, upon the death of the corporation's king, Guillaume Dumanoir II, Louis XIV decided not to continue the office and the title lapsed. It was revived in 1742 for Jean-Pierre Guignon, a famous violinist. Guignon was the last Roi des Violons; he resigned in February, 1773, and the edict finally suppressing the corporation was issued on April 3 of that year.

But minstrelsy was never limited to the professional. From the beginning, the ideal of the well-educated man (and woman) included knowledge of the art. The general assumption of this skill in the gentleman and gentlewoman is found throughout late Medieval and Renaissance writings. A late thirteenth-century poem informs us that

Universality of Minstrelsy

> While Iosian was in Ermonie
> She had learned [the art] of minstrelsy,
> Upon a fidel to play
> Estampies, tunes, and garibles gay.[16]

Note that Iosian is female and that she had been taught to play dance and song tunes and to improvise embellishments. But she was evidently not expected to compose. And a century later, in 1387, "He went on an occasion from a feast much ashamed, for he was asked to sing to the harp, and he could not sing." [17]

[15] Antoine Vidal, *St-Julien-des-Ménestriers et des ménestrels à Paris,* Paris: Quantin, 1878, p. 36.
[16] Quoted in Carter, "Garible," *op. cit.,* p. 162.
[17] Higden, quoted in "Harp, VII, *c,*" *ibid.,* p. 189.

The minstrel was everywhere—in residence at court; traveling from town to town; at banquets, festivals, and other occasions of merrymaking, whether of lowly or high estate. "Noble men use not to make soupers [to dine] wythout harpe or symphony," [18] stated a Cornish historian in 1398. A *symphony* was a small instrument—crwth or bagpipe,—but the word also meant "agreeable sound of music," as did *harmony*; neither yet referred to part music. The Cornishman also wrote, "And diverse Instruments thus serve harmony: drum and bell, harp and psaltery, & nakers [kettledrums—often very small] and also sistrum [a jangling percussion instrument]." [19]

Seldom was one man or instrument mentioned alone, for ideally minstrelsy was various. The poem "King Horn" (c. 1250) speaks of "harperes, Jogelours and fiþelers"; [20] "Arthur and Merlin" (c. 1335) tells of trumpets, fidels, bagpipes, and drums at dinner.[21] Harperes might well be singers, because from ancient times the singer of lays "sang to the harp." Trumpets, flutes, and drums were frequently played at banquets; the New Year's banquet at King Arthur's court was described in the fourteenth-century poem *Sir Gawain and the Green Knight*:

Performance Characteristics

> Then the first course comes, with clamor of trumpets
> That were bravely bedecked with bannerets bright,
> With noise of new drums and the noble pipes.
> Wild were the warbles that wakened that day
> In strains that stirred many strong men's hearts.[22]

Here too the drums were nakers rather than tabors (shallow drums, often with snares).

Performances were naturally compared, and certain minstrels became widely known for their skills; the foremost courts could, of course, employ the most famous performers. A writer spoke of a banquet in about 1400: "They hadde menstrales of moch honours, Fydelers, Sytolyrs, and trompours. . . ." [23] The sytolyrs were players of the citole, a lute-like, flat-bodied, four-stringed instrument that was fretted and played with a quill plectrum. One of the most revealing references to the singing of lays is provided by the Cornish historian. "In that household poets and geste-singers on a balcony performed poems, gestes, and songs, and below were minstrels who mimed the action and deeds that they spoke of in their gestes and songs,

A minstrel with vielle. Many illustrations show a vielle player, the troubadour, accompanying a singer, his jongleur or minstrel. (Courtesy of Photographie Giraudon.)

[18] Bartholomaeus Anglicus, quoted in "Symphonye, II," *ibid.*, p. 437.
[19] Bartholomaeus Anglicus, quoted in "Naker," *ibid.*, p. 318.
[20] Quoted in "Fithcler," *ibid.*, p. 154.
[21] Quoted in "Stiuour," *ibid.*, p. 478.
[22] Marie Borroff (trans.), *Sir Gawain and the Green Knight*, New York: Norton, 1967, lines 116–120. (Courtesy of the publisher.)
[23] Thomas Chestre, quoted in Carter, "Fitheler," *op. cit.*, p. 155.

with bending and turning and posing and stopping of their limbs and their bodies." [24]

We know that the Latin mimus provided a salient part of the heritage of the jongleurs, who were skilled in hand-dancing, an art still very much alive in the Orient. The presentations of the minstrels doubtless comprised a series of musical and other entertainments that we would call a variety show. Of the musical practices, we know the necessary fundamentals: melody was cherished, imagination was a virtue, performances were discussed and compared. We know that the ideal sound was reedy and mildly nasal, with bowed string instruments and voices emulating the clarity and individuality that the sweet reed tone provided. This quality was prized whenever melodic lines were enjoyed individually, either in the monophonic and heterophonic or in the polyphonic techniques. Loudness was not admired except for special effects of pomp or splendor (as in the "clamor of trumpets"). From the passages and broderies in the notations that survive, we know that performers embellished the tunes they sang and played. Evidence of this is also gained from such references as that in the thirteenth-century poem about Iosian, who learned to play garibles on the fidel, that is, flourishes or ornaments added to the written version. And we know that percussion instruments abounded and were generally used in performances; but because percussion parts do not survive and early depictions of performances show drummers, bell ringers, cymbal players, and the like without notated music, we can assume that the rhythmic patterns were provided from a repertoire of figures and devices without separate written parts. Such patterns are still learned by rote, through the use of vocal syllables, in many areas of the world where monophonic and heterophonic arts are practiced.

It is evident that in the performance of Medieval monophony, variety was of primary importance. The chanson de geste, as a story, relied only on the vocal skill of the performer for variety, but, as has been shown, the jongleur might well mime the action of the poem and instruments were certainly used. "Singing to the harp" doubtless meant supporting or doubling the recitation, and many pictures of trouvère performances show a second performer, with fidel or vielle, who must have provided interludes. Many of the poems were very long—some had over 10,000 lines (the famous *Roman de la Rose* had 23,000), more than any voice could present without respite.

But in the lyric, the music shared the importance of the text; and in a popular song, whose words were already known, it may have overpowered the text altogether in certain performances. And we know that instrumental performances of lyric and dance songs, without the voice, were common.

The Medieval concept of instrumentation, like the concept of musical structure itself, was based on the punctus. The principle was of combining, contrasting, and alternating, with the ever-changing qualities particularly savored. In an estampie, for example, the first phrase might have been presented by recorder alone and the second by bagpipe, citole, flute, fidel, lute,

A trobairitz. (Courtesy of Photographie Giraudon.)

[24] Bartholomaeus Anglicus, quoted in Carter, "Gestour," *op. cit.*, p. 164.

vielle, or others of the large number of Medieval instruments; percussion could have been added by drum, cymbal, bell, tambourine, triangle, sistrum, or even clapping or stamping.

Imaginative combining of these sounds produced two additional variables—register and dynamics. Alternating a tenor vielle with a treble recorder, for example, automatically introduced an alternation of register at the fifteenth. The effects of using five or six instruments, all different, could be as various and imaginative as the ingenuity of the performer-producer allowed. At least three registers would be included in the instruments; the basic ones were tenor, alto, and soprano. Variety of number automatically introduced variety of dynamics—one performer alternating with three or four others naturally brought about an alternation between softer and louder elements.

The performer was both arranger and producer in minstrelsy. The performer began with a tune with a definite number of phrases or puncti. The assembled musicians (ideally chosen for variety and skill, but doubtless often accumulated by chance) either would have known the tune or have had a copy of it. Surviving copies are in the tenor register; all performers read in that register (the normal male voice of the time), although they might have played one or two octaves higher.

Role of the Performer

The musicians, once the tune was chosen, planned which phrases each performer would play and which he would not in order to produce a lively and imaginative alternation. Then percussion would be decided on. Soloists (and perhaps even those playing in unison) might embellish the melodies. Undoubtedly, a good deal of experimentation took place on the spot. Certainly, the Medieval audience did not hear the same work done repeatedly in the same way; the art of arranging must have developed with that of composition and must have been relished keenly in a rich and varied art.

❈ Some Composers of Minstrelsy

A sampling of troubadours and trouvères reveals that these poet-composers came from the lower class as well as the nobility; however, their reputations seemingly were not influenced by their origins. Their careers were based on freedom of travel and the assumption of welcome and respect that that freedom implies.

Troubadours

WILLIAM IX, COUNT OF POITOU (1071–1127), called the first troubadour, was a tumultuous fellow who was excom-municated for attacking church properties. He left 7 works, 1 fragment of notation.

MARCABRU (active 1129–1150), a foundling, was taught by his fellow Gascon Cercamon and was known for his pastorelas. He left 45 lyrics, 2 notated.

BERNART DE VENTADORN (fl. 1150–1180), son of a furnace stoker at the castle at Ventadorn, served late in his life in the entourage of Eleanor of Aquitaine in northern France and probably in England. Known as the first to write of courtly love, he left 45 lyrics, 19 notated, and was therefore one of the most important troubadours for musicians.

BEATRITZ COMTESSE DE DIA (fl. 1160), the most famous trobairitz, wrote passionate love lyrics, of which 5 are extant.

GIRAUT DE BORNELH (Borneill) (fl. 1165–1200), of humble blood and a jongleur, was the most famous troubadour at the height of the art and was known as the Master of Troubadours. He left some 80 lyrics, of which only 4 are notated.

RAIMBAUT DE VAQUEIRAS (c. 1155–1205) was the son of a poor knight and minstrel to Boniface II of Monferrand. He left 40 lyrics, 8 with notation.

PEIRE VIDAL (fl. 1175–1215) was the son of a furrier of Toulouse. He left 50 lyrics, 12 notated.

GUACELME FAIDIT (fl. 1185–1215), a jongleur at Ventadorn, wrote a planh at the death of Richard the Lion-Hearted. Known as an eccentric, he waged a fatness contest with his mistress. He left 65 lyrics, 14 notated.

PEIROL OF AUVERGNE (1160–1225) was an impoverished knight known for his love for the sister of the Dauphin. When the Dauphin became jealous of him, he left and became a jongleur. He left 34 lyrics, 17 with notation.

GIRAUT RIQUIER (d. 1294), a Catalan and known as the last troubadour, wrote also in the more módern French. He left 89 lyrics (mostly in French), 48 notated.

Trouvères

BLONDEL DE NESLE (c. 1150–c. 1200) was a trouvère of Picardy. He left 17 notated chansons.

RICHARD THE LION-HEARTED (1157–1199), King of England from 1189 to 1199, was a poet in both Provençal and French, a Crusader, and a patron of other poets. Only 2 of his songs remain.

GACE BRULÉ (c. 1179–1212), a knight from Champagne, was probably associated with the Duke of Brittany and his sister, Marie de Champagne. He was known for his love songs. He left 91 works.

MARIE DE FRANCE (fl. 1181–1216), the greatest poetess of Medieval Europe, was the natural daughter of Geoffrey Plantagenet and thus half sister to Henry II of England. She was best known for her *lais* of courtly love.

GAUTIER DE COINCY (1178–1236), a monk, was known above all for his songs to the Virgin, generally new poems set to tunes, both sacred and secular, that were already popular. There are 25 chansons remaining, most of them with tunes.

THIBAUT IV DE CHAMPAGNE (1201–1253), King of Navarre from 1234, was one of the most famed of trouvères and a sponsor of many others. He left 75 songs, 68 of them notated.

MONIOT D'ARRAS (thirteenth century), a bourgeois from Arras, was the best known of the burgher poets. He left 55 chansons.

ADAM DE LA HALLE (1240–1288), also known as "le Bossu" (the Hunchback), was from Arras. The most famous of the trouvères, he was educated near Cambrai and worked in Paris, Naples, and Sicily. He left 53 chansons and 2 short musical plays.

AGNES DE NAVARRE-CHAMPAGNE, COMTESSE DE FOIX (fourteenth century) was the daughter of Jeanne de France and Phillip d'Evreux. As a writer of lyrics she was most famed for her personal love poems.

GUILLAUME DE MACHAUT (c. 1305–1377), one of the most famous poets in the history of Europe, was secretary to John of Luxembourg, King of Bohemia. In his entourage, Guillaume traveled widely, visiting Germany, Italy, and Russia. He later served the royal family of France. More widely known to musicians as a polyphonic composer, he nevertheless is too substantial a lyric poet not to be included here, and his works were preponderantly trouvère chansons, more than half of them monophonic and most of them dealing with courtly love.

In illuminating the vaults and the walls [of cathedrals] with every diversity of handiwork, and all the hues of the rainbow, you have in a manner shown forth to every beholder a vision of God's paradise, bright as springtime . . . whereby you make men praise God in His creatures, and to preach His wonders in His works. For the beholder's eye knows not where first to rest its gaze: if we look upward to the vaults, they are even as a mantle embroidered with flowers: or if we consider the light that streams through the windows, then we cannot but marvel at the priceless beauty of the glass and the variety of this most precious work. . . . Kindle yourself now to a still ampler scope of art, and set yourself with all your might to fulfil that which is yet lacking to the furniture of God's house, without which the Sacraments cannot be celebrated, nor God be served with due ministrations.

ROGER OF HELMERSHAUSEN *

Sacred Song

PLAINCHANT

3

Another great body of Western monophonic music consists of the song, called *chant* or *plainchant*, of the early Christian Church; it undoubtedly had a strong heritage from both pre-Christian music and secular song. When Christianity began, its rites were not well formed or clearly organized; on the contrary, early Christians struggled for generations—even centuries—in many localities, often as semisecret groups under persecution. They improvised forms of service, making use of whatever music they already knew,

* c. 1280. Quoted in George G. Coulton, *Medieval Panorama*, New York: Meridian Books, Inc., 1955, p. 559.

putting new words to familiar tunes (a practice known as *contrafactum*), or even adapting hymns of converts' previous faiths and giving them new meanings. The heterogeneous and variable music of the early Church has never really yielded to codification; even today many variants of the Roman rite—not to mention the Greek, Russian, Coptic, and others—are found over the world, a pale residue of what must have been a stunning diversity.

Chant must be conceived not only as a musical construction but as an entire esthetic experience, of whose effect part was architectural (relating to the special silence of the stone structure into which the music was projected) and part visual (relating to the effects of light and space). In addition, a large part lay in the listener's attitude, his reaction to the significance of the service and the text, and, of course, his own religious conviction. Chant's seeming austerity is a deception of the printed page, for its line is capable of great subtlety and its sound is innately compelling.

The European heritage of plainchant stemmed from sources parallel to those of the general cultural development. Chant is classified as Old Roman, emanating, it is generally supposed, from Rome; Gallican, used in Central Europe; Ambrosian, used in northern Italy and related to Eastern practice; Mozarabic, used in Spain and influenced by Moorish art; and Sarum, used in the north and named for the Salisbury Cathedral in Britain. Although an attempt at a central codification—named for Pope Gregory the Great (c. 540–604) but actually dating from the climactic years of religious monophony about two and a half centuries later—was made by Rome, it never succeeded completely. However, by the end of the ninth century, a generally accepted body of chant had been brought together, and that, together with new works of the next three centuries, comprises the basic chant of the Roman Catholic Church. Some of it is found today in the *Liber Usualis* ("book of ordinary usage"), a general compilation made in modern times.

The central rite of the Christian Church was the celebration of the Holy Eucharist, a reenactment of the Last Supper, called the *Mass*. It had two parts: the Mass of the Catechumens (for those preparing for Baptism), which consisted of prayers of preparation and praise, reading of the Epistle and Gospel, and finally the sermon, for education in the faith; and the Mass of the Faithful (for which, in early days, only the baptized remained), comprised of the offertory and dedication, Consecration of bread and wine, prayers in preparation for Communion, Communion, thanksgiving after Communion, and dismissal. At the end of the first millennium, the order of the Mass was as follows:

The Mass

Mass of the Catechumens

Prayers in preparation
Introit for the day (entry of celebrants)
Kyrie eleison (prayer for mercy)

Gloria in Excelsis Deo (prayer of adoration)
Prayer for the day's feast
Day's reading from the Epistles
Gradual
Alleluia or tract
Day's reading from the Gospels
Sermon (not liturgically part of the Mass, but inserted here; it generally
    comprised a commentary on the day's readings)

Mass of the Faithful

Credo (creed)
Offertory verse for the day's Mass
Dedicatory prayers
Special dedicatory prayer for the day's Mass
Preface (introduction to the canon)
Sanctus and Benedictus
Canon (central prayers, the same for all days)
    Remembrances
    Prayers of offering
    Consecration
    The Lord's Prayer
    Prayer for peace
Agnus Dei (O Lamb of God, invocation)
    Communion
Communion prayers for the day
Thanksgiving prayers
Ite, Missa est (Go, Mass Is Over—dismissal)
Final blessing

It is important to realize that the Mass had not attained this form early. On the contrary, the form developed gradually and was completed only as the second millennium began. Many prayers are extremely old and from the Hebrew; some, like the Kyrie, are from the Greek. The Sanctus and Benedictus may also be of Greek origin, for they were congregational songs long before becoming part of the Mass. The Agnus Dei, brought into the Roman rite by Pope Servius I (d. 701), a Syrian, took over a century to become established. The Credo, essentially the confession of faith adopted at the Council of Nicea (A.D. 325), did not enter the Mass until 1014, after a long history in Milan, Gaul, and Spain. It was the last addition. Most of the prayers of the present day come from the Psalms, the Old Testament Hebrew songs that formed the basis of early Christian worship.

The year was organized chronologically as a commemoration of the life of Christ—from Advent (preparation for the birth of Christ), Christmas, and Epiphany (the appearance of the Wise Men); through Lent (the penitential preparation for Easter), Passiontide, Holy Week (commemoration of the Last Supper and the Crucifixion, "Passion," of Christ), Easter (celebration of the Resurrection), and Ascensiontide; to Pentecost (descent of the Holy Ghost, also called Whitsunday) and the Sundays after Pentecost (about half the year, devoted to summarizing Christian teaching). This organization of time was called the Liturgical Year, and it ran concurrently with a calendar of saints' days. Some parts of the Mass remained constant from day to day; these were called the Ordinary of the Mass. The other texts, which changed to reflect the character of the day's feast, were called the Propers.

All the Mass was read by the celebrant and certain texts were also sung. Because singing is slower than reading, the singing of the introit, Kyrie, Gloria (except in Advent and Lent, when it is omitted from the Mass), and gradual, with its alleluia or tract, formed a fairly full musical adornment of the priest's reading of the first part of the Mass. The Creed was long and was read only on Sundays and special feast days; it too was sometimes sung. In the second half of the Mass, the singing of the offertory, Sanctus and Benedictus, Lord's Prayer, Agnus Dei, Communion prayer, and dismissal formed a musical accompaniment of the priest's reading. Following are the sung portions of the Mass:

> Introit
> * Kyrie
> * Gloria
> Gradual and alleluia or tract
> * Credo
> Offertory
> * Sanctus and Benedictus
> * Agnus Dei
> Communion
> Ite Missa est

The texts that are starred comprise the Ordinary. The Kyrie, Sanctus and Benedictus, and Agnus Dei were daily items; the Gloria was omitted throughout Advent and Lent (and other penitential Masses), and the Credo was omitted on all weekdays (except special feasts). Thus the musical Ordinary could comprise three, four, or five items, most often three or four. Until the ninth century, the congregation sang the Ordinary, leaving the more difficult Propers to the choir (called the *schola cantorum,* "singing school," or simply the *schola*). In later centuries, when the Ordinary was sung by the choir, this group of texts was to achieve greater significance.

The Divine Office

Of almost equal importance to that of the Holy Eucharist, or Mass, at least in monastic life, was the continuing daily prayer, or Divine Office, of the religious community. For the most part, the Divine Office consisted of chant interspersed with readings, with a much larger proportion of chanted portions than in the Mass.

Music Segments of the Divine Office

Psalm. The 150 Hebrew songs in praise of God, found in the Old Testament, were written in part by King David (1012–972 B.C.), although many predate his reign. The Psalms comprise the bulk of plainchant texts;

their form is generally that of two-part verses, with parallel or contrasting sections mirrored in repeated musical sections. Psalms are often chanted on single notes with beginning and ending formulas, which are called Psalm tones.

canticle (from the Latin *canticum,* "song"). Songs of praise or love of God, excluding the Psalms. (This was established by custom; there really is no distinction between canticles and Psalms except the fact of inclusion in or exclusion from the Book of Psalms.) The Old Testament contains fourteen canticles; the New Testament has three (those in the hours).

antiphon. A phrase or verse sung immediately before and after a Psalm or canticle, suggesting the meaning of the text it surrounds. When introduced into the vocabulary in the fourth century, the word referred directly to the practice of singing by alternate groups. About 1,250 antiphons were authorized by the Church; over 1,000 remain in the *Liber Usualis.*

hymn. A lyric poem set to music, generally a song in praise or adoration and by far the most popular music of the early Christian Church. Although hymns do appear in the Mass, they are far more common in the Divine Office. Of the thousands of hymns written in the first millennium, a few remain in use to this day; 133 are in the *Liber Usualis.* Nonliturgical hymns, such as the secular laude, were sung at private devotions.

Hymns predate the Christian era—two hymns to Apollo survive among the meager musical heritage from ancient Greece. The earliest Christian hymn found is from the Oxyrhynchos papyrus (c. 300), an Egyptian document. The hymn is in Greek and its tune is written in Greek vocal notation. The earliest Western hymns were those of St. Ambrose (d. 397), Bishop of Milan, and his school.

lesson, or lection. A reading from the Scripture or other writings of religious significance. These were sung in the Medieval era.

responsorium. A verse or answering refrain sung after each lesson in the Divine Office and followed by a Gloria Patri (Glory to the Father), called the lesser doxology. This is a short (two-verse) response and should not be confused with the Gloria in Excelsis Deo, or greater doxology, which is the Gloria of the Ordinary of the Mass.

nocturn (Latin, "of the night"). A division of Matins (see below), comprising three Psalms, their antiphons and responses, three lessons and their responses, and a blessing. For simple feasts, three divisions of nine Psalms were read, but Matins usually contained three full nocturns. Originally the term referred to the entire night Offices of Matins and Lauds when they were sung between midnight and 4 A.M.

The Divine Office was divided into seven sessions, or *hours,* to symbolize its complete, circular form.

The Hours of the Divine Office

Matins (night office), the first and most important of the hours, was sung about 2 A.M. It contained nocturns, Psalms, and antiphons.

Lauds (praises) contained four Psalms and the canticle "Benedictus Dominus" (Song of Zacharia) with their antiphons, hymn, lessons and responses, and prayers of the day. It was sung just before sunrise and was followed immediately by *Prime,* sung at sunrise (about 6 A.M.), which contained a short lesson and antiphon.

Terce, sung at about 9 A.M., contained Psalms and antiphons.

Sext, sung at noon, contained Psalms and antiphons.

None, sung at 3 P.M., contained Psalms and antiphons.

Vespers (evening prayer) was sung late in the afternoon. It included five Psalms and the canticle "Magnificat" (Song of Mary) with their antiphons, lesson with response, hymn, and prayers of the day.

Compline (completion) followed Vespers, generally at 6 or 6:30 P.M. but varying with the hour of sunset to some degree. It included three Psalms and the canticle "Nunc Dimittis" (Song of Simeon) with their antiphons, hymn, lesson with response, prayer of the day, and blessing.

The names for some hours—Prime, Terce, Sext, and None—derive from the ancient manner of numbering the hours of the day from 6 A.M., considered dawn. Lauds and Vespers are the long hours; each contains a canticle and several Psalms, all with their antiphons. Since the thirteenth century, Compline has included one of the four Marian antiphons (really hymns but named antiphons because they are sung by alternating groups), rotated by season.

Musically, Vespers is of special importance. It was retained in parish churches as an evening service even after leadership was transferred from the monastery to the cathedral and chapel. In modern times, it is sung in both Catholic and Protestant churches. The "Magnificat," the canticle of Vespers, was to become the most frequently composed text of the fifteenth century and has remained popular ever since.

PLAINCHANT COMPOSITION

By the ninth century, the Divine Office and the Mass had been established and somewhat codified, though far from completely, and composers were turning to the creation of new materials to be added to the liturgy. Great poets and melodists, infused with the new Gaelic lyrical art as well as with Eastern influences, arose in the monasteries and added to the literature of plainchant through the thirteenth century.

The monastery of St. Gall, one of the great cultural centers during the ninth and tenth centuries, was perhaps the most important in the development of sacred monophony. The monastery's early history was written about the year 1020 and tells of the monastic career of Notker Balbulus, who was famous as a minstrel, and of Tuotilo, Notker's friend.

> Notker was frail in body, though not in mind, a stammerer in voice but not in spirit; lofty in divine thoughts, patient in adversity, gentle in everything, strict in enforcing the discipline of our convent, yet somewhat timid in sudden and unexpected alarms, except in the assaults of demons, whom he always withstood manfully. He was most assiduous in illuminating, reading, and composing; and (that I may embrace all his gifts of holiness within a brief compass) he was a vessel of the Holy Ghost, as full as any other of his own time. [Notker was later beatified.] But Tuotilo was widely different.

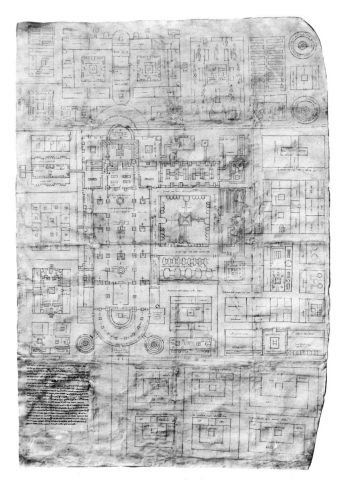

Ninth-century plan for a monastery. From the Chapter Library, St. Gall. (Courtesy of Emile Zumbühl.)

He was strong and supple in arm and limb, such a man as Fabius tells us to choose for an athlete; ready of speech, clear of voice, a delicate carver and painter; musical, with especial skill on the harp and the flute; for the Abbot gave him a cell wherein he taught the harp to the sons of noble families around. . . . In choir he was mighty, and in secret prayer he had the gift of tears; a most excellent composer of poetry and melodies.[1]

The composers (and performers) of chant were human beings seeking a satisfying presentation within an art for which they felt both love and reverence. Inevitably, over the centuries during which plainchant was written, ideas about music changed, swinging from the experimental to the conservative, that is, from the extrovert and ecstatic to the introvert and ascetic. In conservative times, the arts were seen as attempting to supersede the religious experience they were designed to serve and philosophers inveighed against their seductive pull of attention. St. Jerome (c. 340–420) cautioned

---

[1] Quoted in George G. Coulton, *Life in the Middle Ages*, New York: Cambridge, 1954, vol. 4, p. 51.

"the servant of Christ to sing so that he pleases, not through his voice, but through the words which he pronounces." [2] St. Augustine (354–430), who warned of "the peril of pleasure" [3] in plainchant, was also quick to note that "by the delight taken in at the ears, weaker minds are roused up into some feeling of devotion." [4] But it was St. Augustine who spoke so movingly of the *jubilus*, the long florid musical phrase on the final *a* of the alleluia, which was sung on joyful feasts after the gradual in the Mass.

> He who sings a *jubilus*, speaks no words, but it is a song of joy without words; it is the voice of a heart dissolved in joy, which tries as far as possible to express the feeling, even if it does not understand the meaning. When a man rejoices in his jubilation, he passes from some sounds which do not belong to speech and have no particular meaning, to exulting without words; so that it seems he rejoices indeed, but that his joy is too great to put into words.[5]

The cycle of experimental attitude can be revealed by noting that composition enjoyed three peak creative periods—roughly, 850 to 900, 1000 to 1050, and 1240 to 1280. The first introduced the trope, sequence, and other adornments of the Mass Propers. The second produced antiphons, concentrated on the Mass Ordinary, and introduced Marian hymns (hymns to the Virgin, related to the troubadour songs of courtly love), while continuing the interest in the sequence. The third was a culmination of sequence composition, producing both the "Dies Irae" and the "Stabat Mater." These two great monophonic works were related not so much to the monastery, however, as to the secular societies of the Italian religious revival.

Chant is song and, like most song, was rhythmic in early times; it used short *Early Chant* and long notes with the ratio of two shorts to one long, similar to our eighth and quarter notes. The early tenth-century manual *Commemoratio Brevis* said that "all the longs must be equally long, all the shorts of equal brevity, . . . one always twice as long as the other . . . because assuredly every melody is to be carefully measured," [6] in our terms, measured but without meter. Such widely placed theorists as Hucbald (840–930) in Belgium, Guido of Arezzo (c. 990–1050), Odo (d. 982) of Paris, Tours, and Cluny (where, from 927, he was abbot), and Notker Balbulus at St. Gall agreed with this view.

Some early treatises described marks for fast (*c* for *celeritas*), slow (*t* for *trahere* or *tarditas*), and ritard (*x* for *expectare*, "to linger"), but by about 1000 the rhythmic delineation of the chant was on the wane; a generation

---

[2] Quoted in Julius Portnoy, *The Philosopher and Music*, New York: The Humanities Press, 1954, p. 49.

[3] *Ibid.*, p. 50.

[4] *Ibid.*

[5] *Ibid.*, p. 52.

[6] Dom Gregory Murray, *Gregorian Chant According to the Manuscripts*, London: L. J. Cary, 1963, p. 20.

later, Aribo stated that "proportional singing" had been "dead for a long time—even buried!" [7] About 1270, Jerome of Maravia specified that chant was regular and steady and that the pulse was about 125 to the minute; [8] this is a good pace, faster than many performances of recent years.

The first of the three periods of creative activity concentrated on the Mass Propers and can be represented by the offertory "Exsulta satis." Although this offertory was written for a penitential Mass (Ember Saturday of Advent), it is a fairly ornate melodic expression—its free rhythmic and phrase structure reflects the prose text, which is more flexible than a poetic one would be.

The Proper of the Mass

The melody of "Exsulta satis" is average in range—d to d^1, ending on e. The phrase endings reveal a basically falling line, which is further borne out by the placement of the single d^1 toward the end of the long first phrase and the quiet descent over the last nineteen notes.

Decoration appears as repeated notes and as passing or turning figures. A feature of plainchant compositions is the long, almost autonomous phrase, called a *melisma*, sung on the vowel of one syllable. An important means of expression, melismas gave further significance to important words; in Example 11, they are provided for *Sion, Jerusalem,* and *tuus* (thou), with melismatic extensions on *exsulta* and *salvator.*

[7] *Ibid.,* p. 7.
[8] Armand Machabey, *La musicologie,* Paris: Presses Universitaires de France, 1962, p. 66.

Exsulta satis   Example 11
ANONYMOUS

Example 11 (continued)

ec - ce Rex tu - us ve - nit ti
- bi san - ctus et sal - va - tor.

Offertory for the Saturday in Ember Week of Advent. The rhythmic version is from a manuscript from the monastery of St. Gall and represents the rhythmic practice of c. 900. The text reads, "Rejoice abundantly, daughter of Sion: shout joyfully daughter of Jerusalem: behold, unto you comes the King, the Holy One and Savior." (Reproduced from *Gregorian Chant According to the Manuscripts*, Dom Gregory Murray, by permission of the publishers, L. J. Cary & Co. Ltd., London.)

The Alleluia

The most cherished melisma of the Church was the jubilus—the name in itself is a tribute to its power and beauty as an outpouring of joy. It was sung on the last syllable of the alleluia, that joyful shout unto the Lord that followed the gradual in feasts of rejoicing.

The Easter Mass is perhaps the epitome of joy in the Christian heart; the Easter gradual, "Haec dies quam fecit Dominus" (This is a day that the Lord hath made), is relatively long and melismatic itself and is followed by the alleluia.

The Easter alleluia, in its form as sung at St. Gall in about 900, is shown in Example 12. It comprises a long alleluia and jubilus, which is sung twice, and the alleluia verse "Pascha nostrum immolatus est Christus" (Christ our Passover is sacrificed); both are sung responsorially, between the cantor (soloist) and the schola (choir).

The large, high range is typical of the way joy was expressed in plainsong; the work spans the tenth f–a^1, which has both a larger ambitus and a higher tessitura than the offertory "Exsulta satis."

Alleluia, Pascha Nostrum   **Example 12**

ANONYMOUS

Al - le - lu - ia.

Example 12 (continued)

Alleluia and verse for Easter Sunday. The rhythmic version has been made from a manuscript from the monastery of St. Gall and represents the rhythmic practice of c. 900. The text reads, "Christ our Passover is sacrificed." (Reproduced from *Gregorian Chant According to the Manuscripts*, Dom Gregory Murray, by permission of the publishers, L. J. Cary & Co. Ltd., London.)

Sequence and Trope

The Easter gradual was followed by a *sequence*, or *prosa de sequentia* ("further," or "following" text; called a *prosa* in parts of France), which was considered an addition to a gradual prayer. (When a sequence did not follow the alleluia verse, the alleluia was repeated.) Early examples were compositions, called *tropes*, that alternated with the phrases of the introit. Such additions to the Mass were composed as soon as the Mass had achieved definitive form, for the essence of the creative spirit is that it constantly proceeds into new expressions as soon as one expression is established. The new phrases were added to various Mass sections as preludes, interludes, postludes, or running interpolations between verses. Sequences drew the full attention of the composers at St. Gall. They are said to have heard them in about 860, sung by a monk from the Abbay de Jumièges, near Rouen, who was fleeing from the Normans.

The excitement of the sequence lay in its affiliation, through Notker and Tuotilo among others, with the secular lyric. Early sequences were experimental, but they tended toward the double (occasionally triple) phrase, which had two (or three) lines of text sung to one musical element, often with a unique line at the beginning, at the end, or both. Such pairs of text lines imply a psalm-like double-verse structure but do not necessarily mean that a standard length was demanded by all verses; thus it is hard to classify early sequence texts as either prose or poetry. But the double phrase was extremely useful musically and it prospered.

The writing of sequences took on great importance, and, with the encouragement of art and fashion, so many were added to the service that the Mass became unconscionably long and its central meaning deflected. By 1500 there were several hundred sequences; the Church took action. The Council of Trent (1545–1563) eliminated all but four for general use, allowing a fifth for use by the Dominicans in the Mass of the Dominican Rite. A sixth was incorporated in 1727.

Sequences Remaining in the Roman Liturgy
(in their order within the Liturgical Year)

Laetabundus is for Christmas (used in the Dominican Rite). An eleventh-century work, it was a model, not only for a hundred or more sequences, but also for two trouvère works and fifteenth-century German and English songs.

Victimae Paschali laudes is for Easter Sunday; it is an eleventh-century work attributed to Wipo, a Burgundian. A classical form, it opens with a single line and proceeds in pairs of lines of varying lengths. The German chorale "Christ ist erstanden" (Christ is risen) derived from it.

Veni Sancte Spiritus is for Pentecost (Whitsunday, the seventh Sunday after Easter). Called the "golden sequence," it is attributed variously to King Robert the Pious (d. 1031); to Innocent III (d. 1216); to Stephen Langton (d. 1228), Archbishop of Canterbury; and to St. Thomas Aquinas (d. 1274).

Lauda Sion is for Corpus Christi (the Thursday eleven days after Pentecost), which is a feast established in the thirteenth century. St. Thomas Aquinas wrote both the Divine Office and the Mass for this feast, including the sequence, which he patterned after those of Adam of St. Victor.

Stabat Mater is for the feast of the Seven Sorrows of the Blessed Virgin Mary (September 15). Probably by Jacopone da Todi, though sometimes attributed to St. Bonaventure (1221–1274), it was interdicted at the Council of Trent but was reintroduced in 1727, after which it became extremely popular.

Dies Irae is for the Mass for the Dead, obligatory for burial Masses and optional at memorial Masses and the feast of All Souls (November 2).

The most famous sequence is the "Dies Irae," not only because of its beauty and strength of text and music, but also because it was heard so much more often than the others. It is perhaps the most widely known of all plainsong works. The Missa pro Defunctis, or Mass for the Dead (also known as the Requiem Mass, for the opening word of the introit), was sung at all funerals and many commemorations and thus was heard many times during each year, whereas other Masses were sung only once a year or were limited to a season.

The "Dies Irae" is comparatively late, dating from the thirteenth century, and came from Italy. Thus, instead of stemming from a monastically centered time and comprising an experimental prose form, it stemmed from a period of secular revival and lay interest and was a product of a well-established poetic art. Thomas a Celano, to whom the work is ascribed, was deeply involved with the Italian religious revival, which produced sacred and secular works that bent toward each other and shared energy and techniques.

The sequence is addressed to the lay churchman, for its text (Day of Wrath) is hardly one that would mirror monastic thought, in which death was viewed as a happy entrance into heaven. It has remained in the Roman funeral Mass for 700 years, exercising a strong pull on composers of many eras. The melody has been used in modern times by such composers as Berlioz, Liszt, Saint-Saëns, Rachmaninoff, and Cooper.

The Hymn

The hymn is an older form than the sequence and remained popular even after the decline of the sequence. "Ut queant laxis" is a hymn written in the eighth century (c. 770), by John the Deacon, for the feast of St. John the Baptist. It was very popular for several centuries and is still in the liturgy. It displays remarkable subtleties of form.

The stanza form of seven short lines—the refrain, *Sancte Ioannes* ("O Holy John"), is the seventh—is reflected in the musical structure of seven puncti (*a b c d e f*). The total range is the sixth *c* to *a*, a conservative one, and the form is basically an arch with an asymmetrical apex in the sixth phrase. The rise toward the apex is emphasized, not only by the shift

Ut Queant Laxis   Example 13

JOHN THE DEACON

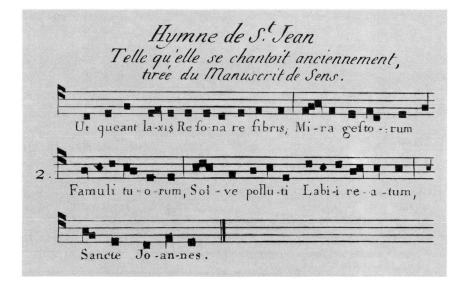

This is a facsimile from Jean-Jacques Rousseau's *Dictionnaire de Musique*, an eighteenth-century dictionary. (Photo by R. E. Kalmbach.)

from the low part of the range in the first and second phrases to the upper part in the sixth, but also by each phrase's beginning on a higher tone, leading to a culmination on *a* in the sixth phrase. The final phrase is set off by its gentle descent and its turn around the final *d* before closing on it.

In general, surviving Ordinaries date from the later periods of plainchant composition—the eleventh and twelfth centuries. The five items of the Ordinary represent long prose texts—Credo and Gloria—and short, repeated invocations—Kyrie, Sanctus, and Agnus Dei.

The Ordinary of the Mass

The Credo is not only long but difficult; it is a complex official confession of faith intended by its authors to be a precise definition of Christian belief—a philosophical statement, not a lyric text. The Gloria, known as the greater doxology, is also long and also prose but is an exalted raising of the heart in joy and praise—much more lyric in essential quality than the Credo. Both are set in long punctus forms, with one phrase for each unit of the text and with little repetition.

The Sanctus, in contrast, is a short, free statement of awe and praise, which begins the Canon.

Sanctus, Sanctus, Sanctus,	Holy, Holy, Holy,
Dominus Deus Sabaoth.	Lord God of Hosts.
Pleni sunt caeli et terra gloria tua.	Heaven and earth are full of thy glory.
Hosanna in excelsis.	Hosanna in the highest!
Benedictus qui venit in nomine Domini.	Blessed is he who comes in the name of the Lord.
Hosanna in excelsis.	Hosanna in the highest.

The Benedictus is contained in the Sanctus but was often separated from it for musical purposes. *Hosanna in excelsis* served almost as a refrain in such cases.

The Agnus Dei, the final invocation of the musical Ordinary before the Communion, is a tighter form.

Agnus Dei, qui tollis peccata mundi, miserere nobis.	Lamb of God, who take away the sins of the world, have mercy on us.
Agnus Dei, qui tollis peccata mundi, miserere nobis.	Lamb of God, who take away the sins of the world, have mercy on us.
Agnus Dei, qui tollis peccata mundi, dona nobis pacem.	Lamb of God, who take away the sins of the world, grant us peace.

At Masses for the dead, *miserere nobis* is replaced by *dona eis requiem* ("grant them rest") and the third response by *dona eis requiem sempiternam* ("grant them eternal rest"). The verses of the Agnus Dei are two-part, Psalm-like structures. Like that of the Sanctus, the text of the Agnus Dei is halfway between prose and poetry, rising, through repetition and emotional force, to a direct, simple eloquence.

The Kyrie is the simplest and most symmetrical of the Mass items, perhaps of all plainsong literature. In contrast to the language of the rest of Roman Church song, which is Latin, its text is Greek.

Kyrie, eleison.	Lord, have mercy.
Kyrie, eleison.	Lord, have mercy.
Kyrie, eleison.	Lord, have mercy.
Christe, eleison.	Christ, have mercy.
Christe, eleison.	Christ, have mercy.
Christe, eleison.	Christ, have mercy.
Kyrie, eleison.	Lord, have mercy.
Kyrie, eleison.	Lord, have mercy.
Kyrie, eleison.	Lord, have mercy.

Its humble petition for mercy without excuse or justification led directly to the prayers on days of sorrow or penitence; on days of joyous feasts, the Kyrie is followed immediately by the Gloria, so that man's petition for mercy is dramatically opposed to his glorification of God in the greater doxology.

The repetitions in the Sanctus and Agnus Dei draw forth musical settings that reflect the texts in musically valid structures. But of all the items of the Ordinary, the Kyrie represents most beautifully the tighter symmetrical forms of plainchant, for the repetitions are so constant and so much the essence of the text that the composer faces a fascinating problem. The whole Kyrie could be composed as one musical phrase in nine statements or with a changed beginning for the *Christe*, but most are much more complex and seek significant patterns of repetition to add artistic counterpart and emotionally well-founded resonance to the stark text. Many forms and expressions were produced for the Kyrie, reflecting the myriad interior recollections that such a prayer can evoke.

Thirty Kyrie settings appear in the *Liber Usualis*; they offer an amazingly wide scope of form, length, and expression. The pattern most often found is that represented by "Orbis Factor," Kyrie XI in the *Liber Usualis*. (A variant version appears as Kyrie X in the chants *ad libitum*.)

In "Orbis Factor," four phrases are used. The first is sung three times, for the first three *Kyrie eleison* lines (indicated by *iij*, the old form of the Roman numeral III); the second is also sung three times, for the three *Christe eleison* lines. The first phrase returns for the second set of *Kyrie eleison* lines but is sung only twice (*ij*), and a longer final phrase, to be sung only once, serves for the last *Kyrie eleison*. In this example, there is not only a return to the opening *Kyrie* but a constant *eleison* for all nine verses (unusual in the settings).

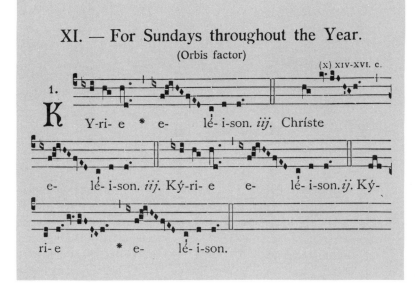

Example 14A. Kyrie "Orbis factor," a facsimile from the *Liber Usualis.* (Courtesy of the Pierpont Morgan Library and Desclée and Company.)

Orbis Factor

ANONYMOUS

Example 14B

The title, "Orbis factor" (Creator of the globe), derives from a trope associated with the tune. Although the trope has long since fallen into disuse, its text remains to identify this particular setting of the Kyrie.

PLAINCHANT STYLE

The scope of form and expression in sacred monophony is astonishing. It is difficult to generalize concerning chant, save to say that it is a rich and marvelous art that continually reveals new insights to those who study it. No summary can convey its variety, and even an attempt to suggest its main forms is dangerous, because this necessitates categorizing an art that is by nature free. Syllabic and melismatic styles; tightly wrought and free forms; answering phrases, variations, and extensions; the prosaic Psalm tone and the melodic parabola—all are there.

The language of chant is a vocal one—not always verbal, as the jubilus demonstrates—and uses the vocal range. Like secular monophony, plainsong is based on the fourth and fifth with an emphasis on any tone within them. The octave is far from sacrosanct but is a good average, and the final is likely to be somewhere within it (sometimes at the bottom, but not at the top), approached most frequently by step from either above or below. Mass IV ends both its Agnus Dei and dismissal with the progression f to d. The Easter Gradual, "Haec Dies," ends on a, approached from c^1. The Church recognized finals on d, e, f, and g, but finals on a, though not frequent, are not uncommon. All phrase finals of the Kyrie "Dominator Deus" are b, with the first eight ending $a–b$, the last $d^1–b$. Within the Divine Office, all finals are found.

The written versions of plainsong are less ornate than secular songs, but we do not know how closely solo performers adhered to the written forms and how much improvised ornamentation or variation they added. However, a good proportion of plainsong was performed in choir, and choral singing would have made improvised ornamentation difficult and unlikely.

Yet plainchant is far from spare; almost all the literature is filled out with surrounding, passing, and repeated notes and cambiata figures, all of which could be decorative in function. The jubilus is really a long and intense embellishment of the alleluia.

PERFORMANCE OF SACRED SONG

The chant of the Christian Church played a vital part in religious life, centering first in the monastery and then, from about the middle of the twelfth century, in the cathedral and the royal chapel. The principles of its performance were parallel to those of secular music of the time, but the chants were conceived for performance in church buildings rather than out of doors or in a castle yard or hall. Like the magnificent structures in which it was brought to life, chant was a marvel of line, color, and contrasts in space.

Even when sung by a single voice, chant was enriched by the reverberations of the sanctuary stones and vaults in the shadowy, candlelit silence by night and in the color-dappled silence by day. And, like its secular counterpart, plainsong was presented with all the variety of sound and effect that its performers could devise.

First in techniques of performance was the alternation of phrases between soloist and group (responsorial) or between equal groups (antiphonal). A monastery choir was generally split into two equal groups facing each other from the sides of a wide central aisle, with the altar at the head of the aisle. For singing the Psalms, a soloist within the choir was chosen. The office was held for only a week (hence the name *hebdomodarian*, from the Greek *hebdomas*, meaning "seven") and was rotated among the members of the choir. The soloist sang the first verse, thus setting the pitch, after which the two sides of the choir alternated verses. The whole choir could, of course, join for certain effects, such as for a unison response to complete a Psalm with a full Gloria Patri. In certain sections of the Mass, the celebrant sang the opening phrase and was answered by half or all of the choir.

Considerable variety was possible. Both monastery and cathedral churches used boys as well as men, which added a higher octave and a contrasting quality of sound. Processions—using complex patterns of entering, walking together in figure eights in the sanctuary, or splitting to go around the church in mirror patterns—introduced motion and enabled added effects by having the sounds emanate from many locations. In the cathedral, the congregation was absorbed into the very center of the music. Many of these practices continue to the present day.

Instruments were also customary both in the choir loft and in procession, except at a limited number of solemn feasts where their silence was symbolic. But because the early Church fathers had outlawed the instruments associated with Roman excesses (of which the organ had been one of the offenders), other instruments, particularly string, brass, and percussion (because of their frequent mention in Scripture), enjoyed the earliest and strongest hold on liturgical performance. By the twelfth century, Pope Calixtus II (1119–1124) wrote of the common use of instruments at Spanish cathedral services, "Some sing to the accompaniment of the cithara, others to the lyre, some to the timbrel [drum], others to the flute, fife, harp, viola, the British and Welsh harp and crwth [a bowed string], and many other musical instruments." [9]

Extramusical effects were common—and often dramatic. In London in the twelfth century, a dove pulling a burning tow, to symbolize the tongues of fire descending on the apostles, was let down through a hole in the vault at St. Paul's during the singing of the hymn "Veni Creator Spiritus" at

[9] Pope Calixtus II, in D. Stevens (ed.), *Spanish Medieval Music*, Decca Record, DL 9416.

Pentecost. At the cathedral of Laon, the Slaughter of the Innocents was acted out liturgically and symbolically. Even earlier, clerics at the priory of La Croix (which was under the administration of the great monastery at Cluny) were acting out the life of Saint Nicholas. In 1080 the practice was suppressed by the prior because "it was not the traditional Cluniac chant, but the playful [*jocularia*] composition of secular clerks"; [10] however, it was soon revived. It is known that such liturgical enactments of episodes from the Scriptures or from the lives of saints gave rise to dramatic forms that are an important antecedent to modern theater art. The Easter Sepulchre (the staging of the Easter-morning discovery of Christ's empty tomb), done at Matins on Easter Sunday, was particularly important in this connection.

In addition, the acted versions of mystery and miracle plays, although actually secular productions (often sponsored, even composed, by local guild members), were given sanction by the Church. Although such productions were presented in monastic churches, the rise of religious drama is more properly associated with the cathedral churches and with town life.

Thus in church music, many effects were sought during the era of plainsong, not only from the alternation and combination of musical forces, but also from the fusion of musical effects with visual and other esthetic elements. At the Easter vigil service, for example, the preliminary rituals began in darkness, the statuary symbolically covered with purple shrouds, instruments silent, the alter stripped, and the vestments somber. The service proceeded to the symbolic lighting of candles (one for each communicant) from the center Easter candle, the pealing of the bells at the Gloria, the change of the clergy to white and gold vestments, the dressing of the altar with cloths and flowers, the removal of the shrouds from the statuary, the burning of incense, the sounding of instruments, and the singing of the Easter vigil Mass with the first sound of the alleluia intoned three times by the celebrant on ever-rising pitches—an ever-expanding revelation of the joy of the Feast of the Resurrection.

[10] George G. Coulton, *Medieval Panorama*, New York: Meridian Books, Inc., 1955, p. 600.

Some Composers of Sacred Song

Composers of sacred song for the most part remained anonymous. Moreover, because of the importance of the texts, the composers were not always mentioned, and those that were may have written only the texts. Of the earlier composers, most of those known were famous for their secular as well as their sacred music. But toward the end of the period of plainchant composition, the anonymity favored by religious dedication gave way to a more worldly pleasure in artistic recognition.

NOTKER BALBULUS (c. 840–912), called the Stammerer, was born near St. Gall at Elgg, Switzerland. He was a monk, teacher, and theorist at St. Gall and renowned as a secular poet. A kind man and much admired in his own day, he was beatified in 1513 and is important as the first great writer of sequences.

TUOTILO (d. 915), a monk at St. Gall and a friend of Notker Balbulus, was a minstrel and stone carver. He is known as a composer of tropes, among them "Cunctipotens Genitor Deus," which gave its name to the Kyrie it once adorned.

WIPO (c. 1000–1048), a Burgundian priest and chaplain to the German emperor Heinrich III, is known as a composer of sequences. Among those he wrote is the Easter sequence "Victimae paschali laudes."

HERMANNUS CONTRACTUS (Herman the Cripple, 1013–1054) was a theorist and composer at the monastery of Reichenau at Lake Constance (Switzerland). A composer of antiphons, he is known particularly for his songs to the Virgin (the Marian antiphons). These include the "Alma redemptoris mater" and the "Salve Regina" (two of the four used at Compline); the latter of these Marian antiphons is one of the most popular prayers of the Church today.

BRUNO, COUNT OF EGISHEIM (d. 1054) was Pope Leo IX from 1048. He wrote a Gloria in the eighth mode, which is one of the few Mass portions whose author is known. It is the first Gloria of the "Cantus ad libitum" in the *Liber Usualis*.

ADAM OF ST. VICTOR (c. 1110–1177) was, from c. 1130, a monk at the Abbaye de Saint-Victor at Paris. He introduced the formal, rhymed, metrical sequence, of which he left over 40 examples.

THOMAS A CELANO (c. 1200–1256), a friend of St. Francis of Assisi and St. Francis's first biographer, was also a composer of sequences. The sequence for the Requiem Mass (Mass for the Dead), "Dies Irae" (Day of Wrath), which is probably the most widely known plainsong melody, is generally ascribed to him.

(ST.) THOMAS AQUINAS (1227–1274), an Italian theologian and teacher, was called The Angelic Doctor by the Church. He taught at the newly founded University of Paris and is known to be the author of the sequence "Lauda Sion" (for Corpus Christi, a new feast for which St. Thomas prepared the Mass) and the hymn "Pange Lingua." Both St. Thomas and Pope Innocent III are thought to be the writers of "Veni Sancte Spiritus," the "golden sequence" (for Pentecost).

JACOPONE DA TODI (c. 1230–1306) was an Umbrian of noble birth and a wealthy lawyer. After his wife's early death, he became a Franciscan monk. He was known as a secular composer as well as a composer of laude and sequences, of which the "Stabat Mater" is the most famous.

Turn and consider this in your mind, that Music and Harmony unite and accord divers things and contrary.

BARTHOLOMAEUS ANGLICUS *

Philosophy and Theory

The study of music was much broader in Medieval and Renaissance scholarship than it is for us today. According to the earlier view of life and the world, existence was a continuing compromise or reconciliation between extreme and opposing forces. To yield to any one of these forces would create imbalance, and to give in entirely would mean destruction. For the human body, the commonly cited opposites were wet-dry and hot-cold, but any extreme—drowning, dehydrating, burning, or freezing—would result in death, whereas life was maintained within a small range between the extremes. Other human forces were recognized: the body versus the spirit or

4

* Thirteenth century. Quoted in H. H. Carter (ed.), "Armonie, III," *A Dictionary of Middle English Musical Terms*, Bloomington, Ind.: Indiana University Press, p. 17.

soul, the active versus the contemplative life, individuality versus conformity (yielding to individuality was conceived of as insanity, called *alienation* until the end of the nineteenth century). In the physical world, there were such opposing forces as action versus inaction, heaviness versus lightness, night versus day, and matter versus energy (the extremes of which were defined as the immovable object and the irresistable force).

Proportion and harmony were the keys to maintaining a viable compromise, and virtually all problems that men faced were defined and attacked with reference to them. The "harmony of heavenly bodies," which has so often been misunderstood, was the belief that the balanced proportion of astronomical forces and counterforces kept the earth in the sky. Alchemy was not a quest for sudden wealth but the philosopher's search for the perfectly proportioned substance (gold) through a harmony of chemical processes.

Music, as we conceive it, was a reflection of the life force and was studied seriously by philosophers for what it might reveal concerning that which it reflected. Most music texts were written by philosophers, who dealt first with *musica divina* (the harmony of God and His creation). Man was seen as a harmony of the angelic and the bestial—the angel was rational but not animate, the beast was animate but not rational. Christ, seen as true God and true Man, was the perfect harmony. Divinity was perfect in another way—being three in one, it contained all in itself and was perfect in proportion. Second, philosophers were concerned with *musica mundana* (the harmony of the earth as a physical body); this study included, among other things, what we now think of as astronomy and geology. Next, there was *musica humana* (the harmony of man as a spiritual and bodily being), which included anatomy, medicine, and psychology. And finally, there was *musica instrumentalis* (perceivable music), in which proportions were audible and physically measurable.

On the one hand, music was viewed as a moral and therapeutic force. Man, while listening to harmonious proportions of sound, would vibrate harmoniously within himself. On the other hand, the science of music could illuminate, by analogy, the more cosmic harmonies and reveal truths about God, the world, and man. "Without music no scientific discipline can be perfect," wrote Isidore of Seville (565–636); [1] he used *music* to mean the search for proportion. Harmony was balanced proportion, either general or musical; musically, it meant the proportion of word and melody, of high and low within the melody, of voice and instrument, of melody and tone quality. It did not imply, directly or indirectly, its modern meaning.

The strength of the pervasive definition of harmony and proportion is not to be underestimated. As late as the eighteenth century, books on musical composition still began with diagrams of astronomical proportions and

[1] Quoted in Paul Henry Lang, *Music in Western Civilization*, New York: Norton, 1941, P. 59.

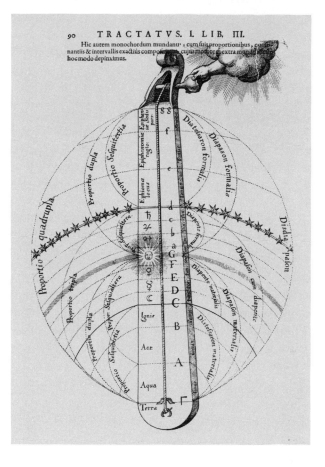

A geometric representation of musical intervals in the Medieval manner, from a seventeenth-century text, *Utriusque Cosmi*, by Robert Fludd. The music of the spheres, or the harmony of creation, tuned by the hand of God, identifies the notes of music with the planets. (Courtesy of Dr. Eugene Helm.)

still likened the harmony of high and low pitches (meaning melody) to the harmony of spiritual and physical man. The treatise *De Institutione Musica*, written by the philosopher Boethius (c. 475–c. 525), was still being used in the nineteenth century as a music text at Oxford University.

Such a philosophy provided secure underpinnings for the delight in contrasts that was the essence of Medieval performance. The carole, the estampie, the rondeau, the antiphonal chants of both the Mass and the Office, and the blending of performing groups, instruments, and locations— all these techniques represent harmonious proportionings of opposing elements.

THE HEXACHORD SYSTEM

Examination of the music of Medieval monophony, both secular and sacred, reveals the sophistication and fluidity of Medieval musical materials. The basic unit was the *hexachord* (from the Greek *hexa–*, "six," and *–chord*, a

The Hexachord

71

"string" or "note")—six notes in which two groups of two whole tones symmetrically surround a smaller interval, a semitone. The entire hexachord was spelled *c–d–e–f–g–a*, or (*c–d–e*)–(*f–g–a*). The semitone was called *diatonic* (from the Greek *dia–*, "between" or "across," and *ton*, "tone").

The hexachord was a subtle structure; it was conceived as tuned from *F* by fifths (*F–C–G–D–A–E*), so that all the seconds were of like size. Each fifth, as the second and third partials of a supposed fundamental, can be mathematically represented 2:3; thus $F–c = 2:3$ and $c–g = 2:3$, so the ninth $F–g = 4:9$ and the second $f–g = 8:9$. All seconds were derived in the same way, with all of them 8:9 except for the diatonic semitone, *e–f*, which is a remainder (27:32). The major thirds could result only from two seconds, each 8:9, and were thus reckoned as 64:81 ($8:9 \times 8:9$), a dissonance. The structure is just the sort of balanced system that the Medieval mind delighted in.

As implied by the use of more than one register, the hexachord could be repeated at the upper and double octaves. Such an extension left a gap between the top tone of one hexachord and the lowest note of the next.

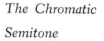

The Chromatic Semitone

The gap between *a* and c^1 (as between a^1 and c^2) was filled by a variable note with two alternative inflections or intonations. One was high, or, as it was then called, hard; the other was low, or soft. We would refer to the two intonations as *B*-natural and *B*-flat, but in the Medieval scale, both were written and named simply *B*. The tone *B* in both inflections, hard and soft, was called the *chromatic*, or colored, *semitone* because of its varying pitch. When taken hard (in Latin, *durum*), it lay a semitone below *C*; when taken soft (in Latin, *molle*), it lay a semitone above *A*; and there was a semitone between its two forms.

This tone was of crucial importance throughout the Medieval and Renaissance periods and was discussed and given special treatment as late as the seventeenth and early eighteenth centuries. The hard *B* (*B*-durum), written ♮, was also called *quadrum* (square); the soft *B* (*B*-molle), written ♭, was also called *rotundum* (round). Separate type fonts were used for the two forms well into the eighteenth century. This convention of notation led to our natural and flat signs, for the ♮-durum and ♭-rotundum were to become *B*♮ and *B*♭ in Western European tradition. But in Eastern Europe and in the German language, the soft inflection became known as *B* and the hard inflection became known as *H*, as it still is. This change (♮ to *H*) may well reflect the fact that the letter *H* in Gothic uncial script was written ♮ . The German terms *dur* (major), *mol* (minor), and *bemol* (flat) also derive from this vocabulary.

The central significance of the tone B is that for a thousand years it had alternative intonations and was apart from the notes in the hexachord. But, although the B was not considered a note of the basic unit, it was a note in the system. It was a colored tone of optimal inflection whose contributions—flexibility and opalescence—to the materials of the art were extremely important to the effect of the music.

As late as 1598, Thomas Morley, in the first chapter of his text *A Plaine and Easie Introduction to Practicall Musicke*, began his definition of the scale with "There be in music but six notes." [2] This may seem strange, because all chromatic tones were in use by then. Yet it is no more strange than to say a Mozart symphony is in C major, to spell the C-major scale, and then to realize that many chromatic tones occur during the course of the symphony. At any rate, to Morley the hexachord was still the scale, whereas B and B-flat were the chromatic semitone.

The fluidity and subtlety of the scale were strong assets, and certainly as an esthetic entity, these Medieval materials would be hard to improve on. The chief difficulty was a practical one—because the two forms of B were used freely, with no distinction of notation between them, individual performers were free to sing B either hard or soft, as they pleased. The result in a choir is easy to imagine.

Guido's Gamut

Just after the turn into the second millennium, Guido d'Arezzo, a monk, devised a system of instruction that could differentiate in rehearsals between the hard and soft B. Guido was of the right generation to organize the musical materials of Medieval music, for notation of music on a staff was becoming a regular practice and the expansion of musical structure in polyphony made the training of choirboys a matter of renewed importance. In his text, the *Micrologus* (c. 1025), Guido set down the whole range of the adult male voice, G to e^2 (bass to countertenor), in a system that has been called *Guido's scale* ever since. This system incorporated the basic concepts of practical musical vocabulary, analysis, and pedagogy that were to be used, with several expansions, at least through the sixteenth century (a considerable heritage still remains). It was Guido's chief purpose to present the choirmaster with a simple, practical means to achieve unanimity in singing and to lessen the time needed to learn new music.

Using the popular hymn to St. John the Baptist, "Ut queant laxis" (Example 13, page 61), whose first six lines begin on the six consecutive degrees of the hexachord, Guido assigned to each tone of the scale the syllable of the hymn text with which each line begins. The six syllables could

2 Thomas Morley, A *Plain and Easy Introduction to Practical Music* (R. A. Harman, ed.), London: Dent, 1952, p. 13.

be used as a teaching aid, for they could stand for a set series of relation-ships (notation had no absolute pitch references at that time).

Whole-step relationships were represented by *ut-re, re-mi, fa-sol,* and *sol-la,* whereas the diatonic semitone was always *mi-fa.* The first syllable, *ut,* was changed to *do* shortly after 1600, when singers began to use the scale not for sight-reading but for practicing vocal patterns (*ut* was not an easy syllable for vocalizing). The seventh syllable, *si* (later *ti* in America, but still *si* in Europe) came into general use at about the same time. It was derived from *Sancto Ioannes,* the refrain of "Ut queant laxis."

With Guido's syllables and using the soft B, or ♭-molle, it was pos-sible to sing the same set of relationships beginning on *f.*

This hexachord, made possible only through the use of the soft inflection of ♭, was called the *hexachordum rotundum* or *hexachordum molle.*

Conversely, by using the hard B, or ♮-durum, it was possible to sing the same set of relationships beginning on *g.*

This hexachord, made possible only through the use of the hard inflection of ♮, was therefore called the *hexachordum quadrum* or *hexachordum durum.* With the introduction of the terms *hexachordum molle* and *hexa-chordum durum,* the original hexachord, on *c,* was called the *hexachordum naturale.* Thus, by designating B to be sung either in the hard or soft hexa-chord, the choir director could achieve unanimous intonation relatively easily.

The notes of the scale consisted of the usual Latin letter names (be-ginning with A) preceded by a single note a whole tone lower, which was called the Greek Γ (gamma). Each note was lined up with its possible uses in the various hexachords.

The full names of the tones consisted of their letter names plus their possible syllabic uses, as read from the top to the bottom of the accompanying representation. For example, the top note, e^2, was called *e-la* (or, as written in Latin, *ela*), whereas the *e* and e^1 were called *e-la-mi* (or *elami*). The lowest *d* was *d-sol-re* (*dsolre*), d^1 was *d-la-solre* (*dlasolre*), and the high d^2 was *d-la-sol* (*dlasol*). Thus, a distinction in register could often be made. A further distinction was made by naming the three octaves, from Γ, *graves*, *acutae*, and *superacutae* (low, high, and very high). Note that *b* and b^1 can be either ♭ *-fa* or ♮ *-mi*, depending on whether it was sung soft or hard; also, the lowest *B* can only be hard. The lowest note of Guido's scale, Γ-*ut* (gamma-*ut*), was the name of the entire system and gave us the word *gamut*.

The Guidonian System

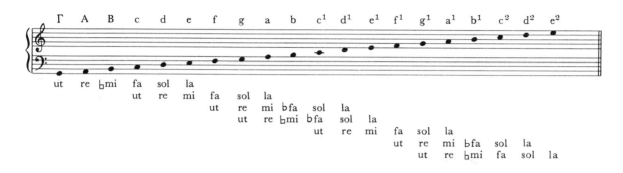

In Guido's system, it was possible to go from the bottom to the top of the gamut by *mutation* from hard to natural to soft hexachords. In a mutation, a note is approached as a member of one hexachord but taken as a member of another. For example, to go beyond the range of the six notes, when singing within the hard hexachord *g* to e^1, the singer would approach e^1 as *la* but sing it as *mi* in the natural hexachord, thus opening his path to continue upward to a^1. If he wished to go even higher, he would take a^1, which he had approached as though it were *la*, either as *mi* in the soft hexachord or *re* in the hard.

Johannes Tinctoris (c. 1435–1511), in his dictionary *Terminorum Musicæ Diffinitorum* (c. 1475), listed eighteen mutations; typical is the one in which *C* is approached as *sol* in the soft hexachord and taken as *fa* in the hard.

Sol fa est mutatio quæ fit in csolfaut et in csolfa, ad descendendum de ♭ molli in ♮ durum.	*Sol-fa* is the mutation that is made on c-sol-fa-ut and on c-sol-fa, in order to descend from the soft to the hard hexachord.[3]

[3] Carl Parrish, *Dictionary of Musical Terms by Johannes Tinctoris*, New York: Free Press, 1963, p. 59.

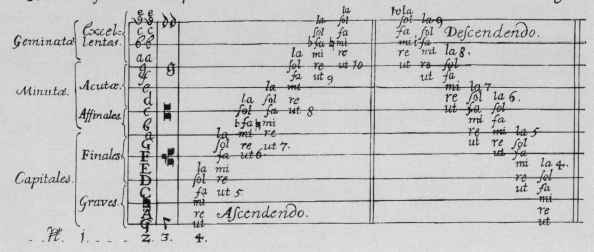

The Guidonian system (the gamut) as taught at the beginning of the eighteenth century. The *B-fa* and *B-mi* were written as flat and natural signs, but the overlapping hexachords were essentially the same as they had been for over 600 years. (J. B. Samber, *Elucidated Music Choralis*, 1701. Courtesy of the University of Michigan Library. Photo by R. E. Kalmbach.)

Note that this mutation is not possible on the low *c*, because *c* cannot be *sol*. The term *sol-fa*, or *solfège*, which is still used to mean the practice of reading music in Guido's system, derives from this mutation.

It is clear that Guido's scale described musical materials as notated rather than as performed. In practice, both men and women sang and treble instruments were exceedingly popular, so notes above *e-la* were certainly in common use. But music was written down in the register of male voices; treble instruments were, in modern terms, transposing instruments.

Even before Guido's time, concepts of register had been considered in relation to the manners in which tunes used particular areas of the gamut. These manners were called *modes*. Three factors had to be considered in regard to mode: What sector of the gamut did the melody use? What tone did it dwell on or center in? And what tone did it end on (in relation to the sector used)? Discussions of sacred chant concerned these factors, and theorists described eight modes; these were never rigidly conceived but were generalizations useful in discussing tunes. Although the modes had no reference to secular music or to polyphonic writing, there were occasional (unsuccessful) attempts to restrict sacred monophony to a conservative, pre-

Mode

76

scribed usage. The Church defined ecclesiastical modes and classified plain-chant accordingly.

The octave, a convenient but by no means definitive range, was thought to have two possible divisions. Neither division was in the center—a concept often encountered in Medieval and Renaissance theory, which enjoyed asymmetry. The *natural division* of the octave, according to the overtone series, was a fifth plus a fourth, such as d–a–d^1; this was also known as the *harmonic* or *authentic* division. The other division was called the *arithmetic* or *plagal* division; in it, the two intervals are reversed to a fourth plus a fifth (d–g–d^1). It does not exist in the overtone series of D but can be deduced simply and logically through mathematical procedures. These two divisions of the octave carry deep implications, because they recognized two ways of using the octave. The harmonic division (d–a–d^1) derives from the funda-mental D and is concerned with that musical reality, defined by the fifth d–a. The arithmetic derives from the fundamental G and is equally con-cerned with that musical reality, defined by the fifth g–d^1. The two manners of dealing with the same range invoke an equal distinction in modern tonal usage.

Second to the concern about the octave and its division was the ques-tion of the tone dominating the melody, generally in the sense of its being sounded most often, either by repetition or by frequent returns. The tendency of a melody to rise and fall—called its *modulation* or *harmony* in early writ-ings—in something like an arch, along with its tendency to stress the division of the octave range that serves as its basis of departure, leads to a natural concentration of force on a note relatively high in the range, in standard usage called the *dominant*. The nature of the dominant was strongly related to the octave division.

The last consideration for the concept of mode was the final tone of a chant, called the *finalis*. This tone was most frequently approached by step, most often from above but also from below. The final and its surrounding notes were to be stable tones (theoretically), and the chromatic semitone was to be avoided. Whether or not for this reason, the finals in conservative ecclesiastical theory (but not in actual practice) were limited to the tones for which this held true—d, e, f, and g. Compositions with finals on a, c, and even b were not uncommon, however; adherents to the modal concept called such practice the *modus lascivus*, the "wanton, unregulated manner"—a "nonmode," so to speak.

In ecclesiastical theory, the modes were numbered from I to VIII; they reveal sibling relationships among themselves through range (lined up by the even and then the odd numbers) and finals (in pairs as listed).[4]

The system of modes represents one more Medieval resolution of op-posing forces: range versus placement of the melodic center and final; har-

[4] Dom Gregory Murray, *Gregorian Chant According to the Manuscripts*, London: L. J. Cary, 1963, p. 24. (Chart, courtesy of the publisher.)

MODE	BASIC OCTAVE	DIVISION		DOMINANT	FINAL
I	d–d^1	d–a–d^1	harmonic	a	d
II	A–a	A–d–a	arithmetic	f	d
III	e–e^1	e–b–e^1	harmonic	c^1	e
IV	B–b	B–e–b	arithmetic	a	e
V	f–f^1	f–c^1–f^1	harmonic	c^1	f
VI	c–c^1	c–f–c^1	arithmetic	a	f
VII	g–g^1	g–d^1–g^1	harmonic	d^1	g
VIII	d–d^1	d–g–d^1	arithmetic	c^1	g

monic versus arithmetic divisions; and, doubtless, even theory versus practice, which would have been considered a reasonable harmony in itself.

Modes I, III, V, and VII are *authentic*, because they use the harmonic or authentic division; modes II, IV, VI, and VIII are *plagal*, because they use the arithmetic or plagal division. The modes with finals in the middle are called *hypo*–, meaning "beneath," and are plagal; their melodies extend below the final. For example, all the tracts (the replacements for the alleluia in feasts of sorrow or penitence) in the *Liber Usualis* are in plagal modes. Conversely, the jubilus, which lies above the final, seems to have been associated with joy. "A jubilus," wrote Tinctoris about 1475, "is a melody delivered with a certain high exuberance." [5]

RHYTHM

As with the scale, the rhythm of Medieval monophony is implicit in the musical examples given so far. The basis of the rhythmic concept lies in the rhythm of the word—in poetry or prose in most sacred monophony and in poetry in the secular. Both forms were rhythmic and both were measured—plainchant only in the first millennium—in the sense that proportions of two or three short notes to one long note were established. But most poetic rhythms were conceived within a pulse, regular or free (and represented in these examples by the dotted quarter note), which probably ranged in speed from a leisurely 50 or 54 per minute, for a slow work such as Giraut's Alba, to 72 or 76, for Raimbaut's sprightly May dance (Examples 2 and 3, pages 22 and 24).

Subdivisions of the pulse could be quite complex, but two things are clear: first, the monophonic song took its rhythmic life from the text, which it both supported and enhanced; and second, as long as practice was fairly

[5] Parrish, *op. cit.*, p. 37.

consistent or easily derived from the text, no notation of rhythmic patterns was necessary. The troubadour and trouvère works that have survived in notation are without rhythmic indication.

In addition to the rhythmic aspects of melody, Medieval rhythm had an important life through the use of rhythm instruments. Percussion is mentioned in virtually all kinds of performances—the drum, tambourine, and cymbal appeared in the sanctuary, in the castle hall, and on the village green. In the dance, time was kept (often by a woman with a hand bell) at least a century before dances were written down.

It is not known which kinds of rhythms these instruments played, but it is more than likely that percussionists based their contributions on independent repeated patterns, called *isorhythms* (*iso*– is Greek for "the same"), which are taught by mnemonics all over the world and which are venerable in tradition. Medieval practice was much more universal than modern practice; Western European art still had much in common with Eastern and folk art, in which isorhythms had always played a significant role. Additional support for such a theory is offered by the absence of notated music for the ubiquitous percussions, even after dances were being written down. It is possible that the patterns of the rhythm instruments were sometimes more complex than those of the melodies they accompanied, because they were not limited to a circumscribed vocabulary of notatable patterns and were doubtless often improvised from a ready vocabulary of isorhythms.

The rhythms of percussion, whatever their nature, were of great importance in Medieval performance. They may have helped to define still another pair of opposing elements—the rhythmic versus the melodic—in the polar reconciliations of Medieval philosophy.

THE IDEALS OF MEDIEVAL MONOPHONY

The era of Medieval monophony was of great length and diversity; long after the development of polyphony, plainsong was still being composed. The trouvère art continued to flourish even longer, alongside the writing of polyphonic songs, and it has never really died. However, in spite of the great time span and the variety of type and function in Medieval music, a few points indicate a common ideal, particularly for the music at the end of the period of monophony.

First, concern with melody and rhythm, basically vocal and expressive, and with forms parallel with the texts.

Second, love of color and brilliant sounds, both for their own sake and for the contrasts available through their alternation and combination. Contrast was often related to spatial elements, as in antiphonal groups within a church or in singing and playing for the dance.

Third, the germ of the ideas of musical (rather than verbal) form, emerging

A Medieval graffito from St. Mary's Church at Lydgate, probably from the late fourteenth century. The graffito is a rebus using four notes in the hexachord—*fa, re, mi,* and *la*—followed by the representation of a die (in Latin, *cater*). The rebus reads, *Well-fa-re-mi-la-dy cater-yne,* or Well fare (farewell) my lady catherine. (V. Pritchard, ed., *English Medieval Graffiti,* New York: Cambridge University Press, 1967, p. 147. Courtesy of Cambridge University Press.)

through the very dependencies of the musical art: the building of song through phrases or verses and of dance through puncti or points; the repetition of strains resulting naturally from the marriage of a tight verse form to a melodic line; and the interest in the bipartite or twofold element, both as two musical units asymmetrically repeated in the virelai, rondeau, or singing of the Psalms and as the pair of contrasting endings to be used at the ends of repeated phrases in the estampie.

Most of these characteristics were to remain for three centuries; they were central to the artistic reality of most Medieval music and may even be said to define it in a general way.

Perhaps the greatest concern of the progressive composer late in the Medieval era was the adornment of plainchant through imaginative presentation. At any rate, it was within this framework that the first vertical organization of chant performances took place. Thus it was adornment of the chant that led to polyphony, a development that was to thrive and change Western music more deeply than anyone could have foreseen.

Organum takes to itself the whole of high and low; it runs forward joyfully like a strong soldier, it bursts into song like a high and powerful prince, sounding all the sweeter for subjugating the cantus to its gracious precedence.

ANONYMOUS *

Gothic Polyphony

EARLY POLYPHONY

5

The performance of plainchant in Medieval churches was based on the alternation and combination of mediums and effects—men's voices, boys' voices, and linear and percussion instruments. The elements produced tonal qualities of a remarkable scope: registers in at least two octaves for voices and three for instruments; differences in volume, through the use of different numbers of performers; rhythmic detail, through the use or omission of percussion; and direction or distance by varying the origins of sound.

* Thirteenth century. Quoted in Hugo Riemann, *History of Music Theory*, Lincoln, Nebr.: University of Nebraska Press, 1962, p. 75.

81

Contrasts were conceived of by complete phrases or sections, consistent with the general phrase-section structure of Medieval music. Thus an entire phrase or verse unit was performed the same way in church, an entire double punctus was performed the same way in the dance, an entire burden (or an entire verse) was performed the same way in the carole, and it is likely that an entire stanza was performed the same way in the short troubadour songs. It is equally likely that two consecutive verses or puncti or stanzas would not have been performed alike if change were possible.

Early Organum

There is little difference between singing in octaves, which is natural for men with boys, and singing in fourths or fifths, which is natural with basses and tenors only. Early theorists told of singing in fourths or fifths, named *organum*, which, as might be expected, was described as characteristic only of single phrases. The organum presented a straightforward performance of the phrase in fourths or fifths above or below the plainchant, singly or doubled at the octave, which required a producer (or organizer) and director rather than a composer. Ninth- and tenth-century texts [1] described this kind of organum, which evidently was a well-established type of improvised singing at that time. The voice singing the authorized plainchant section was called the *vox principalis* ("principal voice") and the one singing the added line, the *vox organalis* ("organizing voice")—terms that reflected the view of organum as being a type of performance rather than of composition.

Early organum in essence comprised an orchestration of single chant phrases; it lent new color to the chant, providing further enrichment in the possibilities of presentation. With the chromatic semitone to provide the alternative soft and hard *B*, the bad fourth or fifth (*f–b*, *b–f¹*), called the *tritonus* (three whole tones), could be avoided without other special rules. The tritonus annoyed early theorists, who could not derive it from the proportions they recognized as consonant.

How early the practice of organum began will probably never be known. As long as it remained simple orchestration of chant phrases, it merited no more attention than singing at the octave. But a fourth or fifth is not quite like an octave; it is more difficult to intone and more difficult to begin on without orientation. Whatever the reason, before long musicians preferred to begin with a unison, expand to the fourth or fifth for the bulk of the phrase, and end with a unison.

The natural leavening of creative ideas led to more complicated effects, until the vox organalis became too involved to sing from the single plainchant written line and a separate part had to be notated for it. It is only from that point that we can trace polyphony with any clarity and at that

[1] The most important of these texts are discussed at length in Hugo Riemann, *History of Music Theory*, Lincoln, Nebr.: University of Nebraska Press, 1962, pp. 11–38.

point that organum became the province of the composer. But the function of organum remained the same. Chant itself was sacrosanct, protected by Church authority and religious tradition; however, although it could not be altered, it could be sung slowly, and it could be covered with embellishments like the altars, choir stalls, and windows. Thus it was as embellishment of the continuing body of plainsong that polyphony was introduced.

As the vox organalis became more ornate in the eleventh century, it naturally took to the higher register, where it was capable of greater fluency and was easier to hear. At its height, organum was a twofold musical fabric, composed of the long, sustained lower tones and the quicker, decorative upper ones.

The entire early development of polyphony can be seen as a gradual enhancement of the plainsong phrase within the Medieval ideal of performance. Over several centuries, the chant remained basically stable, while increasingly ornate parts were added to certain phrases. It is important to understand that polyphony in its early stages—through the thirteenth century—did not supplant monophony but developed and remained as one kind of phrase presentation within the Medieval ideal of successive effects in performance.

It is more important to understand this expansion of linear embellishment than to decide at exactly what point the procedure became polyphonic rather than monophonic. The need for the vox organalis to have a separate written part was crucial, but when this occurred is not so easy to determine. For experimentation must precede definition, and we know that improvisation was universal and continuous in the Medieval era. Improvisation of a countermelody to the plainchant was called *cantus supra librum* ("song added to the book"). The surviving written examples do not follow the rules for improvisation outlined by the theorists; it is likely that great freedom was taken in extemporizing and that an awakening desire for deviation from pure parallelism led to written composition.

At the same time that the first polyphonic experiments were being carried out, the rhythmic tradition of the chant itself was fading. Staff notation had been given a definitive form by Guido, but the rhythmic meanings of the old notation were forgotten. Composers were thus free to slow the chant notes to a succession of long, temporally nondescript tones so as to spin out above it a highly ornate vox organalis. The chant phrase chosen for such decoration was called the *tenor*, later also the *cantus firmus* ("fixed chant"; the plural is *cantus firmi*). The vox organalis came to be called the *duplum* ("second part").

The higher tessitura carried well in the huge stone churches and was clear—even brilliant—in sound. The somewhat reedy voice quality admired for its clarity and dexterity in the Medieval era was easier to cultivate in the upper register, and the tenor and countertenor became the voice ranges of organum. Parts of the plainchant had traditionally been sung by the

The Cathedral of Notre Dame, Coutances, France. The gothic style, with its upward thrust and high windows, furnished the setting for the early fulfillment of sacred polyphony. (Courtesy of Martin Hurlimann.)

choir, who continued to sing most monophonic portions of the services. The organa, on the other hand, were sung by soloists. Contemporary texts tell us that the choirmasters kept natural tenors in their own range and trained the men with lower voices as countertenors by use of falsetto.

By the twelfth century, organum had developed as a great musical art, and centers were recognized at St. Martial, in central France, and at Santiago (St. James) de Compostela, in northwestern Spain; both monasteries had already been known as centers of monophonic song. Doubtless a good deal of organum was improvised even then, but about fifty examples survive in manuscript form, providing our oldest heritage of polyphonic works. By then, organum had become a real two-part composition based on a *cantus prius factus* ("song already made or composed"—the cantus firmus). For although

Later Organum

84

the principle of organum remained that of ornamenting a single section of plainsong and using it as one contrasting section, the notes of the tenor had become longer and a brief phrase had turned into an extended expression.

The feast of St. James was one of the most important of the year, and it was for the alleluia of that celebration at Santiago de Compostela that a vox organalis was written down. The expansion from the plainchant is made clear by the opening punctus with its organum (see Example 15). The cantus firmus is visually the same but is musically transformed by the rhythmic change. The chant is now too slow to be rhythmically generative, and the duplum takes over both the focus of attention and the musical motivation. The duplum is textless and was sung on the vowel of the text it embellished.

Alleluia, plainsong and organum   Example 15
from Santiago de Compostela (excerpts)
ANONYMOUS

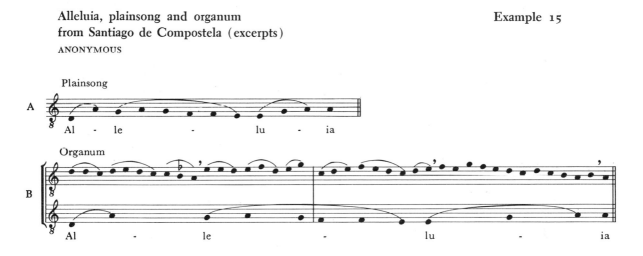

This alleluia is from the feast of Saint James, c. 1150. The full form of the alleluia consists of both alleluia and verse, as in Example 12. The verse of this alleluia is "Vocavit Iesus"; its final melisma is Example 16.

Few rules, for either the use of intervals in vertical combination or for rhythmic progression, impeded the flight of the embellishing duplum. John Cotton, an English theorist at the end of the eleventh century, wrote of the many ways of composing the countermelody and specified a preference for contrary motion as the tenor moves and for ending on the simplest vertical proportion in a deployment largely determined by the practicalities of range.

If the Cantus Firmus ends in a low register, the organizing voice should be above it and rise to the octave; but if the Cantus ends in a higher place, the organizing part must seek the octave below; and when the Cantus concludes in the middle range, the two parts should close in a unison . . . the closes on the unison should be alternated with those on octaves—the former being preferable.[2]

As Cotton suggested, the alleluia, in which the tenor final is the midrange *a*, closes on the unison. In the verse, in which the tenor descends to the relatively low final *d*, the duplum rises to the octave (see Example 16).

Composers considered the intervals at the points where new tenor notes entered as the essential frame of the composition, which was conceived as proceeding from one such interval to the next; the added tones of the duplum were decorative. The essential interval in notation was a *punctus contra punctum* ("note against note")—the origin of the word *counterpoint*. The counterpoints (intervals) of the alleluia are as follows:

The counterpoints provide a summary of the two phrases, outlining the rise of the first and the convergence of the second. They also illustrate a principle of stabilizing phrase beginnings (through use of the perfect consonances) while enjoying freedom between them. Such a frame furnishes a means of understanding the form of the alleluia and also sheds light on the technique of composition. The science lies in the counterpoint; the artistic reality lies in the expanded line of the duplum and in the voice of a skilled countertenor.

"Vocavit Ihesus," the alleluia verse for the feast of St. James, was a long chant to the text "Jesus called James son of Zebedee and John his brother and gave them the surname Boanerges" (Mark 3:17). The verse is fairly ornate, with a long melisma on *Boanerges*. Expansion of the verse through such a style of organum created a substantial composition. The chief problem lay in handling the melisma, because treating it in the same manner as the rest of the chant would overbalance the work. The solution was to tighten the melisma rhythmically by energizing the tenor. The composer introduced a note-against-note descending pattern, which produced an effect quite different from that of the rest of the work. The intensified union of the lines in rhythmic motion and the thick concentration of vertical intervals marked the approaching close effectively.

Interestingly, such a practice was part of the modernity of the works, although the rhythmic aspect of note against note seems akin to the old style of organum. But the difference is greater than the apparent likeness: in the old style, essential tenor tones had been sung one to one with tones of the organizing voice; here, a tenor melisma was set one to one with an-

[2] Quoted in Gustave Reese, *Music in the Middle Ages*, New York: Norton, 1940, p. 261.

Alleluia, Vocavit Iesus

ANONYMOUS

Example 16

Plainsong

Bo - a - ner - ges.

Organum

Bo - a -

ner - ges.

The final melisma and its organum of this alleluia verse, from Santiago de Compostela, written for the feast of Saint James, c. 1150. The word *Boanerges* takes about one-quarter of the plainchant verse, which ends with the melisma slightly longer than the portion given to the text. In the organum, the final melisma, tightened by the note-against-note progression called the *clausula*, is less than half as long as the portion given to the text.

other melisma in a passage that was basically expressive. Later writers gave this type of punctus the name *discantus* or *clausula* (plural, *clausulæ*) and considered it a contrast to pure organum. Discant passages were ordinarily placed, as in the alleluia "Vocavit Ihesus," at a melisma in the cantus firmus; the term clausula (literally "a closing") referred to its placement at the end of a section.

THE SCHOOL OF NOTRE DAME

Both Santiago de Compostela and St. Martial of Limoges were monastic centers, both great schools of monophony (sacred and secular) and of early organum. But during the twelfth century, leadership in the arts gradually shifted from the monastery to the cathedral. This shift represented not only the rise of the great cities of Europe but the new influence of the layman in matters of church art. The cathedral schola performed not only for themselves but for a congregation, a congregation of townspeople—tradesmen, men of the new middle class.

The new spirit brought fresh style to the cathedrals; their construction was a civic work and the cathedral service a civic pride. The hundred years from the start of Notre Dame at Paris in 1163 was a century of cathedrals, with construction begun at Chartres in 1194, Magdeburg in 1209, Reims in 1212, Amiens in 1218, Salisbury in 1220, Beauvais in 1225, and Cologne in 1248, among many others. Instead of the heavy construction of the monasteries, the new churches exploited the vault and the flying buttress, which created lines that soared upward and, by freeing the walls from bearing the whole weight of the structure, allowed the insertion of windows. This new architectural style has come to be called Gothic, which is a convenient word to use to designate the arts that flourished in the cathedrals in the thirteenth and early fourteenth centuries, for the construction of these magnificent cathedrals gave rise to a concentration on the arts that adorned them.

The Gothic era was one of expanding ideas, particularly of a new harmony between the sacred and the secular. In music, fresh styles developed naturally with the changes in liturgical functions that mirrored the new emphasis on congregational and diocesan services. The great popular feast days of the liturgical year (particularly Easter) became more spectacular. Musical composition centered largely in the services of general attendance (particularly Mass and Vespers), and new feasts that reflected the religious revival of the thirteenth century were added to the calendar.

The most popular feast at the height of the era was that of Corpus Christi (Body of Christ). Celebration of the feast included a procession of the Sacrament through the town, and this procession became an important focus for the Medieval love of color and a reflection of the new civic spirit and pride. The clergy, still fully vested, led the procession with the Sacrament under a bright canopy. They were followed by the clerics and the schola, including the boys; trumpeters and players of many other instruments; and prominent citizens, such as the leading guildsmen, knights, and jongleurs, carrying torches, banners, jeweled crosses, and other displays.

The chief forms of Gothic sacred music, besides plainsong (which was still being composed, though waning), were organum, including the discant clausula; processional music, called *conductus*; and the *motet*.

A chief center of creativity for Gothic music was the Cathédrale de Notre Dame (the Cathedral of Our Lady), in Paris. The new popularity of the Virgin was related to the celebration of woman in the courtly love of the trouvère movement, which was at its height during the Gothic era. The city of Paris, already a great center, became the leading cultural seat of Europe with the founding of the university about 1200. The university attracted some of the greatest minds of Western philosophy, among whom was St. Thomas Aquinas, who reconciled Aristotle with Christian philosophy and compiled both the Mass and the Divine Office for the feast of Corpus Christi.

The surviving examples of Notre Dame polyphony testify to its dissemination over a wide area. Works are found in Spanish, Swiss, German, and Scottish manuscripts, and the chief source of knowledge of the school is a treatise by an anonymous Englishman known to scholars as Anonymous IV. This careful scholar not only described the music but also named composers; he called Leoninus (active c. 1160–1180) "optimus organista," the best writer of organum, and Perotinus (active c. 1180 to after 1200) "optimus discantor," the best writer of discant.[3] "Leoninus made a great book of organa (*Magnus Liber Organi*) for the Mass and the Office, to augment the divine service," he wrote. "This book was in use until the time of the great Perotinus, who abridged it."[4] Perotinus also wrote many new discant sections, some of which substituted for Leoninus's. In addition, he added a third part—called the *triplum*—to organum and composed many conductus (the word is both singular and plural) in one, two, and three parts. Finally, he wrote two surviving *organa quadrupla*, great works in four parts, probably between 1198 and 1200.

The early organum of Notre Dame was mainly similar to that of St. Martial and Santiago, but it tended toward rhythmic definition in the vox organalis; like the concentration of the repertoire in the most important feasts of the year, this rhythmic definition reflected the new secular interests. Basic rhythmic proportions were defined, and the ways they were being used were organized as the *rhythmic modes* for purposes of notation. Like the modes of the gamut, they served to provide a technical vocabulary for notating, discussing, and teaching music rather than for prescribing usage to composers. The system of the rhythmic modes comprised a *mensural* (measured) notation, described by the thirteenth-century theorist Franco of Cologne in a text called *Ars cantus mensurabilis* (*The Art of Measured Song*, c. 1260). The rhythmic modes were six in number:

Mode I:	long-short	♩ ♪♩ ♩ ♪
Mode II:	short-long	♪♩ ♪♩ ♩ ♪
Mode III:	long-short-short	♩. ♪♩ ♩
Mode IV:	short-long-long	♪♩ ♩.
Mode V:	long-long	♩. ♩.
Mode VI:	short-short-short	♪ ♪ ♪

Franco assigned proportionate values to two note signs, the longa (long,) and brevis (short,). He also added a third note symbol, the semibrevis (◇), shorter than the brevis but of indefinite value, and a sign for

---

[3] Quoted in William G. Waite, *The Rhythm of Twelfth-Century Polyphony*, New Haven, Conn.: Yale, 1954, p. 3.

[4] *Ibid.*, p. 3.

a rest (/), enlarging the scope of notatable rhythms even further. In addition, he assigned rhythmic meanings to the *ligatures*, symbols of two or more connected notes. The system was very difficult, because the two note symbols used in the six modes actually incorporated proportions, not only of 2:1, but also of 3:1 and 3:2. The confusion can best be appreciated by notating the rhythmic modes as given above with only two time values. Composers compounded the problems by writing music, called *fractio et fusio modi*, that broke and combined modal patterns.

Organum Duplum

The *Magnus Liber Organi* (Great Book of Organa) of Leoninus contains nearly one hundred settings of plainchant for the major feasts of the liturgical year. Leoninus's style of organum—two parts, with the organizing voice based on the first rhythmic mode and the cantus firmus in long tones— came to be called *organum purum*. His setting of the Easter alleluia "Pascha Nostrum" is representative; the style is seen in the opening punctus (Example 17).

The composer had as his heritage the plainchant alleluia, with its jubilus and verse. This he transposed downward by a perfect fifth, maintaining exact interval relationships by invoking the use of the chromatic semitone (i.e., by demanding the soft ♭), a device that created the need for further adjustments—a variable *E*—in the duplum. He set only the solo sections, heightening the contrast so that the performance was an alternation between organum duplum (in solo performance) and plainsong (by the choir), as follows:

ORGANUM (SOLO)	PLAINSONG (CHOIR)
Alleluia	Jubilus (repeated)
Pascha *nostrum* immo*latus* est	Christus
Alleluia	Jubilus

Here, expansion reached its apogee, with 117 notes in the vox organalis compared to only 10 in the plainsong of the alleluia; the effect, of course, was to create a substantial section out of a short phrase. The duplum had not only become more ornate than before but also was given a rhythmic thrust that added to its immediacy. Writers of the time were well aware of the ascendency of the countertenor line. The joy and freedom of the duplum are clear. The problem, as before, came with the plainchant melismata (displayed above in italic type). *Nostrum* had twenty-two notes (eighteen on –*strum*) and had to be turned into two expanded sections comprising some twenty short phrases. And –*latus*, with fifty-five notes (forty-eight on –*la*–), would have been hopelessly long, so a discant section was substituted for organum. Rhythmic organization entered the plainchant melisma, which was speeded up by being measured like the vox organalis (in units of ♩ in the modern notation) and synchronized with it. In the discant section, the ratio of duplum to tenor was close to 2:1 (75:43), a very different effect from the 10:1 (512:49) for the rest of the work and, in its modernity, a very exciting one.

Pascha nostrum   Example 17
LEONINUS

Pas   -   cha

From an organum duplum, the Cathedral of Notre Dame, c. 1160. This opening punctus includes the first word of the alleluia verse (*Pascha*) of Example 12. In this case, the plainsong has been placed a fifth lower. The additional slash on two of the eighth notes in the modern notation indicates a decorative tone called a *plica*. Authorities disagree on how the plica should be rendered in modern notation and also on its musical meaning.

Pascha nostrum   Example 18
LEONINUS

im   -   mo   -

la-

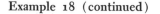

Example 18 (continued)

From an organum duplum of Notre Dame, c. 1160. Beginning of the word *im-molatus*, showing the normal style of organum on *im–mo–* and the start of the long discantus section on *–la–* [*tus*]. The plainchant verse on which this organum is based is Example 12. The plainsong has been placed a fifth lower and in the melisma (on *–la–*), it has been given rhythmic organization as well.

Interestingly, in his revisions, Perotinus furnished new puncti chiefly for *nostrum* and *–latus,* the most crucial and forward-looking sections of Leoninus's organum. Although the text in the revised performance was divided among presentations of plainsong, Leoninus's organa, and Perotinus's substitutions (as above, with the italics now signifying puncti by Perotinus), the alleluia verse was more Perotinus's than the charting of the text would suggest. In his substitutions, Perotinus had taken out 408 of the 460 notes of the original organum for the verse—almost 90 percent. However, most of Perotinus's substitutes were shorter than the originals, so the revision was better balanced.

Organum Triplum

From writers of the Gothic era, we know that part composition was essentially additive, that is, that successive voices were added one at a time. A measured duplum, which could be synchronized accurately, could be joined by a third part, or triplum. "Whoever wishes to compose a triplum must have the tenor and duplum in mind," wrote Franco of Cologne.[5] By 1200 the characteristic organa were *organa tripla*, with both upper parts in mensural rhythm.

The "Haec Dies," from the Easter gradual, was one of the most popular cantus firmi, again a reflection of the attention given to the Easter celebrations. The opening punctus, of two short tenor units, is representative

[5] Quoted in Riemann, *op. cit.*, p. 160.

of organum triplum. The tenor proceeds in measured notes but moves more sedately than the duplum or triplum, which "bursts into song . . . , subjugating the cantus," [6] capturing the attention of the listener in a rich interpenetration of the upper voices. Stratified into middle and higher ranges, the duplum and triplum display individual strength and excitement. The overall structure is that of the phrase, with the unanimous middle cadence giving way to overlapping phrases enhanced by imitation in the second half. As in the two-part works, the upper voices proceed with relative freedom between stable beginnings and endings in which the three voices form a triad of perfect consonances. The 1–5–8 structure, as in the opening sonority, became the standard opening and closing for more than a century thereafter; it was conceived as doubly perfect, that is, with two perfect intervals. To make cadences more effective, imperfect intervals often directly preceded the perfect ones. Rhythmic activity tended to increase before cadence points also, creating a twofold restlessness that the cadence resolved.

Although organa achieved a three-part norm in the generation of Perotinus, the substitute clausulæ remained two-part works; of about 430 such works from Perotinus and his group, some 410 were in two parts.

[6] *Ibid.*, p. 75.

Haec Dics (excerpt)   Example 19
ANONYMOUS

HEC

From an organum triplum, c. 1190. This plainsong is from the Easter gradual and was one of the most frequently decorated sections of plainchant.

A strong reflection of the secular revival of the Gothic era is the large *Conductus* number of surviving processional pieces, the conductus. Informal processions have doubtless always been popular and music a part of them. A Medieval diary noted a small wedding party "led with instruments of music to the Parish church." [7] Pilgrims sang walking songs; one of the earliest known notated walking songs is in one of the manuscripts, dating from about 1140, of St. James of Compostela.

By the thirteenth century, the procession had become an ornate display, incorporating religious, civic, and artistic interests of the time. Naturally

[7] Quoted in George G. Coulton, *Life in the Middle Ages,* New York: Cambridge, 1954, vol. I, p. 86.

Nove Geniture
ANONYMOUS

Example 20

A conductus from Notre Dame, c. 1200. This conductus, for the Feast of the Nativity, has been found in manuscripts in England, Germany, and Italy. The Italian source, from which this version was adapted, includes only a single verse of text, but as many as five verses appear in other sources. Performance may have been completely instrumental or a mixture of vocal and instrumental; vocal performance alone in a procession is unlikely. (Courtesy of Yale University.)

paralleling the increasing practice and sophistication of the processional art was an increased composition of conductus. Formerly monophonic, the conductus in the Gothic era was composed variously as a two-, three-, or even four-part work, usually without a preexisting cantus firmus and with a more unanimous rhythmic motion (as would be expected in a walking piece). It was defined by a theorist, in about 1235, as "a multivoiced consonant composition in one [rhythmic] mode which also allows secondary consonances," [8] in other words, as a mixing of imperfect intervals with the basic perfect ones. The conductus generally used a Latin poem of many stanzas, with the music the same for each stanza.

No brief study can encompass the expansion or the variety of the form. The rhythmic structure of the conductus was vital to its definition. "Nove Geniture," Example 20, is a fully developed work in two voices and can represent the conductus at its height.

At their apex, Gothic forms were defined by distinctions of rhythm and text. Organum was based on a few words of text, disguised both by the slow motion of the tenor and by the ornate, textless upper voices. The conductus was highly rhythmic, and the rhythm was motivating. Thus the sound of the conductus, especially when performed on instruments, was related strongly to that of the secular polyphonic estampie. The conductus was further related to secular composition by the fact that it did not have a cantus firmus.

The thirteenth century produced, in addition to organum and conductus, one of the richest forms of music, perhaps the richest of all multivoiced forms—the Gothic motet. This form emerged as a separate concept when a text was assigned to the vox organalis of a clausula. The duplum was then called *motetus*, indicating the presence of a text different from that of the cantus firmus. The triplum, when present, was first written in the same rhythm and to the same text as the motetus, but it soon became independent in both; however, it retained its name. The Latin word *motetus*, then, served to designate both the whole piece and the second voice in particular. (In this book, the English word *motet* will be used to indicate the whole work and *motetus* to mean the second voice only.)

Motet

The motet had musical and literary aspects. Early motets were musically derived from Notre Dame clausulæ, with both (or all) voices measured and rhythmically related; some motets were in fact clausulæ with words added for the upper part or parts, and others were composed in the same style as the clausulæ. The cantus firmus, still sacrosanct in the order of pitches but without rhythmic obligation, was given rhythmic form in the motet. Often, it was a short pattern that was repeated and set off by rests. As a structural rather than melodic or expressive element, it was of great importance—it led to practices of a highly characteristic nature and the expansion of the tenor to longer and more complex patterns. The rhythmic

---

[8] Jerome of Moravia, quoted in Riemann, *op. cit.*, p. 163.

form of the cantus firmus culminated in the isorhythmic motet of the fourteenth and early fifteenth centuries.

The Gothic motet enjoyed a long development and a singular popularity. More than one hundred manuscripts—some with many examples—contribute to our knowledge of the form. Early works chiefly used Latin devotional texts, often with two upper voices singing about different aspects of the Virgin or some important feast, but after about 1215 the influence of the trouvère art became stronger in both the use of vernacular lyrics and the preference for pastoral and love texts. During the second half of the thirteenth century, most motet poems were in the Marian (Latin) and courtly love (French) tradition, but social and moral subjects were dealt with also, often in superior poetry. Thus the motet, initially a form of sacred music, was increasingly influenced by secular forms and in the end became an artistic form capable of sacred or secular function.

One of the most widely disseminated works of the mid-thirteenth century was the three-part work "O Maria virgo Davitica/O Maria Maris stella/VERITATEM." (It is customary to title Gothic motets by the opening words—*incipits*—of the texts.) This work survives in more than a dozen thirteenth- and fourteenth-century manuscripts—mostly French but also British, German, and Spanish—showing that it remained in the repertoire for well over a hundred years. Because its triplum, with its faster motion, is the type described by Franco of Cologne, it is called Franconian. It is essentially classical in its balanced imbalance, with its thoroughly Medieval ideal of varying components meeting in a harmony of independence and unity.

This motet is representative of the form, in its use of a tenor statement of the plainsong in a repeated pattern of long notes, more varied rhythmic activity in the motetus, and still more varied rhythmic activity in the triplum —a three-speed effect. The individuality of the three voices went beyond our concept of later polyphonic independence. The textual forms were far from the same, and their different lengths and structures were mirrored, not only by the differing speeds required to contain them within the same time span, but also by their independent phrase structure, shown by the rests at the ends of lines. Ranges overlapped (cantus firmus d to a, motetus g to f^1, and triplum g to a^1), with more stratification in practice than the homogeneity of voice types would suggest—though the two upper parts crossed freely enough. Both upper voices sang Marian texts, while the cantus firmus, a section of plainsong, was typically identified by its incipit—in this case, the word on which a melisma occurred in a plainchant gradual of a Mass for the Marian feast.

"Balaam/BALAAM" is a two-part motet. Its tenor is from the plainsong Epiphany sequence "Epiphaniam Domino cananus," from the Sarum rite (Salisbury Cathedral, England). Its poem is a trope of the Epiphany sequence concerning the prophecies of the prophet Balaam. Musically, the work is based on a typical motet rhythmic pattern in the tenor, made from the cantus firmus in a construction often found in fourteenth-century works.

O Maria virgo Davitica/O Maria Maris stella/ VERITATEM Example 21

ANONYMOUS

VERITATEM

Triplum:	O Maria, virgo Davitica,	O Mary, virgin of the house of David,
	virginum flos,	flower of virgins,
	vitæ spes unica. . . .	life's one hope. . . .
Motetus:	O Maria, maris stella,	O Mary, star of the sea,
	Plena gratiæ. . . .	full of grace. . . .

Franconian motet, first of eight puncti, from Notre Dame, c. 1250. This work exhibits the increased motion in the triplum that is associated with Franco of Cologne. (Courtesy of Oxford University Press and Éditions de L'Oiseau-Lyre, Monaco.)

Balaam/BALAAM Example 22

ANONYMOUS

Ba - la - am! pro - phe - tan ti pa - tu - it for - tis ri - no - che-

BALAAM

ro - ta, cu - ius ter - ra mo - ta pe - tris scis - sis la - tu - it to-

Example 22 (continued)

Balaam!
Prophetan ti patuit fortis rinocherota,
Cuius terra mota petris scissis latuit tonitruum in rota,
Ex quo captus fuit a virgine beata,
De tribu Iuda nata.
Nubes iustum pluit mala nostra luit qui caritate fluit;
Unde psallit Abraham, progenies salvata, de quo fatur Balaam.

To Balaam, the prophet, appeared a powerful rhinoceros, under whose tread the
earth shook and the rocks split, covering up the thunder in a wagon, from which
it was taken by the holy virgin, born from the tribe of Judah. The cloud sheds the
just one, purifies our sins, and overflows with charity; of this sings Abraham, his
saved progeny of whom Balaam speaks.

A sacred motet from the thirteenth century. (Courtesy of Hans Tischler.)

At the time when composers used rhythmic patterns structurally, they exploited the contrasting elements of melodic line and rhythmic pattern and reconciled them in an aggressive simultaneous presentation. Emphasizing the independence of the two elements, musicians later gave them individual names—the rhythmic pattern was called the *talea* ("count" or "tally") and the melody was called the *color*.

When the talea and color were the same length, they were simply repeated. But in Example 22 the rhythmic pattern is only three notes long, so the color of twenty-two notes does not come out even with the pattern. Each element proceeds unyieldingly, the two factors producing a new interaction as they continue. When the color is repeated (shown by a double bar in Example 22), it begins on the second note of the pattern instead of the first, so in its second statement, the melodic line appears in a new guise. Conversely, the pattern continues to encounter new melodic embodiments. Musicologists have named such techniques *isorhythmic*.

In "BALAAM," three statements of the color would be required in order for it to end evenly with the pattern, but the composer has inserted a repetition of the penultimate note of the color so as to achieve a final cadence at the end of two statements. The length of the motetus text is doubtless related to this, although it would be rash to assume either that the composer was not also the poet or that the poetry was complete before its musical setting was begun.

Perhaps it is safer to assume that "Hare, Hare/Balaam/BALAAM" (Example 23), a three-part motet whose tenor and motetus comprise the music of the two-part motet of Example 22, is a later expansion of the original two-part work. Moreover, the former sacred text of the motetus has been replaced. The triplum text alludes to the motetus in its reference to the *goud man*, and, by use of punctus exchanges, the triplum melody refers to that of the motetus. Because such an exchange was a British technique, it expands the work's verbal thrusts at the British with musical allusion.

In surviving sources, the two- and three-part works of Examples 22 and 23 appear in two forms—as a two-part devotional work with a Latin motetus and as a three-part secular work with French triplum and motetus. It would be erroneous to think of these forms as a succession in which one supplanted the other, just as it would be erroneous to assume that monophonic music was in any sense replaced by the rise of two-part composition or that either of these was rendered obsolete by three-part works. Even after a three-part texture had attained the status of a norm, monophonic popular music was thriving; two-part motets, conductus, and chansons were being written at the same time as more elaborate works; and organa remained in the repertoire. Every new type was treated as a welcome addition to an art permeated with diversity and contrast. The older textures died slowly—even in the sixteenth century, plainsong was being sung, trouvères were meeting for the puy, and two- and three-part songs were being written. Actually, the simpler forms have never died—the minstrel still sings to his harp,

Example 23A. "Hare, hare / Balaam! / BALAAM," the fac-simile of Example 23B. The parts are separated, with the tenor at the end. Earlier Gothic notation was in score. (Courtesy of the Herzog August Bibliothek, Wolfenbüttel, Cod. Guelf. 1099 Helmst. fol. 197v–198v.)

Hare, Hare/Balaam!/BALAAM

ANONYMOUS

Example 23B

Example 23 B (continued)

Example 23 B (continued)

mi - e.   Or be-vons, ha, hy - e,   de   ce bon vin d'ou - an.

cil Nor-man n'en per - dent la   co - rail - le   qui tant boi-vent "a goud man."

Triplum:

Hare, hare, hye! Goudalier ont fet ouan d'Arras Escoterie.
Saint Andrie!
Hare, hare goudeman et hare druerie!
Caritate crie por Sainte Marie!
Faitez moi demie de poumon et de fye.
Honie soit tel vie!
Mais bon vin sorlie ne mespris je mie.
Or bevons, ha, hye, de ce bon vin d'ouan.

Here, here, hey! The brewers have turned Arras into a second Scotland. Hail! St.
Andrew, my good man, and long live jollity! Cry charity by Holy Mary! Make us
a dish half of lungs, half of liver. A plague on such a life! But wine on the lees I
have never scorned. Let's drink, ho, ho, of this year's good wine!

Motetus:

Balaam! Goudalier ont bien (Ou! An!) leurs tens por la goudale.
Que chascuns en bale,
que en sont Englissemen quant il l'ont bien estale,
demilot a maille por ce il font leur taille.
Si dient: "Bien le vaille!"
Passions l'assaille!
Ele m'est trop male qu'en mes genous m'avale: Merveille ai que cil Norman
    n'en perdent la coraille qui tant boivent "a goud man."

Brewers certainly have time for their beer this year and everyone packs it in, since
the English, after they have had their fill, impose their tax on it at half a penny the
demi-lot. They say "It's worth it." A curse on it! It does me no good since it goes
straight down to my knees. I marvel that those Normans don't burn their intestines,
they who drink so many toasts [to "a good man"].

A secular motet from the thirteenth century. The motetus of the sacred motet
(Example 22) is doubled upon itself in punctus exchanges—as in the opening
material between the motetus and triplum at measure 7 or the material of measure
15 at measure 21. These are played off against the isorhythmic tenor. (Courtesy of
Hans Tischler.)

and the Office is still sung in plainchant in the monastery—though now the language is being changed.

The second half of the thirteenth century witnessed a splendid culmination in the musical arts. Not only was the motet at its zenith, but a last great flowering of plainsong composition was producing sequences as well as chants for the new feasts and the trouvère movement was passing its apogee, with secular poets on the edge of the era of the formes fixes. It was in the richness of forms, colors, and textures, used in effective juxtapositions, that the whole of Gothic art attained a particular vigor. Seldom has a philosophy of man lent itself so successfully to creative discipline. The balancing of intellect and emotion, a Medieval harmony, gave rise to the concept that the artist must consider design before yielding to color. It led to explorations of technique that were to balance but not displace effect.

Gothic art has been defined here as art designed for and inspired by the cathedrals in the era of their construction or, in the case of the motet, as art begun in the cathedrals and retaining reference to that beginning, even in secular forms. But secular music had been inventing its own polyphonic techniques—punctus exchange has already been mentioned—and forms, and these were to join the great musical expression of the thirteenth century, to contribute to the crescendo that, at the end of the century, was to climax in a new art.

PERFORMANCE

The ideals of sound were basically the same for Medieval polyphony as for Medieval monophony. Contrast, both simultaneous and successive, formed the first principle, and imaginative use of the means at hand was the chief ally of the producer, whose role in performance was still a vital one. Notation of the organum, clausula, conductus, and motet—as of the monophonic works—was bare of suggestions for medium or organization, and this was the province of the producer.

In the conductus, only the tenor had a text, so probably all singers sang the words. However, contemporary descriptions of processions speak of a great variety of participating vocal and instrumental musicians. If trumpeters took part, there certainly were fanfares; if drummers took part, there certainly were rhythmic accompaniments or tattoos. Bands of bowed and plucked strings, reeds, and flutes doubtless played conductus, perhaps alternating and joining with the singers. Evidence points to the probability of great freedom—of instruments doubling the singers at the octave, double octave, or both; of instruments on one or two parts with voices on the others; of instruments alternating with the voices or supplanting them altogether. In a long procession featuring a conductus of many stanzas, all these techniques may have had a place.

A miniature of King David, from the Psalter and Book of Hours of Yolande, Vicomtesse of Soissons, c. 1290. David is portrayed twice—at the bottom with his slingshot and at the top at a positive organ. The bellows pumper is peeking around the side of the organ. (Courtesy of the Pierpont Morgan Library, M. 729.)

Within the Gothic church, the colors of windows, statuary, and vestments were equalled by the brilliance of the musical sounds. Testimony to the diversity of instruments in the churches—particularly bowed strings, brass, and percussion (bells, in addition to the more obvious drums)—is varied and convincing. Organum was an alternative form within a basically monophonic service. The schola sang plainchant sections, while soloists sang puncti of organum. But many scholars believe that instrumentalists took over, or at least reinforced, the tenor in organa and that this was an early function of the pipe organ. Other instruments seem more suited to the intricate vox organalis parts; frequently they must have been doubled in the upper registers, because most of the illustrations, in both sacred and secular contexts, of the instruments of the Medieval era show those of high range.

Motets were approached as freely as the conductus; the chief problem was the cantus firmus. In both organum and motet, the long notes of the tenor might well have been sung by the choir. But the motet was not always sung in church, and as the form developed, it became a two- or three-part work for soloists.

Thus, a vocal performance of a three-part motet was a performance of three soloists. But how strictly they kept to the notation is hard to determine, for the art of improvisation remained significant throughout the history of music, declining in the West only during the past two hundred years. All the instrumental enhancements, alternations, and substitutions granted to other forms were potentially part of the motet as well. Most two-part motets would be effective performed by a single musician, singing to the harp in the classic manner of the troubadour or with percussion added by an assistant. Instrumental performances (without any voices) were not uncommon, and by the end of the century the *instrumental motet* (actually a contradiction) was known. A codex found at Bamberg contains several such works, one title of which refers to a viol player.

The Medieval producer would have sought contrasts of medium, range, color, and dynamic level. The modern producer can hardly go wrong. As long as he thinks of the single beat (the dotted quarter in the examples) as the pulse and as long as he conceives of the ideal of resonance rather than loudness and of color and contrast rather than virtuosity, he can clothe these works in whatever sounds he can devise. He is free to make this music as exciting as he wishes.

A vielle player, from the Psalter and Book of Hours of Yolande, Vicomtesse of Soissons, c. 1290. The vielles, along with other instruments of minstrelsy, were freely accepted in the performance of sacred music. (Courtesy of the Pierpont Morgan Library, M. 729.)

There was many a tambourine player,
And many tumblers, which I can well attest
Were skilled in their craft full perfectly.
With subtle art they tossed the tambourines
Up in the air, and then, as often
Caught them fairly and softly on one finger
In such a manner that they never missed.

ROMAUNT OF THE ROSE *

Popular Polyphony

6

The early history of secular polyphonic music is even more difficult to piece together than that of sacred music. Surviving source materials are much rarer and their dates less easy to interpret. Songs were popular for a generation, or fifty years, or even for a century, so the dates of the manuscripts in which tunes come down to us are less likely to represent dates of composition. And undoubtedly some of the most popular tunes were never written down or were lost. However, enough remains to let us know that a lively secular art was thriving and to let us hear sufficient samplings of it to respect and enjoy it.

* From the fourteenth-century translation by Geoffrey Chaucer. (Modern version by the author.)

Study of secular polyphony has added problems. The fact that it was practiced by relatively unlearned musicians means that it was less often written down. Furthermore, the contributions of improvisation to the performance of music in parts means that what appears on paper to be a monophonic song might in actual performance have been sung in two or three parts.

By the second decade of the thirteenth century, the motet was as much a secular as a sacred form. A motet such as "Hare, Hare/Balaam/BALAAM" (Example 23) was composed as a harmony of sacred and secular elements, a blending of the clerical and trouvère traditions. It was not long before secular cantus firmi became common, so a popular song could serve, with as much musical validity as the liturgical tenor, as the spine of a motet. The motet could also be instrumentally conceived, as noted above, by the end of the century.

These techniques are examples of sacred music put into secular usage, but popular music was not merely a rehash of Church practices. Popular musicians had been devising their own polyphonic techniques and forms, which in the thirteenth and fourteenth centuries were to exert a compelling influence on the main stream of musical practice in Europe and the British Isles.

POLYPHONIC DANCES

Instrumental dances were being written in two parts (and occasionally in three). Dances also appeared with duply divided beats ($\quad$ = $\quad$ in modern terms), considered incomplete (imperfect) at that time, instead of the usual perfect beat divided in three ($\quad$ = $\quad$).

The most important dance form continued to be the estampie. An English estampie of five puncti (a stantipes) illustrates some of the trends of thirteenth-century secular music.[1] Each of the five puncti, which were numbered in the manuscript, used the same tune, with ouvert and clos, but presented it each time with a different countermelody. The tune occurred twice in the lower line and three times in the upper. When it was below (puncti 1 and 2), the tune was a fifth lower than when it was above (puncti 3, 4, and 5), a transposition achieved by having the lower part transpose Guido's entire gamut down a fifth, with a signature of B♭. This technique was used often from the thirteenth through the sixteenth centuries. It applied only to the voice or part that had the signature, which was most often the bottom one or, when there were three parts, the bottom two. The flat transposed the Guidonian system down a fifth, so that B was always

[1] This work appears in Harold Gleason, *Examples of Music before 1400*, New York: Appleton-Century-Crofts, 1946, p. 56.

taken soft and $E–E\flat$ was the chromatic semitone. But in English practice, the soft B was much prized, and the signature might appear in all voices. Works with one flat in one or two parts and two flats in another (which indicated a further transposition and caused $A–A\flat$ to become the chromatic semitone) appeared, and further experiments were carried out. In any case, the signatures had no relation to tonality in the modern sense.

POLYPHONIC SONG

The trouvères, continuing in their monophonic art, were also experimenting with polyphony. They must have been in the thick of the popular musical activity, aware of the art of court and countryside alike. Some of these men were learned, some of noble birth, and others occasional or resident members of great households. Certainly they heard organa and motets in churches and private chapels, and they took part in many processions. It would be difficult to ascertain whether a secular motet was in reality a clerical copy of a trouvère song or a trouvère utilization of a church work as a model.

The formes fixes found the motet and conductus textures congenial; the newly developed poetic types had hardly been defined before trouvères tried polyphonic settings for them in the new style—a concurrence of modernities placing these works on the cutting edge of music. Although such works were few (the monophonic art was at its height), their number was to increase.

Adam de la Halle was one of the first to use the new textures in the formes fixes. As in the monophonic form, the ballade, virelai, and rondeau had two kinds of poetic line (a and b), each with a characteristic length and rhyme, paralleled by two musical units. The trouvère performed the poem, using the appropriate punctus for each line and expanding the two musical elements into a complete work. Instrumental doublings or replacements were assumed, as well as the performance by a solo voice (in the top part) with two instrumental lines. No two performances would necessarily have been alike.

English Part-Songs

Although the French language and the trouvère art entered the English court, the vernacular tongue and its musical counterpart continued to flourish throughout the British Isles. Scholars in the Medieval era had high respect for the popular music of the British, which included the Scottish, Irish, and Welsh, as well as the English. The songs of the Irish and Welsh harpers and the pibrochs and marching tunes of the Scottish pipers form long and noble traditions worthy of study. For the general historian of Western music, however, the English forms are the most important, because they were to contribute deeply to the art of the Continent at the end of the Medieval era.

A twelfth-century historian wrote that for the Welsh and English, singing in parts was long established.[2] In addition, the English were known for their fondness for the soft ♭ , as already noted, and for their partiality for harmonic thirds. Whereas on the Continent thirds were still often considered to be dissonances derived mathematically through the circle of fifths, in England, theorists, notably Walter Odington, were looking at the thirds in the overtone series and pointing out that 4:5 is hardly more dissonant than 3:4 and that a major third combined with a minor third composes a fifth. "If the consonance is not found in the numbers, nevertheless, the voices of men bring them together with skill in a pleasing blend."[3] Odington was doubtless legitimizing an already firm fact of British musical life.

English lyrics such as "Edi beo þu"[4] illustrate an early concentration of harmonic thirds in a practice that later theorists called *gymel*, "twin song" (in Latin, *cantus gemellus*), which flourished in the thirteenth century and possibly earlier. Consecutive thirds, being of different sizes, are parallel only on paper. To the ear the effect is a blend of colors, essentially different to the Medieval musician from the concentration on perfect intervals.

Perhaps the most famous of all Medieval polyphonic songs is the *rota* (round) "Sumer is acumen in," found in a manuscript dating probably from the end of the thirteenth century. The song is a remarkable work, amazingly zestful, and still a joy to sing. It comprises a four-part round over a repeated bass (*pes*, "foot") in two parts. Instructions were given for both the rota and the pes, implying that a literate musician was not expected to know how to perform the work, which may attest to its modernity.

The *rondellus*, as described by Walter Odington (with an example evidently of his own composition),[5] had the form of two thoroughly exploited punctus exchanges, a type of construction called *Stimmtausch* by German musicologists. This work, which was true and complete Stimmtausch, had punctus units as follows:

a	b	c	d	e	f
b	c	a	e	f	d
c	a	b	f	d	e

Each group of three phrases represented three identical harmonic statements, but when the three lines were carried through with contrasting tone qualities

[2] Giraldus Cambrensis, quoted in F. M. Padelford (ed.), *Old English Musical Terms*, Bonn: P. Hanstein's Verlag, 1899, p. 15.

[3] Quoted in Hugo Riemann, *History of Music Theory*, Lincoln, Nebr.: University of Nebraska Press, 1962, p. 99.

[4] This work appears in Dom Anselm Hughes (ed.), *New Oxford History of Music*, vol. II, *Early Medieval Music up to 1300*, Fair Lawn, N.J.: Oxford University Press, 1954, p. 342.

[5] Riemann, *op. cit.*, pp. 167–169; Gleason, *op. cit.*, p. 46.

Example 24A, "Sumer is icumen in," a facsimile from a late twelfth-century or early thirteenth-century British manuscript page. (Courtesy of the British Museum, Harl. 978, fol. 11ᵛ.)

Sumer is icumen in

Example 24B

ANONYMOUS

Su - mer is i - cu - men in, Lhu - de sing cuc-cu; Grow - eth sed and blow - eth

med, and spring the wu - de nu. Sing cuc - cu. A - we ble - teth af - ter lomb, lhouth

af - ter cal - ve cu. Bul - luc ster - teth, buck - e ver - teth, mu - rie sing cuc - cu.

Cuc - cu; Cuc - cu, Wel sing - es thu cuc - cu; ne swik thu na - ver nu.

Four companions can sing this rota, which should not be performed by fewer than three, or two, in addition to those who sing the pes. It should be sung thus: the others remaining silent, one begins with those who sing the pes, and when he reaches the note after the cross another starts, and so on with the others. Each one pauses at the rests (/), but nowhere else, for the space of one long (♩.).

Example 24B (continued)

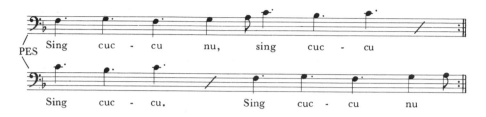

PES

Sing cuc - cu nu, sing cuc - cu

Sing cuc - cu. Sing cuc - cu nu

One performer repeats this as often as needed, counting a rest at the end; the other sings this, with a rest in the middle, but not at the end, where he repeats the beginning once more.

A rota from a late thirteenth-century manuscript. (Translation of rubrics courtesy of W. W. Norton & Company, Inc.)

—say, lute, viol, and recorder—each statement was unique in sound. Phrase *f* was given a text: *Ave mater Domini* (Hail, Mother of the Lord). If three men sang the work, using vocalise except for *f*, the production would have been effective. But both voices and instruments might well have been used in performance.

The English Carole

The English carole, of all Medieval secular forms, was to remain active— though changing in style—through the centuries to the present day. Originally a dance related to the virelai, the carole soon became a song form. Most surviving Medieval examples are found in fifteenth-century manuscripts, but many probably had an earlier origin. As the form took on successive styles, it continued to incorporate new techniques and idioms, but its essential form of alternating elements is Medieval in character. Therefore, in spite of the relatively late date of the surviving manuscripts, caroles properly belong to the Medieval era.

The polyphonic dimension served to increase the potential of contrasts. Like the monophonic example (Example 9), polyphonic caroles [6] were based on alternation of burden and verse, beginning and ending with the burden. The burden, with three parts, and the verse, with two, offered a contrast in texture that was typical of the carole at that time. However, the number of voices was not standardized and it was not particularly desirable for the thicker texture to appear in the burden.

The inclusion of Latin phrases was common in the poems. Christmas caroles were the most popular, but caroles were used to celebrate many holi-

[6] The most complete source is John Stevens (ed.), *Musica Britannica*, vol. IV, *Mediæval Carols*, London: Stainer and Bell, 1952. "Nowell sing we" (p. 5) best represents the type of carol discussed here.

days (such as May Day) and to commemorate great occasions. One of the most famous examples, "Deo gratias Anglia," celebrated the English victory at Agincourt in 1415.

Harmonically, the many burdens used the practice, called *English discant*, of writing in thirds and sixths. A discant phrase typically began and ended with the standard 1–5–8 doubly perfect triad, with harmonic concentration between the triads on the shifting colors of major and minor thirds and sixths, creating basically consecutive motion. Such practice appears to have been a later development of gymel, which had centered in the major and minor thirds. It was characteristically English, not only because it developed in the British Isles, but also because extended use of harmonic imperfections was still spurned on the Continent. Both gymel and discant were evidently often improvised, which makes it more difficult to establish their development from written documents. The middle voice, called the *meane* in English secular writing, was assumed.

Characteristically, polyphonic caroles included proportional rhythmic shifts from the standard beat, represented in modern notation by the dotted quarter (♩. = ♪♪♪), to a larger beat of a dotted half note (♩. = ♩ ♩ ♩) and a smaller beat of a dotted eighth note (♪. = ♪ ♪ ♪), which became common rhythmic vocabulary in the fourteenth and fifteenth centuries. Both

A banquet scene from a fifteenth-century manuscript, *Le Miroir de l'Humaine Salvation* (Mirror of Human Salvation.) The musicians are in attendance and so is the jester, whose name and office descended from the jongleur and the singer of *gestes*, songs telling of great deeds. (Courtesy of the Newberry Library.)

these shifts were called *hemiola* ("one-and-a-half") proportions. In the first case, the shift from the basic beat ♩ to the subdivision   (of ♩. = ♩ ♩ ♩) was taken so that the long ♩. was one-and-a-half of ♩ ; in the second case, the shift from the subdivision ♪ of the basic beat ♩. was taken so that the whole beat ♪. (in ♪. = ♪ ♪ ♪) was one-and-a-half of ♪ . In modern terms, the first hemiola, ♩ ♩ ♩ , proceeded as a $\frac{3}{4}$ measure, not as a syncopation in $\frac{6}{8}$ and the second hemiola, ♫♫ , proceeded as two measures of $\frac{3}{16}$ and not as a syncope within $\frac{3}{8}$.

PERFORMANCE

Aside from the basic principles of Medieval sound, which are clear, a good deal of detail concerning performance techniques must be a matter of speculation. How much performance was instrumental is hard to estimate. This is true of all music to some extent, even of today's popular songs, but it is doubly true for the music of the Medieval era—absence of a text in a manuscript did not rule out a vocal performance and the presence of a text did not guarantee one. But working within the principles of contrast of medium, register, and origin of sound, the producer could work out many kinds of performances within the Medieval ideal. Because the Medieval pitch system was one of relationships rather than absolutes, works could be freely transposed to suit instrumental conveniences. Instruments could be combined freely and in combinations unusual to the modern ear, avoiding the obvious blends we are used to striving for.

If a man has to lay the foundations of a house, he does not set a rash hand to the work: the inward line of the heart measures forth the work in advance and the inner man prescribes a definite order of action; the hand of imagination designs the whole before that part of the body does so; the pattern is first the prototype, then the tangible. . . . The inner compasses of the mind must encircle the whole quantity of material beforehand.

GEOFFREY DE VINSAUF *

Ars Nova

7

Even as Gothic forms were defined and refined, musical language was expanding with idioms and techniques representative of the forces of modernism and secularism. Conservative musicians rejected these techniques, however, possibly because traditional notation could not cope with them. Modernists such as Petrus de Cruce (Pierre de la Croix) were straining the notation with ornate melismatic triplum lines using 5:1, 7:1, or even higher rhythmic proportions.

Every generation regards itself as modern and its art as new, but a generation that requires fresh symbols and a new vocabulary proclaims its art as

* C. 1280. Quoted in J. Harvey (ed.), *Gothic England*, 2d ed., London: B. T. Batsford Ltd., 1947, p. 162.

new with a particular fervor. At the turn into the fourteenth century, the secular rhythms found their spokesman in the priest-poet-musician Philippe de Vitry (later the Bishop of Meaux), who worked out a system of rhythmic notation capable of dealing with the developing complexities of the new language. His treatise, dated about 1320, was called *Ars nova* (The New Art) and it named an era.

It is probably true that before any practice can attain a definitive position and exercise influence on the main stream, it must first be assimilated into the written tradition. However, this art was doubtless new more to the notator than to the improviser of music. Practitioners of the Ars nova saw themselves as bearers of a new wisdom, and they looked back on the musicians of the thirteenth century as hopelessly old-fashioned. They called the older practices the *Ars antiqua*.

It is always difficult to sort out the cause and effect of practice and notation, for the practice must exist in order to make the development of notation necessary, but once established, the notation itself shapes future musical thoughts. In any case, the fourteenth century saw the most complex rhythmic notation in the history of Western music. Vitry's system, when fully expanded over several generations, offered such an array of proportions that, in addition to stems, flags, and empty and solid noteheads, two colors of ink were required to indicate the possible relations. This notation is extremely lovely to look at, and its use coincided with a great period in the illumination of manuscripts. The notation was also well suited for the music it served. The new style dealt with each part as an independent force, leading to interactions so complex that it was no longer feasible to notate them with visual alignment. The tenor, however, which tended to remain more conservative, sometimes maintained the old notation, emphasizing its heritage and its derivation from the Ars antiqua—in sacred music a testament to its venerable authenticity.

By the end of the century, extreme rhythmic complications had developed. They were made possible by the independent proportioning of each part to a coordinating tactus, to which each performer adjusted as though to a metronome. Such proportional involvements do not readily lend themselves to translation into our metric notation, because tactus was not the same as accent. The musician of today who plays this music must do his best to find relative note lengths in the modern notation and to use the bar lines only to synchronize parts; he should approach the rhythmic language of each voice as independently as he can.

The Ars nova rejected the rhythmic assumptions of the past and many of the theories that had justified them, particularly the assumption that the triply divided beat was essential for the basic unit of forward motion. Secular music had long acknowledged the duple beat, but with the invocation of the Trinity to give a theological as well as theoretical approval to triple proportions, the twofold division had been regarded as incomplete (imperfect) at best and sacrilegious at worst. The Ars nova claimed equal validity for imperfect time, and the duple division gradually assumed more importance—it was to become the standard beat of the Renaissance. Acceptance of duple proportions carried with it tacit acceptance of secular idioms in general—the secular motet was already well established, of course—and, along with it, the rejection of the automatic superiority of sacred music.

The trouvère was ready to step in or, more properly, had already entered. The French claim Adam de la Halle as the first composer of the Ars nova, and to the extent that he wrote trouvère forms in motet textures, this is true. But Vitry's treatise appeared about 1320 and Adam had died in 1288. The treatise dealt chiefly with the isorhythmic motet, which continued to carry the bulk of liturgical composition, whereas the great forms of the Ars nova were the formes fixes of the trouvère tradition.

The pattern is clear—the trouvère became the chief figure at the cutting edge of music, and the trouvère forms took over the techniques of modernity. The trouvères adopted the idioms of the motet, centering their harmonic language in the 1–5–8 double perfection as beginning and ending, the cadence preceded by the double leading tone. The concept of perfections and imperfections was to prosper through the Renaissance and then to carry over, with new meaning, into the Baroque and beyond. The three-part norm also carried through from the Ars antiqua and formed a definitive aspect of late Medieval music, though this does not mean that works in two or four parts were considered radical. Melodic ideals were another carry-over from the Ars antiqua, but the rhythmic explorations inevitably involved faster, more melismatic lines. We shall probably never know to what extent these had been prefigured as garibles or other improvised additions in the thirteenth century.

The new art, then, represented a rejection of the liturgical centrality of musical forms and a reduction of the dominance of Church authority in matters musical, while continuing the development of the essential musical fabric—harmonic and textural—of the thirteenth century. But times had changed. The Gothic era had been one of hope, experiment, and religious fervor, symbolized by the building of cathedrals, founding of great universities, and exploration in the Orient. The fourteenth century, by contrast, was an age of fear and disintegration, symbolized by the scourges of the Black Death, the divided papacy, and the decline of Church authority in all matters temporal. The poet Eustache Deschamps called his century an "age of tears, anxiety, and torment; time of weariness and damnation." [1]

Perhaps the very violence of the era called forth the classical balance of strict poetic forms. In any event, the political and moral upheaval gave birth to resplendent poetry, for this was the age of Machaut and Petrarch, Chaucer and Boccaccio. That the cultural infusions in fourteenth-century music reflected the weakening of the Church as a body of civil authority is

[1] Quoted in André Maurois, *A History of France*, New York: Evergreen Books, Grove Press, Inc., 1960, p. 105.

clear. But social differences, chiefly the new individuality of the composers, stemmed from positive rather than negative influences. Merchant economies were beginning to replace feudalism; the state (city or nation) was becoming a strong focus for loyalty—loyalty that brought new dimensions (and new wars) to European politics. For the first time, real power could be exercised by the wealthy, and wealth was not altogether dependent on nobility. Thus a respect for man's ability as well as for his genealogy was developing. Man began to see himself less as creature and more as creator, a concept to blossom in the Renaissance as *humanism*.

FRANCE

Throughout the fourteenth century and well into the fifteenth, the trouvère chanson maintained its leadership in composition on the Continent. The trouvères used French for their poems, so a chanson, wherever composed, had a French text. Moreover, Vitry was French, so the Ars nova, as a movement, was of French inception.

The trouvère poem itself was a lively incorporation of cultural focuses. Love texts were formalized and were often songs of veiled religious devotion; political songs, often parodies, were also popular.

The Ars nova in France produced one of the great poet-musicians in the history of Europe. Although Guillaume de Machaut is studied more in literature than in music courses, he was one of the great composers in our heritage. A priest and secretary to King John of Bohemia, Machaut was widely traveled and widely respected. And he was extremely influential on succeeding generations of poets and musicians. (He met Chaucer, for example, and affected that poet's later development.) Like Vitry, Machaut was from Champagne. He retired as canon of Reims, where he evidently supervised the collection of his musical works, in seven volumes arranged chronologically.

He wrote about two dozen motets early in his career, probably before 1340. Three-quarters of them were French, one-quarter Latin (most of them isorhythmic—one of them in all parts). They yielded place to his growing interest in the secular forms, of which he left 115 examples—42 ballades, 33 virelais (many monophonic), 21 rondeaux, and 19 lais (2 of which were hunting songs). He also wrote the first polyphonic Ordinary of the Mass known to come from one composer as a musical entity. It is one of the great works in the history of music and one of the most remarkably individual.

Machaut was a trouvère and his most representative form was the lyric, with or without its musical setting. To the degree that his works from the middle of the century incorporated the best of the Ars nova, he was its ideal ambassador.

In Machaut's works, the essential growth of the form lay in the size of the poetic-musical concept of the formes fixes. Whereas the elements had begun as single lines and single musical phrases, the units have expanded here into small interior multiline verse sections and cognate musical units. The stanza forms are often subtle and complex.

"Je puis trop bien," an expansion of the *aaB* ballade form, is interestingly structured with a balanced imbalance characteristic of Medieval structures: seven of the eight lines have ten syllables; the first line of the B section has seven. The last line of the poem is the refrain. The poem actually had three stanzas and used the same rhymes for all. As before, the performer sang the poem, using the appropriate musical element for each section. The ouvert and clos (first and second endings, related to the double punctus of the estampie) were often necessitated by the expanded form, because a stronger cadential delineation became essential to maintain clarity of structure in longer works.

Like the form itself, the rhythmic language was expanding. Rhythmic sophistication took the form of broken phrases (hocketing, see page 122) and

Je puis trop bien   Example 25

GUILLAUME DE MACHAUT

A.

Example 25 (continued)

que fist Py - ma - li - on.   que

Me - de - e Ja - zon.   Li   folz   tou - dis la pri -

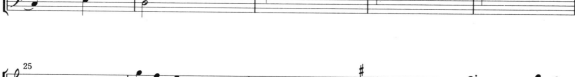

oit   Mais l'y - ma - ge riens   ne li re - spon - doit.   Eins - si   me

fait   cel - le   qui mon cuer font,   *Qu'a*

Example 25 (continued)

des la pri et riens ne me re-spont.

a	Je puis trop bien madame comparer A L'ymage que fist Pymalion.	a	My lady, well may I compare you To the image [of Aphrodite] which Pygmalion made.
a	D'yvoire fu, tant belle et si sans per Que plus l'ama que Medee Jazon.	a	It was of ivory, so lovely, without equal, And more beloved to him than was Medea to Jason.
b	Li folz tou dis la prioit, Mais l'ymage riens ne li respondoit. Einssi me fait celle qui mon cuer font, Qu'a des la pri et riens ne me respont.	b	As though mad, he prayed to the image endlessly, But it answered not. Thus does she treat me who has caused my heart to melt, For though I beseech her ever, she answers not.

TRANS. BY JON RINKA

A polyphonic ballade in the trouvère tradition. (Courtesy of Breitkopf & Härtel, Wiesbaden, Germany.)

independent proportions, along with the added complexities of a greater number of note values. The tenor of the ballade, for example, was told by the opening proportion sign (a broken circle in the original) to use a duple beat per half tactus (up and down were each a half tactus), whereas another sign (the perfect circle) told the countertenor and triplum singers to use a triple proportion. Red ink was used to indicate the occasional triplets in the tenor line. Translated into modern terms, with the triplets shown in grey, the tenor might read as follows:

Looking at such a version of the part, it is easier to understand the approach of the singer. If we set a metronome at 60-72, each back-and-forth movement can serve as the down-and-up of the tactus. The sign tells us that each half note of the part is to be proportioned to each half tactus, with a division of two quarters (rather than three) to the half, and a subdivision of two eighths (rather than three) to the quarter, except when the notation is red (when the subdivision is triple). The grouping of notes into phrases is to be accomplished and decisions concerning the chromatic semitone are to be made without reference to bar lines or to visual synchrony with the other parts. They, in turn, are proceeding in the same way, synchronizing to the tactus without reference to us.

Melodic and harmonic developments were less pronounced. The two-part texture was concerned with relatively conservative juxtapositions of consonance and dissonance. Most cadences were achieved through progression in contrary motion from imperfection to perfection, a concept that allowed considerable variation and imaginative figuration. The three-part texture had more potential for variety in the fabric of the musical language, but cadences were, by definition, less free. They were continuing to use 1–5–8 as the ideal final triad toward which imperfect consonances strove. In the characteristic cadence, the 1–5–8 final was preceded by a twofold imperfection—third and sixth over the superfinalis (2–4–7 when the tenor final was 1).

Theorists specified the use of major intervals even when the pitch had to be heightened by altering pitches of Guido's scale by introducing such tones as $g\sharp$ and $c\sharp^1$ when the tenor descended to a cadence on d. Indications for the alterations were generally omitted in the original notation, because the practice was taken for granted and singers were expected to modify the appropriate tones without their being labeled. These tones had been called *musica falsa* in the thirteenth century, but by the beginning of the fourteenth century the theorist Philippe de Vitry preferred the term *musica ficta*. "It is not false music," Vitry wrote, "but true and necessary." Since in modern theory these high intonations leading upward are called *leading tones*, theorists call this formula the *double leading-tone cadence*; it was significant in musical form throughout the rest of the fourteenth century and into the fifteenth, and even then its influence was not so much surrendered as transformed.

Horizontal and vertical elements were beginning to exert the tensions of concurring but still independent elements so representative of the Medieval sense of structure. Melody was still the focal element. The notation of individual parts on separate areas of the manuscript pages shows that only the second part (of two) or the triplum (of three) was given a text, except in the motet, where separate texts over a cantus firmus tenor persisted. Thus the chanson had become a solo song with one or two accompanying parts, presumably to be played on contrasting instruments. Such performance inevitably brought virtuoso qualities to the solo line. It not only exploited the rhythmic and melodic freedoms of the era, but introduced harmonic decorations, chiefly the *appoggiature* and other dependent dissonances, in increasing numbers. Evident in Machaut, these characteristics climaxed in an overproliferation, called *mannerism,* in the next generation of French composers.

THE NEW ART IN ITALY

At the beginning of the Ars nova, vernacular art songs were written mainly in the French of the trouvère. But through the late fourteenth and the fifteenth centuries, secular interests, local (civic or national) rather than international (Church) loyalties, and individual rather than corporate artistic expressions all reinforced one another in the cultivation of local vernaculars. By the height of the Renaissance, national forms would be definite and strong.

Perhaps the earliest development parallel to the French Ars nova and soon a great new art in its own right, was the Italian poetic art, the *dolce stil nuovo* ("gentle new style"). The French art, having begun as a courtly expression, had a tendency toward oversophistication and mannerism—the totality of the rhythmic complication was never exported. The Italians and the English tended to reserve the hocket, for example, for hunting pieces and other works in which such truncations and interjections could serve good (and good-natured) purpose.

In France the trouvère was the composer of the new art for the first two-thirds of the century. In Italy, the composer was a specialist sooner, the separation of poet and musician more distinct. The original formes fixes were not native to Italy, and the Italian poets developed their own forms. These were characterized by a greater regularity of line length, such as in the sonnet, in which a pattern of rhymes is worked out in a series of fourteen lines of equal length. The Italian forms were the *madrigal* (plural, *madrigali*) and the *caccia* (plural, *cacce*). The Italians also used the virelai form, which they called the *ballata* (plural, *ballate*). The French ballade and rondeau forms were not popular in Italy.

The madrigal developed early—in 1313 a theorist mentioned the form as one "qui de novo emergunt" [2] (that was newly emerging), and it was used by Dante, Petrarch, and Boccaccio. A forme fixe, the madrigal had two or three stanzas of three lines followed by a two-line refrain in contrasting rhythm. Early examples of its musical settings abounded in fifths and octaves, which were often parallel and were generally melismatic. The musical set-

[2] Francesco da Barberino, quoted in Nino Pirrotta, "L'Ars nova italienne," in *Histoire de la musique 1, Des origines à Jean-Sébastien Bach, Encyclopédie de la Pléiade,* Paris: Librairie Gallimard, 1960, p. 786.

tings of the madrigal form were parallel to the settings of other verse-refrain types.

The caccia was more unusual. It was a two-part vocal canon (deployed as $\begin{smallmatrix} a & b & c & d & e \\ a & b & c & d \end{smallmatrix}$ etc., rather as in English punctus exchange) over a slower, instrumental tenor. The name means hunting song, the same as the French *chasse*, which enjoyed less popularity but which was parallel in concept (Machaut left two of them). The hunting text, with its cries and interjections, was ideal for the lively exchanges of the canon and for the introduction of the truncated rhythms of hocket.

Hocket had been described by Walter Odington toward the end of the thirteenth century as "chopped singing," [3] that is, as alternate notes and rests spelling out a melody in brisk exchange between two parts. The exchange of parts carried through until the cadence formula began. Hocket was widely practiced and evidently very popular. Sections in hocket appeared in all schools, but hocket was especially beloved in those of the Italian and English.

The greatest figure of the Italian Ars nova was the blind organist Francesco Landini. A famous portrait [4] shows him holding a portative organ, a treble instrument whose exact function is disputed—it may have doubled the voice in a monophonic song or provided a countermelody, or it may have been used for simultaneous variation (heterophony), a practice that recent research has revealed to have been common in the fourteenth and fifteenth centuries.

Landini's art, as illustrated in Example 26, represents the Italian style as Machaut's does the French. Landini combined greater regularity of poetic line with greater coloratura in the solo voice, though with fewer proportional sophistications. The style was already Italianate in its rhythmically forthright yet vocally ornate solo line, for the upper line was definitely a solo part in spite of the presence of words for both lines. The appoggiature in quick two-note patterns within the melismas foreshadowed the vocal style of the Italian Baroque.

The final cadence, in which the major sixth to octave progression was decorated by a descending tone in the countertenor, was characteristic of Landini among the Italians of his time (though it appeared in Machaut and many other composers) and is called the *Landini cadence*. Its defining element was a final countertenor progression of 7–6–8 (measured from the tenor final) instead of the usual 7–8. The same progression occurred in three-part textures. It was actually a decorative form of the imperfection-to-perfection cadence over the standard 2–1 tenor, with an escape note embellishing the leading tone to final—a cadence in use for over a century by Landini's time.

---

[3] Quoted in Hugo Riemann, *History of Music Theory*, Lincoln, Nebr.: University of Nebraska Press, 1962, p. 167.

[4] Norbert Dufourcq, *Larousse de la musique*, Paris: Librairie Larousse, 1957, vol. I, p. 48.

Example 26A, "Amor con fede," by Francesco Landini, a facsimile from the Squarcialupi Codex, fifteenth century. The faster countertenor is at the top, the slower tenor at the bottom, and in each part the two musical elements are clearly marked off. The remaining text is given between the two parts. (Courtesy of the Biblioteca Medicea-Laurenziana, Firenze, Med. Palat. 87, c. 130. Photo by Guido Sansoni.)

Amor con fede

Example 26B

FRANCISCO LANDINI

Example 26B (continued)

Example 26B (continued)

A	*Amor con fede seguito, sperando* *Graçia da lucid' ochi che mi fanno,*	*Trust follows love, and I give thanks* *for those true eyes which give me hope.*
b	Ma s'umiltà contra dureca vale Innamar sempre con sincero core.	Humility is victorious over callousness and always loves a sincere heart.
b	Pur piegherà l'alter cor quello strale Che prenda a sensi el perduto vigore	Even the cold heart will yield to love's arrow as it draws forth tender feelings from melting resistance.
a	Et la virtù dell' eccelso splendore Renderà pace al mio molesto affano.	And virtue of the highest splendor will bring peace to my sorrowing soul.
A	*Amor con fede seguito, sperando* *Graçia da lucid' ochi che mi fanno.*	*Trust follows love, and I give thanks* *for those true eyes which give me hope.*

TRANS. BY JON RINKA

A polyphonic ballata (virelai) of the Italian school, based on the trouvère tradition. (Courtesy of The Medieval Academy of America.)

THE AVIGNON SCHOOL

The city of Avignon, in the south of France, could be expected to feel the cultural forces of both France and Italy. The papal court, located there for most of the fourteenth century, brought forth an international school of music composition in which the techniques of the Ars nova reached a culmination. The composers writing in and for the papal court were called *mannerists*, because they completed the rhythmic explorations of the Ars nova and used up the complex mannerisms of its notation. But they also pointed the way toward a new and simpler art.

Like the mannerists in the visual arts, who were concerned with arabesques, parabolas, and decorative designs mixed in a bewildering display of colors and symbols, the musical mannerists were producing their works for a dying feudal nobility who were going to extremes in dress, way of life, and cultural interests. It is worth noting that while the difficult, fussy musical practice was fashionable at court, minstrelsy was flourishing outside. A puy was held at Avignon in the fall of 1390, on the subject of constancy.

Of the arts in general, only the vernacular literary output, a rising rather than a culminating art, escaped the extremes of mannerism. Within the musical art, liturgical compositions—motets and Ordinaries of the Mass, of which about two dozen remain in two, three, and four parts—escaped also, aided by the papal bull of 1324–1325, which had spoken out against the secular techniques used in Church compositions. The art of the mannerists centered in the secular song.

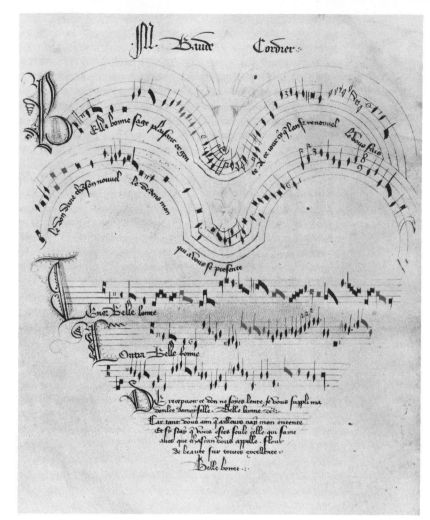

A chanson by Baude Cordier, in the shape of a heart. The upper part, the cantus, is not named, but the two lower parts are labeled "tenor" and "contra." Rhythmically the tenor is the simplest part; the contra and cantus are much more complex, with about a dozen shifts in proportion in the cantus. Sharp signs appear in all parts. (Courtesy of Musée Condé, Chantilly, Ms. 1047, and Photographie Giraudon.)

Like their predecessors, the composers of the Avignon school were primarily interested in the ballade, virelai, and rondeau. As a group, these composers delighted in the virtuoso notation (and hence in the reading skills) for which the school was known; therefore the music is dependent on the original notation for full appreciation.

In general, works of the Avignon school were rhythmically complex and relatively conservative in harmonic decoration, blending both French and Italian details. In addition, they frequently used northern French and Flemish linguistic forms in the texts. The extreme examples were concerned with virtuoso aspects of notation and with flamboyant rhythmic intricacies more pleasurable to the skilled performer than to the listener. When the possibilities of the notation were exhausted, composers had to turn to new, simpler materials, but they left a literature of songs that speaks with renewed vitality to musicians of the twentieth century.

ENGLAND

England was late in turning to the new art, and even when it did, British composers used the Ars nova more as a fund of new idioms to incorporate into the British musical style than as a new basis of composition. For one thing, a relatively late interest in sacred polyphony led to the fourteenth-century flowering of the Gothic motet, which was directly influenced by the last examples of the Notre Dame school. For this reason, the style of the English motet is often called *Petronian* after Petrus de Cruce, whose works had presaged the rhythmic niceties of the Ars nova. English motets tended to maintain rhythmic freedom in all parts, rejecting isorhythmic structures to enjoy a variety of pattern.

The English also avoided the dichotomy between secular and sacred styles that had characterized the Ars antiqua. The conductus used the punctus exchange technique of the rondellus and, in addition, was given instrumental preludes and interludes, long part of the minstrels' art but slow to enter the tradition of notated music. Both types, as well as such secular forms as the carole (then in its heyday), flourished in the fourteenth century in England. Minstrelsy was a strong force both at court and in the towns.

Although English adoption of the polyphonic motet and conductus came late, their practice of these forms was robust. By 1400, they maintained the strongest musical art in the Western tradition and were ready to supply the new materials that the depleted Ars nova required. As early as 1375, the view of English superiority appeared in critical writing.

> The French ditty outranks the Latin;
> Likewise the English surpasses them both.[5]

British fourteenth-century composers centered their interests in sacred polyphony, notably the motet, the Mass, and the trope, particularly with Marian texts. Composers turned to the polyphonic Ordinaries of the Mass (except for the Kyrie, which the English preferred as monophony) and brought significant creative energy to them before Continental composers did. Although the English Church was ruled by Rome, the rite (called Sarum use) was of the cathedral of Salisbury and was strongly related to the old Gallican practices of France. The English Gothic focused even more strongly on the Blessed Virgin Mary (B.V.M.) than the Continental had; the English cathedral typically devoted a chapel to her, called the Lady Chapel, where Lady Masses and special Marian Offices were performed.

---

[5] Quoted in Henry Holland Carter (ed.), "Ditty," *A Dictionary of Middle English Musical Terms*, Bloomington, Ind.: Indiana University Press, 1961, p. 129.

During the fourteenth and fifteenth centuries, England was involved in the long struggle with France known as the Hundred Years' War, a debilitating and draining conflict fought on French battlefields. The effects, which were devastating on the Continent, doubtless contributed to the feeling of musicians that the Ars nova was in decline. In England, musical opinion was divided into two schools of thought. Those composers who remained in the British Isles, constituting an insular school, continued their work in developing sacred polyphony in the English taste, using secular idiom as it pleased them. Those who worked on the Continent, chiefly in France and Italy, constituting a Continental English school, turned to the chanson and to sacred works, particularly the motet, in the Continental style.

About three dozen English composers of this time are known to us, most of them only by their names. However, over two hundred English works appear in surviving European manuscripts, a considerable testimony to the respected place English composers held in Continental opinion. And one work, "O Rosa Bella," [6] an Italian poem set to music by an English composer, was one of the most popular songs of the fifteenth century.

John Dunstable, the best known and probably the greatest of the composers, is representative of the English school of the first half of the fifteenth century. His place as a transitional figure is implicit in the variety of forms and styles in which he worked, whereas his essentially Medieval style is attested to by his use of three-part texture and the techniques associated with it. He used gymel and discant, along with isorhythmic structure, representing both English and French heritage. But the fulfillment of Dunstable's art lay in his bringing the three-line texture with solo, developed in the chanson of the French Ars nova, to the motet. The English approach contributed further developments to the motet—the borrowed tune, often embellished, put into the top solo voice over a liturgical cantus firmus and, particularly, a rhythmic organization that followed the text. This type of motet was called *declamatory*; it was, in a sense, the inevitable result of the accommodation of a French secular form to a sacred Latin text by an Englishman used to isochronous verse.

The chanson itself was not unknown in the English school; it was used by many composers. But the motet, with solo top part, is probably the most representative form of the English school on the Continent. The motet "Quam pulcra es" [7] was a compendium of late Medieval idioms and techniques—cambiata and related figures, discant techniques, declamatory passages, the double leading-tone cadence, large and small hemiola, the exploitation of the chromatic semitone (here E and $E\flat$), and the transposition of Guido's scale to achieve the soft $\flat$. The modernity lies in its being

---

[6] This work appears in Archibald T. Davison and Willi Apel, *Historical Anthology of Music*, vol. I, *Oriental, Medieval and Renaissance Music*, rev. ed., Cambridge, Mass.: Harvard, 1962, pp. 65–66.

[7] This work appears in Arnold Schering, *Geschichte der Musik in Beispielen*, Leipzig: Breitkopf & Härtel, 1931, pp. 29–30.

a motet built like a chanson and in the mixture of techniques associated with a variety of schools.

THE BURGUNDIANS

The Hundred Years' War included periods in which English and French interactions were common on all levels: Henry V of England married a French princess; English musicians were included in the retinues of princes and ambassadors (Dunstable with the Duke of Bedford in Paris, for example); English choirs came to France; and English music—such as the carole "Deo gratias Anglia," [8] written in celebration of the English victory at Agincourt in 1415—was known to musician and layman alike. But the war sapped resources, leaving France and England too exhausted, physically and economically, to take the lead in cultural matters. Strength lay in other quarters, specifically in the Burgundian dynasty, whose dukes drew great men around them and turned the Burgundian courts into an international cultural center. Painting, dancing, literature, and, of course, music were all supported and cherished. It was a transitional time, and the Burgundian school produced the last great expression of the Medieval genius, while also developing the new forms and techniques that were to define the coming Renaissance.

The geographical center of the Burgundian school was the group of provinces whose names even now ring with the memory of splendor—Flanders, Brabant, Holland, Zeeland, Hainaut, Namur (now Belgium, the Netherlands, and the northeastern provinces of France). During the fifteenth century, the northern provinces were held by the dukes of Burgundy. Burgundy itself, in eastern France, was less important to the dukes than the northern centers such as Bruges and Brussels, where trade flourished and could support a sumptuous life. Philip the Good (1396–1467) became an active patron of the arts, drawing to his courts a dazzling group of artisans and artists. Color was a byword; the new art of oil painting was introduced by Jan van Eyck (c. 1370–1441). Artisans developed architectural and interior styles that, along with the flamboyant costumes of the courts, illustrate our fairy tales to this day. Entertainments were lavish and, in the manner of minstrelsy, combined vaudevillian and musical elements with flair. Dinner and after-dinner entertainments were traditional during the Medieval and Renaissance eras (as they still are). One of Philip's dinners featured "a pie within which were 28 live persons, playing various instruments, each when his turn came." [9]

[8] This work appears in *Musica Britannica*, vol. IV, *Mediæval Carols*, London: Stainer and Bell, 1952, p. 6.
[9] Quoted in Henry Leland Clarke, "Musicians of the Northern Renaissance," in Jan La Rue (ed.), *Aspects of Medieval & Renaissance Music*, New York: Norton, 1966, p. 71.

But music was, as always, more than entertainment, and the Duke's practice of populating his courts with gifted men from many places was to produce a musical cross-pollination of significance to the entire succeeding art of music in the West.

The native lowlanders of the generation born about 1400 were surrounded by diversity as well as by brilliance. Surviving Burgundian manuscripts include English, French, and Italian works. Composers could draw on forms as different as the chanson, the carole, and the caccia, and on techniques as variable as those of discant, punctus exchange, or mannered notation. The challenge of forging such divergent elements into a new musical language brought forth the men to accomplish it—three generations of composers as transcendently gifted as any in our heritage. Eventually, they were to move southward and disseminate throughout Europe the style that would form the basis of the new music of the Renaissance.

Gilles Binchois and Guillaume Dufay, considered the greatest of their generation, complemented each other. Binchois is remembered chiefly as a traditionalist composing in the formes fixes; Dufay is remembered as a modernist, one of the great modernists in the history of music, who wrote at the cutting edge for over half a century.

Although the chanson continued to be written in its Medieval guise for decades, well into the Renaissance, its last truly Medieval flowering was at the courts of Burgundy. The specialization of the artist, already seen in Italy, is evident in the Burgundian chanson, where poet and musician were as often two men as one (Binchois had a reputation as a poet but Dufay did not). One of the loveliest works in the history of song, for instance, is Dufay's setting of Petrarch's sonnet "Virgine Bella"; [10] here a unique work was produced by the concurrence of two great specialists.

More typical of the late Medieval chanson are the works of Binchois, whose rondeau "De plus en plus" (Example 27) is representative. The work is an expressive and graceful solo with instruments. In three separate lines and in triple proportion (with large and small hemiola freely used), it ranges Guido's scale and enjoys that scale's chromatic semitone and musica ficta. In an expanded forme fixe, with a total verse form of twenty-one lines, its poem is made of a lines of nine and b lines of eight syllables—the A section scanned aab, whereas B was ba. The musical elements parallel the poetic form in phrases and large units but with independent musical shape and logic. The work is an almost perfect reconciliation of polar elements—text and music, voice and instruments, English and French melodic idioms (the opening melodic thirds were typically English), originality and tradition (as evidenced in the cadences completing the two sections, A, personal, and B, a Landini formula).

Of interest is the cadence at the end of the first punctus, where the

[10] This work appears in Heinrich Besseler, *Dufay: Opera omnia*, Rome: American Institute of Musicology, 1964, vol. VI, pp. 7–9.

countertenor (on the bottom staff) lies below the tenor and proceeds up an octave as the tenor descends to the phrase final, here interrupted by an eighth rest. Such a countertenor progression, reckoned as 5–5 (measured from the tenor final), became a standard formula in popular music (as in Example 30); it is called the Burgundian cadence, the 5–5 cadence, or the Dufay cadence.

Guillaume Dufay is best represented by his sacred music, which was culminative for its genre as was the Binchois chanson for the formes fixes.

De plus en plus
GILLES BINCHOIS

Example 27

Example 27 (continued)

B.

Ce me fait le très grand dé - sir Que j'ay de vous o-

ir nou - vel - le.

A	*De plus en plus se renouvelle,*	A	*More and more does my wish to be with you*
	Ma doulce Dame gente et belle,		*Renew itself, my sweet lady,*
	Ma volunté de vous véir.		*Beautiful and kind.*
B	*Ce me fait le très grant désir*	B	*From this springs my great desire*
	Que j'ai de vous ouir nouvelle.		*To hear all news of you.*
a	Ne cuidiés pas que je recelle—	a	Do not fear that I disguise the truth.
	Comme à tous jours vous estes celle		You are as ever she whom I would obey
	Que je vueil de tout obéir.		In everything I do.
A	*De plus en plus se renouvelle,*	A	*More and more does my wish to be with you*
	Ma doulce Dame gente et belle,		*Renew itself, my sweet lady,*
	Ma volunté de vous véir.		*Beautiful and kind.*
a	[Lost]	a	[Lost]
b	[Lost]	b	[Lost]
A	*De plus en plus se renouvelle,*	A	*More and more does my wish to be with you*
	Ma doulce Dame gente et belle,		*Renew itself, my sweet lady,*
	Ma volunté de vous véir.		*Beautiful and kind.*
B	*Ce me fait le très grant désir*	B	*From this springs my great desire*
	Que j'ai de vous ouir nouvelle.		*To hear all news of you.*

TRANS. BY JON RINKA

A polyphonic rondeau in the trouvère tradition, as practiced at the Burgundian court. (Courtesy of Breitkopf & Härtel, Wiesbaden, Germany.)

(Dufay afterward moved ahead to the new style.) The late Medieval style, particularly in England, developed the Mass (meaning the Ordinary) and the motet in the chanson texture. Although complete Masses were a late development, to become central to Renaissance music, more and more complete Masses appeared in manuscripts during the fifteenth century. At the beginning of the century, most manuscripts offered all the Kyrie movements, all the Gloria movements, and so on, in separate sections, leaving the producer to select items to make up the complete Ordinary. By the end of the century, most manuscripts contained unified complete Ordinaries. Dufay was one of the first to write Masses in the new style, with four parts (adding a bass beneath the tenor). During his career, the new style was practiced alongside the old, the new gradually increasing its strength, eventually to overpower the old.

The chanson texture, with an embellished cantus in the solo line, appeared in late Medieval Mass and hymn settings, of which Dufay wrote many.[11] The settings incorporated a melodic decoration of an almost universal type, common to both exotic and Western music; such a decoration is as much at home in a Bach organ variation on a hymn tune and a jazz version of a popular tune as in Dufay. Harmonically, the hymns were often related to the fourteenth-century English practice of discant and used both the double leading-tone cadence (at the end) and the Burgundian formula (5–5).

In late Medieval English practice—often extemporization at sight from a written tenor—imperfect intervals were used, juxtaposed for the sake of their sounds. When the sound was brought to the Continent, the procedure was reversed, with the cantus on top and the accompanying parts beneath—a radical departure from the long tradition of building upward from the tenor. On the Continent, the technique was called *fauxbourdon*, "false bass," which indeed it was, in traditional terms. Fauxbourdon was widely used during the fifteenth century, and, although it was soon superseded as a definitive technique, it long remained in the vocabulary and idiom of Western music and appeared frequently in brief passages throughout the Renaissance.

THE FIFTEENTH CENTURY

The fifteenth century was a period of transition, during which the whole philosophy of man and his institutions was being revised. The great book of the century (and, next to the Bible, the second-best seller of all time) was *The Imitation of Christ*, written about 1420 by Thomas à Kempis, a churchman from the diocese of Cologne. The work was a bold study of man's ability to be Christlike through the power of his own will as well as

---

[11] Rudolf Gerber (ed.), *Das Chorwerk*, Wolfenbüttel: Möseler Verlag, 1937, vol. 49. Two of the settings—no. 2, pp. 5–6, and no. 15, p. 15—appear in two versions, in fauxbourdon and with a countertenor part marked "Contra sine Fauxbourdon" added when the fauxbourdon was not sung.

through grace. The political structure of Europe was changing, shifting from feudal to financial (merchant) bases, with a resultant increase in city population. The central importance of the Burgundians was broken with the death of Charles the Bold in 1477. His dying without a son caused the partition of his lands—the northern provinces went to the Habsburg dynasty through the marriage of his daughter Mary to Maximilian of Austria. In Italy, the city-state was thriving as a political unit. And even where feudalism had not disappeared, nobles built city houses and centered their lives more and more in urban settings, thus keeping their country holdings as secondary establishments.

But the chief result of the new developments was the creation of a new kind of citizen—the man of means. In a valid sense, this man was to be the hero of the Renaissance. For the first time, there were men who lived in houses and had livingrooms (neither castle nor hut, huge stone hall nor dirt-floored single room), time for study, and money to hire tutors and copyists. This new man of means sought out ways to provide himself with knowledge; the invention of movable type in the West, associated with the Gutenberg Bible of 1453, assured its availability. The man of means also needed the services of the architect, the artist, the tutor, and the musician, giving rise to a host of new professions and professional men. The printer, the instrument maker, the carpenter, the mason turned from private to public service and entered the body politic as citizens in their own right and as consumers of music.

It took time for these changes to occur; their fruition was to be the animating spirit of the Renaissance. The fifteenth century was the time of gradual change; the century began in the Medieval era and ended in the Renaissance. Art and music rose to transcendent heights at the end of the century. Leonardo da Vinci (1452–1519), an embodiment of the "new man," is listed in the dictionary as "Italian painter, sculptor, architect, musician, engineer, mathematician, and scientist." His sketchbooks show that he worked on designs for everything from time machines to airplanes, fountains to parachutes, cathedrals to gardens. Michelangelo Buonarroti (1475–1564) is listed as "Italian sculptor, painter, architect, and poet." [12]

Great musicians were carrying on a parallel Renaissance art, with Josquin des Prez and Heinrich Isaac as illustrious in music as Leonardo and Michelangelo were in the plastic arts (though musicians tended more toward specialization). The new music was the product of long development of new materials, beginning with the Burgundians and continuing largely through the Franco-Flemish heritage. But during the development of the new style, which, at its inception, was mainly limited to the professionals, the Medieval style continued to flourish, so that popular and learned music formed quite distinct styles in the third quarter of the century. Although the popular music retained the conservative tradition of musical materials, it derived its excite-

[12] *The American College Dictionary*, New York: Random House, 1947.

ments from the contributions of the performer in arranging, producing, and staging. An account from 1469 vividly illustrates this point—the chronicler described an entertainment for Louis XI, who was visiting Paris.

> Upon his entry, the herald, Loyal Cœur, presented him with five noble ladies who represented the five letters of the name *Paris*, and each of them made a speech of welcome. The horses were caparisoned with cloth of gold lined with sable, with velvet lined with ermine, and with cloth of Damascus mounted with goldsmith's work. At the fountain of Ponceau were three very pretty girls in the role of sirens, all naked, and one could see their lovely breasts, separate, round, and firm, which was a very pleasant thing, and they sang short motets and bergerettes [pastoral songs]. And near them were playing several low [soft] instruments that sounded many tunes. A few paces off, there was a Passion represented by people in dumb show [pantomime], God stretched upon the Cross and the two thieves to right and left. On the Pont au Change, the birdsellers, who have a monopoly in selling their birds on the Place du Chatelet [they still have it], set free two hundred of their wares, brilliant of plumage. . . . [Later, when the Queen arrived by boat], a great and notable number of counselors and burghers of the aforesaid city came to meet her, also in boats that were all richly covered with beautiful tapestries and silken drapes. And in them were the little choir-boys of the Sainte-Chapelle, who sang beautiful virelais, chansons, and other bergerettes very tunefully. And there were also a great number of clarinos, trumpets, singers, high and low [loud and soft] instruments of diverse kinds, who played all together most melodiously.[13]

The quotation is of interest, for it tells of three treble voices singing a motet in the old style, that is, three voices in similar range. It also records the performance in public by women, a practice in which the French were often exceptional, and it certainly illustrates the juxtaposition of elements and the overall love of color and spectacle so beloved in the Medieval philosophy of the arts.

The most popular tune of the century was a French song, a soldiering tune called "L'homme armé" (The Man-at-Arms or, simply, The Soldier, Example 28). The tune is strong and motivating—as soldiering tunes often are—and very French, with its interest in fourths and fifths. How the tune was originally arranged and performed is a matter of conjecture. It is a fine fife-and-drum tune, of course, and doubtless had many a performance in that medium. But by the fifteenth century, two- and three-part textures were popular and standard, and groups of people singing and playing together may have improvised parts. Also open to conjecture is how the gentler popular tunes—still in the heritage of courtly love—were sung. The poignant "A the syghes" (Example 29), though English, may well have been familiar on the Continent, for at this time English choirs were singing in France and their informal music must have been as familiar as the formal.

---

[13] Quoted in H. Biehn, *Les fêtes en Europe*, Paris: Editions Albin Michel, 1963, pp. 89–91.

L'homme armé   Example 28

ANONYMOUS

L'hom - me, l'hom - me, l'homme ar - mé, l'homme ar - mé,

l'homme ar - mé doibt on doub - ter. On a fait par

tout cri - er Que chas - cun se viengne ar - mer D'un

hau - bre - gon de fer. L'hom - mé, l'hom - mé, l'homme ar -

mé, l'homme ar - mé, l'homme ar - mé doibt on doub - ter.

The man-at-arms is not to be trusted; everywhere it is announced that we should armor ourselves with hauberks.

This tune was at its height of popularity in the second half of the fifteenth century. Like most popular music of that time, it was widely sung but seldom written down.

We know more about the performance of the love songs popular through the end of the century, because these were written out in separate lines (generally three), sometimes with words for all parts but more often with a text for the cantus only.

The chanson "Amor con l'arco tesso" (Example 30) is an interesting mixture of elements. The lyric has a complex yet balanced *axaaya*/787979 structure, in Italian rather than French. The song was included in the *Chansonnier Cordiforme,* one of the most famous of fifteenth-century manuscripts. It is a heart-shaped book and one of the loveliest of the handwritten musical volumes of an era known for its excellent scribes and illuminators.

The musical form is simply *abcdef.* The song's spare rhythmic language may be deceiving, for accounts of popular singing described embellishments

Example 29A, "A the syghes," a facsimile from a British fifteenth-century manuscript. The music is simple to read; the C clef, the B-flat signature calling for the soft hexachord so beloved of the British, and the sign for imperfect time are all quite clear. The fermata is used to mark the end of the puncti. (Courtesy of the British Museum.)

A the syghes

ANONYMOUS

Example 29B

A the syghes that come fro my hert they greve me pas-sing sore Syth I must fro my love de-part ffare well my Joye for e-ver-more.

A the syghes that come fro my hert
They greve me passyng sore
Syth I must fro my love depart
Ffare well my Joye for evermore.

Oft to me with hir goodly face
She was wont to cast an eye
And now absence to me in place
Alas for woo I dye I dye.

I was wonte hir to beholde
And takyn in Armes twayne
And now wyth syghes manyfolde
Fare well my Joye and welcome payne.

A methynke that I schud yete
as wolde to Gode that I myght
There myght no Joyes compare with hyt
Unto my hart to make hyt lyght.

A popular English tune of the fifteenth century.

that were not part of the notation. Yet block progression, in which all parts were based on a single rhythm and imperfect intervals featured, was extremely popular with Italians, who appreciated the beauty of the vertical

137

combinations even over melodic grace. Such rhythm was said to be in the *familiar style*, and its directness and simplicity were typical of Italian popular songs in the last third of the century. In another generation, such works, characterized by the use of punctus forms without repetition and by the familiar style, would be the most popular in the country. Their freedom from the formes fixes and their harmonic joy would be typical of the Renaissance style.

The countertenor part of "Amor con l'arco tesso," with its range G to d^1, lies generally below the tenor, though at cadences it seeks return to its usual high ground. For vocal classification, such a part, by then commonly found in both modern and conservative music, had to be distinguished from the traditional countertenor, because the new part required another voice range. The two types were therefore called the high and low countertenors, or *contratenor altus* and *contratenor bassus*. Usage would shorten the words to *contr'alto* and *contra'basso* (both Italian terms of a century later) and to the further shortened *alto* and *basso*, which came to stand for these ranges in general. *Countertenor* persisted in England (where the voice was much loved) as an indication of the high male range.

The cadences of this work are of interest. As usual, the final cadence is the most formal and represents the standard type of the style, in this case, the 5–5 cadence (see page 131), in which the countertenor crosses the tenor. The interior secondary cadence (on *primo*) is the same. Most of the others are weak, with repeated sounds rather than progression to a final tone; but the second stop, on *asferera*, looks forward to harmonic progressions of the Renaissance.

The proportion is doubly duple—the song has duple division and duple subdivision of the beat, both of which were standard by then, as they would be throughout the Renaissance. The opening rhythmic pattern of long-short-short on repeated notes became a cliché for the chanson and was to have a significant life as an opening motive.

Such works as "Amor con l'arco tesso" represented both the last of the Medieval ideal and the first strong breath of the Renaissance. The music lay within Medieval concepts, however, with performance intended by contrasting qualities; the combination of voices and instruments was held to be the perfect harmony. By 1500 such a work in Italy was called a *frottola* (plural, *frottole*).

In addition to the performances of such chansons, singing to the lute (or another instrument) became extremely popular again, in emulation not of the troubador, for Gothic ideas were increasingly in disrepute, but of the ancient Greeks, who had sung to the lyre. The famous lutenist-singer Pietro Bono sang alone early in his career, accompanying himself on the lute, but later he employed an instrumentalist, called a *tenorista*, who plucked a viola; presumably the tenorista performed the tenor while the soloist sang the cantus. The great men of secular music—Pietro Bono, Seraphino Aquilano, Lawrence of Cordoba—were improvisers whose music is lost in the long past

Example 30A, "Amor con l'arco tesso," a facsimile from the *Chansonnier Cordiforme*. The three parts are set across two open pages, many of which have miniatures showing scenes of courtship. (Courtesy of the Bibliothèque Nationale, Rothschild 2973, Folio 14ᵛ–15.)

Amor con l'arco tesso   Example 30B

ANONYMOUS

A - mor con l'ar - co tes — so   del co - re me   as - fe - re -

139

Example 30B (continued)

Love, like a drawn bow, grips my heart. The strong chain of the first love cannot be broken, with its hold that is leading me to great suffering.

A popular chanson of the Italian period of transition between the trouvère tradition and the Renaissance. It evinces characteristics of both. (Courtesy of the American Institute of Musicology, Rome.)

of unwritten sounds. Leonardo, too, was known as an improviser (he favored a viola-like instrument called the lira da braccio). He wrote that music could not be imprisoned in time, that it should be improvised and thus lost to the future.[14]

The reconciling of independent elements that retained their individual character, a central ideal in Medieval music, was dying out as a creative philosophy. Yet the dances in the book of Marguerite of Austria (the daughter of Maximilian I and Mary of Burgundy and the final figure of the brilliant lowland courts) demonstrate the joy in such reconciliation even after 1500. The dance "La Margarite" was thirty-eight beats (long notes or full counts) long—the musical phrase structure of the tune was $2 + 6 + 7 + 6 + 7 + 10$, whereas the dance steps proceeded as $2 + 8 + 6 + 8 + 6 + 8$. The dance was monophonic, notated as a single line of thirty-eight notes. It was to be given rhythmic detail by the players and be organized as minstrelsy, with contrasting instrumental types and registers, or as improvised heterophony. (Pictures of court dances show a variety of linear and, often, percus-

[14] Emanuel Winternitz, "Leonardo's References to Music," unpublished paper read to the American Musicological Society, Washington, D.C., 1963.

The basse danse "La Margarite," from the *Dance Book of Marguerite of Austria.* The manuscript was notated with gold and silver ink on black parchment. Each note of the dance represents a musical unit comparable to the initial pitch of each measure in $\frac{12}{8}$ time, to be filled in by the players. Beneath the music are letters representing dance steps. (Courtesy of the Bibliothèque Royale de Belgique, Ms. 9085, fol. 8ʳ.)

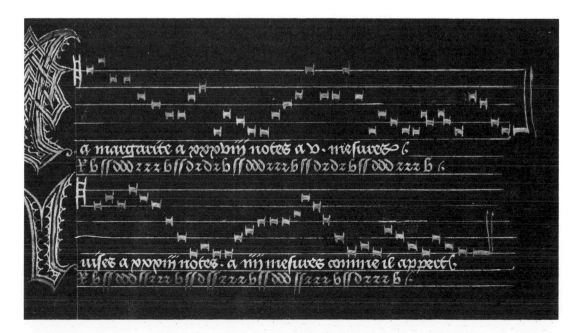

"Dancing on Christmas Eve," by Hartmann Schedel, a woodcut from *The Nuremberg Chronicle*, 1493. For a free scope of embellishment or for wide-ranging melodies, a longer flute than the three-hole pipe was needed. The flute and drum became a two-man combination of instruments. (Courtesy of the Pierpont Morgan Library.)

sion instruments.) Such design incorporated the harmony of polarities to create a balanced imbalance that stamped the Medieval genius with the unique energy and beauty that was vital to Medieval music.

❀ *Some Composers of the Fourteenth and Fifteenth Centuries*

The initial impetus of the Ars nova was centered in France, particularly in Philippe de Vitry (c. 1291–1361) and Guillaume de Machaut (see page 48). A survey of representative composers from the fourteenth and fifteenth centuries shows that the location of musical leadership was shifting throughout the period but that a flow of creative energy was nevertheless maintained through travel and international exchange.

Italians

GIOVANNI DE CASCIA or DE FLORENTIA (active c. 1340–1350) was from Florence. His works, written mainly in two parts, are found in many manuscripts. He left ballate, cacce, and madrigali, to which he is said to have given the definitive form.

JACOPO DA BOLOGNA (c. 1300–c. 1365) worked in Florence, Bologna, and Milan and was influenced by Vitry. He wrote madrigali, cacce, and ballate, in two and three parts. His single motet is the only surviving Italian secular motet of this period.

FRANCESCO LANDINI (c. 1325–1397) of Florence was the greatest of the composers of the Italian school. A blind organist and composer, he left 1 caccia, 12 madrigali, and 140 ballate, mostly in two parts. He was influenced by Machaut.

The Avignon School

ANTONELLUS DE CASERTA (active c. 1375–1400), a Frenchman, may have worked in Modena, where religious compositions of his have been found. Of his Avignon works, 5 ballades, 10 virelais, and 2 rondeaux remain.

JOHANNES CICONIA (c. 1335–1412) was from Liège. In Avignon by 1350, then in Italy, he wrote madrigali and ballate as well as French works. From 1372 to 1401 he was in Liège, where he concentrated on Masses and motets. After 1401 he returned to Italy, and he died in Padua.

MATHEUS DE PERUSIO (active c. 1380–1410) was one of the modernists of the group. Looking forward to Dunstable and Dufay, he is credited with the introduction of instrumental interludes in the chansons. He was prolific and influential, and further investigation may show him to have had a vital role in the transition from the French to the Burgundian styles. Remaining are 4 ballades, 7 virelais, 10 rondeaux, and 1 canon.

BAUDE CORDIER (active c. 1400–1420), from Rheims, has left 1 three-part Gloria and 10 chansons. His rondeau "Belle, bonne, sage" fused the ballata and the French forms. He is known for heart-shaped and circle formats, chansons notated so as to form imaginative shapes on the page (see p. 126).

English

THOMAS DAMETT (died c. 1430), a royal household musician, was perhaps involved in training the choirs that toured the Continent. His motet "Salvatoris Mater" is isorhythmic, and surviving Mass movements are in the chanson style.

LEONEL POWER (died 1445), a musician of Christ Church, Canterbury, was known as a composer and theorist. (He wrote a treatise on English discant.) About 50 Mass fragments survive, along with 1 cyclic Ordinary, 2 settings of the Ave Regina, and 1 Salve Regina.

WALTER FRYE (died c. 1450), known to have been at the papal chapel in 1428, is thought to have centered his career at the Burgundian courts, where most of his surviving works have been found.

His Ave Regina exists in thirteen manuscripts; he also left 3 Masses (2 in three parts, 1 in four), 5 motets, and 7 chansons (2 in English). He was an important and influential figure.

JOHN DUNSTABLE (c. 1370–1453), a mathematician and astronomer, was one of the greatest musicians of the century. He served the Duke of Bedford, the regent in Paris, and was said by the generation following him to have been the founder of modern music. Surviving are over 70 works, including motets (some of them isorhythmic), Mass movements, and chansons.

Burgundians

NICOLAS GRENON (c. 1375–c. 1450) was a choir master at Cambrai from 1404 and, hence, probably a teacher of Dufay. Specific dates of his activity are 1421 and 1427. He left 5 chansons, 1 Gloria, and 4 motets.

PIERRE FONTAINE (c. 1380–c. 1450) was a choirboy in Rouen. From 1404 to 1420, he was at the courts of the dukes of Burgundy; from 1420 to 1427, he was at the papal chapel; and from 1427, he was at the duke's court at Dijon as chaplain. Surviving are 7 chansons—6 rondeaux and 1 ballade, 6 in three parts and 1 in four.

HUGO DE LANTINS (active c. 1420) was from Liège. Surviving works include 8 Mass fragments, 5 motets, 14 rondeaux, and 4 ballate (an international group of works).

GILLES BINCHOIS (c. 1400–1460) was a soldier in France and then a priest. He was in Paris in 1424, and from 1430 he served Philip the Good. He left Mass fragments, motets, and a Magnificat but is best known for his chansons, about 40 of which survive, almost all rondeaux.

GUILLAUME DUFAY (c. 1400–1474) was, from 1409 to 1414, a choirboy at Cambrai, where his career was to center in spite of trips—to Italy in 1419 to 1426 and (for the papal chapel) in 1428 to 1433, to Savoy in 1433 to

1435, and then to Florence and Bologna in 1435 to 1437. He served the dukes of Burgundy from 1445 with occasional trips such as one to Besançon in 1458 to judge a puy. Dufay was a modernist all his life, working in both the old and new styles even in his seventies. About 9 complete Masses and 37 Mass fragments remain, along with 5 Magnificats, 32 motets, 44 hymns and liturgical pieces, and more than 90 chansons (84 in French) in forty-seven manuscript sources. Prolific, universally revered, and called "Luna totius musicæ" ("the moon of all music"), Dufay is among the handful of the transcendently great composers in our history.

Part Two

THE RENAISSANCE

A goodly song we here have writ
For singing in four parts—to wit,
The Tenor, Cantus, Alto, Bass
A courtly text do interlace
And prettily together fit,
In sweetest concord sounding it
To lift up hearts in glad content.
'Twas Amphion did the song invent.

HANS SACHS *

At the Height
of the Renaissance

8

The four-part polyphonic Ordinary of the Mass was the most important musical form at the opening of the sixteenth century. The fifteenth century had been a period of two practices—the old three-part and the new four-part textures had existed side by side during a long transition. Ordinaries in four parts were composed from the second quarter of the fifteenth century, when Dufay and other modernists of the Burgundian group were experimenting in the new style. However, the new style was the province of the avant-garde until the end of the century, by which time it became strong enough to become standard for all music. As the new style became more firmly estab-

* Sixteenth century. "The Singers." Trans. by Christiane Cooper.

lished in sacred music, the old texture became more exclusively associated with the popular. Dufay cultivated both styles from his middle years, contributing splendid works to both.

The new style was defined by the addition of a fourth part, a low countertenor (contratenor bassus), set below the tenor and given increasing recognition as a motivating element in vertical structures. Its eventual domination, even over the tenor, was to herald the Baroque ideal, but at the High Renaissance period, the contratenor bassus was what its name indicated—a low-ranged line written against the defining tenor and, in general, below it. Thus it was not only the four-part norm of the Renaissance that comprised a change from the three-part norm of the Medieval era; it was the total range of the parts and, in particular, the redeployment of the tenor from the bottom to the inner areas of the total sound that comprised a more significant change.

Even more definitive was the new concept of total sound, which viewed the polyphonic work as one that used the four parts to create a unified and expressive harmony of voices. Although the parts were conceived separately and were still usually composed one by one, beginning with the tenor, the vertical element was being redefined. The importance of the vertical in polyphony at the beginning of the sixteenth century was indicated in many manuscripts. One writer in the first decade of the century wrote of the recent change, "The simple [unison or octave] performance in the high register used in the old days would be joined by related sounds from the low register, and from the latter a combined symphony [a sounding together] would flourish more richly, . . . by which the sense of the ear can best be filled with perfect sweetness." [1] This comment defines the change from the Medieval to the Renaissance ideal, and the writer, like his contemporaries, was well aware that he was a member of a special generation.

The generation was, in fact, an apex of the Renaissance; it was the generation of Leonardo and Michelangelo. The Renaissance was an exhilarating time whose catholic interests centered on man. Medieval man had seen himself as creature, created by and, at his best, reflecting his Creator; Renaissance man saw himself as the noblest creation of God and, further, as a creator in his own right. He explored the world and claimed it as his own. He explored himself and gloried in what he found. He speculated on everything, and he refined the arts of observation and measurement. His greatest achievements lay in the visual arts and architecture, which could portray, honor, and commemorate man.

The enormous wealth that existed in private hands created an era of sponsors of artistic splendor and consumers of lavish personal adornment. It is no coincidence that the Renaissance produced Benvenuto Cellini (1500–1571), the world's most famous worker in precious metals and gems, or that Cellini's most famous piece was not a chalice or a reliquary, as a Medieval

[1] Quoted in Nino Pirrotta, "Music and Cultural Tendencies in 15th-Century Italy," *Journal of the American Musicological Society*, vol. 19, no. 2, p. 153f., Summer, 1966.

artisan's might have been, but a salt cellar for the private table of Francis I. Nor is it a coincidence that whereas the Medieval metalworkers were anonymous, Cellini was so renowned that he wrote his autobiography, which is still widely read. The generosity of the patron was a considerable spur to artists and musicians. As early as the 1470s the writer Joannes Tinctoris made note of this.

> Since the singers of princes, if their masters are endowed with the liberality which makes men illustrious, are rewarded with honor, glory, and wealth, many are kindled with a most fervent zeal for this study. At this time, consequently, the possibilities of our music have been so marvelously increased that there appears to be a new art, if I may so call it, whose fount and origin is held to be among the English, of whom Dunstable stood forth as chief. Contemporary with him in France were Dufay and Binchoys, from whom directly succeeded the moderns. . . .[2]

[2] Quoted in Oliver Strunk (ed.), *Source Readings in Music History*, New York: Norton, 1950, p. 195.

Benvenuto Cellini, "Salt Cellar of Francis I." A superb example of the Renaissance crafts, created between 1530 and 1543. (Courtesy of the Kunsthistorisches Museum, Vienna.)

The new music flourished in private chapels, which were not so much a strong religious force as a symbol of status and power. As the place of daily assembly for Mass and the Offices, the chapels became a convenient focus of social gathering, of entertainment, and of welcoming and impressing visitors and ambassadors. Music was part of this panoply of self-esteem. Chapel personnel, in addition to performing religious functions, formed a corps of secretaries, bookkeepers, and political officers. The chaplain was often a personal adviser in matters of public weal, and members of the chapel were legates, ambassadors, and even ministers of state.[3]

Italy, ahead of Northern Europe in the development of merchant duchies and city-states, could best support chapel activity. Italian dukes and doges bore the names of Medici, Sforza, Este, and Borgia, dynasties whose power could command the greatest talents of the day and bring them to Italy. The papal chapel had been increasing its roster during the fifteenth century— from nine singers in 1436 (when Dufay left) to twenty-four by 1500. And some private chapels rivaled the papal chapel.

Franco-Flemish composers furnished musical leadership in a number of Italian centers—Florence, Milan, Padua, Venice, Ferrara, and many others. These musicians were a cosmopolitan group; they traveled widely and drew together many strands of musical influence to create the new style. They emerged as somewhat free-wheeling men who knew they were in demand and could fashion careers of interest and importance. They were examples of the new man of means who was to dominate the cultural developments of the next century, less spectacularly but, in the long run, more significantly than the dukes they worked for.

THE POLYPHONIC MASS

The musical setting of the Mass Ordinary had expanded into a significant and autonomous musical work. By the year 1500 the Mass was a substantial musical statement. Like any other creative movement, the one that gave rise to the new style of the Renaissance had rejected much from the past—the very sound and texture of the musical fabric—but retained much of past technique. The tenor continued to provide a structural basis for composition and, through the use of the cantus firmus, to invoke the authority of established melodies. The Renaissance view of the whole man made it possible for composers to include secular songs among these melodies— many Masses were based on popular songs and the more sophisticated chansons. In fact, Mass titles were the names of the previous works on which the works were based—Dufay's *Missa Se le face ay pale* (chanson) and Josquin's *Missa Pange lingua* (plainchant hymn) are representative.

[3] For a discussion of the chapel of Maximilian of Austria, see Louise Cuyler, *Emperor Maximilian I and Music*, Fair Lawn, N.J.: Oxford University Press, 1971.

Other Masses were called *Missa sine nomine* (Mass without a name); these were freely composed without reference to a stated cantus prius factus. And still others used a *soggetto cavato* (carved subject), in which the vowels in a name or phrase were made to represent sol-fa syllables—*a–e–i–o–u* became *fa/la–re–mi–sol–ut*. This latter technique is represented in Josquin's "Missa Hercules Dux Ferrarie." The composer dedicated the work to one of his patrons, Hercules, duke of Ferrara; he reduced the duke's name to the vowels *e–u–e / u / e–a–i–e* or *re–ut–re–ut–re–fa–mi–re*, which he then used as a cantus firmus. Ockeghem produced a *Missa Mi–Mi*, in which the various hexachords and their transpositions provided a liberal set of variants for the syllables. In short, cantus firmi could derive from the most imaginative sources.

Experiments in pitch materials and rhythmic proportions also abounded. Johannes Ockeghem was well known for these; he composed both a *Missa Prolationum*, with double proportional canons, and a *Missa cuiusvis toni* (in any mode), with alternative performances made possible by using different clef signs in the same parts. However, the techniques were more common as internal devices in cantus firmus Masses.

No less free than the derivation of the cantus firmus was its treatment. Whatever the composer's ingenuity could devise to serve the unity of the work, the enjoyment and appreciation of the listeners, or the progress of musical exploration in the new style was introduced and tried. Tunes were put in the tenor, as suggested by the old motet tradition, in the top part, as suggested by the Burgundian style, or (rarely) in any other part. One tune or phrase of plainchant was used throughout all the movements of the Ordinary or a different phrase was used for each movement—a plainsong Kyrie for the Kyrie, a plainsong Gloria for the Gloria, and so forth—or even for sections within movements. A whole four-part motet or chanson could be paralleled in all four parts of a Mass movement, possibly with variations, or its cantus or tenor alone could serve as a cantus firmus. The skill of a composer was demonstrated in his use of variety in source and technique. Therefore no standard usage, only the ideal of imaginative and various incorporations of elements into the new ideal of sound, can be adduced from the Renaissance Mass literature.

The most popular tune of the fifteenth century was probably "L'homme armé" (Example 28). It was certainly the popular song most frequently used in the polyphonic Mass. Over thirty composers based works on it, drawn perhaps by the tune's concern with fourths and fifths as well as by its popularity—from Dufay and Josquin to Palestrina and Carissimi. Its commemoration of the "common man" makes its choice significant.

The first of Josquin's two Masses on "L'homme armé" (Example 31) provides an excellent summary of Renaissance style and technique. It was among the earliest sacred works published (1502) and comprised the full five movements of the Mass Ordinary. The Kyrie, Sanctus-Benedictus, and Agnus Dei comprised the constant movements; the Credo was reserved for

Sundays and high feasts; and the Gloria was omitted in Masses of penitential character (including all those during Advent and Lent). Thus, in spite of the fact that there were five musical movements in the Mass Ordinary, in practice many Mass celebrations used only three.

Probably the most obvious characteristic of the work is its sweep of size. Each movement was extensive and fully developed. Although various sections were in two and three parts, the norm was four parts, all male voices: the tenor, countertenor parts above and below the tenor (contratenor altus and contratenor bassus), and the *superius* (literally, the part above) on top. (The same superius was called the *cantus* when it had the principal part or tune.) In range, the four parts were a basso (G to c^1 with one extension up to d^1 and one down to F), two tenors (c to g^1 with extensions to a^1), and a countertenor (a to d^2). These were standard.

The five movements represented an imaginative, systematic extension of the tune "L'homme armé." The extension began successively on the six tones of the hexachord—on C in the Kyrie, D in the Gloria, E in the Credo, F in the Sanctus, G in the first Agnus, and A in the last. The tune was lodged in the tenor until the last Agnus, when it rose to the top voice in a special effect perhaps related to the sense of climactic power characteristic of final movements.

The new sound of the Renaissance focused on the effect of the voices together, a change from the traditional soloists or mixed vocal and instrumental sounds. Thus, emphasis was placed on the timbre of a choir with two or three men singing each part, often with instrumental doublings, and on the symphony of combined tones they produced. Variety of structure was the keystone—perfections were seasoned with imperfections, and, among imperfections, major varied with minor. The final double perfection 1–5–8 was still standard, with an added third not infrequent in interior cadences. The approach to the cadence final was not stereotyped but was still largely experimental, with the final cadences of the various movements comprising a catalogue of possibilities within the inherited cadence vocabulary and the scope of the new emphases. As might be expected, the final cadence of the Mass, that closing the last Agnus, was the most representative of the coming norm. The defining elements were the descent from 2 to 1 in the tenor, the 5 to 1 progression in the bass, and the suspended leading tone (still derived as musica ficta in the sixteenth century) proceeding to the final. In Josquin's generation, the unanimous perfection was normal for the final chord; but inclusion of the third was becoming more frequent and in the next generation would be standard. The cadences of two-part sections are personal and in some cases unique.

If Josquin's harmonic language was representative of his time, his use of the cantus firmus was not, except insofar as imaginative and unusual procedures were in themselves representative. In addition to the systematic placement of the tune on all degrees of the hexachord, unique in this work, the cantus firmus procedure in the first *Missa L'homme armé* included a backward version of the tune. The Gloria (not given in Example 31) employed the tune in long values in the tenor; it was followed by instruction to repeat it backward, from last note to first. Because such a practice comprised, with the aid of instruction, two musical versions from one printed line, it was properly a canon—even when the two versions were to be performed successively in one part. (The instruction was the canon.) A backward version was called *retrograde* or *cancrizans* (crab motion). In modern notation, cancrizans readings require separate written versions; however, this was not the case in proportional notation, where each note stood separately and bar lines did not interrupt the flow of the individual parts. It was quite simple to read a Renaissance part backwards.

Missa l'homme armé: Kyrie, Sanctus, and Agnus Dei   Example 31
JOSQUIN DES PREZ

Example 31 (continued)

Example 31 (continued)

Example 31 (continued)

Example 31 (continued)

Example 31 (continued)

Example 31 (continued)

Example 31 (continued)

Example 31 (continued)

Example 31 (continued)

Example 31 (continued)

Example 31 (continued)

Example 31 (continued)

Example 31 (continued)

Hosanna ut supra. [Repeat the Hosanna as above, page 162.]

Example 31 (continued)

Example 31 (continued)

Example 31 (continued)

Canon at the
fifth and
octave: bassus,
altus, and
superius

Example 31 (continued)

Example 31 (continued)

Example 31 (continued)

Example 31 (continued)

Example 31 (continued)

Example 31 (continued)

Example 31 (continued)

Example 31 (continued)

One of two Masses by Josquin on the tune "L'Homme armé." It was published in both Italy and France, and this version was adapted from the A. A. Smijers edition, which was based on the Petrucci edition of 1502.

The essential fabric of High Renaissance polyphony is well represented by the Josquin *Missa L'homme armé*, which proceeds in a four-part vertical design built from a defining tenor. Such a concept did not mean that the tenor had always to be present but, more significantly, defined the work so that when the tenor was absent, its absence itself was definitive; sections without the tenor had the effect of either introductions, postludes, or interludes.

The Kyrie, for example, comprises one full statement of the cantus prius factus. The tune itself is A–B–A in structure, a form easily mirrored in the Kyrie, where the threefold *Kyrie eleison* is recapitulated after a threefold *Christe eleison*. The entire movement is thus defined by the tenor in length and in formal structure but not in the use of mode or in the rhythmic language. The scale, with its chromatic semitone and its use of musica ficta, is still Guido's. Although the added voices accommodate to the tenor, the tune does not imply a specific final chord. The tune's final is C (the *modus lascivus*), whereas the cadences of the three sections fall on A, E, and D, almost as though Josquin had set his imagination to the task of stretching the implications of the tune in a series of puns on it. Certainly the tune was recognizable, announced as it was by a suggestion in the contratenor bassus and then presented directly in the superius before its more stately appearance in the tenor. Its conclusion, in both the first and second sections, as an imperfect tone added to the final double perfection, must have been a fairly startling modernism. The tune was built on a frame of perfect intervals; their use as color tones was a primary effect of the Kyrie and Sanctus. In the

final Agnus, the perfect intervals returned to an expected vertical context to provide the last movement of the Mass with stability. The tune was also made slower in the last Agnus, adding nobility and strength to the finale, a matter of importance in so long a work.

The Mass is also representative of the rhythmic ideal of the time. The independence of individual voices is best appreciated by writing them out without the (modern) bar lines. Rhythmic patterns accrued freely within each part, and the natural groupings are not hard to discern behind the rigidity of our notation. For example, the opening countertenor rhythm ♩ ♩ ♪♩ ♪♩ (4+3+3+2) contains the composite of 3+3+2, which, with its variants 3+2+3 and 2+3+3, abounds in Renaissance polyphony.

Rhythmic activity was used significantly in creating the overall shape of the Mass. The opening Kyrie, for example, is fairly complex, but the Christe is relatively quiet, as was traditional by Josquin's time. The final Kyrie balances the first with a return to greater density and quicker motion. Such rhythmic reinforcement of the larger aspects of form was found throughout Renaissance music and was a significant concern of composers and performers. In this work, the rhythm of the final Agnus is particularly notable, for the slower, more obviously broadened statement of the tune is set off by an increasingly complex and active rhythmical language in the polyphony, in which the intense overlapping of figures in imitative appearances approaches a climactic force.

The melodic language was still couched in Guido's gamut and still made frequent use of the cambiata figure. From a basic melodic unit of a fourth, divided into a major second and a minor third and used freely in direction and rhythm, the cambiata had become a descending figure with an initial interval of a second; the two notes most frequently had the time values of a dotted eighth and sixteenth (in modern terms). The third tone lay a fourth below the first and was free to have any note value and to progress at will.[4]

K 26　　　　　　K 32　　　　　　　　S 40　　　　　　S 93　　　　　　　K 15

The bringing of the cambiata figure into an era with strong vertical interests gradually led to the concept of a free tone whose vertical definition need not be measured. The second tone of the figure came to be called the cambiata tone.

---

[4] In the musical progressions illustrated, K stands for Kyrie, S for Sanctus, and the numbers for measures in Example 31. Thus, "K 26" indicates that that progression is found at measure 26 of the Kyrie.

Serving as interludes in the Josquin *Missa L'homme armé* are three sections of two and three lines—the *Pleni sunt coeli* of the Sanctus, the Benedictus, and the second Agnus. The *Pleni sunt coeli* ("Full are the heavens") is an intense, modern movement of substantial length, in which the three countervoices offer imitations of melodic figures and overlapping rhythmic patterns in a fullness of content that sounds all the busier without a mediating tenor. The Benedictus is a series of three short phrases, each of which is a unison mensural canon at the ratio of 2:1 rising from the first in the contratenor bassus, through the second in the contratenor altus, to the third in the superius. The spare two-part phrases are surrounded by the rousing *Hosanna in excelsis*, in which the tenor tune is at its least restrained. The final interlude is a three-part mensural canon beginning simultaneously on the double-perfection triad 1–5–8 and proceeding in the ratio 2:1:3; again the tenor is absent. This interlude, relatively quiet in both rhythmic and melodic content, directly precedes the final Agnus, preparing for its noble proportions. It is probable that all the interludes were sung by smaller contingents, possibly by soloists.

Another common form was that of the alternate verse Mass, in which phrases of plainchant alternated with polyphonic phrases, a practice called *alternatim*. Such a technique had the advantages of shortening the total work and providing a showcase for the use of cantus firmi. The Kyrie of the Heinrich Isaac *Missa Martyribus* [5] illustrates the technique; like Josquin's work, it is highly personal. Isaac's cantus firmus is the plainsong Kyrie illustrated as Example 14, whose paraphrases are all the more clearly heard in their juxtaposition with the original. The successive movements are written on separate cantus firmi drawn from parallel plainchant movements, and thus the longer ones lack the repetitions that are implicit in the Kyrie text.

Here the paraphrases present a shape, an overall design. The opening phrase is plainsong so of the three Kyrie phrases, only the second is polyphonic; it systematically develops the opening of the plainsong phrase in the four voices. Both the first and the third statement of the Christe are polyphonic; traditionally the Christe is relatively subdued, as here with the voices reduced to three, then two. The first Kyrie is again plainchant; the second represents the climax of the movement, both in its return to four voices and its use of rhythmic proportions, which provide urgency and lead the final section readily to its greater size. In general, the rhythmic language in this work is less complex than in the Josquin work, but its focus is often harmonic, upon that "combined symphony . . . by which the ear can best be filled with perfect sweetness." [6]

[5] This work appears in Louise Cuyler (ed.), *Five Polyphonic Masses by Heinrich Isaac*, Ann Arbor, Mich.: The University of Michigan Press, 1956, pp. 97–100.
[6] Quoted in Pirrotta, *op. cit.*, p. 154.

THE MOTET

Second only to the Mass in defining the new style was the motet, which was free to embrace the new sound and to develop new methods of composition. The motet could be as short as a single punctus or as long as an entire Psalm or canticle; it was versatile, experimental, modern. The composer of a short motet might be interested in one vertical combination and exploit it with rhythmic thrust and vocal drive, or he might develop a melodic figure. Motets were monotextual, and the modernists were using their musical vocabulary to service the text.

Isaac's introit "Exaudi Deus" (Example 32), in spite of its close interior imitations, centers on a triad on D, with its fifth and a third, and works over the tones of that combination with forcefully intertwining figures in the

Exaudi Deus   Example 32

HEINRICH ISAAC

Example 32 (continued)

Motet from the *Choralis Constantinus III*, first published in 1555. The text is an introit from the Common Feast of a Martyr and reads, "Hear my prayer of supplication, O God. From the fear of my enemy, deliver my soul." (Courtesy of the University of Michigan.)

upper parts. It is extremely direct, with little embellishment save for the accented neighbor tones, and builds from the opening plainchant phrase to a four-part final statement.

The tract (Example 33) is more elaborate and, in particular, more telling in its interpretation of the text "Blessed is the man [*vir*] who fears God." The text, which originally pointed to God, is given a more Renaissance emphasis on the word *man*, which appears in a hocket-like exchange in the upper voices so that it is singled out almost as a proclamation—a technique used elsewhere by Isaac on the same word.

Beatus vir

HEINRICH ISAAC

Example 33

Example 33 (continued)

Example 33 (continued)

Motet from the *Choralis Constantinus III*. The text is an alleluia verse from the
Common Feast of a Martyr: "Blessed is the man who fears the Lord: he takes
great delight in His commandments." (Courtesy of the University of Michigan.)

POLYPHONIC SONG

Song has always flourished, but at the height of the Renaissance, it came to a particular flowering. The part-song, basically in the familiar style, had been the chief popular form of the late fifteenth century. Thus when the new four-part texture turned toward the chanson, it was influenced by the song's simplicity and directness and, in turn, brought to the chanson some of the sophistications of the motet.

By the end of the fifteenth century, polyphonic song had become a splendid reflection of the Renaissance spirit. It incorporated the continuing popular music in such a versatile concept that national and regional characters could be expressed and fulfilled. Because French texts were used by the Franco-Flemish composers, who were in the position of leadership, the chanson was the archetype. But the frottola was already competing with the chanson in Italy, as was the *Lied* in Germany. The *Liederbuch* (book of songs with German text) had appeared as early as 1450, when the Lied reflected the Medieval three-voice norm for popular music of that day. By 1500 the Lied had achieved the four-part Renaissance norm and had incorporated many of the techniques of sacred polyphony. The frottola too had changed toward the new ideal, though retaining its relative simplicity of style. The Venetian printer Petrucci published eleven books of frottole between 1504 and 1514. The humanism and nationalism of the Renaissance inevitably led to the particularization of songs by country and type.

Some Renaissance Song Types

strambotto was an Italian free solo song with instruments, often with instrumental interludes. Petrucci used the term also to specify certain couplet forms among the frottole of 1504 and 1508.

canzona was an Italian song, generally to a serious text of several eight-line stanzas. But the term was often used generally to indicate a song of gentle, lyrical quality. A *canzonetta* was shorter, lighter in mood.

canti carnascialeschi (carnival songs) were Italian humorous songs often grouped into comic scenes and presented as *mascarades*—celebrations that were to develop into the *masque* (and ballet), on the one hand, and into the *masquerade* (masked ball), on the other. Isaac was known as early as the 1480s for his canti carnascialeschi for the Medici.

villancico, a Spanish and Portuguese strophic form, consisted of a stanza (*copla*) alternating with a refrain (*estribillo*). It was related both to the carole and the virelai and was very popular early in the Renaissance. Examples before 1500 were polyphonic, though simple in texture and mostly in the familiar style. After 1500, the villancico was composed also as a solo song with lute.

quodlibet (Latin, "what you will") was a humorous song that included snatches of several popular tunes, often with each voice singing the music and text of a separate fragment. The quodlibet was popular in Germany and, under the name *fricassée*, in France.

ballad, an English form, was originally a dance but, from the fourteenth century, a song. The ballad form was basically a couplet or quatrain stanza type, with or without refrain. Soon after the beginning of the sixteenth century, the ballad became popular as a song printed on ballad sheets sold by street vendors. These songs often told stories of topical interest, in the form of contrafacta of already popular tunes, and served somewhat the function of newspapers.

vaux de vire (later *vaudeville*), a French street song, was kin to the Italian villanella and the English ballad. It was a popular song, gay of tune, often topical and satirical in text, and often written as contrafactum.

villanella, or *villanesca*, was an Italian rustic song, often a street song. Unlike the vaux de vire and the ballad, the villanella was a parody in which musical roughness and solecism, rather than textual content, was the source of wit. Generally in three or four parts, the villanella was popular in the late fifteenth and early sixteenth centuries.

The chanson at the beginning of the sixteenth century was an eclectic work, synthesizing the directness and simple phrase (point) construction of the Italian frottola with the learned style of the Franco-Flemish experimenters. As popular forms so often do when they come into special focus, the polyphonic song of the High Renaissance, once it was well established, drew forth a large group of practitioners. The chanson as a form of the Franco-Flemish (international) tradition gave way to the French (national) chanson as other national forms developed. The Franco-Flemish group were absorbed as naturalized citizens, musically and often politically.

"Bergerette savoyene," by Josquin, is a Franco-Flemish chanson that uses imitation internally and focuses as much vertically as horizontally. The opening rhythm, by the sixteenth century a cliché of the chanson, is common to the three songs in Examples 34, 35, and 36. It was standard but not mandatory.

"Isbruck, ich muss dich lassen" is a Lied by Isaac; it was one of the most popular songs of the Renaissance. Its nostalgia for the lovely city of Innsbruck (the text, popularly attributed to the Emperor Maximilian, begins "Innsbruck, I must leave you"), more than a superficial courtly formality, has kept the work in the repertoire ever since. Largely in the familiar style, the song is ambiguous in rhythmical groupings; in modern terms, it is as much in $\frac{3}{2}$ as in $\frac{2}{2}$.

"Je n'ose être content," by Certon, is a later chanson, reflecting developments in the generation after Josquin and Isaac. Many two-, three-, and four-voice chansons were written as the form began to take on a specifically French character. Here, imitation is generative rather than internal and decorative. The punctus, generated by imitative entries of the participating voices, was called an *imitative point* and its use characterized a style as *learned*.

Example 34A, "Bergerette savoyene," a facsimile from
Petrucci's *Odhecaton* (1501).
The cantus (not labeled) and
tenor are on the top of the
page, and the altus (a shortened
form of contratenor altus) and
bassus (a shortened form of
contratenor bassus) are on the
bottom. The two-section dance
form is set off with repeat marks
and a fermata at the end of the
first section. (Courtesy of the
Library of Congress.)

Bergerette savoyene

Example 34B

JOSQUIN DES PREZ

Example 34 B (continued)

Example 34B (continued)

The title means "shepherd song of Savoy," but *bergerette* referred also to a simple punctus structure used in dances. No text appears with the original.

Isbruck, ich muss dich lassen   Example 35

HEINRICH ISAAC

Is - bruck, ich muss dich las - sen, ich far da-hin

Is - bruck, ich muss dich las - sen, ich far da - hin

Is - bruck, ich muss dich las - sen, ich far da-hin

Is - bruck, ich muss dich las - sen, ich far da - hin

mein stras - sen in frem-de Land da - hin. Mein freud ist mir ge - nom -

mein stras - sen in frem-de Land da - hin. Mein freud ist mir ge-nom -

mein stras - sen in frem-de Land da - hin. Mein freud ist mir ge - nom -

mein stras - sen in frem-de Land da-hin. Mein freud ist mir ge - nom -

Example 35 (continued)

Isbruck, ich muss dich lassen,
ich far dahin mein strassen in fremde Land dahin.
Mein freud ist mir genommen,
die ich nit weiss bekummen,
wo ich im elend bin,
wo ich im elend bin.

Innsbruck, I must leave you,
Traveling long roads away
Into a strange land.
My joy is taken away
That I knew not how to enjoy,
And now I am in misery.

Tradition ascribed the poem of this Lied to Maximilian I of Austria (1459–1519),
for whom Isaac worked.

The three songs share a basic concern with polyphony as horizontally and vertically significant. Those in four parts use color tones within the 1–5–8 triad most of the time, showing a preference for the perfection combined with imperfection. The suspended leading tone at the cadence and the final chord with added third are both standard. The harmonic language was becoming richer but, in consistently using the third, was also becoming less various.

The Renaissance chanson was more stratified than earlier polyphony. The countertenor range, the cantus in secular works, still represented the high voice, indicating continuing performance by men; but, unlike sacred music, where two or three men might double a part, the chanson was conceived for soloists. Together, the three songs suggest the spirit, versatility, breadth, and individuality of several thousand works by scores of composers.

Je n'ose être content   Example 36

PIERRE CERTON

Example 36 (continued)

Je n'ose être content de mon contentement,
Ne voulant désirer plus grande aise en ma vie,
De peur de perdre plus que ce dont j'ai ennuie;
Car qui demande trop pour plaisir a tourment;
Car qui demande trop pour plaisir a tourment.

I dare not be happy with my contentment,
Not wishing to desire greater ease in my life,
For fear of losing more than that which is tedious;
For he who seeks too much pleasure
is also tormented.

TRANS. BY JON RINKA

A popular French chanson of the national rather than international (Franco-Flemish) tradition. (Courtesy of the Theodore Presser Company for Music Press.)

They comprise a great literature of polyphonic songs, which were a central fulfillment of Renaissance style.

FOLK SONG

In the sixteenth century folk songs also were given renewed vigor by the new humanism. The folk ballad, a song telling a story, became the gossip column of the people, relating tales of the common man as well as of royal or heroic figures. With the rise of literacy in Great Britain, English ballads were printed on separate sheets, called *broadsheets* or *broadsides*, and hawked on the street by ballad sellers. On the occasion of any local excitement, from marriage to murder, broadsides were hastily put together, often as contrafacta on tunes already popular. One of these was titled "the vvofull Lamentation of *William Turcas*, vvho for murtherin his Mother at *Thaxted* in *Essex* was executed at *Chelmsford*. To the tune of, *The rich Merchant*." [7] Many broadsides were attractively printed and included an illustrative woodcut.

Our knowledge of folk songs begins with their sixteenth-century written forms. But their tunes were often not new; in fact many were old even before they were notated. The age of a tune is easier to assess if it has survived with its original text. For example, a number of ballads may well have dated from the fourteenth-century plague years, when songs and dances of death were most prevalent.

[7] Quoted in Percy A. Scholes (ed.), *The Concise Oxford Dictionary of Music*, Fair Lawn, N.J.: Oxford University Press, 1952, p. 43.

Drawings on a sixteenth-century manuscript of popular songs. (Courtesy of the Bibliothèque de la Ville de Cambrai, France. Photograph by M. Delcroix.)

One such ballad is "Death and the Lady." The poem, particularly its opening line, is representative, as standard as "once upon a time." Its direct dialogue is characteristic, as is the disengaged, objectively detailed relating of the tale of death. The five-line stanza is set as a five-punctus arch form, musically based on partials of C and with *c* as its final.

The song "Brimbledon Fair," or "Young Ramble Away," is not a ballad; this type of text, a glorification of the free life, appeared in many versions with different details or substitutions. Its four-line stanza was typical, though ballads generally used second and fourth lines that were one accent shorter than the first and third. The tune is based chiefly on the fifth *c–g*, ending on *d*.

The sailor chanty was a song in a strong dance rhythm, most frequently the *hornpipe*. "The Rambling Sailor" is not a hornpipe (its earliest words

Death and the Lady

ANONYMOUS

Example 37

I said, Old man, what man are you?
What country do you belong unto?
My name is Death; hast heard of me?
All kings and princes bow down unto me,
And you, fair maid, must come along with me.

I'll give you gold, I'll give you pearl,
I'll give you costly rich robes to wear,
If you will spare me a little while,
And give me time my life to amend,
And give me time my life to amend.

I'll have no gold, I'll have no pearl,
I want no costly rich robes to wear;
I cannot spare you a little while,
Nor give you time your life to amend,
Nor give you time your life to amend.

In six months time this fair maid died;
Let this be put on my tombstone, she cried:
Here lies a poor distressed maid;
Just in her bloom she was snatched away,
Her clothing made of the cold earthern clay.

The text of this folk ballad is related to the fourteenth-century plague texts. Tradition also places the tune in the fourteenth century.

ANONYMOUS

As I was a-rid-ing to Brim-ble-don Fair, I saw pret-ty Nan-cy a-curd-ling her hair, I gave her a wink and she roll'd a dark eye, And said I to my-self: I'll be there by and by.

I watch'd and I watch'd, all the night in the dark
For to ask pretty Nancy to be my sweethart.
But all that she said, when I saw her next day:
And are you the young rogue they call Ramble-away?

I said: Pretty Nancy, don't laugh in my face,
But she answer'd by slipping away from the place.
So to find her I rambled thro' fair Lincolnshire,
And I vow'd I would ramble, I did not care where.

Come all you young maidens, wherever you be,
And find pretty Nancy and bring her to me,
And all you young ramblers you mind and take care,
Or else you'll get brimbled at Brimbledon Fair.

A folk song typical of English country tunes of the sixteenth century.

were about a soldier), but it is typical in its strong accents—the upbeat and downbeat on each of its eight counts. It is a vigorous, wide-ranging tune, on a C fundamental, and it could be played on a bagpipe with C and G drones. (It is *on* C but not *in* C.) Like most chanties, its melodic action centers in the fundamental and its fifth, flat seventh, and octave (c-g-$b\flat$-c^1).

These three tunes are variations of punctus or phrase structure, the most important technique of folk tunes in England and elsewhere. Many tunes had no repeated phrases but created their shapes by juxtaposition, in an *ABCD* or *ABCDE* form. "Death and the Lady" is an *ABBxCD* form, "Brimbledon Fair" is *ABBxA* (with *x* being an extension), and "The Rambling Sailor" is *AABA*; other common arrangements were *AABBC* and *AABBxCD*. Repetition was more likely to occur in middle phrases. Refrains were found occasionally, as in these songs, but nonsense syllable refrains were also used.

Folk tunes were both songs and dances and were sung by street per-

The Rambling Sailor
Example 39

ANONYMOUS

I am a sailor stout and bold, long time I've plough'd the ocean; I've fought for king and country too, Won honor and promotion. I said: My brother sailor I bid you adieu, No more to the sea will I go with you; I'll travel the country through and through, And I'll be a rambling sailor.

If you should want to know my name,
My name it is young Johnson.
I've got permission from the king
To court young girls and handsome.
I said: My dear, what will you do?
Here's ale and wine and brandy too;
Besides a pair of new silk shoes,
To travel with a rambling sailor.

The king's permission granted me
To range the country over;
From Bristol Town to Liverpool,
From Plymouth Sound to Dover.
And in whatever town I went,
To court young maidens I was bent;
And marry none was my intent,
But live a rambling sailor.

A chanty typical of British tunes of the fifteenth and sixteenth centuries.

formers called *buskers*. Many children turned to busking rather than begging and, for instruments, used the comb-and-paper, *eunuch flute* (a mirliton pipe, also called the *onion flute* and the *kazoo*—in French, the *chalumeau eunuque*), recorder, bagpipe, an array of percussion instruments, and their voices—in short, the universal instruments.

Practice was international; many tunes and poems traveled from one country to another. "Death and the Lady," for example, appeared in many versions in virtually every country in Europe. Early versions of the popular ballad "Lord Rendal" have been traced in Great Britain, Ireland, Germany, Italy, Iceland, Sweden, Hungary, Denmark, Czechoslovakia, Holland, and, of course, the American colonies as soon as Europeans were living there.

THEORY

The materials of music, as defined in the Gothic era, had expanded but had not changed in essence during the Ars nova and the fifteenth century. During the Renaissance, the long-assumed definition of musical materials was slowly becoming more inadequate. Such changes required, not the further expansion of traditional concepts, but the development of new ones— a development that was to require more than a century. The sixteenth century was truly transitional insofar as the basic theoretical concepts of music were concerned, for theorists searched to explain the new concepts but had to do so within the vocabulary of the old.

Very early, at the end of the Gothic era, tuning had presented problems, and as time had passed the problems had multiplied. In the Renaissance, the pitch system remained Guidonian, though greatly expanded, and the basic unit remained the hexachord. Medieval theorists had already transposed Guido's gamut down a fifth, using a B♭ signature and creating the chromatic semitones E–E♭. By the early part of the fifteenth century, signatures of two and three flats were used in individual voices (seldom in all), each flat representing an additional transposition and thus creating new chromatic semitones and requiring additional leading tones as well. By 1412, a treatise [8] proposed transposing the hexachord through flats to A♭ and through sharps to B, resulting in acknowledgement of seventeen tones to the octave—C, D♭, C♯, D, E♭, D♯, E, F, G♭, F♯, G, A♭, G♯, A, B♭, A♯, and B, from lower to higher. Later in the century the theorist John Hothby (c. 1418–1487) [9] extended the transpositions to D♭ downward and F♯ upward. Such an array of transpositions, with their attendant chromatic semitones, created a scale of twenty-one notes to the octave—C, D♭, C♯, D, E♭, D♯, F♭, E, F, E♯, G♭, F♯, G, A♭, G♯, A, B♭, A♯, C♭, B, and B♯. Hothby supported Pythagorean tuning, in which fifths are 2:3 so that the circle of fifths is actually a slowly sharpening helix rising about a quarter step for each enharmonic (twelve steps on the circle). Hothby had opponents, and shortly after his death, arguments on practical tuning flourished, but no solution would have satisfied musicians who were so much in transition and who could not define what they wanted.

Rather than accept equal temperament, which would vitiate rather than underline chromatic subtleties, composers continued to explore the chromatic implications of the Guidonian system. By the middle of the sixteenth century,

---

[8] Quoted in Hugo Riemann, *History of Music Theory*, Lincoln, Nebr.: University of Nebraska Press, 1962, pp. 233–238.
[9] *Ibid.*, pp. 260–261.

quarter steps were not only discussed but used. Nicola Vicentino (1511–1572), an Italian priest who studied in Venice and worked in Rome, sought an answer to current problems by reading the Greeks of the classical age. Studying the diatonic, chromatic, and enharmonic Greek scales, he applied certain Greek theories, or Renaissance concepts of them, to the Guidonian system. He built a two-manual harpsichord (and an organ) with thirty-one steps to the octave and taught a group of students to sing enharmonic works of his own composition. The chromatic expansion of the madrigal, a significant development in the final third of the sixteenth century, was thus not a radical but a compromise technique using extreme but not experimental materials.

Meanwhile, modal considerations were complicated by both old and new problems. The modes, basically a description of a range and tessitura of a plainchant melody, had no meaning in the polyphonic additions to the cantus firmi or in motets and chansons. Transpositions raised such issues as whether a final G, in a transposition of one flat, was mixolydian or dorian. The increasing use of the soft B and the consistent use of the leading tone in cadences tended toward lessening modal color, so the system was becoming more uniform in practice. And this uniformity was leading to a breakdown of the already flimsy distinctions among the modes, which were inoperative in polyphonic voices in any case. The theorist Heinrich Glarean (1488–1563) tried to clarify modal confusion by attempting to legitimize the already common use of A and C as finals, naming them Aeolian and Ionian, respectively.[10] In addition, a final on B, called Locrian, was hypothesized, but the nature of the chromatic semitone made such a mode inacceptable, although B had been used as a final. It was soon realized, however, that the creation of more modes was not the answer, because the whole modal concept was moribund. Thus, the Aeolian and Ionian modes were never added to the Church list, which remains eight in number.

Meanwhile, experiments in chromaticism continued. One question of the sixteenth century concerned which theory would eventually win out. The increasingly uniform practices of the scale were no longer being regulated by the tenor but were developing largely under the influence of the relatively new contratenor bassus, soon called the *bassus* or, in Italian, *basso*. Intervals above the basso, or measured from the lowest sounding voice, were thought more and more to combine into significant triads—1–5–8, 1–3–8, 1–6–8, and, increasingly, 1–3–5 and 1–3–6. The 1–3–5, along with its alternates (1–1–5, 1–5–5, 1–5–8, etc.), was called a "chord of the fifth"; whereas 1–3–6, along with its alternates (1–6–6, 1–1–6, 1–6–8, etc.), was called a "chord of the sixth." Because the former, when its third was major, was contained in the overtones series as 4:5:6, the chord of the fifth ranked above the chord of the sixth; it contained one perfect and one imperfect interval and therefore was a fine balance of elements. The chord of the sixth was still con-

---

[10] Quoted in Strunk, *op. cit.*, pp. 219–227.

sidered a double imperfection and was still variable—either major or minor sixth and either major or minor third. The theorist and composer Gioseffo Zarlino (1517–1590) [11] discussed these two basic triads and, by considering both the chords of the fifth and the sixth as implying the presence of the third, laid the groundwork for the concepts that were to serve music for the next hundred and fifty years. The basso was generative—D–F–A was a "D chord of the fifth," as was D–F♯–A, whereas D–F–B♭, D–F–B, D–F♯–B, and D–F♯–B♭ were all examples of a "D chord of the sixth." The former was more stable, the latter more various.

The emphasis on vertical composites led to rhythmic simplification and to a definition of both dissonance and embellishment as defined by the composites. The tactus was held to begin on a consonance equated with a strong beat and to continue with a free tone, either another consonance or a passing dissonance, but in any case equated with a weak beat. The normal rhythmic language became a duply proportioned beat defined as strong-weak (*Xx Xx Xx*), with *X* indicating consonance. A triply proportioned beat was strong-weak-weak (*Xxx Xxx Xxx*). The suspension became an important asset, because it threw an accented dissonance into the scheme (*Xx XX xx*), lending rhythmic bite to an otherwise somewhat bland structure.

Duple proportion, which was standard in the sixteenth century, left us a heritage in modern practice—a reduction from the many possible proportions to a few. At the end of the sixteenth century, the English composer Thomas Morley, in his *Plaine and Easie Introduction to Practicall Musick*, was still teaching the whole system of proportion. In the dialogue section of his text, he had the student react to the table of thirty-odd proportions with the following remark. "Here is a table indeed, containing more than ever I mean to beat my brains about. As for music, the principal thing we seek in it is to delight the ear, which cannot so perfectly be done in these hard proportions." [12] The master, far from chastening his student, continued to outline the simpler major and minor modes (division into 3 or 2) and the greater and lesser prolations (subdivision into 3 or 2). The circle was the sign for triple division; the dot, for triple subdivision; the broken circle, for duple division; and a slash mark (vertical or slanted), for duple subdivision. Thus ⊙ represented 3 × 3; ⦶ represented 3 × 2; ℭ represented 2 × 3; and ¢ represented 2 × 2. These signs can be associated with the later meter signs as follows:

$$\odot \,(3 \times 3) = \frac{9}{4} \text{ or } \frac{9}{8} \qquad \mathfrak{C}\,(2 \times 3) = \frac{6}{4} \text{ or } \frac{6}{8}$$

$$\Phi \,(3 \times 2) = \frac{3}{2} \text{ or } \frac{3}{4} \qquad \mathit{¢}\,(2 \times 2) = \frac{4}{4} \text{ or } \frac{2}{4}$$

[11] *Ibid.*, pp. 229–261.
[12] Thomas Morley (R. Alec Harman, ed.), A *Plain and Easy Introduction to Practical Music*, London: Dent, 1952, p. 58.

Further signs (Ͻ, ꝑ, ₵3, etc.) were used to indicate more complex proportions. However, the use of proportions was already on the wane.

The last of the signs in the chart above has remained in use, along with the sixteenth-century term *alla breve*. Alla breve was a directive to apply the breve (a short note comparable in notation to our whole note, which is still called a breve in England), rather than the longer note, to the half tactus. The term had a meaning roughly equivalent to the current term *cut time*.

The concept of the cambiata also changed. By the middle of the sixteenth century, the three-note figure was defined as an embellishment of consonance, escape note, and consonance, written most often as long-short-long (see *a* below). A variant figure was that in which the third was filled in so that the fourth was bridged, not with the cambiata note, but with two passing tones (see *b* below).

PERFORMANCE

The Renaissance concept of harmony—the "combined symphony . . . by which the sense of the ear can best be filled with perfect sweetness" [13]— was a matter of performance as well as structure. The concept was one of vertical unity and charm, in which a blend was achieved both in the combination of intervals and in the balance of sound. Instead of the Medieval ideal of simultaneous contrasts, which had emphasized the individuality of the

[13] Pirrotta, *op. cit.*

A chest of Krummhorns (cromornes), sixteenth century. Removed from their chest, they would be used as a consort. (Courtesy of the Musée Instrumental du Conservatoire Royale de Musique, Brussels.)

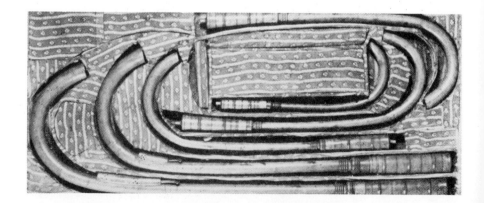

separate lines, the Renaissance ideal became one of combining elements into a sonorous and unified total sound.

An important aspect of the new sonorousness was the development of the choir. A famous late-fifteenth-century miniature shows a choir of nine men in front of a lectern on which is a large music book; one man—thought to be Ockeghem—is keeping the tactus. Early in the Renaissance, sacred music was written, in the choir-book notation developed during the Ars nova, on large vellum sheets bound into one volume or codex. After the invention of printing techniques for music, part books were published. From then on, it is more difficult to assess the size of choirs, because their size was no longer limited to the number who could read from one book. To reinforce the choir, it was customary to use brass or reed instruments, doubling the voices (and using the same part books). In cantus firmus works, sometimes the tenor alone was doubled so that it might be heard clearly.

In contrast to the relatively large contingent of voices often used in the chapel, a smaller group prevailed in the court and in the newly developed livingroom of the Renaissance man of means. The four-voice chanson was conceived for a matched group of voices or instruments known as a *consort*. The early polyphonic chanson, also published in part books, could be performed by instruments as easily as by voices—more easily if it was to be performed by a group unacquainted with French. In either case, one performer for each voice line was standard. Consorts of either recorders, viols, or Krummhorns (capped reeds), called *low* (meaning "soft") *music*, were in use, as were groups of open double reeds and brasses. The latter groups, considered *high* (meaning "loud") *music*, were used mainly out of doors or in

The Lutenist, by Michelangelo da Caravaggio (c. 1565–1609). The lute is a typical sixteenth-century Italian instrument. It was generally double-strung, each pitch being served by two strings, but in northern lutes, the top string was often single, resulting in an eleven-string instrument. The picture presents the common method of holding the unwieldy instrument, that is, on a table and is typical in that it portrays the music in detail. Missing parts to incomplete works have been restored through such precise representations. (Courtesy of the State Hermitage Museum, Leningrad.)

larger halls. The brass instruments were combined with kettle drums, particularly in cavalry music, because since the fifteenth century, when Polish kettle drummers had ridden with the troops into the West, kettle drums had been associated with mounted drummers. Consorts of recorders were particularly popular in England, where clear treble voices have always been admired. The vocal consorts also strove for blend, unity, and clarity. At home and at court, women joined the men in singing, so the top voice, or cantus, quickly attained a true soprano range in the Renaissance chanson. Like the instrumental consort, the vocal consort consisted of a group of soloists, and lightness and agility, sweetness and suppleness were the ideals of both voices and instruments.

During the first years of the sixteenth century, interest in the lute as a consort instrument developed. Within the Medieval ideal, the lute had been used for delineation of a single line, as other instruments were used for other lines. However, the new emphasis on total sound led to the performance of all four parts of a chanson on the lute, or, in a modern version of the Burgundian technique, of the cantus as a vocal solo, with the other three voice lines played on the lute. The lute was ideally suited to the livingroom of the Renaissance man, and it entered a period of vogue unprecedented for a single instrument.

✿ Some Composers at the Height of the Renaissance

The elder generation was led by a large group of Netherlanders who fanned out through Europe to fill virtually every important musical post from the North Sea to the Adriatic—an unprecedented monopoly of leadership. In the sixteenth century, men of other countries built on the Netherlanders' leadership and created their own national schools. But the Church maintained sacred music as an international art, so the national styles were initially seen only in secular music, particularly in the polyphonic chanson.

Franco-Flemish Composers

JOHANNES OCKEGHEM (c. 1430–1495), a Flamand, was a great teacher as well as a great composer. He is associated with the development of the larger choir. A choirboy at Antwerp and later in Cambrai under Dufay, he served the Kings of France in Paris from 1452, spending forty-three years in their service. He left 19 Masses (and other fragments), 9 motets, and about 20 chansons. He was known for writing canons.

JACOB OBRECHT (c. 1452–1505), a Netherlander, was ordained a priest in 1480. He was in charge of choirboys at Cambrai from 1484 and sang at Utrecht, Ferrara, Antwerp, and Brussels. He returned to Ferrara in 1504. Obrecht's reputation was that of a mystical, somewhat romantic composer. He left 24 Masses, 22 motets, several chansons, and a Passion.

JOSQUIN DES PREZ (c. 1445–1521), probably from Picardy, was brought up in the choir school at St. Quentin. The most celebrated and widely performed composer of his age, he would have been great in any era. He had a remarkable career, working in Rome,

Florence, Modena, Paris, and Condé for such patrons as the Vatican; the Italian dukes of Sforza, Este, and Ferrara; the French duke of Lorraine; and King Louis XII. Of his prolific works, 22 complete Masses and 129 other sacred pieces (motets, hymns, and Psalms) remain. In addition, 86 secular pieces are known.

HEINRICH ISAAC (c. 1450–1517), a Lowlander, was second to Josquin in contemporary opinion. He worked for Lorenzo de Medici, the duke of Ferrara, and Maximilian of Austria and spent his last years in Florence. He left 23 Masses and many motets and Psalms and is most renowned for the *Choralis Constantinus*, his huge collection of motets for the entire liturgical year. He also wrote more than 80 secular songs with texts in German, Italian, French, and Flemish.

PIERRE DE LA RUE (c. 1460–1518), born probably in Tournai, centered his life in the north, where he worked for many luminaries—from Maximilian of Austria and his daughter Marguerite to Philip the Fair, in Malines. He also served at chapels in Bois-le-Duc, Courtrai, and Namur. He left over 30 Masses, as many motets, 7 Magnificats, and about 40 chansons.

Composers Who Contributed to the Nationalization of Renaissance Song Forms

BARTOLOMEO TROMBONCINO (c. 1470–c. 1535), an Italian writer of frottole, carried his art to the courts of Mantua, Ferrara, and Florence. Many of his works were published by Petrucci in his nine books of frottole (1504–1514); 29 were published in lute tablature in 1509. He also left 9 lamentations and one Benediction service (in three voices).

CLÉMENT JANEQUIN (c. 1480–1560), a French composer celebrated for his chansons, worked in Paris and possibly in Bordeaux and Spain. He honored

and depicted in chansons the exploits of the martial figure the Duc de Guise. Janequin wrote 2 Masses, a volume of motets (of which only one copy survives), and four volumes of sacred music, chiefly Psalms and spiritual songs. But it was for secular songs, published as chansons and intabulations, that he was justly renowned—between 1520 and 1559, he published more than ten volumes that included 275 works in three and four voices.

LUDWIG SENFL (1488–1543), the Swiss master of Renaissance polyphony, was a student of Heinrich Isaac, whose works he compiled after Isaac's death. Senfl worked for Maximilian of Austria and at the courts of Bavaria and Brandenburg. Sympathetic to the Protestant movement, he was praised by Luther, but he remained until his death at the court of Bavaria, which was Catholic. He left both sacred and secular works, including Masses, motets, and German Lieder. (His large output of Lieder led to his being called "the prince of German music".) He was known for his quodlibets.

CLAUDIN DE SERMISY (c. 1490–1562), a French composer in both sacred and secular traditions, worked for the great Renaissance monarch Francis I, centering his activities at the Sainte-Chapelle in Paris but accompanying the king in his travels. Of sacred music he left 11 Masses (all with four voices), four books of motets (three to six voices), a Passion, and miscellaneous works, such as lamentations, as well as about 150 chansons.

JACOB ARCADELT (c. 1510–c. 1560), a Flemish composer, worked in Florence, Rome (at the papal chapel from 1538 to 1546), and then in France. He left 3 Masses, one book of motets (1545), 3 lamentations, and a volume of Psalms. But it was as a secular composer that Arcadelt was renowned and influential. Between 1539 and 1544 he published over 250 Italian frottole and madrigals and, after he moved to France, wrote chansons that strengthened the Italian influence in the French tradition.

PIERRE CERTON (c. 1510–1572), a French musician whose career centered in Paris, worked at Notre Dame and then at Sainte-Chapelle, where he was master of the choirboys from 1548. His early publications date from 1533. Although he produced a substantial amount of music for the Church, including 8 Masses, 50 motets, and 50 Psalms (1555), it was in his approximately 300 chansons that he showed most talent. In the development of the chanson, his work was of signficant influence.

I am not pleased with the Courtier if he be not also a musician and, beside his understanding and cunning upon the book, have skill in like manner on sundry instruments. . . .

Methinks [part song] is a fair music, so it be done upon the book surely and after a good sort. . . . But singing to the lute with the ditty is more pleasant than the rest, for it addeth to the words such a grace and strength that it is a great wonder.

BALDASSARE CASTIGLIONE *

At the End
of the Renaissance

9

Music in the last third of the sixteenth century was different from that in the first third in degree more than in kind and especially in its underlying attitudes and function. The main forms of the High Renaissance—the Mass, the motet and its extended forms, and the polyphonic song in its nationalistic types—continued to prosper throughout the century. But by the end of the century the sacred polyphonic forms were declining in influence and, in general, were as conservative as they had been experimental a century earlier, while the cutting edge of modernity had in great part shifted again to the secular forms. Secular polyphony could serve the new sound well and could

---

* 1528. Quoted in Oliver Strunk (ed.), *Source Readings in Music History,* New York: Norton, 1950, p. 282.

involve the man of means in his own home, allowing him to enter the musical sphere of influence.

In addition to sacred and secular polyphony, which continued through the sixteenth century, three new kinds of music were coming into focus as the century progressed. Protestant sacred polyphony and spiritual songs were used for private worship. Instrumental music achieved autonomous stature at least theoretically equal to that of vocal music. And solo vocal music with instrumental accompaniment—called *monody*—became the most important focus of modernity at the end of the century; it would serve as the forerunner of the coming Baroque style.

Music in the sixteenth century clearly reflected the political and cultural developments that were at work in Europe as the result of the Renaissance redefinitions of man and the world. Man gave himself the right to move freely through the culture of his world and to exert whatever influence he could through his own personal vigor, his intelligence, and his skill. Seen in this light, the rise of the Protestant faiths was one aspect of the Renaissance belief that man has the stature to confront God directly and to work out his own salvation, an idea that could not have achieved wide popularity two centuries earlier. The Protestant churches also fulfilled the desire of men to learn, to worship, and to express themselves in their own tongue. The ramifications of this desire were felt in virtually every aspect of sixteenth-century life. For the new Protestant churches, it meant defining not only new liturgical forms, but also forms for private worship, and it meant devising musical types suitable to serve both.

Countering the Protestants, the Roman Catholic Church called a general council, which met, in the northern Italian city of Trent, for a number of sessions between 1545 and 1563. The Council of Trent took a long look at Church doctrine and practice, and the Church undertook to reform itself. Among its actions was the paring down, particularly at Mass, of extraneous musical materials. Special attention was given to sequences, and all but five for church use were abolished (a sixth was added in 1727; see page 60). A strongly conservative half-century followed, in which the philosophy of "music as handmaiden to the word" was reintroduced.

Much of Renaissance development was tied to the constantly growing skills of printing and publishing, an industry that, by supplying books, created an ever-increasing demand for them. Men took pride in knowledge, and the new man of means typically maintained a small private museum, called a *gabinetto* (small room), in which he gathered new-fangled inventions, botanical specimens, exotic items (perhaps from the Orient), or other oddities. Musical instruments were often included in the gabinetto and generally classified among the new-fangled inventions.

Finally, man's consciousness of himself as both creator and reactor led to an emphasis not on universal feeling but on personal feeling, not on love or suffering but on "I love" and "I suffer." Emphasis on the personality as individual and worthy of observation, a concept that was also a product of

Renaissance humanism, coincided with the full definition of the new sound. In the last third of the sixteenth century, the expanding language and techniques of Renaissance music were put to the service of expressing affections and *word-painting*, an art that was based on the word not as initiating structural shape and features but as informing mood and eliciting response through expression.

CONTINUING POLYPHONIC FORMS

Throughout the sixteenth century, the Mass and the motet continued as the important forms in the service of the Catholic Church. The forms retained the general techniques and basic effects that had served them so beautifully at the height of their period of definition, but as they continued, their harmonic language became richer and their rhythmic scope more restrained. Enrichment of the vertical structure was encouraged by the more frequent use of thirds and often by the use of five or six voice lines instead of four. Five-voice texture was the standard of the second half of the sixteenth century. The added part was called *quinta pars* (fifth part) at the middle of the century, but as the voice designations came to have a primary sense of range, the fifth part was often named according to its range, such as *cantus II*. The fuller texture of the five-voice norm can best be understood through comparison. In Rome, an anonymous fifth part has been found for the final Agnus of the Josquin *Missa L'homme armé*, an addition that italicized the special character of that movement as a finale.

Mass and Motet

Comparing excerpts of the Agnus with the fifth part (Example 40) to the four-part original (Example 31) not only reveals the textural expansion but also points out the direction that the concept of vertical structures would take during the last decades of the century. The example also demonstrates how much change the addition of one line could effect, resulting in a modern sound of full chords and almost seamless overlapping texture.

The addition of the cambiata (*a–g–e*) at the final cadence of the Agnus turns the original cadence formula, so representative of the High Renaissance, into one equally representative of the late Renaissance. The cambiata, already redefined in harmonic terms, was now further modified within the more conservative melodic and rhythmic ideals of the younger generation. The cambiata tone in Example 40 skips downward a third to a weak beat and is followed by a resolution upward to the tone skipped in the downward leap. The reverse (upward) progression was no longer acceptable.

The best way to investigate the new harmonic art of the sixteenth century is to examine part of a late Mass written in four voices. Although the Sanctus and Agnus Dei of Victoria's *Missa in Dominicalis* are old-fashioned in their use of four instead of five, six, or more voices, they are modern in harmonic language.

Victoria was a master of color, exploiting the potential of the Guidonian system, with its chromatic semitone and musica ficta, in a rich fabric; C and C♯ , F and F♯ , ♭ and ♮ , are put together for contrast, sometimes creating friction by juxtaposition. Far from insisting on the constant use of chords of the fifth with added third, usually major, as did the more conservative contemporary composers, Victoria gave the variable chords of the

Agnus, Missa l'homme armé (excerpts)   Example 40

JOSQUIN DES PREZ

Example 40 (continued)

The example includes the "Quinta pars" (Fifth part), which was added later, anonymously. It was found in the Vatican Library.

sixth full play. Through the use of both major (M) and minor (m) forms of the third and the sixth, successive chords of the sixth were capable of producing an almost opalescent color:

M_6 plus M_3
M_6 plus m_3
m_6 plus M_3
m_6 plus m_3

Victoria also used the cadence of the double perfection, 1–5–8, though omission of the third was becoming rare in late Renaissance style. This spare sonority, combined with his rich use of the variable imperfect intervals, created a fabric of exceptional scope.

The Agnus, though directly harmonic, was composed as polyphony and was based on the plainsong of Mass XVIII. Here the plainchant shifts to the superius, but the phrases still follow it closely. Vertical analysis of the Agnus reveals the full Renaissance vocabulary of chords of the fifth and sixth, used simultaneously with suspensions to create a remarkably sophisticated harmonic fabric. Certainly the final Agnus, which, of all the phrases, casts off the cantus firmus and simply presents its own harmonic expression, displays the intense musical feeling that was associated with the works of Victoria.

The motet, less tied to the past by technique and tradition, continued in many ways to be more modern than the Mass. Many motets were composed without a cantus prius factus and relied on means developed in the chanson to achieve musical form.

Sanctus and Agnus

Example 41

TOMÁS LUIS DE VICTORIA

Example 41 (continued)

Example 41 (continued)

These movements were combined with an earlier Kyrie by the same composer to make a short Mass called *Missa in Dominicalis*. (Courtesy of Breitkopf & Härtel, Wiesbaden, Germany.)

In the late Renaissance, the motet was most often constructed by means of the imitative point, a staple of Renaissance polyphony after 1525 or 1530. By 1550, the imitative point was so thoroughly worked out and so accepted that the practice was already subject to variation and further development. In order to create a longer span, one point often overlapped another; thus, to define the points, one must find the new line of text as it appears in each voice.

The Renaissance motet comprised a literature of surpassing greatness.

The chapel musicians of the duke of Bavaria, led by Roland de Lassus, a Netherlander. The heterogeneous mixture of the chapel music provided a contrast to the consort ideal of popular music. (Courtesy of the Bayerische Staatsbibliothek, Munich.)

It was experimental in defining the polyphonic art and then conservative in order to hold that art, which was bending before the excesses of secular polyphony on the one hand and the increasing pressure of a change of style on the other. The chief excess of the Renaissance motet after its fruition was the expansion of the number of voices, an excess in which the Mass joined. The size of the choir increased not so much in the number of persons singing each part as in the number of parts themselves. Palestrina's Masses include several in eight voices, while both Lassus and Victoria wrote for twelve. Thomas Tallis (c. 1510–1585), an English composer who worked for both Catholic and Anglican Churches, was more sparse in his Anglican settings, but his Latin motet "Spem in alium" was composed for forty voice parts. And Orazio Benevoli, an otherwise unimportant composer, wrote a Mass in fifty-three parts for the consecration of the Salzburg Cathedral in 1628. But by then the new music of the Baroque had made such flamboyance academic.

Protestant Music

The Protestant movement was a powerful force in virtually all aspects of sixteenth-century life, and music was not the least of these. The many publications of devotional music directed to the nonprofessional and the number of editions that many of these publications enjoyed indicate a wide musical literacy. New musical types developed in the countries with established Protestant churches, and a new vernacular vocabulary came into prominence, because a tenet of the churches was that every man should worship in the language of his daily life.

Each country invented its own liturgical music and music for private worship. Early services comprised direct translations of the Mass and the Hours, the latter simplified into Morning and Evening Prayers and retaining the canticles. Martin Luther (1483–1546) brought out in 1526 the *Deutsche Messe und Ordnung Gottesdienst* (German Mass and Order of the Service of God), which, along with other works, outlined the services and sacraments that were to be basic to Lutheran worship. The Anglican *Book of Common Prayer,* the sacramental and liturgical guide of the Church of England, was published in 1549.

Most important in the history of musical development, however, was the Protestant commitment to private prayer and the expansion of the hymn to include participation by the congregation in church. At home the singing of spiritual songs became a lively part of private worship. It is important to distinguish between sacred and secular music in this new sense. A sacred work was written for and performed in church in liturgical function. A secular work was written for use outside the church; such a work might have a religious text but was still secular.

In Holland and Germany, Latin Psalms and hymns were translated and new vernacular hymns were written. Often the tunes were already popular, but some were newly composed. Luther attached considerable significance to the hymn tune, in Germany called a *chorale*, and he is thought to have composed a few himself, of which the most famous is "Ein feste Burg ist unser Gott" (A Mighty Fortress Is Our God). Publications as early as 1524 included both chorales and spiritual songs. The songs, for three to five voices, were in the style of the day, with the tune in the tenor and the other voices added around it. By the end of the century, the chorale was firmly established in German music and German hearts.

Complete vernacular verse translations of the Psalms were not long in coming. The earliest musical version—the *Souterliedekins* (Psalter Songs), a Dutch publication—appeared in 1540. As might be expected, the concentration of effort was still focused on the texts and the fact that they were being sung for the first time in the vernacular. *Souterliedekins* was a collection of popular songs (tunes only) whose phrases matched the verse forms of the translations. Later, tunes were set in three and four parts and were designed for performance in the home. It is evident that the family group, made up of high and low male and female voices in equal numbers, would favor the four-part tune with two parts each for males and females. Thus the Protestant spiritual song and Psalm may be credited with the modern four-part concept, very different from the four voices of the High Renaissance or the five- and six-part norms then current in the Catholic countries. The Protestant Hymnal was established.

A sixteenth-century table knife on which is scored one part of a musical grace to be sung in parts before meals. (Courtesy of the Musée Cluny, Paris, and Éditions Robert Laffont.)

A facsimile of an early contra-factum of the popular song, "Isbruck, ich muss dich lassen," by Heinrich Isaac (Example 35); the title means "O World, I Must Leave Thee." The con-trafactum is from a seventeenth-century hymnal, the *Geistreiches Gesang-Buch* (*The Spiritually Rich Book of Songs,* 1676), compiled by Christoph Bernhard. The measured rhythm is typical of the chorale at that time. (Courtesy of the British Museum.)

The French Psalm settings were related to those of the Dutch. Although France remained a Catholic country, the Huguenots (the Protestant minority) were strong and their faith prospered in spite of persecution. However, their literature could not be published in Paris, so Amsterdam and Geneva became the French Protestant printing centers. The spiritual song, called *cantique* or *air spirituel*, soon appeared, not only in Protestant, but also in official Catholic publications (as part of the Counter Reformation).

In England, the service of Holy Communion comprised the translated Mass, and Morning and Evening Prayers incorporated the canticles and other items from the Hours. The antiphon, called *anthem* in English, took the place of the motet in the Anglican service. The Great Service was written in the learned style, but the Short Service was preferred, because for the most part it was in the familiar style and the words could be understood. By the end of the century, composers were writing more Morning Prayer services than Holy Communions. The Communion, though basically a translation of the Mass, used only the Kyrie, Gloria, Credo, and Sanctus. (The Benedictus and Agnus Dei were added in the nineteenth century, chiefly to allow English

215

INNSBRUCK. 7 7 6, 7 7 8.   HEINRICH ISAAK, *cir.* 1450–1527

Quietly, with movement

1. O Bread of life from heav - en, To wea - ry pil - grims giv - en,
2. O fount of grace re - deem - ing, O riv - er ev - er stream-ing

O Man - na from a - bove! The souls that hun - ger feed thou, The
From Je - sus' ho - ly side! Come thou, thy - self be - stow - ing On

rit.

hearts that seek thee lead thou, With thy most sweet and ten - der love.
thirst - ing souls, and flow - ing Till all their wants are sat - is - fied. A-men.

3 O Jesus, by thee bidden,
We here adore thee, hidden
'Neath forms of bread and wine;
Grant, when the veil is riven,
We may behold in heaven
Thy glorious countenance divine. Amen.

A later contrafactum on Isaac's "Isbruck." The title attests to the tune's origin, and the figures following the title indicate the number of syllables in each line of the stanzas. (Courtesy of the Commission on the Liturgy and Hymnal of the Lutheran Church in America and the Oxford University Press. Photo by R. E. Kalmbach.)

versions of Masses composed to the Latin Ordinary.) The composers of the new religious music were generally versatile men known for other music also, but a few devoted themselves primarily to religious works.

Chanson and Madrigal

The harmonic language of the hexachord system had expanded through experiments in composition, tuning, and word-painting. The system had been established with twenty-one notes to the octave, and quarter-tone and micro-tone composition was the next logical step.

   The freedom within materials of the system, with pull toward the finalis limited basically to the superfinalis and leading tone, had not been redefined or essentially changed, even though an increase in the number of notes naturally made a great difference in sound. But freedom brought its difficulties. Chromaticism in the intense form it was to take at the end of the century presented problems of tuning that have never been solved and that are probably insoluble if heightened rather than equalized effects are considered desirable.

The churches resisted the use of experimental music, so the experiments were most fruitful in secular forms. Nevertheless Vicentino, one of the most radical chromaticists (who worked with about thirty tones to the octave) was a priest and wrote chromatic and enharmonic motets in the 1550s.

The art of music, becoming more and more nationalistic during the sixteenth century, turned increasingly toward Italy; it was in Italy that the new musical style of the Baroque was chiefly to be defined. Italian patrons combined artistic acumen with money to take chances on new art and to indulge in the status game of being lavish with novelties. The chapel continued, of course, but emphasis shifted to the hall or salon (in Italian, *camera*, a vault and hence a vaulted room), where secular music was performed and where the musical entertainment of important visitors increasingly centered. As the differences between sacred and secular music widened, musicians became specialized into those of the *capella* (chapel) and those of the camera.

The most prominent late-sixteenth-century polyphonic secular form was the madrigal. This fourteenth-century term was revived, possibly because the frottola had too strong an association with the old formes fixes and the Burgundian solo performance, whereas the new madrigal was polyphonic and as much of the learned as of the popular tradition. Its sense of being a particular poetic form had been lost, and the name had no metric or linear association. The term *madrigal* was used in Italy shortly after 1530, and by the middle of the century, the new form was enjoying great popularity there; it continued to do so for two generations.

England imported the madrigal with the publication, in 1588, of *Musica Transalpina* (Music from Across the Alps), a publication that both stemmed from and encouraged an English vogue for things Italian. The English madrigal emulated the Italian but nevertheless had a distinctive sound. The French continued to write chansons, incorporating certain features of the Italian style, but they did not use the term *madrigal*. And at the end of the century, a few German composers wrote madrigals but used Italian texts. Thus before 1588, a madrigal was Italian, and, after that, it was either Italian or English.

Madrigal texts were generally undistinguished and as stereotyped in their emotional yearnings, love pangs, and death wishes as the Medieval song of courtly love was in its distant adoration. The focus of the troubadour work was on the beloved, that of the madrigal on the lover, who was usually rejected or bereaved.

Madrigals were composed in a style that combined both familiar and imitative techniques. The great madrigal writers wrote for three to eight or more voices, but the norm was five. The five-voice texture did not necessitate the constant presence of all voices, but the relative thickness militated against chords without thirds. In the interests of linear independence, parallel progressions of perfect intervals were not considered desirable, and within such strictures, even four lines are hard to manage without thirds. Harmonic richness was highly prized, however, and incorporated all the materials of the Guidonian system, with chords of the fifth, chords of the sixth, and dissonances—chiefly the suspension—often combined to stunning purpose.

The famous "Moro lasso" of Carlo Gesualdo provides a representative structure.[1] Its opening chords are a $C\sharp$ chord of the fifth, a $C\natural$ chord of the sixth (M_6 plus M_3), a B chord of the fifth, and a B chord of the sixth (m_6 plus m_3).

They illustrate the harmonic principle very well, showing a clear bass progression with alternating chord forms attained through transposition of the gamut. In addition, it is clear that in order to enjoy these harmonies fully, both rhythmic and melodic interests have been sacrificed. These, in turn, come into play in the imitative section, where the scale materials tend to stay within the untransposed gamut. The growing association of the learned style with diatonic scale materials, rhythmic thrust, and melodic vitality and, conversely, the association of the familiar style with the expanded chromatic vocabulary was definitive. In addition, the chromatic vocabulary was used in the service of emotional and depictive texts.

The English madrigal tended more distinctly toward a simple harmonic language and a centripetal organization in which the final was anticipated during most of the work. English emulation of things Italian led the English madrigal writers into imitation of the Italian texts. Because Italian is characterized by *ah* and *oh* vowels and feminine endings, the English invented the *fa–la–la* and *non–nonny–nonny* (the *os* were hard) refrains and allowed the texts to utter vapidities in order to achieve feminine endings, which are unnatural to the English tongue. The present participle and the gerund became indispensable, so that "the month of May" became "the month of Maying," and the short supply of English names such as Sally (who, of course, liked to dally) soon yielded to Italian and Latin ones, which served well in a general Renaissance return to classical concepts. Queen Elizabeth—an impossible name for a madrigalist—was praised as the goddess Oriana in

[1] William J. Starr and George F. Devine, *Music Scores Omnibus*, part I, Englewood Cliffs, N.J.: Prentice-Hall, 1964, pp. 37–39.

a collection of 1603, *The Triumphs of Oriana,* in which twenty-six composers were represented. The English madrigal was populated with shepherds, shepherdesses, and lesser deities, who would remain popular for another century and a half. Hundreds of such works appeared between 1590 and 1620, in madrigals of from two voices (often called canzonets) to eight or more voices.

But the English also found a compromise between the sometimes inane but often charming pastoral text and the sad, suffering Italian text of the forlorn lover, for there were great poets in England and amusement could not represent them adequately. The polyphonic madrigal, which tended to hide the text in imitative sections, served serious verse less often than did the solo song.

The love of the English for their language, which, because of its multiple heritage, is rich in puns as is no other, led them also to develop the round canon, called a *catch.* The repetitions and relationships between voices incorporated puns, often extremely coarse and very funny, into the text of the catches, and they frequently used hockets (or even belches) in pursuit of hilarity. The first book of catches (*Pammelia,* 1609) initiated a fad that would last a century and more. The English loved them so much that "catch clubs" were formed for singing them. Because these were men's clubs (the coarse nature of the texts making them less suited to performance by the delicate sex), catches tended to be unison rounds (see Example 53). The most famous publication was the series *Catch That Catch Can* (1625–1658); the most famous club, the Nobleman and Gentlemen's Catch Club, was founded in 1761 and still meets once a month.

A later development, perhaps in reaction to the free-wheeling catch, was the more sedate *glee,* a term revived from English minstrelsy. The glee was typically a men's part-song in familiar style, composed in the punctus form and with each line reflecting its text. The glee was popular from about 1750 to 1830, and the term *glee club* continues to be used to denote a men's singing group, particularly in university life.

An interesting related activity was barbershop music, which flourished in Europe and England during the sixteenth and seventeenth centuries. In *Don Quixote* (1604), Cervantes wrote that "most [Spanish barbers] are players on the guitar and song makers." [2] The typical barbershop had a banjo-like cittern on hand for customers to play and sing to while waiting, so singing has long been associated with the barbershop. Although this activity declined in England in the eighteenth century, it thrived in America. In 1860 a Boston musician wrote of a man he had met that because "he had been a barber he knew how to play the guitar." [3] Barbershop quartet singing —using High Renaissance voice types with countertenor—still thrives in the United States, where the literature, dating mostly from 1870 to 1925, is still

[2] Quoted in Percy A. Scholes (ed.), *The Concise Oxford Dictionary of Music,* Fair Lawn, N.J.: Oxford University Press, 1952, p. 46.

[3] *Ibid.,* p. 47.

sung. The Society for the Preservation and Encouragement of Barbershop Quartet Singing in America (S.P.E.B.Q.S.A.) still holds local and national conventions and contests, a modern heir of the medieval puy.

Monophonic song, with its punctus structure, had offered instrumentalists a natural basis for orchestration; it is not an exaggeration to say that minstrelsy was as much an instrumental as a vocal art, especially at its culmination. The estampie, with its double punctus and twofold endings, was in fact a very successful instrumental form.

Instrumental Music

At the turn of the sixteenth century, two concurring factors had provided the groundwork for experimentation with polyphonic instrumental forms. The ideal of sound had turned toward the consort, and the new style had established workable techniques in the motet and chanson. Both factors were concerned, in an unprecedented manner, with the vertical elements in music.

The immediate and obvious experiment with instruments was the development of instrumental consorts, equal to their vocal counterparts. The making and playing of balanced sets of instruments, of like kind but of different sizes to emulate the different vocal ranges, became a modern musical ideal. Such a set of instruments was called a *chest*. Henry VIII of England (1491–1547), for example, had chests of recorders and viols. Chansons were often presented by a consort instead of a group of voices.

Another experimental channel, and a crucial one for later instrumental music, was the performance of vocal polyphony on a single instrument, such as the organ or lute, that could manage all the voices with a single player— a one-man consort. The small organ, sounding four voices on one manual, was in itself a unity. It may have been the first consort instrument to be recognized, for German examples survive from the middle of the fifteenth century.

But the lute, above all other instruments, was the instrument of the Renaissance. The consort of viols was expensive and required that a group of people rehearse and play together. The organ was expensive and clumsy and also rather loud for the livingrooms of the men of means. But the lute furnished a gentle, bright sound, capable of subtlety and eminently suited to performance in small rooms. "[Lutes] are judged to have the most delightful impact on the ear," said a writer of 1510, "for that sure-fingered playing, now repetition, now stopping [rests], now lessening and almost interlacing of sounds, are in the habit of creeping easily into the minds of men with their exquisite sweetness." [4]

The lute soon began a life of its own. A notation for the instrument was developed, in which six staff lines represented not musical space but the six strings of the lute and numbers or letters on the lines indicated not pitches but frets behind which the performer would place his finger. Any such notation, which visually represents the instrument rather than musical space,

[4] Quoted in Nino Pirrotta, "Music and Cultural Tendencies in 15th-Century Italy," *Journal of the American Musicological Society*, vol. 19, no. 2, p. 153, Summer, 1966.

is called a *tablature*. The early publications for lute were *intabulations* of chansons, the notating in tablature form of chansons from part books.

The popularity of the lute had many ramifications. An increasing amount of music intabulated for lute was published, and the instrument was studied by more and more people. Method books were introduced and the *luthier* (lute-maker) had more work. Professional lutenists rose to the challenge of competition in performance and to the demand for private tutoring. Thus a perceptive, receptive audience—an audience who appreciated the skills of the lutenist through personal experience—was created.

Early instrumental forms developed naturally from the new style, while retaining idiomatic techniques from the fifteenth-century skills of improvisation and variation. In general, early forms worked out either systematic or free alternations between chordal (familiar) and imitative (learned) puncti, which were interspersed with sections of runs and other figures called *passages*. (This term meant "passing notes" in earlier times and was related to improvisatory techniques; later it became *passage work*, referring to fast idiomatic but nonmelodic materials.) Early titles mirrored these alternatives.

Instrumental Forms

organ prelude was originally a punctus improvised before a vocal work to indicate the pitch to performers (the French verb *préluder* meant "to improvise"), but written examples from the middle of the fifteenth century have been found. Later, the prelude came to be an opening piece, performed either before a vocal work or as the first in a series of pieces in a suite.

organ hymn was an early development in organ composition—as early as the establishment of independent instrumental forms. The use of hymns as cantus firmi, in embellished form, dates back to Dufay and earlier. Examples of such hymns, often close to paraphrases, occurred as early as they were printed in the sixteenth century (1511, 1512). Later examples (from 1542) expanded the form to include imitative techniques. An organ hymn or a shorter *versel* might be alternated with choral verses in performance.

ricercar (plural, *ricercari*) was an experimental piece of many types for lute, organ, or consort (viols). The term derives from *ricercare*, "to search." The earliest examples (1507) were for the lute and consisted of alternate chords and passages; the early organ ricercar (from 1523) was similar. The instrumental ricercar (for a consort; from 1547) paralleled the vocal forms, using alternate learned and familiar phrases and a tendency to center in imitative points. The later organ ricercar (1550 to 1740), in exploring imitative possibilities with one idea, became virtually synonymous with the *fugue*. This later type was called *tiento* in Spanish and *tento* in Portuguese.

fantasia (plural, *fantasie*) was a free instrumental form related to improvised techniques of the sixteenth century. (The term meant "imagination" in Latin.) The lute fantasia (from 1535) demonstrated the skill of the new professional lutenists in the virtuoso skill of polyphonic (learned) improvisation in alternate slow and fast puncti. Toward the end of the century, the fantasia became a popular form with the English virginalists, who wrote so freely that only an examination of the many examples can reveal their variety.

toccata (plural, *toccate*) was a free composition for keyboard, much like the ricercar and fantasia in its alternation between learned points and passages. The verb *toccare*, "to touch," was the technical term meaning to play a keyboard instrument, so *toccata* refers to the idiomatic passages that characterized the form. Early examples, with puncti of varying speeds, resembled the fantasia; later examples, such as those in the Frescobaldi *Fiori Musicali* (1630), revealed the expansion of the puncti into sections alternating between chordal and imitative styles.

canzona (plural, *canzone*) was an Italian instrumental work based on the chanson and incorporating the typical long-short-short repeated note opening of the vocal form. Early canzone were instrumental versions, or even paraphrases, of specific chansons and were called *canzone francese* ("French chansons") or *canzone alla francese* ("in the French style"). But soon, the form branched off into idiomatic types for lute (from 1536), organ (from 1542), and consort (from the 1570s). Like the other early instrumental forms, the canzona was based on alternating learned and familiar styles and expanded into multisectional works with contrasting tempos.

variations began to be written down in the sixteenth century, perhaps because of the need for teaching materials. Certainly the variation was a principal teaching means through the seventeenth century. The chief kinds of variations were the following:

grounds were repeated bass patterns over which varied figures were improvised or composed (from 1522).

paraphrases were enhanced repetitions of whole sections or pieces, especially dances or songs. Often the paraphrases were in a different proportion (later, meter). Such paraphrases were called *differencia* or *glosa* in Spain, where they were included in organ and lute treatises (1543, 1553, etc.). Another term for a paraphrase repetition, particularly of dance movements, was **double.** Typically, all voices were involved in the paraphrase.

divisions were the embellishment of the chief melodic line of a song or piece, often with no change in the other voices. Because such embellishment involved breaking longer note values into shorter ones, improvising was called *dividing*. Division technique is associated with solo linear instruments, and the early practice, called *diminutio*, is lost. Like the other techniques, division began to be written out (1511) chiefly for teaching materials.

Because the derivation of instrumental forms was largely from an improvised, undocumented tradition, the emergence of these forms seems sudden. Their earliest composers are difficult to ascertain. It is clear, however, that fine instrumentalists were flourishing at the beginning of the sixteenth century, as they had been in the fifteenth.

As the sixteenth century progressed, leadership in instrumental forms centered more and more in Italy, with the continuing development of organ forms and the invention of the *canzona*; and by the end of the century, the canzona was strongly associated with the Cathedral of San Marco (St. Mark's) in Venice. At the same time, the influence of organ forms began to expand. The verset and the organ Mass and Magnificat, many set only in alternate verses, were basically old concepts of punctus construction; although they did not die out, they ceased to be modern. The toccata and the organ canzona, however, could benefit from continuing experiments in the new techniques, and so they developed longer lines, proceeding from the punctus to sectional structure as the formes fixes had done before them. The free forms, particularly fantasia and toccata, developed into longer, somewhat discursive works of improvisational character, whereas the ricercar continued to represent the more learned style.

Protestant churches needed new instrumental forms, chiefly works to encourage meditation before services. Composers turned to the hymn (chorale) for material and to the variation or paraphrase for techniques. The *prelude*, based on a hymn tune, was inevitable in both England and Germany.

But the most popular instrumental music of the Renaissance was dance music. Guglielmo Ebreo (William the Jew, c. 1440-c. 1500), a dance master who had been a ghetto letz in northern Italy, laid the foundation for modern social dancing and ballet. In his treatise, he worked out a notation for dance and proposed that the *basse danse* ("low dance"), in which leisurely gliding steps kept the feet close to the floor, be the basic social form. The competing *saltarello* ("leaping dance") was shocking the courts by the middle of the century, but the basse danse maintained its popularity. Although many local dance types, each with a different rhythm, became popular in a succession of fads through the sixteenth and seventeenth centuries, they were merely rhythmic variations within one standard form.

A woodcut of a positive organ, from *Spiegel der Orgelmacher und Organisten* (Mirror of the Organ Builder and the Organist, 1511), by Arnold Schlick, a German organist. The organist is participating in a performance of mixed instrumental color. (Courtesy of Three Lions, Inc.)

Some Late Renaissance Instrumental Forms

instrumental dance. Dances for lutes and consorts became popular in the sixteenth century and were too numerous to itemize. The most popular were the *basse danse, pavane, volta, galliard, courante, recoupe, allemande, gavotte, tordion, bransle* or *brawl, passamezzo,* and *saltarello.* Like dance musicians today, sixteenth-century musicians grouped dances by twos or threes, often in slow-fast order (good for social dancing), such as *pavane-galliard, passamezzo-saltarello,* or *basse danse-recoupe-tordion.*

concerto ecclesiastico ("sacred concerto") was a composition for church performance (but not liturgical). The word *concerto* derives from the verb *concertare,* "to vie together" in Latin and "to accommodate" in Italian. Early uses of the term (1587, 1595) refer to the combining of independent vocal and instrumental elements, as distinct from doubling vocal lines with instruments in a capella practice. The works, for the most part, were sacred songs; they were written in Germany, as *Geistlichen concerten,* through the seventeenth and into the eighteenth century.

organ chorale or *chorale prelude* was a Protestant organ piece based on a hymn tune (chorale). Originally, the organist played the tune before the congregation sang it, as a means of teaching. In the early seventeenth century, new organ versions proliferated; by the end of the century, the form had expanded into an independent work based on a chorale and using whatever techniques (including imitative and ornamental) the composer's imagination could bring to bear on the practice. The climax of the form came during the two generations before and after 1700.

fugue was a later development of the learned style, growing out of imitative techniques. Related to both the canzona and ricercar at the beginning of the seventeenth century, its first known use was in 1607 in a publication by Bernhard Schmid the Younger (born 1548) titled *Fugen, oder wie es de Italiener nennen, canzoni alla francese* (Fugues, or What the Italians Call Canzone in the French Style). The fugue form was to become the polyphonic working-out of a single subject and was to remain a principal organ form well into the eighteenth century.

fancy, an English form, was popular, at the turn into the seventeenth century, with the virginalists, for whom the form was free and improvisatory. It was popular for a much longer time with the amateur viol players, who comprised a lively musical force throughout the century. The fancy was written for a consort of viols and emulated the canzona more than the fantasia, of which the term *fancy* is a translation.

Perhaps the most significant development for the coming history of the single movement was the definition and standardization of the two-part dance form. The standard dance type is well represented by the "Dance" and "Double." These dances comprised two puncti in a decorated familiar style, each repeated as a double punctus reminiscent of the estampie (though these particular dances do not include ouvert and clos endings). The form can be summarized *aabb,* or *a* :||: *b* :||. In the dance *Laura gentile* (Example 44), the two puncti end on different finals, F and D.

By the end of the century, the form had expanded to two sections, each with several puncti, and this double section with repetitions was to be a standard instrumental form well into the eighteenth century. Even then, it

A lute dance, with its double, from the end of the sixteenth century. The original tablature is here transcribed at pitch. (Courtesy of G. Ricordi & C.)

was not dropped but further expanded and transformed to become once more a standard of a new music.

Vocal composite forms were basically Masses, motets, chansons, or madrigals extended to accommodate long texts. The organ Mass and Magnificat basically can be put in the same category. The chief instrumental composite work of the latter part of the sixteenth century was a series of dances called a

Musical Composites

225

dance suite. Musicians performing instrumental music for social dancing naturally offer contrasting speeds and types, and some combinations are used over and over. In the sixteenth century, pairs such as a pavane and a galliard were composed together, often with the second as a variation of the first, either with a different rhythmic proportion for the same notation or with a double. When instrumentalists began to perform more for listeners, they naturally turned to the dance literature with which they were already familiar and made suites of dances.

The dance suite had many advantages, the first of which was the ease of achieving a desired length. Six or seven (or fewer or more) short movements could create a work of substantial length. A second advantage was the already proven popularity of the forms. They were direct, simple (hence, susceptible to embellishment), and, as individual dances, in public favor. And a third advantage was the adaptability of the two-punctus form and its ease of combination with other movements and types.

Thus, series of loosely related movements, under a variety of titles, constituted an important form early in the seventeenth century. As well as writing suites, composers assembled them for publication or published extended groups of dances in the same key. This furnished a pool from which a performer could select contrasting items to make a suite according to the dictates of his skill, time, or taste.

Once the Renaissance forms were well established, there began a long period of expansion in both their length and number of performers. A five-voice norm had supplanted the four-voice norm of the High Renaissance by the middle of the century, and soon six- and eight-part motets were, if not standard, at least no longer surprising. At the end of the sixteenth century, many of the basic assumptions of three or even four hundred years—notably rhythmic proportion and the Guidonian pitch system of expanded hexachords —were being supplanted by new concepts.

Performance

Inflation of the medium of performance occurred by increasing the number of parts rather than by using additional performers in the standard number of parts. It is recorded, for example, that Thomas Warwick, the organist of Westminster Abbey, composed a song in forty parts, which, about the year 1633, was performed before Charles the First by forty singers.[5] Given the ideal of the consort plus the architecture of the churches and the prestigious history of antiphonal practice, the use of eight parts as two groups of four rather than one consort of eight was a logical application of late Renaissance ideas. Italy seems to have been the center for the development of the twofold group, or double consort, which was called the *coro spezzato* ("split choir"; plural, *cori spezzati*). A performance in coro spezzato took place in Padua as early as 1522, but development of the technique, particularly in the instrumental canzona, is associated more with Venice at the end

[5] Thomas Busby, A *General History of Music*, London: G. and W. B. Whittaker, 1819, vol. II, p. 155.

An air view of St. Mark's Cathedral in Venice, showing its five domes and its Greek-cross design. (Courtesy of Foto ENIT Roma.)

of the century. The architectural design of St. Mark's Cathedral was based on a Greek rather than a Roman cross (square rather than elongated), which gave it a double choir loft, one on each side of the altar and about 10 feet above the floor. Such an arrangement comprised a readymade stage for the new kind of antiphonal productions, although plainchant antiphony was a hallowed tradition and doubtless formed a reassuring precedent.

The new coro spezzato techniques were vocal as well as instrumental, and double motets, as well as double canzone, became popular in the second half of the century. The architectural placement of performers became crucial again, and the true modernist was in reality the producer. Decisions about instruments—which ones, how many, and where—became essential to balance and contrast, the basis of double-choir performance. In the Medieval era, these decisions had been made without written directives, but in the late Renaissance, composers began to specify additional aspects of their music in the notation. Register was often indicated by varying the clefs, but such notations have never been complete. Organists, for example, consider registering to be their own prerogative, even though registers are occasionally specified, particularly when clarification of the bass (and thus the harmonic structure) is involved. However, register could be controlled by specifying an instrument whose range would make it necessary to sound a given line higher or lower than the written pitches.

The *Sonata Pian' e Forte* of Giovanni Gabrieli, dating from about 1600, was an eight-part canzona of two cori or consorts.[6] Coro I called for a cornetto (a wooden instrument with fingerholes, bound in leather and having an ivory mouthpiece) and three trombones; Coro II called for a violin and three

[6] This work appears in Archibald T. Davison and Willi Apel, *Historical Anthology of Music*, vol. 1, *Oriental, Medieval and Renaissance Music*, rev. ed., Cambridge, Mass.: Harvard, 1962, pp. 198–200.

trombones. The work was significant not only because it specified the instruments as part of the notation, but also because it used *piano* and *forte*. The dynamic contrasts were produced by natural means—a single choir is softer than the combined sound of numbers—without reference to change of tone on the part of the performers. The passages of alternating cori tend to be lower in range and less active rhythmically, so the aggregate reverberations are heightened by tessitura and rhythmic density.

But the consort had undergone some redefinition—neither coro of the *Sonata Pian' e Forte*, for example, is a true consort. The consort, the instrumental joy of the central Renaissance, had given way to the broken consort and the mixed consort. The *broken consort* was a consort with a substituted instrument, frequently on top. Although such substitutions doubtless had always been made because of necessity, it is clear that at the end of the century, they were made purposefully for the effect of the contrast. The *mixed consort*, as its name implies, was made up of a mixed group of instruments. In order to be musically successful, such a mixture had to be consistent in dynamics. The mixtures were considered generally as either loud or soft, with brasses (including the cornetto) and double reeds as the basis for the former and flutes (including recorders), Krummhorns, and viols as the basis for the latter. Dynamic levels were considered analogous to those of speech, in which *high* and *low* mean "loud" and "soft," respectively. The mixed brass and reed consort was called *high music*, whereas the consort for viols and recorders—often high in our sense—was *low music*. The violin was louder than the viol and thus could appear in a broken consort of high music.

The end of the Renaissance saw a further development. From the coro spezzato, which might be called bichoral, it was but a small step to the combining of a number of consorts or vocal groups in polychoral techniques. The characteristic polychoral type was the instrumental ensemble (today sometimes called the Renaissance band); it was made up of several consorts and included solo harmonic instruments, notably lutes. As with the larger instrumental groups of minstrelsy, the instrumentation was the producer's bailiwick; Gabrieli was exceptional in calling for specific instruments. A simple

Cornetts: treble, tenor, and bass. The bass cornett was given the appropriate name "serpent." A consort of "high music" might consist of two trebles, two tenors, and a bass. (Photo by R. E. Kalmbach.)

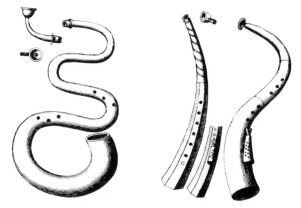

four-part dance might be performed by a number of consorts—complete, broken, and mixed. A consort of viols and one of recorders (both low music), a broken consort of three trombones and violin, and a mixed group of reeds and brasses and perhaps an organ would play in alternation, in a variety of combinations, and finally in total aggregate (in Italian, *tutti*). Percussion would also have been added (a further similarity to earlier instrumental practice), most frequently in dances and in connection with high music.

The consorts were placed as units, so the total effect (focus and contrast) was spatial as well as instrumental. The Renaissance band had no set format. Ideally it was an assembly of consorts, each complete and all different, and was composed of as many as thirty or thirty-five players, so that the tutti sections attained considerable power. Such ensembles represented the culmination of the expansion of Renaissance polyphony for instruments. Thus to perform the works of the first three decades of the seventeenth century, which were written for such groups, in a single blended group affords only a pale reflection of the colorful and various effects of the original.

MONODY

Expansion of polyphonic techniques was the central characteristic of the Renaissance. The results—an increased interest in harmony and a relative disinterest in rhythmic complexity—turned polyphony toward the extremes of size represented by twenty-four- to forty-part motets and the Benevoli Mass in fifty-three parts. Such works at their best achieved a solid majesty, but coordination was difficult and subtlety was impossible; thus the result was often musically turgid and textually chaotic.

Countering this polyphonic expansion was an interest in the simple single line and a reaction against the learned style, the imitative point, and the complexity that had obscured musical focus and ceased to delight in its design and virtuoso skill. The modernists thus rejected the extremes of their contemporaries, which they felt had been used up.

At the same time, the new definitions of harmony and harmonic functions remained at the cutting edge, and interest in emotional expression and word-painting continued to grow. The sixteenth century was eminently literary, for such surpassing poets as Torquato Tasso (1544–1595) in Italy and William Shakespeare (1564–1616) in England were producing texts worthy of clear, expressive settings. In addition, during the second half of the sixteenth century, there developed a passion for the theater, first in Italy, then in England. Performances, often of newly translated classical plays, were unbelievably lavish, with splendid settings, costumes, and a good deal of machinery.

In 1585 the Teatro Olimpica opened in Vicenzo, near Venice, with a production of *Oedipus Rex*, by Sophocles. One of the audience described the

L'Ouïe (*Hearing*), an anonymous painting based on an engraving by Abraham Bosse (1602–1676). The voice, lute, and gamba were an important combination in the lute song and the early ideal of monody. (Courtesy of the Conservation des Musées, Tours, and Photographie Giraudon.)

play, which ran from 7:30 to 11 P.M., in a letter that reflects the enthusiasm of a knowledgeable viewer. The letter tells of the many aspects of the production, the excellence of the participants, including the musician Andrea Gabrieli, and the relative place of music in a production striving to reach its audience through every possible channel.

> The theatre can easily accommodate 3,000 spectators. . . . The eyes of the laymen receive the overall impression of an incredible loveliness. . . . Angelo Ingegneri, capable of such things, has directed this tragic business. The choral music was composed by Andrea Gabrieli, organist of St. Mark's. The settings were designed by Vicenzo Scamozzi, architect of Vicenza. The costumes were by Maganza. . . . There were eighty stage costumes. . . . Two of the players, the King and the Queen, were magnificently dressed in gold cloth. . . . When the time had come to lower the curtain, a very sweet smell of perfume made itself felt to indicate that in the city of Thebes, according to the ancient legend, incense was burned to placate the wrath of the gods. Then there was a sound of trumpets and drums, and four squibs exploded. In a twinkle of an eye the curtain fell before the stage. I can hardly express in words, nor can it be imagined, how great the joy was, and

the infinite pleasure felt by the spectators, when they, after a moment of stunned surprise, watched the prologue, and when the sound of harmonized voices and divers instruments could be heard from a distance behind the scenic facade. . . .[7]

The modernists wanted to use music more directly in dramatic utterance. They sought a dramatic style for the madrigal and developed the *solo madrigal* (the *lute song*, in countries other than Italy). At its greatest, the solo madrigal was a fine poem, sensitively set and performed by a singer-lutenist, with a reinforced bass line often added by a second performer playing a *viola da gamba*.

The lute and voice together comprised a combination similar to a broken consort—one that in its very sound delighted the experimenters. The standard-sized lute, by now strung in double courses, was joined by larger sizes, an important one of which was the *theorbo*. The theorbo was an *archlute* (a large bass lute), developed in Venice about 1575, that provided six or eight additional bass strings from a second pegbox (placed beyond the first to provide greater length). The added strings could be variously tuned to provide for the demands of individual pieces but were not set over the fingerboard and could not be fingered—once tuned, they remained at the set pitch. The large size of the theorbo and cumbersome technique of playing it denied to the theorbist the passage work and brilliant technical display possible for the lutenist but afforded him a depth and resonance, along with a reasonable amount of manipulability in the upper section, that was ideal for accompaniment. Just before 1600, the instrument appeared in France, where, as in England, interest in the lute song followed Italy's by a generation.

By the end of the century, singing to the lute was practiced with great popularity in Italy, France, Spain, and England—virtually throughout Europe. A generation of composers turned to the writing of solo songs with lute.

Although international in practice, the solo song with lute maintained national characteristics. In France, the lute song took the name *air*, a term that covered songs in general, both solo and polyphonic. The two main types were the *air à boire* ("drinking song") and *air de cour* ("court" or "formal song"). Both were lighter and less associated with the learned style than was the chanson. The air de cour was the rage at court during the seventeenth century, with the guitar becoming as popular as the lute. (Louis XIV took daily guitar lessons.) Collections of *airs sérieux et à boire* ("serious and drinking songs") were published yearly well into the eighteenth century. In Spain, the popularity of the lute song continued throughout the seventeenth and into the eighteenth century as a song with guitar accompaniment. In England, in an age of supreme poetic attainment, the *ayre* was written to lyric rather than either dramatic or formal texts. The English lute song was

---

[7] Quoted in A. M. Nagler, *A Source Book in Theatrical History*, New York: Dover, 1959, pp. 83–86.

Facsimile of an air from *Airs de différent auteurs*, a collection from about 1600. Such songs were used for dancing in court ballets as well as for singing. (Courtesy of the Eastman School of Music, University of Rochester.)

able to reach unequaled depth and artistic fulfillment, because the real love and respect of the British for their fine poetry created the basis for a total unity and effect amounting almost to a mystique. The English writer of lute songs was often a poet-composer-singer-lutenist. The immediate appeal of the solo voice, magnetic in any era, was joined to the lutenist's art, resulting in a subtlety and perfection attainable only by a single performer.

John Dowland's "Flow my teares," a countertenor solo, is a lovely work, which well represents the full achievement of the English lute song. The five stanzas of the poem are set as two repeated sections plus a final one that stands alone. The harmonic usage, though less chromatic than in some ayres, is representative. Its climactic e^2 (measure 39), the high point of the piece, is set off by a preceding rest and emphasized by its length and its expansion of meaning as a suspension. The rich vocabulary, a compromise between extreme chromatic and conservative diatonic usage, is exploited through a juxtaposition of two forms of a note (as with g^1 and $g\sharp^1$ in measure 10) and through reliance on the singer to maintain color tones. In particular, thirds, which often sound to bare fifths in the lute, were left to the voice to temper them as the fretted lute could not.

The form of this piece is not standard but is representative in its clear heritage from the past. The repeated sections are related to the double punctus, and the final section is kin to the trouvère ballade, especially in its use of the cadence (last four measures) from the first repeated section (measures 12 to 15).

Interpretation of the song within a metrical system leads to rhythmic distortion of the original. As the solo reads, the text is hoisted into unwelcome accentuations, yet a singer who is aware of the proportional concept and particularly of hemiola (large and small) will see that the solo is actually a precise rhythmic representation of the text as it would be recited naturally.

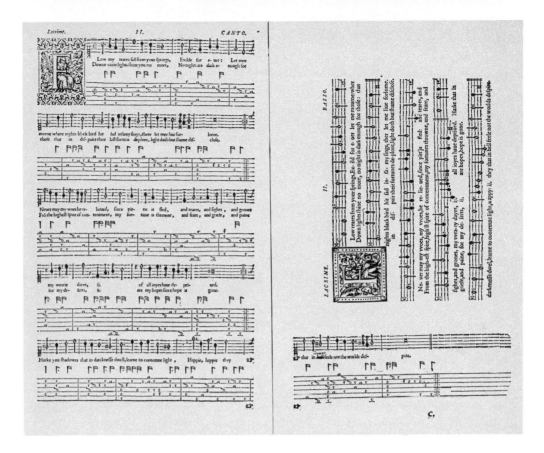

Example 45A, "Flow my teares," by John Dowland, a facsimile from the *Second Booke of Songes or Ayres*, 1600. The English lute was tuned g[1], d[1], a, f, c, G; the letters indicate activation of the string—a for open string, b for the first fret, c[1] for the second fret, and so forth. The letters beneath the lines of the tablature represent the added strings of the theorbo. (Courtesy of the Henry E. Huntington Library and Art Gallery.)

Flow My Teares

JOHN DOWLAND

Example 45B

Example 45B (continued)

Example 45B (continued)

This English lute song is from the poet-composer's *Second Booke of Songes or Ayres,* published in both tablature and parts in 1600.

The text *hir sad infamy* is a small hemiola; *shadowes that in darknesse* (final phrase, not shown) is a large hemiola. The Renaissance rhythmic language was a fine means to show subtleties of texts, especially effective in a one-man performance. In the original, a bass part was provided but was optional.

Flow my teares fall from your springs...

Where nights black bird hir sad in - fa - my sings...

Nev - er may my woes be re - liev - ed...

Well into the sevententh century, French, Spanish, and English composers continued using tablature, doubtless keeping their works more accessible to the great number of amateur lutenists. The Italians, still centering on dramatic goals, had different performance conditions. They wanted the singer to act out a text on a stage while being accompanied by other musicians. Thus the singer did not accompany himself, nor was the lute (even the theorbo) the ideal balance to heightened dramatic utterance. As continuous support for the singer and to balance his part, the Italians developed an accompaniment with a linear bass written out as a melody in its own right. Reflecting this focus on the singer and the effectiveness of the melodic bass in supporting the solo line, it soon became customary for the bass line to be written out and the harmonies to be indicated by figures and signs, which were relatively easy for harpsichordists and theorbists to read, while the melody was played also on a viol. Such a bass was called a *basso continuo* ("constant bass") and was played by at least two people. Thus a solo madrigal or *aria* ("air") was often performed by three people, in contrast to the English or French air, which was most often performed by one, or by two when a viola da gamba was used for added support.

Composers of vocal music with basso continuo called it the *stile nuovo* ("new style") or the *stile espressivo, stile rappresentativo,* or *stile recitativo* ("expressive," "realistic," or "declamatory"). In contrast to monophony and polyphony, this new texture of solo and basso continuo was called *monody.* The great early publication of monodic songs was Giulio Caccini's *Le Nuove Musiche* (1602). One song, "Amarilli," uses a pastoral text typical of the solo madrigal and is set with the clarity of focus that is the particular virtue of that form. Like the English lute song, it uses Renaissance harmonic and rhythmic idioms. The numbers over the bass are the intervals, measured up from the bass note, that are played by the harpsichordist or theorbist. (Absence of figures indicated a chord of the fifth on the bass note.)

Amarilli

GIULIO CACCINI

Example 46

Amarilli mia bella
Nó credi ò del mio cor dolce desio d'esler tu
L'amor mio?
Credilo pur
È fe timore t'affale
Prendi questo mio strale
Aprim'il petto
È vedrai scritto il core:
Amarilli, Amarilli,
Amarilli, e'l mio amore.

Amarilli, my beautiful one!
Will you not believe that I long for you to be
The darling of my heart?
Ah, but believe:
If fear and doubt assail you
I will seize an arrow,
Gash open my breast,
And engrave on my heart:
Amarilli, Amarilli,
Amarilli is my beloved.

TRANS. BY JON RINKA

A facsimile from *Le Nuove Musiche* (The New Music; 1602), which was the pioneer in the use of figured bass. Notated in the baritone clef (middle line *f*), the bass used both interval numbers and sharp signs. The numbers 11 and 10 were soon reduced to 4 and 3, respectively. The book was printed in movable type, in which one section of staff, with one note, is juxtaposed to the next. Thus the staff lines, which have a characteristic unsteadiness, were accumulated. For a summary of Caccini's preface on embellishments, along with a discussion of performance of the solo madrigals, see H. Wiley Hitchcock, "Vocal Ornamentation in Caccini's *Nuove Musiche*," *Musical Quarterly*, vol. LVI, no. 3 (July, 1970), pp. 389–404. (Courtesy of the Library of Congress.)

DRAMMA PER MUSICA

With the establishment of monody as a mature technique, the *dramma per musica* ("drama in music"; plural, *dramme per musica*) became practicable. To it were brought the techniques and styles of both music (old style as well as new) and the theater. Traditional music contributed the techniques of the motet, madrigal, canzona, dance forms, and occasional types such as fanfares and processional music. The theater contributed the accumulated experience of plays, ballets, and entertainments, all of which had used music either incidentally (as the plot required) or, in the ballets, as suites of dances or short songs (but not in dialogue). In addition to being used in plays, music had been presented between the acts, typically as an *intermezzo* ("set between"; plural, *intermezzi*). The intermezzo was most often a light or comic diversion, sometimes comprising a group of madrigals loosely strung together with a spoken text. All these techniques were retained in the dramma per musica.

But it was monody that defined the new form. The concept of the solo balanced by the basso continuo, with its rhythmic flexibility and its focus on the singer, allowed the creation of free declamatory monody. Applying the style to dramatic texts, monodists rejected the use of repetition and let the text be reflected in a continuing free form. The whole was devoted more to theatrical than musical ends; the singer was urged by Caccini to "a noble disdain of melody" [8] combined with an interpretation of the text. In free monody, an irregularly accented prose text could be set in a natural style or a poetic text given high dramatic emphasis, which afforded ample scope for interpretation by the singer. Such monody, the recitativo type, constituted the very life of the dramma per musica.

The earliest dramme per musica were produced in Florence by members of an experimental group called the Camerata Florentine (Florentine Cameraderie). Several such groups flourished at the end of the sixteenth century; the Camerata met at the court of Count Bardi fairly regularly from about 1576, when Caccini became the count's secretary. The group comprised not only musicians but speculators in several of the arts and sciences, among which our current differentiations were neither clear nor sacrosanct. Rhetoric and poetry figured prominently in their concerns, and their search for a declamatory or realistic style of performance was not purely musical. Early works were based on mythological, allegorical, or classical stories, of which *Orpheus and Eurydice*—the legend of the Greek musician who followed his wife to the underworld—was the most often used. Two of the earliest dramme per musica, one of them by Caccini, were produced in 1600 in Florence, and productions soon followed in other cities. The most

[8] Quoted in Curt Sachs, *Our Musical Heritage*, Englewood Cliffs, N.J.: Prentice-Hall, 1948, p. 207.

famous was *La Favola d'Orfeo* by Monteverdi, which was produced in Mantua in 1607. Monteverdi's dramatic music was the summit of the late Renaissance achievement.

The greatness of Monteverdi's art can be recognized by noting that his work in the stile nuovo is free of the tentative effect that so often attends experimental writing. On the contrary, Monteverdi brought the skills of the old style to bear on the new, so his recitativo evinces the subtlety characteristic of the English lute song as well as the dramatic force of the new style. Although sacrificing nothing of the power of music, he wrote that "harmony, from being the mistress, becomes the servant of the words."[9] The singer should not keep rigidly to the tactus but should follow the soul's affection. At the performance of the famed "Lamento" from his opera *Arianna* (1608), the audience was so moved that they wept. It is no wonder that of all the early composers of the dramma per musica, Monteverdi is the one whose works are still performed by opera companies today.

The dramma per musica was based on the free monody, or recitativo, which carried the action forward. But alternating with the recitativo were choruses written in motet or madrigal style, dances in the double-punctus form and played by consorts (singly and combined), and instrumental interludes, often based on the canzona. The instrumental forces in some productions were impressive; Monteverdi listed thirty-eight players, to be used as consorts that would alternate according to the mood or action of the drama, in his own score of *La Favola d'Orfeo*. His imagination and originality are demonstrated by his specifying such effects as tremolo and pizzicato for the violins. Although such experiments in instrumental technique are characteristic of the Baroque period, the concept of the musical composite and the instrumental ensemble of combined consorts is representative of the late Renaissance art. *Orfeo* was a work of consummate skill and imagination that reveals the art of music as it poised for a new era.

[9] Quoted in Strunk, *op. cit.*, p. 407.

❀ *Some Composers of the Late Renaissance*

Nothing can better illustrate the sweep of change in the hundred years from 1525 to 1625 than a survey of the work of representative composers. Most worked in more than one style or medium, but as time passed, the styles grew farther apart so specialization was the norm, and a variety of output the exception. Few musicians at the end of the Renaissance were equally well-known for work in more than one aspect of music, but they achieved a more sharply focused fame than did their predecessors. The influence of the Netherlanders was still potent throughout the sixteenth century, but the growing importance of the Italians is clear.

Masses and Motets

CHRISTOBAL DE MORALES (c. 1500–1553) was a great Spanish composer of sacred music. Born in Seville, he worked in

Avila and Rome (papal choir 1535–1540), then Toledo (1545–1547) and Malaga (1551–1553). He was widely respected by his contemporaries, who called him "the light of Spain in music." Two books of his Masses (including two on "L'homme armé") were published in Rome in 1544. In addition, he left many motets, including longer works such as Magnificats and lamentations.

GIOVANNI PIERLUIGI DE PALESTRINA (1526–1594), an Italian whose conservative sacred polyphony became the model of later emulation, began as a choirboy at Santa Maria Maggiore in Rome. In 1544 he was music director at the cathedral in Palestrina, whose bishop became Pope Julius III. The Pope brought Palestrina to Rome, where he variously prospered and bided his time. The new decrees on simplifying sacred music found fruition in Palestrina's forthright style. His output was prodigious, including over 100 Masses (in four to eight parts), about 600 motets and other large liturgical settings (Magnificats, litanies, lamentations, etc.), 42 Psalms, about 200 madrigals (both spiritual and profane), and 9 organ ricercari.

ROLAND DE LASSUS (1531 or 1532–1594) was the last great Netherlander of the polyphonic tradition. He began as a boy soprano and led a life if international adventure and fame during his first quarter century. In 1556, already dubbed "The Prince of Music," he entered the service of the dukes of Bavaria in Munich, where he was raised to the nobility. His incredible output of over 2,000 works, not yet completely counted, comprises a virtual summary of late Renaissance polyphony, both sacred and secular. His sacred works include 53 Mass ordinaries (from four to eight parts), 23 Magnificats, 4 Passions, an array of Psalms (including a complete setting of the 7 Penitential Psalms), lamentations, vigils, and well over 500 motets (from two to twelve parts). His secular works are a testimony to his international-

ism—French chansons (he won a trouvère contest at a puy in southern France), Italian madrigals, German Lieder. Of the latter alone, 93 examples remain (from three to eight parts).

TOMÁS LUIS DE VICTORIA (c. 1549–1611), the greatest of the Spanish polyphonists, devoted his life and his art to religion. He was a Roman Catholic in the midst of the developing Protestantism, on the one hand, and the rising secularism, on the other. Much of his early and later years are obscure, but it is known that his early training was in Avila, that he entered the Collegium Germanicum in 1565 to study for the priesthood, and that he succeeded Palestrina as music master at the Collegium in 1571. Ordained in 1573, Victoria remained in Rome in a number of capacities. The last fifteen to twenty years of his life were spent in Spain, at the convent of the Descalgas Reales in Madrid. He left 21 Masses (four to twelve voices), 46 motets (four to eight voices), 35 hymns, and 19 canticles, plus Psalms, Litanies, and other sacred works. (He left no secular music.) He is known for the *Hymni Totius Anni* (published in Rome in 1581 and in Venice in 1600) and a Requiem Mass of 1605, for which he wrote an organ accompaniment that was a forerunner of future Baroque practice.

JACOBUS GALLUS (1550–1591), from Carniola, in an area that is now in western Yugoslavia, was chapel master for the Bishop of Olmutz in Prague and traveled widely in Eastern Europe. He was a militant Catholic, considered the equal of Lassus and Palestrina in music, and was the most zealous of the musicians of the Counter Reformation. He wrote 19 Masses (four to eight voices), mostly based on other compositions in all parts (called *parody* by modern scholars) and many motets and occasional pieces. Four volumes of motets, titled *Opus Musicum*, were published between 1586 and 1591.

Protestant Music

JOHANNES WALTHER (1496–1570), a German composer who defined the early direction of Lutheran devotional music, worked as a basso singer for the duke of Saxony. He founded the first known society for German song, and, as a friend and counselor of Luther, he prepared, in 1524, the earliest spiritual songbook of the Protestant movement, the *Geystliche Gesangk-Buchleyn*. Walther left many motets and chorale melodies, a Magnificat, a Passion, and miscellaneous instrumental pieces.

CLAUDE GOUDIMEL (c. 1505–1572), a French composer who became a Protestant, wrote a Huguenot Psalter that is one of the great monuments of the early Reformation. Born in Besançon, he worked in Paris, Metz, and Lyon, where he was killed in the massacre of St. Bartholomew. His *Les CL pseaumes de David, nouvellement mis en musique à quatre parties* (150 Psalms of David, newly set to music in four parts) was published in Geneva in 1564. He also left a significant production of 5 Masses, 3 Magnificats (before his conversion), and several volumes of motets, most published in his lifetime.

THOMAS TALLIS (c. 1510–1585), an important English composer, worked at Waltham Cathedral, near London, until its dissolution in 1540. He was Gentleman of the Royal Chapel under both Henry VIII and Elizabeth I. In 1575, in partnership with William Byrd, Tallis was granted a monopoly on music printing. The polyphonic versions of the plainsong responses for the Church of England that are still in use were written by Tallis, as were several services, many hymns, 18 anthems, and three books of Psalms. In addition, he left, for the Anglican services, 2 Masses and, for the Catholic Church, 52 motets, most of which were early works, plus 2 Magnificats and 2 lamentations.

CLAUDE LE JEUNE (c. 1528–1600), a French Protestant, worked for the duke of Anjou (brother of Henri III), the Vicomte de Turenne, and, from 1594, King Henri IV. His early settings of the Psalms into French, dating from 1564, established his reputation. The great body of his work was published after his death by his sister and his niece—150 *Pseaumes* (four voices) in 1601 and five other volumes, including another set of Psalms in three voices and miscellaneous songs, both sacred and secular, from 1601 to 1612. A later edition of the 150 *Pseaumes* (1613) was circulated internationally and translated into German and English; some copies even found their way to the New World.

WILLIAM BYRD (c. 1540–1623), when a young man, was organist of the Lincoln Cathedral. In 1572 he went to London and joined his teacher, Thomas Tallis, in the Royal Chapel, where he became a chief founder of the English modern style. One of the great masters of the Renaissance, Byrd was also one of the most versatile, and English tolerance enabled him to enjoy his versatility. Of sacred music, he left important works for both Roman and English services—chiefly Masses and sacred songs for the former and services, Psalms, and anthems for the latter. Of secular music, he contributed to the song and madrigal and, more significantly, to instrumental forms, notably over 100 pieces for harpsichord, plus works for organ and for viols.

Secular Vocal Polyphony

COSTANZO FESTA (c. 1495–1545), a Roman-born Italian, is credited with bringing the nationalistic elements of the sixteenth century into Italian music, both by bringing the Franco-Flemish tradition into Italy and by developing the early madrigal. In the papal chapel from 1517, he centered his life in Rome. He wrote a four-voice *Te Deum*, which is still in the literature of the papal choir, a volume of three-voice motets, and a Magnificat. But he was renowned chiefly for his madrigals, three books of which he published, c. 1535, 1537 (both in three voices), and 1539.

CIPRIANO DE RORE (1516–1565), a Netherlander, studied in Antwerp and Venice and worked in Ferrara and Parma. He published eight books of madrigals, the first of which, in five voices, appeared in 1542. One of the most illustrious of the lowlanders in Italy, he was known for his experiments with chromaticism, particularly the incorporation of chromatic elements as part of the expressive technique of the madrigal. He also left 3 Masses (in five and seven parts—1 on a *soggetto cavato*), three books of motets, a Passion, and a few instrumental works.

LUZZASCO LUZZASCHI (1545–1607) was an Italian organist and composer at the Court of Ferrara, where, as a child, he had studied with Cipriano de Rore and where he, in turn, taught Frescobaldi. He wrote seven books of madrigals (two are lost), which were published from 1575 to 1604 (all in five voices), sacred songs, and a volume of madrigals from one to three voices with organ accompaniment (1601). He also left a number of organ works, chiefly toccatas and ricercari.

LUCA MARENZIO (1553–1599), an Italian singer and composer, served the Este family, the King of Poland, and others before returning to Rome to serve the papal court. His prodigious output covers virtually all the vocal forms current in his lifetime. He wrote entertainments for court celebrations, motets (four, eight, and twelve voices), and sacred songs (five to seven voices) but is best known for his eighteen books of madrigals, including one of *Madrigali*, *Spirituali* in four, five, and six voices. (Nine books are in five voices.)

THOMAS MORLEY (1557–c. 1603), English organist and composer, was a Gentleman of the Royal Chapel but was famous for his secular music. He wrote madrigals (some with Italian texts), canzonets, ballets, and lute songs and was famous for the consort lessons for mixed instruments, a collection from different composers. He is known for having furnished music for the first performance of Shakespeare's plays, including *As You Like It*.

CARLO GESUALDO DI VENOSA (1560–1613), Italian lutenist and composer, was a nobleman who grew up surrounded by the fine musicians of his father's court. His second marriage, to Eleanora d'Este, sister of the future duke of Modena, brought him into contact with Luzzasco Luzzaschi, from whose counsel he benefited. He published six books of madrigals for five voices (1594–1611) and left a group for six voices. The five-voice works were published in 1613 and the six-voice works in 1626.

Instrumental Music in the Sixteenth Century

ADRIEN WILLAERT (c. 1480–1562), born possibly at Bruges, studied law in Paris but switched to music. He returned to Flanders and then emigrated to Italy. He was in Rome, Ferrara, Urbino, and possibly Hungary before he found his metier—as director of music at San Marco in Venice, where he remained (except for two visits home) from 1527 until his death. Willaert founded one of the great musical schools—San Marco remained an important musical center for a century afterward. Although he wrote motets, Masses, hymns, villanesce, chansons, and madrigals, Willaert was most important for his instrumental fantasie and ricercari.

MARC'ANTONIO CAVAZZONI DA BOLOGNA (c. 1490–c. 1560), an Italian organist and composer, worked in Rome (for Leo X) in 1520 but settled in Venice in 1522. In 1523 he published *Ricercari, Motetti, Canzoni*, the first known use of the term *ricercari* for organ works. His son, GIROLAMO CAVAZZONI, continued to explore instrumental forms, including organ Masses, hymns, ricercari, and toccate.

FRANCESCO DA MILANO (1497–1543), an Italian lutenist of great skill and fame known as "il divino," worked in Rome under Paul III. In addition to being one of history's surpassing lutenists, Milano was pivotal in his development of new forms. Seven books of his lute works were published from 1536; these include many intabulations of chansons and motets but also present ricercari, fantasie, and a toccata, perhaps the first published example. Although he is known to have improvised on dance tunes, no dances or variations survive.

ANTONIO DE CABEZÓN (1510–1566), a blind Spanish organist and composer of noble birth, was organist of the royal house of Castille at sixteen. Under Charles V, he was a master of the royal children and professor of music. Widely traveled, even in his peripatetic generation, Antonio was known and respected for his harmonic gift and his versatility. His works were published, after his death, in a compilation called *Obras de musica* (Musical Works), in which he is listed as *musico de la camera y capilla del Rey* ("musician of the chamber and chapel of the King"). He is known for his instrumental works, including preludes, ricercari, canons, and organ Magnificats. He left 1 vocal polyphonic work, a five-voice litany.

ANDREA GABRIELI (c. 1510–1586), a Venetian composer and organist, was associated with the great school of San Marco, where he was second organist from 1564, first organist from 1584. A prolific composer, Andrea left about a dozen books of madrigals and other secular vocal works, chiefly in five or six voices; several volumes of sacred songs, Psalms, and Masses; and a half-dozen books of instrumental works (canzone and ricercari). He was influential in his day (many of his works appeared in several editions during his lifetime), not only as a composer establishing the instrumental forms, but also as a teacher.

BALTAZARINI (c. 1540–1585), called BEAUJOYEUX, an Italian composer and violinist, brought a troupe of violinists to France under the aegis of the Marechal de Brissac. Influential and ubiquitous, Baltazarini served Catherine de Medici, Mary Stuart (later Queen of Scots), Charles IX, and Henry III—all in the capacity of chamber violinist. Well known for his compositions of ballets (with which early use of the violin was associated), he was also an entrepreneur and producer. He was best known for one of the most influential productions in the history of music, the *Balet Comique de la Royne* (The Queen's Comic Ballet), which was given in 1581 for the marriage of Henry III's sister.

EUSTACHE DU CAURROY (1549–1609), a French singer and composer, was associated with the Royal Chapel from 1575. In 1595 he became a chamber musician as well. Versatile and productive, he left about 50 motets (four to seven voices), about 60 chansons and Psalms (four to six voices), and a Requiem Mass (five voices), all of which are conservative. He is much more important for his 42 instrumental fantasie (in three, four, five, and six voices), which were influential in the developing forms, leading the theorist Mersenne to write (in 1636) that "all composers in France hold him to be their master."

Instrumental Music at the End of the Renaissance

GIOVANNI GABRIELI (1557–1612) was brought up by his uncle, Andrea, a Venetian organist and composer. He succeeded Andrea as second organist at San Marco when the latter became first organist in 1584. From 1575 to 1579, Giovanni served in Munich as assistant to Roland de Lassus. Both he and his uncle were great teachers, and, although less prolific than his uncle, he nonetheless contributed vocal and instrumental forms, both secular and sacred. With Andrea, he brought out concertos (six to sixteen voices) and a volume of organ works; by himself, he wrote madrigals (four voices), sacred songs (four to six voices), and three volumes of instrumental works (from three to twenty-two voices). His works are still widely performed.

JAN PIETERSZOON SWEELINCK (1562–1621) was a Dutch organist and composer who ranked with Obrecht in the history of Dutch music. Sweelinck worked for forty years in Amsterdam, where he was renowned as both a performer and a teacher. (So many Germans went to Amsterdam to study with him that he is often considered the founder of the seventeenth-century German organ school.) His influence in the history of forms for the keyboard was equally profound; his 19 fantasie, 13 toccate, and 24 chorales for organ were definitive. Yet he left over 250 vocal works, including 22 chansons, 153 French Psalms, 37 Latin motets, and 4 Italian madrigals.

JEHAN TITELOUSE (1563–1633), a French organist and composer, was organist at the cathedral in Rouen from 1588. Born in the Spanish Netherlands, he became a French citizen in 1595 and a church canon in 1610. In the same year he published *Hymnes pour Toucher sur l'orgue avec les fugues et recherches sur leur plain chant* (Hymns for Playing on the Organ with Imitations and Searchings [ricercari] on Their Plain Song [melodies]). His organ Magnificats appeared in 1626. Titelouse's works are polyphonic, belonging to the Renaissance concept of the learned style, and idiomatic, being for organ, not "keyboard." He was also known as an authority on organ construction and as a minor poet.

HANS LEO HASSLER (1564–1612), a German organist and composer in Italy in 1584, was a student of Andrea Gabrieli in Venice. Returning to Germany, he worked in Augsburg and Nuremberg, from 1595 at the court of Rudolph II in Prague, and finally in Dresden, as organist for the Elector of Saxony. An enterprising man, he was both a librarian and a maker of musical clocks. His historical importance centers in his sacred music—*Cantiones sacræ* (four, eight, and more voices, 1591), *Sacri concentus* (five to twelve voices, 1601), *Psalmen und Christliche Gesang* (1607), *Kirchengesang: Psalmen und Geistlich Lieder* (1608), and *Litaney Teutsch* (seven voices in coro spezzato, published posthumously in 1619). Hassler also published one volume of canzonette and two of madrigals.

MICHAEL PRAETORIUS (1571–1621), a German composer and theorist, was in the service of the duke of Brunswick at Groningen from 1589 and Wölfenbüttel from 1604. He brought out many volumes of sacred songs, which included over 1,200 simple songs in the familiar style; he named them *Musæ Sionæ*, and his famous "Lo, how a rose ere blooming" is an example. In addition, he published a great number of motets, madrigals, and litanies. He contributed to instrumental literature with his publication of dances, *Terpsichore* (1612), and by his great treatise *Syntagma Musicum* (1615–1620), the second volume of which dealt with instruments and is a valuable musicological source.

ORLANDO GIBBONS (1583–1625), last and most illustrious of a family of English musicians associated with Cambridge and Oxford Universities, was born at Oxford but began his career as a choirboy at Cambridge. From 1605, he was organist of the Royal Chapel and a Gentleman of the Chamber as harpsichordist. He composed 2 Anglican services, about 40 anthems, and madrigals (secular and spiritual), mostly in the old style. Considered one of the greatest of the English virginal school, he left dances, variations, and fancies and is known also for his 9 fancies for viols.

ENNEMOND GAULTIER (c. 1575–1651), a French lutenist and composer, was known as Gaultier le Vieux (The

Elder) or Gaultier de Lyon. He was in the service of the duchess of Montmorency and, then, of Marie de Medici, regent of France. Surviving are only isolated works, including the first French chaconnes for lute and the "Tombeau de Mezangeau," one of the earliest commemorative pieces. His cousin DENYS (1603–1672), called Gaultier le Jeune (The Younger) or Gaultier de Paris, came to Paris as a composer and teacher. He left a greater number of works, including the *Rhétorique des Dieux* (62 pieces), published by a friend to preserve Gaultier's "inexpressible" art.

GIROLAMO FRESCOBALDI (1583–1643), a versatile performer and composer, was known chiefly as an organist. He was born in Ferrara but studied in Rome and went to Brussels. From 1608 he was organist at St. Peter's in Rome, where he settled his family and pursued his career, though he spent time in Florence and elsewhere. He published many volumes of his own music, including five-voice madrigals (1608), motets, and miscellaneous vocal works, but was known for his experimental works in the developing instrumental forms—toccate, canzone, ricercari, versets, and hymn paraphrases. His master work was the *Fiori Musicali* (Musical Flowers, Venice, 1635).

JOHANN HERMANN SCHEIN (1586–1630), a German composer and scholar, was the son of a Lutheran minister. He studied law as well as music and served first as a professor of music at Leipzig, then as chapel master at Weimar (1615), and finally (from 1616) as cantor at the Thomaskirche in Leipzig. He published a tremendous number of volumes of both vocal and instrumental music—secular and sacred songs, sacred concertos, dances, Italian madrigals, and many occasional works. Most important was a miscellany called the *Banchetto Musicale* (1617), containing 20 dance suites in the polyphonic style (five voices).

SAMUEL SCHEIDT (1587–1654), a German organist and composer, studied with Sweelinck, remaining in Amster-

dam several years. Returning to Germany, he worked at Halle and Brandenburg as master of the chapel to the Margrave. Although he was known to his contemporaries as a vocal writer (39 cantiones sacræ, 100 Psalms), in retrospect he seems more important for his instrumental pioneering. His playing founded a great German school, and his composition was highly influential in defining the new forms. He left collections of dances, sacred concertos, and three volumes of a great variety of forms—figures, toccate, variations, Psalms, dances, hymns, etc.—called the *Tabulatura Nova* (The New Tablature, 1624).

Lute Songs, Airs, and Solo Madrigals

MIGUEL DE FUENLLANA (dates unknown) was a blind Spanish lutenist from Madrid who served the Spanish court as musician to Isabella of Valois, Queen to Philip II. His works include virtually all the important lute forms of the second half of the sixteenth century. His famous publication, *Orphenica Lyra* (1554), included transcriptions of chansons and villancicos for solo voice and vihuela.

GIULIO CACCINI (c. 1548–1618), a Roman singer, theorbist, and composer, was credited by his contemporaries as being "the father of a new style." He began by writing madrigals in the old style and from 1564 served the Tuscan court. His experiments in singing to the lute, in which he strove for a natural declamation, led to his book of solo madrigals and airs, which was definitive in the stile moderno. The book was called *Le Nuove Musiche* (The New Music) and was published in Florence in 1602 and in Venice in 1607 and 1615; it contained a preface dealing with the new style. Caccini, who was also much involved with the theater, is included in the roster of the earliest composers of dramma per musica. His daughter FRANCESCA (1588–c. 1640) was also a composer.

FRANCIS PILKINGTON (c. 1565–1638), an English singer, lutenist, and composer, took his degree at Oxford and was known chiefly for his secular ayres and madrigals, even though he took minor orders and was associated with the Chester Cathedral from 1602 until his death. His *Book of Ayres* (1605) and two books of madrigals (1614 and 1624) were much admired. The latter were published in alternative forms— as four-part polyphonic madrigals and as vocal solo with lute and viol.

JOHN DOWLAND (1562–1626), an Irish composer, lutenist, and singer, worked in France, Germany, and Italy, at the royal court of Denmark, and finally as lutenist to James I of England. He studied at Oxford and married an English girl. Undisputed as the greatest British lutenist and held by many to be the greatest of his age, he left a surpassing literature of ayres in four books (1597, 1600, 1603, 1612). Some were published in alternative versions, for singing in parts or for solo singing with lute and viol; others were conceived solely as lute songs. The introduction of dance forms into the ayres and chromatic innovations are attributed to him. His first book included a dance "for two players upon one lute."

CLAUDIO MONTEVERDI (1567–1643), an Italian composer who was a master first of the traditional style and then of the new, was one of the great composers (and one of the great modernists) in the history of music. His prodigious output was representative of the shifting tastes of a transitional time. Although his travels took him north to Flanders and east to Hungary, he is chiefly associated with Venice, where he worked from 1613 to 1643. He left nine books of madrigals, which reflect the unfolding of his long stylistic development, several volumes of sacred songs and spiritual madrigals, a Mass, a Vesper service (1610), and three books of canzonette and other secular songs. Monteverdi's fame today is based largely on his dramatic works, of which he wrote about 15. The most famous are *La favola d'Orfeo* (1607) and *L'incoronazione de Poppea* (1642). Also a great teacher, he was known in his time as "il divino Monteverdi."

PIERRE GUÉDRON (c. 1570–c. 1620), a French singer and composer, was choirboy for Cardinal Guise in 1583 and, from 1590, a regular in the Royal Chapel. He wrote many ballets under Henry IV and Louis XIII and published six books of airs de cour (1602 to 1620); many of his lute songs appeared in collections during the same years. His works were very popular and internationally known.

ANTOINE BOESSET (1586–1643) was a French singer, lutenist, and composer. He was also a nobleman, a secretary to Louis XIII, and Louis's favorite musician. He married Guédron's daughter and succeeded him as Master of the King's Music in 1622. Boesset left nine books of airs in four and five parts and five books of lute songs. In addition, many of his songs were used in ballets and appeared in collections of the time. He was the most famous composer of airs de cour.

The multitude, the grandeur and the beauty of [their] buildings [is remarkable], for they are so many in number and so many are the parts of the country where they are found, and so well built are they of cut stone in their fashion, that it fills one with astonishment. . . . [They have books of science and biography, theology and legend,] cures of diseases, and antiquities, and how to read and write with letters and characters, . . . songs in meter, . . . farces, . . . and comedies for the pleasure of the public.

BISHOP DIEGO DE LANDA *

America

10

Renaissance views on the glory of man were brought into brilliant focus by explorations into the unknown world. Europeans were discovering the Southern African peoples as they circled Africa in their voyages. The Congo was already known. In 1491, Portuguese emissaries attended a funeral of the Congolese king and took an organ as a gift. They commended the music of drums, ivory trumpets, and string instruments "in good tune with each other." [1] And Vasco da Gama, putting into an East African port in 1498,

---

* C. 1560. Quoted in Alvin M. Josephy, Jr. (ed.), *The American Heritage Book of Indians*, New York: American Heritage Publishing Co., Inc., 1961, p. 21f.
[1] Quoted in Robert Stevenson, "The Afro-American Musical Legacy to 1800," *The Musical Quarterly*, vol. 54, no. 4, p. 478, October, 1968.

was met by a king with a musical retinue. "[The King of Mylynde] brought with him many Shagbuts [sacbuts], and two Flutes of Ivorie, which were eight spans of length each of them, they were very well wrought, and vppon the same they played by a little hole that is in the midst thereof, agreeing and according well with the shagbuts." [2]

In 1591, the Congo's ambassador in Rome, a European who had lived at the Congolese court from 1568 to 1587, published a book about the Congo. The book contained descriptions of Congolese instruments, such as those used in war, for love songs, and at feasts. Of particular interest were guitar-like instruments with a belly of stretched skin and strings "made of the woode of *Palme-Tree*" and "of the *Elephantes* tayle"; [3] these instruments he reported to be "very strong and bright." Tiny pieces of silver and iron were hung on the strings for an added tingling sound.

> Those that play vppon this Instrument, doo tune the strings in good proportion, and strike them with their fingers, like a *Harpe*, but without any quill very cunningly. . . . Besides all this (which is a thing very admirable) by this instrument they doo vtter the conceites of their mindes, and doo vnderstand one another so plainely, that euery thing almost which may be explained with the tongue, they can declare with their hande in touching and striking this instrument. To the sounde thereof they do dance in good measure with their feet, and follow the just time of that musicke with clapping the palmes of their handes one against the other. They have also in the Court, Flutes and Pipes, which they sound very artificially [skillfully], and according to the sounde they daunce and moue their feet. [4]

Explorers in America also discovered established civilizations. Although North America was rather sparsely settled, with small, often nomadic groups in the north and cities only in the south, South America was more populous, with cities along the coasts and rivers, where the land was free of the jungle. Permanent settlements most frequently took on the characteristics of empires in the areas that are now occupied by Mexico, Central America, and Peru.

Description of the many empires is impossible, but their scope can be suggested by a few facts. Several hundred languages have been identified as native to North America—estimates of the total number range up to a thousand—and South America had more. Although the peoples lived in separate small groups, they were definitely not primitive or undeveloped. For a thousand or more years before Columbus, trade, war, and empire gave the Western Hemisphere as complex a history as that of Asia, Europe, or Africa.

[2] *Ibid.*, p. 481.
[3] *Ibid.*, p. 479.
[4] *Ibid.*

THE TOLTECS, THE INCAS, AND THE AZTECS

The Toltecs, who preceded the Aztecs as a great empire in what is now Mexico, were at their peak at the end of the ninth century—their King Toplitzin was contemporary with Charlemagne. Located at the center of a trade empire that included both land and sea routes, the Toltecs had paved roads extending several thousand miles; slave caravans (there were no horses in the hemisphere until the Spanish brought them) used the isthmus and west coast roads in order to reach South America. Seagoing canoes (twenty-five paddlers) carried goods across the present Gulf of Mexico to the Mississippi and up the river as far as Wisconsin. Their trade included only those items that were native to the Western Hemisphere—items that now comprise 60 percent of the world's agriculture. They also exported salt, chewing gum, rope, yarn, obsidian sword blades, paper, pottery, paints, dyes, and, of particular interest here, flutes. Some of their musical instruments seem to have been already old—flutes, drums, ceremonial rattles, bells, and marine-shell trumpets are virtually universal. The marimba, documented later, was named the *zapotecano*, after the Zapotecs, whose heyday was earlier than the Toltecs'. Details are scarce, but the evidence makes a musical tradition certain.

The Inca and Aztec empires both reached their apex with fifteenth-century emperors. The Inca empire stretched for 2,500 miles along the west coast, and its capital was located near modern Lima (Peru). Although the culture of the Incas was at a high point by the fourteenth century (their national music school was founded about 1350), their most advanced monarch was probably Pachacuti, who reigned from 1438 to 1475. His 350,000–square-mile kingdom had terraced farming (with irrigation), a regular census, good roads and mail service, fine metallurgy, and a textile art considered by some authorities to be the greatest textile art ever produced anywhere.[5] The Incas' medical skill was well developed, and surgery was practiced. They were a highly organized people who loved ceremonies and games, and Pachacuti, aside from busying himself with administration and philosophy, was said to have written many songs. As in Africa and the Orient, references link certain instruments and songs with particular rituals, often with almost obsessive precision. The Incas knew the Toltec instrumental types and, in addition, may well have used the friction drum, a cylindrical drum whose membrane head had a hole in the middle and which was sounded by rubbing with wet hands or a wet stick.

[5] Alvin M. Josephy, Jr. (ed.), *The American Heritage Book of Indians*, New York: American Heritage Publishing Co., Inc., 1961, p. 49.

The Aztecs began their rise with the fall of the Toltecs in 1168; by the fifteenth century, they had stretched their empire from the Pacific to the Atlantic. King Nezahualcoyotl ("hungry coyote") reigned from 1428 to 1472 and was not unlike his Inca contemporary—he too concentrated on composing songs (sixty remain). A school of music had long functioned at Texcoco, the empire's artistic and intellectual center, which in Nezahualcoyotl's time had a population of 300,000 (versus London's, then, of 120,000). In addition to schools of the arts and observatories (the Aztec calendar was more accurate than ours), the Aztecs maintained religious and medical centers. But the center of wealth and power was not in Texcoco but in Tenochtitlan, a city of canals and floating gardens, which is now Mexico City.

The Aztecs' culture was rich in music, and the names of many of their musical instruments are known. Reports of their religious ceremonies (based

This illustration is from an early account of the arrival of the Spaniards in the New World. The Indians are dancing with ceremonial staff rattles, called chicahuatl, to the music of a Spanish bagpiper. (Courtesy of the Arents Collection, New York Public Library, Astor, Lenox and Tilden Foundations.)

on human sacrifice like those of the Incas and the Toltecs) form the chief documentation for specific musical usage but tell little about the type of performance and, aside from what is implicit in knowledge of instruments, nothing of the sound of the music. It is known, for example, that the Aztec armies marched to war with a band of marine-shell trumpets, fifes (clay), and drums of two tones, while the warriors added their cries to summon the gods and frighten their enemies. It is also known that large groups of musicians performed at ceremonial occasions and that antiphonal effects were used. Preliminary studies of existing documents indicate that one Aztec musical scale was probably based on five tones to the octave without semitones, comprising two cambiata patterns. This is close to a universal scale, and its presence in pre-Columbian America is more a matter of interest than surprise. The main musical interests of the Inca and Aztec peoples were the same, and their vocabularies shared names for the basic types of song (e.g., *harahui*, "a sad love song") and instruments. Some of their lyrics survive; one example is the Aztec song below.

Aztec Song

We only came to sleep
We only came to dream
It is not true, no, it is not true
That we came to live on the earth.
We are changed into the grass of springtime
Our hearts will grow green again
And they will open their petals
But our body is like a rose tree:
It puts forth flowers and then withers.[6]

Some Pre-Columbian Instruments
of the Aztec and Inca Peoples

alumnaxkaki was a panpipes of ten to twelve pipes.
teponaztl, a drum, had an H-shaped slit that formed two tongues, each of which was pitched. The large instruments were played on the ground, the small ones on tripods.
tetzilacatl was a percussion trough played with beaters.
tlapiztalli was a beaked whistle flute, of bone or clay, with four finger holes.
tepuzquiquiztl, a marine-shell trumpet, was blown at one end.
ayacachtl, a gourd rattle, was called *maraca* in Amazon groups.
zapotecano was the marimba.
cocoloctl, a small whistle flute, was made of bone or clay and had four finger holes.

---

[6] *Ibid.*, p. 87.

chicahuatl, the ceremonial staff rattle, was several feet long and was one of
the most important instruments throughout both South and North
America. The ceremonial rattle was of wood, but the pellet bell rattle,
also common, was of metal.

huehuetl, a clay drum, was played with the hands.

tlapanhuehuetl was a larger war drum, of wood, and was played vertically.

Most of their instruments were common throughout the hemisphere,
but the panpipes were distinctive to the Inca; these were well developed, with
some pipes as tall as men. String instruments were also used; the musical bow
is still played in South America and seems to have been known in North
America as well. Song, in the troubadour sense of singing a poem, and dance
were common, as in the rest of the world, and it can be assumed that the
musical art was refined and sophisticated, since its history was long and its
practice honored. The existence of Inca and Aztec schools of music indicates
that a separate instrumental practice existed, aside from a vocal one, because
separate instruction for instrumentalists requires its own literature. We know
that the Aztec music school had its own building, for it was the crumbling
of a wall in the music school [7] that King Moctezuma II (Montezuma,
Nezahualcoyotl's son-in-law) saw as the first omen of disaster before the
arrival of the Spaniards.

THE SPANIARDS AND THE INDIANS

The Spaniards arrived in 1516, and by 1544 the Aztecs were conquered.
Being Renaissance men, the Spaniards were humanists who felt the world was
theirs for the taking if they had the courage to take it. Cupidity drew
some of them, but the adventurous spirit of the sixteenth century drew
many others—they crossed the ocean to see for themselves what was on
the other side and to savor what must have been one of the greatest adventures of all time.

Numerous groups of Indians covered the Western Hemisphere, and
each had its own culture. The diversity was astounding—some nations were
warlike, some were nomadic, and some were settled and cultivated in the
arts of peace. For example, the Hopi, whose name meant "the peaceful ones,"
were a settled people with a highly developed architecture. They dwelt in
pueblos, which were extensive apartment cities whose separate homes, ball
courts, ceremonial areas, kitchens, and storerooms testify to a lively civilization. One pueblo, whose construction has been estimated, by tree-ring dating,
at A.D. 919 to 1067, had over eight hundred rooms. Arriving in Hopi territory

[7] *Ibid.,* p. 79.

in 1539, the Spaniards were in awe of the imposing city, which comprised a continuous 3-acre complex.

For nine thousand years, the Indians of the Arizona-New Mexico area had enjoyed an unbroken culture, possibly the longest in the earth's history. They had a fine artistic heritage, including painting and sculpture, and a literature of legends, religion, and enjoyment. The Hopi were also a musical people. Their philosophy of harmony with nature and the forces of life had produced a multitude of rituals, songs, and dances that showed a way toward consonance with the world and gave them an unusually rich musical literature. Their music, which was based on dance and song, was rhythmically sophisticated and melodically lyrical; atypically, it used a low rather than a high tessitura.

The Hopi sang to their crops to make them want to grow and, having cleaned the storerooms in their honor, brought them in at harvest time with grateful but informal ceremony. They explained to the Spaniards that such ceremonies were carried out "so the corn will be glad that we are bringing it in."[8] They also used ceremonial songs during the process of corn grinding.[9]

But the Spaniards viewed the Indians primarily as pagans. Like all Europeans, they loved music; however, they rejected Indian music and established the European tradition in Mexico. Within three years after the fall of Tenochtitlan (Mexico City), a Spanish music school was being formed. There the Indians were taught plainchant and the musical aspects of the Roman rite. Secular and instrumental arts were also introduced, and the making of instruments was begun. In Spain the art of the lute and vihuela was reaching its first peak, so the lute, which was easily portable, can be assumed to have arrived in the New World quickly. In 1538 a good cathedral choir with a choirmaster was sent from Spain. And dancing had always thrived. Mexico City became a modern city, and in 1556, the first printing of music, a Mass Ordinary, was accomplished in the New World and that art became established.

But there was little reciprocity. A few Indians were taken to the Spanish court to entertain as jugglers and to demonstrate the games they played with the strange bouncing balls. But exploration continued to be a superimposition of European culture on the native peoples, whose music was not only associated with pagan practices, but based on exactly those musical elements—rhythmic sophistication and monophonic song—from which Renaissance culture had specifically turned away in embracing the new harmony of sounds. Europeans of the fourteenth century might have been able to appreciate the art of the slit drum and the clay flute, but the sixteenth century ideal made

---

[8] *Ibid.*, p. 117.
[9] Bruno Nettl, *Folk and Traditional Music of the Western Continents*, Englewood Cliffs, N.J.: Prentice-Hall, 1965, p. 152.

appreciation by the Renaissance Spaniards impossible. The literature of Mexican Indian music was perpetuated only in the folk art of obscure groups. However, the exploration of South America is far from completed, and the more knowledgeable and less judgmental explorers of today are traveling with cameras and tape recorders. It may be that the songs of the ancient peoples are not completely lost.

Part Three

THE BAROQUE ERA

Let a Singer have a Fund of Knowledge sufficient to perform readily any of the most difficult Compositions; let him have, besides, an excellent Voice, and know how to use it artfully; he will not, for all that, deserve a Character of Distinction, if he is wanting in a prompt Variation.

PIER FRANCESCO TOSI [*]

The New Style in Italy

11

During the Renaissance, the lower classes in Europe had remained illiterate, and although the nobility were literate, they were dedicated to generality of learning. A nobleman eschewed ignorance as being unbecoming but avoided acquiring depth in any subject, which he considered fit only for persons of lower birth. Therefore the Renaissance had witnessed the development of a new citizenry, classed between the noble lord and the servant or worker and thus called the middle class—the seventeenth century saw this middle class rise to a position of strength.

The time was one of intense energy; there was a drive toward discovering, mapping, and measuring. Thus it was an age of instruments, of machines

[*] 1723. *Observations on the Florid Song,* London: William Reeves, 1926, p. 4.

—telescopes, microscopes, navigational instruments, clocks, chronometers, architectural tools, surgical instruments, thermometers, and domestic machinery. Machines were also important in entertainment—mechanical toys, clocks (particularly the great tower clocks with moving figures of men or animals that were activated on the hour), and above all, theatrical machines of staggering number, complexity, and expense. The arts in general were concerned with man's possessions, his attainments, and his character; they sought to exploit contrasts, to bring together groups of elements and to give them order and meaning through juxtaposition and interrelation.

It was a time of extravagance—extravagance of idea, imagination, and enterprise. In a sense, the seventeenth century was the century of transition between the Medieval and modern modes of thought, still living with the old, yet investigating the new. The century produced work of contrasting or even conflicting nature—texts in both the old astrology and the new astronomy, the old alchemy and the new chemistry, the old theological and the new scientific treatises on man. René Descartes (1596–1650) presented his philosophy *cogito ergo sum* ("I think, therefore I am") in a time when the persecution of witches was at its height; mathematicians interested themselves in parabolas, formulating algebraic equations for a study of curves, in a time when numerology was still considered a science. That time is now called the Baroque Era, a name given later, in retrospect, by more conservative thinkers for whom *baroque* meant "extravagant" or "flamboyant"; but today, grandeur and energy are the essential associations of the term.

THE NEW IDEAL OF MUSIC

Monody was the new and experimental structure in music. Although the lute song was an international form and rose to rare heights in England, monody was a thoroughly Italian art. The theatrical elements of both its concept and performance, along with its focus on the singer, were the essence of the Italian Baroque.

Thus it was in Italy that the new music flourished first, and Italian innovators maintained their position of musical leadership throughout the seventeenth century. The new vocabulary of key tonality, with its structural principles, was announced in Italian works, so the traditional musical vocabulary of the succeeding centuries was Italian—even after Italy relinquished leadership.

Throughout the seventeenth century and into the eighteenth, the theater flourished in all its forms, and all of them used music incidentally or centrally. The Carnival of Venice, a yearly celebration comparable to New Orleans's Mardi Gras, which brought many travelers to the city, was a rowdy affair. It was described by a French visitor of 1678.

Nothing can be more singular, than to see in a manner all the City in Masquerade, the Mothers carrying in their Arms their little children in Disguise. . . . The Place of Saint *Mark* is the great theater, upon which is to be seen the great Appearances [performances] of the *Carnaval*; for there is scarce a Masque in *Venice* that does not come here about an Hour before Sunset.[1]

Alongside these lusty traditions the relatively sedate, mechanized, and formal theater flourished. "There are very few Cities in Italy which have not more than one Theatre," wrote an Italian observer sixty years later. "The Italian theatres are magnificent. . . . In Venice one may see a Comedy for sixteen Sols of Current Money, which is paid at the Door." [2]

The *dramma per musica*, soon called the *opera*, provided a counterbalance to carnival and comedy. The opera's appeal as a composite work of visual and aural splendor made it an apogee of the Baroque idea. An Italian observer described a performance in Venice in 1701; the work was *Catone Vticense* by Tomaso Albinoni (1671–1750).

Cato of Utica is the Subject of an Opera presented upon the Theatre of St. John Chrysostome [theaters were named for the parishes in which they were built] in the Year 1701. As Caesar with his Army is supposed not to be far from the Scene where the Action is laid . . . the Ground of the Stage represents a Field, towards the Middle of which there was hung in the Air a Globe, resembling that of the World; this Globe was observed by degrees to advance towards the Front of the Stage, to the Sound of Trumpets and other Instruments. . . . In the Moment when it comes opposite to Caesar, it opens into three Parts, representing the then three known Parts of the World. The Inside of the Globe shines all with Gold, Precious Stones, Metals of all Colours, and contains a great Number of Musicians.[3]

This was theater, a grandeur to which all arts contributed but any one was secondary.

The Voice

The singer was not secondary, however. The voice was now the subject of measurement, of theories of physiological and mechanical structure and function, and of experiments in mutation and technique. And the singer became a specialist, for singing required all his energies. He became a *virtuoso*, a marvel to his audiences, who thrilled to his *bravura* art—a term incorporating technical skill, daring, and brilliance.

The new concept of vocal technique began in Italy as the *buen canto* ("good singing") and developed into a European tradition of *bel canto*

1 Limojon de St. Didier, quoted in A. M. Nagler, A *Source Book in Theatrical History*, New York: Dover, 1959, p. 262.
2 Luigi Riccoboni, quoted in *ibid.*, p. 269.
3 *Ibid.*, p. 270.

("beautiful singing"), which remained Italian in essence. The vocal ideal was summed up in a French treatise of 1705.

> A perfect voice should be sonorous, of wide range, sweet, exact, lively, flexible. . . . I reduce the merit of a singer to three things: accuracy, expression, cleanness. . . . The first thing required of a singer is correct pitch. . . . Expression on the part of a singer consists in entering, in a spirited and appropriate manner, into the feeling of the verse he sings, to inform them with passion. . . . Cleanness is that great mass of small attentions . . . [such as] to open the mouth, to produce tones in the right way, to prepare, ornament, and finish a cadence, etc.[4]

These ideals produced the fleet, manipulable voices that were the glory of the Baroque era.

The Italians had been using both female and male singers, but soon the dramatic demands on the performers became too great for the normal voice, so the castrato came to be in demand. *Castrato* was the name applied to a boy singer who was castrated before puberty; he retained his soprano (or contralto) range for life and characteristically developed an enlarged barrel chest, which provided unusual breath supply and control. Castrati had been used in chapel choirs in the sixteenth century; in the 1630s, they entered opera and soon became the rage of Italian vocal performance. It is estimated that in Italy in the second half of the century about four thousand boys were subjected to castration each year. Castrati sang all over Europe, many amassing personal fortunes, and by 1700 were the most popular, adulated performers in Europe. In 1702 a French writer wrote of the art of the castrati.

> No man or woman in the world can boast of a voice like theirs; they are clear, they are fleet, and affect the soul itself. . . .
> These pipes of theirs resemble that of the nightingale; their long-winded throats draw you in a manner out of your depth and make you lose your breath. They'll execute passages of I know not how many bars together, they'll have echoes on the same passages and swellings of a prodigious length, and then, with a throb in the throat, exactly like that of a nightingale, they'll conclude with cadences of an equal length, and all of this in the same breath. . . . But the greatest advantage the Italians receive from these castrati is that their voices hold good for thirty or forty years.[5]

Considering the traditional love of the French for males and females on the stage, the writer's response to the sexless character of the castrati is interesting:

> Add to this that these soft, these charming voices acquire new charms by being in the mouth of a lover; what can be more affecting than the expressions of their sufferings in such tender passionate notes; in this the

---

[4] Le Cerf de La Vieville, quoted in Oliver Strunk (ed.), *Source Readings in Music History*, New York: Norton, 1950, p. 501.

[5] François Raguenet, quoted in *ibid.*, p. 483.

Italian lovers have a very great advantage over ours, whose hoarse masculine voices ill agree with the fine soft things they are to say to their mistresses. Besides, the Italian voices being equally strong as they are soft, we hear all they sing very distinctly. . . . Our upper parts are usually performed by girls that have neither lungs nor wind, whereas the same parts in Italy are always performed by men whose firm piercing voices are to be heard clearly in the largest theatres without losing a syllable, sit where you will.[6]

The castrato voice was the ideal emulated by all other voices of the time. Bel canto, in general, sought for a tone quality that was sweet and clear, rather than forceful and vivid, and that penetrated a balanced instrumental component through purity and cleanness of attack, rather than by volume.

The Violin

The study of the voice as a mechanism and as the ideal instrument for musico-dramatic projection was not divorced from the study of musical instruments per se. The seventeenth century saw the development of an instrumental ideal based on the vocal model. The instrument of the Baroque era was, above all, the violin. A linear treble instrument, capable of sonority, sweetness, clarity, and flexibility over a wide range, the violin was as close to the soprano voice as science and art could make it. The *luthiers* ("lute makers"; the name now means "violin makers") gave their attention to the new instruments, and their science rose to transcendent heights with the legendary Nicolo Amati (1596–1684), Antonio Stradivari (1644–1737), and Giuseppe Guarnieri (del Gesù, 1683–1745), only three of the illustrious luthiers who translated the new ideals into physical terms. They emulated the vocal quality, striving for its subtleties and dramatic potential, and balanced the tone through the design of the bridge and placement of the sound bar.

The Italian passion was the solo treble line, represented by both the soprano voice and the violin. The clarino trumpet, generally a long trumpet with bore and mouthpiece designed to exploit the upper register, also grew popular in Italy at the end of the century. But in France, instrumental color and contrast were greatly cherished, so there the oboe, the hunting horn, the flute, and the bassoon were being defined as members of the instrumental ensemble. Our heritage of Italian terms clearly represents the Italian leadership in matters of form, vocal technique, and the violin family of instruments, but the woodwind terms are French.

The French developed a variety of vocal types: for women, the *dessus*, "soprano," which was often divided into first and second; and for men, the *haute-contre*, "countertenor," the *taille*, "middle," and the *basse*, "low." During the Baroque, the five-part norm of the late Renaissance was maintained in France, where choruses were made up of first and second dessus, contre, taille, and basse. Such groups were extremely practical in the theater— the natural balance of the voices enabled an equal number of men and women to provide a perfect vocal component.

[6] *Ibid.*

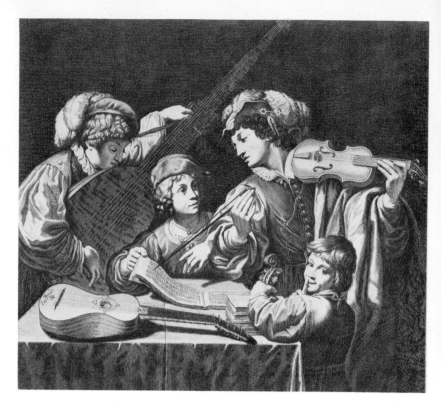

"Symphonia," an etching by S. Picard Romanus, from a painting by Domenico Zampiere, early seventeenth century. The etching, which contains old and new instruments, represents a harmony of the old and new styles. The violin and guitar are shown in transitional forms. The great size of the chitarrone (bass lute), which was larger than the theorbo, is clearly depicted, as are the instrument's two sets of strings; the short strings are those with their pegs at the player's left hand in the picture, and the long ones, unfingered, are those with their pegs at the top edge of the picture. (Courtesy of the University of Michigan Library, Stellfeld Purchase, and Musée du Louvre. Photo by R. E. Kalmbach.)

Cultivation of a greater number of instruments gave the French leadership in matters of instrumental color but denied them an early development of the violin technique that was the rage of Italy in the last quarter of the seventeenth century. When the Italian violin sonatas were brought to France, about 1695, and Louis XIV wanted to hear them, there was not a violinist in France who could manage their difficulties, so singers performed them for the king in vocalise. In a sense, this episode sums up the international and national character of the seventeenth-century musical ideal.

As the voice and violin epitomized the new Baroque ideal of musical sound, the basso continuo, which motivated and balanced the solo line, epitomized the new ideal of musical fabric. This new fabric incorporated the polar concept that had turned the polyphonic ideal inside out. In Renaissance theory, music had been conceived as expanding from the tenor line outward; in the Baroque, the concept was that of propulsive outer lines with a harmonic interior.

The Basso Continuo

The new style shifted focus to the outer elements by balancing the solo line with a bass of two functions. First, it formed the polar melodic line, which pulled the listeners' attention to the bottom as the solo line pulled it to the top. Second, it motivated and defined the harmonic progression. Perhaps no period in the history of music has been so clearly defined by a single practice as the Baroque era by the basso continuo.

Almost inevitable was the development of a system of notation that would make clear both the focus on the outer parts straddling a harmonic middle ground and the unimportance of that middle ground as voices in the polyphonic sense. This was the *figured bass*. The melodic bass was written out separately and entirely, and above it were placed figures of various kinds indicating its harmonic implications but not always specifying the exact notes to be played. The figures included numbers, sharps, flats, dashes, slashes, and other signs. Most aspects of figured bass were standard and have survived in harmony textbooks; a few details were highly individual, varying from country to country and even from composer to composer.

Performance of the basso continuo also emphasized its twofold function, because its two aspects were entrusted to two separate musicians. The bass melody was played on a linear bass instrument, generally a viola da gamba (later a cello) but sometimes a bassoon or other instrument. The realization of the figures required a harmonic instrument, the most common of which was to be the harpsichord, though an organ, theorbo, or some other chordal instrument could also serve.

The keyboard performer played the bass line with his left hand, doubling the melodic bass instrument, and with the right hand he realized the harmonic structures demanded by the figures. His job was to be competent and inconspicuous, to complete the harmonic dimension of the music without taking attention from the primary parts above and beneath. He used a relatively small range—seldom below *a* or above g^2—and kept fairly much to the rhythm of a bass or a simplification of it, with two or, for emphasis, three or four notes added to the bass.

The basso continuo was ideally suited to working out the polar concept, because by avoiding questions of specific inner voices, it enabled the composer to concentrate on the issues vital to his creative life—the impelling of music forward by rhythmic impetus, the use of chord progression, and the centripetal pull toward a tonal center. During the century and a half of Baroque musical language and form, the basso continuo was assumed to be a constant and necessary presence. As late as the middle of the eighteenth century, a teacher, listing balanced instrumental ensembles, did not include the harpsichord but stated "I assume that the *harpsichord* will be included in all ensembles, large or small." [7] Interestingly, in the largest ensemble (twenty-one string players), he specified a second harpsichord and a theorbo.

The basso continuo incorporated a contrast of quality as well as function. In fact, contrast was the underlying principle of Baroque form, both in the fabric and between successive sections. It was prefigured in the ensemble of consorts, used in alternation and combination. The continuing principle of contrast, in which the combining of mediums drew forth musical appositions of structural significance, was called the *stile concertato*, the "concerted style."

[7] Johann Joachim Quantz, in Edward R. Reilly (trans. and ed.), *J. J. Quantz on Playing the Flute*, London: Faber, 1966, p. 214.

At the end of the Renaissance, musical form had been defined in textual terms, either through use of a lyric or through techniques in which the imitative point and dance punctus were analogous to poetic lines. At the end of the Baroque, the means would be firmly established for the creation of viable musical forms independent of textual guides and analogies. The accomplishment of this sweeping change was the drama of music in the Baroque era.

ITALIAN LEADERSHIP

In a time of European instability, Italy was relatively secure and, with the wealth of her trading cities, could support an experimental art. Moreover, because Italy had not taken part in the Protestant Reformation, the need to develop a new liturgy had not deflected the focus of Italian composers. On the contrary, the Roman Church, in mounting the Counter-Reformation, put the new style to use, furthering its development and adding ecclesiastical approval to popular appeal.

Secular theater was not the only focus for monody. Chamber concerts presented short monodic works, under such titles as *concerti* (originally referring to combining voice and instruments), *scherzi, canzonetti,* or simply *musiche,* which were as much the vogue as the polyphonic madrigal had been before. The singer was the key figure of the new style; as early as 1601, one of the monodists of the *Camerata fiorentina* wrote about the singer's contribution.

> I have come to believe that it is the only [style] our music can give us to be adapted to our speech. ... For this reason . . . I demonstrated this new manner of singing, which gave the highest pleasure . . . not only to [some] learned gentlemen (for music flourishes today among the nobility), but also to that celebrated lady whom one may call the Euterpe of our age, Signora Vittoria Archili. This lady, who has always made my compositions seem worthy of her singing, adorns them not only with those trills and those long windings of the voice, simple and double, which the liveliness of her talent can invent at any moment (more to comply with the usage of our times than because she considers the beauty and force of our singing to lie in them), but also with those elegances and graces that cannot be written or, if written, cannot be learned from writing.[8]

It is clear that this composer felt his works to be enhanced—even completed—by the singer's art, which he admired more than he directed.

The new style was used in both chamber and church, in both secular and sacred concerts. In the sacred concert (not always held in a church), the Roman Church found an excellent vehicle. Sacred concertos and semi-

---

[8] Jacopo Peri, quoted in Strunk, *op. cit.,* p. 375.

dramatic performances—even operas—were given to edify and strengthen the populace in the faith.

By the middle of the century, some vital new musical definitions had been achieved and were reflected in the vocabulary. A work for voice and basso continuo was called a *cantata*; a dramatized musical work was called an *opera*; a quasi-dramatic work on a Biblical text was called an *oratorio*; and a totally instrumental work, cognate with the cantata, was called a *sonata*. These were nascent types that continued to develop through the century; they were joined finally by the *concerto grosso*, the most instrumentally conceived and perhaps the most innovative instrumental form of the Baroque era. Their names reflect their mediums rather than their structure, for the central underlying principle of contrast, the stile concertato, was the informing breath of them all.

In addition, certain Renaissance forms persisted, redefined, through the seventeenth century into the eighteenth century and beyond. Solo lute, organ, and harpsichord music could not adapt to the new practice because they could not use the basso continuo; outdoor types such as the high (loud) music (reeds and brasses), which was associated with parades, mounted forces, and civic panoply, also could not adapt. These retained the suite, canzona, prelude, toccata, and fugue, bringing to bear on them the new concepts of harmony and key. Organ forms prospered, particularly in Germany with the development of the Protestant churches.

In England amateurs continued to delight themselves with consorts and improvising of divisions, particularly with the viols, for which the great texts appeared in the second half of the century. And catch clubs prospered. Of these amateur activities, improvising divisions was the one that accommodated the basso continuo. Certain bass patterns became internationally popular

"Musical Instruments," by Bartolommeo Bettera, c. 1600. Like many such representations in the seventeenth century, this musical evocation includes an hourglass to suggest the temporal aspect of music, which was essential to the Baroque ideal. (Courtesy of the Museum of Fine Arts, Boston.)

and were used over and over as the basis for improvised variations above. A pattern was called a *basso ostinato* (obstinate bass) in Italy, but the English used their own term, *ground* (basis). The art of variations on a ground was most popular in England at the end of the seventeenth century.

Developing the forms of the new style required many decades and was the mutual concern of three generations of composers. The Italians took the lead.

Vocal Forms in Italy

In three generations, the cantata grew from a short continuing monologue in the stile recitativo to a work with gradually differentiating selections of recitativo and aria. At the beginning of the century, Monteverdi's monodic *Lamento d'Arianna* had made listeners weep,[9] and to professional musicians monody offered a way out of "the confusion and babel of words arising from the long and intricate imitations [of the learned style]." [10] But the recitativo, after an initial period of enthusiasm for its clarity of text, had begun to pall because of its lack of form and musical cohesion. By 1626, Domenico Mazzochi was writing of "the tedium of the recitativo." [11] The *arioso*, a more melodic monody, flourished briefly as a transitional type, but within a decade, the aria da capo had been invented. In the second half of the century, the aria da capo was to become the most important vocal form, and it was to remain so for the next three centuries.

Aria da Capo. The *aria da capo* was an air in a tone (key) with a definite beat and meter, followed by a section contrasting in melody and tone but generally in the same meter; at the end of the contrasting section, the air was to be repeated from the beginning. The name of the form derives from the composer's method of notation; he notated only the air and the contrasting section, and at the end of the latter, he wrote the directive *aria* (the air) *da capo* (from the beginning). The aria, like the recitativo, generally began and ended with a phrase, called the *ritornello* (plural, *ritornelli*), for instruments alone.

The aria da capo pleased everyone. The composer was provided with new forms of contrast, rhythmically between the impelling beat of the aria and the freely interpreted rhythm of the recitativo and tonally between the stable aria and the uncommitted, often meandering recitativo. In addition, the internal contrasts of the aria da capo offered him the possibility of using tone as a basic aspect of form, of using tonic-contrast-tonic as a principle of structure.

The performer could exploit these same contrasts, punctuating the dramatic recitativo with the aria, during which he could put aside the

[9] Curt Sachs, *Our Musical Heritage*, Englewood Cliffs, N.J.: Prentice-Hall, 1948, p. 198.

[10] Agostino Agazzari, quoted in Strunk, *op. cit.*, p. 430.

[11] Quoted in Sachs, *op. cit.*, p. 224.

exigencies of the action and devote his art to the presentation of a beautiful song. In addition, the repetition of the aria provided him with a vehicle for ornament and variation.

The listener was given the best of both worlds. He could enjoy the dramatic and the lyric ability of the singer and could more clearly discern the singer's elaborations in the da capo because he had already heard the aria; and he could enjoy the strengthening place of music as a force in the opera.

By the eighteenth century, critics dismissed Italian opera as a "bundle of airs"; [12] their acceptance of "ornaments, cadenzas, *da capos*, and all the Gothic barbarous and extravagant things that have been introduced into our music" [13] showed that music would reverse the "noble contempt of singing" [14] and reduce the drama to subservient status once again.

In the change from the domination of the text to that of the music, which took place gradually over a century and a half, the last third of the seventeenth century represents a point of relative balance, of equal tensions, between dramatic and musical forces. The period of balance was relatively brief; almost as soon as the aria reached maturity as a form, attention to the recitativo began to decline.

Cantata. The cantatas of Alessandro Scarlatti are representative of the culminating form of the cantata in Italy. The form was eventually standardized at four movements—recitativo-aria, recitativo-aria. The two types were effectively played off against each other: the recitativos were effective rhetorically, with the harmonic and rhythmic freedom that enables the performer to approach them as declamation; the arias, within the concepts of tone and meter, worked out more purely musical designs.

Scarlatti's *Bei prati, freschi riui* typifies the Baroque cantata. For solo soprano and basso continuo, it is in the standard format of a love text set musically as two pairs of recitativo-aria. The recitativo is vocally active and dramatic, the bass consisting of a series of chords ranging from $B\flat$ major to $C\sharp$ major and pointing to a constantly shifting variety of tonal centers. It ends on A (traditionally taken as a major chord) as dominant. The aria, in d minor with cadences to F major and g minor, reverses the two parts in rhythmic motion, giving the motivating subjects to the bass. The aria is no less active harmonically than the recitativo, but is focused, rather than restless, both in subject and in tonal balance.

As the form of the cantata was expanded toward the end of the seventeenth century, composers sought further contrasts. The addition of a solo instrument—often a violin or flute—enabled them to enlarge the opening and closing instrumental ritornelli and allowed the singer to engage in imitative repartee with the solo instrument. A second solo singer could be used

[12] *Ibid.*, p. 242.
[13] Raniero Calzabigi, quoted in *ibid.*, p. 287.
[14] See Chapter 9, footnote 9 (page 239).

Bei Prati, fresci riui

ALESSANDRO SCARLATTI

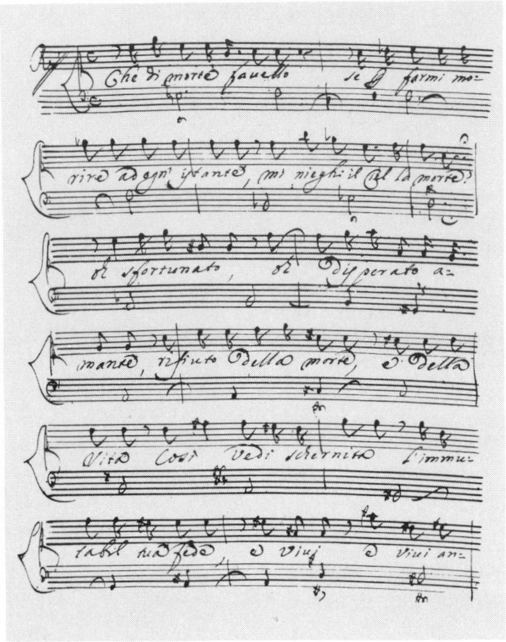

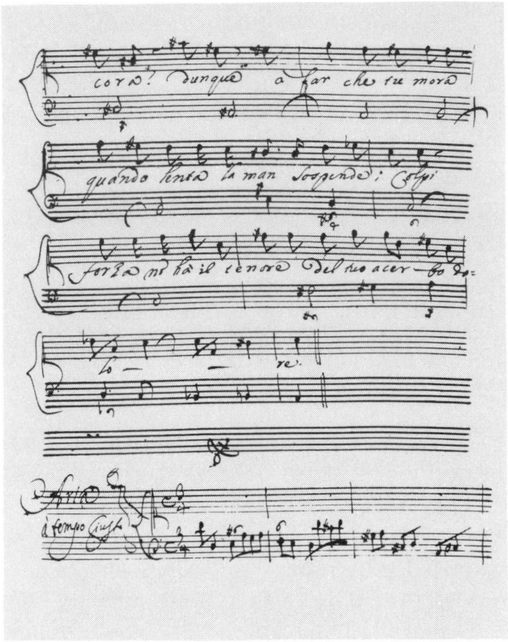

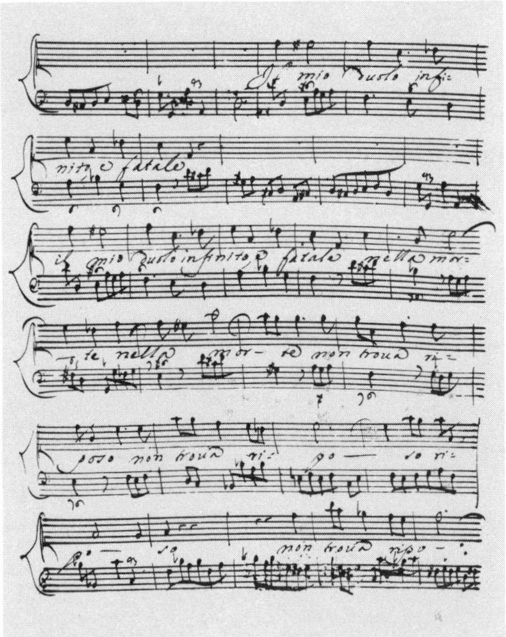

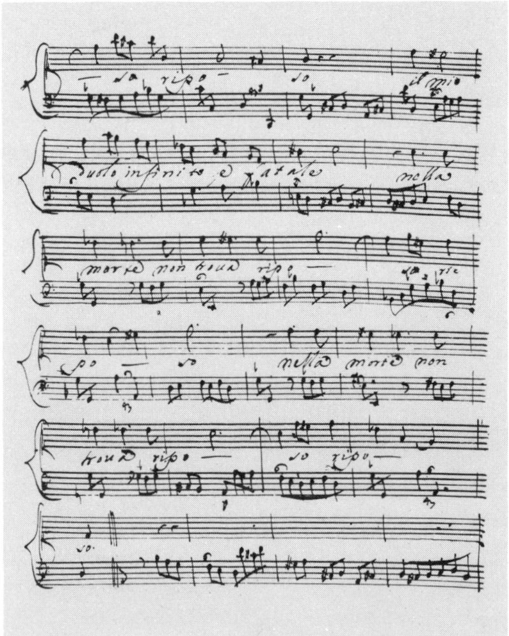

Re[*citativo*]:

Che di morte favello se farmi morire ad ogni istante, mi nieghi il ciel la morte? Oh, sfortunato, oh disperato amante, risputo della morte, e della vita, così vedi scernita l'immutabil mia fede, e vivi, e vivi ancora? Dunque a far che tu mora quando tenta la man sospende. Colpi forza non ha il tenore del mio acerbo dolore.

Recitativo:

Since the stroke of death can finish me at any moment, why does heaven deny that death to me? Oh wretched and hopeless lover, giver of life and death, do I see thus that my dauntless faith is a mockery and that I must continue to love? Then I shall strike you down even as your hand is raised against me. But the strength of my blow will not have the clinging might of my relentless sorrow.

Aria:

Il mio duolo infinito e fatale
Nella morte non trova riposo,
E dir posso con vanto odioso
Che il mio duolo m'ha reso immortale.
Il mio duolo infinito e fatale
Nella morte non trova riposo.

Aria:

I find no rest from endless, fatal grief
At the thought of death,
And I can say with odious boasting
That my grief has made me immortal.
I find no rest from endless, fatal grief
At the thought of death.

TRANS. BY JON RINKA

The example includes the second recitativo and aria from the cantata *Bei Prati, fresci riui*; it is written in a contemporary hand, possibly the composer's. Characteristic is the "6" on its side (on the opening note of the recitativo) and the single sign for "4-3" (measure 5 of the aria). It was customary to end the recitativo with a major triad as the dominant in order to prepare the coming tonic. The harmonically restless recitativo and the highly motivated aria formed one of the essential pairs of contrasts in the Baroque. (Courtesy of the University of Michigan Library, Stellfeld Purchase. Photo by R. E. Kalmbach.)

by alternating solos and introducing duet arias. (Recitativo, though often alternating between two performers in dialogue, was not suited to duet.) Other instrumental forces were occasionally added, such as the trumpet and strings in the Scarlatti cantata *Su le sponde del Tebro*. A chorus was also added, but only rarely until the end of the century and even then the choral cantata was not really an Italian form.

Oratorio. Oratorio and opera were the results of greater expansions within the same principles. The oratorio, a chief musical form of the Counter-Reformation, told a Biblical story. With a narrator and indirect action, it was quasi-dramatic, in contrast to the opera, which had no narrator and presented the action directly. The recitativo was sung by the *historicus* ("narrator"; in Italian, *testo* meaning "text"), and individual quotes became solo arias. References to crowds used chorus and instruments and those to sleep, battles, or storms became popular as instrumental ritornelli. Battle pieces were the rage from time to time—good ones were still being written at the end of the eighteenth century. Storm music continued even longer— Rossini's overture to *William Tell* (1827) can be seen as a Romantic era version of the old convention.

The oratorio used as many as four or five solo voices, either singly or in combination, as the story suggested. The form reached its first culmination in the middle of the seventeenth century, with the works of Giacomo Carissimi. His oratorio on the Old Testament story of Jephte illustrates how the Baroque artists used features of a story to provide contrasting elements for the stile concertato. Jephte was a general who, in return for victory in the coming battle, pledged to God to sacrifice the first person of his household whom he would see upon returning home. He was victorious and when he returned home, he saw first his beloved daughter who had run out to welcome him. For Carissimi, Jephte, the daughter, and the historicus provided natural contrasts in voice range, whereas Jephte's army and the household servants formed choruses. The dramatic prayer, the battle, and the equally dramatic confrontation afterward provided natural vehicles for recitativos, arias, and choruses—the battle itself was conveyed by a highly active movement for a six-part chorus, which is reminiscent of the polyphonic chanson. The work, which dates from 1650, is earlier than the Scarlatti cantata—at that time, recitativo still comprised the majority of the musical life and arias were much less distinct, while the instrumental ritornelli comprised only a phrase or two.

Opera. In addition to enjoying popular support, the operatic form was at the same time in the forefront of experiment. Operas, of course, contained even more elements than oratorios, but many of these elements were not musical; costumes, scenery, and the beloved machines were still primary to these productions, which, at their height, were theatrical spectacles. Other elements, such as processions, dances, and whatever entertainments and displays the plot gave rise to, were partly musical.

Claudio Monteverdi was the single great composer of operas in the first half of the seventeenth century—at least the one whose operas are still in the repertoire. *Orfeo* (1607) had been a remarkable synthesis, accomplished in the new style by a master of the old. But Monteverdi continued with his innovations, and his later works, notably *Il Combattimento di Tancredi e Clorinda* (1624) and *L'Incoronazione di Poppea* (1642, when he was seventy-five), were equally remarkable.

Florence is acknowledged as the city where monody was first presented, but the dramma per musica flourished in other Italian cities, such as Mantua, Parma, and Venice, and Monteverdi's theatrical works were produced in all of them. Venice was the site of the first public opera house, the Teatro San Cassiano, which opened in 1637; there Monteverdi's *L'Incoronazione* and the first opera of Marc Antonio Cesti were produced. But Rome was leading in operatic experiments at the middle of the century, and it was in Rome, between 1620 and 1660, that the aria developed. Mazzochi developed a livelier style in declamation, which he set off by arioso sections and in which he had the solo singer accompanied only by a basso continuo. It was called *recitativo secco* (dry), as opposed to the more fully accompanied solos of the earlier monodists, called *recitativo stromentato* (instrumental). The distinction between the two types would remain for well over a century. Both Mazzochi and Luigi Rossi were important in the development of the aria, whose significant early successes date from the 1640s.

Mazzochi's vocal works represent Roman diversity; he produced motets, madrigals, cantatas, and theatrical works, including not only opera but sacred opera, comic opera, and oratorio. The musical comedy *Chi soffre speri* (Who Suffers May Hope), on which Mazzochi collaborated with another composer, was presented in Rome in 1639. Mazzochi also experimented with expression markings, using ◁ and ▷ for *crescendo* and *diminuendo* and *p* and *f* for *piano* and *forte* in one of his works, explaining their use in a preface.

By the middle of the seventeenth century, earlier experiments in opera were taking on definite characteristics. The late Renaissance aspects of Roman opera—particularly the chorus, based on the polyphonic ideal, and the composite orchestra—began to die out, and theatrical spectacle took over the center of attention from dramatic focus. Inevitably, the operatic ideal became distinct by itself and, in the end, was divorced from the *rappresentazione sacra* and from Church support, which was strongly associated with the old ideals, both musical and dramatic.

The center of operatic leadership moved to Venice, where a long-established love for the theater, for civic panoply, and for secular diversions such as the carnival soon helped to clarify operatic goals. The chorus, which had been a significant part of Roman opera, virtually died away; but it was not missed in the flamboyant productions that made the Venice opera famous all over Europe for its stagecraft, its use of machinery, and its gala exhibitions. Opera librettos became complex elaborations of mythological, historical, and pastoral subjects in a series of scenes that would provide the basis for the theatrical and musical arts. Comic scenes became popular and were frequently introduced between the acts of serious works.

Opera had developed from a new form produced in private theaters only for wealthy and knowledgeable noblemen, through a period of experiment and diverse example, to a culmination as a somewhat set, highly fashionable theater piece belonging to an enthusiastic public. No other entertainment approached the popularity of the opera at the height of the Baroque era.

Parallel in some aspects of development to vocal forms, and inevitably in constant interaction with them, were the instrumental forms.

Instrumental Forms in Italy

The term *sonata,* in the beginning a loose designation of a piece sounded by instruments (sometimes even including voices), changed through various early uses and finally meant a piece for solo treble and basso continuo, particularly for violin. Still later, the most popular form of the sonata—and, by sheer force of numbers, the most popular instrumental form of the late Baroque—was that for two treble instruments and basso continuo. This was the *trio sonata.* The word *trio* indicates three written parts, but the most common performing group for the trio sonata in Italy comprised two violinists for the treble solos and a gambist (or cellist) and harpsichordist for the basso continuo, a total of four players.

Not long after the establishment of the trio sonata as a viable form, the *concerto grosso* was introduced, and it too became an important and popular form. Because it was designed for a grand or concert occasion, however, the concerto grosso was not so universally or so frequently performed as the trio sonata; the latter could be effective in a small salon and thus became the form of the instrumental amateur. But the concerto grosso, because of its professional and, in the sense of exploration on the cutting edge, more serious character, was perhaps the most significant instrumental form to be developed during the Baroque era. It was the concerto grosso that would lead into the later classical concept of the orchestra and hence to the symphony.

Sonata. Development of the sonata was spurred by the convergence of the new style with the new interest in instruments (particularly the violin), using the principles of construction already at hand. *La Gardana,* the sonata of Marini's opus I (1617) [15] and perhaps the earliest sonata in the new style, was written in a punctus form made of contrasting phrases, seven in a sixty-four–measure work. The solo part was marked *violino o cornetto* ("violin or cornett")—the same instrument that Gabrieli had used in the *Sonata Pian' e Forte* (see page 227), and another association of the violin with high (loud) music. The bass was marked *basso continuo,* but the instruments were

---

[15] Arnold Schering, *Geschichte der Musik in Beispielen,* New York: Broude Brothers, 1951, pp. 212–213.

unspecified. The work proceeds, in the manner of a Renaissance toccata or fantasia, to present alternating phrases of familiar style and passage work.

Within a decade, Marini's concept had expanded; in his *Sonata per il violino per Sonar con due corde* ("Sonata for the Violin to Be Played on Two Strings"—referring to the use of double stops in the second section) of 1626,[16] the sections were substantially longer, seven of them consuming 158 measures. As in the earlier work, the sections alternated slow-fast-slow, beginning and ending with a slow section; but in contrast to *La Gardana*, each section in the 1626 work was made up of more than one punctus and approached the status of an independent movement, with double bars to set it off. Marini used indications of tempo—*tardo* ("slow") and *presto* ("fast") —in quick alternation in the long (thirty-two–measure) third section and added embellishing terms—*groppo* ("trill"), *affetti* ("ornaments"), and *forte-piano* (to indicate an echo).

By 1640 the trio sonata had appeared, though it would not reach its height of popularity for another generation. Monteverdi's *Scherzi musicali* had presented two tenors and a basso continuo in three-line structures, and the added voice offered the same possibility of increased contrast to the instrumental as it did to the vocal composer. Early examples of the sonata were written by instrumental specialists (as the early cantatas were written by vocal specialists), but the second half of the century found the basic forms sufficiently defined for active composers to work in both vocal and instrumental forms. Giovanni Legrenzi was one of these.

By Legrenzi's time, sonatas were being performed both in church and in private concerts; it was natural for the differing backgrounds and functions of the two locales to produce a difference in the works themselves. The trio sonata thus was either a *sonata da chiesa* ("church sonata") or a *sonata da camera* ("chamber sonata"), a distinction more practical than musical but having musical implications.

The sonata da chiesa was played at high Mass (before, during, or after) or at another service. Its association with the sanctuary made secular associations inappropriate, so the designations for the sections of the work, telling the kind of motion or movement required, were abstract. *Adagio* ("slow," "leisurely") and *allegro* ("fast") were the two most important kinds of motion—neither was extreme. The extremes were *grave* ("slow") and *presto* ("fast"), but even these were not extreme in the modern sense. The middle speed, neither fast nor slow, was called *largo*; *andante* was similar, being the speed of a comfortable walk. Legrenzi favored a four-movement group of allegro-adagio-largo-allegro, a kind of symmetry that was effective in capturing attention and in ending forcefully.

Allegro movements in the mature sonata made good use of the two-section dance form (*a* :||: *b* :||), which, with its two finals, prefigured the possibility of tonal relationships. The rhythmic motivation of meter was equally important, particularly in modulation, where it aided in resetting

---

[16] *Ibid.*, pp. 213–217.

tonal balances. A chord weak in one key could be placed on a strong beat and taken to a new leading tone, thus demanding resolution to a new tonic. Such a procedure must have been breathtaking to early audiences.

The adagio and other slow movements of the sonata were often in a free punctus structure and were generally short. The adagio and allegro in the mature sonata formed a pair analogous to the recitativo and aria in the cantata, though the adagio was not as free rhythmically as the recitativo. The sonata da chiesa in the 1680s settled into a four- or five-movement scheme, with a simple adagio-allegro-adagio-allegro the most common. Slow-fast movements were often paired, with the adagio ending on the dominant to prepare for the coming allegro. The latter were often fugal, but polyphonic aspects of the music became secondary to harmonic function. Nonetheless, such movements retained their inheritance from the imitative point and the polyphonic canzona.

The sonata da camera did not have to disguise its closeness to secular forms, so many chamber sonatas were dance suites in arrangement, and the dance titles could be affixed, as they could not be in the church works even when dance rhythms were being used. The two-part dance form was more prominent (fugal movements less so), and the dance title made tempo designations unnecessary, since each dance had its traditional speed.

Chiesa and camera were designations mainly of performance and only secondarily of musical differences, which were never categorical and which disappeared in the eighteenth century. The typical jig of the final movement might be labeled *giga* in a chamber sonata and *allegro* in a church work, but the musical difference was virtually nil. The chief musical differences lay in the greater number of movements and greater variety in slow movements in the chamber sonata and the tendency in the church sonata toward using the techniques of the learned style.

The last quarter of the seventeenth century found Italian music ready for a man who could bring the new forms to an early culmination. This man was Arcangelo Corelli, whose genius at the center of Italian Baroque instrumental music made him one of the most influential musicians in history. He was doubtless a great violinist, bringing to the solo violin sonata the expression of the passions that the singers valued and improving the melodic lines with embellishments and variations (see page 704). He was called *virtuosissimo di violina, e vero Orfeo de nostri tempi* ("the greatest violin virtuoso and the true Orpheus of our times"). Corelli lived in Rome from about 1675 at the palace of Cardinal Ottoboni, mingling with the aristocracy and producing concerts.

Throughout Europe, Corelli's art, as both performer and composer, was held to be the height of artistic attainment. And both these capacities were enhanced by his skill as a producer. His Monday afternoon concerts were famous, a center for visitors, including northerners on the "grand tour." In 1728, an English amateur reminisced about the coming of the Italian taste to England.

One of the chief [factors] was the coming over of the works of the great Corelli. Those became the onely musick relished for a long time, and there seemed to be no satiety of them, nor is the vertue of them yet exhaled, and it is a question whether it will ever be spent, for if musick can be immortall, Corelli's consorts will be so. Add to this, that most of the young Nobillity and Gentry that have travelled into Itally affected to learne of Corelli, and brought home with them such favour for the Itallian musick, as hath given it possession of our Pernassus. . . .[17]

It was Corelli, above all others, who served to reconcile the forces of instrumental technique with the developing concepts of meter and key. Stradivari's first violins date from 1666, when Corelli was thirteen, so the productions in Rome must have been astoundingly modern in sound as well as form.

The *Trio Sonata in C major*, opus III, no. 8 (Example 48), is representative of the sonata da chiesa, which was typically of four movements, largo-allegro-largo-allegro, with the third movement in a contrasting tone, *a* minor. Key contrast within a movement was taken for granted, particularly in punctus construction, where the Renaissance tradition of cadencing on a variety of finals was translated into the new style.

In the sonata da chiesa, the slow-fast movements were typically conceived as pairs. Many slow movements ended on a dominant triad to prepare for the coming tonic. But when the second slow movement was in the relative key and ended on the dominant, the return to tonic became a piquant juxtaposition of chords with roots a third apart. Such a progression confirmed the Baroque view of *tone* as interrelating with scale materials in which *a* minor is closer to C major than to A major, in contrast to the later view of *key*, in which the relationships would be reversed. In the present example, the *a* minor largo ends on its dominant, E major, and proceeds to the final allegro, which is in C. The cadence to the dominant, called *Phrygian* because of its resemblance to progressions to a Phrygian final, and its return to the tonic a third below is an idiom that sums up much of the transitional nature of the Baroque concept of harmony.

Equally representative of the Baroque musical language is Corelli's rhythmic and melodic idiom and the kind of interplay that characterizes the use of the three parts, two in the treble in mutual polarity with the bass. Chains of upward-reaching melodies overlap in the violins, producing a dialogue—sometimes leisurely, sometimes brisk—between them. The beginning of the third movement illustrates such a chain.

The individual lines are highly metric, and the beat itself is their informing element. In the allegros, the incisive beat is emphasized by the downbeats, which receive both the fresh tones and the long values either as sustained tones or as repeated notes. For example, the bass figure at the

[17] Roger North, quoted in John Wilson (ed.), *Roger North on Music*, London: Novello and Company Ltd, 1959, p. 358f.

start of the final allegro, through strong rhythm and octave leaps, couches a simple descent in a robust, vigorous progression.

The suspension moved easily from the proportional to the metric system, which, by producing expectations of regular accents, automatically opened the way for off-accents, rhythmic surprises such as syncopations larger than the single beat, and the *sforzando* (sudden accent). The suspension of the leading tone, already familiar in modal cadences, continued as an essential of the standard cadential formula, with the progression from supertonic to tonic now in the top line. Embellishments of the cadences were expected, particularly on the supertonic note, where a performer was to provide a trill whether it was notated or not. Often the same part adds an anticipation of the tonic note, which sounds against the leading tone. These abrasions were heightened, not minimized, in performance and were standard.

Corelli's personal idiom involves a further delay of the leading tone, prolonged so that it is only a sixteenth note long. When the other violin is descending to tonic by step from above, it often uses an anticipation of the keynote, thus creating a progression of consecutive seconds, which Corelli seems to have enjoyed. It is known as the "Corelli clash."

Elements carried over from the old tradition include the punctus construction, fugal techniques deriving from the imitative point, the idea of alternating sections, the use of passage work, and the Phrygian cadence. The

Trio Sonata, opus 3, no. 8   **Example 48**
ARCANGELO CORELLI

By the nineteenth century, figured bass as a form of musical notation had become obsolete; it was used only as an exercise in four-part harmony. Thus, the figures indicating
the harmony, which previously had been placed above the bass line, were transferred to
below the bass in order to make room for the tenor part. (Courtesy of Augener & Co.,
London.)

hemiola appears in cadences in triple time, now a device for approaching the close of a movement. The bass rhythm ♩ ♩ ♩ ♩ | (measures 27 and 28) was variously notated as one long $\frac{3}{2}$ measure, ♩ ♩ ♩ |, with or without a change in signature, or even ♩ ♩ ♩ |, which was fairly common at the end of the century. It is not a syncopation.

Concerto Grosso. If it was Corelli the violinist and composer who contributed so much to the definition of the sonata, it was Corelli the producer who was the prime creator of the concerto grosso. Separating his players, Corelli built on a lively tradition of divided choir performances. The concerto grosso was a compound performing group, of which one section was called the *concerto grosso* ("large consort") and the other the *concertino* ("little consort"). The concerto grosso in the sense of a large consort was a new kind of group, made of strings and basso continuo, in which more than one player played the same part on the same kind of instrument and at the same register. The Italians also called a large group a *concerto ripieno* ("reinforced consort"; plural, *concerti ripieni*) and used two or three instruments to a part.

But one of the chief elements in the Baroque style was contrast, and the concerto ripieno, while satisfying a desire for robust acoustical display, did not in itself provide a vehicle of contrast. Corelli is given credit for combining a trio sonata and a concerto grosso into a twofold group. Details of his concerts, which date from about 1682, are unknown, but it is known that both the small group and the reinforced group used a continuo and that Corelli was very careful to place the groups at the best distance for optimum interplay and contrast. The term *concerto grosso* really has three meanings: the large, reinforced group, the combination of the concerto grosso and concertino; and a work of music designed to exploit the possibilities of juxtaposing the two. (This triple definition makes the term a difficult one to use.)

The possibilities implicit in such a juxtaposition lie basically in the contrast of sound through alternation. A concerto grosso might involve fourteen or fifteen people—four in the concertino and ten or eleven in the concerto grosso. The large group was louder by dint of numbers and fuller by dint of the broad, intense quality of the reinforcement. Contrast could be achieved through alternation in an expansion of the punctus construction principle; balance was sought by demanding more dexterity and fluency of the concertino players to compensate for their smaller number.

The concerto grosso was a most satisfying form to a Baroque audience. It contained the essential contrasts—in sound and in speed—that they cherished. In 1701, a German writer told of his encounter with the form in Italy.

> The idea of this ingenious mixture first occurred to me some time ago in Rome, . . . where I heard, with great pleasure and astonishment, several concertos of this sort, composed by the gifted Signor Arcangelo Corelli, and

beautifully performed with the utmost accuracy by a great number of instrumental players.[18]

He savored the contrasts in both dynamics and tempo.

> For by exactly observing this opposition or rivalry of the slow and the fast, the loud and the soft, the fullness of the great choir and the delicacy of the little trio, the ear is ravished by a singular astonishment, as is the eye by the opposition of light and shade.[19]

The early concerto grosso used the form of the sonata da chiesa—slow-fast-slow-fast. But as the virtuoso aspects of the concertino came into greater prominence, the opening slow movement was more often omitted, enabling the "singular astonishment" to focus at once on bravura performance. Given the dramatic flavor of the concept and the human nature of the virtuoso, the three-movement fast-slow-fast form of the concerto was no doubt inevitable. So was an expansion of virtuosity in the concertino.

Even at its height, from about 1690 to 1720, the concerto was already in a state of flux. In Bologna, composers such as Giuseppe Torelli were writing works using clarino trumpets, specializing in the high octave where the partials were close enough together to allow virtuoso passage work. Trumpet concertos were extremely popular; it was to the "sweet trumpet" that Corelli's violin tone was likened, and many of Corelli's fast movements present materials for the violins that derive from the trumpet idiom (see the last movement of Example 48). The trumpet was associated with royalty and pomp and was used in the theater to support plots dealing with marital or majestic subjects (which means most of them).

The culminating figure of the concerto in Italy was Antonio Vivaldi, whose prolific and splendid works center in his more than 450 concertos, probably written from about 1690 to beyond 1730. His concertos were extremely varied; the concertinos ranged from six or more soloists down to one —most often a violinist. Always inventive, Vivaldi had a natural springboard for variety in his position as director, from 1703, of the *Ospitale della Pietà* (Conservatory of the Pietà) in Venice. The concerts at the Pietà were famous for over a quarter of a century and evidently occasioned a great bulk of his output. It is easy to imagine his furnishing works for gifted students as well as for himself. Interestingly, the Pietà was a girls' school and many of Vivaldi's performers were female. He wrote concertos for solo bassoon, oboe, and flute and even for the newly invented clarinet. He also included in his concertino sections such instruments as mandolin, harp, guitar, and lute.

The concertos for two instruments (often two violins or two trumpets) were perhaps a middle ground between the solo and concertino. They formed a substantial segment of Vivaldi's works. Being a producer as well as a com-

---

[18] Georg Muffat, quoted in Strunk, *op. cit.*, p. 449.
[19] *Ibid.*, p. 451.

poser, Vivaldi, like Corelli, was careful of the placement of players in performance. Some works survive with his annotations on placement. One of his concertos for two violins directs one violinist to stand away from the concerto grosso and specifies that the second is to stand off on the other side, under the clerestory; this is comparable to a modern instruction to play from the wings.

Vivaldi's concertos were in three movements, fast-slow-fast and often used the two-part dance form (a :||: b :||). Interactions with vocal and theatrical forms had brought the aria da capo into occasional use in an instrumental slow movement, but, in addition, the nature of the concerto gave rise to the ritornello principle.

Ritornello. Along with his contemporaries, Vivaldi sought contrasts. Basic to the concerto were the contrasts among movements and between the solo instruments (often groups of winds) and the concerto grosso. Composers exploited these contrasts, building works upon them. The concerto as a musical structure was based on the alternation of those sections dominated by the solo players with those in which the larger group participated extensively, called *tutti* or *ritornelli*. It was not a tidy division of forces but an endlessly variable one. The soloists presented more intricate materials, more delicate coordinations, and more ornate embellishments (written or added) than the concerto grosso. Wind players could add a different technical idiom. The materials for the two groups were inevitably different and frequently were farther separated stylistically by the composer's knowledge that the soloists would be skillful players and that the ripieno players might not be. At their best, the simpler, more forthright ritornelli presented the structural solidity required of a longer work, while the solo sections served as their foil, offering contrasting *episodes*. Often the ritornelli contained the subject and the solo sections dealt with passage work, technical displays, or simply contrasting materials.

The typical allegro movement opened with a ritornello presenting the subject, which, in keeping with the Baroque ideal, was centrally concerned with key or tone and with the beat. But Vivaldi's allegros often presented the beat itself in an intense, almost compulsive energy, sometimes italicized by repeated notes. In working out the form, he proceeded much like his contemporaries and based the subject on the tonic, dominant, and mediant of the tone in either the authentic (1–3–5–8) or plagal (5–1–3–5) tessitura. Such a subject centered harmonically in the tonic and dominant triads, so the ritornello was generally harmonically stable. Departure from the tone was usually accomplished in the succeeding episode, most often through a sequence around the cycle of fifths.

The circle sequence was vital to Baroque form. The cycle of fifths, which rises slowly at 2 percent per interval when the fifths are perfect (not tempered), is in reality a helix or screw thread; it is tonally neutral, and a true sequence around the cycle would carry the music into keys too distant for practicality. To reconcile the freedom of the circle sequence to the ambitus of closely related scale materials and to prevent the music from going too far from the key center of the movement, composers included within the sequence one diminished (or false) fifth. In addition, the sequence brought a variety of harmonic colors into play, especially when it was comprised of seventh chords. Both major and minor thirds and sevenths would take their turn, contrasting the restless major third–minor seventh combination with the gentler minor third–minor seventh and the biting major third–major seventh (*Mm, mm,* and *MM,* respectively) and spicing the whole with the diminished fifth, most often in combination with minor third and seventh (*dm*).

For all its effectiveness in both variety of harmonic color and satisfying strides of the bass through the cycle of fifths, the circle sequence was not difficult to manage. Generally, composers let the sequence go one or two strides too far and then return in a reverse motion to establish one of the fundamentals as dominant. By progressing directly from the lower to the upper dominant, omitting the tone that lay between them in the cycle of fifths, the composer set up the demand for that tone, much as clock hands pointing to, say, 2 and 4 would create an angle for the bisection of 3. In addition, the progression from lower to upper dominant incorporates the lowest and highest notes of the scale (as they appear in the cycle of fifths)—first the subdominant tone in the bass, then the leading tone in one of the upper parts over the dominant bass. Those two notes, the tritone, defined the tone very clearly.

Departure from the tonic, maintained by setting the second ritornello in a contrasting tone, would be extended by the ensuing solo episode and might be continued in a third ritornello in a third tone. Each additional ritornello section presupposed an additional solo section. The final ritornello often comprised a return to the opening ritornello of the work, as a da capo when exact repetition obviated the need to write it out.

The principle of alternation was basic; the number of ritornelli varied and, dependent on this, so did the number of solo episodes. Allegros of four ritornelli (with three alternating episodes) were standard, as were those of five ritornelli (with four alternating episodes).

The solo concerto used the same forms as the concerto grosso, but the spotlight on the soloist tempted him to more brilliant displays of his art and took him farther from the style and content of the ritornelli, so the later solo concertos tended to be simpler in form. The solo violinist developed techniques that enabled his part to stand dramatically alone against the larger group. Double stopping, relatively simple on the viols, was a virtuoso technique on the violin. And composers learned to take advantage of the capacity of the violin for playing wide leaps and used leaps in a single melodic line to present complete harmonic units. Arpeggiation was useful, but larger leaps—tenths, twelfths, and double octaves—were no harder to play and were much more impressive. The technique of accumulating chords in such a way was called *breaking;* a violinist could play one line but give the effect

Concerto in C for Two Oboes, Two Clarinets, and Concerto Grosso: First Movement

ANTONIO VIVALDI

Example 49

The example includes the first four pages of the score, possibly in Vivaldi's own hand, and shows the opening ritornello, the first episode, and the start of the second ritornello. The opening ritornello serves, atypically, as an introduction, while the main subjects form the basis of the second ritornello. (Courtesy of the Biblioteca Nazionale di Torino. Photo by Chomon–Perino.)

of two when the line was skillfully broken, or he could exploit the breakings for the sake of their textural effect.

Ritornello structure was simply a design—any design—that used as a motivating principle the contrasts of medium implicit in the use of two groups. The concerto grosso thus summed up the fabric and forms of the Baroque ideal, using freely what had been developed in other mediums and forms, yet also developing its own characteristic ritornello structure and instrumental techniques.

✻ Some Composers of the Italian Baroque

The development of the forms that were to be basic to music for the following two centuries can be traced in the works of the Italian innovators of the seventeenth century. Such men as Giovanni Gabrieli (see pages 243–244) and Claudio Monteverdi (see page 246) were masters of the old style who sought the contrasts that defined the new.

Vocal Music

LUIGI ROSSI (1597–1653), an Italian singer, guitarist, organist, harpsichordist, composer, and producer, was known for his skill in improvisation. Born in southern Italy, he studied at Naples and worked in Rome. There he married a harpist and, from 1633–1635, was organist at the French church of Saint-Louis. After six years in Florence at the Medici court, he became a chamber musician, in Rome and Bologna, to Cardinal Barberini; in 1642 he produced an opera in the Barberini theatre. When Barberini went to Paris, he called Rossi to the French capital, and in 1647, Rossi's opera *Orfeo* was performed at the palace, stimulating French interest in opera. Rossi was known as the "new swan" for his singing. He left some 385 cantatas and other vocal works, of which only a few were published during his lifetime.

DOMENICO MAZZOCHI (1592–1655) was a Roman lawyer who composed music.

He was an imaginative innovator and wrote in both the old and new styles. His madrigals of 1638 were polyphonic (for five voices) but contained experimental expressive markings. He also composed cantatas (sacred), motets, an oratorio (1641), and operas with both standard texts (1626, 1641) and sacred texts (1626). He collaborated with the composer Marazzoli in composing the first musical comedy in the new style.

PIER FRANCESCO CAVALLI (1602–1676), an organist and composer trained in Venice, was the organist at St. Mark's Cathedral from 1640 (director from 1668). He composed a substantial amount of sacred music, such as a Requiem Mass, but is remembered chiefly for theatrical works, including over 40 operas. In his operas, he made increasing distinction between recitativo, the vocal staple of his early works, and aria, more important in his later works.

GIACOMO CARISSIMI (1605–1674), an Italian organist and composer, was the son of a cooper in Marino, near Rome. A singer at the cathedral in Tivoli in 1623, he became organist there in 1625. In 1629 he became the music director of the Church of San-Apollinare of the German College in Rome, where he remained until his death thirty-five years later. He was renowned as the greatest composer of oratorios, of which some 16 remain; *Jephte* (1650) is considered his greatest work. His contemporaries credited him with the creation of recitativo and the cantata, of which numerous examples survive (with both French and Italian texts) in spite of the dispersal of his manuscripts after his death. He left also 3 books of motets and Masses (including one on "L'homme armé"), along with other miscellaneous works.

MARC' ANTONIO CESTI (1623–1669), a Minorite monk, studied with Carissimi in Rome and proceeded to a series of prestigious posts as singer (tenor) and *maestro di capella*—at the Medici court in Florence (1647–1651), at the court of Ferdinand-Charles of Austria in Innsbruck (1651–1663), and at the court of Leopold I in Vienna (1666–1669). Much in demand as a composer, Cesti wrote cantatas, motets, and operas. It is said he wrote about 100 operas, but only 12 remain. These works, important in the bel canto tradition, were produced in Florence, Venice, Innsbruck, and Vienna. Perhaps the most famous was *Il Pomo d'oro* (*The Golden Apple*), first presented in Vienna in 1667.

ALESSANDRO STRADELLA (1645–1681), a Neapolitan singer and composer, brought melodic gifts to bear on opera in Venice and Rome. He was a prolific and important composer whose works are found as far apart as Oxford, Paris, Dresden, Vienna, and Brussels. His stormy personality filled his life with amorous adventures and eventually led to his murder. In addition to oratorios and operas, Stradella left a number of motets, cantatas, and songs, along with trio sonatas and other instrumental chamber works. He was later (1837 and 1844) to be the subject of two romantic operas.

AGOSTINO STEFFANI (1654–1728), an Italian organist, composer, priest, and diplomat, was of great renown in his own time and was influential in both vocal and instrumental music. His career was international. Beginning as a choirboy in Padua and Munich, where he became organist in 1675, he worked in Paris in 1678 and 1679. In addition, he produced 3 of his 20 operas in Düsseldorf, where he was also privy councillor and papal representative, thus combining his creative life with diplomacy. Aside from his operas, in which he developed advanced instrumentation, he left five volumes of cantatas, including works for two singers and basso continuo (1683), trio sonatas (1679), and well over 100 works of diverse types. In 1706 he was consecrated bishop.

ALESSANDRO SCARLATTI (1660–1725) was a Sicilian composer and producer who studied in Rome (possibly with Carissimi) from 1672 to 1678; shortly thereafter he became chapel master for the exiled Queen Christina of Sweden. From 1680 he was in Naples, and in 1684 he was appointed to the royal court. He was virtually the founder of the Neapolitan school, a term referring chiefly to operas, of which he wrote about 115. In addition, he left over 1,000 cantatas (about 750 of them for solo voice and basso continuo), 200 Masses, about 20 oratorios, and 6 madrigals. Of instrumental music, he left 12 concerti ripieni, along with miscellaneous sonatas, suites, and harpsichord works.

Instrumental Music

SALOMONE ROSSI (c. 1565–c. 1628), a composer at the court of Mantua, was innovative in the writing of instrumental music and is credited with writing the first instrumental trios in the new style. He collaborated with Monteverdi in writing the sacred drama *Maddalena* (1617) and wrote other theater works as well. He published eight volumes of secular vocal music, including five books of madrigals for five voices and basso continuo (1600 to 1622), and four volumes of sonatas for from three to five parts (1607 to 1623). A Jew, he added *Ebreo* ("Hebrew") to his name and published 28 *Salmi e Cantici ebraici* (Psalms and Hebrew Songs) for four to eight voices for the Jewish liturgy. His sister, known as Madama Europa, was a singer of reputation; she sang in Monteverdi's *Arianna* in 1608.

BIAGIO MARINI (c. 1595–1665), a violinist and composer, was born in Lombardy (northern Italy), studied with Monteverdi, and in 1617 and 1618 was a violinist at San Marco in Venice. His career led him to posts in Brescia (1620), Parma (1622), Neuburg (1623 to 1645), Milan (1646), and Ferrara (1654); he died in Venice. He left twenty-two volumes of music, to which he gave *opus* numbers, the first known use of this term. He was also the first to use the term *sonata*, for his opus I (1617); the sonata is called *La Gardana*.

GIOVANNI LEGRENZI (1626–1690) was born near Bergamo and was organist at the Cathedral of that city in his youth. After a short tenure in Ferrara, he moved to Venice in 1664, and it was in this city that his career culminated. He was director of the Conservatorio de'Mendicanti from 1672 and maestro da capella at San Marco from 1685. A composer and teacher of great influence, he wrote music for church, theater, and chamber. He published nine volumes of motets, Psalms, litanies, and Masses (double chorus), along with a handful of oratorios; he produced some 20 operas; and he wrote some of the earliest and finest sonatas (both church and chamber), and concertos.

ARCANGELO CORELLI (1653–1713), an Italian violinist, composer, and producer, was born near Bologna of a wealthy family. Trained in his teens in Bologna, he spent most of his life in Rome with sponsors of the highest rank. His reputation was international and his influence paramount in instrumental music. Known for stunning performances and enlarged techniques for the violin, he produced concerts on Monday afternoons at the palace of his patron, Cardinal Ottoboni (nephew of Pope Alexander VIII). He left only six volumes of his music—four of trio sonatas, one of solo sonatas, and one of concerti grossi.

GIUSEPPE TORELLI (c. 1650–1708), an Italian violist and composer, pursued his career in Bologna from 1684 to 1695 and from 1701 until his death. He was also in Vienna (1695–1698) and at the Brandenburg court (1698–1701). Torelli was in the forefront of writers of the concerto (both solo violin concerto and concerto grosso) and works using trumpets. His *sinfonia* for trumpets and strings influenced the violin style of later composers as well as the double concerto for trumpets.

ANTONIO VIVALDI (c. 1676–1741), a Venetian priest, violinist, teacher, and producer, was associated with the Conservatorio della Pietà, where Vivaldi's concerts were a prime tourist attraction for more than a quarter-century after his appointment there in 1703. Known as "il prete rosso," "the red (headed) priest," Vivaldi was famous throughout Europe, and his influence was widespread and continuing in the art of instrumental music. His prodigious output is still not completely known—at least 75 trio and solo sonatas, 45 operas and oratorios, and about 40 large sacred works (including 12 Magnificats). But his concertos are the basis of his fame and influence. Of the 454 known surviving, 96 were published in his lifetime; the set known as *The Seasons* remained in the repertoire for a half-century. Some 50 of the concertos, for strings without soloists, presaged the symphony.

The first scene represented a chariot of singers composed of the rarest voices that could be procured. . . . A masque representing fire was admirable; then came a Venus out of the clouds. . . . But the glory of the masque was the great persons performing in it, the French King, his brother the Duke of Anjou, with all the Grandees of the Court, the King performing to the admiration of all. The music was twenty-nine violins, vested *à l'antique*, but the habits of the masquers were stupendously rich and glorious.

JOHN EVELYN *

The New Style in Europe

FRENCH MUSIC
IN THE SEVENTEENTH CENTURY

12

France was probably the least divided of the European monarchies of the seventeenth century. Its music inevitably reflected royal taste, for although the court was not the only musical center, the other centers were reflections of it. Both Louis XIII and Louis XIV loved music and supported it well; the century of their combined reigns (1610–1715) was a time of musical splendor.

*1651. Eric Blom (ed.), *The Music Lover's Miscellany*, London: Gollancz, 1935, p. 354. The event was a performance of the *Ballet des elemens*, and the king was the twelve-year-old Louis XIV.

The French predilection for instrumental color and the dance informed the early decades of the century. From 1581, when the *Balet Comique de La Royne* was produced, to the death of Louis XIII in 1643, over two hundred ballets were produced in France. The French considered the ballet the perfect art form, because it included virtually all the elements of art. (They have retained their loyalty to this concept through the centuries.)

Louis XIII was the founding patron of both the French Académie and the famous string group known as Les Vingt-Quatre Violons du Roy (The King's Twenty-Four Violins), usually written as Les 24. Known also as the Grande Bande, Les 24 had the five-part makeup of the French chorus. The membership in 1630 was six each of *dessus* (sopranos) and *hautes-contres* (countertenors) and four each of *tailles* (tenors), *quintes* (fifth part players, from the Renaissance *quinta pars*), and *basses de violon*. The upper two were violins, the quintes were similar to violas, and the tailles might be either; the basses de violon were cellos with the low string tuned to $BB\flat$.

Louis XIV, in a seventy-two–year reign (1643–1715) that has been labeled the "Age of Magnificence," gave a glory to the French nation that still transfixes our attention. His energy was prodigious, his interest in the arts keen and knowledgeable. He kept the nobility, whom he did not trust, in a state of enervation through command attendance at one court spectacle after another. He supported a galaxy of artisans and artists (and established the *Prix de Rome* to train them), ennobled the best of them, and led the taste of a nation that still looks back on his royal figure with awe.

Louis XIV continued his father's sponsorship of ballets (in which he himself danced until 1669), of Les 24, and of the Académie de Musique, which concentrated on opera when the King no longer danced. He revised the chapel music administration in 1683 and sponsored development of the choral motet for performance at his daily Mass. And he became increasingly interested in chamber music after his second marriage, at the age of 45.

Musical Theater

In the first half of the seventeenth century, French music centered in the *ballet*, the musical *divertissement* (entertainment), and the *air de cour*, which in some cases was a song already known from a ballet. Monody developed slowly in France—for the first four decades of the century, many songs were intabulations (for solo and lute) of polyphonic chansons. The lute solo, also popular, was often a dance suite or a set of variations on a dance or song tune. Toward the middle of the century, the *clavecin* (harpsichord) and guitar became popular instruments. Louis XIII was particularly interested in the clavecin; Louis XIV continued the custom of listening to a *claveciniste* virtually every evening, but he danced often to the lute and for many years had a daily guitar lesson; the royal children studied the clavecin.

Like the Italians, the French enjoyed lavish stage effects. In addition to the machinery of the stage, however, they enjoyed outdoor spectacles. Mounted maneuvers, called *carrousels*, presented patterns in the palace courtyard. Water galas used fanciful boats or artificial islands built in the lagoons of the formal gardens. Ballets were held in the garden or tennis court and

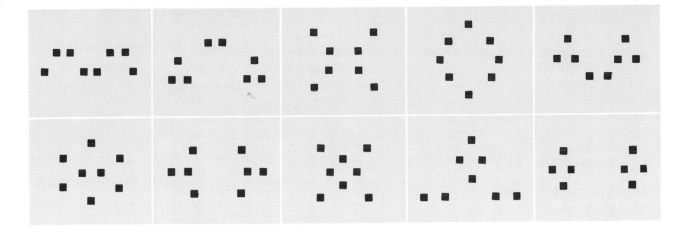

Ballet patterns, formed by groups of dancers, were seen from the balcony. At the beginning of the dance illustrated, eight dancers stood as statues. The dance proceeded with the dancers moving according to the figures shown. (From *Des Ballets Anciens et Modernes*, 1682. Courtesy of the Bibliothèque Nationale.)

were watched from balconies; the dancing consisted of "steps" and "figures," designs achieved by the position of the dancers on the floor, more similar to band positions during a half-time display at a football game than to the classical ballet as we know it. But the ballet was a splendid amalgam in which the costumer, set designer, machine architect, composer, poet, singer, reader (for not all the poems were sung), instrumentalist, and dancer all took an important part.

In the third quarter of the century, opera came to Paris and was added to the extravaganzas of the court. Rossi's *Orfeo* was brought to Paris with enormous success, but the French composers bent the musical language, particularly the recitativo, to the French tongue. And although the French had entertained Italian monodists at court in 1601 and 1605, the extreme emotionalism of the stile rappresentativo was not to the French taste. The natural subtlety of the French language led many composers to conclude that French recitativo could not be developed, but others felt the difficulties were not insurmountable. The controversy between Italian and French style —or Italian and French taste, as the writers stated it—continued to be a lively issue well into the eighteenth century.

But the difference was more than language; the Frenchmen's taste in theater was basically different from that of the Italians, with a strong preference for the scene and the dance. The many classifications of musical theater in France give an idea of the variety of tastes that existed—the heroic ballet, the pastoral ballet, the heroic pastorale, the divertissement, the ballet mascarade, the comic ballet, the tragic ballet, and the *ballet à entrées* (a group of short dances). Opera was a further development of the same categories; tragedy was the most usual, but the pastorale, ballet, ballet opera, and, rarely, a production called simply an opera appeared, some fifty of them by 1700.

The element that set opera apart from ballet was the recitativo. Development of the French recitativo is attributed to Jean-Baptiste Lully, the Italian-born composer-producer who championed the French taste. His answer to the rhythmic problem was to use freely changing meters—many of Lully's recitativos changed meter signature for virtually every measure. Such a scheme could structure emphasis and yet maintain the essential contrast with the measured airs and dances.

Lully's ballets were on allegorical or mythological subjects, such as *The Seasons* and *The Birth of Venus*. The operas were the same; they included *Psyche, Alceste, Le Triomphe de l'Amour* (The Triumph of Love), and *Amadis* (his favorite). In his last and perhaps his most influential work, *Acis et Galatée,* he revived the pastorale, which had fallen out of popularity in the previous generation.

Lully was an imaginative, knowing entrepreneur who knew how to please the king and who won for himself virtual dictatorship in the musical

Acis et Galatée, Act I (excerpt)   Example 50

JEAN-BAPTISTE LULLY

theater. He put strong emphasis on dance and instrumental color and was an innovator of instrumental techniques. He introduced uniform bowing in Les 24 and used horns, trumpets, flutes, oboes, and bassoons in various instrumental sections (called *symphonie* or *ritournelle*). The operas abound in dances—210 in the double-punctus dance form, 91 of which were minuets.

Perhaps Lully's most important contribution was the opening symphonie, or *ouverture* (called *sinfonia* in Italy), which consisted of a majestic first section and a fugal second section, often with a final slow section. The form was exported and was known as the *French overture*. In France the majestic section was associated with dotted figures, which became idiomatic in the French overture, and dotted figures found their way into the preludes of suites, marches, and other works striving to convey pomp and display. The overtures were published in short score, as though for trio sonata, often with no indication of the instrumentation. But publications of operas were com-

GALATÉE: I thought to find here my beloved nymph. I will reproach her for being so late.

ACIS: Without that nymph, alas! Is there nothing, O charming shore, that can give you any pleasure?

GALATÉE: I am delighted by the charms of this place. But my joy would have been greater had this shore offered to my eyes a vision of the nymph that I seek.

ACIS: Ah, if you knew of the misery which the absence of my only love causes me, would you not have pity on the torment to which the gods of Love expose me?

GALATÉE: Be done with such talk. Can you only speak of matters of the heart?

ACIS: Alas! Can the pain I suffer without her be hidden even for a moment?

TRANS. BY JON RINKA

The commemorative edition of the opera was printed, in movable type, in a large score. The instrumental ritornello is a sarabande; although it is notated as a trio sonata, it may have been performed by wind instruments as well as strings. The final cadence of the ritornello elides with the opening chord of the recitativo. The opening figure of the vocal line, plus the tied-over bass tone that becomes a suspension, are French idioms of the period. In French figured bass, the diminished fifth was common; it was indicated (as 5♭ over *e* in measure 2 of the recitativo) whether or not it required alteration of the upper tone.

The French violin clef (bottom-line G) is used in the ritornello. The clefs for the two soloists are the soprano (bottom-line C) for Galatée and countertenor (now the alto, middle-line C) for Acis. In the bottom system of the first page, the singers' clefs have been reversed in a misprint; the notes are correct for the correct clefs. The modern bass clef is used throughout. The small *t* on the top line indicates a trill. (Courtesy of the University of Michigan Library. Photo by R. E. Kalmbach.)

memorative rather than practical, and the addition of other lines and instruments is known from examination of instrumental parts and payrolls.

Musical theater was exclusively a royal entertainment at the beginning of the reign of Louis XIV, but the Académie de Musique, which was the French opera, subsequently offered productions to the public that initially had been presented at the court. By 1685, provincial productions began.

The French court extended its love for lute and guitar solos to the harpsichord solo. France was the leader in the modern keyboard style and in the development of the *pièce de clavecin*. Chambonnières and his students based the new keyboard pièces on the lute style, using arpeggiations and other effects idiomatic to lute and guitar. An abundance of embellishments (*agréments*, or graces) were indicated by abbreviated signs that they called *ornements surajoutés* (superadded ornaments), which were semi-exact in designation. The French enjoyed a highly decorated texture in all contexts. A theorist of 1687 wrote about ornaments.

Pièce de Clavecin

> Ornaments are to the voice and to instruments what decoration is to an edifice, and as ornaments are not necessary to the structure of the building, but serve only to render it more pleasing to behold; thus an Air for the voice and a Piece for instruments can be basically strong and yet not satisfy the ear if it is not adorned with suitable Ornaments; and the same as a too great quantity of decoration produces a sort of confusion that makes the edifice less pleasing, so confusion of ornaments in Airs and in Pieces serves only to lessen the beauty. . . . One can say further that Ornaments are a melodic Salt which seasons the singing and gives it taste, without which it would be tame and insipid, and which, like Salt, must be used with prudence, so that there will be neither too much nor too little.[1]

The book *Pièces de Clavecin* (1689) by Jean-Henry d'Anglebert is representative of the genre. Like most books of pièces de clavecin after 1680, it grouped many pieces in a single tone or key, with the intention that the player could use them to make up a suite. "I have put into this collection pieces in only four tones," he wrote in the Preface, "though I have composed in all the others. I hope to give the rest in a second book." [2] (He did not.)

The pieces in G are Prelude, Allemande, Courante (with double), 2nd Courante, 3rd Courante, Sarabande, Gigue, Gaillarde, Chaconne, Gavotte, and Menuet. Three, four, or five might make a suite.

D'Anglebert's Prelude, like many French preludes from the 1630s to about 1710, was written without meter and was to be performed in a spontaneous manner; association of the prelude with free rhythm was traditional. The verb *préluder* (to prelude) meant "to improvise." The notation, which is easy to read, suggests quite clearly which tones are to be held to accumulate chords. The absence of key signature is representative of the refusal of the

[1] Jean Rousseau, *Traité de la viole*, Amsterdam: Antiqua, 1965, pp. 74–75. (Facsimile reprint.)

[2] Jean-Henry d'Anglebert, *Pieces de Clavecin*, New York: Broude Brothers, 1965, folio *d*. (Facsimile reprint.)

Prelude and Courante, from Pièces de Clavecin　　　　　Example 51

JEAN-HENRY D'ANGLEBERT

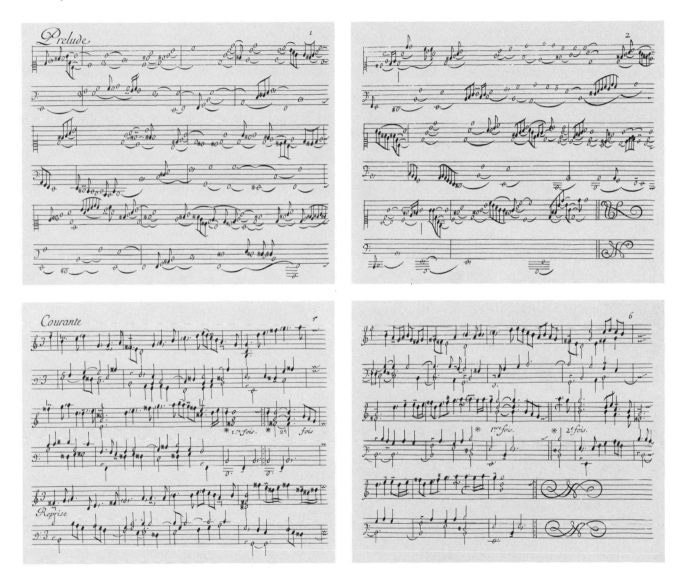

The Prelude is unmeasured and suggests only its order and cumulative effects. The Courante is a representative French incorporation of the two-section Baroque dance form. The second ending of the second section includes repetition of the last three-and-a-half measures, which the French called the *petit reprise*. The use of treble and baritone (third-line *F*) clefs was standard. D'Anglebert's table of embellishments appears on page 706. (Photo by R. E. Kalmbach.)

seventeenth-century artist to be regimented in details of notation. The chaconne is in the rondeau form, an instrumental form in which an opening double punctus (the rondeau proper) is performed twice and then alternated with short sections called *couplets* (verses). If R stands for the rondeau double punctus and numbers stand for the couplets, the form is R :‖ 1R2R3R etc. The two-part dance form and the rondeau were the basis of the French suite. The Gigue was often used as a finale.

By the last years of the seventeenth century, the pièce de clavecin, though still based on the dance and rondeau forms, was more and more often a character piece. Many of Couperin's pieces had evocative titles—battles, animals, well-known people. The double-section form became the vehicle for increasingly complex and allusive keyboard pieces. The unmetered prelude disappeared, the suite was written as an obligatory succession, and the style was increasingly idiomatic, with less of the lute-generated figurations and more of the techniques of the coming keyboard style—crossing of hands, quick repeated notes in alternation (called *batterie*), octaves, and others.

Many French predilections pointed to the coming Classicism, but French composers developed one form that was so thoroughly Baroque that it placed them in the main stream. This was the *grand motet*. From its early maturity late in the seventeenth century and for the seventy-five years of its life, the form was widely practiced and highly popular in France and highly respected abroad.

Grand Motet

The grand motet, or its full name, the *motet à grand chœur* ("motet for full chorus"; plural, *grands motets*), was a work for soloists, choir, and instruments. It was much like the oratorio but based on a Psalm, Canticle, or other text without a plot and hence did not have a *historicus*. A grand motet was customarily performed during the daily royal Mass, a low Mass in the Royal Chapel at 10 A.M. Sébastien de Brossard, the writer of the first French dictionary of music (1703) wrote that "the motet style is varied, complex, and susceptible of all the embellishments of art."[3] Its resources were truly splendid, for the French used both the full five-voice chorus (soprano, alto, tenor, baritone, and basso) and a small choir, generally of three or four parts with one singer to each line, called the *petit chœur* (small choir).

The master of the grand motet was Michel-Richard Delalande. His *De Profundis*,[4] for example, is a string of movements contrasting in medium, tempo, texture, and dynamics—symphonie, basso solo, full chorus, small choir (SSAT) basso solo, small choir (SAB), soprano solo with oboe obbligato, small choir (SST), tenor solo, full chorus with sections for duo (SS), tenor solo, and a grand fugue for full chorus. Strings, organ, flute, oboe, and bassoon were specified. The grand motet contained as many movements

[3] Sébastien de Brossard, "Motet," *Dictionaire de musique*, Amsterdam: Antiqua, 1964. (Facsimile reprint.)
[4] A modern edition was edited by Alexandre Cellier, Paris: Editions Salabert, 1944.

as the text had verses, but the *De Profundis* is unusual in not adding the two final verses, the "Gloria Patri" (Glory be to the Father) and "Sicut erat in principio" (As it was in the beginning), which form the culmination of most grands motets.

Other Forms

The seventeenth century saw French music make a slow and never complete transition from Renaissance to high Baroque ideas. The opera, though extremely Baroque in concept, was not really a separately defined theater type but overlapped and interacted with the ballet and divertissement and even with the comic play.

At the end of the seventeenth century, interest was rising in chamber performances and in the smaller forms suitable for the salon. The King had married a religious woman and was becoming less interested in the theater. The decline in royal enthusiasm and Lully's death in 1687 turned the opera more and more to public sponsorship. Many smaller salons gradually replaced the court, so music as an art was both decentralized and smaller in scope.

The turn into the eighteenth century saw the establishment of the new chamber forms, particularly the sonata and the cantata, both of which were brought from Italy in the middle 1690s. These were seized upon by the great number of French harpsichord amateurs; they popularized the trio sonata, taking pleasure in the realization of the figured bass and often hiring professional musicians for the solo parts.

Both popular songs and lute and guitar solo work were strongly supported well into the eighteenth century. The annual publications of *chansons serieux et à boire* continued, now with a *basse continue* (basso continuo).

As the eighteenth century began, France was ready to bring her genius to bear on the creation of chamber music, using the forms that had been popular in Italy for a generation. She would redefine these forms in her own image and make herself a strong influence in the coming Classicism.

ENGLISH MUSIC
IN THE SEVENTEENTH CENTURY

England's political life in the seventeenth century, and particularly the break in the monarchy between the execution of Charles I in 1649 and the accession of Charles II in 1660, formed the frame within which English social and artistic life was worked out. The Puritans, elevated to authority in the Commonwealth, had long been opposed to both drama and music (even in the Liturgy). Roger North (c. 1651–1734), a lawyer and ardent gambist and consort player, described the final days under Charles I and the fallow period after his death:

> Amongst other arts, Musick flourished, and exceedingly improved, for the King, being a vertuous prince, loved an enterteinement so commendable

as that was, and the Fantazia manner held thro' his reigne, and during the troubles; and when most other good arts languished Musick held up her head, not at Court nor (in the cant of those times) profane Theatres, but in private society, for many chose rather to fiddle at home, than to goe out, and be knockt on the head abroad; and the enterteinement was very much courted and made use of, not onely in country but citty familys, in which many of the Ladys were good consortiers; and in this state was Musick dayly improving more or less till the time of (in all other respects but Musick) the happy Restauration.[5]

In 1672, there appeared in the *London Gazette* a "Notice, that at Mr. *John Banister's* House, now called the Musick school, over against the *George* Tavern in White Fryers, this present Monday, will be Musick performed by Excellent Masters, beginning precisely at four of the Clock in the afternoon, and every afternoon for the future. . . ." [6] North said that the musicians (both vocal and instrumental) played on a raised box curtained off from the customers, who sat at tables in alehouse fashion. These may have been the first modern public concerts.

The Pretender had been entertained by the French King for a decade before the Restoration, and at his return as Charles II in 1660, he brought French predilections with him. He had instituted his own "24 violins," an English band numbering six sopranos, countertenors (both violins), tenors, and basses. The music of Lully was imported; it was "most frequently used," wrote North, "and Lully was thought a muse imortall." [7]

Then the Italian forms arrived to triumph over those of the French. North continues, "Then came over Corelly's first consort [trio sonata] that cleared the ground of all sorts of musick whatsoever. By degrees the rest of his consorts and at last the conciertos came, all which are to the musitians like the bread of life." [8]

North wrote as a string player whose pride lay in being a "compleat, ready, and dexterous thro-bass man." [9] The great harpsichord music of the virginal school had also flourished early in the century, in a particularly English art, along with the consort music for viols and the dividing on a ground that North cherished. After the Restoration those instruments fell into disuse—the virginals rather quickly and the viol gradually—theater was revived, and the masque gradually yielded to the opera. And songs (now with basso continuo)[10] and catches were at an apogee late in the century.

[5] John Wilson (ed.), *Roger North on Music*, London: Novello and Company Ltd, 1959, p. 294.

[6] Robert Elkin, *The Old Concert Rooms of London*, London: Edward Arnold, 1955, p. 18f.

[7] Wilson, *op. cit.*, p. 301n.

[8] *Ibid.*, p. 310.

[9] *Ibid.*, p. 26.

[10] The great collection of songs in England at the end of the century was Purcell's *Orpheus Britannicus*, 2 vols., 1698 and 1702. Both volumes have been reprinted in facsimile by Broude Brothers, New York, 1965.

The decades before "the troubles" had witnessed the culmination of the English late Renaissance style, notably the lute song, lute solo, and music for the virginal. Many publications presented "select lessons upon the lute," or "lessons upon the virginals." (The term *virginals*, or even *a pair of virginals*, was idiomatic.) A *lesson* meant simply a piece of music. Collections of lessons found the popular dances basic.

Other English music types included the intabulation or keyboard version of songs (many with variations), one-phrase pieces called *points*, pieces based on London cries or street tunes, and *Innomines*. Innomines were pieces for viols, harpsichord, or organ based on the setting of the words *In nomine*

The Virginal School

Pavane and Galliard   Example 52

WILLIAM BYRD

These dances, which were written for the Earl of Salisbury, were originally published in the *Parthenia* of 1612. The two six-line staves use F and G clefs. The bottom line of the treble and top line of the bass are both c^1. The use of the proportional signature for the galliard was not unusual; it is comparable to a metric $\frac{3}{2}$ signature. (Courtesy of the British Museum.)

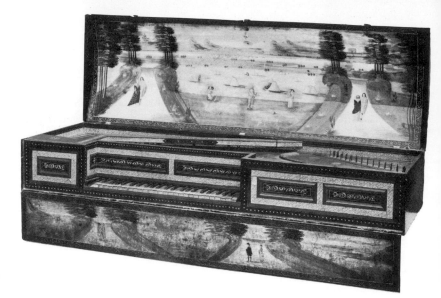

A virginal by Thomas White (c. 1642). The virginal was a table harpsichord. (Courtesy of the Victoria and Albert Museum.)

Domini of the Benedictus of the *Missa Gloria Tibi Trinitas* by the sixteenth-century English composer John Taverner (c. 1495–1545). The tradition of the Innomine had been popular at the end of the sixteenth century, was renewed in the seventeenth, and reached a new high point in Purcell's generation. But these works were continuations of the Renaissance ideal and were gradually and inevitably supplanted by the new Baroque interest.

Chief among the new interests was the musical theater, which flourished as the court masque in the first half of the century and as the masque and opera after the Restoration. The most famous masque of the early decades was *Comus*, with the text written by John Milton (1608–1674) and the music by Henry Lawes. It was produced at Ludlow Castle in 1633, with Lawes in the cast. Five songs are still in existence, including the well-known "Sabrina Fair."

Musical Theater

As in France, the distinction among various types of theatrical entertainments in England was never clear. The fifty-odd productions to which Purcell contributed music varied from plays for which he wrote only two or three incidental pieces to *Dido and Aeneas*, which is completely set to music, with no clear demarcation of types. As Milton is associated with Lawes, John Dryden (1631–1690) is associated with Purcell—they created works of dramatic integrity, such as *King Arthur* (1691). Dryden defined opera in a Preface in 1685: "An Opera is a poetic tale, or fiction, represented by vocal and instrumental music, adorned with scenes, machines, and dancing." [11] Shortly afterward, in 1690, Purcell wrote of the musician's share in opera: "Musick is the exaltation of poetry. Both of them may excell apart, but surely they are most excellent when they are joyn'd, because

[11] Eric Blom (ed.), *The Music Lover's Miscellany*, London: Gollancz, 1935, p. 442.

nothing is then wanting to either of their proportions; for thus they appear like wit and beauty in the same person." [12]

The British musical art maintained its national integrity until the end of the seventeenth century, when the Italian craze displaced the native style; then opera was sung in Italian, and the English idiom was absorbed or superseded. Boys in the northern countries maintained their adolescent treble much longer than those in Italy and Spain; Italian boys' voices broke at twelve or thirteen, but many English boys could still sing soprano at eighteen. Thus the British could train a boy and use him as a seasoned treble for five or more years. One result was that the British did not cultivate the castrato voice, so the castrati had to be imported from Italy, which meant also importing the entire bel canto literature and tradition.

Henry Purcell was aware of the Italian Baroque influence but felt that music was coming into its own as an eclectic art. "Musick is yet but in its Nonage," he wrote, "a forward Child, which gives hope of what it may be hereafter *in England*, when the Masters of it shall find more Encouragement. 'Tis now learning Italian, which is its best Master, and studying a little of the *French* Air to give it somewhat more of Gayety and Fashion." [13] Purcell's *Dido and Aeneas* was Baroque and international in its central concern with recitativo, aria, instrumental pieces, and French dances, staged with imaginative use of scene, costume, and machinery. But it also was English, with Purcell's exquisite subtlety in setting English text and his ability to use the forms and techniques of his heritage to illuminate the emotional realities, which were so often obscured by the familiarity of those techniques. The best known aria from *Dido and Aeneas* is Dido's Lament at the departure of Aeneas.[14]

The *Lamento* was an Italian convention. The descending chromatic bass, particularly as a constantly repeated figure—*basso ostinato* in Italian or *ground* in English—and characteristically in triple time, was international but so beloved of the English (who translated the *lamento* as *lament*) that it is tempting to call the ground a national technique. Dido's Lament is not really an example of the divisions on a ground that appeared so often in English—the divisions were sets of variations. The repetitions in the Lament, necessary to the beautifully contained sorrow, kept it from being a systematic set of "diversifications" but enabled it to enter the realm of the truly theatrical.

With Purcell's death, England lost its musical momentum. Roger North described Purcell admirably in a moving tribute: "The Orfeus Britannicus Mr H. Purcell, who unhappily began to shew his great skill before the

[12] *Ibid.*, p. 105f.

[13] A. K. Holland, *Henry Purcell*, Baltimore: Penguin, 1948, p. 61f.

[14] Robert Stevenson, *Music before the Classic Era*, New York: St Martin's, 1958, pp. 95–96, 198–199; Archibald T. Davison and Willi Apel, *Historical Anthology of Music*, vol. 2, *Baroque, Rococo, and Pre-Classical Music*, Cambridge, Mass.: Harvard, 1956, pp. 144–145.

reforme of musick *al' Italliana,* and while he was warm in the persuit of it, dyed; but a greater musicall genius England never had." [15]

GERMAN MUSIC
IN THE SEVENTEENTH CENTURY

All aspects of German life had suffered in the Thirty Years' War (1618–1648); it left the already divided German States devastated by the traffic of soldiers and by the death of eight million of their population of eighteen million. The land was wasted, the treasuries depleted, and the people exhausted.

The division of Germany is difficult to imagine. At the end of the century, about three hundred small units made up the German-speaking states. Their courts imitated the French magnificence of Louis XIV, but the German courts were miniatures, and their artistic displays could not match the gala spectaculars at Versailles. Instead of the giant splendors of the French, the small courts produced masquerades and costume dances. The cities were more truly German than the courts. While the courts were copying France, the cities, and particularly the churches, were developing a genuinely German musical art.

Organ Music

The church music director was in a position of musical leadership in seventeenth-century Germany. He was generally in charge of both church and civic music and was the town music teacher. Church music was based on the organ and choir and civic music was based on the wind band, which performed in processions, from the towers of churches, and in town halls. Neither the organ (as a solo instrument) nor the wind band used the continuo.

The organ served the function of enhancing the religious experience—introducing the service and preluding (improvising) on the chorales of the service. Hymnals customarily contained only the hymns (poems) or the hymns plus the tunes, and the organist was expected to harmonize the tunes himself. The notation, often without measure bars and always without added harmonic suggestion, left the tunes open, so the creative drive of German musicians found a particular fruition in chorale-based composition.

At their simplest, these compositions were direct harmonizations, probably to teach the tunes or to support the congregation's singing. But they served also as a musical commentary on the hymns and, at their best, provided direction for meditation. Chorale tunes were still being written throughout the seventeenth century and into the eighteenth, when the approximately five thousand tunes began to be standardized and put into regular meters.

The chorale prelude was a characteristically German fruition, one in which the imagination could explore any avenue of presentation. Tunes

[15] Wilson, *op. cit.,* p. 307.

Chamber organ. Although this sketch of the organ face dates from the middle of the eighteenth century, it shows a seventeenth-century organ style. The top of the console is shown at the bottom of the photograph. (Courtesy of the University of Michigan Library, the Stellfeld Purchase. Photo by R. E. Kalmbach.)

were divided, set polyphonically, treated fugally, used in the bass, written as canons, used as a basis for variations, fragmented in a fantasia, or treated in any other way a composer could think of, in a remarkable interaction between the techniques known to the organists and the melodies familiar to them and their congregations. The chorale prelude came to a climax in the works of Diedrich Buxtehude and Johann Pachelbel.

Organists also continued to use the old polyphonic forms, notably the toccata, fantasia, and fugue. The toccata and fantasia expanded into multi-section works, and the fugue became a tonal structure. Although basically these were Renaissance forms, Baroque composers saw them anew within the concept of key tonality. In addition, they paired contrasting movements, generally one free and one learned, both in the same tone. The pairing of movements achieved contrast of texture and type, afforded new musical meanings through juxtaposition, and fostered an increasingly idiomatic technique. The prelude and fugue and the toccata and fugue can well represent the late seventeenth-century development. Buxtehude and his contemporaries arrived at a balance of elements that represent the German Baroque ideal in its first flowering.

The Cantors (music directors) of the German churches turned to the cantata as the harbinger of the new music. Instrumentalists were already included on the church rolls, and singers were eager to try the Italian innovations. The stile nuovo was adapted to the needs of the German churches. The cantata became a choral form, utilizing the forces available in the churches—choir, soloists, organ (or harpsichord, or both), and instruments.

The Cantata

In the Baroque manner, the verses of text became separate movements—recitativo, solo aria, duo or trio, chorus (singing a chorale or a free chorus), and instrumental ritornello—providing the contrasts that nourished Baroque forms. The congregation often joined in singing the chorales.

As in Italy, the cantata grew from a single aria for solo with basso continuo. The spiritual song (in German, *Geistliches Lied*) had easily adopted the basso continuo. Heinrich Schütz studied in Italy, and the techniques he brought back contained the various traditions he had learned—monody, traditional polyphony (both sacred and secular), plainchant, polychoral style, and the multiconsort sacred concerto form. His voluminous output juxtaposed styles and textures in splendid array. The *Passion according to St. John* (1666), for voices only, juxtaposed the plainsong of the historicus and of Christ, with madrigal-like settings for the *turbo* (crowd) and slower harmonic choir pieces to interpolate statements of faith or response. His *Christmas Oratorio* used recitativo and aria, with an instrumental contingent built on the basso continuo. Selected instruments in the manner of the late Renaissance band—recorders for the shepherds, viols for the angels, trombones for the priests—aided the symbolism of the Christmas story.

Other composers continued in the new style, translating Italian practice into German usage; many mid-century titles show a mixture of Italian and German terms. Adam Krieger's work is representative. The full title of the *Arien* was *Arien von einer, zwey, und drey Vokal-Stimmen benebenst ihren Ritornellen auff zwey Violinen und einen Violon samt dem Basso continuo* (Airs for One, Two, and Three Vocal Parts together with Their Ritornelli with Two Violins and a Bass [Viol] with Basso Continuo). In the title, Krieger took pains to explain the work with details that a composer in an established style would find unnecessary. The Italian terms *aria, ritornello,* and *basso continuo* appear in the title, but the first two were given German endings.

By the end of the century, the cantata had developed its multi-instrument form and had fully absorbed the modern style. The form assumed a central position in the music of the Lutheran church. A cantata, often fifteen or twenty minutes in length, was performed at the midpoint of the Lutheran service, after the reading of the Gospel and just before the sermon.

Lute and Harpsichord Music

The German courts found the lute particularly congenial to their social, artistic, and financial needs. Most courts were too small to support a band of violins, but they could maintain a court lutenist and singer and a chapel organist. The lutenist was usually a product of the French school, and French lute tablature soon supplanted German tablature in most of the German states.

Lutenists provided lute songs, both spiritual and secular, and lute suites, many of them demanding considerable virtuosity. The solo lute suite, which was based on the French model, sometimes opened with an improvisatory prelude and basically comprised a group of dances in the two-section dance form.

Procession in Brussels, by Denis van Alsloot, c. 1615, detail showing a consort of "high music." The polyphonic canzona was long maintained in processional and tower music, where a basso continuo was impossible. The group illustrated, which is composed of bombardes, cornetts, and trombone, was conservative; at the end of the seventeenth century, cornetts were still in use and trumpets had been introduced. (Courtesy of Ampliaciones y Reproducciones MAS.)

The keyboard suite fared less well in the German states until the end of the seventeenth century. Its chief German practitioner in the middle of the century was Johann Froberger, an international rather than a German musical figure. His suites were important to the coming German tradition, but they were not published until the last decade of the century, a generation after his death, and therefore influenced only the eighteenth-century German composers. The Froberger suites were generally in four movements—allemande, gigue, courante, and sarabande or allemande, courante, gigue, and sarabande. The free opening prelude was omitted by Froberger but was retained by many other composers. By the end of the century, considerations of effect led performers to prefer ending with the gigue, which was lively and could create a brilliant finale.

The German suite at the beginning of the eighteenth century was likely to have seven or eight movements. Typically it began with a prelude, toccata, or other free movement and continued with an allemande, courante, sarabande, and gigue; optional movements (gavotte, bourée, minuet, etc.) were inserted before the sarabande or, most typically, before the gigue. Ending with the gigue was so well established by the last decade of the seventeenth century that Froberger's suites, all of which had ended with the sarabande, were published with the gigues at the end. The volume published in France in 1693 was annotated *mis en meilleur ordre* (set into better order).

Opera

With few exceptions, the musical theater in the German states was Italian opera or French ballet, imported or written by Italian and French composers at German courts. The Hamburg public opera house opened in 1678 and soon became the center of opera in Germany. The Italian term *dramma per musica* was translated as *Singspiel* (literally a sing[ing] play or drama; plural, *Singspiele*), and the opera company's corps of native German composers was open to both Italian and French influences. The culminating composer of German opera was Reinhard Keiser, an eclectic who combined Italian recitativo and aria, German Lied, and French overture and dance pieces in a work with a German text. His Singspiel *Croesus* (1711, revised version 1730) was typical of his art, which a critic, writing at the time of Keiser's death, characterized as having "surprising inexhaustibility of invention." [16]

THEORY

As in all periods in which new sounds and new musical aims are defined, in the seventeenth century composers were thinking about the new with the vocabulary of the old. The Guidonian system—the gamut—was still being taught as the basic vocabulary for the performer, meters were being taught as rhythmic modes, and metric time values were being taught as proportions.

The opening decades of the seventeenth century had seen the overlapping of old and new concepts in virtually all areas. The philosophy of the essential harmony of opposing pulls was still accepted. John Donne (1573–1631) spoke of the "subtle knot that makes us man," [17] and John Milton stated that the purpose of education was to make men "Christian and musical." [18]

In the musical art, the first half of the seventeenth century marked the culmination of the development of Medieval-Renaissance musical materials and techniques. But by the middle of the seventeenth century, the stile nuovo had proposed a new concept of materials, and the cycle was beginning anew. The sciences of mathematics and acoustics were called on to explain (and justify) the new materials.

Speculative Theory

Two important theorists—Marin Mersenne (1588–1648) and Athanasius Kircher (1602–1680)—represented musical thought during the long transition period between the Renaissance and Baroque eras. Both men were priests and philosopher-scientists who regarded music as one important science among others. Both believed in the assumption that the harmony of music was a reflection of the higher harmonies and thus a superior means of approaching knowledge in the inclusive sense. Mersenne, a French Franciscan who lived in Paris and held court for many of the prominent intellectuals of his time, was concerned with theological and astronomical analogies and, through these, with acoustics. Kircher, a German Jesuit, was

[16] Johann Mattheson, quoted in *Histoire de la musique. 1. Des origines à Jean-Sébastien Bach, Encyclopédie de la Pléiade*, Paris: Librairie Gallimard, 1960, p. 1804.
[17] John Donne, *The Essay on Man.*
[18] John Milton, *Paradise Lost.*

a practical naturalist, known as an archeologist and collector for the *gabinetti* (small museums) that were characteristic of the century; his approach was more empirical.

Mersenne's *Harmonie Universelle* (Universal Harmony) was published in various forms between 1627 and 1648; the definitive two-volume version appeared in French in 1636–1637. Kircher's *Musurgia Universalis* (Universal Art) was also a two-volume work, published in Latin in 1650. Both works dealt only partly with music but have proved very useful to modern musical scholarship because of their authors' interest in musical instruments. Consistent with the passion for measurement so important in that day, the authors included detailed studies of the instruments plus accurate drawings.

El Oido (*Hearing*), by Pieter Brueghel (the Younger), c. 1620, detail. This painting displays the love of diversity in the early Baroque; it includes a lute, viols, and a cello, as well as a harpsichord, drum, trombone, shawms, cornett, and a kit (dance master's fiddle—beneath the lute). In the upper left, a consort of singers and instrumentalists gathers around a table. (Courtesy of Ampliaciones y Reproducciones MAS.)

Seventeenth-century speculation was a charming mosaic of ancient, Medieval, Renaissance, and Baroque concepts, juxtaposed generally through means of analogy. When Mersenne spoke of diatonic, chromatic, and enharmonic melodic categories, he related them to the Father, the Son, and the Holy Ghost and incorporated classical Greek and Christian theological ideas in his explanation. Diatonic melody was like the Father, for it contained the other two (through transposition of the hexachord); chromatic melody, like the Son, was a balance of extremes that Mersenne equated with wisdom; and the enharmonic was like the Holy Ghost in its rational and suprarational qualities. But the meaning of these terms was technical—diatonic referred to tone or key, chromatic to borrowed notes outside the tone, and enharmonic to progressions exhibiting false relations.

The series of partials was viewed as a rational progression from the fundamental through the audible (lower) partials to the inaudible (higher) partials. By analogy, the fundamental was like the earth, the audible partials like man, and the inaudible partials like the angels. Such an analogy had a practical application—theorists could use it to explain why the fundamental, though generative, was seldom used on brass instruments (on which it sounded slowly or not at all), why the music that men most enjoyed centered in the first twelve partials, and why the higher partials, though inaudible to man, had a considerable influence on the quality and beauty of the sound.

More important in practical terms was Mersenne's basic statement that "sound is the principal stuff of music. . . . Motivation of sounds with each other, and the manner of using them in songs and in all kinds of compositions, is the formal means of music." [19] The direct motivation of tone was of primary importance; the idea of forward motivation residing in tones themselves was a new one, replacing the concept of text as being basic to form.

Practical Theory

It took a long time—well over a century—to translate the new concept into practical materials. The organist-composer-theorist Guillaume-Gabriel Nivers (1632–1714) published his *Traité de la Composition de Musique* (Treatise on Composing Music) in 1667; it was reprinted in 1688, 1694, and 1712 in Paris, published in 1697 in Amsterdam, and copied by other theorists both in France and abroad. A modernist, Nivers began by saying that "the true rules of composition are doubtlessly none other than those which are generally practiced by all the excellent masters of this century." [20]

Nivers listed the tonal materials of music as twelve pitches, each with its duplication in all registers—C, C♯, D, E♭, E, F, F♯, G, G♯, A, B♭, and B♮. (The B♭ was still printed—even by Brossard and Walther—with a round ♭.) A few theorists expanded the number to thirteen, to include

[19] Warren Dwight Allen, *Philosophies of Music History*, New York: American Book, 1939, p. 18.
[20] Albert Cohen (trans. and ed.), *Guillaume-Gabriel Nivers: Treatise on the Composition of Music*, New York: Institute of Mediaeval Music, 1961, p. 4.

A♭, and the other enharmonics were known and were available by transposition.

All intervals were built with whole tones and semitones. The semitone was either major or minor (retaining but redefining the old terminology), the major spanning two staff degrees (such as F♯–G) and the minor but one (G–G♯). The whole tone could be "true" or "false"; a true whole tone was a second divided into one major and one minor semitone (F♯–G♯, C–D, etc.), and a false whole tone was two major semitones (G♯–B♭). In speaking of a whole tone, one assumed it to be true; in speaking of a semitone, one assumed it to be major.

All other intervals were computed by their constituent whole tones and semitones. The perfect fifth, for example, comprised three whole tones and one semitone, e.g., C–G was C–D–E–F♯–G. Distinction was made between the augmented fourth (three whole tones) and the diminished fifth (two whole tones and two semitones)—for example, between B♭–(C–D–)E and E–(F♯–G♯–A–)B♭, the latter of which could not be three whole tones because the whole tone G♯–B♭ was false.

Such false intervals as the augmented second, diminished third, and diminished fourth, though banned from interval building, were used in composition. "On certain extraordinary occasions, the ear tolerates them agreeably, and in this manner all the most excellent masters practice all the false relations, of which the use or the avoidance on such occasions depends purely and simply on the ear and on the good taste of the composer." [21] Further, Nivers encouraged melodic progressions of false intervals or of two consecutive leaps spanning a false interval. He questioned the narrow Renaissance view on this: "Tell us, oh philosopher of olden times, on what ground have you absolutely prohibited the use of two consecutive major or minor thirds [e.g., C–E–G♯ or E–G–B♭] . . . .?" [22]

Tone

Nivers used his twelve pitches in twelve *tones* or *modes* (in a new sense), each with a final, mediant, and dominant that he considered different from the final and dominant of the "modes of former times." [23] These tones were *d* minor, *g* minor, *a* minor, *e* minor, C major, F major, D major, and G major; the *e* minor tone was irregular, having certain characteristics of *a* minor and perpetuating the exceptional nature of the cadence to E, which was already familiar from Phrygian usage. Tone was both key center and a characteristic mediant (major or minor).

The cadence was defined as "a certain melodic conclusion which occurs when the parts have come to rest and end on a chord which the ear appears to expect in a natural way." [24] This was the typical Baroque dominant-final cadence, called *authentic* or *perfect*. The concept of expectation of a final,

[21] *Ibid.*, p. 23.
[22] *Ibid.*, p. 4.
[23] *Ibid.*, p. 19.
[24] *Ibid.*, p. 23.

in which the entire movement centered, was basic to the idea of tone. The term *tone* would produce the concept of *key tonality* [25] as a system exploiting that expectation. Nivers also described *modulation*, which was still a modernism.

> After having constructed several cadences essential to the Tone, one can build others and endeavor to obtain a beautiful melody on borrowed notes and notes foreign to the Tone (for example, if one passes from a flat to a natural, and vice versa), which is called "Leaving the Mode." But it is necessary to take heed to leave at an opportune moment and to return in good time. This is practiced only among the learned.[26]

The rules of composition centered in the linear idea, which Nivers termed the *subject*. "A subject is a tune, created by the force of the imagination, which conforms to one of the Modes and is for one part, from which afterwards all the other parts are composed." [27] The subject was most often in the treble, but wherever it was, "one must begin to compose the remaining parts always with the Bass, which is the foundation and the basis for all composition." [28] The discipline of learning to compose had seven steps, the first six of which concerned the subject and the bass. The seventh was *fugue*, the "step of perfection"; [29] it comprised imitative entries over a harmonic progression. The old harmonic (1–5–8) and arithmetic (1–4–8 or, in tonal terms, 5–1–5) divisions of the octave were invoked to keep the imitation within one tone. The fifth C–G (1–5), for example, was to be imitated by the fourth G–C (5–8) to complete the tonal definition of C, rather than by G–D, which would be "Leaving the Mode." [30]

Subject

Interestingly, Nivers did not discuss the practice of the basso continuo. Although his statement about the essential Bass is very clear, the Italian technique was not yet firmly established in France. By the end of the century, however, the practice was common throughout Europe.

Figured Bass

Figured-bass technique held that the bass note was always 1; an unfigured note was assumed to call for a fifth and a third above. Order and register were not important; an unfigured G would call for a D and either B or B♭, whichever the signature indicated. The figure 6 displaced the 5, and the figure 4 displaced the 3. Other figures were added to the 5 and 3; one of these was 7, which displaced neither the 5 nor 3 but was added to them.

Alterations could be demanded by such designations as ♭6 or ♯7— the flat or sharp alone indicated a raised or a lowered third. The use of flat and sharp as relative signs to indicate raising and lowering rather than abso-

---

[25] I am indebted to Robert Donington for the phrase "key tonality."
[26] Cohen, *op. cit.*, p. 24.
[27] *Ibid.*, p. 17.
[28] *Ibid.*, p. 20.
[29] *Ibid.*, p. 25.
[30] *Ibid.*, pp. 42–43.

lute tones made the natural sign unnecessary. To change a *B♭* to a *B♮*, the sharp sign was used, that is, the *B♭* was sharpened, raised, by a minor semitone. The natural sign was used only occasionally, generally to cancel a previous alteration.

Voice leadings were suggested by consecutive numbers. A delay (suspension) from the fourth above the bass to the third above was indicated by 4–3; 7–6 was a similar progression, different from the 7 alone.

A chord was conceived as a group of notes, and consonance and dissonance were accepted as polarities almost in the Medieval sense. Brossard defined harmony as follows.

Harmony

> In Music it is that which results from the union of several Pitches heard all together. In such manner that those which are Dissonant, very far from smothering the Consonances or hindering their sweetness and good effect, serve on the contrary to make them all the more sensitive and brilliant, through the happy and wise opposition of these two contraries.[31]

The concept of the need for dissonance was old—what was new was the definition of dissonance. By the end of the seventeenth century, the dissonant note was defined as one that was not a member of the chord with which it was sounded. Embellishing tones were gradually given the same definition, that is, as nonchord or nonessential tones. Such a view was based in the secure definition of an underlying harmonic progression as being essential to the fabric of music.

Chord, composition, and progression were all part of the bass and its motivating effect. The bass note defined the chord as it had in the Renaissance. The note *B♭*, for instance, was the fundamental tone of any chord built from it, the essential chords being a *B♭* chord of the fifth (unfigured), a *B♭* chord of the sixth (figured 6, the 6 displacing the 5 but not disturbing the 3), and a *B♭* chord of the seventh (figured 7, the 7 added to the 5 and 3). The bass melody defined the harmonic progression and motivated the form of the music, with particular reference to the tone. The bass notes were related to function within the tone, but the chords built on them were not separately defined. Thus *B♭* as the mediant in g minor served, in the bass, to motivate the progression toward *C* or *D*, the lower or upper dominant. Whether a chord of the fifth, sixth, or seventh (or the first two at once, figured ⁶₅) was built on this tone was immaterial—it was still a *B♭* chord and was defined by the mediant function of the bass.

The functional aspects of Baroque form were carried out by means of the basso continuo. Bass functions were of three main types—static, active, and cadencing. The static bass reflected the Baroque enjoyment of the reality of the tone. It had three aspects—the bass tonic note, the rhythmic motivation in some pattern incorporating the beat and meter, and the

---

[31] Brossard, *op. cit.*, under the entry "Harmonie."

exploration of the main notes of the tone by the other instruments above the bass. The most characteristic kinds of subjects were the trumpet tune and the interlocking imitation, most effective when the answering instruments were spatially separated. This static bass, directly reveling in the tone, tempo, and instrumental diversity, comprised a virtual statement of the musical Baroque essence of being.

The active bass reflected the Baroque enjoyment of chord types and bass functions. It included several types. Progressions from the tonic to the upper or lower dominant and back (1–5–1 or 1–4–1) in chords of the fifth were the simplest. More active was the melodic bass incorporating mediant tones (upper and lower), supertonic, Neapolitan, subtonic, leading tone, and leading tone of the dominant. The active bass, when in constant eighth-note motion (as it often was), generally used passing tones as well. Other active basses used the rhythm of the subject in imitative or even fugal manner. The step sequence could appear in an active bass within the tone. Finally, the active bass might decorate an otherwise static line with runs, octave leaps, or whatever the imagination of the composer led to.

Leaving the tone would most probably be preceded by a circle sequence. This was generally couched in slow harmonic motion, in a spacious, even majestic striding around the circle of fifths with chords of the fifth or seventh (including the one diminished fifth). The step sequence could also be used to leave the tone, most frequently through a series of leading tone–tonic pairs in a chromatic progression. And finally, the active bass types included occasional modulatory bases that presented a subject and effected a modulation; this was done by introducing a new leading tone in a free pattern, most often in conjunction with the other member of the tritone of the new key.

The cadencing bass reflected the Baroque enjoyment of suspensive arrival. The traditional formula was still standard for final cadences; it incorporated a descent from the supertonic to tonic in the solo line, over a bass of dominant to tonic, with a 4–3 suspension over the dominant tone— a suspension of the leading tone in one of the inner voices. The open cadence on the dominant was also common. Its function was twofold—at the end of a slow movement to heighten the expectation of an ensuing allegro and, internally, to serve as a less conclusive cadence, perhaps at the end of a solo section anticipating the entrance of a ritornello. The first of these functions could be accomplished by a simple bass descent from tonic to dominant, through either major or minor forms of the intermediate notes—and sometimes by a chromatic line incorporating both forms. This was sometimes called a Phrygian cadence. Other cadences to the dominant were variously approached, without formula. Final cadences would have been decorated as a matter of course. The cadential $^6_4$, a double suspension of the dominant, appeared only occasionally in notation, but it may have been more common in practice.

Baroque harmonic theory assumed the necessity of meter, for the function of the bass was dependent on unequivocal rhythmic focus and clarity. Whether the upper parts duplicated or departed from the strongly metrical bass, they derived from it, for a counterrhythm is dependent on the rhythm it counters. The hemiola disappeared from the Baroque rhythmic fabric, save for the large hemiola which survived as a device at the cadence in triple meter. The cadential ♩ ♩ | ♩ ♩ was really a switch from ♩ ♩ ♩ to ♩ ♩ ♩, a true change of proportion; the late seventeenth-century practice of notating it ♩ ♩ ♩ or as a single $\frac{3}{2}$ measure in a $\frac{3}{4}$ context (without change in signature) clarified the rhythmic intention. This functioned as a reining in, a *ritard*, far different from a *syncope* ♩ ♩ | ♩ ♩ |, which was an offbeat counteraccent, generally a dissonance; the syncope was given both dynamic and agogic stress.

Meter

As might be expected in an age of measurement, both time and pitch were being subjected to scientific examination. The theorist Etienne Loulié (c. 1650–1702) invented both a chronometer (metronome) and a sonometer; both were intended for measuring the speed of the beat (particularly for dances) and for tuning the harpsichord. In addition, the French physicist Joseph Sauveur (1653–1716) discovered a means of measuring absolute pitches; his discovery was presented to the Académie des Sciences in 1700 by the writer Fontenelle (1657–1757!), who read the paper for Sauveur, a deaf-mute.[32] Sauveur also wrote about tempered tuning, which was under discussion everywhere. The increasing use of modulation had made temperament a lively issue—equal temperament would become the inevitable solution.

Machines

The acoustical theory of tone quality was not given attention in the Baroque era. The instruments of measurement could define the mathematics of interval relationships, but the tonal spectrum of the oscilloscope would have to await another era. Although quality was of interest to the performer and of course to audiences, musical theory ignored the concept of quality for the next two and a half centuries, an omission that would be as crucial to the theory of key tonality as any factor it was to include. Baroque audiences were moved—even transported—by tone quality itself, but a physical analysis of tonal beauty still lay in the domain of the angels or the inaudible partials that the angels symbolized.

Tone Quality

[32] Sauveur's principle was simple enough. It was based on the traditional mathematical study of interval proportions. Knowing that the difference between a minor and a major third was 24:25, he set up organ pipes for E♭, G♭, and G♮. The latter two vibrated as 24:25, with each twenty-fourth cycle of the G♭ coinciding with each twenty-fifth cycle of the G♮ as a sudden loudness, which he called a *beat*. When precisely four beats occurred in one second, the G♮, with twenty-five vibrations to the beat, could be measured at exactly 100 vibrations per second. Sauveur's method of determining exact frequency opened the door to a new scientific era in acoustics.

A keyboard, from a text of the early eighteenth century. Tuning problems generally centered around the G♯-A♭ key, which was often left as a variable to be tuned between pieces, according to the intonation demanded. Such a note was called the *howler* or *wolf*. On the keyboard illustrated, the solution was to tune the G♯, omit the A♭, and have the howler on D♯-E♭, with a double key in the center register to afford both pitches in that one octave. In addition, double keys appear in the lowest register, providing a variant of the "short octave"; this was generally a diatonic octave in the space of a fifth that was created by using the black keys. The use of ♮ and ♭ for B and B♭ is a Guidonian residue. (Courtesy of the University of Michigan Library. Photo by R. E. Kalmbach.)

PERFORMANCE

Two basic types of performance—corporate and solo—were important in the Baroque period, and two styles of music were needed to fulfill them. A clear, sensitive style was required in corporate performances and a virtuoso, interpretive style was desired in the soloist.

In a corporate performance, each performer was one entity of the total. A work for twelve instruments, for example, could create a dynamic shape by using a few, then several, then all the players. Whether the forces were small, as in a trio sonata, or large, as in an oratorio or a grand motet, the actuality of the music lay to a large extent in the management of those forces, a specification of action and interaction that was at the same time a precise control of dynamic level. Such works demanded a simple, straightforward style of performance that would delineate separate lines and enable the scheme of interaction to become manifest with clarity and verve.

The beat was a basic excitement of Baroque music. Because it was essential and motivating, a right tempo was vital. The beat informed all other aspects of the work—even an adagio had this motivation, which was a matter of impulse rather than speed. The old style had proportioned each line to a tactus, a stable coordinating beat around which the polyphonic lines accommodated themselves. The Baroque style reversed this, changing the beat itself, a procedure that must have astounded audiences at first.

312

Surface texture was the second vital element in Baroque corporate performance. Clarity was attained through a light, nonlegato attack. The mid-century theorist Johann Joachim Quantz told the violinist to use "short and articulated" bow strokes.[33] He stated that fast tempos "require a lively, very light, nicely detached, and very short bow stroke," whereas a "slow and melancholy piece . . . requires the greatest moderation of tone, the longest, most tranquil, and [more sustained] bow-strike." [34] Wind players needed to use "lively tonguing," [35] particularly for fast notes. Singing required a separate impulse for each note.

Phrasing, the shaping of a line as a series of units, was the third vital element of Baroque corporate performance. The motivic unit, the subject, was to be characteristic and recognizable. "If in an Allegro the principal subject frequently recurs it must always be clearly differentiated in its execution." [36]

The solo keyboard player had the same ideals, because organists and harpsichordists dealt with combined forces. The larger instruments were able to command more than one manual and a number of stops and thus could be used for corporate performances. But the harpsichordist of the basso continuo, one of a group, was no soloist. According to Quantz, he was to remember that the outer lines should predominate and that the harmonic middle part, which he provided, "should be heard least of all." [37] Yet balance was vital, so his "manner of playing is most important" [38]—he was to use the idiom of his instrumental technique in realizing the bass. "Passages marked Piano on the instrument may be improved by moderating the touch, and by decreasing the number of parts, and those marked Forte by strengthening the touch, and by increasing the number of parts in both hands." [39] But the harpsichordist must never destroy the essential polarity or compete with the soloists. "How can a composition sound well if the principal parts are drowned out and suppressed by the bass or even the middle parts?" [40]

Soloists, particularly singers and violinists, worked in the same basic technique as did the members of a performing group but expanded it by virtuosity and rhetoric or expression. The virtuoso aspect of performance was related to the expanded technical competence that gave the soloist greater dexterity, speed, range, or control than other performers. He was not accommodating himself to the others but was being accommodated by them, and he was free to demonstrate his skill through the addition of embellishment and expression.

[33] Quoted in Edward R. Reilly (trans. and ed.), *J. J. Quantz on Playing the Flute,* London: Faber, 1966, p. 230f.
[34] *Ibid.,* p. 231.
[35] *Ibid.,* p. 133.
[36] *Ibid.*
[37] *Ibid.,* p. 214.
[38] *Ibid.,* p. 253.
[39] *Ibid.*
[40] *Ibid.,* p. 214.

In notation, French music seems to have been more highly embellished than the Italian, but Quantz pointed out that Italians omitted embellishments from the notation. "Almost no one who devotes himself to the study of music, particularly outside France, is content to perform only the essential graces; the majority feel moved to invent variations or extempore embellishments." [41] Such embellishments were the first characteristic of expression, the infusing of music with moods or *passions*. "Since music should now rouse the passions, now still them again, the utility and necessity of these graces in a plain and unadorned melody is self-evident." [42]

The longer embellishment, a parenthetical solo improvisation during a *fermata* (pause) in the accompaniment, was called a *cadenza* because of its original appearance at the cadence. The effectiveness of the cadenza lay in its simultaneous italicizing of both the technical and expressive elements in a spontaneous climax that transcended the intellectual aspects of skill. "Because of the necessity of speedy invention, cadenzas require more fluency of imagination than erudition. Their greatest beauty lies in that, as something unexpected, they should astonish the listener in a fresh and striking manner and, at the same time, impel to the highest pitch the agitation of the passions." [43]

Occasional slurring and tonguing were also devices of expression. The performer was taught to connect appoggiaturas to their resolutions and to introduce "slurred and close intervals" [44] (i.e., conjunct motion) for tenderness in slow pieces. Couplet slurs were becoming more important, a lively part of the slurring, tonguing, and bowing, salient elements of a "good execution" which was "indispensable." [45]

Expression was not a matter of occasional embellishment only, but had to pervade an entire movement. "Good execution must be *expressive*, and *appropriate to each passion that one encounters*. In the Allegro, and in all the gay pieces of this type, liveliness must rule, but in the Adagio, and pieces of this character, delicacy must prevail." [46] The allegro and adagio types, in spite of variant moods, were basic and were useful in presenting the summary of performing techniques. "[Expressive] passages in the Adagio must not be attacked too rudely with the stroke of the tongue and bow, and on the other hand joyful and distinguished [characteristic] ideas in the Allegro must not be dragged, slurred, or attacked too gently." [47]

A movement's characterizing mood was most easily determined by its tempo mark but could also be discerned by its use of note values and intervals, by its tone, and by its use of dissonance. Short note values, leaps, the major

[41] *Ibid.*, p. 136.
[42] *Ibid.*, p. 98.
[43] *Ibid.*, p. 186.
[44] *Ibid.*, p. 125.
[45] *Ibid.*, p. 121.
[46] *Ibid.*, p. 124.
[47] *Ibid.*, p. 125.

keys, and consonance were associated with the allegro; longer note values, conjunct motion, minor keys, and telling dissonances were characteristic of the adagio.[48]

The role of dissonance in Baroque style tends to be underrated. Embellishments that served to introduce and emphasize dissonance were savored as the most compelling of devices. Appoggiaturas were lingered over, always to at least one-half and more often to two-thirds or three-fourths of the note they embellished (though they were not precisely measured). Appoggiaturas, in turn, were given the added embellishments of vibrato and slurred resolution. Trills were always begun from the note above, even when repetition of that note was needed, and were defined as series of falling appoggiaturas, with the emphasis on the dissonant upper tone. Like all embellishments, trills were supposed to take on the character of the movement in which they occurred—slow in a slow piece and lively in a fast one—as part of the essential fabric. "The passions can be excited much more effectively with a few simple intervals, skillfully mingled with dissonances," Quantz wrote, "than with a host of motley figures." [49]

[48] *Ibid.*
[49] *Ibid.*, p. 186.

❧ Some Composers of the Seventeenth and Early Eighteenth Centuries

The new style of Italy was imported slowly into France, England, and Germany by means of interaction. Italians visited in the north, and the other nationals studied in Italy and returned to their homelands to incorporate elements of the new style into their own traditions. Thus the various national styles were both unified and individual, resulting in one of the most fascinating eras of style counterpoint in the history of music.

France

JACQUES CHAMPION DE CHAMBONNIÈRES (1602–1672) was a French harpsichordist to Louis XIV. His grandfather had been harpsichordist to Louis XIII and his father an organist who succeeded to that post. Chambonnières was wealthy, leading a life of musical ease and prominence. He danced in court ballets, directed his own private concert series, and emulated the life of the nobility. His playing, improvising, and composing were legendary, and his harpsichord works (of which few survive) were still selling in 1750—an unprecedented tribute. He was famous also as a teacher and was the virtual founder of the great French harpsichord school.

ANTOINE AND ETIENNE MOULINIÉ (dates unknown) were Gascon brothers who were singers, dancers, and composers at the royal court. Antoine, the elder, served as chamber musician from 1619 to 1655, when he was killed in an accident. He brought Etienne to Paris, and they both appeared in court ballets, in which Antoine particularly was esteemed as bass singer and composer. Etienne was more prolific, publishing five books of airs de cour and four of airs au luth, as well as a Requiem Mass (1636), some chansons spirituels, and a few pieces for viols. From

1628 to 1660, Etienne worked as singer, composer, and producer of concerts for Gaston d'Orleans, the King's brother. He organized a series of concerts in Paris in the 1650s that were (justly) famous.

JEAN-BAPTISTE LULLY (1632–1687) was an Italian-born violinist and entrepreneur; he came to France at the age of fourteen as a page. In 1652 he joined the household of the sixteen-year-old Louis XIV and became his companion in music and the dance; he remained high in royal favor. He first appeared in court ballets, then composed and produced them. In 1672, he was granted a monopoly for the production of French opera. He was imaginative, musical, well organized, and a good businessman who attained a sizable fortune for himself. His 22 ballets and 18 operas formed the basis of French musical theater, and his recitativo defined that idiom in the French tongue. He also composed religious choral works.

JEAN-HENRY D'ANGLEBERT (1628–1691) a Parisian harpsichordist and organist and a student of Chambonnières, was harpsichordist to Louis XIV and hence a most influential figure in French music. He published *Pièces de Clavecin* (including 60 works) in 1689. His son, JEAN-BAPTISTE-HENRY (1661–1747), was Lully's godson; he succeeded his father, by special agreement with the King, in 1674.

MARC-ANTOINE CHARPENTIER (c. 1636–1704), a French composer and music director, came from a family of painters and went to Rome to study art. There he became a music student, possibly of Carissimi, whose style he emulated during his long activity in France. Charpentier was a strong partisan of the "Italian taste," in contrast to the Italian-born Lully, who was equally determined to develop the "French taste." Charpentier worked for the Dauphin and for the Princesse de Guise, for whom he produced "continuous music" until her death in 1688. He was maître de musique at the Jesuit chapel, at the Sainte-Cha-

pelle, and for the duc d'Orléans. His output was large; it included secular entertainments (12 divertissements and about 70 instrumental pieces), theatrical works (16 operas, incidental music for Molière and Corneille, ballet music), and religious works (including 100 motets, 30 hymns, 32 anthems, over 40 Psalms, 12 Masses, 9 litanies, and 24 Latin oratorios, which he called *histoires sacrées*). He also wrote treatises on accompaniment and composition.

ANDRÉ DANICAN PHILIDOR (c. 1643–1730), called l'Aîné (the Elder), was a member of a great musical dynasty, a drummer and wind player (oboe, cromorne, and trumpet), and a composer of chamber and theater works. He became the librarian of the royal library in 1684, and his manuscripts comprise a treasury of French and Italian works. His son ANNE-HYACINTHE DANICAN PHILIDOR (died 1728) was an oboist, violinist, and composer and wrote flute sonatas, a Te Deum, and a few pastorale operas; he also founded the Concert spirituel in Paris in 1725. Another son (from a second marriage), FRANÇOIS-ANDRÉ (1726–1795), became a chess champion and popular theater composer.

MICHEL-RICHARD DELALANDE (1656–1726), an organist and composer, was connected with important church posts from 1678 and in 1683 was appointed to the Royal Chapel. He became the favorite composer of the middle-aged Louis XIV, for whom he produced 72 grands motets, the majority before 1700; these form the great body of his fame. He also wrote about 20 theater pieces and a small but important group of instrumental works, including concertos for trumpets and timpani and the famous *Symphonies pour les soupers du Roi*. One of the great composers of the Baroque, Delalande was held in esteem abroad as well as at home. His grands motets comprised a staple of the concerts in Paris until the revolution—a unique example of musical longevity before the nineteenth century.

FRANÇOIS COUPERIN (1668–1733), a harpsichordist and composer, was the most illustrious member of a great musical dynasty; he was called "the great" even in his own time. His uncle, LOUIS COUPERIN (1626–1661), a student of Chambonnières and one of the great organist-composers of his day, had established the family's reputation. François studied with his father and at the Royal Chapel, publishing two organ Masses in 1690 and in 1693 becoming an organist in the Royal Chapel. He was also the harpsichord teacher to the Dauphin. He introduced the Italian sonata into France (c. 1695) and contributed many works to the royal chamber music, including the 4 *Concerts Royaux* and the 10 concerts called *Les Goûts Réunis* (the styles united). Of delicate health, he renounced his official duties in 1723 but continued to compose. Besides the chamber music, he left over 30 vocal works (motets, cantatas). But it is for his 240 harpsichord pieces, which appeared in four books of pièces de clavecin (1713, 1717, 1722, 1730), that he is chiefly remembered. His *L'Art de Toucher le Clavecin* (The Art of Playing the Harpsichord, 1716) was an important text in his own day and in modern times comprises an important source of knowledge of Baroque practice.

England

JOHN JENKINS (1592–1678), a famous viol player, was chamber musician to both Charles I and Charles II, spending the period of the Commonwealth (1649–1660) in private service in Norfolk. He was a prolific composer, important especially for his consort music, which he was still composing late in life—121 of the fancies have been collected, some of them with two movements. In addition, he wrote a considerable number of suites and about 200 single dances, which he called *rants* or *ayres*. Most of the consort music was for five viols, in the Renaissance concept. Toward the end of his life, Jenkins turned to the new style, composing for violins and voices with basso continuo. His songs were included in many popular collections during his lifetime.

JOHN COPERARIO (c. 1575–1626), an English lutenist and viola da gamba player, was born John Cooper and changed his name when he studied in Italy. Master of music for Charles I, he was the chief proponent of the new Italian style, which he hoped would enlarge rather than supplant the English style. He wrote numerous songs and dances for court masques, contributed fancies and suites to the repertoire of the consort of viols, and authored *Rules How to Compose* (c. 1610). He was influential as a teacher. Miscellaneous works include lute songs, anthems, spiritual airs, and organ fantasies.

HENRY LAWES (1596–1662), a student of Coperario and a Gentleman of the Royal Chapel from 1626, was the most renowned of English vocal composers of his day. Poets praised his rhythmic sense and sought him for lyrical and theatrical collaboration. His publications included three volumes of *Ayres and Dialogues for 1, 2, and 3 Voices* (1653, 1655, 1658) and music for the masque *Comus* (text by Milton, 1633). He was prolific, producing a considerable number of Psalm paraphrases for voice and thorough bass (1637) and for three voices and thorough bass (1648), as well as several masques and numerous songs, which appeared in virtually every anthology of the time. He lost his post at court when Charles I was executed in 1649 but regained it in time to compose *Coronation Anthem* for Charles II in 1660.

MATTHEW LOCKE (c. 1630–1677), an English singer and composer, was particularly known for his theater music but was in fact a versatile man who wrote in many mediums and in both the old and new styles. He left polyphonic suites for three and four viols; airs and dances with basso continuo;

a series of pieces for six winds (cornetts and sacbuts), played at the coronation of Charles II (1660); a group of anthems; a considerable quantity of incidental music (he wrote part of the masque *Cupid and Death*, 1653); and *Melothesia, or Certain General Rules for Playing upon a Continued Bass* (1673), the first known English work on basso continuo.

JOHN BLOW (1649–1708), an organist and composer, was a member of the Royal Chapel from the restoration in 1660, an organist at Westminster Abbey, and then master of the choristers of Saint Paul's Cathedral. He left numerous songs, including a collection of 50, called *Amphion Anglicus* (1700); 110 anthems; 13 services; 14 large choral Psalms and odes; 4 suites for harpsichord; and a number of theater pieces. Of the latter, most are short contributions to collaborations, but he composed the entire *Masque for the Entertainment of the King: Venus and Adonis* (c. 1684), his most famous work.

HENRY PURCELL (c. 1659–1695) was the most illustrious of a great musical family and one of England's finest composers. The son of a Gentleman of the Royal Chapel, he himself was a Composer in Ordinary for the Chapel Orchestra in 1676, organist at Westminster Abbey in 1679, and at the Royal Chapel in 1681. His compositions were great in number and scope. His sacred music included anthems, services, and organ voluntaries, among others, and for the court he wrote 29 odes and welcome songs. For both court and public he wrote music for over fifty theater productions, from incidental music to a complete score, *Dido and Aeneas*, c. 1689. In addition, he left many songs and catches. His most famous publication was the *Orpheus Britannicus* (1698), two large volumes for one, two, and three voices with thorough bass. He was no less important for his instrumental works; these include 22 trio sonatas, a volume of *Choice Collection of Lessons for the Harpsichord or Spinet* (8 harpsichord suites), *Fantasies* (for three and four viols, 1680), a fantasia on one note, plus assorted Innomines, chaconnes, pavanes, etc.

The German States

HEINRICH SCHÜTZ (1585–1672) was an organist and composer who, after studying law, went to Venice where he studied with Giovanni Gabrieli from 1609–1612. When he returned, he brought Italian ideas northward. Centering in Germany (Dresden) and Denmark (Copenhagen), he produced a great body of compositions in which the polychoral style of Gabrieli, along with monodic innovations, was translated into the German language and Lutheran religion. His work has been called the foundation of the German Baroque. His compositions include Psalms (1619, for choirs and instruments and using the stile recitativo), oratorios, *Cantiones sacræ* (1625), *Geistliche Konzerte* and *Symphoniæ sacræ* (1628, 1636, 1639, 1647), and *Geistliche Gesänge* (1657). His opera *Dafne* (1627) is lost. In his seventies he composed a Christmas oratorio (*Historia der Geburt Jesu Christi*, 1664) and three *Passions* (1665–1666) and in his mid-eighties, the *Deutsches Magnificat* (1671), which returned to the polyphonic tradition of the double choir.

JOHANN CRÜGER (1598–1662) was a Prussian organist, composer, and theorist who studied at the Lutheran seminary at Wittenburg, turned to music, and after study and travel returned to accept the post of organist and Cantor at Saint Nicholas Church in Berlin. From this position, which he held for forty years (from 1622), he exercised a powerful influence on German Lutheran music. He published books on liturgical musical methods, and his music provided a foundation for chorales and geistliche Lieder, upon which German organ and choral music flourished. His most important work was the *Praxis Pietatis Melica* (Piety's Practice in Song), which was published in about forty editions between 1647 and 1736.

JOHANN JACOB FROBERGER (1616–1667) was an organist and composer, whose father and four brothers were chapel musicians at the court in Stuttgart. Froberger worked at the court in Vienna from 1631 to 1637, went to Rome to study with Frescobaldi until 1641, and then returned to the Viennese court. He later traveled to Brussels, London, and Paris (where he made a "triumphant" appearance in 1652) and returned to Vienna until 1657. Although he was one of the most famous organists in Europe, he did not publish his works. Two collections appeared after his death (1693 and 1696), including toccatas, canzone, and fantasie for organ and keyboard suites.

ADAM KRIEGER (1634–1666) was a Prussian organist and a renowned composer of songs. He studied with Scheidt and Schütz and worked briefly at Saint Nicholas Church in Leipzig. In 1657 he became chapel organist of the court of the Elector of Saxony, at Dresden. In that same year he published his important volume of songs, the *Arien*. In spite of the brevity of his life, Krieger was an important and influential figure in the history of the Lied, both spiritual and secular; many of his secular *Arien* were short German cantatas in the Italian manner.

ESAIAS REUSNER (1636–1679), a lutenist and composer, studied lute with his father and later, when he was a valet at the Radziwill court in Breslau, with a French lutenist there. He worked in Liegnitz, Brieg, Leipzig, and finally, from 1674, at the Brandenburg court in Berlin. He published many volumes of lute pieces and chamber music between 1667 and 1676 and, before his death, a volume of 100 spiritual lute songs.

JOHANN CHRISTOPH PEZEL (or Petzold; 1639–1694), a violinist, trumpeter, composer, and writer, was at Leipzig from 1664 to 1681 and then at Bautzen. His reputation was widespread, and his many publications include concerted works (one volume for voices and instruments in 1678). But he was most important for polyphonic wind music, including the *Hora Decima* of 1670 (40 sonatas for five wind players), *Intraden 2 4* (1683), and *Fünffstimmigte blasende Musik* (five-voiced wind music; 1685). He was a theorist of some interest—his treatises include the *Musica politico-practica* (1678).

DIEDRICH BUXTEHUDE (1637–1707), an organist and composer, is associated primarily with Saint Mary's Church in Lübeck, where he was organist from 1668 until his death. During these four decades, Buxtehude directed the famous Abendmusiken (evening concerts) begun by his father-in-law in 1641. (These concerts were later continued to 1810, and then from 1890 to World War II.) Buxtehude's works, not yet completely collected, centered in organ and vocal compositions for concerts—chorales, sets of preludes and fugues, cantatas, geistliche Lieder, and sacred concertos. He also wrote some harpsichord suites and trio sonatas.

HEINRICH BIBER (1644–1704), an Austrian violinist and composer, was chapel master at Salzburg from 1684 and was so well thought of that he was ennobled in 1690. He was an important composer of violin works, including sonatas on the *Fifteen Mysteries of the Virgin Mary*. Biber used double stops and *scordatura* (tuning a string to a different pitch to make double stops easier in certain keys or progressions).

JOHANN PACHELBEL (1653–1706), an organist and composer from Nuremberg, held several posts of importance —in Vienna (1674), Eisenach (1677), Erfurt (1678), Stuttgart (1690), Gotha (1692), and Nuremberg (1695). A few of his works were published during his lifetime—variations for keyboard (1683), trio sonatas (1691), and chorale preludes

(1699)—but more, including motets and cantatas, organ toccatas, fugues, chaconnes, and harpsichord suites, remain in manuscript. Generally conservative, he was nevertheless a strong influence in German music.

REINHARD KEISER (1674–1739) gave an early impetus to German opera. The son of the organist of Weissenfels, he studied in Leipzig from 1685 to 1692. In 1693, he produced his first opera at the Brunswick Court and the following year, moved to Hamburg, where he remained. He contributed about 120 operas (116 with German texts) to the Hamburg company, of which he was co-director from 1703. (Unfortunately, fewer than 20 of his operas have been found.) He organized concerts, expanded the concerts to other cities (in Germany, Denmark, and Russia), and in 1728 became cantor of the Hamburg Cathedral. In addition to operas, he wrote oratorios, Passions, motets, Psalms, and cantatas, as well as serenades and sonatas.

His feet flew over the pedal-board as though they had wings, and powerful sounds roared like thunder through the church. This filled Frederick, the Crown Prince, with such astonishment and admiration that he drew from his finger a ring set with precious stones and gave it to Bach as soon as the sound had died away.

CONSTANTIN BELLERMAN *

At the End of the Baroque

13

The eighteenth century was, in general, a leveler—raising some nations, humbling others, and redefining the political balance. France lost much of her political luster with the death of Louis XIV and the accession of his great grandson. Spain, with her new ruling house founded by a grandson of Louis XIV, returned to prominence. Austria was the greatest empire in Europe at the end of the century. The archduchess Maria Theresia (1717–1780) became a symbol of fiscal stability, and she is recognized to this day by the continued minting of her thaler (dollar), all with the date 1780. Germany began the slow process of unification, reducing the huge number of

* A description of a performance of Johann Sebastian Bach in Kassel, 1714. Karl Geiringer, *The Bach Family*, Fair Lawn, N.J.: Oxford, 1954, p. 145.

states and creating a few powerful kingdoms; the Prussian kingdom, whose capital was Berlin, became the nucleus of the modern German Empire. Frederick the Great (1712–1786) ruled with a despotism that has tinged the word *Prussian* ever since. England was ruled by the House of Hanover, whose four Georges were on the British throne from 1714 to 1830. In Russia, Peter the Great (1672–1725) and Catherine the Great (1729–1796) bracketed the eighteenth century with reigns that helped bring Russia into the European cultural mainstream. Other nations, including Italy, the Netherlands, Switzerland, and Sweden, prospered and continued on a more even keel. And America became an entity, a cultural branch of seventeenth-century nationalities, linguistically English, domestically Dutch, and increasingly polyglot as each crisis in Europe sent boatloads of emigrants to the New World.

The common coin of music was still Italian in vocabulary and basic practice and French in instrumental techniques and theoretical speculation. The international craze was Italian opera. The international practice was the basso continuo, which unified European composition. The international impetus was the constant importation of musicians and teachers. And the international form was the trio sonata—how many thousands of them were composed in the first half of the eighteenth century has never been determined. The smaller national fads were for folk instruments, particularly the vielle, guitar, and hurdy-gurdy; professionals concertized with violin, flute, bassoon, and even the stentorian *tromba marina*, popular in Paris in the 1730s.

The men who had invented the new types of composition and who worked out a definition of structure that could bring the new music to fruition had brought the Baroque art to its first culmination: these men had made the forms ready for the next generation, which would expand the forms and carry them to their height. This new generation, writing in the first decades of the eighteenth century, was richly gifted. They were international, not only deriving from a variety of nations, but also achieving international fame.

Tromba marina (marine trumpet or nun's fiddle). This instrument, of one, two, or even three strings, had a trombone-like, powerful voice. It was played as a series of partials or harmonic tones and bowed above the left hand. Large sizes were placed on the floor with the top on the shoulder, but earlier representations show smaller sizes held on the lap, both peg up and peg down. (Courtesy of the University of Michigan Library. Photo by R. E. Kalmbach.)

VOCAL FORMS

The whole art of singing and of composing for the voice was exported from Italy; Italian singers were singing everywhere, and Italian teachers went abroad to teach the art in other countries, as Italian violinists had done before them. Italian composers produced Italian operas in foreign cities. Germans composed operas in Italian, and the German opera declined and eventually died out. Even the English critics could not squelch the Italian craze in spite of their sometimes devastating digs at the posturing castrati and outlandish plots, which still dealt mainly with gods and heros.

In Italy operas were produced in cities as well as at courts. Venice continued to outproduce Naples three to one but with lesser composers, so musical influence centered increasingly in Naples, where opera reached an apex under Alessandro Scarlatti and Giovanni Battista Pergolesi and their followers. The apex was reached in the 1720s, when almost two hundred new operas were produced in Italy, as compared with about forty in France and Germany, about thirty-five in Austria, and thirty in England.

Outside of Italy, France alone had its own opera, and the "war" of Italian and French taste continued, rekindled in 1746 by an appearance of the Italian comedians in Paris. The main composer of French opera was Jean-Philippe Rameau, a theorist-composer who turned to the theater at the age of fifty. He became one of the great innovators in eighteenth-century opera, particularly in instrumentation, always a special French skill.

A countermovement developed of lighter fare, in which homely action and the language of the people were central. Enjoyment of language is associated with humor, and the vernacular operas of the eighteenth century were often witty. In general, they used spoken dialogue punctuated by songs in the popular style rather than recitativo and formal arias. They were not always funny, so *comic opera* is not an entirely satisfactory name; *light opera* is perhaps better.

A ballad opera was a play with interpolated songs, many of which were already familiar to the public. The form prospered in England, with important hits starting in 1727. Their titles still delight the ear: *The Devil to Pay, or The Wives Metamorphos'd* (Charles Coffey, 1731), *The Merry Cobbler* (Coffey, 1735), and, above all, *The Beggar's Opera* (John Pepusch, 1728), which has been imitated in this century by Kurt Weill as *Dreigroschen Oper* (1928) and the *Threepenny Opera* (1954). The masque died out by mid-century. *Alfred*, by Thomas Arne, one of the last of the genre, was produced in 1740 in the garden of the Cliveden residence of the Prince of Wales. "Rule, Britannia!" a patriotic song from the finale, became extremely popular in both Great Britain and the United States, where it appeared in a contrafactum of 1794 as "Rise, Columbia!" After the decline of support for the masque, there developed a kind of chamber opera, called *English opera*, similar to the ballad opera but using newly composed materials. Most of Thomas Arne's works were of this type.

Separate arias and dances from popular operas were published continually, but songs were popular as well, and the market for them was growing. From the middle of the century, glees were at their height. These straightforward part-songs, generally for three or four solo men's voices, were simple sectional works that had much in common with the ancient forms of *gleoword* ("minstrel's song"), from which the name derived, in both their punctus structure and the social nature of their performance. The catch remained unchal-

The Puzzle

JOHN HILTON

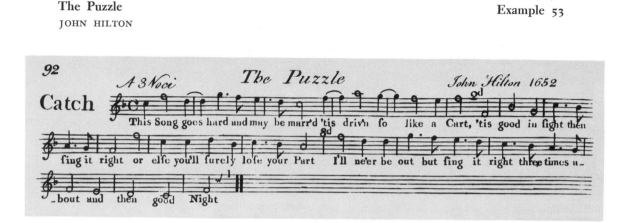

A puzzle catch with a clue in the second and third lines of the text—"then sing it right or else you'll surely lose your Part; I'll ne'er be out but sing it right three times about." These lines mean that the catch will not end correctly unless each person sings it three times and does not drop out to complete the final measure, that is, the second round begins on a different part of the measure than the first. (Courtesy of the University of Michigan Library. Photo by R. E. Kalmbach.)

lenged in the hearts of Englishmen, performed in men's clubs whose principle function was the support of singing.

Music engravers did a lively business—popular songs and ballads, songs and dances from theater productions, political ditties, sailor chanties (or shanties), and love songs were published in separate sheets and in collections. French songs, much like the English ones, continued to be published in separate sheets and collections. However, instead of publishing *chansons sérieux et à boire* ("serious and drinking songs"), which would have paralleled the English catches, the French changed to the more general *recueils* ("collections," "miscellanies"), which were published annually in Paris and elsewhere. They included tunes from popular entertainments—and occasionally from court entertainments—and the light operas, as well as separate songs (*chansons détachées*), both serious and humorous.

In Germany, the composition of chorales was declining and the literature was complete by Bach's day; there were about 5,000 tunes (not all of which survived). Bach did not compose original chorale tunes, but he left 371 harmonizations, in four parts, which so completely incorporated both the old —polyphonic—and the new—harmonic—practice that they became in the nineteenth century the consummate model for the emulation of theory students. In addition to the chorales, the German Lieder, or Arien, continued

Critique

Example 54

ANONYMOUS

A traveler who gads 'round the world
Is soft in the head, and what's more,
He can ride the carousel of the globe
And see nothing he's not seen before.
Let him traverse the sea and the shore,
After a thousand round trips he will know
It's the same thing wherever you go.

In England what will he find?
Youngsters, fun-crazy and sly,
Grown men with their quarrels and wars
And not a dotard who'll give up and die.
People are people, say I.
Are savages worth less than we?
It's the same thing where'er you may be.

TRANS. BY JON RINKA

This song is typical of the humorous chanson of French collections; it is printed
in movable type and there is no indication of an author. (Courtesy of the Bibliothèque Nationale.)

in the seventeenth-century tradition, with spiritual songs, simple ballads, and, increasingly, folklike songs. The latter, popular in the second half of the century, were to become significant as the Romantic ideal increased in importance.

The cantata, oratorio, and grand motet found their fullest embodiment in the first half of the eighteenth century. In an age of extremes and contrasts, these forms offered potential for the imaginative juxtapositions so desirable in the Baroque ideal, and they did so without the huge expense for costumes, sets, and machinery that limited opera production to the great cities and courts of Europe.

Larger Vocal Forms

The three forms were featured at public concerts, in churches, or, increasingly, in special halls. Several prominent French musicians had held public concerts and recitals in their own salons through the second half of the seventeenth century, but the Concert spirituel, which opened in 1725 with a Christmas Eve concert, offered what may have been the first concerts presented consistently in the same public hall—the Tuilleries—devoted to nothing but music. The Concert spirituel utilized the same personnel as the Opéra but presented programs of sacred and abstract music suitable for times when the Church forbade the performance of opera—about sixty days a year.

The German Lutheran cantata, particularly in the hands of Johann Sebastian Bach, achieved a culmination in the early decades of the century. Frequently featuring a chorale associated with a particular feast day, the German cantata combined the forces of organ, orchestral instruments, and a four-part chorus, generally with soloists. It presented the chorale, often following it with a fugal chorus based on one or more of the chorale phrases. The techniques of the era abound in Bach's cantatas; like the French grands motets, Bach's cantatas comprise a definition of the Baroque ideal.

The oratorio, particularly the Passion, was popular well into the eighteenth century in Germany and England. Oratorios were substantially longer than grands motets, the comparable works in France; they can be considered the culminative works of the stile concertato and the supreme examples of the Baroque style in music.

In Great Britain the oratorio was associated with George Frideric Handel, who built on the heritage of Purcell as well as that of his Italian and German predecessors. Handel had been a daring and imaginative entrepreneur of operas but turned to oratorio when the production of operas became financially hazardous for him. His productions of concert choral works with scriptural texts achieved tremendous success. Handel's transcendent achievement was his *Messiah*, an oratorio based uniquely on selected Old and New Testament texts in English. It was produced, in 1742, in Dublin, a productive musical center throughout the century, and, in 1743, in London. The work took the British by storm and has maintained its prime position in musical enterprise in the Anglo-Saxon world ever since.

INSTRUMENTAL FORMS

The Sonata

By sheer numbers, the trio sonata must be considered the most popular of Baroque musical types. It may also have been the most international. An early Baroque projection, the form had reached maturity in Italy in the third quarter of the seventeenth century but established itself outside of Italy only at the end of the century. Its era of greatest popularity in Europe was the first half of the eighteenth century.

Seventeenth-century music patrons might have been kings and noblemen but the new eighteenth-century patrons, who outnumbered the nobility, were the not-so-humble, often very rich, citizens; they were classified as "lesser nobility" and were called "gentlemen." They patterned their education, daily life, and manners on those of the more highly born and made it the ideal of the European world to be considered "true gentlemen." For gentlemen and gentlewomen, music was a suitable and edifying pastime, and the trio sonata was an excellent vehicle for performance in their homes. Four players could gather together to play either for themselves or for a small gathering of friends. It was during the eighteenth century that the term *chamber music* took on its modern meaning, that is, of music for a few players without duplication of parts.

Other trio sonatas were composed for professional concerts at court or in public. In France, the flute and violin were friendly rivals; the two were often pitted against each other in virtuoso performances, which the *Mercure de France* (a newspaper of the day) called an *espèce d' assaut*, a "kind of bout." [1] Thus the gentleman could perform a trio sonata at home and then listen to another at a concert. By offering him music for both functions, composers created one of the most perceptive public audiences that European music has ever enjoyed.

Keyboard and vocal works were central to the gentleman's musical literacy, and these two diverged into concert and domestic types at the end of the Baroque. This divergence created a distinction between music of a simple, direct nature and that of a relatively complicated structure. The complicated music had involved textures, fugal techniques, imitative sections, or intricate relationships among the instrumental lines; it was called *worked* and its kinship to the Renaissance learned style is obvious. The parallel between the simpler style, which was called *free* or *unbound*, and the Renaissance familiar style is less clear. The forthright rhythmic motion characteristic of the familiar style in 1500 had become basic to most music by 1700.

The trio sonata was often a mixture of free and bound movements. A five-movement sonata might comprise a polyphonically textured adagio, a

[1] *Mercure de France*, April, 1745, p. 140.

fugal allegro, a free aria, a free dance, and a quick imitative gigue. Two points were significant: the contrast between worked and free styles was used as a further means of contrast in the stile concertato; the complex movements tended to be placed at the beginning and the simpler movements toward the end, in a natural response to the way people listen.

As the impact of the gentleman's market for music for himself and his lady to play made itself felt, inevitably the association grew between the simple style and the gentleman, or, as he was called by both French and German writers, the *homme galant*. As early as 1713 the theorist Johann Mattheson (1681–1764) wrote a book, *Das neu-eröffnete Orchestre*, for the newly emerging gentleman. The full title of the book is instructive.

> The Newly-Inaugurated Orchestra, or Universal and Basic Introduction on How an *Homme Galant* May Acquire a Perfect Understanding of the Loftiness and Majesty of Noble Music, Form His Taste Accordingly, Understand the *Technical Terms* and Argue Cleverly about This Admirable Science.

The homme galant was expected to be a connoisseur of all the fine and practical arts, but he was no match for a professional at his own game. As a musician, he played either for his own delight, and was a *dilettante*, or because he loved it, and was an *amateur*. These terms, basically complimentary, soon became negatively charged with connotations of dabbling and superficiality. However, the distance between the gentleman and the professional musician was unbridgeable. To inform the gentleman of the differences between styles, Mattheson said, "The greatest difference exists between church, theatre and chamber music, and that is enough for an *homme galant*." [2]

The solo sonata, also an important Baroque type, served both amateur and professional and widened the distance between them by developing a virtuoso style. The virtuoso violinist built on the legacy of Corelli. Virtuoso solo sonatas were often very difficult, but their notated form can only suggest the technical wizardry of performance, because it omits whatever "improvements" the artist added on the spot (see pages 703–704).

In 1738 the *Mercure de France* printed a long article characterizing over two dozen French and Italian virtuoso violinists, from Leclair to Vivaldi, and comparing their compositions and their styles of performance. The Italians were the most sought after; like Italian opera singers, they fanned through Europe and created a legendary art. Easier sonatas were available to gentlemen; the *Mercure* article noted that the violin had been so "ennobled" in its new flowering that "it is no longer shameful for honest men to cultivate it." [3]

In 1725, not too long after Mattheson's book was published, the theorist Johann Joseph Fux published, in rebuttal to the new style, a text on polyphonic writing called the *Gradus ad Parnassum* (Steps to Parnassus). In this book Fux returned to the use of a cantus firmus, rejected the basso

[2] Ruth Halle Rowen, *Early Chamber Music*, New York: Columbia, 1949, p. 108.
[3] "Notes for a History of Instrumental Music," *Mercure de France*, June, 1738, p. 1113.

continuo, concerned himself with the ecclesiastical modes, and wrote in Latin, attempting to return to what he conceived to be the style of Palestrina (who had been recommended for emulation by Pope Gregory XIII). Fux did not know about proportional rhythmic motivation, nor did he have Palestrina's works to study—and in any case Palestrina's works were not representative of the Renaissance style—but Fux's system of the orderly progression through rhythmic *species* of counterpoint was thorough and provided a good counter-discipline to the work with subject and bass. His book appeared through the eighteenth century in German, Italian, English, and French. In modernized versions, his theory continued to be studied through the tonal era, as *strict* or *species counterpoint*. Some theorists today prefer a more authentic study of sixteenth-century style, but others feel that the Fux discipline's very abstraction from any specific historical style makes it generally relevant to *all* styles. Its application to twentieth-century techniques is giving the discipline new life; it is still widely practiced.

Both Mattheson and Fux were widening the gulf between amateur and professional, the one by providing special fare for the gentleman and the other by working out a deeper study for the apprentice. If the trio sonata reflected this gulf, the music for keyboard incorporated it. The harpsichord and, particularly in Germany, the clavichord were the instruments of the private citizen. In England the virginals were replaced by the spinet, either the rectangular or the graceful "leg o' mutton" shapes. Both harpsichord and clavichord were keyboard string instruments, but their difference was tremendous. The harpsichord produced a musical tone by *plucking* the string with a *plectrum* in a jack mechanism, whereas the clavichord produced a tone by *touching* the string with a *tangent*.

Keyboard Music

The Harpsichord. The harpsichord jack was attached to a bar at a right angle to the end of the long key, so depression of the key at the keyboard end

English spinet in the leg-o'-mutton shape, by John Crang (c. 1758). (Courtesy of the Victoria and Albert Museum.)

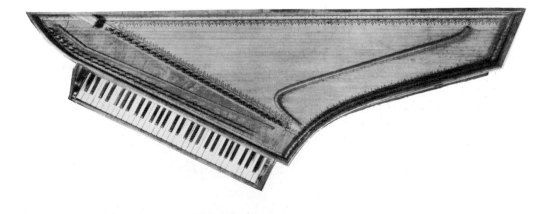

would cause the bar to rise at the other. The plectrum was hinged in such a way that it engaged the string on the way up but slid by, soundless, going down. A damper mechanism allowed the string to vibrate as long as the key was down and stopped the vibration upon release of the key.

The total harpsichord mechanism, culminating in the concert instruments, some of which were over 10 feet long, was complex and versatile. The performer could command a number of options with two manuals and often with two or three sets of strings (including those that sound as written, 8 feet, and an octave higher, 4 feet). A number of hand levers enabled him to engage or disengage sets of jacks, to move an entire set of jacks to a new point of contact with the strings, and to couple the manuals so that by playing on one he could activate both. By engaging all the jacks at once and coupling the manuals, the harpsichordist could produce the resonance of four or five sets of strings, both 8 feet and 4 feet, sounding together. On a sizable instrument the effect was stunning.

Selection of the mechanical setup for each movement was called *registration*. To register a piece, that is, to decide what stops to use in it, was an important aspect of a harpsichordist's skill; and the more complex the instrument, the more imaginative the result could be.

Equally important was the variety of finger control, called *touch*; *touching a harpsichord* was the technical term for playing it. Degrees of detachment could bring out a line with greater or lesser force, make a figure stand out, or give the effect of a small crescendo. The technique required both dexterity and strength, not only because the use of couplers necessitated a deep, clean, hard attack so that the separate strings would not sound separately and give

A two-manual concert harpsichord. The photograph is of a modern version, by Christopher Bannister, of an eighteenth-century instrument. Pedals were a late Baroque mechanism for changing stops and were never damper devices. This harpsichord, which was very powerful, was radically different from the spinet—more so than a grand piano is from an upright. The harpsichord was a double instrument, with several stops, and its strings were longer, making it different in tone quality as well as appearance. (Courtesy of Christopher Bannister. Photo by Gene Wieland, Jr.)

a ragged sound, but also because most effects depended on a precise release of the key as well as a precise engagement.

The greatest harpsichordist of the eighteenth century was probably Domenico Scarlatti; he held Europe spellbound with his virtuosity. Many harpsichordists, in France especially, had captivated the public in the past century, but Scarlatti arrived on the scene when the cult of the virtuoso was in full cry. As a young man in Naples, he astounded his audiences with daring virtuoso feats at the keyboard. One account described a fast opening passage beginning at the extremes of the keyboard and comprising contrary dashing runs. Scarlatti began it with crossed hands on two manuals and continued converging the lines until his hands were in the normal position. Crossed hands, wide skips, runs, and figurations had long been commonplaces of the French harpsichord school, but Scarlatti's techniques could go beyond them to include such innovations as chord clusters.

Scarlatti wrote separate movements, which he called *essercizi* ("studies" or "exercises"). They were couched in the two-part standard Baroque dance form, and Scarlatti played them in contrasting pairs. The essercizi form a unique body of works that are at once thoroughly Baroque and highly personal. Their driving momentum was not effected as a repeated guitar-like pattern, as the German prelude often was, nor as a working-over of a short subject; it derived from the consecutive introduction of several ideas, united by the single-minded beat and by the overall scheme of contrasting tones.

Essercizo in *a* minor   **Example 55**
DOMENICO SCARLATTI

A facsimile from *Essercizi per gravicembalo*, 1738 (L. 366, K. 1). (Courtesy of the Library of Congress.)

The Clavichord. The clavichord was as introvert as the harpsichord could be extrovert; it had a much smaller scope of function, mirroring its smaller dynamic range. But within its small range the clavichord was so versatile, so open to imaginative effects that it was held in special regard by its practitioners. A small and relatively inexpensive instrument, it was especially popular in Germany.

The clavichord had the simplest and most direct action of all the keyboard instruments. The long key, when pushed down at the keyboard, pushed up at the other end. A small blunt metal blade, called the *tangent,* was attached at right angles at that far end and, upon depression of the key at the keyboard, was pushed directly onto the string, remaining in contact with the string until the key was released. Because the tangent stayed in contact with the string, the vibrating length of the string extended from the tangent to the bridge, rather than between two bridges as in other European stringed instruments.

The ramifications of this were enormous. First, the tangent, by touching the string within its sounding length, damped the sound. The result was a sound so delicate that the instrument could not be used in a public place.

A late Baroque clavichord, by **Barthold Fritz** (c. **1751**), front view and interior seen from above. This is a full clavichord, with one string for each key. It was common in earlier instruments to let one string serve more than one pitch—generally adjoining chromatic tones, which would not be sounded together. This was accomplished by touching the string at different points. A half step was about the same length as it was on a lute—the distance of a fret —so such a clavichord was said to be *fretted.* (Courtesy of the Victoria and Albert Museum.)

Although greater pressure at the keyboard produced a louder tone, the dynamic range was very small; however, within its range, the clavichord was incredibly supple and responsive. It was played alone, and it could be heard by only a few others—it was truly a private instrument.

Second, the clavichord tangent activated not only the sound but also the pitch. Greater pressure at the keyboard stretched the string, and the pitch changed accordingly. Thus, intonation could be heightened for certain tones according to the desire and skill of the player. Further, such heightenings could be inaugurated *after* the key had been depressed, so the player could alter the quality and intonation of a tone after it had been activated. By moving the key up and down while the tangent was on the string, he could produce a true vibrato, called a *shake* (*Bebung* in German).

The popularity of the harpsichord and clavichord required the composition of a new kind of music—music not for an audience but for the nonprofessional practitioner, the gentleman. In France, he was likely to be one of the lesser nobility and to play the harpsichord; in England, he was likely to be one of the landed gentry or a city professional and to play the spinet; in Germany, he was more likely to be a well-to-do burgher and to play the clavichord.

German Keyboard Music

Because of the central position of the Cantor in German musical life, German keyboard forms owed much more to the organ than did the forms of other countries. Tuning had always been a problem, for the octave contains more notes than can be put into it comfortably. Tuning a clavichord was fairly simple and created no more problem than tuning the theorbo, which had a minimum of seventeen strings. (The small harpsichord was no more difficult.) But the organ was another matter. Two or three manual organs plus a pedal organ, each with several ranks of pipes, made possible the contrasts and qualities that were such a delight to the Baroque man, but the instrument was architectural, and voicing the pipes was a huge, cumbersome, tedious job. However, German composers, whose work centered in their positions as royal or civic *Kapellmeister*, based their compositions in the learned style and were concerned also with problems of temperament. Thus they turned to the problems of key and of tuning, and it was in the German school that the successful compromise of equal temperament was carried out.

French suites were also studied by German composers, who made copies of them for their libraries and composed suites in the French style. The four volumes of keyboard music by Johann Caspar Ferdinand Fischer, who was in the service of the Margrave of Baden, illustrate the juxtaposition of French and German styles and the influence of the French theorists on the German expansion of key. The four volumes, which were probably composed from 1695 to 1715, were preceded by his collection of French airs and ballets for instrumental ensemble, called *Le journal du printems* (Springtime Journal); this collection shows Fischer's thorough absorption of the French instrumental style.

The first of Fischer's volumes of keyboard music, the *Blumen-Strauss* (Bouquet of Flowers, published in 1732), contains eight groups of pieces, each in a single tone or key and each comprised of a *præludium*, six fugues (Fuga I, Fuga II, etc.), and a finale. The separate items are short (the median length is eleven measures), and the fugal technique is not consistent. The format is unusual, perhaps unique, and supports the probability that it was composed early.

The second volume, the *Pièces de Clavessin* (Harpsichord Pieces, published in 1696), contains eight suites in the French style, each in a different tone. They vary in length from two movements (prelude and chaconne, of the French rondeau type) to seven movements and include the standard items—prelude, courante, allemande, gavotte, sarabande, and menuet—and a few less common ones, such as branle, plainte, and canaries.

The third volume, the *Musicalischer Parnassus* (Musical Parnassus, published in 1702), in spite of its German title is also a series of French suites —nine of them, each named for one of the Muses of Greek mythology. These suites are longer than the others, varying in format from five to eleven movements, and they use English as well as French items. The nine suites are in nine different tones, and, as in the *Blumen-Strauss*, all dance movements are in the double-punctus Baroque form and the preludes are free.

The fourth volume, the *Ariadne Musica* (published in 1715), is a series of twenty pairs of preludes and fugues. The movements are a bit longer than those in the *Blumen-Strauss* (the median length is thirteen measures), and the fugues are more regular. The twenty pairs are in twenty different tones, and the title of the work, suggesting the labyrinth in which Ariadne was imprisoned, indicates that the composition negotiates the intricacies of temperament as Theseus had negotiated the labyrinth in rescuing Ariadne. The reference was quite clear to Fischer's contemporaries, who knew their mythology, and the point was well taken.[4]

The tonal explorations of the *Ariadne Musica* can best be appreciated as the culmination of a continuing development beginning with Nivers's list of tones. The expanding concept can be seen by noting the tones of Nivers and then those of Fischer's four books. Major tones are in capital letters, minor ones in small letters, and the exceptional Phrygian *e* is indicated with an asterisk.

Nivers:	*d, g, a, e*, C, F, D, G*
Blumen-Strauss:	*d, g, a, e*, C, F, D, G*
Pièces de Clavessin:	*d, F, a, C, e, D, g, G*
Musicalischer Parnassus:	*C, G, a, B♭, e, F, g, D, d*
Ariadne Musica:	*C, c♯, d, D, E♭, e*, e, E, f, F, f♯, g, G, A♭ a,*
	A, B♭, b, B, c

The *Blumen-Strauss* series of tones is identical to Nivers's, including the Phrygian *e**. The series in the *Pièces de Clavessin* has a new order, alter-

[4] Ernst V. Werra (ed.), *Johann Kaspar Ferdinand Fischer: Saemtliche Werke Fuer Klavier und Orgel*, New York: Broude Brothers, 1965.

nating major and minor tones, and brings *e* into the regular minor type. The series in the *Musicalischer Parnassus* reshuffles these and adds *B♭* to make the ninth tone. The *Ariadne Musica* more than doubles the number of tones, adding ten new ones, and also (interestingly) includes the Phrygian *e** of Nivers along with *e* minor and the new *E* major.

Key signatures were not standardized: the *A♭* had three flats; *e* had two sharps in the *Ariadne Musica* but only one in the Parnassus (*e** had no signature). In general, the minor tones had one flat fewer or one sharp more than the modern conventions. Codification of signatures was beginning, however, and the standard would be arrived at by the middle of the century. Nevertheless, the minor mode involved so many alternative intonations that any minor signature was a compromise, and a variety of minor signatures was maintained longer than that of major ones. Nineteenth-century editors changed the older signatures to conform with their own, but now editors are keeping them as the composers wrote them.

St. Thomas Church, in Leipzig, in the time of Johann Sebastian Bach. (Courtesy of the Museum for the History of the City of Leipzig.)

Seven years after the publication of the *Ariadne Musica*, Johann Sebastian Bach, the Cantor of the city of Leipzig at the Thomaskirche, brought out a volume, *Das wohltemperirte Clavier* (The Well-Tempered Keyboard), that had an additional five tones. This made a total of twenty-four, including major and minor tones for all the key centers that Fischer had used (Bach omitted the Phrygian *e**), thus completing the integration of the keyboard. Like Fischer, Bach chose to write a pair, prelude and fugue, for each tone; his pieces were two or three times as long as Fischer's, and they represent the culmination of the development of this type of composition. Like Bach's *Inventions*, his preludes and fugues reflect a concern with form and pedagogic qualities rather than with instrumental idiom. The preludes introduced the standard types of opening movement, some of them little changed from their Renaissance progenitors except in harmonic content; these standard types included improvisatory free forms, lute or guitar figurations (written as chords by Fischer, some with titles suggesting figuration), idiomatic keyboard figurations, and toccatas. The fugues introduced a remarkable variety of subjects and demonstrated an absorption of French rhythmic freedom that in the Fischer books was characteristic only in the French suites. In Fischer's preludes and fugues, by far the bulk of the movements (seventy of eighty-seven) were in duple time, whereas, in his suites, the division was equal (fifty-one duple, fifty-three triple).

More important than the variety of meters in the French style, however, was the greater variety of rhythmic patterns within the music itself. The German style tended toward a steady forward motion that is not so much rhythm as figuration; the French style tended toward changing patterns within the impelling meter, a modern concept. Fischer's works Germanized the French movements, ironing out the rhythmic elements; Bach brought French elements into the German style, imparting to his preludes and fugues a rhythmic vitality that crowns his work in *Das wohltemperirte Clavier* and makes it a supreme achievement.

As the title *Well-Tempered Keyboard* implies, the technical and formal aspects of the work were primary, whereas the question of whether the movements were intended for the clavichord, harpsichord, or organ was left open. Bach's keyboard works intended for professional performance were much more idiomatic. The *Concerto in the Italian Taste*, for example, was a harpsichord work in the fast-slow-fast format associated with Vivaldi, in which the designations *solo* and *tutti* were used to indicate that a single stop was pitted against the coupled full registration of the instrument in a two-manual performance. The suites reflected French idiom as well; the longer suites, which Bach called *partitas*, were more eclectic, a fine culmination of international elements of the Baroque.

Bach displayed a particular mastery in his organ works, and they remain a basic literature for organists everywhere. His seven substantial volumes of these works include short preludes and fugues and a set of short chorale preludes, called the *Orgelbüchlein* (Little Organ Book); these were supposed to cover the liturgical year (but were only one-third completed at the time

Prelude and Fugue in C major

Example 56

JOHANN SEBASTIAN BACH

Example 56 (continued)

Example 56 (continued)

The example is a facsimile from a book (published before 1815) of six preludes and fugues. The prelude displays characteristics, such as the accumulation of chords, that are associated with the French unmeasured prelude. (Courtesy of the Library of the Riemenschneider Bach Institute, Baldwin-Wallace College, Berea, Ohio.)

of his death) and were intended for students. The title of the *Orgelbüchlein* continues: *In which a Beginner at the Organ is given Instruction in Developing a Chorale in many divers ways, and at the same time in Acquiring Facility in the Study of the Pedal.* Like *Das wohltemperirte Clavier*, these student works remained in use after Bach's death. In addition, he left longer, more difficult works that challenge the organist at the highest level of technique. Pairs of prelude-fugue, toccata-fugue, fantasy-fugue, and so forth, provide a summary of Baroque tradition. The chorale preludes form an equal summary of techniques using the German Protestant chorale. Bach also wrote six organ trios (not trio sonatas), that is, three-line works in the polyphonic sense, designed for performance on two manuals and pedals.

The German Kapellmeister, in general, dealt with the organ and with church styles and therefore was the music master of a conservative tradition. In writing within the old forms, Bach was looking backward, because the new Classical style was already burgeoning in Europe. His important contribution was working out the old forms within the harmonic language of the late Baroque.

A Baroque organ, showing the console and architectural details of the instrument. (Courtesy of the University of Michigan Library. Photo by R. E. Kalmbach.)

Pipes of the organ (1737) of the St. Bavo Church in Haarlem, Netherlands. (Courtesy of Drukkerij Van Boekhoven Photography.)

A worker soldering organ pipes. Two ranks of pipes are illustrated—those marked "N" are conical, and those marked "M" are cylindrical. (Courtesy of the University of Michigan Library. Photo by R. E. Kalmbach.)

The concerto grosso was the quintessential Baroque form, incorporating the producer's concern for spatial contrasts, the composer's interest in instrumental music in general and in the new abstract (i.e., nondance) formal techniques in particular, and the performer's desire to present himself in heroic virtuoso terms. During the early decades of the eighteenth century, the concerto was a free and experimental type that flourished in a joyful variety of mediums and groups. The concertos of Antonio Vivaldi can serve to outline the directions in which composers were turning. Concertos were of four main types—the concerto grosso, the solo concerto, the concerto for four or five instruments, and the concerto for a larger group of players. All used the basso continuo, of course.

The concerto grosso pitted the concertino against the concerto grosso. The concertino of the *Concerto in d minor* (opus 63 no. 2) is a viola d'amore and lute; that of the *Concerto in F major* (opus 64 no. 2) is violin, oboe, bassoon, and two horns. The first of these works instructs the concerto grosso to use mutes, to allow the delicate solo instruments to be heard. The second, with its expansion of the number and heterogeneity of sounds, uses the solo players not as a single concertino but as a changing series of solo-duo-trio combinations. The double concerto, for a two-instrument concertino, can be considered as having a very small concertino, or as being a halfway house from the concerto grosso to the solo concerto, or as being simply a concerto for two virtuosos. It was probably put in all three categories at one time or another.

The solo concerto pitted a single instrument against an instrumental ensemble, either large or small. In some cases, the solo—oboe, flute, violin, cello, bassoon, or lute—played against a trio sonata; in others, against a true concerto grosso with *ripieno* (doubling) instruments. As the cult of the virtuoso gained momentum, the solo concerto became more frequently used by performers in pursuit of public acclaim. The solo played against a small contingent was not as glamorous as the solo played against the larger ensemble, because the soloist had to balance the more powerful sound with his command of technique.

The concerto for four or five instruments comprised a substantial number of works in the first decades of the eighteenth century. The instruments used in a small solo concerto and a concerto for four or five instruments were virtually the same when strings were used; the difference lay only in the difficult solo part. Vivaldi's Opus 59, *Concerto per due violini e leuto* (Concerto for Two Violins and Lute), implied only three parts in its title; the basso continuo, always present but seldom mentioned, was a fourth part. This work, in essence a trio sonata plus a solo lute, required two violinists, a cellist, a harpsichordist, and a lutenist for performance. If the lute part had provided a contrast in degree of difficulty and had given the lutenist the glamor of the starring role, the work would have been a small solo concerto, but in fact, it is a charming integration of its elements and alternates the prominence of sound and technique.

The concerto for a larger group of players was a work in four or five parts that doubled some or all of the parts. Vivaldi customarily called his works of this type *concerti per ripieno* or *concerti ripieni*; the French called them *grands concerts* ("large concertos"). Basically such a work was a concerto grosso without a separate concertino. The larger group of players generally comprised a dozen or so, though several groups had more members for special occasions. Alessandro Marcello called for thirteen in a concerto grosso in 1738—six violins, three violas, two cellos, one harpsichord, and one cello or bassoon; this grouping was representative at that date. The orchestra of San Marco in Venice was always large; it numbered twenty-three in 1708—ten violins, four violas, one string bass, three theorbos, one cornett, two trumpets, one trombone, and one oboe—but it is unlikely that the entire membership would have been combined except for occasions of great pomp.

All four forms of the concerto were popular at concerts. The solo concerto depended on the performer, and it is not surprising that the violin was most popular. Of Vivaldi's approximately one hundred and fifty solo concertos, about one hundred are for the violin and thirty-seven for the bassoon. He made almost exclusive use of the fast-slow-fast format, with its forceful beginning and ending, which is so rewarding for the virtuoso. The trend in the concerto in Italy was toward the large solo concerto and the large concerto ripieno, a twofold reaching for a more substantial sound. This was not the Baroque sense of the grand, which had evidenced itself in mammoth performances, but a desire for a new kind of sound in which doublings would be standard.

In France the large sound was less welcome, for the French preferred the joys of suppleness and subtlety. French modernity lay in new ideas of texture and construction, not in the definition of the concerto ripieno. In 1738 the *Mercure de France* reported that the large concertos, including one, by Mondonville, for three groups, were to be heard at the Concert spirituel.[5] But the French were also producing some of the most enlightened works in the smaller chamber forms and were experimenting with new instruments in the theater and private orchestras; as always, they were in the forefront in the use of instrumental color. The German Johann Mattheson wrote that the French were, "because of their inborn liveliness, great masters of instrumental music."[6] The French were to make a vital contribution to the coming Classical style.

Although Great Britain received the concerto late, the Italian style penetrated deeply into British taste. London established an academy in 1710 and several gentleman amateurs were well versed in the performance of the Italian style. Francesco Geminiani (1687–1762), an Italian violinist and

[5] *Mercure de France*, September, 1738, p. 2080.
[6] Rowen, *op. cit.*, p. 3.

student of Corelli, was established in London from 1714 and also spent some years in Dublin; he brought out five volumes of concertos between 1732 and 1746. The French school was represented in England by such men as Jean-Baptiste Loeillet (1680–1730), a Flamand who established his reputation in France and settled in London in 1705 as a performer, producer, and teacher. A flutist and oboist, he introduced the transverse flute, long popular in France, into England, which had been a bastion of the recorder. Vivaldi was also known in Great Britain; his Opus 3, known as *L'Estro Harmonico* (Harmonic Whim), which was twelve concertos for various instruments, appeared there in 1715.

There were others, of course, but it was George Frideric Handel who most influenced the English taste. Handel was a true eclectic with an instinct for public taste; his works show the influence of Lully and Purcell as well as Corelli and Vivaldi. He used improvisatory types, dances, popular songs, the French overture, the German fugue, the dramatic vocal style, and the German tradition of the French suite. His work ranged from pieces for outdoor concerts at the Vauxhall Gardens to his eighteen organ concertos for church performances, from the *Water Music* (1717) to the music for the *Royal Fireworks* (1749). Unlike the *Water Music*, which achieved size by his stringing together twenty short movements into a long suite, the concertos of Opus 6 search out a musically logical series of four, five, or six movements that seem spontaneous yet are inevitably linked.

Vivaldi had a direct influence in the German States through his visits, as well as through Germans who had studied with him or who (like J. S. Bach) had copied out and studied examples of his music. In addition, a large Saxon group was directly connected with Vivaldi through study in Venice.

Johann Sebastian Bach's contribution to the concerto tradition, representative of German techniques of instrumentation, were the six concertos he wrote in 1721 for the Margrave of Brandenburg, six organ concertos, and about twenty concertos for other instruments. The *Brandenburg Concertos* can be seen as a summation of the instrumental possibilities of the concerto grosso. They display a variety of instrumental contingents, with concertino wind, string, and keyboard instruments, and call for a total of from six to twelve performers.

Representative of the new direction in Germany was Georg Philipp Telemann, whose long life and good health account in large measure for what may be the most prolific output in the history of music. His natural exhilaration and fecundity of idea, which appealed to his public, have brought him into renewed popularity today. He wrote at least 170 concertos (the full number is not yet known), and they well represent both the diverse traditions that had been infused into the concerto concept and the diverse directions toward which it was pointing. Telemann was a well-traveled man, internationally connected and nationally of immense reputation. His activity as the founder and producer of public concerts in Leipzig, Frankfurt-am-Main, and Hamburg kept him in the public eye.

In Telemann's works, the concerto grosso was represented by such compositions as the *Suite in F* for two horns, two violins, and concerto grosso and the *Concerto in D* for three trumpets, two oboes, and concerto grosso. His solo concertos included works for trumpet, horn, flute, recorder, oboe, oboe d'amore, harpsichord, viola, and, of course, violin. Of his double concertos, the *Concerto in e minor for Flute, Recorder, and Concerto Grosso* was unusual, not only in his juxtaposition of those two instruments, but also in his using a four-movement (slow-fast-slow-fast) format.

The small concerto was well represented in Telemann's works. The *Concerto in F for Recorder, Horn, and Basso Continuo*, the *Concerto in D for Trumpet, Two Oboes, and Basso Continuo* (he also wrote one for trumpet, two violins, and basso continuo), and the *Concerto in G for Flute, Oboe, Violin, and Basso Continuo* were representative of this genre. The small concerto provided the most convenient and appealing form for *Tafelmusik* ("table music," music for performance at a banquet); such a piece was generally titled with the word *suite* and was less associated with the learned style. The *Suite in F for Three Horns, Two Violins, and Basso Continuo* was typical.

The large concerto was represented not only by Telemann's works that were titled *Concerto Grosso* and were without concertino, but also by his French *Ouvertures*, which are, for practical purposes, concertos both large and small. Of these he wrote over six hundred. The *Concerto for Violin, Two Trumpets, Two Horns, Two Flutes, Two Oboes, Two Bassoons, and Concerto Grosso* is a grandly conceived, variable concertino work with seven movements—presto, corsicana (un poco grave), allegrezza, scherzo, gigue, polacca (polonaise), and minuetto—a suite format.

What the diverse concertos of the late Baroque had in common was the stile concertato ideal and the restless search for an embodiment of the modern spirit, which could not be satisfied by the techniques of the Baroque.

❀ *Some Important Composers of the Late Baroque*

A culminative period, the late Baroque was truly international. Travel both encouraged and was encouraged by an easy interchange and open understanding among men, based on mutual goals. Many composers were equally active in vocal and instrumental composition, sacred and secular forms, theatrical and concert music. Except in opera and vocal techniques, Italian influence was generally on the wane, while aspects of the coming Classicism were beginning to exert a pull toward French, German, and Austrian leadership.

ANTONIO CALDARA (1670–1736), an Italian singer, cellist, and composer, studied with Legrenzi at San Marco in Venice and traveled to Rome and then to Spain. From 1716, he was at the Royal Chapel in Vienna under the directorship of JOHANN JOSEPH FUX (1660–1741), the noted contrapuntist. Caldara was a fecund composer whose influence on subsequent generations was profound. He left 87 theater works and entertainments, 31 oratorios, and a great number of Masses, motets, cantatas, madrigals, and vocal canons. In instrumental forms, he left keyboard works, sonatas for one or several instruments, and some early symphonies. Some of his church music is still in use.

BENEDETTO MARCELLO (1685–1739), a Venetian theorist and composer, lawyer and politician, was called "the prince of music" in his own day. His great work was the *Estro poetico-armonico* (Poetic-Harmonic Whim), a setting of paraphrases of the first fifty Psalms for one to eight voices with basso continuo (published in 1724–1727 in eight volumes). He wrote prolifically in virtually all the forms popular early in the eighteenth century and left several hundred cantatas, a volume of concertos, several sonatas, oratorios, motets, and Masses. In addition he produced three theater works and wrote a satire on the decadence of opera, *Il Teatro Alla Moda* (1720). His brother ALESSANDRO (1684–1750) was also a composer.

JOHANN CASPAR FERDINAND FISCHER (died 1746), a German organist, harpsichordist, and composer, was Kapellmeister from 1695 at the court of Baden. His works, incorporating current tastes and interests, were important in his own day. He left four volumes of keyboard works, including the *Ariadne Musica* (1715), *Vesperæ seu psalmi pro toto anno* (Vesper Psalms for the Entire Year, 1701), and a later *Litaniæ Lauretanæ*; the latter two volumes were for four-part chorus and basso continuo with instruments. Fischer also left an instrumental work in the French style—*Journal du Printems, consistant en airs et ballets à 5 parties et les trompettes à plaisir* (Springtime Journal, Consisting of Airs and Ballets in Five Parts with Optional Trumpets, Opus I, 1695). Other works remain in manuscript.

JOHANN SEBASTIAN BACH (1685–1750), a German organist, church music director (*Cantor*), and composer, was a member of a great musical dynasty and was one of the great composers in the history of music. His prodigious output paralleled the demands of his various jobs—court musician, civic

church organist, and, finally (from 1723), municipal music director for the city of Leipzig where he centralized his activities as organist and Cantor at the Thomaskirche (St. Thomas Church). Bach's early works were mainly instrumental forms for the court—the *Brandenburg Concertos* (1721), instrumental suites, and solo and double concertos for violin and for harpsichord, as well as numerous short pieces, of which the most famous are probably the 48 preludes and fugues of *Das wohltemperirte Clavier* (Well-tempered Keyboard) and the two- and three-part *Inventions*. His sacred music includes over 200 cantatas, 5 Passions, *Missa in H-moll* (Mass in *b* Minor), 2 Magnificats, and a group of motets. The organ works center in the older forms (particularly the fugue), which are generally paired with a preceding contrast (prelude, fantasy, toccata, etc.) and range from fairly simple to virtuoso demands, and the organ chorale, of which he left 371 harmonizations and several volumes of chorale preludes. It is hard to assess the relationship between these works and Bach's own performing repertoire, for he was known as an improvisor of exceptional skill. Although his skill was appreciated in his own day, his great fame as a composer dates from only a century ago, when he was rediscovered.

GEORGE FRIDERIC HANDEL (1685–1759), a naturalized English organist, composer, and entrepreneur, was born in Saxony. After a stint as ripieno violinist at the Hamburg opera, and already a composer, he went to Italy at the age of twenty-one. There he came into contact with the giants of Naples, Rome, and Venice (including the Scarlattis and Corelli). He accepted a post in Hanover in 1709 and visited London in 1710, where he produced an opera. Handel made London the chief locale of his subsequent career, producing operas and concerts, working in many jobs, and sustaining the many ups and downs inevitable in the public theater. An internationalist, Handel adapted his output to British tastes and is claimed by the English as one of their greatest composers. His output was staggering. His instrumental works included 44 sonatas and three books of harpsichord pieces, 30 concertos (including 12 for organ), and works for specific performances, including the *Water Musick* (1717) and the *Royal Fireworks Musick* (1749). He also left 40 operas (1705 to 1741), 122 cantatas (for one, two, and three voices), 2 Passions, and 32 oratorios to both secular and sacred texts. The oratorio *Messiah*, which Handel produced in Dublin in 1741, became (and remained) a mainstay in the British choral repertoire.

DOMENICO SCARLATTI (1685–1757), son of Alessandro, a Neapolitan harpsichordist and composer, was organist and composer at the Neapolitan court at the age of sixteen and had his first operas produced at eighteen. From 1709 he was in Rome, working at the Roman court of the Queen of Poland; later he was at the Vatican, where he wrote choral works, including a Mass (for four voices), *Miserere*, and *Stabat Mater* (for ten voices). From 1720 he was in Lisbon and Madrid, in the service of Juan V of Portugal. When the Infanta Maria Barbara married Fernando, Prince of Asturias, in 1729, she took Scarlatti to her court in Madrid. In 1746 Fernando became King, and the Queen appointed Scarlatti Maestro de Camara. Although he composed numerous operas and choral works, Scarlatti's place in the history of music centers in his originality and imagination in performing and composing for the harpsichord. His skill at that instrument was widely known in his early years, when he exploited its idiom and astounded his hearers with his virtuosity. The 555 of his harpsichord works that remain were written down after he entered the service of Maria Barbara; a few were published as *Essercizi per gravicembalo* (Studies for the Harpsichord) in 1738, 1742, 1749, 1752, and 1757. His last work was *Salve Regina* for chorus and instruments.

JEAN-MARIE LECLAIR (1697–1764), a famous French violinist, was a dancer and dancing master in Torino as a young man. In Paris by 1723, he published his first book of solo violin sonatas in that year. He later married a music engraver, appeared successfully at the Concert spirituel, traveled to Holland, and returned to Paris in the service of the duc de Grammont, for whose theater he produced several works. He left several books of solo sonatas with basso continuo, and several shorter volumes of trio sonatas, concertos, and other miscellaneous works. One of the great violinists of the century, he is considered a definitive figure in the history of violin virtuosity in France.

JEAN-PHILIPPE RAMEAU (1683–1764), a theorist and composer, made his early reputation as a philosopher of music; his *Traité d'harmonie* (1722) became a foundation of harmonic thought for the next century and a half. His early works were *Pièces de clavecin* (1706, 1724, 1731), 5 grands motets, and several cantatas. At the age of fifty, Rameau turned to the theater and between 1733 and 1764 produced 26 operas and ballets which rank with Lully's. The operas are notable for their advanced instrumental usage, in which Rameau was imaginative and original. His theoretical output continued, with thirty-five publications after the treatise of 1722.

JEAN-JOSEPH MOURET (1682–1738) was a singer and composer from Avignon who became one of the most influential composers in the history of French music. In Paris from 1707, he was central to virtually all the musical developments of the early decades of the century. He was the director of music for the duchesse du Maine, wife of the favorite son of Louis XIV, at her estate at Sceaux; there he inaugurated the famous entertainments (cantatas, ballets) called *Les Grandes Nuits de Sceaux* (Grand Nights of Sceaux). He conducted the Opéra orchestra (1714–1718), was the artistic director to both the Concert spirituel (1728–1733) and the Comédie Italienne, the predecessor of the Opéra Comique (1716–1737), and sang in the king's chamber music (from 1720). In addition, he was an innovative and fecund composer. In theater works, of which he wrote 7 operas and ballets, he invented the lyric comedy, which would prove so important throughout the century. His solo and duet petits motets were the rage of the early programs of the Concert spirituel, and his 2 *Suites de symphonies* (1729) were among the earliest works leading to the development of the symphony. He left six volumes of *Divertissements,* numerous chamber works, and many popular songs and vaudevilles. His contemporaries called him "le musicien des grâces."

JOSEPH BODIN DE BOISMORTIER (1689–1755) was born in the south of France and came early to Paris, where he remained. His output was prodigious in both variety and amount but is still uncounted. He is credited with the introduction of the three-movement concerto to France. He contributed sonatas, concertos, pièces de viole, ballet-operas, cantatas (including *Diane et Actéon,* long attributed to Rameau), harpsichord suites, and many volumes of popular music. His grand motet for Christmas, *Fugit nox* (1742), remained popular for twenty years.

GIOVANNI BATTISTA PERGOLESI (1710–1736), a Neapolitan composer and violinist of great influence and output, was a consumptive who spent his brief life in Naples and Rome. From a poor family, he was educated at the Naples city conservatory and became a competent violinist and a composer in great demand. His works have yet to be completely collected and authenticated, but they were varied, including about 15 serious operas, comic operatic intermezzi, concertos, trio sonatas, and miscellaneous sacred works. The last of his works, *Stabat Mater* for two treble voices and instruments, was revered throughout Europe—it was performed at the Paris concerts every year until the revolution. His comic intermezzo, *La Serva Padrona,* was produced in Naples in 1733 between the acts of one of the composer's serious operas and again in Paris in 1746 and 1752, when it created a furor; this work was basic to the foundation of the *opera buffa.*

GEORG PHILIPP TELEMANN (1681–1767) was a German composer but nevertheless studied law in Leipzig. Although he had been a gifted child and had written an opera in the style of Lully at the age of twelve, he was largely self-taught in music and, unusual for his time, was not known as a performer. Telemann devoted his energies almost entirely to composition and became the most famous German composer of his time and one of the most prolific in the history of music. His output is fairly staggering—40 operas, 44 Passions, about 3,000 cantatas, over 100 services, and a great number of instrumental works, including over 170 concertos, trio sonatas, and harpsichord suites, 600 overtures, and numerous miscellaneous works. He was a versatile man, whose career took him to many posts and led him to many friendships and interests. The leading modernist in Germany, Telemann was a friend of Johann Sebastian Bach (whose Leipzig post he had been offered and refused) and Handel. His *Pimpinone* (1725) was an early example of comic opera. Telemann was also an author; he wrote some of his own librettos and published two autobiographies (1731 and 1740). In addition he was an engraver and engraved some of his own works.

THOMAS AUGUSTINE ARNE (1710–1778), the son of a London upholsterer, became the most successful English composer of his time. A versatile writer, his output included 7 trio sonatas (1750), 2 oratorios, 2 Masses (lost), organ concertos, symphonies, and keyboard works, as well as the masques and English operas on which his fame rests. He composed about a dozen operas for the public theater, furnished incidental music for 28 plays, and wrote a large number of songs, catches, and glees. He introduced program notes at the Drury Lane Theatre in 1768. His son MICHAEL (1741–1786) was a singer and harpsichordist, who made his debut at the age of nine and remained on the boards, chiefly as the composer of about 19 operas. He also wrote popular songs, of which "The Lass with the Delicate Air" is still in the repertoire.

JEAN-JOSEPH CASSANÉA DE MONDONVILLE (1711–1772), a Gascon violinist, composer, and entrepreneur, was known in his thirties for his brilliant virtuosity and his playing of harmonics (he was the first to publish, in 1738, instructions for playing them). He was also known for his experiments with instrumental texture; in two volumes of chamber music, he dispensed with basso continuo and combined the techniques of violin sonatas and harpsichord pieces, melding the Italian and French styles. His opera *Titon et l'Aurore* (1753) was a huge success, and his grands motets were famous internationally. For a generation before retiring in 1762, he directed the Concert spirituel in Paris. He left five volumes of chamber music, 5 theater works, 16 *grands motets*, and 2 French oratorios.

There was likewise a merry song made, which, to make their Revells more fashionable, was sung with a Corus, every man bearing his part; which they performed in a daunce, hand in hand. . . .

THOMAS MORTON *

The New World

14

If the sixteenth century in the New World belonged to Spain, the seventeenth century belonged to France and Great Britain. The Virginia colony began in 1607 with the arrival of 900 British colonists at Jamestown. Swamps, disease, and the Indians (encouraged by the Spaniards to the south to raid the settlement) all made colonizing perilous—750 of the original settlers died within three years. But the remainder of the starving Englishmen were saved; Captain John Smith wrote that "it pleased God (in our extremity) to move the Indians to bring us Corne to refresh us, when we rather expected they would destroy us." [1]

* About 1640. Quoted in Gilbert Chase, *America's Music*, New York: McGraw-Hill, 1955, p. 11.
[1] Alvin M. Josephy, Jr. (ed.), *The American Heritage Book of Indians*, New York: American Heritage Publishing Co., Inc., 1961, p. 165.

The seventeenth century was Baroque, not Renaissance, and the attitude of the settlers was very different. The new spirit was not exploration for the glory of God or king, but exploration for the founding of commercial empires. It was the century of the East India Companies, of the importation of coffee and spices from the East, of the beginnings of the scientific views of exploration. The fur trapper and the tobacco grower were the North American pioneers of the seventeenth century. The English wanted neither to save the Indians' souls nor to enslave them for labor but to take the land. Plymouth, the Massachusetts colony, and other British settlements throughout the northeast were acquired by simply taking possession.

The Dutch and Swedes bought their land—the Dutch bought Manhattan in 1626—and were interested for the most part in fur trading. The French were interested both in the fur trade and in the saving of souls; they concentrated their settlements in the north and sent explorers to penetrate southwest via the water routes, notably the Great Lakes and the rivers, including the Mississippi. In 1672, Louis XIV commissioned Louis Joliet "to discover the south sea" and follow the Mississippi, "which is believed to empty into the California Ocean." [2] Joliet took the Jesuit priest Jacques Marquette with him; they set out from Mackinac Island, traveling via Green Bay and the Fox, Wisconsin, and Mississippi Rivers, and reached as far south as the present site of Saint Louis—"an unbroken wild of timber, a continuous waste of forest, with its trees kissing the very wave." [3]

Of all the European ways of looking at life, the Baroque ideal was the one that was capable of seeing the Indians for what they were. To an ideal that tried to measure and assess man and see him whole, the Indian, the Turk, the Chinese, the South Sea Islander, and the African were evidences of multiplicity, which in itself was good.

Observers were more interested in physical than esthetic evidence, more interested in ritual than in art. Only a few remarks on Indian music remain from the Baroque era. In 1634 William Wood said of the singing of the Massachusetts Indians, "to hear one of these Indian's unseene, a good eare might easily mistake their untaught voyce for the warbling of a well tuned instrument. Such command have they of their voices." [4] The French reported in 1632 that the Huron Indians were musical. [5]

It is known that the tribes in the northeast used antiphonal techniques and punctus construction in songs. The construction of songs accruing from two musical elements was emphasized by separate parallel percussion accompaniments. A typical arrangement was *A A B A B*, with the *A* strains accompanied by the high trilling rattle and the *B* strains by the lower, more

[2] Robert Silverberg, *Mound Builders of Ancient America*, Greenwich, Conn.: New York Graphic Society, 1968, p. 20.

[3] *Ibid.*, p. 22.

[4] Josephy, *op. cit.*, p. 26.

[5] *Ibid.*

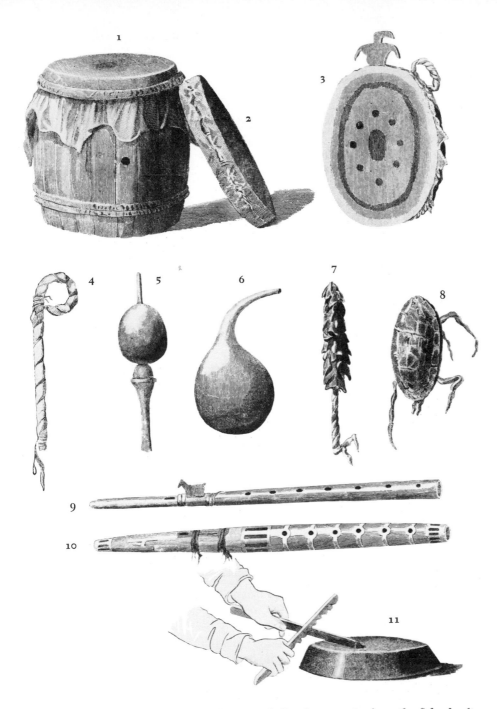

Traditional American Indian instruments, from the *Schoolcraft Report*, 1844. Key: 1–3, drums; 4, drum stick; 5, 6, gourd rattles; 7, rattle made of deer's hooves; 8, turtle-shell knee rattle; 9, 10, flutes; 11, scraper. (Courtesy of Mr. and Mrs. R. A. Rubovits. Photo by R. E. Kalmbach.)

A skin painting showing a dance, by Naiche. (Courtesy of the
Oklahoma Historical Society Photograph Collection.)

incisive drum, as was used in the Iroquois Eagle Dance.[6] Many Indian
songs were based on the cambiata figure of minor third plus major second,
often with a second on each end $(g–a–c^1–d^1–e^1)$.[7]

The colonists through the seventeenth century were able to maintain a
basic respect for the Indians, though from a position of assumed superiority.
They thought the Indians would recognize the higher culture and entrust
themselves to Anglo-Saxon tutelage. In 1636 the founders of Harvard College
stated in the charter that the school was instituted "for the education of the

[6] Bruno Nettl, *Folk and Traditional Music of the Western Continents*, Englewood Cliffs,
N. J.: Prentice-Hall, 1965, p. 161.
[7] *Ibid.*, pp. 160–162; Gilbert Chase, *America's Music*, New York: McGraw-Hill, 1955,
pp. 409–431, especially the Ojibway songs on pp. 411–412.

English and Indian youth in knowledge and Godliness." [8] The aim of educating Indians as well as white men was also stated at the founding of the College of William and Mary and, as late as 1769, at the founding of Dartmouth College. Dartmouth's charter included a clause setting forth the goal of "instruction of the youths of the Indian tribes in this land." [9]

The towns were small versions of towns in England and Holland and afforded a surprising amount of domestic comfort. The Dutch skill in home furnishings along with the English talent in the arts of earthenware and

[8] John L. Stoutenburgh, Jr., *Dictionary of the American Indian*, New York: Philosophical Library, 1960, p. 99.
[9] *Ibid*.

"Bull dance of the Mandan Indians," by George Catlin (c. 1832). (Courtesy of the National Collection of Fine Arts, Smithsonian Institution.)

pewter provided amenities at an early date. Intellectual life also paralleled that in the home countries, and printing presses arrived at the turn of the century to feed it. Benjamin Franklin (1706–1790) was the model intellectual, combining a versatile and ready mind with the manly, simple virtues that glorified life of the new world. He was a scientist and inventor who was and is famous for his experiments with electricity—but he also invented a musical instrument, the glass harmonica, a stove (known as the Franklin stove) that was a standard kitchen appliance as late as the twentieth century, and bifocal lenses for eyeglasses. In addition, he ran a printing press in Philadelphia and published *Poor Richard's Almanack* from 1732.

CHURCH MUSIC IN THE COLONIES

Most of the musical activity in the English colonies was of three types— singing in church, formal concerts presented on the European model, and informal musicmaking of a basically simple if not folk type. Church singing is the best documented; the Psalm books of the late Renaissance were brought to the New World by the settlers, as was the Anglican *Book of Common Prayer*. Maryland had been ceded to the Lords Baltimore, who were Roman Catholic, so the Roman Missal, already brought over by the Spanish and French, was part of English colonial life also, as was the music of the Mass and devotional domestic exercises.

In addition to the Puritans, Anglicans, and Roman Catholics, smaller sects were attracted to the new lands, in which they could establish religious practices as they choose. German Pietists came in 1694, the Swedish Gloria Dei group about the same time, the German Seventh Day Dunkers in the 1720s, and the German Moravians in 1741. Many of these groups settled in eastern Pennsylvania, near Philadelphia, and developed musical arts in their churches, homes, and communities parallel to the music they had left. The Pietists and Dunkers sang chorales and developed a large literature of their own; in 1730, Benjamin Franklin printed the Dunkers' *Ephrata Hymn Collection*, which was named for their communistic community, the Ephrata Cloister. The Moravians introduced the more complete instrumental art that was popular in Europe by 1740. Their community, at Bethlehem, Pennsylvania, became a center of concert life and was kept somewhat up to date with music brought by new arrivals. And the Swedish Gloria Dei church imported an organ.

The Puritans had left England at the point of transition between Renaissance and Baroque practice, when the multiple-line anthem was reaching a point of excess but the stile nuovo was not yet defined. Their rejection of music in church, save for the simplest Psalm singing, can be related to the general rejection of excess as a concept. Their disapproval of social dancing can be viewed in the same light, for the court dances in England reflected the same excess and had shocked many who were far from puritanical. Once in the New World, the Puritans were cut off from the musical redefinitions of the seventeenth century and, to some extent, from other communities in the colonies. Separation led to the necessity of teaching the tunes from memory and by rote, which resulted in each community's developing its own individual practice. Thus, musical separatism was the rule through the seventeenth century. Attempts to worship jointly, when choristers were at a loss to reconcile differing versions of the same hymns, led to controversy over the need to standardize the tunes. Around 1720 two books appeared that attempted to solve the problem,[10] but too many variants had developed—variants that singers felt comfortable with and that they therefore believed must be right—to make standardization easy. It would be two generations before a vigorous native art of tune writing and singing, in which *note* had been substituted for *rote*, was achieved.

The Anglican and Roman Catholic communities had fewer problems, because they were branches of European churches and could be kept abreast of practices abroad without undue hardships. In about 1715, an organ was brought over by the King's Chapel parish of Boston, and by the end of the Baroque era, a few organist-choirmasters were being hired directly from England to supervise the musical aspects of services. In 1753 Trinity Church in New York brought over the organist-choirmaster of Bristol Cathedral. By the end of the decade he was busying himself with community choral concerts in the English tradition, and in 1770 he produced the first performance in the Western hemisphere of Handel's *Messiah*.

SECULAR MUSIC IN THE COLONIES

In general, it can be assumed that the church musicians were involved in starting regular concerts, either by producing them or by arranging for the appearance of touring groups. Charleston, South Carolina, was the most active American city in musical matters in the decades after 1730. A local finishing school for young ladies included music in the curriculum by 1730, professional concerts began there in 1732, and in 1733 a song recital was presented, perhaps the first in the New World. In 1735 the ballad opera *Flora, or Hob in the Well*, an anonymous work that had been produced in London in 1729, was presented. It was followed, in 1736, by Charles Coffey's *The Devil to Pay* (London, 1731); this work was later offered in New York (1751). In addition, a series of amateur concerts, followed by "Country

[10] John Tufts, *A Very Plain and Easy Introduction to the Whole Art of Singing Psalm Tunes*, Boston: Samuel Gerrish, 1720; Thomas F. Walter, *The Grounds and Rules of Music Explained*, Boston: F. Franklin, 1721.

Dances for the Diversion of the Ladies," was presented in 1732; the concerts became popular, and the *South Carolina Gazette* reported "a fine appearance of good company"—a review of the audience rather than the musicians.[11]

Other towns were not so active as Charleston, which had the highest reputation for refinement and social graces throughout the Colonies. But in Boston, the earliest known concert, "a Concert of Music on Sundry Instruments," was announced in 1731. Boston's Fanueil Hall was soon used for "Concerts of Musick," and a concert hall, presenting performances of "Vocal and instrumental Musick to consist of Select Pieces by the Masters," [12] was opened in 1754. Philadelphia's musical life centered in the domestic concert, which was more consistent with the Quaker philosophy. Yet a dancing teacher was able to make his living there in 1710. Public concerts began only in 1757, and the attendance of George Washington at the second one gave prestige and respectability to the idea, which neither the Puritans nor the Quakers wholly trusted.

The informal music of the colonies must be reconstructed largely through conjecture, but this should not belittle the substantial place it surely had in the daily lives of the settlers. Townspeople knew the popular songs of England, such as "Sally in Our Alley" and "The Girl I Left Behind Me," the ballad opera favorite "The Vicar of Bray," and Arne's "Rule, Brittania!" In the country areas, the reciprocity between settlers and Indians was considerable. New England colonists were quick to adopt Indian foods, from succotash to baked beans, and soon were joining in Indian games as well. An English trader wrote that the Indians "exercise themselves in gaminge, and playing of juglinge tricks, and all manner of Revelles, which they are delighted in." [13] Indian clambakes were often attended by settlers, and the Algonquin dance party, actually a dancing match, which they called a *cantico*, became popular. As a contemporary writer put it, "many a time Indians and settlers cut a cantico together." [14] In addition, the custom of a Thanksgiving ceremony after harvest had long been practiced by the Indians of the northeast, and it was soon shared. Some of the Indian Thanksgiving songs notated by twentieth-century scholars are lyrical and compelling.

In turn, Indians often came to the settlers' parties, which included dancing to songs, percussion, and fiddles. (Violins were brought to the New World, as were any small instruments that a man could play easily in the wilds—notably the Jew's harp, also called the jaw's harp and juice harp.) Such parties were common, because putting up the roof of a house or a barn involved a community effort. After a new arrival had finished the preliminary work on a building, the neighboring men came to help finish the job and the women came to prepare food for all. Barn dances originated in such commu-

[11] Shirley Mackie, "Secular Music in America," *The American Music Teacher,* September-October, 1967, p. 30.

[12] John Tasker Howard, *The Music of George Washington's Time,* Washington, D.C.: United States George Washington Bicentennial Commission, 1931, p. 51.

[13] Josephy, *op. cit.,* p. 163.

[14] *Ibid.,* p. 173.

nity gatherings; after the roof was up, a dance would be held on the barn floor, before stall partitions, lofts, and other fittings were added. The expression "raising the roof" also derives from these parties.

People sing, make music with instruments, and dance everywhere, and they always have, so the musical life even in isolated families probably ranged from occasional to intensive. The hills of the Appalachian range, where many colonists settled and then were cut off to a large extent, provide even today a lively repository of English folk songs and dances from the seventeenth century; such songs as "Barbara Ellen" (or "Barbary Allen") and "Lord Randall" are heard in both England and America. Moreover, the mountain people still play the violin as it was played in the seventeenth century, against the chest and with little vibrato.

It has often been pointed out that amusements were few and that it was for this reason that music and dancing were so popular, but song in its fullest sense is a poem sung, and folk ballads give people some feeling of community through a shared literature of legends, experience, and emotions. The American folk song was born of the common goals of the settlers, their trail stories, and, above all, the particular loneliness of men facing and trying to conquer a vast landscape. It was recognition of a man's worth in combatting nature, a concept different from any European concept, that captured the Old World imagination; and nowhere was it more poignantly evoked than in the lonely figure of a man riding into an unmeasured wilderness singing "I'm a Poor Wayfaring Stranger" or, with his Jew's harp, humming a slow tune whose folk character tinged it with the sadness of universality. Such a picture was Baroque only in its contrast of smallness and simplicity with the vastness of the country and the man's purpose; it was nonharmonic, and it was a unity of expression. It was closer to the Indian camp than to the court salon.

But Europe was entering a new era of humanism and was enamored of the "natural man," so books on the New World proliferated. The impact of the New World on the Old centered in natural history and new imports. At the opening of the seventeenth century the rage for tobacco took hold in Great Britain, and the literature of the lute song benefited from the many odes to tobacco and the joys of smoking. Studies of ethnic groups were rare; it was the single plant, animal, or artifact that was the desired item for an exhibit in a private gabinetto. Thus the author Filippo Bonanni in his *Gabinetto Armonico* (Musical Museum; 1723) [15] illustrated European art and folk instruments, plus fourteen Turkish, six Chinese, nine African, and three American Indian instruments—the coiled bark trumpet of the Florida Indians, the seed-filled gourd rattle of the Virginia (Shawnee) Indians, and the arm and leg rattles of the Brazilian Indians. But the illustrations were not accurate; one even pictured a female Indian dancing in a Greek tunic.[16] However, Bonanni was more interested in the instruments than the music;

[15] Frank L. Harrison and Joan Rimmer (eds.), *Filippo Bonanni: The Showcase of Musical Instruments*, New York: Dover, 1964.

[16] *Ibid.*, plate 125.

he made no attempt to understand the music or the sociological aspects of its presentation. Such a focus was entirely consistent with the Baroque intellectual life as a whole; it was also a natural result of the inevitable frustration that resulted (and still results) from attempts to notate Indian music within the European concepts of pitch and meter. A fourteenth-century musician, with his grasp of complex temporal proportion and his respect for monophony, would have been better able to succeed; in the early eighteenth century such attempts were hopeless.

Part Four

MUSICAL CLASSICISM

He who wishes to devote himself to composition must have a lively and fiery spirit, united with a soul capable of tender feeling; a good mixture, without too much melancholy, of what scholars call the temperaments; much imagination, inventiveness, judgement, and discernment; a good memory; a good and delicate ear; a sharp and quick eye; and a receptive mind that grasps everything quickly and easily.

JOHANN JOACHIM QUANTZ *

The Modernist Generation

What had begun as delightful multiplicity ended as irritating confusion. The most obvious characteristics of the Baroque musical art were the bass-treble polarity and the freewheeling use of musical instruments within the concertato principle. The stringing together of contrasting movements had provided a formal bulwark to composers who faced the question of how music could achieve size without guidance from text, dance, or cantus firmus. Now composers were turning away from the bass-treble polarity and from the concertato principle as a means of expanding musical form. Instead of contrasts *between* movements, composers were seeking variety *within*

15

* Edward R. Reilly (trans. and ed.), *J. J. Quantz on Playing the Flute*, London: Faber, 1966, pp. 12–13.

movements. And instead of seeking contrasts through the jousting of musical forces, they were beginning to seek it through the manipulation of musical ideas. Composers were also seeking to sort out the multiplicity of instruments and settle on a superior and reliable few. Instruments, which had been various, were to become standardized; the texture of music, which had been standardized, was to become various. Thus the elements of stability and variety would be reversed. Although the change may seem small to the modern musician, the difference to audiences must have been huge and exciting.

In the middle of the eighteenth century the heart and head were equally acknowledged. A text of 1751 began, "The Intention of Musick is not only to please the Ear, but to express the Sentiments, strike the Imagination, affect the Mind, and command the Passions." [1] These five aims—the five verbs are instructive—sum up the ideal of musical function at the middle of the eighteenth century.

THE CLASSICAL STYLE

By 1760 the continuo harpsichord was optional, and its use in the symphony doubtless depended more on social than musical considerations. The contracts of eighteenth-century musicians with their patrons were legally firm and morally binding. The continuo harpsichordist who had given good service for twenty years would not be fired, but after 1760 few were replaced. Decline of the basso continuo was not the result of filling in the middle parts and thus not needing the notes of the harpsichord; it was the result of rejecting the concept of the polar bass-treble fabric and the continuing bass part that this concept implied. The essence of the new style was a redefinition of musical texture and a concern with texture as the new element of contrast and motivation.

The new ideal made use of three basic registers—top, middle, and bottom—equally definite and equally able to share the three musical functions of presenting a subject, providing the harmonic structure, and offering a countersubject. The new style centered on the introduction of many textures within a constant meter. A short subject might present one texture and be followed at once by another subject with another texture. Instead of an apposition of performing groups, the new style focused on an apposition of textural formats.

Basic to the quick contrasts of the new style was the companion contrast of *attacks*, manners of addressing the instruments, which is another kind of texture, a *surface texture*. In the Classical style few notes were slurred, and these were generally *couplets* or two-note groups, which were to be

---

[1] Francesco Geminiani (David D. Boyden, ed.), *The Art of Playing on the Violin*, Fair Lawn, N.J.: Oxford University Press, 1952, p. 1.

played *legato* ("ligamented," "bound"). The appoggiatura, already in the Baroque vocabulary, was the most important of these couplets and was given both a special notation (the first tone as an added small note) and a special emphasis. The appoggiatura meant a "leaning" note; it displaced the normal tone, delaying its arrival and setting up the need to attain it in a *resolution*. The slow appoggiatura was called a *sigh* (in German, *Seufzer*; in French, *sanglot*, "sob"). An English writer called appoggiature "binding notes or emphatical discords" and instructed his reader on their proper performance: "Those notes should be prest hard; for the elegance and surprise excites a great attention, as if the auditors were upon [tip-toe] to know what would become of this business." [2]

Also popular was the two-note dotted figure, either a dotted eighth plus a sixteenth (♪. ♪) or its reverse (♪♪.). It was a separate entity in performance, detached from what followed. A popular rhythmic figure in the Classical style, the reverse figure was sometimes called the "Lombardy figure" or, rarely, the "Scottish snap." A variation substituted two thirty-second notes for the sixteenth (♪. ♫ or ♫♪.).

Contrasts of surface and structural texture became inseparable when two registers, or all three, combined, each with its own style of attack. Passage work in the violins might be combined with eighth or quarter notes in the bass while a single long note was being sustained in the middle; a threefold texture was representative of the full Classical subject. Horns and oboes were particularly suited to the holding of a note—most often the dominant of the key—while detached effects were presented and exchanged elsewhere. The sustained tone, like a constant thread or clothesline, could serve at once as a basis for contrast and a means of unity.

Mannheim

The court of the prince elector at Mannheim was a primary center in the definition of the symphony. By bringing the modernist Johann Stamitz to the court in 1745, the elector made Mannheim famous for its new music. In the following twelve years, Stamitz produced about seventy-five symphonies and gathered around him a coterie of young men who contributed to the large literature of the *Mannheimer Stil* ("Mannheim style").

The instrumental staff at Mannheim was large and by 1756 numbered about forty-five; this was almost as many as were on the Paris Opéra staff—and that staff also served the Concert spirituel. (The Mannheim musicians were called an *orchestra*, whereas the Opéra still spoke of the *symphonie*.)

The Mannheim style was radical. It not only redefined the instrumental ensemble, it experimented with the kinds of sounds the orchestra could produce and developed a vocabulary of orchestral techniques that were to become basic idioms of the Classical style. Most were not new but were used in new, often stunning, ways. For example, string tremolos had been used by Monteverdi, and mutes on trumpets and strings had not been un-

---

[2] Roger North, quoted in John Wilson (ed.), *Roger North on Music*, London: Novello and Company Ltd., 1959, p. 219.

common in the seventeenth century. Crescendos and diminuendos were natural vocal stocks-in-trade, and the solo madrigal had used dynamic shades. Bel canto singers used all the dramatic effect they could produce, and solo violinists imitated vocal fervor in expressing the passions. What was new and startling was a crescendo by an entire orchestra, an effect that seems to have begun in Rome and been carried northeast by the traveling Italian composers. The orchestral crescendo, *subito piano* (a sudden piano at the end of a crescendo), and other devices were not introduced in Mannheim but were often expanded there. For example, the *tirata* (an embellishment in which a quick run connects two notes of a melodic leap) was given to the entire violin section in an extended upward-sweep form (a twelfth or fifteenth) and played with a crescendo. This effect must have been astonishing; it was given the name *Racket* ("rocket," "Roman candle") or "Mannheim rocket."

Such flamboyant techniques were representative of the intensely experimental Mannheimers. Like so many crusaders, they exaggerated the effects they sought, so although the techniques were not forgotten, they were adopted elsewhere with considerably more circumspection. Typically, the other orchestras of Europe were half as large and only half as daring as that in Mannheim. However without the extravagance of the Mannheim group, the momentum that was vital to Classicism could not have been so strongly established.

The city of Paris was the intellectual hub of Europe in the eighteenth century, serving as a center for the discussion of musical philosophy, both formal and practical. It drew visitors from many directions and was a chief center for music publishing, not only of French music, but also of the new instrumental music of other countries. Foreign composers came to Paris to be heard at the Concert spirituel, to hear the private orchestra of the rich tax collector and music lover Le Riche de la Pouplinière (1693–1762), and to have their music published and thus establish themselves in their profession.

Paris

But the French were making their own contribution to the new style. The concerted keyboard work, particularly the sonata for harpsichord and added instruments, was a distinctively French musical type that had developed in Paris during the first decades of the eighteenth century. At first, the additional instrument did little more than enhance, in the manner of a ripieno, the upper part of a solo harpsichord piece. Then in 1734, Jean-Joseph Cassanéa de Mondonville brought out the *Pièces de clavecin en sonates*, a set of six works in which the harpsichordist played the solo pièce (as before) but the violinist played an independent line, as though he were performing a solo sonata. The partnership of two equal soloists was unprecedented.

The new form was adopted by other composers. In 1741 Rameau presented a larger instrumental force that created a union between the pièce and the small concerto. His publication was the *Pièces de clavecin en con-*

certs avec un violon ou une flûte et une viole ou un deuxième violon (Harpsichord Pieces in the Manner of Concertos, with a Violin or Flute and a Viola da Gamba or a Second Violin).

Johann Schobert brought the tradition to its climax. His works, all titled *Pièces de clavecin*, were variously subtitled *Sonata* (some with further subtitles of *Quartetto* and *Sinfonia*) and *Concerto*. The sonatas used a single violin or violin and cello in addition to the keyboard, those marked quartetto used two violins and cello in addition to the keyboard, and those marked sinfonie used a violin and two horns in addition to the keyboard. The six concertos used a larger string group (two violins, viola, and bass— meaning cellos and perhaps a contrabass) and flute, plus oboe or horns. In his sonatas, Schobert used Mannheim symphonic techniques and formats, producing three- and four-movement designs similar to those of the symphonists.

> Allegro assai, Siciliano, Tempo di Menuetto.
> Allegro, Andante assai, Allegro assai, Menuetto.
> Allegro, Adagio lamentabile, Presto.

Schobert's works were widely performed in Paris and thus were heard by larger and more cosmopolitan audiences than could have been assembled in any other center. From November, 1763, to March, 1764, Leopold Mozart and his family were there, on the first of the international tours that Leopold arranged for his gifted children. Nannerl was eleven and Wolfgang almost seven when they arrived in Paris; during their stay, the children played for the royal family and for the Prince de Conti, and Nannerl played some of Schobert's works. Wolfgang's tributes to Schobert were twofold. While in Paris, Wolfgang composed his first publication, which was brought out in the spring of 1764—*Sonates Pour Le Clavecin Qui peuvent se jouer avec l'Accompagnement de Violon* (Sonatas for the Harpsichord That Can Be Played in Company with a Violin). And in his first piano concertos, Wolfgang used Schobert subjects.

But modernism was declining in French music. Even while Mozart was in Paris, listening to Schobert at the palace of the Prince de Conti, the modernists were being heard only by the connoisseurs. The mass audiences were going to the theaters, and the war between ornate Italian opera, dramatic opera (these two at odds themselves), and popular opera began to dominate the French public scene. It was to do so until the time of the French revolution.

Keyboard Music

At the midpoint of the eighteenth century, the clavichord, harpsichord, and pianoforte (called the *fortepiano* in Germany) were all being used; each had its own musical potentials and social functions. The harpsichord was the instrument of the professional on the concert stage, serving as both the continuo instrument and virtuoso vehicle. The smaller harpsichord (in England,

A pianoforte, by Johann Zumpe, c. 1765. (Courtesy of The Metropolitan Museum of Art, The Crosby Brown Collection of Musical Instruments, 1889.)

the spinet) was the most common home instrument in every country but Germany, where the rage for the clavichord was still powerful. And pianos were the rich man's luxury; they were very scarce, except in the few courts whose royalty spent money generously on the art of music.

One such court was that of Frederick the Great in Berlin, which, in addition to housing two Silbermann pianos, also housed Carl Philipp Emanuel Bach. Bach, the court's keyboard virtuoso and teacher, was chief among the many composers who sang the praises of the clavichord and furnished material for it. He centered his music in the techniques of the clavichord and pianoforte and sought to put drama into his compositions by using the stylish *Empfindsamkeit* ("expressiveness"), so beloved of the amateurs. In addition, he concerned himself with the parallel problem of internal structure, exploring intramovement coherence in a remarkably modern way.

Bach's central accomplishment in form was to redefine the function of the musical subject or motif. He used repetition with variation, referring to a previously stated subject but changing it by new textural details. Two important results of his technique were to have enormous implications for his successors: first, as a movement progressed, Bach could make a subject more important by singling it out for such presentation; and second, he could demonstrate relationships between two subjects and justify their appearance within the same movement.

The Silbermann pianos in Frederick's court were similar to those of Bartolommeo Christofori (1655–1731), who, in the beginning of the eighteenth century, had built some of the earliest successful models. The pianos were long instruments in the shape of concert harpsichords. However, whereas in the harpsichord the string was plucked by a plectrum and on the clavichord it was touched by a tangent, on the piano the string was *struck* by a *hammer*. The process was more like that of the harpsichord than of the clavichord in that the activation of the string was momentary; both the plectrum of the harpsichord and the hammer of the piano engaged the string for an instant and then left it, whereas the tangent of the clavichord stayed in contact with the string, simultaneously damping the sound and allowing for unique expressive possibilities. The piano did resemble the clavichord in its response to finger pressure, but the freedom of the string to vibrate fully after the hammer attack allowed it greater resonance. The piano could be played in a dynamic range considerably greater than that available to the clavichord and could be used in public. It was not as loud or as brilliant as the concert harpsichord, however.

The problem with the early pianos lay not in starting the tones but in ending them. The damper action was faulty or even absent in the piano, and the instrument was incapable of the good articulation of other keyboard instruments, unless the player used the harpsichord technique of releasing the string as precisely as he struck it. But because the pianoforte entered the picture as a new kind of clavichord, not harpsichord, few of the amateurs could manage it. As late as 1783, a critic complained that the pianoforte was "a defective instrument on which the tones run into each other with bad effect unless the player has an elastic spring in each finger." [3]

It was not the concert pianoforte but the smaller, rectangular instrument called the *square piano* that ensured the popularity of the new instrument. The square piano could fit into the rooms of the amateurs; it was less expensive, within the range of the middle-class families upon whose predilections music was becoming increasingly dependent. And, perhaps most important, it was much less expensive to maintain than a harpsichord because the pianoforte stayed in tune longer and did not have to be requilled. The square piano was being made in the 1740s, but its manufacture began in England only in the late 1750s; it became popular there in the 1760s. By 1770 it was being manufactured in France, and by 1780 it was a universal instrument.

INSTRUMENTAL FORMS

By 1730 the new directions of the concerto were becoming clear. The title *concerto grosso* was increasingly rare, while *concerto* might indicate a small group of soloists, a larger group with doublings, or a traditional con-

[3] Johann Baptist Cramer, quoted in Sister M. Romana Hertel, O.S.F., "The Keyboard Concertos of Johann Wilhelm Hertel" (unpublished doctoral dissertation, Catholic University of America, Washington, D.C.), University Microfilms, 1964, no. 65–5556, p. 128.

certino—more and more likely to be a solo—and larger ensemble. The use of such terms as *symphonie, sonata, overture, suite,* and *ritornello* in an almost equal manner created a confusion that bothered the Baroque musician far less than it bothers the modern scholar. Each of these terms had a generalized meaning that overlapped and was used interchangeably with one or more of the others. But the terms provided a readymade vocabulary for the musicians who flourished from 1730 to 1760; they did not have to invent new terms, they only had to agree on the meanings of the old ones.

They began by being more specific in designating a quartet, quintet, and so forth, and by using the term *divertimento* (in French, *divertissement*). The word meant "diversion," in the sense of both a digression, as in the episode of a ritornello movement or a fugue, and an entertainment.

As the divertimento became popular, it too took on additional names. *Serenade,* an old troubadour title, meant "evening music"; *cassation,* a term of obscure derivation, may have meant a "farewell" piece. But by whatever name, the divertimento retained its relationship to the suite, being a free succession of movements, often including dances.

The term *concerto* continued as a designation for works in which the rivalry between two entities comprised a motivating force. As the orchestra

"Mlle. de Charolais Playing the Guitar," anonymous, c. 1715. The guitar remained an instrument of cultured amateurs through the eighteenth century. (Courtesy of the Conservation des Musées, Tours. Photo by R. Arsicaud et Fils.)

Group of ancient instruments. *Plate 1*. Nolan Amphora, attributed to Brygos. An Attic, red-figured amphora on which a cithara player is depicted. (Courtesy of the Museum of Fine Arts, Boston, the John Michael Rodocanachi Fund.) *Plate 2*. Egyptian flute, A.D. third century. The instrument is made of wood covered with bronze. (Courtesy of the University of Michigan, Kelsey Museum of Ancient and Mediaeval Archaeology.) *Plate 3*. Mural from an unknown tomb in Thebes, eighteenth dynasty. (Courtesy of Hirmer Fotoarchiv, Munich.)

4

Plate 4. The Minnesinger Heinrich Frauenlob (upper left) in a German miniature of the late thirteenth century. He is portrayed as king of the minstrels surveying a group of performers. Two singers (with their hands in position for beating the tactus) are surrounded by musicians with drums, a straight flute and tambourine (called a *galoubet*, a Provençal type similar to the pipe and tabor), a tenor vielle, a chalumeau, a treble vielle, a dulcimer, and a musette (small bagpipe). The shield and crest (heraldically meaningless) represent the subject of Frauenlob's songs (his name means "praise of women"). (Courtesy of Photo Lauros, Paris.)

Plate 5. A late fifteenth-century miniature, of Flemish origin, depicting musicians at a church portal. The variety of instruments is representative of minstrelsy and implies that the sound was comparable to the vivid colors of the miniature itself. From the left, the instruments are pipe and tabor, triangle, a wind instrument (probably a shawm), buzine trumpet, harp, small lutes, a group of treble shawms, psaltery, and a tenor shawm; at the right foreground is a portative organ. (Courtesy of the British Museum.)

Plate 6. A performance of Leonardo da Vinci's *La Contesa dei numi*, painted by Giovanni Paolo Pannini, 1729. The lavish setting is a private theater in the palace of the Cardinal de Polignac at Rome. The orchestra, shown in tiers on the stage, was unusually large. (Courtesy of La Réunion des Musées Nationaux, Paris.)

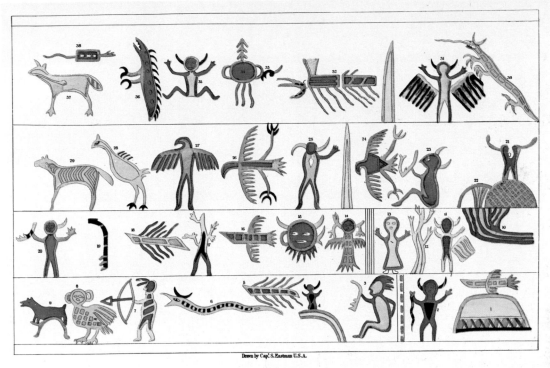

7

WABENO SONGS.

Indian songs. *Plate 7.* Wabeno songs. (Drawings by Captain S. Eastman, U.S.A., for the *Schoolcraft Report.* Courtesy of Mr. and Mrs. R. A. Rubovits.) *Plate 8.* War and love songs. (Drawings by Captain S. Eastman, U.S.A., for the *Schoolcraft Report.* Courtesy of Mr. and Mrs. R. A. Rubovits.)

WAR AND LOVE SONGS

Plate 9. "Interior of the Park Theatre in New York, November, 1822," a watercolor by John Searle. (Courtesy of the New York Historical Society.)

9

Romantic scenes. *Plate 10.* An American cowboy playing the banjo, a watercolor by Thomas Eakins, 1890. Like the minstrel with his harp and the Elizabethan singer with his lute, the Western balladeer with his guitar or banjo joined the universal art of songmaking. (Courtesy of the Metropolitan Museum of Art, Fletcher Fund.) *Plate 11.* Castle of Neuschwanstein, built for King Ludwig II of Bavaria (1845–1886). Architecture such as this, which was an evocation of the romance of the Medieval era, was an important aspect of the nineteenth-century ideal. For Ludwig, who was Richard Wagner's patron, architecture was a vital part of the ideas of the *Gesamtkunstwerk*, as defined by Wagner. (Courtesy of Duncan Edwards, F.P.G.) *Plate 12.* "Reverie," by Sir Frank Dicksee, 1895. Painted when the Romantic concept of the piano was at its height, this work summarizes the ideal of music as personal, suprapersonal, philosophical, and, above all, evocative. (Courtesy of the Walker Art Gallery, Liverpool.)

10

11

12

13

Plate 13. "The Promenades of Euclid," by René Magritte, 1955. The painting lives in its own time and space, raising questions of illusion and reality. It evokes the color and even the architectural type of Medieval illumination, not to reproduce them Romantically, but to add them to the total resonance of the experience. (Courtesy of The Minneapolis Institute of Arts.)

was defined, the concerto remained with it, so a new designation might be "concerto for violin and orchestra."

The divertimento was a popular form designed to amuse large numbers of listeners—both amateurs and the unlearned. Its performance was frequently out of doors and informal. The concerto was also popular, but the greater formality of its performance gave it a lesser, though generally more enlightened, audience. The symphony, at the cutting edge of music in the second quarter of the century, was the province of the professional, the avant-garde, and the connoisseur.

The orchestra was now under the direction of the Kapellmeister, a title that had become a general term for any music director—at court, in public, or in church. He was, of course, the *Konzertmeister* ("concert master"), but he also played in the orchestra, most often as a violinist or a harpsichordist. If he was a violinist, he led the first violin section and conducted by exaggerated bowings from where he played. If he was a keyboard player, he directed from the keyboard. Exceptionally, the French Académie in Paris used a separate conductor.

In both London and Paris composers were writing symphonies by 1750. William Boyce in London and François-Joseph Gossec in Paris were composing in the new form and were representative of the experimentalists there and elsewhere. *The Symphony*

Stamitz, Boyce, and Gossec had in common the mixed Baroque heritage of contrasting movements. Their symphonies were eight or ten minutes long and, with considerable leeway, were typically of three movements. The Boyce formats were representative.

> Allegro assai, Vivace, Presto
> Allegro, Vivace ma non troppo, Gavot
> Largo-Allegro, Larghetto
> Andante-Spiritoso, Moderato, Jigg
> Allegro ma non troppo, Tempo di Gavotta, Tempo di Menuetto

Gossec often preferred a simple fast-slow-fast format, as did Stamitz, who often ended with a minuet or added a fourth, more sprightly movement. Stamitz's *Sinfonia a 8*, in D major, had a four-movement format of Presto, Andante non Adagio, Menuetto, and Prestissimo.

Like most popular types, the divertimento was conservative in form but experimental in certain aspects of sound. In the divertimento, composers experimented with combining instruments. They combined instruments of variable range, sometimes of similar type but more often of mixed types. The introduction of new instruments (such as clarinets) or new usage (such as the horn as a melodic instrument) was often accomplished in the divertimento; it was the only rival to the opera in the introduction of new sounds. *The Divertimento*

Austria was a center for the divertimento, which flourished in good-natured abundance, at about the middle of the eighteenth century, in Augsburg, Salzburg, and Vienna. A leading composer of popular instrumental music in Austria was the violinist Leopold Mozart. Under the title divertimento, cassatio, serenade, or even symphony, he produced some of the most popular music of the time—the *Military Divertimento*, the *Hunt Symphony*, and the *Cassatio in G,* which made use of toy instruments from the famous toy factory at Berchtesgaden. (The third, fourth, and seventh movements of this work, played separately, were formerly attributed to Joseph Haydn as the *Toy Symphony*).

Typical of Leopold Mozart's divertimenti is his *Divertimento in F* (called the *Musical Sleigh Ride*), which was first performed at an Augsburg inn in January of 1756. Mozart advertised the coming performance with a movement-by-movement description of the work.

The beginning makes an *Intrada* of a pleasing *Andante* and a magnificent *Allegro*. This is followed by an *Intrada* with trumpets and timpani. Now follows the Sleigh Ride with the tinkle of the sleigh-bells and all the other

Mozart, at the age of eight (1763), playing the harpsichord at a tea party, by Michel Ollivier. The salon is representative of the high-ceilinged halls of the period. Behind the harpsichord is the famed French tenor Pierre Jelyotte of the Opéra and the Concert spirituel, who also sang to the guitar. (Courtesy of the Musée du Louvre, Cliché des Musées Nationaux.)

instruments. After the end of the Sleigh Ride one hears How the sweating horses shake themselves. A pleasing entertainment [divertimento] follows with the chorus of the oboes, horns, and bassoons, as the former sound their entrance and the latter their march in an alternating fashion. The company alights and goes to the ballroom. One hears an *Adagio* which shows the lady trembling with cold. The ball is opened with a *menuetto* and a *trio*. One tries to warm up with German dances until the end draws near at last. The whole company betake themselves with an *Intrada* of the trumpets and timpani to their sleighs to return home.[4]

The scoring is for four string parts (two violins, a viola, and a cello); pairs of oboes, bassoons, horns, and trumpets; and, in addition to the timpani that accompanied the trumpets, five pitched sleigh bells (on c^3, d^3, f^3, g^3, and a^3) and "two persons with courrier-whips," the great snapping lashes that sounded rather like popping a paper bag.

The divertimento, traditional in form and modern in instrumentation, was the Classical complement of the symphony, for the symphony was experimental in form and, once the standard of oboes, horns, and strings was arrived at, conservative in the introduction of new instruments. The importance of divertimenti in the final definition of the symphony was substantial.

THEORY

The art of Classicism was defined in a period in which the ideal was a full measure of both heart and head. A good musician required both emotional fire and intellectual skill. Johann Wilhelm Hertel put it very well.

> Principally it is bountiful nature which must produce the first aptitude for an able composer and must give that which Horace referred to as *"Deum in nobis"* [God within us]; . . . that nature without industry produces nothing but a wild vine, but industry without nature only a forced, dry fruit; . . . and finally, that only he who combines persistent industry with a fine talent and a mind trained by the sciences, a soul full of emotion, and who seizes the right opportunity to gain momentum, can hope at some time to gain honor in this pursuit.[5]

Such a philosophy of art was not the Medieval harmony of polarities. The concept was cumulative rather than proportional; it comprised a mutually necessary pair, each half of which was to be cultivated to the greatest possible extent. The list of qualities necessary for making a good musician had such dimension that, in practical terms, it was impossible to achieve, but it was still serviceable as a set of ideals to guide the young.

---

[4] Quoted by Ernst Fritz Schmid, in annotations for *Leopold Mozart: Musikalische Schlittenfahrt* and *Cassatio ex G*, Archive Production recording ARC 3093.
[5] Quoted in Hertel, *op. cit.*, p. 127.

The eighteenth century was a time of musical culmination, when creative teachers found materials sufficiently defined to support new methods. During the years 1700 to 1775, the books that were to be basic to the teaching of music for the next two centuries were written. J. J. Quantz, Leopold Mozart, and C. P. E. Bach were three of the many theorists who wrote about the new music.[6] Their texts made up a trilogy, the sort of concurrence of giants that comes whenever a high point is marked in history. Although each of them dealt with one instrument in particular, they all saw the subject of music in its entirety, were composers of recognized excellence, and were remarkable teachers. They were part of the growing consciousness that the next musical leadership would come from the musicians who could successfully absorb differing national styles.

The general theory book that pulled the harmonic thought of the century into a concept acceptable throughout Europe was the *Traité d'harmonie*, by Jean-Philippe Rameau—music theory would be based on it until the twentieth century. Rameau was a controversial figure in Paris, and in eighteenth-century terms it is easy to see why. Although he came to Paris as a performer, his bent was toward the scientific study of music.

Rameau had no entree into the scientific world, but his theories reached the public through his apologists, notably Jean le Rond d'Alembert (1717–1783), who was an encyclopedist and a member of the Academy of Sciences (in mathematics and acoustics)—a man with the right credentials. D'Alembert's book *Elémens de musique* claimed to present Rameau's principles in a "clarified, developed, and simplified" manner; it went into six French editions and was issued in German in 1779.

In the second edition of the *Elémens* (1762), d'Alembert added a Preliminary Discourse, which began with a statement of the Classical view of music.

> One can consider Music either as an Art one of whose principal objects is to please the senses or as a science through which that Art is reduced to its principles. It is the double point of view under which it is propounded that it be treated in this Work.[7]

The author ended the Discourse with an equally Classical view.

> Is it necessary to add that it is not enough to make good Music, to be thoroughly familiar with the principles set forth in this Book? One can learn only up to a certain point the mechanics of the Art; it is up to nature to do the rest; without her, one will not compose better Music for having read these *Elémens*, any more than one will write better verse for having read the

[6] Johann Joachim Quantz, in Edward R. Reilly (trans. and ed.), *J. J. Quantz on Playing the Flute*, London: Faber, 1966. Leopold Mozart, quoted in Editha Knocker (trans.), *A Treatise on the Fundamental Principles of Violin Playing*, Fair Lawn, N.J.: Oxford University Press, 1951. Carl Philipp Emanuel Bach, quoted in William J. Mitchell (trans. and ed.), *Essay on the True Art of Playing Keyboard Instruments*, New York: Norton, 1949.

[7] *Elémens de musique théorique et pratique*, 2d ed., Lyon: Jean-Marie Bruyset, 1762, p. j [i].

dictionary. These are, in a word, *Elements of Music*, and not *Elements of Genius* that I propose to give.[8]

Rameau's principles were based in the nature of the single chord. He demonstrated that a fundamental together with its third and fifth partials creates a natural triad, which he called the *common chord*. This, of course, had been the basis of Renaissance and Baroque harmonic concepts, but Rameau went further in his contemplation of the common chord. He proposed that its elements were essentially immutable in their function, which was the function of the fundamental. The theory of the invertibility of *structure* was not new; it had been published in the seventeenth century. It was the invertibility of *functions* that was Rameau's contribution to the theory.

The practical result was the acceptance of the notion of *invertibility*, that the triad C–E–G turned upside down was a C triad still. In Rameau's sense, the acceptance of invertibility meant the recognition that the root of the chord functioned in any position. This, in turn, created three primary triads—common chords built on the lower dominant (subdominant), dominant, and tonic—with which most subjects could be adequately harmonized without having to concentrate harmonic activity in the bass. For example, the E chord of the sixth, written in figured bass as E with a six over it and spelled E–G–C in Baroque theory, had taken its meaning from the bass function of E within the tone in which the chord appeared. In the C major tone, for example, the E chord of the sixth had a mediant function and was most likely to appear in a progression leading (perhaps from C) up to F or G. In the new theory, the same chord would have C as its fundamental tone and would be considered tonic.

Rameau's theory focused attention on the vertical element of the musical language and clarified the essential identity of major and minor modes with the same tonic—the small but crucial difference between tone and key. The original twelve tones had included both g minor and G major, for example. But to Classical composers, g and G were the minor and major modes of the single key of G, with the primary fundamental bass tones of C (subdominant or IV), D (dominant or V), and G (tonic or I) and with the F♯ leading tone essential to both modes. All other scale tones could vary. At the middle of the century, Blainville, another theorist, suggested a "third mode." This was the free use of both major and minor scale materials, a concept embraced by many French composers a good deal earlier and by Classicists everywhere. It is now called *bimodality*.

Rameau's theory of chord structure was the accepted theory of harmony through the nineteenth and into the twentieth century and, in conservative enclaves, to the present time. Its value in furnishing a clear, simple statement of tonal function and a vocabulary for discussing music in a key was incalculable.

---

[8] *Ibid.*, p. xxxv.

PERFORMANCE

The basis of the Classical style was variety of texture, both structural and surface. Clarity was paramount; the standard attack was detached, approximately three-quarters of the written value of notes. Exceptions were generally for embellishment or contrast. The formal embellishments, such as the appoggiatura, the trill, the mordent, and the tirata, were slurred. Pairs of notes, such as the dotted figure, were also slurred. The upbeat was generally detached but had an occasional switch in steady rhythms, such as the eighth notes in $\frac{2}{4}$ or $\frac{6}{8}$ time, when an upbeat might be slurred across the bar line and all other notes detached. The detached type, called the *dry upbeat*, was a hallmark of the Classical style.

The Voice

In every era, the human voice has, almost mystically, been recognized as an embodiment of the ideals of the era. To the Medieval mind, the qualities of man and the angels could be sensed in a perfect voice, which was almost literally considered inspired. The harmony of text and voice gave song a particular glory. To the Renaissance man, the voice was man's own instrument, and even when he was singing to the glory of his Creator, he was aware of the excellence of the created. In the Baroque ideal, the voice was the perfect medium because it was the most complete contrast to the bass and because it was the ideal instrument for the expression of the passions. To the Classicist, the voice was the instrument with the most intimate relationship to both heart and head, and a beautiful voice was, as always, greatly esteemed. But in the age of head and heart and of the common man, the castrato was too unnatural and extreme. Thus the art of the castrato was on the way out.

The Classical style, with its desire for human simplicity and its need for a high surface texture, was not the ideal basis for serious vocal music, except in the opera, where it could join the other elements in the service of a mutual goal. This goal the Classicist, with his balanced, cumulative view, defined as dealing effectively with all aspects of opera; he attempted to do so by making the dramatic and musical aspects equal and by sacrificing the excesses to produce a work in which all the facets were abundantly represented.

Song was to share the same ideal; both text and melody were to be fully exposed. Simple, folklike songs began to gain in popularity, both in private concerts and in the musical theater. The setting of good poetry came back into style, and, as always in an era that values the text, humor came strongly to the fore. The humorous song, using the high texture to its own ends, enjoyed a superior place in the Classical popular art. In many comic or character pieces, rests abounded with the frequency of the Medieval hocket. (Hocketing had also been put to frequent use in good-natured and humorous music.) Popular songs in the late eighteenth century, which ap-

An anonymous engraving of the Vauxhall Gardens, about 1730, showing the orchestra during a performance. (Photo by R. E. Kalmbach.)

peared singly and in copious collections, were leavened with high surface texture and humor in a happy unity.

Unlike pieces evincing the broader Baroque humor, Arne's "The Stammering Lover" was neither salacious, obscene, nor merely a setting for a clever poem on the joys of liquor, tobacco, or coffee. It was a parody as much of the musician as the lover. Musical and verbal humor were separate but were also one; diction, clarity, simplicity were necessary for effective performance but also for characterization. In short, though a good clear presentation was necessary, the song could not succeed if the singer did not put a good deal of spirit into it.

The popularity of the glee form had been growing. As the new ideal of musical directness and simplicity took hold, everything that hinted of the learned style fell into disrepute in England. The straightforward glee supplanted the involved catch, and by 1775 the glee club was more stylish than the catch club. Gentlemen met regularly at inns or taverns to sing glees by such composers as Luffman Atterbury (died 1796). Glees, with their simple punctus construction in the familiar style, were to be important tutors of the harmonic language in the coming Romantic era, and they would remain

THOMAS AUGUSTINE ARNE

This example is a facsimile from a collection of Arne's songs called *The Vocal Grove*, published in 1774. (Courtesy of the University of Michigan Library. Photo by R. E. Kalmbach.)

in favor because they were ideally suited for the musical expression of the tender sentiments. The Romantic glee would be at its height in the first third of the nineteenth century.

The ideal Classical medium was a single entity that contained variety but was not ruled by it. The suitability of the piano was self-evident, that of the voice was subtler but still self-evident. But to people brought up on Baroque

The Orchestra

Tell Me Then the Reason Why   Example 58

LUFFMAN ATTERBURY

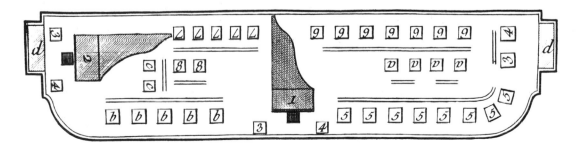

(Courtesy of the University of Michigan Library. Photo by R. E. Kalmbach.)

Seating chart for the Dresden Opera orchestra under Johann Adolph Hasse. Key:
1. harpsichord of the Maitre de Chapelle; 2. harpsichord for accompaniment;
3. violoncellos; 4. double basses; 5. first violins; 6. second violins, with backs to
the audience; 7. oboes, the same; 8. flutes, the same; a. violas, the same; b. bassoons; c. horns; d. a platform on each side for trumpets and timpani. (From Jean-
Jacques Rousseau, *Dictionnaire de Musique*, Paris, 1768. Photo by R. E. Kalmbach.)

Instrumental Personnel
of Some Eighteenth-Century Orchestral Centers

Leipzig Konzert Gesellschaft (Concert Society), 1746

17 strings
    10 violins
     3 violas
     4 basses (unspecified distribution)
3 flutes and oboes
2 bassoons
2 horns
1 harpsichord
—
26

Opera theater of the Florentin, Naples, 1754

18 strings
    12 violins
     2 violas
     4 basses (2 each of cellos and contrabasses)
2 oboes
2 trumpets (implying timpani)
1 harpsichord
—
23 (24 with timpani)

The Château de Fontainebleau, 1754

20 strings
    14 violins
     6 basses (all cellos)
4 bassoons
2 horns
1 trumpet
1 timpani player
1 harpsichord
—
29

The court of Mannheim, 1756

30 strings
    20 violins
     4 violas
     6 basses (4 cellos and 2 contrabasses)
1 flute
2 oboes
2 bassoons
4 horns
4 trumpets
2 timpani players
1 harpsichord
—
46

The court of the Archbishop of Salzburg, 1757

16 strings
    10 violins
     2 violas
     4 basses (2 each of cellos and contrabasses)
3 flutes and oboes
4 bassoons
2 horns
—
25

The Foundling Hospital, London, 1759

20 strings (unspecified)
4 oboes
4 bassoons
2 horns
2 trumpets
1 timpani player
—
33

La Pouplinière, Paris, 1762

7 strings
    5 violins
    2 basses (1 each of cello and contrabass; the contrabassist doubled on horn)
1 flute
1 oboe
2 clarinets
1 bassoon
2 harps (1 doubled on horn)
1 harpsichord (2 horns if the contrabass and 1 harp were unused)
—
15

The Académie de Musique, Paris, 1775

42 strings
    24 violins (13 firsts, 11 seconds)
     4 violas
    14 basses (10 cellos and 4 contrabasses)
2 flutes
3 oboes
2 clarinets
4 bassoons
2 horns
2 trumpets
1 timpani player
—
58

Esterháza, 1783

19 strings
    11 violins
     4 violas
     4 basses (2 each cellos and contrabasses)
2 oboes
2 bassoons
2 horns
—
25

ideas, to define the orchestra as a Classical entity was quite another thing. However, in a sense, the orchestra was the most ideal of all. Like the passionate and emotional faculties of the composer, the orchestra's separate choirs were seen no longer as opposed segments whose tensions produced vitality but as ingredients to be used sometimes equally but always joined in one reality and in the service of one goal.

The Classical orchestra of oboes, horns, and strings was standard rather than rigid, ideal rather than actual. It was composed of a diverse group of instruments—a basic component of strings plus added winds. Orchestras were drawn from the available personnel and can be assessed from surviving payrolls. However, in a group as active as the Académie de Musique in Paris, a rotation system was used, so that the orchestra seldom, if ever, comprised more than two-thirds of the personnel.

❀ *Some Composers Active in the Modernist Generation*

Men in many European centers took part in defining musical Classicism. Still international in training and interaction, the composers of the middle of the eighteenth century demonstrated the shift from Italian to German and Austrian leadership.

WILLIAM BOYCE (1710–1779), a Londoner, was a choirboy and apprentice organist at St. Paul's. He held private teaching posts and, from 1758, was Organist of the Royal Chapel and Master of Music for George III. He wrote, in addition to the anthems and organ voluntaries expected of a chapel musician, several theater works, a series of song books (*Lyra Britannica*, 1745–1755), and a substantial number of instrumental works, including 12 trio sonatas, 12 overtures, and 8 symphonies (1750). From 1760 to 1778 he collected and published English sacred music from two centuries, a valuable collection called *Cathedral Music*.

CARL PHILIPP EMANUEL BACH (1714–1788), the third son (fifth child) of Johann Sebastian Bach, was the most famous of his family in the eighteenth century and one of the most influential pedagogues of history. His career centered first in Berlin, where, from 1740 to 1767, he was harpsichordist and chamber musician to Frederick the Great, then in Hamburg, where he succeeded Telemann (his Godfather) to the post of civic music director. Bach was prolific as a composer, writing about 260 keyboard works, including the so-called *Prussian Sonatas* (1742), the *Wurtemberg Sonatas* (1746), and about 50 concertos. His six books of sonatas, fantasie, and rondos for amateur pianists (1779–1787) formed an important contribution to the beginning of the art of piano playing. His *Versuch über die wahre Art das Clavier zu spielen* (Essay on the True Art of Playing Keyboard Instruments, 1753) was one of the great texts of the century. In addition to keyboard work, Bach left many small concertos (mostly wind trios and quartets), 18 symphonies, and many vocal works (22 Passions, a Magnificat, cantatas, and more than 250 songs).

JOHANN STAMITZ (1717–1757), a Czech-born violinist and composer, was, from 1745, Kapellmeister at the court of Mannheim; he became famous throughout Europe as director of the orchestra there and pioneer in the new orchestral style. He left about 75 symphonies, 12 solo violin sonatas, some unaccompanied violin sonatas, a dozen violin concertos, many orchestral trios, and a few vocal works (such as a *Mass in D*). His works were published in Paris, Amsterdam, and London. Stamitz's son KARL (1746–1801) was a famed virtuoso of the viola d'amour and lived a good deal of his life in Paris. He left 70 symphonies and many other works. Another son, ANTON (1754–1820), also settled in Paris, as violinist in the royal orchestra. He left over 75 works, including 13 symphonies.

LEOPOLD MOZART (1719–1787), an Austrian violinist, teacher, and composer, was trained as a choirboy at Augsburg. He spent most of his career, as violinist, orchestra director, and court composer, in the service of the Archbishop of Salzburg. Mozart wrote sacred and instrumental music (12 oratorios, 18 or more symphonies, keyboard works, etc.), but his major contribution lay in popular forms, particularly the divertimento. He was one of the century's great teachers, and his book *Versuch einer gründlichen Violinschule* (Treatise on the Fundamental Principles of Violin Playing, 1756) was one of the most widely used texts in the history of music.

JOHANN SCHOBERT (c. 1735–1767) was born in Silesia (now Poland) but was in Paris, in the service of the Prince de Conti, for most of his brief but brilliant career. A harpsichordist and pianist of renown, he left twenty volumes of music, including 6 sets of keyboard concertos, 9 of keyboard-violin sonatas, 2 of keyboard-violin-cello trios, and 2 of quartets for two horns, violin, and keyboard, which he engraved himself.

JOHANN WILHELM HERTEL (1727–1789), a German harpsichordist, pianist, and composer, studied with a student of Johann Sebastian Bach in Eisenach, and, for a year, with Carl Philipp Emanuel Bach in Berlin. At twelve years of age, he toured with his father, a gamba virtuoso, and at eighteen he joined his father at the Strelitz court in Mecklenburg; from 1754 he was at the Schwerin court. He was influenced by the Italian school and developed a Classical style early. His keyboard concertos are of particular interest, for several were written for his patrons to play and therefore avoid extreme technical demands. He left 60 symphonies, 55 concertos (almost all solo, including 15 for keyboard and 16 for violin), 29 keyboard sonatas, 17 violin sonatas, and many miscellaneous works, including German and Italian songs, sacred and secular cantatas, and choral Psalms. In addition, he wrote several theoretical books and his autobiography.

FRANÇOIS-JOSEPH GOSSEC (1734–1829), a northern Frenchman, was a choirboy in Antwerp from 1743 to 1751, after which he went to Paris. His long life was one of honor, and he seems to have taken France's political upheavals in his stride. He conducted La Pouplinière's orchestra until 1762, then served as music director to the Prince de Conti. He founded the Concert des amateurs (Music Lovers' Concerts) in 1770 and conducted the Concert spirituel from 1773 to 1777. He joined the Opéra management in 1775 and became its director in 1782. During the revolution, Gossec conducted the band of the National Guard, and in 1795 he was a founder of the National Conservatory. Under Napoleon he was made a Chevalier of the Legion of Honor. His more than 100 instrumental works, including many symphonies, came early in his career. A number of the symphonies were written before 1762; they were followed by the operas. His larger choral works, including 6 revolutionary hymns, came later. He wrote his *Messe des vivants* (Mass for the Living) at the age of seventy-nine.

I have had to compose a symphony for the opening of the Concert spirituel. It was performed on Corpus Christi day with great applause, and I hear, too, that there was a notice about it in the *Courier de l'Europe*, —so it has given great satisfaction.

WOLFGANG AMADEUS MOZART *

The Classical Generation

By 1760, the time was right for a definitive generation, and, as always, gifted men were ready. The preceding generation had produced some of the finest teachers of music history, and they had written definitive books. It was now possible to learn to compose music on one's own, through a combination of eye and ear, book study, and direct musical experience. Franz Joseph Haydn, deciding in 1750 to become a composer, continued his own education with a book on basso continuo practice, Fux's *Gradus ad Parnassum*, and Mattheson's *Der volkommene Capellmeister*, plus the early keyboard sonatas of Carl Philipp Emanuel Bach, which he studied to learn their secrets.

16

* From a letter to his father, dated July 3, 1778. Quoted in Eric Blom (ed.), *Mozart's Letters*, Baltimore: Penguin, 1956, p. 107.

Musically, the 1760s were exciting years. The new piano style was reaching a height in the solo works of C. P. E. Bach, the trios and quartets of Schobert, and the concertos of J. C. Bach, Hertel, C. P. E. Bach, and Dittersdorf. Johann Christian Bach gave the first public piano recital and the square piano began to be widely manufactured and distributed. For the public, opera—still the rage—entered a new and controversial phase, but for composers, the string quartet and the symphony were the forms at the cutting edge of music. In this respect, the composers were distant from the public, who found them too experimental. But in the divertimento, professional and public met at the heart of the new style.

INSTRUMENTAL FORMS

The 1760s were the peak years for the divertimento, and its focal point was in Vienna, where Joseph and Michael Haydn and Karl Ditters (von Dittersdorf only from 1773) lived and worked. Ditters combined spontaneity with experiment. He liked to use pairs of oboes and clarinets or oboes and horns with a single bassoon, that is, a five-instrument group. He also employed a five-movement form—an opening allegro, a minuet and trio, a slow movement, another minuet and trio, and a finale. Michael Haydn's works were similar. His *Divertimento in D major* has six movements—the five movements of Ditters's works preceded by an andante marcia—and is a quartet for flute, oboe, horn, and bassoon. The use of an overture or entry piece at the beginning and especially of the term *finale* for the last movement implies a concern with the work as a whole. This was an important part of the Classical concept.

The Divertimento

The Joseph Haydn *Divertimento a nove stromenti* (nine instruments) can represent the works of the early 1760s, though they are extremely diverse. The work, which has been dated as late 1761, was scored for two clarinets, two horns, two violins, two violas, and basso continuo. It is made up of six movements—Allegro, Menuetto, Recitativo, Andante, Menuetto, and Finale—but because each minuet alternates with its trio or second minuet and the Finale is a three-movement Allegro, Andante, and Allegro molto, the work seems longer.

The third movement is a true recitativo stromentato as practiced in light opera. The first violin takes the part of the voice, presenting the free *fioratura* over chords held by fermate, with a long appoggiatura (the sob) and a stock cadential formula. The middle section of the Finale presents a Turkish tune in *c* minor with frequent *f♯*, always unharmonized (the tune is harmonically enigmatic in Classical terms), and played in unison or in octaves in the low and middle registers. The rage for things Eastern had been fairly constant for a century, and Turkish dances, particularly the *tam-*

bourin (a swirling dance in duple time over a drone bass with tambourine percussion), were popular.

But more important in the *Divertimento a nove stromenti* than its particularities of subject are its tonal designs—large and small—and its use of the Classical minuet. The minuet had begun as a simple Baroque two-part dance form that could be schematized A :||: B :|| or, tonally, *x-y* :||: [*y*] ⤳ *x*:||. In the Classical ideal, return to the original key involved restatement of the original material to underscore it, as A :||: BA :||.

An even more sophisticated design occurred in the opening allegro, which is representative of the growing concentration on allegro movements. In shorter works, a simple modulation and return raised little problem, but in a longer movement, problems abounded. The most frequent solution lay in an expansion of tonal function.

Such a movement used a tonic key to begin and conclude the movement but gave a strong secondary role to another key, most often the dominant. A sturdy subject was most often associated with the home key because of its forceful initial appearance there. The second key level might have its own materials, and when it did, these were likely to be less stable, built on inversions or introducing variable figures. Characterization of the second key level with unstable musical elements had been a French technique of the early *pièce en concert*; by the height of the Classical style, it was vital to the larger forms. The third section, or recapitulation, required great skill. It must be essentially unified tonally, yet not lack tonal interest; it must repeat large sections of the first section, and yet remain fresh. The entire movement should be suffused with the inventiveness of many textures and many musical ideas. Often one such subject was primary, but the embodiments of the Classical form were so diverse that any generality on the role of the subject in the Classical instrumental movement—except to say that its spirit and design informed the music of its solution—would be misleading.

The individual movement was a tonal design that worked out a balance around a key center—and so was the entire work. As the key center was defined in the smaller sense by the lower and upper dominants, it was defined in the larger sense by a balance of activity to the sharp and flat sides of the home key of the work.

Of the divertimento's six movements, the first and last pairs are in the home key, C, whereas the third and fourth movements (the Recitativo and Andante) form a less stable pair. The Recitativo progresses through a number of keys, with one cadence to D and a second in G. The Andante, in G major, proceeds to its own dominant, D major, to present the brightest key of the work at its midpoint. To counter this activity to the sharp side of C, the first, second, and last movements contain extended sections in *c*, *g*, E♭, *d*, F, and *f* (lower case letters indicate minor keys). The trio of the first minuet (second movement) uses a tonal plan *c*-E♭ :||: E♭-*f* ⤳ *c* :||, the longest excursion to the flat side in the divertimento. The first and last movements are especially well balanced, containing materials on both sharp and flat sides, and the second minuet is the most static. The total form can be generalized:

I	II	III	IV	V	VI
Balanced	Flat side	Active	Sharp side	Static	Balanced

String Quartet

Haydn wrote sixty-six divertimenti for various instruments. Further, he wrote eighty pieces of a type that would have been a small concerto or divertimento a generation earlier, a type singled out for special attention by the composers of the Classical generation—the quartet for two violins, viola, and cello, known as the string quartet. This combination was homogeneous in tone quality but had the subtle differences in quality and technique that inevitably accompany differences in register and physical size. The viola was newly emerging as a potentially equal member of the quartet, for although the Baroque concept of polarity had given an unspecific character to the middle range, the Classical style gave it an important place in textural structures. The viola was therefore as indispensable to the string group as it had been unnecessary to the trio sonata. In the Classical concept, the middle range, given full participation, could not be left to chance.

Composers were interested in working out the interrelations of four such highly manipulable instruments. String quartets began to appear in large numbers in the 1760s, in the early works of Dittersdorf, Luigi Boccherini, André-Modeste Grétry, and Joseph Haydn. These men saw the string quartet as a medium through which the investigation of Classical techniques could be carried out. The small component of players made the quartet practical for immediate performance—composers could meet for sessions of playing and talking. The home of Stephen Storace (1763–1796), an English composer and arranger then living in Vienna, was one location for these sessions and Michael Kelly (1762–1826), an Irish singer, actor, and theater director, wrote of being present at them in 1786. Kelly, with wry wit, made the most of it.

> Storace gave a quartett party to his friends. The players were tolerable, not one of them excelled on the instrument he played; but there was a little science among them, which I dare say will be acknowledged when I name them.
> The First Violin: Haydn
> The Second Violin: Baron Dittersdorf
> The Violoncello: Vanhall
> The Tenor: Mozart
> . . . I was there, and a greater treat or a more remarkable one cannot be imagined.
> On the particular evening to which I am now especially referring, after the musical feast was over, we sat down to an excellent supper, and became joyous and lively in the extreme.[1]

[1] *Reminiscences*, New York: J. & J. Harper, 1826, p. 151.

Both the music making and the "joyous and lively" discussions were part of the interchanges, and remarkable ones they must have been. The four composers who played quartets that evening were the cream of the Viennese musical world—Joseph Haydn, then fifty-four and famous throughout Europe as the greatest living composer; Karl Ditters von Dittersdorf, forty-seven and a baron, a master of the lighter style; Johann Vanhall, the same age as Dittersdorf and one of the most important of the Classicists, who himself wrote over a hundred string quartets; and Wolfgang Mozart, then thirty (always the youngest).

The string quartet held a strong attraction as a vehicle for continuing exploration, and composers turned it into an almost perfect embodiment of Classical form. The quartet was musical design in its purest, most exhilarating form, and the Classicist was a man so in love with music that he could take it neat.

The Symphony

In the period from, roughly, 1760 to 1780, the symphony was nurtured only at courts known for superior music and in a very few cities. The most notable of these was Paris, where symphonies were heard in private concerts or, in public, as preludes to the large choral works that were still the mainstay of concert programs. Yet the definition of the symphony took place during those years. It was the Classical generation who led the symphony from the closed interest of the connoisseur and professional to the public enthusiasm it slowly began to gain in the 1770s. Joseph Haydn wrote seventy-two symphonies between 1759 or 1760 and 1781. Most of these were composed for pairs of oboes and horns in addition to the strings, with the assumption that bassoons might be used in *tutti* sections as ripieno players for the cellos. He dropped the oboes or horns in a few works and added trumpets and timpani or, occasionally, a flute. The symphonies toward the end of that period (1778 to 1781) gave the bassoons separate materials.

Repetition and direct contrast were redefined. In the Baroque style, repetition for the most part had been either exact or sequential, either an extension of the subject in the momentum of the beat or a means of leaving the tone. In the new style, the presentation of a subject was more likely to be succeeded at once by a contrasting subject, and then followed by a repetition of the pair to emphasize the contrast. But repetition in the Classical style was not bound to literal, sequential, or decorated restatements—a subject could be the same and different at the same time. Because the various aspects of a subject were now conceived as being separable, one aspect could change while the others did not: it could be repeated with a different rhythm or a different harmony, even within a different tonal context; it could appear in a different register without having to change its function; and it could redefine itself through changes in other elements. Such repetition with variation, in which a subject could be presented newly garbed or led through a series of changes in a continuing revelation of its potential, became known as *development,* and this technique lay at the core of the Classical experiment. With its elements of surprise and suspense and its excitement of revelations, development fulfilled the Classical desire for full participation of head and heart.

In an art requiring time for its realization, techniques of repetition are essential to form, and in a form concerned basically with the abstract musical elements of space and time, they were crucial. It was in the symphony of the 1760s and 1770s that the Classical generation carried on much of the experimentation that defined these techniques and put them into viable structures that would prove indispensable to composers and delectable to listeners for the next century and a half.

The music of Wolfgang Amadeus Mozart spans the years of musical Classicism. By 1773, at the age of seventeen, he had amassed as much musical experience as many men gain in a lifetime. He was in Salzburg and was writing in a variety of forms, chief among which was the symphony. By this time, the symphonic form was at the height of its Classical embodiment, and Mozart's symphonies are surpassing examples of the pure Classical style.

The fifth of the seven symphonies he wrote that year (and about the thirtieth of his composition) was in $B\flat$ major. Through its abundant reflection of the idioms and techniques of the Classical style, it can well represent the Classical symphony. Like all such works, in form it is unique, developing its materials in a successful structure within the Classical ideal. The work has three movements—Allegro Spiritoso, Andantino Grazioso, and Allegro.

Although the opening Allegro Spiritoso uses the techniques of the Classical style, it is not to be construed as a typical design, for a design was seen as one unique result of the application of the techniques to particular materials. The tonal plan was a three-section one that presented stability at more than one tonal level, continued with a contrasting unstable (modulatory) section, and culminated with a recapitulation of most—or all—of the first section, now tonally loyal to the key of the movement.

These three sections—*statement, development,* and *recapitulation*—became basic to an opening allegro movement. It could be preceded by an introduction or followed by a coda or both. This particular example can be scanned as follows:

Section		Measures	Function
Statement I	**A:**	1–17	Subjects in $B\flat$
	B:	17½–36	Modulation to F
	C:	37–49	Subjects in F
Development II	**D:**	49½–66	Modulatory (F, g, d; d, c, $B\flat$)
	E:	67–75	$B\flat$ cadencing (open)
Recapitulation III	**A:**	76–92	Restatement of A ($B\flat$)
	B¹:	92½–118	Modulatory, returning to $B\flat$
	C¹:	119–131	Transposition of F subjects to $B\flat$
Coda IV	**F:**	131½–146	Cadencing (closed) and final assertion of $B\flat$.

Upon these sections are superimposed about a dozen subjects and characteristic figures, which give a rich, lively fabric to the whole. Contrast of subject was basic to the Classical style. The ideal of direct contrast is illustrated many times in the Mozart Bb Major Symphony, but the first pair of subjects (measures 1 to 8) can serve as a model.

First Subject (1–2, 5–6)	Second Subject (3–4, 7–8)
All instruments	Violins only
Incisive attack	Standard attack
Expansive range $(d\text{–}bb^2)$	Narrow range $(c^1\text{–}eb^2)$
Stable harmony	Unstable harmony
In octaves and unisons	In sixths
One note per beat	Many notes per beat
Spare line	Ornate line
Falling line	Rising line
Three registers	One register

The contrasts provided variety and motivation and filled in the structural frame with materials and stable and unstable subjects to support an arching overall scheme.

The second movement of the Mozart Symphony in Bb Major is the most modern in fabric but uses the French rondeau form accommodated to the ideals of tonal balance. Using R for the rondeau proper, e for episode, and c for coda, the movement can be scanned as R :|| e R e R c ||. The tonal plan is based on Eb major, the key of all statements of the rondeau strain and the coda. The first episode is in Bb; the second is in Eb with an opening nod to Ab (27) and a brief cadence in Bb.

The fabric is of great interest. The rondeau strain, as the title of the movement suggests, is leisurely and gracious. Use of mutes in the violins and pizzicato in the bass was not unusual, nor was substitution of flutes for oboes (very possibly with the same players), but retention of four wind instruments in a slow movement was exceptional. Even more so was the sustained unity of the phrase, which is built of a single long arch rather than of contrasting subjects. The structural texture is unusually thick for a quiet movement, and an almost murmuring restlessness is maintained by the second violin part. The large amount of activity, with all instruments in use, would normally produce a substantial sound, but the designation *piano* at the start indicates a dynamic effect not supported by the music itself, as was standard, but superimposed on it by the performers. The effect of suspensive quiet is reinforced by the somewhat enigmatic nature of the opening measure, which seems introductory but in its reappearance serves almost as a resolution. The effect must have been stunning. The rondeau proper can be called a *theme* rather than a subject, an innovative concept whose origin in the modern definition was part of the Classical achievement.

The final Allegro is a rollicking, energetic movement, bursting splendidly into life with an almost Baroque sense of key ($B\flat$ major) and beat (a fast $\frac{3}{8}$, taken as one beat to the measure). Its single subject, though typically Classical in articulation, is used in an old-fashioned jousting between tutti and small groups.

The form of the movement is the same as that of the rondeau, but the entire episode-rondeau-episode-rondeau-coda, as well as the opening statement of the rondeau, is repeated: R :‖: eR eR c :‖. The repetition of the rest of the movement serves to extend its length without further complication so that it can provide an adequate balance to the weightier first movement without entering into as intricate a structure.

As a whole, the symphony presents three very different movements in a balance of type of subject, techniques of form, and, above all, an overall tonal logic and listening plan. That the intellectual meat resides in the first movement is logical, because the listener is fresh and ready to attend to it. The intense opening movement is naturally followed by a less demanding, relaxed, though modern movement, and that, in turn, is naturally followed by a movement of simple vigor and animal spirits, the least intellectual and the most kinesthetic.

This plan of movements served many works of the Classical era. It was perhaps the one most commonly in use at the inception of the Austrian symphonic form, although many early symphonies included a minuet between the slow movement and the finale, as though a more genial movement could make a kinder transition from the restful to the rousing. In general, such a movement was included more often as the symphony expanded in size. By 1780, the four-movement plan had attained the status of being a standard format.

The tonal plan of the Mozart $B\flat$ Major Symphony, though unique in detail, incorporates a balance so successful with many kinds of subjects that it was used over and over again. In this plan, the first movement, in spite of some balancing thrusts to the subdominant, spends so much time in the dominant that the movement is pulled to the sharp side. The use of the subdominant as the key of the second movement provides a balance to the concentration of the first movement, mirrors the relaxed mood with the regressive key, and, at the same time, makes the ensuing Allegro seem brighter. The Minuet, when there was one, was generally in the tonic, often with the trio in the parallel or relative minor. The modulation of the Minuet to the dominant was thus balanced by the darker materials of the trio.

None of these tonal generalities were seen as rules or as indications of what ought to be. Rather, they comprised the most natural working out of tonal balance. Where the materials of the work led into different tonal areas, the individual problem was individually solved. Haydn, for example, liked adventuresome tonal juxtapositions, both in developmental sections and between movements. Therefore, he generally exploited the variable tones of the minor colors even within major movements, often using an entire sec-

Example 59 (continued)

Example 59 (continued)

Example 59 (continued)

Example 59 (continued)

Example 59 (continued)

Example 59 (continued)

Example 59 (continued)

Example 59 (continued)

Example 59 (continued)

Example 59 (continued)

Example 59 (continued)

Facsimile of the first edition, c. 1880, K. 182 (166ᶜ). (Courtesy of Breitkopf &
Härtel, Wiesbaden, Germany. Photo by R. E. Kalmbach.)

tion in the parallel minor, setting it off with double bars, and marking it
MINORE. Mozart was more likely to introduce tonal color through chromatic embellishments or to use diatonic and chromatic materials as part of
the aspects of contrasting subjects.

The Mozart B♭ Major Symphony is an excellent hunting ground for
Classical idioms. The first of these was *air*, the clarifying and enlightening
element invoked by the generally detached style and by the rests written
into the score, both of which produce the high surface texture so essential
in performance. In the full Classical style, both the subject, which was standard, and the theme, which was occasional and special, were used. (The
importance of theme increased in the 1780s and 1790s.) Contrasts of textural
elements, both simultaneous and otherwise, were the very life of the fabric
and involved the use of variable function and rhythmic motion in three
registers.

Natural dynamics, produced by the orchestration, were standard; most
effects were still the province of the composer rather than the performer.
More subtle effects were also possible. Accents resulted from the addition of
instruments for one or two beats [2] (I:62, 64—these are also harmonic accents) or from the use of violin multiple stops (I:1, but more particularly
I:5). A *subito forte* was achieved through rhythmic means (II:52, 54, the
fifth sixteenth accented by slurring). Exceptions were few but significant; in
this symphony, they occur in concurrence with other modernisms in the
theme and coda of the second movement.

Other idioms were the unanimous statement of a subject without added
harmony, dry upbeat, orchestral tremolo, Lombardy rhythm, sustained wind
notes, tirata, couplet slurs among detached notes, long skitting runs, breaking, and such embellishments as the trill and the appoggiatura.

MUSICAL THEATER

Just as the symphony drew the fire and intellect of the instrumental
composer in the 1760s, the musical theater drew the fire and intellect of the
vocal composer. In addition, it drew the fervor of the public, who had always been ready for stars and styles but who now entered wholeheartedly
into a decade of redefinition and new directions.

In the 1750s, Paris was a center for controversy over operatic matters,
a controversy that continued from old arguments about French versus Italian
recitativo, and theater and theater music were much in the public mind.
Rameau was in his operatic prime; though an old man, he was making immense and unique contributions to the musical meat of opera, particularly
in harmonic and instrumental elements. *Les Indes galantes* (an opera ballet,

---

[2] In these references, the Roman numeral indicates the number of the movement; the
Arabic numeral, the measure. Thus I:62 indicates movement I, measure 62.

1735), *Castor and Pollux* (an opera, 1737, with over 250 performances in its first fifty years), and *La Princesse de Navarre* (an opera ballet on a text by Voltaire, 1745) were landmarks in the history of the musical theater and of orchestration as well. However, Rameau's overall concept was traditional and geared to extravagant stage setting and costumes and to the traditional heroic subjects.

But even in Rameau's time other winds were blowing. Mondonville, as though to confound the arguments about French and Italian tongues, produced a highly successful opera in the Provençal dialect. And in 1752, Jean-Jacques Rousseau produced *Le Devin du Village*, a work based on the English ballad opera and which the author called a "lyric play." It was produced in London in 1766 in an English version called *The Cunning-Man*.

The heated arguments over the merits of the French versus the Italian style, which had been going on for a century, became confused with other issues. The style war was brought to a peak by the production of Italian comic opera—opera buffa—in Paris. Giovanni Battista Pergolesi's *La Serva Padrona* was performed in Paris in Italian in 1746 and in a French version a year later, causing a furor. It was not only simple, with no machinery and a cast of only two singers and a mime, but also was in the older, pure Italian Baroque style. It leaned heavily on recitativo and dealt with current rather than historic or mythological figures.

By the middle of the eighteenth century, the controversy was much more than a debate on the relative merits of the Italian and French tongues in musical settings. It concerned the whole operatic philosophy, including questions of production, the suitability of plot and character types, and, particularly, the importance of the singers versus that of the composers, directors, dramatists, librettists, producers, machinists, choreographers, cos-

An opera scene at Esterháza, about 1770. The identification of the harpsichordist as Joseph Haydn is questionable. (Courtesy of the Theatermuseum, Munich.)

tumers, and set designers. The entire history of opera can be seen as a continuing fluctuation of the degree of influence exerted on musical-theater production by the varying forces of these professionals, and the operatic style of any period or school can be easily assessed by discovering which group held the greatest power and made the most money. It has seldom been the composers. To the late Baroque mind, the answer clearly was that the singers were at the top, with the machinists not far behind. It was customary in 1760 to compose arias for particular singers; they could accept or reject the arias at will and would use those they accepted as a framework for their own improvisations in performance. In Italy, which was Baroque at heart until the nineteenth century, the singers' importance was approached only by the machinists and set designers, while in France the choreographers and costumers joined the opposition. The dramatic and literary elements were at the bottom of the heap.

Such a state of affairs had to be unacceptable to the Classical ideal of equalized forces of head and heart, rational and artistic elements. Paris, always an intellectual hub, was the center of the Classical upheaval in opera. The issues were multiple, and the proposed answers reflected them by defining, in the 1760s, four types of musical theater. These types remained through the Romantic era.

> *Grand opera* was a mitigated but still magnificent presentation of pomp, vocal art, and often a story of tragedy in high places. It was a child of the Italian late Baroque (Neapolitan) tradition, and its key words were *production* and *performance*.
> *Serious opera* was a large production using the forces and subjects of grand opera but deploying them logically toward the subject matter to attain an artistic unity. It was a child of the Classical reform, and its key words were *drama* and *music*.
> *Light opera* (opéra comique, opera buffa, Singspiel, ballad opera, English opera) was a small production with reduced cast, sets, orchestra, and length, likely to portray lesser personages in either serious or comic plots. It was a child of public enthusiasm and its key words were *lyricism* and *stage business*.
> *Composite entertainment* was made up of songs, dances, skits, *tableaux vivants*, acrobatic and animal acts, and even short monologues or serious dramatic scenes. It was a child of the troubadour art, the street vaudeville, and the marketplace show, and its key words were *variety* and *entertainment*.

Grand opera was to remain both Italian and French, but the Italian language would continue to predominate. It is still the Italian tradition that comes most readily to mind in association with the term *opera*.

Serious opera was to become a German tradition in the nineteenth century. Its key words gave rise to the term *music drama* and the even more integrated *Gesamtkunstwerk* ("complete art work"). Both grand opera and serious opera were sung throughout, without spoken dialogue.

Light opera was to flourish, particularly in France and England. (The term *operetta* would be introduced in England in the nineteenth century to succeed the term *English opera*.) Although not always comic, light opera was always produced to capture the public fancy and was an ideal medium for social and, at times, political satire. It used spoken dialogue and featured separate songs that could enter into the popular tradition outside the theater. Light opera was supposed to be understood directly by the public; it was typically in the vernacular (in both language and idioms), of topical interest, and of relatively simple, conservative musical content. Its practitioners have generally been the most universally famous composers of their times.

The composite entertainment, whose lineage is honorable but whose reputation is spotty, has flourished everywhere and always. It was never a musical production, but music was always essential to it—to unify it and keep it moving as well as to provide one of its primary pleasures. Such theatrical entertainments could be entirely made up of musical performances or of acts using a musical background (dance, pantomime, acrobatic routines, magic, or animal acts, all of which required music for momentum). In the nineteenth century, the type would range from the French spectacle, the English music hall, and the American minstrel show to such nonmusical entities as the state fair show and the circus. Perhaps the supreme example of this tradition is the Folies Bergère of Paris, whose sumptuous costumes, lavish tableaux, ballet *entrées*, topical and salacious skits, and popular singing are at once the heir of both the court spectacle and the street vaudeville.

In the 1760s and 1770s, the new definitions were emerging through productions of a number of opposing camps. They can be examined most easily by studying individual leaders, each of whom had many followers.

The Opéra Comique

In the early years of the eighteenth century, divertissements or *spectacles forains* ("exhibitions of the fair") were given at the *foires* ("marketplace fairs") of Paris. Through the 1730s, they were tent shows featuring magicians, acrobats, marionettes, singers, and troupes of players and dancers. All the spectacles featured musical numbers, of which the most popular was the *vaudeville*, a typically French type of topical satire that had been popular since the trouvères. A writer in 1721 described a production of the *Théâtre de la Foire*, a nonopera or even antiopera (at least anti-Académie), that was wryly dubbed *opéra comique*: "These works are characterized by the *vaudeville*, a sort of poetry peculiar to the French, esteemed by foreigners, and loved by everybody, being the most suitable means to exhibit witty sallies, to point up the ridiculous, and to improve morals." [3] In addition to the vaudevilles, comic scenes (some set to music as duets) and dances (some handsomely costumed) were featured. Parodies were also important; these were sections (sometimes single arias) with new, often satiric, texts.

Charles-Simon Favart (1710–1792), who became a producer in the 1730s, deepened the musical content, worked with good composers, and in-

[3] Alain-Réné Lesage, quoted in Paul Henry Lang, *Music in Western Civilization*, New York: Norton, 1941, p. 550.

fused real comic art into a previously crude, though often amusing, genre. A "real comic art" was a new concept, an art between low buffoonery and high tragedy, and required a permanent theater building—the foires had none. Favart therefore leaned toward the legitimate theater, but with more thoroughly planned productions that eliminated much of the improvisations of the spectacles. Favart's contributions included turning light musical entertainment from haphazard to fully realized productions, seeking a rapprochement with the Italians, and, in 1762, effecting a merger of his *Théâtre de la Foire* with the *Comédie Italienne*, using the latter's theater and calling the company the Opéra Comique. A building specifically for this company soon followed, and by the time of Favart's death, he had seen the Opéra Comique become firmly established and himself honored by their naming the new playhouse the Salle Favart.

Not only was Favart a luminary of the popular musical theater of Paris, he was also a considerable influence elsewhere. He chose superior composers, such as the younger Philidor and André-Modeste Grétry, and he was the director and organizer, and often the librettist, for a host of works that glorified one of the busiest theatrical eras in the history of France.

Grand Opera Reforms

Another war was being waged in Paris, this one between the proponents of Italian opera in the grand style and the movers toward reform. Neither of the chief proponents was French and Paris was not the only battleground, for the quarrel was international.

Italian opera had been taken over by the arts of the castrati and the machinists, and as early as the 1740s a French critic spoke of its "tediousness" and of "arias pinned to the end of every scene, not really connected with the action. . . . One does not go to the opera for the subject, but for the accessories of music and the spectacle." [4] Everyone seemed to agree that the Italian opera needed reform but differed about the direction reform should take. The leaders of the two main camps were Niccolò Piccini and Christoph Willibald Gluck.

Piccini, an Italian, felt that opera buffa should contribute to serious opera its modernity of subject matter and its response to the public's concern for humanism, along with its more lyrical and less embellished music. His most popular opera was an adaptation of the English novel *Pamela* (1740), by Samuel Richardson; Piccini produced it in Rome in 1760 as *La Buona Figliuola* (The Good Girl), a startling title to those used to only mythological heroics or low-class parody. The opera ran for two years, and its rousing success made the composer famous as an exponent of a modernized but still basically Italianate production. Such hybrid terms as *opera semiseria* ("semiserious opera") and *comédie larmoyante* ("tearful comedy") were coined to support the Piccini reforms.

[4] Charles de Brosses, quoted in *ibid.*, pp. 553–554. (The two sections of the quote have been reversed.)

Gluck was a German who was trained in Prague and Italy and led an international life. In the 1760s and 1770s he produced operas in fifteen cities, but his interests centered in Paris and Vienna, two cities that became allied in 1770 through the marriage of the Habsburg princess Marie Antoinette to the Dauphin of France.

Gluck's position was that opera should return to the classical Greek concept of drama, particularly that of tragedy. His invocation of the Classicism of the Greek drama paralleled that of the Italian monodists; they had turned to the same source at the end of the sixteenth century. In Gluck's view, the drama itself was primary, and the other elements of the production should serve it. Of necessity, the corollary was that music was secondary. "I have striven to restrict music to its true office of serving poetry," he wrote.[5]

His most famous reforming works were a trio of operas on subjects from Greek mythology—*Orfeo ed Euridice* (1762), *Alceste* (1767), and *Paride ed Elena* (1770)—all produced in Vienna to Italian librettos by Ranieri di Calzabigi (1714–1795). In the 1770s, Gluck turned to Paris. *Orphée*, a French version of *Orfeo ed Euridice* in which the castrato lead was rewritten for tenor, was produced there in 1774 and played forty-seven performances. In the same year Gluck produced *Iphigénie en Aulide*, using another mythological subject, to a libretto based on the tragedy by Jean Racine (1639–1699).

Gluck's five years in Paris capped his career. Secure in his Paris position, with Marie Antoinette as his protector, Gluck had his partisans bring the unsuspecting Piccini to Paris into the warmth of controversy. Piccini's reforms were of subject matter and of the quality of the set pieces, but not of the basic musical plan. Therefore, Gluck planned to produce *Iphigénie en Tauride* on the French libretto used earlier by Lully and had his supporters suggest that Piccini set the same libretto. In this way, Gluck thought to establish his superiority over the younger man, because the text, both in its subject and its seventeenth-century format, was just Gluck's forte. Produced in Paris in May, 1779, Gluck's opera was perhaps his finest work, proved immensely successful, and represented the peak of his career. Piccini's opera, produced in Paris in January, 1781, was late, so in the controversy between the "gluckistes" and the "piccinistes," Piccini's supporters lost by default. Though it was successful, Piccini's opera was less so than Gluck's had been.

Actually, neither composer had lost; there was no one simple answer to opera reform. Both Gluck and Piccini wrote fine works and saw their reforms begin to take root (their innovations were later fulfilled in lasting traditions). Gluck did not demean the musical element in opera, but he did set the composer above the singer; he did not do away with arias, choruses, dances, and orchestral interludes, but he did demand librettos that offered natural opportunities to introduce them and thus provide a musically balanced whole. And he used an overture as a true introduction—to present the mood and even

[5] Quoted in Alfred Einstein, *Gluck*, London: Dent, 1936, p. 98.

offer some of the materials of the work that was to follow. Gluck's overtures are satisfying works in themselves and a few are still in the symphonic repertoire. In contrast, Piccini aimed for lyricism (an immediate "singable-ness"), a modern concept associated with the new humanism; lyricism would be the watchword of Italian opera throughout the nineteenth century. And although Piccini did not achieve a marriage of opera buffa and opera seria, these types would never be so distant from each other again.

A central problem of the whole operatic upheaval was the insistence of the Académie and the gluckistes on the concept of *tragédie*. Tragédie was thoroughly formalized, with conditions and regulations; the academic mind accepted as tragédie only that which completely fulfilled the dramatic specifications. Thus tragédie was a technical rather than a subjective concept; it was precisely defined, whereas nothing else was defined at all. It was simple to the académicien—tragédie was tragédie and everything else was "comédie." This gave the term *comédie* so broad an application that it was virtually meaningless in regard to subject matter or even mood. Although the origin of the difficulty was French and lay in the eighteenth century, the problem would continue into the nineteenth and even the twentieth century.

Johann Adam Hiller was the central figure in the establishment of German opera during its Classical rebirth. Hiller was a modernist, a strong advocate of the new humanism, and an important musician in the musical life of Leipzig. There his career centered from 1758, and there he exerted an influence of multiple aspects for more than forty years. His many-faceted interests made him an ideal man for the musical theater. *Singspiel*

The new humanism centered in Germany, and the opposition to Classical tragedy centered in the theater. The opposition was embodied in a series of translations and productions of William Shakespeare, a humanist in the Renaissance tradition whose plays roamed freely in all three of the elements that the Classicists would restrain. *Antony and Cleopatra*, in addition to its covering a variety of actions over a long and not continuous period of time, had thirty-eight scene changes.

Johann Wolfgang von Goethe (1749–1832), probably the most respected man in Germany for the next fifty years, was impressed with the fluidity and versatility of Shakespeare's technique; he referred to it as "the technique of the curiosity box." [6] In 1773, Goethe published a play, *Götz von Berlichingen*, with fifty-four changes of scene, each of which required some change of stage setting. Rejection of the unities in the theater was carried even further by Johann Friedrich von Schiller (1759–1805); he wrote the play *Die Räuber* (The Robbers, 1781), which was to be read, "without seeking the dubious advantage of stage adaptation." [7] Shakespeare's "on your imaginary forces work" [8] was the watchword; excitement imagined was

[6] Quoted in Vera Mowry Roberts, *On Stage*, New York: Harper & Row, 1962, p. 354.
[7] *Ibid*.
[8] Prologue, *Henry V*.

thought more vivid than excitement enacted. The heroic and exaggerated view of man captured the idealistic aspect of the German character. In 1776 Friedrich Maximilian von Klinger (1752–1831), a soldier-author, produced a play called *Sturm und Drang* (Storm and Stress); the title was seized on as a name for the movement, which fact in itself denotes the highly charged atmosphere.

The middle of the century had produced a generation of fine actors who had broken away from formalized gestures and stereotyped costumes; they propounded a new kind of acting, one based on feeling instead of diction, on gesture instead of posture. Instead of the "sonorous line" and the "studied grace of deportment" desired by the Classicists, the young actors aimed for a natural style deriving from character study rather than elocution. David Garrick (1717–1779), the manager of the Drury Lane Theatre from 1747, is still a legend in England, as is Friedrich Ludwig Schroeder (1744–1816) in Germany. In support of the new mood, these producers ended the practice of seating members of the audience on the stage. In France, parallel changes were taking place in the ballet, always a central art in French hearts. The great Parisian dancer-choreographer Jean-Georges Noverre (1727–1810) became the ballet master at the Paris Opéra in 1776. He had been at the Court of Wurttemberg from 1760 to 1767 and thus was also an influence on opera production at Stuttgart, the capital of Wurttemberg. In 1760 he published a treatise against the geometric figures and independent routines of the formal ballet. "Renounce cabrioles, entre-chats, and over-complicated steps," he exorted; "abandon mincing airs to study sentiments, artless graces, and expression. . . . Be original; form a style of your own." [9]

The new philosophy comprised a revolution not just in method but in the entire goal of the theater. Goethe's view went a step beyond natural realism. "The player must consider that he should not only imitate nature," he wrote, "but also portray it ideally, . . . uniting the true with the beautiful." [10] Opera, Goethe felt, possessed not literal truth but "a certain interior truth, which arises from its completeness as a work of art. . . . When opera is good, it creates a small world of its own, . . . which must be judged by its own laws, felt according to its own spirit. . . ." [11]

Goethe went further still. To him, this "small world of its own" was a superior world, the product of a superior man, and could be appreciated on its high level only by the "connoisseur." So the cult of the ideal gave rise to the cult of the superior genius. "A work of art can seem to be a work of nature only to a wholly uncultivated spectator; . . . he can be satisfied only when the artist descends to his level; he will never rise with him, when,

---

[9] Quoted in A. M. Nagler, A *Source Book in Theatrical History,* New York: Dover, 1959, p. 361.
[10] Quoted in *ibid.,* p. 429.
[11] Quoted in *ibid.,* p. 438.

prompted by his genius, the true artist must take wing." [12] Here is abstract adulation of genius, the mystical sorting of the lesser from the higher man. A hierarchical ranking was thus produced: the uncultivated spectator, who sees only the literal; the connoisseur, who grasps the higher truth that transcends the literal; and the Promethean genius, who creates that higher truth.

It was with these ideas as background that Hiller carried out his many projects in Leipzig. That city, with its eastern location, was musically important; like Vienna, it was open to the great influx from Bohemia and the Slavic countries, which, at the middle of the century, were so prominent musically. The Classical ideal was eclectic, drawing musical materials from many directions and enjoying the excitement of putting them together in newly effective ways. Leipzig maintained a great university, was a publishing center, and was the most international market town in Germany. It was, in addition, the German center for modernism and youth, and the Sturm und Drang movement was one of youth—Klinger wrote *Sturm und Drang* at the age of twenty-four, Goethe wrote *Götz von Berlichingen* at twenty-four, and Schiller wrote *Die Räuber* at twenty-two.

The rebirth of German opera was an international project, for it involved Italian, French, and English elements. English plays were already popular, and in 1743 the ballad opera *The Devil to Pay* (1731), by the Irish entrepreneur Charles Coffey, had been produced in Berlin as *Der Teufel ist Los!* (The Devil Is on the Loose!), presumably with Coffey's original songs. Interestingly, it was a new translation of that same work, from a roundabout source, that Hiller reset to music in 1766 for the Leipzig audience to enjoy in their new theater. The poet Christian Felix Weisse (1726–1804) had for some time been interested in the new types of theater, particularly the hybrids such as the comédie larmoyante and the opera semiseria. He went to Paris and there saw for himself several lyric plays, including Rousseau's *Devin du Village* and a French adaptation of Coffey's *The Devil to Pay* called *Le Diable à Quatre*. Weisse made a new version in German from the French, adding nineteen songs and using the former German title, *Der Teufel ist Los!*

Favart's influence on Hiller was strong and can be seen most clearly in Weisse's adaptation of three of Favart's libretti. Hiller set them to music, calling most of them "lyric plays," as Favart did, but one of them he set completely, using recitativo (secco) and the more formal da capo arias— this one, a modern humanist story, Hiller called a *romantic opera*. A *romance* (*roman* in French) was a novel, and the novel was a new literary form active in the cause of humanism. But the term was not unrelated to the coming Romanticism, for it is from the romance that it would take its name.

Hiller called his new type of lyric play the Singspiel, which was close to the French and also invoked the Hamburg heritage of Keiser's German operas (though the Hiller works were of a very different genre). The Sing-

---

[12] *Ibid.*

spiel, like its French counterpart, the opéra comique, came to be defined on technical grounds—basically on the presence of spoken texts.

Classicists who wanted to use serious or seriocomic subjects in production of artistic and musical seriousness had problems of which the verbal confusions were only a pale symbol. The opera and the popular theater were not merely different artistic concepts; they were separate performing organizations housed in different theaters, with different managements, different singers, and different techniques. A work that fell between definitions had to be performed at either an opera house or a popular theater. In the Classical generation, composers did write such works—Mozart's output of the 1780s comprises an outstanding example. After the Classical generation yielded to the Romantic ideal, the problem subsided, for Romantics were generally happier with categories and were content with opera and operetta.

Hiller's legacy was not as firmly institutional as Favart's, but it was much broader musically, and through his other projects, its influence extended far beyond the theater. More of an eclectic than Favart, who remained French in outlook, Hiller knew the English theatrical tradition, musical and otherwise, and the Italian style as well. "The Italian style is nearer to the German," he wrote, "but in fact the French have it over the Italians in their bent for the dramatic." [13] He was a Lieder composer of substantial gifts and filled his Singspiele with songs that achieved popularity almost as folk songs did—he was one of the first to compose in imitation of the natural folk style. Hiller often put such songs into the parts of the common man, ennobled through the purity and directness of the *volkstümliches Lied* ("folk-like song"), and left the high-flown aria for the portrayal of the nobility. In *Die Jagd* (The Hunt, 1770, also from a French source), the rustic milieu allowed for the complete yielding to the natural style; this opera proved to be Hiller's most outstanding attainment in the Singspiel. He achieved a German style to which the public could respond, and in this accomplishment lay a vital impulse for the coming Romantic ideal.

ENGLAND

During the 1760s and 1770s, Great Britain was still musically reverberating from the expansive sonorities of Handel and contenting herself with imported instrumentalists and grand opera stars. Her two great capitals, London and Dublin, centered their native talent in the theater. David Garrick was bringing acting to its first modern height, and Thomas Augustine Arne, now known as Dr. Arne because of an honorary doctor of music degree awarded to him by Oxford University in 1759, was writing English operas,

[13] Quoted in Norbert Dufourcq (ed.), *Larousse de la Musique*, Paris: Librairie Larousse, 1957, vol. I., p. 448.

keyboard works for amateur harpsichordists, and popular songs. The most important musical figures in London in those years were Dr. Arne, John Bach (Johann Christian), and William Boyce. Bach, who was in London from 1762, enjoyed a career as a pianist, composer, teacher, and sometime entrepreneur in the production of Italian operas of his own composition. Boyce had put his English opera productions behind him and was concentrating on his book *Cathedral Music* (three volumes, 1760–1778), a collection of church music of the previous two and a half centuries.

All three men wrote symphonies in the new style, but only Bach, a generation younger, wrote for the piano—sonatas, concerted chamber works on the French model, and piano concertos. His innovative presentation, in 1768, of the first public piano recital was not assessed by its hearers as a significant step toward a new art. It seems to have been considered a single musical diversion among a multitude of diversions and certainly not as stylish as hearing Arne's latest popular song. The symphonies of Arne, Boyce, and Bach had to await rediscovery in the twentieth century; the English were not interested in them. It was as though the British, suspended in the knowledge that a new era was at hand, were content to let the past settle, to listen to comfortable music, and to leave the definition of the new musical style to composers elsewhere.

❀   *Some Important Composers of the Classical Generation*

The men of the Classical generation were the sons of the teachers of the late Baroque. The fathers had analyzed and defined the musical art and produced the pedagogical basis for the future. With a unique combination of the new style and sure training, the younger men rose to a particular brilliance that has kept their works in the repertoire ever since.

(FRANZ) JOSEPH HAYDN (1732–1809), an Austrian composer, was one of the splendid figures in the history of music. He was a choirboy at St. Stephens, in Vienna from 1740 to 1748 and evidently turned to composition late, for his earliest known works date from his nineteenth year. He taught himself thorough bass and counterpoint and gradually entered the musical mainstream. From 1761 to 1790 he was in the service of the Princes of Esterházy and from 1766 was the Kapellmeister in charge of a fine and famous orchestra. Already internationally famous by the time of the Prince's death, he subsequently went to London for extended periods. His works were very influential and reflect his career to some extent; the bulk of the divertimenti were from his formative years, and the large choral works were from the last period (*The Creation*, 1798; *The Seasons*, 1801). He left a huge amount of music, the study of which continues, but numberings of his works vary so much that any summary can only be approximate—104 symphonies, 80 string quartets, 60 divertimenti, 50 piano works (most of them sonatas), 30 concertos (15 for piano), 65 trios, 24 operas (*seria* and *buffa*) and *Singspiele*, 14 Masses, and about 250 other works, including 50 vocal canons, about 40 Lieder, and 32 pieces for musical clock. His brother (JOHANN) MICHAEL (1737–1806), at Salzburg, left, among other works, about 30 Masses and 30 symphonies, also of high caliber. He also founded a school for the teaching of musical composition, where he taught successfully and with influence.

JOHANN CHRISTIAN BACH (1735–1782) was the eleventh son (eighteenth child) of Johann Sebastian Bach. He studied in Berlin with C. P. E. Bach, his half brother, from 1750 to 1755 and then in Italy, where he was organist of the Cathedral in Milan from 1760 to 1762. In 1762 he went to England and enjoyed huge success, first with the opera *Orione* (1763) and then with a concert series. He reigned in London for over a decade as teacher, producer, composer, and performer and was an early and lasting influence on the young Mozart. In 1768, Bach gave the first piano recital on a square Zumpe piano he had bought for 5 guineas. His larger works were of considerable influence. His 13 operas premiered in London, Mannheim, and Paris, and 2 piano concertos were published at Riga. He left about 40 piano concertos, over 40 symphonies, an oratorio, about 20 piano sonatas, and a substantial amount of chamber music, including 6 quintets (Op. 11) for flute, oboe, violin, viola, and cello.

CHRISTOPH WILLIBALD GLUCK (1714–1787), a German composer for the theater, was educated in Prague and Vienna, where he was chamber musician to Prince Lobkowitz. In 1736 he went to Milan in the entourage of Prince Melzi. He remained in Italy and from that time produced 107 operas, 4 ballets, and many comic operas (mostly in French). His early works, which were Italian operas in the grand style, were produced in Milan, Venice, Paris, London, Vienna, Prague, Pillnitz, and Rome. Beginning with *Orpheo ed Euridice* (in Italian), which was produced in Vienna in 1762, he championed a return to a primary dramatic importance in opera. In addition to his theater works, he wrote about 10 symphonies, a dozen

sonatas, a *De Profundis*, and other miscellaneous pieces.

NICCOLÒ PICCINI (1728–1800) was the most famous member of an Italian family that contained important partisans of Italian opera and opera buffa through the first half of the nineteenth century. His first work, an opera buffa produced in Naples in 1754, inaugurated a career of over 130 productions that made him popular in both France and Italy. His son LOUIS (1766–1827) followed his father in dividing his career between Paris and Naples. Louis also served briefly in Sweden but settled permanently in Paris after his father's death.

JOHANN ADAM HILLER (1728–1804), a German composer and producer, was trained in Dresden and then (in law) in Leipzig, where his long career was centered. Although Hiller composed instrumental works and three books of songs for children, he was most famous for the management (from 1763) of the Leipzig concerts, which Telemann had organized, and for the Singspiel, of which he wrote several. His most famous Singspiel was *Die Jagd* (The Hunt, 1770), which was produced at Wiemar. Hiller also supported the new style by publishing works of his German and Italian contemporaries.

KARL DITTERS VON DITTERSDORF (1739–1799), an Austrian violinist and composer, was trained in his native Vienna in the orchestra of Prince von Hildburghausen. In 1763, he accompanied Gluck (who had just produced *Orfeo* in Vienna) to Italy. Highly prolific and highly successful, Dittersdorf was made a baron in 1773. Of his works, about 50 symphonies were published in his lifetime. In addition, he left about 85 other symphonies, 150 piano works (including 12 sonatas for four hands), 22 concertos, and many divertimenti of significant influence in the formation of a Viennese style.

ANDRÉ-MODESTE GRÉTRY (1741–1813) was a choirboy at Saint-Denis and was drawn early to instrumental forms—

6 symphonies date from 1758 and his quartets and concertos from the early 1760s, when he was studying in Rome. Deciding that his career lay in the popular theater, Grétry returned to Paris and, from the late 1760s, produced over 60 works at the Opéra-Comique. The most famous of these were *Zémire et Azor* (1771) and *Richard Cœur-de-Lion* (1784). Grétry also wrote his memoirs (published in 1789, with two additional volumes published in 1797). His observations about the effects of music on the human pulse comprise an early example of experiments that led to such modern fields as music therapy.

LUIGI BOCCHERINI (1743–1805), an Italian cellist, guitarist, and composer, studied in Rome, played in the theater orchestra at Lucca, and appeared in Paris at the Concert spirituel in 1768. He published 6 string quartets and two books of sonatas and then went to Spain, where he became a member of the Spanish royal chamber music. He went to Germany in 1782 and returned to Spain in 1799. In addition to his works for cello, he left 120 string quintets (many with guitar), 100 string quartets, 20 symphonies, 60 trios, 21 violin sonatas, an opera, and several cantatas.

JOHANN WILHELM HÄSSLER (1747–1822), a German pianist and composer, was the son of a hatter. Although apprenticed in his father's trade, he studied music with an uncle (a student of J. S. Bach) and became the organist at the Barfüsserkirche in Erfurt at fourteen. He traveled widely from 1771 to 1780, went to England in 1790, and then to Russia, where he remained. His works, all for the keyboard (including some for four hands), are as yet uncollected, but many were published in Russia. They are personal works of charm and strength.

ANTONIO SALIERI (1750–1825) was an opera composer and director who studied in Venice and settled in Vienna, where he was Kapellmeister at the imperial chapel and a conductor (later director) of the opera. He held a position of great influence, both professional and personal, and was a teacher of high repute. After conducting the court and public concerts from 1790, he retired from conducting in 1818 and from the imperial chapel in 1824. The fiftieth anniversary of his arrival in Vienna was celebrated by a concert of works by his students, including a cantata by Schubert. Salieri wrote 39 operas, many sacred choral works (4 Te Deums, a Passion, etc.), 30 offertories, and a number of instrumental works. Among his students, in addition to Schubert, were Beethoven and Liszt.

WOLFGANG AMADEUS MOZART (1756–1791), an Austrian composer and pianist, was one of the great creative men of Western music. A prodigiously gifted child, Wolfgang was born when the new eclectic art was at the beginning of its crest. He had a superior education, both from his father, Leopold, who was in the service of the Archbishop of Salzburg, and in his extensive childhood travels to Italy, France, England, Germany, and the Austrian imperial court in Vienna. His music was a true synthesis of styles, at a time of unique equilibrium between the invention and fulfillment of forms. Mozart left over 600 works, which were catalogued in 1862 by Ludwig von Köchel. The catalogue includes 40 divertimenti, 55 concertos (including 29 for piano and 14 for violin), 49 symphonies, over 100 chamber works (25 string quartets, 45 duos for piano and violin), about 75 piano works (23 sonatas), 69 church works, over 100 songs and detached arias, and 25 operas. Mozart's heart lay in his operas, but he was never able to find the niche that his talent yearned for. Of tremendous intelligence and energy, to this day he remains a figure of fascination, to musicians and nonmusicians alike.

MUZIO CLEMENTI (1752–1832) was born in Rome into a family of artisans and musicians. Prodigiously gifted, he studied keyboard instruments, voice, and composition as a boy. At the age of nine, he held an organ post, and at fourteen, he was creating a sensation in Italy as a keyboard virtuoso. A personable youth, he was adopted at fourteen by an English aristocrat and educated as a British gentleman. To the influences of his early training, which had included the works of Scarlatti and C. P. E. Bach, he added the influences of Johann Christian Bach and, through trips to Paris, Johann Schobert. His music ranged widely but focused in the piano forte, and his career was international but was based in London. His concert career was one of the greatest in the history of music, and he laid the foundation of modern piano techniques, particularly of fingering. As a composer, he was held in high esteem (Beethoven preferred Clementi's sonatas to Mozart's), but many of his works are lost. Still, over a hundred piano sonatas survive (almost half in the French style, with accompanying instruments), along with sonatinas, a few symphonies, and several volumes of incidental piano pieces, including waltzes, toccatas, and caprices. His most famous work, *Gradus ad Parnassum*, one hundred études for piano, was originally published in 1817; it is still a basic volume for pianists. Clementi was also a publisher, a piano manufacturer, and a teacher; his students included Johann Baptist Cramer, John Field, and Ignaz Moscheles.

Went to meeting in the afternoon and heard the finest singing that ever I heard in my life; the front and side galleries were crowded with rows of lads and lasses, who performed all their parts in the utmost perfection. I thought I was rapt up; a row of women all standing up and playing their parts with perfect skill and judgment, added a sweetness and sprightliness which absolutely charmed me.

JOHN ADAMS *

They lightened their labour by songs, one of which was composed extempore; for I was myself the subject of it. It was sung by one of the young women, the rest joining in a sort of chorus. The air was sweet and plaintive, and the words, literally translated, were these: "The winds roared, and the rain fell. The poor white man, faint and weary, came and sat under our tree. He has no mother to bring him milk; no wife to grind his corn. Chorus—Let us pity the white man; no mother has he."

MUNGO PARK †

America and Africa

AMERICA

17

In America the years before the Revolution were characterized by exploration, settling in, and the kinds of adventures that folk ballads are made of. The names of landmarks and localities recall Indian legends, men of courage, and lands back home. Settlers came from many nations, bringing their own instruments and sustaining a multiple heritage of song. Of these national arts, perhaps the most important for the future, though the most

* 1771. Quoted in Alan C. Buechner, "New England Harmony," New York: Folkways Records and Service Corporation, 1964, p. 6.
† 1799. Quoted in Samuel Charters, *The Bluesmen*, New York: Oak Publications, 1967, p. 7.

scantily documented, were those of the Africans who were being imported as slaves. The music of black Africa was always admired, but it was part of the informal tradition, ignored in the concert hall.

On the frontier, there was little time for formal music, but we know that in New York subscription concerts were started in 1760 and open-air concerts (parallel to the garden concerts in England) in 1765. In 1763, a new concert hall opened in Boston; it claimed the finest organ in America. Charleston's St. Cecelia Society was founded in 1762 and within a decade became a focus for musical and social gatherings. In 1772, a visitor from Boston noted in his diary that

> the music was good—the two base viols and French horns were grand. One Abercrombie, a Frenchman just arrived, played the first violin, and a solo incomparably better than anyone I ever heard. He cannot speak a word of English, and has a salary of five hundred guineas a year from the St. Cecelia Society. There were upwards of two hundred and fifty ladies present, and it was called no great number. In loftiness [of coiffure], these ladies stoop to the daughters of the north,—in richness of dress, surpass them. . . . The gentlemen, many of them dressed with richness and elegance, uncommon with us: many with swords on. We had two Macaronis present, just arrived from London.[1]

Like the concert review a generation earlier, the comment dealt as much with the audience as with the music. Macaronis were dandies who put on airs of foreign elegance; the term itself was the latest slang and was immortalized in the verses, which were written about that time, to the tune "Yankee Doodle."

Immigrants with musical ability and enterprise could furnish a good concert, but music was caught between the Baroque and Classical styles and the new definitions were not yet known to the colonials. Perhaps the most ambitious organizer of those years was John Gualdo, a wine merchant who came to Philadelphia from London in 1767. He began to sell music and musical instruments and to give lessons on the flute, guitar, and violin. In 1769 he organized a concert series, one program of which is known.

Act I

Overture composed by the Earl of Kelly.

"Vain is Beauty, gaudy flower," by Miss Hallam.

Trio composed by Mr. Gualdo, first violin by Master Billy Crumpto.

"The Spinning Wheel," by Miss Storer.

A German flute concert, with Solos, composed by Mr. Gualdo.

A new symphony after the present taste, composed by Mr. Gualdo.

[1] Josiah Quincy, quoted in Gilbert Chase, *America's Music*, New York: McGraw-Hill, 1955, p. 108.

Act II

A new Violin concerto with solos, composed by Mr. Gualdo.

A song by Mr. Wools.

A Sonata upon the Harpsichord, by Mr. Curtz.

Solo upon the Clarinet, by Mr. Hoffman, junior.

Solo upon the Mandolino, by Mr. Gualdo.

Overture, composed by the Earl of Kelly.[2]

The overture was probably the opening movement of a symphony; such a movement, generally the most substantial of the symphonic form, was so designated in programs of the time. It would later be replaced by the opera overture and the one-movement orchestral piece. The Earl of Kelly is unidentified. Miss Hallam, Miss Storer, Mr. Wools, and Mr. Curtz were performers, not composers. As for Mr. Gualdo, he had come from London almost at the height of Johann Christian Bach's popularity there, and his knowledge of the latest British musical fashion would have assured him a position of advantage. It is not known how old he was, but his compositions used the Baroque basso continuo—trio sonatas and other chamber music, all with thorough bass. Gualdo's modernity lay more in the "new symphony after the present taste," but assessment of the work is not possible because it has not been found. Philadelphia's concert life might have been greatly enhanced by his talents, but he soon became ill; he died in 1771.

The colonial gentleman, like his English model, would have considered himself lacking if he were not musically literate—knowing how to play the flute, guitar, or harpsichord, to "read from the notes," and to dance the minuet and gavotte as well as the reel, jig, and square dance (also called the contradance and the quadrille). The respected advances of the English scene were mirrored in the New World as much as the colonists could manage. Geminiani's *The Art of Playing upon the Violin* appeared in an American edition in 1669, and the new square piano was imported soon afterward. By 1775, Philadelphia had two active piano makers.

The Singing School

In the less heavily populated areas, the singing school was the social and educational event of the year. Musicians, like portrait painters and often grammar school teachers, were itinerant, traveling from village to village and offering their services to the residents as they went. Journeymen musicians taught music in sessions of six weeks to three or four months, depending on the location. In the larger centers, a newspaper ad sufficed to announce the singing school and to begin a subscription list. By the 1760s, such schools were functioning as an accepted part of life in both rural areas and towns in the English colonies. The purpose of the schools was ostensibly the prep-

[2] Quoted in John Tasker Howard, *The Music of George Washington's Time*, Washington, D.C.: United States George Washington Bicentennial Commission, 1931, p. 6.

aration of the young to sing in church choirs, but approved social events for young people were rare, and doubtless the singing schools were cherished as courting places and occasions for social enjoyment. Most descriptions of the singing schools date from the period of their greatest popularity, which was twenty years later, but the descriptions serve the period from 1760 to 1774 as well. One, of a singing school in 1788, is delightfully revealing.

> A singing school was got up about two miles from my father's house. In much fear and trembling I went with the rest of the boys in our town. Quite a number of young ladies and gentlemen had come to the school. We were soon paraded all around the room, standing up to boards supported by old fashioned kitchen chairs. The master took his place inside the circle, took out of his pocket a paper manuscript, with rules and tunes all written with pen and ink, read to us the rules, and then said we must attend to the rising and falling of the notes. . . . The books contained only one part each, bass books, tenor books, counter books, and treble books. The good master began, "Come boys, you must rise and fall the notes first and then the gals must try." So he began with the oldest. . . . Then the gals had their turn to rise and fall the notes. "Come gals, now see if you can't beat the boys." . . . A good number of tunes were learned in this school, and were sung very well as we thought. . . . I attended some kind of singing school every winter but two until I was twenty-one years old.[3]

The system taught was a Guidonian form of syllable reading called *fa-sol-la* or *fasola*. It located the half step between *mi* and *fa* and thus pointed to key, for *mi* defined the leading tone, not the major mediant.

The church tunes that were taught in the singing schools were no longer limited to the Psalm settings brought from Europe but were now being composed by native composers. The tune book was soon to be a prominent and distinctly American publication. The first known native publication of a book of tunes was in 1761, but in the next half century, almost three hundred tune books, containing over four thousand tunes, were published. An important composer of tunes was William Billings, a self-taught Bostonian. His first book, the *New England Psalm Singer* (engraved by Paul Revere) was issued in 1770; it contained two of his most famous tunes, "Chester" and "When Jesus Wept," and gave him an early reputation. *The Singing Master's Assistant* followed in 1778, when Billings was choirmaster of Boston's Brattle Street Church. At his death, Billings was said to have been a "self-taught man" who "spoke and sung and thought as a man above common abilities." [4] He stands as one of many composer-choirmasters (about two dozen are known) who made the pre-Revolutionary decade memorable for its choirs. The men of this group are known now as the "New England school" (though the singing school customs extended far beyond the boundaries of New England). They were primitives in the technical sense, unschooled and self-

---

[3] Moses Cheney, quoted in Alan C. Buechner, "New England Harmony," New York: Folkways Records and Service Corporation, 1964, p. 3f.

[4] William Bentley, quoted in *ibid.*, p. 9.

taught, using books (for the most part, fifty years old) of choirmastery from England and using Renaissance Psalms as their models. They set their Psalms and hymns in four parts with the tunes in the tenor. As directors, they strove for a natural voice, which we would consider nasal, and used seating arrangements that placed the choir in the gallery of the church, along both sides and the back of the sanctuary in good late-Renaissance opposition. The art of choir singing was cherished.

The tunes of Billings and his followers were of three main types—hymn tunes, fuging tunes, and anthems or part-songs. The hymns were metrically identified according to the number of syllables in the stanzas. *Common meter* (C.M.), *short meter* (S.M.), and *long meter* (L.M.) were the most frequently used; they were all four lines long and had syllable counts of 8.6.8.6, 6.6.8.6, and 8.8.8.8, respectively. Categorizing by meter enabled one to sing a hymn to any tune of the same meter. In addition, one could use any of the meters twice to make up an eight-line stanza; the meters were then said to be "double." A full eight-line stanza of 8.6.8.6.8.6.8.6. was labeled *common meter double* (C.M.D.). These meters made up the great majority of the hymns. In Billings's work, however, close to a fifth of the tunes were in *particular meter* (P.M.), of which the composer's favorite was a short-line stanza of 6.6.6.6.4.4.4.4, often called the *hallelujah meter* (H.M.). Billings liked *long meter, long meter double*, and *hallelujah meter* (of which he wrote eleven examples) more than did his contemporaries. Other meters were considered irregular and had no names; they were indicated by the syllable count (see Example 43, page 216).

Hymn tunes were independently titled, generally with a one- or two-word name such as "Chester." This tune, for which Billings had written the poem, first appeared in the *New England Psalm Singer* of 1770. "Chester" is a stirring tune, a punctus structure with one musical phrase for each line of text. The tune proper, in the tenor, could well be analyzed in the same manner as an early monophonic tune, and it clearly relates to a single fundamental. It is straightforward, rhythmically direct, and well structured melodically.

Harmonically, the hymn tunes of Billings's school present the primitive style at its most individual. The suave mid-eighteenth-century harmonic accommodations of the European style were necessary for clarity when tonal-harmonic progressions and modulations functioned in working out the form. But the New England school avoided elegance of harmonic detail, though they embraced the concept of key (in the Baroque sense of tone). The double-perfection, 1–5–8 triad, unsweetened by the third but strong functionally, was common, as was the arrival at chord positions through polyphonic means rather than through harmonic formula. The result was a marvelous structural strength that disregarded the amenities of modern harmonic progression. As an incorporation of a forthright people who rejected the macaronis of the salon, the hymn tune of the New England school came close to a portrait of the frontier American.

Chester

Example 60

WILLIAM BILLINGS

This song was included in *The New England Psalm Singer*, published in 1770; the volume was engraved by Paul Revere. (Courtesy of the Library of Congress.)

Kedron

Example 61

ANONYMOUS

From Amos Pilsbury's *The United States Harmony*, 1799. (Courtesy of the Library of Congress.)

Such tunes as the anonymous "Kedron" demonstrate the ready harmonic strength of the singing school hymn tunes. Vertical power, rather than melodic grace, informs the whole; the text is beautifully fulfilled.

Rounds and catches had come to the New World with the English settlers and were popular as easily learned and often jolly, if not lewd, songs in the tradition of tavern and club music. Billings saw the potential for expression in the round and wrote one of the loveliest works of the American heritage—a short four-part canon on his own poem—for his 1770 *New England Psalm Singer*. The round "When Jesus Wept" relied on the power

When Jesus Wept   Example 62

WILLIAM BILLINGS

From *The New England Psalm Singer*, published in 1770.
(Courtesy of the Library of Congress.)

of the fifth and was based on two fifths with roots a third apart. It was a perfectly matched union of a lovely poem of direct and honest awe and a musical setting of uncommon beauty. Rounds were not associated with sacred practice, however, so Billings transcribed the work as a regular hymn tune for his 1778 *Singing Master's Assistant*; it appeared only as a hymn tune, with the title "Emmaus," thereafter.

Most of the hymn tunes of the New England school had straightforward settings, in four voices, of a four-line stanza in a four-punctus structure in the familiar style. But a large minority (about 25 percent) of the tunes contained one line of text set as an imitative point. Such a point was called a *fuge*, and a tune containing such a point was a *fuging tune*. The fuging tune might contain a point of separate but not imitative entries—still one punctus in the learned style—instead of the imitative point.

Billings wrote thirty-six of the more than one thousand fuging tunes known to have been written in the first fifty years of the tune books, and at the time of his death, he was acknowledged to have been the first in the New World to write them. He called his hymns *Psalms* and his settings *Psalm tunes*, not because they were paraphrases of the Old Testament Psalms (for some were not), but because they were in verse or, as he put it, in meter. But Billings also wrote (and selected from other authors) free-verse or nonmetrical lyrics. Most were extended texts that produced a type of music he called the *anthem*. "I think," Billings wrote, "any piece of divine music, that is not divided into Metre (excepting canons and chanting pieces) may with propriety be called an Anthem." [5] His anthems, of which he left over fifty, were extended works, with independent musical designs that derived more from interrelations with the texts than from the punctus structural concept. A good deal of textual repetition extended the anthems even further than their longer texts indicate. Important and particularly emotive words or phrases ("Mourn, Mourn," for example), set off by rests, were often repeated by all four voices—sometimes in four or five statements. Billings exploited prose rhythms in his anthems and changed meter signature as often as did Lully in a recitativo. In the *Funeral Anthem* [6] (1778), Billings changed the meter ten times in twenty measures. At one point he alternated it between ⊃[$\frac{2}{2}$] and $\frac{3}{2}$ every measure for nine measures to emphasize the text *for they rest [from their labors]*, which appeared four times. The effect of the statements, each of which was couched in the two-measure rhythm ⊃ ♩ ♩ | $\frac{3}{2}$ ○ ▬ , is of a series of interpolations in $\frac{5}{2}$ at a high point of the text. Like the fuging tunes, most anthems contained both familiar and learned points. The anthems had a broader scope, however, presenting contrasting points for one or two voices as well.

Set pieces were choral works with secular texts. They were not so common as Psalms and anthems but were far from rare. Billings was a man of humor, and his set pieces allowed him to parody the foibles of his beloved art. In *Modern Music*, he poked fun at the newest techniques of the day—shifts of mode and meter to create moods, the garbling of words in the imitative point—and included jibes at the vanity of singers and even at the

Fuging Tune, Anthem, and Set Piece

[5] Hans Nathan (ed.), *The Continental Harmony*, Cambridge, Mass.: The Belknap Press, Harvard University Press, 1961, p. xxxii.
[6] Buechner, *op. cit.*, p. 17.

responses of the audience.[7] The text incorporated the confusion of the Renaissance, Baroque, and contemporary vocabulary of the self-taught New England composer.

In the decade and a half before the Revolution, the American colonial gentleman came close to equaling his European counterpart in elegance and the amenities of his home. But the colonists born in the American cities during the 1730s and 1740s were brought up in an increasingly individual culture, for no matter how much they emulated the British way of life, the realities of the New World affected the new rationalist humanism in a way that stamped the Americans with an unmistakable character. The young men in the 1760s and 1770s had a twofold heritage—European and frontier—that combined with the new concept of man to create a vigorous independence of mind. American heroes were explorers and inventors—the American gentleman might be either or both of these in his leisure hours.

The American gentleman was a well-rounded and often homespun version of the British gentleman. The Baroque model was Benjamin Franklin (1706–1790), one of the most influential figures of the century. He was a man of his time and had a Baroque mind, that is, a mind of no small intellectual capacity and of seemingly universal curiosity. He was a scientist, whose experiments with electricity were respected in Paris; an epigramist and publisher, whose wit was admired in London; a tinkerer and inventor, whose inventions were found everywhere; a thinker, whose political skill was crucial to the colonial decision to fight for freedom; and a man of energy, honesty, and charm, who was one of the first Americans to influence European thought.

Franklin was interested in the science and philosophy of music and in musical instruments. His speculations were more than mere reflections of the views of his day, however, for he seems always to have been young and modern and he espoused new ideas all his life. More than this, he was an original and imaginative man. He speculated on the relation of melody to harmony, concluding, as did Rameau, that melody itself incorporates chords.

In 1761 Franklin worked out a practical mechanism for musical glasses that was to be given international recognition for the remainder of his life. "Of all musical inventions," a German magazine stated in 1782, "the one of Dr. Franklin of Philadelphia has created perhaps the greatest excitement." [8] Musical glasses had been popular in Europe for a hundred years but had always been difficult to tune and clumsy to play. The procedure necessitated partially filling glasses with water and playing them by touching the rims with wet fingers. Franklin put glass discs in graduated sizes on a spindle, which, held horizontally, was then half immersed in a trough of

[7] W. Thomas Marrocco and Harold Gleason, *Music in America*, New York: Norton, 1964, pp. 114–118.
[8] Quoted in Chase, *op. cit.*, p. 89.

water and turned by a foot treadle, thus keeping the discs wet. A gentle touch sufficed to activate the ethereal sound of the glass discs. Franklin called his new mechanism the glassy-chord but soon changed the name to the armonica; the instument finally became known as the glass harmonica. The glassy-chord was popularized in England and then in Europe by two lady musicians; one was a blind girl named Marianne Kirchgassner, for whom about a dozen composers, including Mozart and Beethoven, wrote solo and chamber works.

George Washington (1732–1799) was the gentleman model of the Classical generation; more than that, the people held him high in a popular esteem that bore more than a passing resemblance to the hero-worship of the German literary movement of the *Sturm und Drang*. But Washington was a man of his generation, and his entire concern was for balance—balance between the emotional cry for liberty and the practical considerations of making the war a success and producing a viable new government. As a musician, he was a typical gentleman—he loved music and dancing and was said to excel in the latter. Having married Martha Custis, a widow with young children, he saw to it that the children had music lessons—singing, harpsichord, and guitar.

Thomas Jefferson (1743–1826) was much more of a musician than Washington. Like Franklin, Jefferson wrote books of maxims and observations, and he also experimented with a variety of mechanisms, including a four-way music stand for use by a string quartet. From his youth, he was a devoted chamber music player (he played the violin), and he ordered a piano from London in 1771. In a letter of 1778, he noted that he regretted

The glass harmonica, an invention of Benjamin Franklin. (Courtesy of Photo Lauros, Paris.)

that "the bounds of an American fortune will not admit the indulgence of a domestic band of musicians." [9] He wished he could hire a gardener, a weaver, and other workers who could also play instruments, so that he could have "a band of two French horns, two clarinets & hautboys and a bassoon" at no extra expense.[10]

The years of the Revolution and the establishment of the Republic were lean years for culture, and the popular tunes reflected it—political and war tunes were the dominant music of the time. In the 1760s, "The Girl I Left behind Me" and "The British Grenadiers" were popular, but as the incidents leading to the Revolution began to increase, new protest songs, often contrafacta on favorite tunes, began to appear. The "Liberty Song," a contrafactum on the tune "Hearts of Oak" (1759), by William Boyce, was printed in the Boston Gazette in 1765; it warned the British in a rousing call to the colonists.

Music during

the American Revolution

> No tyrranous acts shall suppress your just claim,
> Or Stain with dishonor America's name.

A parody soon followed and then a rejoinder, "The Parody Parodised," which was even stronger, advising the British to renounce their tyranny and "Prevent the fierce conflict which threatens your fall!" After the Boston Massacre (1770), more contrafacta appeared, but the Boston Tea Party (1773) brought on a spate of original tunes, including "The Taxed Tea" and "The Blasted Herb." The British had taunted the Bostonians in 1770 by calling them Yankees and had enjoyed disrupting the colonists' church services by loudly singing "Yankee Doodle" when the Americans were singing hymns. In the first American rout of the British (from Lexington in 1775), the Americans raced after the British, singing "Yankee Doodle" in triumph, thus making that song American and ensuring its popularity. During the war it continually acquired additional verses. And in 1784, it appeared in George Colman's ballad opera *Two for One* to the words "Adzooks Old Crusty, Why so Rusty?"

Only in New York City, which remained a British town, was formal musical life unbroken by the war tunes' ascendancy. There the chamber concerts continued; in 1775 the most popular piece of music was the Boccherini "Minuet" from his *Quintet in A Major*. In Boston, band concerts began in 1771, when the Sixty-fourth Regiment (British) gave a concert of "vocal and instrumental musick accompanied by French horns, hautboys, etc." [11] The Philadelphia Regiment in 1756 had maintained a band "with Hautboys and Fifes in Ranks . . . [and] Drums between the third and

[9] *Ibid.*, p. 802.
[10] *Ibid.*
[11] Quoted in John Tasker Howard, *The Music of George Washington's Time*, Washington, D.C.: United States George Washington Bicentennial Commission, 1931, p. 9.

fourth Ranks," [12] but the war band consisted of the fife and drum corps and dispensed with the oboes, probably because no fighting man could have kept an oboe reed in condition. The fife major and drum major positions were highly respected ones in the Continental army. Undoubtedly new march tunes were being written, but the fighting men were well content with the tunes they already knew. "God Save the King," the British national anthem, was subject to contrafacta as early as 1775, when a new text, beginning "God save America," was written. And Billings's "Chester" was even more popular.

Aside from the patriotic tunes and the singing school music, the most representative American music during the Revolutionary years was native music on the European—particularly the British—model. Of the imitators, the most notable was Francis Hopkinson, who had been composing since the late 1750s. He was a lawyer in Philadelphia and, like Benjamin Franklin, an inventor and a statesman. He was abnormally short, but his intelligence

[12] *Ibid.*

Toast to Washington   **Example 63**
FRANCIS HOPKINSON

This is a photograph of the original (1778), written in Hopkinson's own hand. (Courtesy of the New York Public Library, Special Collections.)

and social art were undisputed. His songs, like his other works, were British in character, like those of Arne rather than those of his journeyman compatriots. In 1778, he composed both the words and music for the "Toast to Washington"; in this song, he used a more than usually robust English style to adulate the hero of the Americans.

Many of the colonial amateurs were aware of another enrichment of the American musical art, an enrichment achieved from the music of the slaves. The first black slaves in the Western Hemisphere had come with the Spanish, but the founding of the tobacco plantations shortly after 1600 led the owners to turn to slave labor, and by 1620, the first blacks were being imported directly from the West African lands. By 1700 about 50,000 blacks were in the plantation colonies in the South; by 1750 about 120,000, including several thousand freedmen, were in the colonies.

The Slaves

It was clear from the beginning that the Africans were possessed of a remarkable gift for musical invention. Early comments on the music of the black slaves were in the Baroque tradition, reflecting an interest in the culture and instruments of another people. Later comments grew comparative, judging everything in relation to the current European musical style. African music was much more intricate rhythmically than the European, highly knowledgeable in heterophony (which European music was not), much less interested in harmony, and not at all interested in any kind of key tonality or chord progression. In addition, greater value was placed on melody in the European tradition. No music can focus on all these elements.

The Baroque observer was happy to comment on the singing skill displayed by the blacks. At the middle of the eighteenth century, a minister who devoted his work to the slaves wrote of the response of about three hundred of them whom he had taught to read, write, and sing. He introduced them to the American singing-school hymns, with which he said they were "exceedingly delighted."

> They have a kind of ecstatic delight in psalmody; nor are there any books they so soon learn, or take so much pleasure in, as those used in that heavenly part of divine worship. . . . All the books were very acceptable, but none more so, than the Psalms and Hymns, which enabled them to gratify their peculiar taste for psalmody. Sundry of them lodged all night in my kitchen; and sometime when I have awaked at two or three in the morning, a torrent of sacred psalmody has poured into my chamber. In this exercise some of them spend the whole night.[13]

Thomas Jefferson represented the later, Classical attitude, which still acknowledged the innate gift of the Negro but was impelled to compare it, particularly in reference to harmony, to the European skills. "In music they are more generally gifted than the whites, with accurate ears for tune and time, and they have been found capable of imagining a small catch. Whether

[13] Quoted in Chase, *op. cit.*, p. 80.

they will be equal to the composition of a more extensive run of melody, or of complicated harmony, is yet to be proved." [14] The attitude is essentially condescending; it simply never occurred to Jefferson that if "rhythm" were substituted for "harmony," the same doubt could well be expressed about him.

Slave music was a lively art and was already beginning to exert influence on the American musical scene. It is a tribute to a brave people that they brought to a foreign soil, under abominable moral and physical conditions, an art so vigorous that it could survive and thrive in—and ultimately inspire —a hostile world.

MUSIC IN BLACK AFRICA

Over seven hundred groups existed in Africa, each with its own culture, and none is known that did not have a sophisticated artistic and musical life long before the Europeans invaded Africa's coasts and forests. The literature of the Gabon pygmy people, for example, is highly developed, some of it lyrical and extremely lovely. One of their early traditional songs invoked the guardianship of the night sky.

Glittering stars of the white night,
    Moon shining on high,
Piercing the forest with your pale beams,
Stars, friends of white ghosts,
    Moon, their protectress! [15]

No summary of African cultures can present the variety of that continent in the eighteenth century. The African heritage was a rich one, but a few generalizations can be made about it. In any continent, musical practices are various, but in Africa, music was honored to an unusual degree, and virtually all the African cultures were rich in poetry, song, sculpture, ritual, and dance. In general, African groups saw the arts as a means of being in harmony with life, God, earth, animals, plants, and other men; certain instruments and certain songs were connected with particular facets of life. For example, in Ruanda, just east of the Congo, the *ndamutsu* and *nchabagome* were two drum types among many. The first was played only at the appearance of the king, and the latter only at an announcement of a court verdict of guilty.

Tone quality, rhythm, and texture were (and are) the basic focuses of African music, and from these many of the other elements can be seen to

[14] *Ibid.*, p. 66.
[15] Quoted in C. M. Bowra, *Primitive Song*, New York: Mentor Books, New American Library of World Literature, Inc., 1963, p. 198.

have derived. African culture has a history of thousands of years and African music is of unknown age, influenced to an undetermined degree by contact with Near- and Far-Eastern traditions. African music seems to have changed little, whereas European music became interested in the definition of discrete harmonic units and their implications in progression. But harmony was reported in Africa as late as 1497, when the explorer Vasco da Gama landed there and was met by Hottentots. A description of the occasion by one of his men was translated into English in the sixteenth century.

> The Saterday next after came to the number of two hundreth blacke men: and more, some little, some great, bringing with them twelue Oxen and foure sheepe, and as our men went on shore, they began to play vpon foure Flutes accordingly with foure sundry voyces, the Musicke whereof sounded very well, which the Generall [da Gama] hearing, commaunded the trumpets to sound, and so they daunced with our men.[16]

It is fascinating to speculate on the similarity of esthetic principles in Africa and in Europe in the centuries of the Medieval era. Certainly the African musical art had much in common with European Medieval techniques and concerns. The vocal art was poetic and often religious, and the instrumental art was highly rhythmic and assumed percussion. The basic harmony was of the word and its setting, of the music and its social usage. In both continents, the polyphony often was improvised, used hocketing techniques, and included isorhythmic structures; and improvisation of word and music took place in public contests. The rhythmic language was complex and centered in a steady beat conceived proportionally, with frequent use of such counterrelationships as the hemiola. And the concept of sound involved quality, with a splendid number and variety of instrumental types and sizes at hand for the delight of performer and listener.

In addition, the Africans tended toward more universal participation. Some groups assumed that all members would compose music, so each man sang only his own songs. Special instruments were made for the children, who in general were given more attention than those in Europe. And the Africans had developed an amazingly rich vocabulary of vocal techniques, including yodeling used as embellishments before and after beats, often as a slide so fast as to be perceived as a different quality rather than a pitch change; portamento (slower slide), also used as an embellishment; accents, presumably derived from imitations of animal sounds; and a rich vocabulary of tone qualities. Like the Medieval European voice ideal, the African ideal was (and still is) nasal, clear, and penetrating; this has probably been the ideal throughout the world wherever outdoor performance has predominated.

Most of the slavers in the American trade took blacks from the western coastal areas now defined by the crescent extending from the Congo to Ghana and including Gabon, Cameroon, Nigeria, and Dahomey. That area

---

[16] Quoted in Robert Stevenson, "The Afro-American Musical Legacy to 1800," *The Musical Quarterly*, vol. LIV, p. 479, October, 1968.

of Africa, large as it is, shared a generally homogeneous musical esthetic and used many of the same instruments, even though the musical art was full of variation. The practices of the peoples from that area, notably those of the Ashanti, Bantu, Dahomey, Yoruba, and Bini groups, were of greatest importance in the New World.

African Musical Instruments

The West African tribes used most of the musical instruments known in Africa, the number and variety of which rivals any other culture. It would be impossible to list even the main types in detail; the percussion contingent is well known, but even that is underestimated.

In our culture, where drum types are limited, the drums of Africa are difficult to conceive. They could be classified physically by shape, by the head, and by the manner of playing. Shapes included the cylinder, cone, barrel, goblet, kettle, frame, mushroom, beehive, and hourglass. The body could be made of wood, carved tree trunk, metal, clay, bone, ivory, or gourd; and the head could be made of antelope or other hide, parchment, lizard skin, elephant ear, or resin. The drum head could be glued, nailed, or laced to the body. There might be one or two heads. If two, they could be the same or different in size or material or both; if there was only one head, the other end could be open or stopped.

Each drum was played in a specific way. Some were held vertically—on the ground, on a stand, or strung on the body of the player. Others were held horizontally—on the ground, in the lap, or on a stand. Some were played by one person, others by two or more persons according to the length of the drum. Some were played by the hand, which could produce several effects through the use of the fingers, fists, flat palm, or heel of the hand. Most often the effects were mixed in quick, imaginative patterns. Others were struck by beaters; the beaters might have rubber, hide, sinew, resin, or wooden ends, and they might be flexible or sturdy, single or compound, straight or fan-shaped. In addition, the size and proportion of the drums could alter their tone; they varied from those made of gourd or clay, which were smaller than the hand, to tree-trunk drums that have been measured

African drum from the Belgian Congo. (Courtesy of the American Museum of Natural History.)

as large as 30 feet. A cylinder or cone could be tall and narrow or short and squat. Further refinements included slits, tongues, sound holes, membranes, variable thickness of the body, enclosure of some rattling object such as a pebble, and the use of tuning paste on the head.

In the social context, the variations were even more numerous. Certain drums were played only by women, others by children, by the chief, or by some other official; some were associated with specific rituals or social events; some were played only in the presence of the chief; many were used in specific dances or were in the service of one god. Drums were instruments of the free men, forbidden to their slaves.

In short, to speak of "a drum" is to say very little. A few examples must suffice to suggest the vast scope of the art of the drum in Western Africa.

> *dikubila,* a small hourglass drum with two hide heads nailed on. The body was carved, and a sound hole was cut on the side and covered by a thin membrane as a mirliton. It was a Balunda instrument of the Congo. A similar drum (16 to 20 inches) of the Bambala people had two wooden handles.
>
> *dindo,* a squat wide barrel drum about 2 feet tall, with two skin heads tied on in an interlacing that covered the entire body. Played by men for dancing, it was an instrument of the Gombe people (Congo). A smaller version of this drum, with a palm nut sealed inside, was called the **dindo moana.**
>
> *lingita,* a barrel drum of squat proportions with two laced heads of lizard skin and a pebble sealed in. It was played vertically with a stick, by the chief or a high-ranking nobleman, who applied tuning paste to the skin. It was of the Gombe people (Congo), but the Bapote group (also of the Congo) called it the **ngundu.**
>
> *ndembo,* a large kettle drum with a sculptured wood body and an antelope-hide head nailed on. It was made in different sizes. The ceremonial instrument of the chief of the Mayombe people (Congo), it was used only on formal, ritual occasions.
>
> *ndungu,* a small drum made from a hollowed gourd fruit of the baobab tree. It had a single hide head laced on. The gourd fruits were of substantial size and the drums could measure up to 15 inches. The ndungu was an instrument of the Dunde people (Lower Congo).
>
> *nkole-nkole,* a slit drum with a dumbbell-shaped slit; of the Wangota people (Congo). The similar **nkoko** and **nkonko** were slit drums of the Vili (Lower Congo). The first was large, up to 6½ feet long, and boat-shaped; the second was small, 8 or 10 inches, most often with a carved wooden handle, and was played with a small stick. For the Wangota, the nkole-nkole was a general-purpose instrument; for the Vili, the nkonko was a ritual dance drum.
>
> *ntumpani,* a two-drum pair used jointly as a two-tone talking drum. The ntumpani were slightly bowed cylinders with heads of elephant ears that were laced to pegs on the body. The drum was played with sticks, generally by a chief at a ceremonial or court occasion, and it was played alone. It was an Ashanti instrument.

Talking drums were characteristic of the western groups, whose languages were labial, rhythmic, and inflected in from two to four high and low pitch areas (called tones). In tonal languages, the pitch of a syllable is as much a part of its definition as its vowel-consonant aspects, and the same syllable has different, and often unrelated, meanings in three different inflections. The number of vowel-consonant combinations can thus be smaller than in a nontonal language. The talking drums directly represented the rhythms and tonal levels of the language and could be understood as speech; they were often considered to be the heightened speech of God or an ancestor speaking through the chief.

Slit drums had no heads. They were generally tubular and could be made in various proportions, with length, overall diameter, and wall thickness the significant dimensions. They could be struck anywhere on the tube but were most generally struck along the slit, where the wall thickness was carefully varied to produce different pitches. The potential of such an instrument for representing a language that was both tonal and percussive was tremendous.

Other percussion instruments of Western Africa included a variety of rattles, scrapers, concussion sticks, shakers, and such intermediate types as bells and bull roarers. Less well known are the traditional African string and wind instruments. Of the latter, trumpets, horns, and flutes were the most common. Trumpets and horns included both end- and side-blown types and were made of horn, ivory, and wood. Flutes were conical or cylindrical, stopped or unstopped, and end or side blown. In addition, panpipes and whistles of two or three pitches were used. The string instruments included

Harp, native to Mangbetu, Congo. (Courtesy of the American Museum of Natural History.)

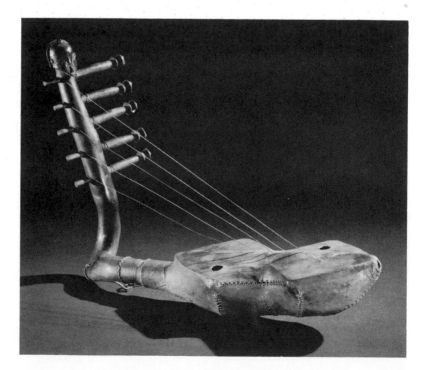

both arched and angular harps, lyres, and zithers. The zither appeared in many types, some of them unique to Africa. The board, trough, tube, raft, and stick zithers were the most common. They were made of strings or canes and in many sizes, from a single cane and resonator played with a stick (a dulcimer, in the European classification) to a large frame with eighteen, twenty, or more strings plucked, with or without a plectrum (a psaltery). The mirliton, though properly a device for modifying rather than engendering musical tone, should be listed as well, because mirliton membranes were used with several instruments; a few mirlitons, such as the box-shaped *mbanakum* of the Fang people, were used as separate instruments. More important were the specifically African and West African instruments that were not only original to the continent but also most widely used.

sansa, a hand instrument with tongues made of cane or metal and fitted over a bridge so that the end toward the hands was free. The tongues, which could be tuned, were depressed by the thumbs and then allowed to spring back, activating the tone. The sansa was made in many sizes and types, for public and private use. Large gourd resonators were added for carrying power in public, and small instruments without resonators were for playing when alone. An average instrument had ten to thirty tongues and was capable of virtuoso technique. The instrument is sometimes called the **thumb piano,** and more than sixty other names are known for it.

marimba (probably from the Bantu *imba,* "song"), a xylophone, each slab of which was provided with a gourd resonator. By the seventeenth century, when marimbas were first observed by Europeans, many sizes and kinds were in existence. A *mbila* (Congo) had a single slab mounted over a calabash and was played with a rubber-padded stick. A *malimba* had seventeen hardwood slabs of different sizes (or pitches) mounted parallel in order of size; each slab had its own gourd resonator, and each of these was also graded in size. In addition, the gourd resonators were furnished with small side holes covered with a fine animal membrane to serve as a mirliton. The malimba was played with sticks gummed with resin. Other marimbas were even larger or had different proportions to emit different tone qualities. Some used drum supplements or varied the mirliton by using spider-egg tissue for a finer membrane. The names for marimbas are uncounted.

musical bow, an instrument of ancient lineage (see page 252), constructed like a simple bow weapon but which evidently could be used for musical purposes. It was played by tapping the string with a stick or by plucking or rubbing it with a plectrum. When the bow had no resonator, the player could hold the string to his lips or actually pass it through his mouth. Varying the mouth position strengthened different overtones, similar to the manner that tones were varied with the Jew's harp. The player could place the bow against a pot or gourd (detached or affixed) for further resonation. Subtleties of bow technique included harmonic string tones (attained by depressing the bow gently at a nodal point and rubbing it with the plectrum), combining the voice with the bow, and using carved notches on the bow as a scraper, which added percussion as well. Over 220 names, most of them African, are known for the instrument.

pluriarc, a name coined in the twentieth century for a bow lute. This was really a multiple musical bow, with from two to eight bows attached to a common box-shaped resonator. About three dozen names are known for it, most of them from Western Africa, to which the instrument is indigenous.

banjar, banger, or *banjo,* a plucked string instrument with a circular frame body and parchment stretched over the top side (open at the bottom). The strings varied in number; originally the banjar had four, but in the eighteenth century, experiments were made with five, six, seven, and nine strings, and frets were added. The neck was detachable in early banjars. The instrument was a combination of a drum and a plucked string and was West African.

The sansa was an informal and a generally, rather than ritually, played instrument. It was widely known and used by many people, a few of whom attained virtuoso skill, in both solo and ensemble performance. The Bantu said that it was a good instrument to play while on a journey or before a hunt, and it was also used by singers to accompany themselves. As early as the sixteenth century, various types were mentioned by Europeans—the Portuguese who explored Mozambique in the 1580s described the *ambira*, a sansa of nine tongues. The instruments were analogous to the European lute in their ability to be used as an accompaniment for singing as well as in solo performance, in their relative portability, and in their potential for private enjoyment. A twentieth-century French listener to sansa playing described the performance.

> The sansa is played only by the two thumbs, no matter what the number of tongues; the polyphony is necessarily reduced to two parts, but it happens that the musician works them *prestissimo* and with so perfect an independence one from the other than certain sansa pieces are veritable masterpieces of instrumental technique. They demonstrate, if there was need for it, that in Africa as elsewhere, virtuosity resides in music as a permanent temptation.[17]

The marimba was also a product of Africa and, along with the banjo, was brought into the European tradition through its use by blacks in the Americas. In Africa, it was an instrument of great versatility. Generally, several marimbas were combined in a formal group to provide a large musical range and a thorough working-out of the total fabric—some marimbas had attached drums; some players wore bells on their wrists. The marimba was also used in musical games. In the most popular of these games, two players sat cross-legged on either side of a marimba; one began to improvise and the other followed in canon, the first trying to outwit the second. Such a game not only required quick wit, instrumental skill, and a well-developed musical imagination, but also dexterity on the instrument regardless of whether the higher pitches were to the player's left or right.

[17] Gilbert Rouget, *Histoire de la musique: Encyclopédie de la Pléiade*, vol. I, *Des origines à Jean-Sébastien Bach*, Paris: Librairie Gallimard, 1960, p. 223.

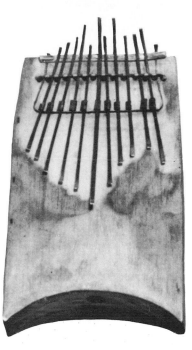

Sansa, which is played by plucking the upturned tongues. (Courtesy of the American Museum of Natural History.)

The musical bow was less common in the west than in the southeast of Africa, though it was used throughout the continent and was found also in Asia, the South seas, and America. The multiple bow, or *pluriarc*, on the other hand, was characteristic of West Africa. These instruments were known in Europe by 1600 and were described, with an illustration of the pluriarc, by Michael Praetorius in his writings on instruments. In general, the musical bow was more a private than a public instrument.

The banjar was known primarily as an instrument used by the blacks in America, and for that reason, some scholars have doubted its African origin. But in his *Notes on Virginia*, Thomas Jefferson wrote of the musically gifted blacks, "The instrument proper to them is the Banjar, which they brought hither from Africa";[18] this presents the view of an observer

[18] Quoted in Chase, *op. cit.*, p. 67.

Musical bow from the Wa'husha tribe. The strings are split from sections of the cane from which the instrument is made. (Courtesy of the American Museum of Natural History.)

close to the origins of black music in the New World. The banjar may have originated as a pluriarc with a shallow drum resonator. Or it may have been the "guitar-like instrument" seen in the Congo in the sixteenth century. If it was created in the New World by the slaves, it represents an incredible achievement for a subjugated people.

Baroque observers of the world were interested in musical instruments, as evidenced by surveys such as Praetorius's *Syntagma* and Bonanni's *Gabinetto Armonico*. Bonanni depicted nine African instruments, including the sansa, musical bow, gourd rattles, iron double bells, wooden single bell, long drum, gourd drum, and marimba,[19] but showed little concern for the music itself. The marimba appeared in two examples, both decently described but poorly depicted. The first, Bonanni labeled "Instrumento Africano"; the second, "Instrumento detto [called] Marimba." The latter type he illustrated as a frame dulcimer carried by a black with the help of a neck strap, and he called it "the sweetest and most agreeable of all African instruments."

African Musical Materials

Information on African music in the eighteenth century is sparse. The usual approach is to study the music of today, concentrating on those forms least likely to have been influenced by foreign cultures or by time. Like Oriental music, West African music holds to tradition, and it is probable that twentieth-century traditional music can reveal many details of eighteenth-century style.

A modern Bapende marimba group is representative of an instrumental contingent.[20] The group consists of three marimbas in an intricate fabric that comprises an expanding sonority of range, pitches, and qualities. The piece begins with two marimbas in the range ab to Bb^1 (using a scale roughly comparable to the black piano keys but with a low gb^1). After a few minutes, the range expands by a note in each direction, enlarging it from G to c^2. Later, the third marimba enters, adding the lower octave, with emphasis on Bb, C, and D. And at the end, vocal interjections are added. The piece is polyphonic in the sense that several independent units are operating simultaneously; and it is harmonic in its obvious delight in vertical combinations. But it is not harmonic in the European sense of chords as separate frames of a motion picture; rather, the entire tonal potential of this particular set of tones in this particular quality creates a single sonority that is explored freely by the performers. Improvisation is a vital element. Another set of instruments would present another sonority; another fabric would present another sound.

Such combined sounds, independent but within a single sonority, are generally called *heterophony* but is in fact a polyphony of elements. In the African concept, performance includes separate rhythmic entities, independently deployed but synchronized by a steady tactus. As the piece progresses,

---

[19] Filippo Bonanni, *The Showcase of Musical Instruments*, New York: Dover, 1964, plates 77, 78, 91, 92, 120, 121, 124, 144, and 145.

[20] A comparable improvisation has been recorded on Ethnic Folkways Library Record, no. FE 4427.

the fabric becomes more complex, while the expansion of range and number of instruments shapes the work. Some larger groups comprise twenty or more instrumentalists, which, in essence, means a heterophony of twenty units within an enveloping ground of a largely conceived sonority.

Drum music is much the same. A polyphony of six drums means six different kinds or sizes of drums in independent action, synchronized by a steady pulse common to all—a pulse felt and assumed as a *basis organizandi* but not always present. The organization can be both proportional and metric, with independent entry of parts, of rhythmic materials, and of inter-actions between two or three of the ensemble. Many drums are tuned, and when octave or perfect-fifth pairs are used, they may relate specifically to-gether as a pair within a larger contingent. The same effect can be attained with a single drum by having two hide heads tuned an octave or a fifth apart. A piece may begin with a solo drum and add layers of sound one by one. The Bambala people of the western Congo, for example, have used a pair of drums, one with the two pitches d and d^1 and the other the single pitch g.[21]

Music was necessary in virtually all the symbolic acknowledgments that Bambala men made in life—decisions to hunt, to battle, or to marry; and important events, such as the birth of a baby, the arrival of a guest (friend or enemy), the sorrow of death or loss, or the joy of success in a project of construction, embassage, or war.

Vocalise, vocal music without text, was one aspect of a vocal art that enjoyed many facets. The polyphonies of melodic instruments were paral-leled by polyphonies in vocalise, in a variety of types, with and without verbal sounds—with syllables, vowel sounds, yodels, and clicks.

Instrumental polyphony was also practiced; the Bambali used flute duos and trios and multiple trumpets, which were excellent mediums for the short-phrase mosaic construction characteristic of the melodic elements. A German explorer reported a century ago that he had heard West African en-sembles of over a hundred trumpeters playing "remarkable" music.[22] The present use of wooden and short ivory trumpets, on which the partials from four to eight are strong, may be related to the African predilection for thirds—the major, minor, and small third of the ratio 6:7—along with a large second 7:8. The pluriarc (called the *usambi*) of the people south of the Congo was a four-bow instrument played with a plectrum. It was tuned $a\flat$, f, $e\flat$, c; in many modern groups the $e\flat$ is low, so that the cambiata figure f–$e\flat$–c is tuned to the ratio 8:7:6. Thus the West African melodic scales were often very much like the older European gamut.

West African lyric song was related to the general philosophy of life and to the poetic art, which was at a high level, and the literature includes both ballads and lyric songs. The typical ballad is of the stanza type, with long

*West African
Lyric Song*

[21] *Ibid.*
[22] Georg August Schweinfurth, quoted in Rouget, *op. cit.*, p. 220.

melodic phrases. A story might be serious, describing heroic exploits or parts of the long history of the group (most clans had official historians), or light, dealing with human foibles or comic incidents. One lengthy song tells of a young man who had to choose a wife from among three candidates from three different villages. The song depicts his journey to the three villages, interspersed with comments on the girls—the first girl is a good fisherwoman and fills her basket but cannot cook the fish well; the second girl is a terrible fisherwoman ("The fish laughed under her nose, the crab pinched her for amusement") and her mother has to catch the fish, but the girl makes up for it by cooking them excellently; the third girl can neither fish nor cook but is marvelous at making love. The young man carefully weighs the girls' relative merits and, after considerable suspense, finally decides which one to marry.[23]

The lyric songs tend to be made up of short units, highly rhythmic and put together in tight forms. The characteristic fabric is responsorial, with a solo unit answered (often exactly) by the group to build up sections. The overall form is typically an *ABAB* or *ABABA* type. A traditional Bakwesi song (western Congo) used three units.[24] The first, *a*, is relatively long. The

Bakwesi song, elements (X)   Example 64A

ANONYMOUS

a/A Bakwesi song

main section of the song is made up of four statements of this unit—soloist, choir, soloist, choir. In scanning, this can be represented as *a A a A*, with small letters for the soloist and capitals for the group. The whole section can be called X.

The contrasting section is made up of two units, one for the soloist (*b*) and one for the group (*C*). In the next section, *b* and *C* alternate (or overlap, with the accented tones coming together) in *b C b C* presentation, to make a section called Y. The two sections are repeated, so the whole is *a A a A b C b C a A a A b C b C* or, overall, a four-section form, *XYXY*. But in all units, the different texts create variations in the music, melodically and rhythmically. Therefore the units are conceived as flexible (and hence this notation is approximate), even though the repetitions are not changed

---

[23] Bowra, *op. cit.*, pp. 179–180. (The young man selected the third girl.)
[24] The Bakwesi song was recorded on Ethnic Folkways record FE 4427, *Folk Music of the Western Congo.*

Bakwesi song, elements (Y)

ANONYMOUS

Example 64B

enough to be called variations. Although the embellishment in this song was limited to text-related differences, the embellishment of many songs was much livelier and included portamento, yodel before and after beats, and variable pitches.

More complex is a Basuku song of similar construction.[25] The main section uses units A, b, and C (again, small letters for solo and capitals for group performance), and the second section uses d and E. A, b, and C are

Basuku song, elements

ANONYMOUS

Example 65

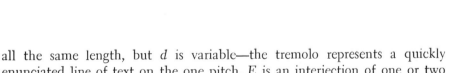

all the same length, but d is variable—the tremolo represents a quickly enunciated line of text on the one pitch. E is an interjection of one or two syllables of approximate register, at two levels, by the group, which is divided in two. Perhaps of greater importance, the ab^1 of d is flatter than the ab^1 of b, with the distinction particularly clear at the return of b in the main section. In general, a four-beat count results from the repetitions, which make five sections, as follows:

I (X)	II (Y)	III (X¹)	IV (Y¹)	V (X²)
$b\,A\,\begin{smallmatrix}b\\C\end{smallmatrix}\,A\,\begin{smallmatrix}b\\C\end{smallmatrix}\,A$	$\begin{smallmatrix}d\\C\end{smallmatrix}\,\begin{smallmatrix}d\\E\end{smallmatrix}\,\begin{smallmatrix}d\\E\end{smallmatrix}\,\begin{smallmatrix}d\\E\end{smallmatrix}\,\begin{smallmatrix}d\\E\end{smallmatrix}\,\begin{smallmatrix}d\\E\end{smallmatrix}$	$b\,\begin{smallmatrix}A\\C\end{smallmatrix}\,\begin{smallmatrix}b\\C\end{smallmatrix}\,A\,\begin{smallmatrix}b\\C\end{smallmatrix}\,A\,\begin{smallmatrix}b\\C\end{smallmatrix}\,A$	$\begin{smallmatrix}d\\{}\end{smallmatrix}\,\begin{smallmatrix}d\\E\end{smallmatrix}\,\begin{smallmatrix}d\\E\end{smallmatrix}\,\begin{smallmatrix}d\\E\end{smallmatrix}\,\begin{smallmatrix}d\\E\end{smallmatrix}\,\begin{smallmatrix}d\\E\end{smallmatrix}$	$b\,\begin{smallmatrix}A\\C\end{smallmatrix}\,\begin{smallmatrix}b\\C\end{smallmatrix}\,A\,C$

25 *Ibid.*

439

BLACK MUSIC IN THE NEW WORLD

It is erroneous to picture the slaves as living totally without cultural interaction with the whites, particularly in regard to music. The informal music of the slaves, the popular and folk music of the whites, and to some extent the music of the Indians maintained an interaction, while the formal music of the concert hall and the drawing room remained aloof from any but European influence.

Black musicians were part of the European scene, however. Joseph Boulogne, Chevalier de Saint-Georges (c. 1739–1799), for example, was a French officer (organizer of the American hussars), violinist, composer, and poet, whose sonatas, symphonies, and comedies made him a musician of importance in Paris from 1766 to his death. His two volumes of string quartets (1773 and c. 1781) made him one of the first French composers to write in that genre.

In America the two decades before the Revolution, for the most part, were years of musical ferment at the informal level and of imitation of European formality in the salon and concert hall. Not many blacks were involved in American concerts, but a great many took part in informal music. A number of advertisements for slaves mentioned their ability in European music. One ad of 1753 spoke of "an orderly Negro or mulatto who can play well the violin [and also] a young healthy fellow . . . who [plays] extremely well on the French horn." [26] Some of the best dance fiddlers were blacks, both slaves and free men. In the South, the most famous was Sy Gilliat, the official fiddler of the state dances at Williamsburg. He was described as wearing the most elegant of silks and having manners "as courtly as his dress." [27] More important, he was held by many to be the best fiddler in the Colonies.

But the war years were a time of cultural status quo: few cultural matters were thought about; no ships were docking with the latest clothes, books and music, or visiting musicians; and life was so devoted to the establishment of a new nation that music was used only in the service of the war and the political struggle. However, the war must have provided an intensification of song sharing, for singing is a traditional form of socializing around a campfire. Moreover, wherever men have gathered in song, they have singled out the beautiful voice and outstanding singer, regardless of his race—and the white, black, and red man were all in the war. About five thousand colonial blacks, plus about seven hundred Haitians, fought in the Continental Army. Even the fife and drum corps had its contingent of free blacks. Thus it is probable that the blacks did more than their share of singing. At home, too,

[26] Chase, *op. cit.*, p. 76.
[27] *Ibid.*

women, old men, and children must have sung together. Unfortunately, however, the songs that were sung around the army campfires and in the homes the soldiers had left are unknown.

❀ Some American Composers of the Eighteenth Century

In the eighteenth century America's first native composers in the European tradition worked to bring a full musical life to the Colonies. Amateurs were eager and inventive; professionals, most often with other business activities by which they made their living, were primarily associated with churches and singing schools.

FRANCIS HOPKINSON (1737–1791), a Philadelphia-born statesman, writer, inventor, and composer, was a lawyer in Philadelphia and was much involved in politics (he was the first Secretary of the Navy). He was composing music in his teens (*Ode to Music*, 1754) and published *Songs for the Harpsichord*, that is, with harpsichord accompaniment, in 1788. In addition, Hopkinson wrote an "oratorical entertainment" (*The Temple of Minerva*, 1781), of which only the text has been found. He invented a metronome, called the Bell-Harmonic, and a keyboard attachment for Benjamin Franklin's glass harmonica, and he worked out a new way of quilling harpsichords.

WILLIAM BILLINGS (1746–1800), a Boston tanner, taught himself music and ran singing schools in addition to his tannery. He was the author-composer of some of the most popular music in the United States during and after the Revolution and was choirmaster of the Brattle Street Church (Boston) during the Revolutionary War. He published six volumes of hymns, anthems, and set pieces (including secular concert choir pieces), containing over 250 hymn tunes and 50 anthems: *The New England Psalm Singer* (1770), *The Singing Master's Assistant* (1778), *Music in Miniature* (1779), *The Psalm Singer's Amusement* (1781), *The Suffolk Harmony* (1786), and *The Continental Harmony* (1794). The last volume contains a substantial introductory text.

DANIEL READ (1757–1836) was a Massachusetts-born composer who began as a farm worker and a surveyor. He started to write tunes when he was a private in the Revolutionary War. After the war, he settled in New Haven, Connecticut, where he manufactured combs, was co-owner and director of a book publishing and printing business, ran a singing school (from 1782), published a magazine (1786 to 1787), and composed. *The American Singing Book* (1785) and *The Columbian Harmonist* (1793), the second of which expanded the first, were put out in several editions until 1810; they comprised two of the most influential early books in the United States. Read left over 400 compositions.

> The best thing of all is when a good composer, who understands the stage and is talented enough to make sound suggestions, meets an able poet, that true phoenix.
>
> WOLFGANG AMADEUS MOZART *

Music in the 1780s

18

Mozart dominated music in Europe in the 1780s. This view is in part retrospective, but nobody in Europe who was at all interested in music could have been unaware of his presence. His instrumental works during the decade were amazingly diverse—piano sonatas, violin sonatas (still titled "sonatas for the harpsichord or pianoforte with accompaniment for the violin"), piano quartets and quintets, divertimenti, and works for wind instruments, of which he was particularly fond. The quintet for horn and strings dates from 1782; the quintet for clarinet and strings, from 1789; the four great string quintets, from 1787 to 1791. In 1785, Mozart published his first string

---

* From a letter to his father, dated October 13, 1781. Quoted in Eric Blom (ed.), *Mozart's Letters*, Baltimore, Penguin, 1956, p. 184.

quartets in over a decade and dedicated them to Joseph Haydn. "He goes too far in his attempt to be new," a critic wrote. "His new quartets, dedicated to Haydn, are too strongly spiced—and what palate can stand that for long?" [1] But Haydn appreciated the meaning of the gesture and, with his gift for continued growth, learned from the man young enough to be his son. Haydn, in his string quartets of the late 1780s and 1790, brought the Classical concept of that music to a culmination with a maturity and delight very much his own. The Mozart quartets display a maturity of style and man; they are urbane, knowledgeable, modern. Haydn's have the more comfortable maturity of long experience; they are modern more in their relationships and design than in their materials.

No musical form had a shorter Classical life than the concerto, which seemed to slip from the Baroque to the Romantic concepts of virtuosity with only a handful of works in between. Virtuosos continued to write concertos, of course, but these were beginning to show off the soloist more and more and to use the orchestra less and less, while continuing in the Baroque tradition of ritornello-solo construction. The Classical concerto was an orchestral concept, dramatic rather than theatrical, and symphonic in form. It is an oversimplification to say that Mozart alone defined the purely Classical concerto, but it is not too much to say that he embodied its potentials and brought the form to perfection in a series of works that rank with his greatest. The fifteen piano concertos that he composed between 1782 and 1786 represent the summit of that form.

In opera, too, Mozart created works of transcendent power, including *Le Nozze di Figaro* (The Marriage of Figaro, 1782), *Don Giovanni, ossia*

[1] Anonymous reviewer for *Der Magazin der Musik*. Quoted in Max Graf, *Composer and Critic: Two Hundred Years of Musical Criticism*, New York: Norton, 1946, p. 134.

Eighteenth-century engraving of a hurdy-gurdy player (left) and a bagpiper. (Courtesy of the University of Michigan, the Stellfeld Purchase. Photo by R. E. Kalmbach.)

il Dissoluto punito (Don Juan, or The Libertine Punished, 1787), *Così fan tutte* (All Women Are Like That, 1790), and *Die Zauberflöte* (The Magic Flute, 1791). His most successful works were the most innovative; they brought to bear the full panoply of orchestral and vocal techniques on the dramatic elements of character and motivation and produced dramas of incredible balance and power. They were at the edge of public interests, incorporating both the new humanistic ideas and Turkish elements—the disguises in *Così fan tutte* were Turkish, and *Die Zauberflöte* was a statement about the brotherhood of man involving Masonic and Egyptian symbolism. In a letter to his father while working on an opera, Mozart told of a dramatic musical shift he had just injected into a scene of rage; it reveals both his consummate theatrical skill and his fully Classical view of it.

> For just as a man in such a towering rage oversteps all the bounds of order, moderation and propriety, and completely forgets himself, so must the music too forget itself. . . . Passions, whether violent or not, must never be expressed in such a way as to excite disgust, and . . . music, even in the most terrible situations, must never offend the ear, but must please the hearer, or in other words, must never cease to be music.[2]

DANCE AND SONG

Although opera was extremely popular in Vienna, the craze for dancing —in particular, for the waltz—was even greater. The city had a population of about 85,000 in the 1780s, double that number if the suburbs were included. It had always been a city of pleasures, but dancing was the rage of the day, and every composer of any repute, including Haydn and Mozart, wrote dances to feed an insatiable public. It is hard to believe, from descriptions of Vienna in 1786, that the waltz mania was still in its early stages.

> The people of Vienna were in my time dancing mad; as the Carnival approached, gayety began to display itself on all sides, and when it really came, nothing could exceed its brilliancy. The ridotto rooms, where the masquerades took place, were in the palace, and spacious and commodious as they were, they were actually crammed with masqueraders. I never saw, or indeed heard of, any suite of rooms, where elegance and convenience were more considered; for the propensity of the Vienna ladies for dancing and going to carnival masquerades was so determined, that nothing was permitted to interfere with their enjoyment of their favorite amusement—nay, so notorious was it, that, for the sake of ladies in the family way, who could not be persuaded to stay at home, there were apartments prepared, with every convenience, for their accouchement, should they be unfortunately required. . . . For my own part, I thought waltzing from ten at

---

[2] Quoted in Eric Blom (ed.), *Mozart's Letters*, Baltimore: Penguin, 1956, p. 181f

night until seven in the morning, a continual whirligig; most tiresome to the eye and ear,—to say nothing of any worse consequences.[3]

Concerts were long and mixed, seldom devoted to one performer or one medium. A singer, a pianist, an orchestra, and a chamber group might appear on one program, and song was almost always a feature. Classical song was by nature transitional, a halfway house between the Baroque and Romantic concepts. Popular songs were still printed as two lines, solo and bass (with or without figures). The most popular song in Europe was the "Air de Marlbourouck," supposedly sung as a lullaby to the French dauphin in 1781. Over a dozen versions followed within the next four years, some called "Malbrouk," including a set of variations for keyboard. This tune became a phenomenon, retaining popularity in the nineteenth century in England as "We Won't Go Home Until Morning" and "For He's a Jolly Good Fellow," and in the twentieth century in America as "The Bear Went Over the Mountain."

In the New World, song served the purposes of patriotism and religion, both of which sustained the colonists during the Revolutionary War. After the war, music rapidly recouped its place in the life of the Americans, with a continuing emulation of the European social scene, though not British-centered as it had been. The most popular song was "Drink to Me Only with Thine Eyes," but the patriotic songs, particularly those honoring Washington, were a special rage; these included marches, such as "Washington's March" and "Washington's March at the Battle of Trenton." Original composition was confined to a few songs for domestic performance, notably the *Songs for the Harpsichord*, which Francis Hopkinson wrote and published (1788).

The songs of American composition that flourished most widely in the 1780s, aside from the folk songs of the frontier and slave compounds, which cannot be traced, were the singing school tunes. These were not only the true music of the English colonial heritage but were still the bulwark of the singing schools, which continued to be of great significance in the life of the new nation. The fuging tunes of Daniel Read, a New Englander, were extremely popular, and his tune "Sherburne" was one of the most popular of the first hundred years of the nation's history—well into the twentieth century in some rural areas.

The United States was a dancing country also. The minuet and quadrille (square dance) were popular everywhere, and barn dancing was popular in the frontier country, which was more extensive as the eighteenth century came to a close. Moreover, frontier dances were popular in the cities, as country dances were in the cities of Europe. A dance in Virginia (though in 1774) was typical.

[3] Michael Kelly, *Reminiscences*, New York: J. & J. Harper, 1826, p. 131.

Sherburne

DANIEL READ

Example 66

One of the most popular of the fuging tunes. It was published in a collection
called *The Easy Instructor* (1802), which was printed in *shape notes* (also called
buckwheat notation). (Courtesy of the Library of Congress.)

About seven the Ladies & Gentlemen begun to dance in the Ball-Room—
first Minuets one Round; Second Giggs; third Reels; and last of All Coun-
try-Dances; tho' they struck several Marches occasionally—The Music was
a French-Horn and two Violins—The Ladies were Dressed Gay, and splendid, & when dancing, their Skirts & Brocades rustled and trailed behind
them! [4]

The reel was so popular in Virginia that it was to take the name of the state.

At the highest level of the popular dance were governors' balls, comparable to court or state balls in Europe. The most famous dance musician

[4] Arthur Loesser, *Men, Women and Pianos*, New York: Simon and Schuster, 1954,
p. 439.

was still Sy Gilliat, the black fiddler who had made his reputation in Williamsburg before the war. He moved to Richmond after Virginia became a state and took on an assistant, another black, a clarinet and flute player named London Brigs. A nineteenth-century journalist, recalling his youth in Richmond, still remembered these two musicians. "To the music of Gilliat's fiddles and 'London Brigs' flute all sorts of capers were cut. Sometimes a 'congo' was danced and when the music grew fast and furious, a jig would wind up the evening." [5] The "congo" is unexplained, but it could only have been an African-inspired dance. (It was not the same as the conga, which originated later in the Indian-Spanish-Negro Southern Hemisphere.)

Instruments were imported after the war, because the American manufacturers were not yet back in production. John Jacob Astor, that enterprising merchant who was in business in New York, ran an ad in 1786 describing goods just arrived from London. "An elegant assortment of Musical Instruments, such as piano-fortes, spinnets, pianoforte guittars, the best of violins, German flutes, clarinets, hautboys, fifes, the best Roman violin strings, and other kinds of strings, music books and paper and every other article in the musical line." [6] The "spinnets" were harpsichords and the "pianoforte guittars" were keyed guitars, an invention that was briefly popular at the end of the century (its general type has continued in the autoharp, now used chiefly in schools).

In general, the 1780s were years of folk tradition and the importation of instruments, music, and musicians. Interaction with the Indians was dwindling, and the decade marked the brief climax of interest in Indian music. In 1784 an Indian melody was published in London. It enjoyed a brief vogue in Great Britain and America and was titled, "Alknommook (Alkmoonok), The death song of the Cherokee Indians, an Original Air, brought from America by a gentleman long conversant with the Indian tribes, and particularly with the Nation of the Cherokees. The Words adapted to the Air by a Lady." [7] The song had been put into a regular rhythm and furnished with a figured bass.

THE PIANO SONATA

The popularity of the pianoforte was a phenomenon of unprecedented proportions. The Viennese composers, notably Haydn and Mozart, were writing piano sonatas in which the Classical allegro, with its high texture, contrasting tonal levels, and development of subject, was being introduced to the keyboard forms. But in the hands of the German keyboard writers,

[5] Mordecai Samuel, quoted in Gilbert Chase, *America's Music*, New York: McGraw-Hill, 1955, p. 76.

[6] Loesser, *op. cit.*, p. 443.

[7] Willi Apel, "American Indian Music," *Harvard Dictionary of Music*, Cambridge, Mass.: Harvard, 1950, p. 26.

the sonata owed more to the clavichord and the concept of *Empfindsamkeit* ("expressiveness") than to the orchestral experiments of Paris and Vienna. These composers were still following the tradition of Carl Philipp Emanuel Bach; they were able to transfer clavichord techniques to the pianoforte fairly easily.

One of the finest of Bach's followers was Johann Wilhelm Hässler (1747–1822). He published several student works—works of tremendous value in educating the new piano-playing public. For the most part, the German sonatas had two movements (as compared with three or four for the Viennese) and were conservative in form, because their focus may lay in the fabric itself. Hässler's 1790 publication of *Sechs leichte Sonaten fürs Clavier oder Piano-forte*, Six Easy Sonatas for the Keyboard (here meaning "clavichord") or Pianoforte, was his fourth volume of the same title; the sonatas are charming and represent the German tradition very well.

Hässler's Sonata in C displays simplicity of construction and tonal design contrasted with complexity of texture and fabric, plus the careful and suggestive editing associated with the clavichord technique. The two movements are Baroque in their relationship, that is, juxtaposition of contrasts—slow-fast, major-minor, expressive-direct.

Sonata in C major   Example 67

HANS LEO HÄSSLER

Example 67 (continued)

Häßlers 6 leichte Sonaten, 4ter Th.

Example 67 (continued)

(Courtesy of the University of Michigan Library. Photo by R. E. Kalmbach.)

The easy sonatas of Hässler were bought and played by the awakening European public. The change in the previous thirty years can be gauged by comparing Hässler's sonatas with the works written for the amateur of a generation earlier. In 1761, the British novelist Oliver Goldsmith (1728–1774) had one of his characters speak archly of the stylish ladies who "would talk of nothing but high life, . . . pictures, taste, Shakespeare, and the musical glasses" [8]—an excellent summary of the latest fads of the 1760s. But by 1788, a Frenchman was so disturbed by the keyboard skills of French ladies that, in a decidedly candid reaction to the lesser art of a Boston drawing-room concert, he wrote, "God grant that the Bostonian women may never, like those of France, acquire the malady of perfection in this art! It is never attained but at the expense of the domestic virtues." [9] Between Goldsmith's giddy ladies and the serious amateurs whose efforts threatened the Frenchman's domestic comforts had risen the art of the Classical generation.

[8] *The Vicar of Wakefield*, quoted in Curt Sachs, *The Commonwealth of Art*, New York: Norton, 1946, p. 170.
[9] Loesser, *op. cit.*, p. 445.

Part Five

ROMANTICISM

Music discloses to man an unknown realm, a world that has nothing in common with the external sensual world that surrounds him, a world in which he leaves behind him all definite feelings to surrender himself to an inexpressible longing.

E. T. A. HOFFMANN *

The Romantic Classicists

19

It was a time of huge energies and huge concepts, of admiration for the individualist—even the eccentric—and a huge longing for the unattainable, the indefinable, and the inexpressible. Ernst Theodor Amadeus Hoffmann (1776–1822), one of the most articulate of the Romantics, wrote that this longing was the essence of the movement. Further, he specified instrumental music as the single complete embodiment of Romanticism, because it could not be verbal. In 1813 he defined his position.

When we speak of music as an independent art, should we not always restrict our meaning to instrumental music, which, scorning every aid, every

* 1813. Quoted in Oliver Strunk, *Source Readings in Music History*, New York: Norton, 1950, p. 775f.

admixture of another art (the art of poetry), gives pure expression to music's specific nature, recognizable in this form alone? It is the most Romantic of all the arts—one might almost say, the only genuinely romantic one—for its sole subject is the infinite.[1]

Hoffmann found "a sweet melancholy yearning"[2] in Joseph Haydn and wrote of Mozart that he "leads us into the heart of the spirit realm" with "an intimation of the infinite, . . . inexpressible longing."[3] But it was the generation following the Classicists that led music into the Romantic era; although trained in Classical techniques, they served the Romantic movement.

PIANO MUSIC

In the 1790s, the piano became a common denominator, seemingly essential everywhere. It was the amateur instrument in the home. It was the virtuoso instrument, overtaking the violin as the chief focus for heroics in the concert hall. It was the basic instrument of theater and dance orchestras, replacing the continuo or even serving alone. It was the instrument of accompaniment, and it joined with the solo voice to put forward a new art of song.

By the end of the eighteenth century, the idea of the great piano virtuoso was well established. Ludwig van Beethoven was ideally endowed to be a focus in the new ideas about man and music—he was a pianist, an iconoclast, versed in the old traditions but able to turn his art toward the ideals of Romanticism. As early as 1791, a commentator wrote that Beethoven's playing "differs [so] greatly from the usual methods of treating the piano, that it seems as if he had struck out an entirely new path for himself."[4] Another commentator, writing in retrospect of Beethoven's later appearances, defined his innovations. "All music performed by his hands' appeared to undergo a new creation. These wonderful effects were, in a great degree, produced by his uniform legato style, which was one of the most remarkable peculiarities of his playing. . . . In every movement, Beethoven varied the tempo according as the feelings changed."[5] A "singing tone" was basic to the new concept, along with the freedom of the beat that was the Romantic *rubato*. In 1796, Beethoven wrote to a leading piano manufacturer that "providing one can feel the music, one can also make the pianoforte

[1] Quoted in Oliver Strunk, *Source Readings in Music History*, New York: Norton, 1950, p. 775.

[2] *Ibid.*, p. 776.

[3] *Ibid.*, p. 777.

[4] Carl Ludwig Junker; quoted in Harold C. Schonberg, *The Great Pianists*, New York: Simon and Schuster, 1963, p. 73.

[5] Anton Schindler, quoted in *ibid.*, pp. 76, 84.

sing." [6] Descriptions of his playing center in the emotional. "The moment he is seated at the piano he is evidently unconscious that there is anything else in existence. . . . The muscles of his face swell and its veins stand out; the wild eye rolls doubly wild; the mouth quivers; and Beethoven looks like a wizard overpowered by the demons he has called up." [7] Anton Reicha left a vivid sketch of Beethoven performing a Mozart piano concerto in 1795 or 1796. The sketch is fully Romantic in the sense that Reicha saw the performer as dominated—even overpowered—by the art that had seized him. "He asked me to turn pages for him. But I was mostly occupied in wrenching the strings of the pianoforte which snapped, while the hammers struck among the broken strings. Beethoven insisted on finishing the concerto, and so back and forth I leaped, jerking out a string, disentangling a hammer, turning a page, and I worked harder than Beethoven." [8]

The piano sonata benefited from concurrence of interests and meanings at the end of the eighteenth century. The piano was the heir to the harpsichord and clavichord, and to other domestic instruments, such as the guitar and harp, as well. In addition, the piano became a means for promulgation and study of the new tonal forms, particularly the large, multimovement

[6] *Ibid.*, p. 87.
[7] *Ibid.*, p. 88.
[8] *Ibid.*, p. 74.

Sonata Pathètique, Opus 13, First Movement   Example 68
LUDWIG VAN BEETHOVEN

Example 68 (continued)

Example 68 (continued)

Example 68 (continued)

This early edition (c. 1800), published by N. Simrock of Bonn, is marked in detail to clarify surface texture and dynamics. (Courtesy of the University of Michigan Library. Photo by R. E. Kalmbach.)

work, the piano sonata, which was comparable to the symphony and string quartet. It was Beethoven who completed the definition of this form, bringing the Viennese and north German techniques together, using improvisational techniques within symphonic forms, and arriving at a four-movement symphonic standard so as to be able to concentrate on the fabric. The standardization of the opening allegro movement was so definitive that it was given the name *sonata allegro* (sonata form).

Beethoven was important also in the Romantic redefinition of the piano concerto. The virtuoso concept, in pulling the concerto away from a twofold medium and toward a one-man exhibition, had worked against the musical aspects of the form. In 1802, a lexicographer wrote that the virtuoso concerto was a "hocus pocus," without artistic significance. In it, he said, "musical expression becomes the art of rope dancing. . . . A well-wrought concerto [is] one in which the orchestra is not merely present as accompaniment, but in which a passionate conversation takes place between the soloist and the orchestra, which is on a par with him." [9]

The Concerto

But the piano concerto, equally a symphonic and pianistic work, incorporated the current orchestral and pianistic techniques well into the nineteenth century. Beethoven, who contributed significantly to both piano and orchestral forms, wrote five piano concertos, three of which are still basic to the repertoire. The slow movement of his *Concerto in G Major* (1808) summarizes the intense dialogue, and the aggressive allegro of the *Emperor Concerto* (E♭, 1811) summarizes the dramatic virtuosity of the Romantic ideal.

The arch-Romantic virtuoso was the violinist Niccolò Paganini (1782–1840). He defined modern violin technique, introducing pyrotechnical devices such as left-hand pizzicato, enlarging on old techniques such as double-stopping, and reviving other techniques such as *scordatura*. (He tuned strings up a step to attain greater brilliance of tone.) In addition, he is regarded as the inventor of the *perpetuum mobile*, an exhibition of skill suited to the particular form and technique of the violin—an instrument that imitates the voice but does not have to breathe. Paganini encouraged scandalous legends about his life and kept to himself the secrets of his art, which were often as simple as lengthening the fingerboard of his violin to increase string tension and permit higher notes. He specialized in theatrical effects such as working himself up to a peak of excitement, cutting three of the violin strings with long scissors, and then completing his performance on the single remaining string, which he had tuned up a step for brilliance.

Virtuoso concertos were descendents of the Baroque rather than the Classical style, so it is not surprising to read of ritornello rather than development. The violin was the instrument of the Baroque, and the violin concerto

[9] Heinrich Christoph Koch, quoted in Sister M. Romana Hertel, O.S.F., "The Keyboard Concertos of Johann Wilhelm Hertel" (unpublished doctoral dissertation, Catholic University of America, Washington, D.C.), University Microfilms, 1964, no. 65–5556, pp. 135–136.

retained its older heritage long after piano works had embraced the Romantic ideal. Comparison of Beethoven's one violin concerto with his piano concertos reveals the two influences clearly.

The Symphony

At the end of the eighteenth century, symphonic form was ready to be standardized and expanded. The desire for a larger orchestra had already taken hold, along with pleasure in works of greater length. The last great symphonies of Mozart (1788), a high point in the literature, were much longer than the earlier ones, and the increased length justified a larger instrumentation. The growth of the public's enjoyment of symphonies led to larger audiences and hence to larger rooms. As early as 1781 the increase of instrumental forces was under way; Mozart wrote to his father in that year of a performance of one of his symphonies, "There were forty violins, the wind instruments were all doubled, there were ten violas, ten double-basses, eight cellos, and six bassoons." [10] Expansion was accomplished by doubling the whole contingent, thus retaining the high contrasts of string and wind color. But such increases were unusual in 1781, only occasional in 1791, and not standard for another two decades or more.

In the 1790s Joseph Haydn was considered the greatest living composer, and in 1791 and 1794 he made trips to London at the invitation of Johann Peter Salomon (1745–1815), who had organized a concert series there. Haydn went to London as a celebrated guest, and his visits were triumphs of mutual esteem. He wrote of "This mighty and vast town, its various beauties and marvels causing me the most profound astonishment.[11] And the English toasted Haydn as a great man as well as a great composer. Salomon increased the orchestra in Haydn's honor, providing forty musicians in 1791 and sixty in 1794; Salomon was the concertmaster, playing a Stradivarius violin that had once been Corelli's, while Haydn held forth at the keyboard (harpsichord in 1791, pianoforte in 1794). The effect, according to one observer, was "electrical," and the British responded with "such a degree of enthusiasm as almost amounted to a frenzy." [12]

Haydn composed a dozen symphonies for his London concerts. Written under conditions of excitement rather than pressure and when Haydn was at the climactic years of his long creative span, they comprise a high point in the history of the symphony. The "London symphonies," as they are called, represent a standardization of form, comparable in their influence in the nineteenth century to the early piano sonatas of Beethoven. Typically, the opening allegro movement which worked out both thematic and tonal concepts, was preceded by a short introductory adagio. The second movement

[10] Frederick Dorian, *The History of Music in Performance*, New York: Norton, 1942, p. 169.

[11] Quoted in Karl Geiringer, *Haydn: A Creative Life in Music*, Garden City, N.Y.: Doubleday, 1963, p. 105.

[12] Charles Burney, quoted in *ibid.*, p. 115.

tended to be lightly lyrical, characteristically in the major mode with a section in the parallel minor that was set off in the score with double bars and labeled *Minore*. The third movement was a minuet and trio, frequently with a musical joke in the trio. And the finale, though far from standardized, was characteristically fast, direct, and often rollicking, using the Classical allegro or rondo forms.

After his London visits, Haydn returned to Vienna, where he turned to the large choral works that comprised still another phase in a career of seemingly inexhaustible creativity. Prince Nicholaus Esterházy, Haydn's patron, had died in 1790, and his successor had cut the musical establishment, though retaining Haydn as Kapellmeister and giving him an increase in salary. The new Prince Esterházy asked for Masses, and the English combined-choir performances inspired Haydn's writing of oratorios, including *The Seasons* and *The Creation*. The composer gave performances of these works to raise money for musicians' families.

Beethoven's nine symphonies carried on the Haydn tradition. As the form grew in length, the opening allegros became complex movements, frequently regarded as philosophical. The slow movements tended to be lyric rather than dramatic. The third movements retained their allegiance to Baroque sectional structures and to the relaxed ease of the dance, though not always to the dance itself. Beethoven enjoyed the *scherzo*, which was related to the minuet in form and in triple time but was faster—often of daemonic or humorous energy. The finales grew as well, being rollicking less often as the third movements took on a more energetic character—the last movements still had to serve the whole and often had a substantial coda as a means of balance.

Other symphonists were also at work during Beethoven's career—Dittersdorf well into the 1790s, Michael Haydn until after 1800, Schubert until his early death in 1828. Their works, along with Cherubini's one known symphony (1815), formed an important part of the literature. The older men retained the divertimento heritage, writing more popular works, but Schubert was a true son of his time. His works, like Mozart's, derived a large part of their style from his concentration on vocal writing. His symphonies were not influential, because they were little performed, but their thematic invention and rhythmic power make them outstanding examples of the early Romantic art.

As the symphonic ideal expanded, so did the ideal of the orchestra, but this expansion was evidenced less in number than technique. Haydn had conducted an orchestra of forty in 1791 and of sixty in 1794, but these were exceptional in those years. In the first decade of the nineteenth century, however, forty was, unusually, both a standard and an ideal. Increased numbers meant increased distances on stage and a resulting lack of focus for players and audiences alike. The very nature of Romantic techniques, particularly the new sense of the free beat, compounded the hazards. In many

The Pavilion at Brighton, England, 1800–1933. Public buildings mirrored the Romantic love of the exotic and imaginative. (Courtesy of the Director of Entertainments & Publicity, County Borough of Brighton.)

cases, both concertmaster and keyboard player conducted, but the solution lay in a single conductor, easily visible to all and not burdened by instrumental performance. The whole idea of a public concert of orchestral music was relatively new; eighteenth-century concerts had mixed orchestral, chamber, and vocal works, and a program devoted to one person or one medium was a rarity. The public was new in spirit after 1800—the American and French revolutions, the Napoleonic wars, and the new sciences of industrialism were creating an urbanized middle class. By 1820 this new class was beginning to support concert and orchestral societies, and musicians were beginning to think about careers in the public concert life instead of in the salon of a wealthy patron.

An interaction had been established. A new public, having been taught new listening techniques in the last two decades of the eighteenth century, was ready to support symphony concerts in ever increasing numbers. Composers, having been given the techniques of symphonic composition by their

462

predecessors, were ready to expand the symphony itself and demanded larger orchestras and more skilled orchestral musicians to keep pace with the form. Instrument makers were ready to supply more powerful tone capacities and teachers to instruct players in the new techniques. And entrepreneurs and journalists were ready to stimulate interest in musical events by offering virtuoso appearances and by supplying dramatic accounts of artistic temperament and creative fervor.

Into this spiral stepped a new musical figure—the virtuoso conductor. At first, he was a violin or keyboard conductor who left his instrument in order to stand where all could see him—only later did he become a virtuoso in his own right. Ludwig Spohr (1784–1859), an important violinist-composer of the generation of the Romantic Classicists, was one of the first to appear as a conductor in the new style. In his memoirs he recalled his appearance in London, in 1820, where he had gone to play violin concertos with the London Philharmonic. He was supposed to conduct from the violin section while the regular keyboard conductor would conduct, at the same time, from the piano.

> Mr. Ries took his place at the piano, and he readily agreed to surrender the score to me and to remain wholly excluded from participation in the performance. I then took my position with the score at a separate music desk in front of the orchestra, drew from my pocket my directing baton, and gave the signal to begin. Quite alarmed at such a novel procedure, some of the directors would have protested against it; but when I pleaded with them to grant me at least one trial, they became pacified. . . . Incited thereby to more than usual attention, and conducted with certainty by the *visible* manner of beating time, they played with a spirit and correctness as until then they had never been heard. Surprised and inspired by the result, the orchestra immediately after the first movement of the symphony expressed aloud its unanimous assent to the new way of conducting, and thereby overruled all further opposition. . . . The result in the evening was still more brilliant than I could have hoped for.[13]

Spohr was no virtuoso of the baton, but the electricity of his London appearance was real and the baton was there to stay. Virtuosity in the Romantic sense meant heroism, charisma, the strength to dominate by sheer power of will and genius. A virtuoso conductor would require a full-blown Romantic symphonic style, a larger orchestra, and an audience no longer surprised by the conductor's art but well versed in its appreciation. The time would not be long in coming.

Both symphonies and overtures (along with string quartets and even piano trios) were published in piano transcriptions for two or four hands. For every person who had heard such a work in an orchestral performance,

Piano Transcriptions

[13] Quoted in Schonberg, *The Great Conductors*, New York: Simon and Schuster, 1967, p. 86.

Ludwig van Beethoven, Overture to *Coriolanus.* Illustrated is the first page of a four-hand piano version, c. 1820. (Photo by R. E. Kalmbach.)

many had gotten to know it through an edition for piano. Thus the piano became a crucial instrument in the dissemination of the larger works of significance as philosophic statements of the Romantic movement. The advantages of using the widely popular piano were substantial—its large range, its ability to present complex structural textures, particularly when two people joined in four-hand performance, and its variety of dynamic effects. The disadvantages were unobserved or, if observed, not seen as disadvantages—they lay in the limiting power of the piano as a single medium. Formal elements in music became divorced from tone quality; composers began to write without reference to medium, orchestrating their works later; and instrumental quality took on the rank of embellishment, secondary in the assessment of structure and often in the process of composition as well. The second disadvantage was a loss of appreciation, in the Classical sense, of high texture. The piano is not by nature lyrical and to make it "sing" required the holding of tones, the cultivation of legato, and the accumulation of tones spread too far to be sounded as one by the hands through the use of the damper pedal. It had been the essence of harpsichord technique that the performer controlled both the attack and release of tone; the pianist for the most part concerned himself only with attack. Once a tone entered, it joined the body of sound, to be released not by the finger but by the next pedal action.

But learning a symphony through performance at the keyboard was an

464

extremely thorough method. No matter how many times someone heard a symphony in orchestral performance, he could not approach the depth of knowledge of its form that was available through practicing it several times and working it through to a reputable reading. Themes were clarified by notation, structure was made visible, and a young musician could learn more without a teacher than had ever been possible before.

The four-hand transcriptions were very popular. They made difficult passages negotiable to the amateur and allowed them to stand without the oversimplication that amounts to distortion. In addition, the four-hand performance was a companionable occupation, whose opportunities for socializing were not lost on the younger generation. And gaining a respectable skill at the piano was considered edifying by the older generation. Thus it is not surprising that many symphonies were published first in piano transcriptions and only later in full score.

SONG

It was the song, of all musical forms, that had remained closest to the Baroque type throughout the Classical transition. The polar format of solo voice and basso continuo had been so successful an embodiment of musical

465

forces that the appearance of most published songs at the end of the eighteenth century differed hardly at all, aside from the omission of figures in the bass, from their appearance at the start of the century. And the two-part polar format was to continue well into the nineteenth century in popular song.

True Romantic song could not emerge until the Romantic poem was established as an important expression of the era. Poetry had developed in two directions—the simple short lyric and the substantial work comparable to a play or a novel. The first was to become the song lyric, and the second, of which Goethe's *Faust* (1808, 1833) was the great example, would form the basis for the Romantic opera libretto.

In addition to *Faust*, Goethe had written lyric poems and ballads based on the Medieval form, and many of them were set by numerous composers during the century. *Nur wer die Sehnsucht kennt* ("None but the Lonely Heart") is a lovely poem of yearning and was one of the most popular short poems of the century. *Der Erlkönig* ("The Elf King") was also extremely popular; it was an imitation of the Medieval folk ballad and told a tale of the supernatural. The chief elements of this poem are all essentially Romantic: its atmosphere, in which the natural world contains and even merges with the supernatural forces of evil; the story, which is more an incident than a story; the characters, unidentified except for the elf king; the vague motivation of the ride, more symbolic and mystical than actual; the directly dramatic depiction of the encounter of father and son with the elf king; and the simple conclusion, without commentary, which is so eloquent in leaving recognition of the father's grief to the imagination.

Early settings of *Der Erlkönig*, such as that of Carl Friedrich Zelter, had been basically strophic, with modifications for special emphases and effects. But the full implication of the Romantic text needed one more facet—the piano as an equal member to carry the symbolic, subconscious, or supraverbal elements. By 1800 the piano was ready to participate in such a partnership.

Schubert's Lieder pulled together the forces previously unfocused in the song or developed elsewhere. His setting of *Der Erlkönig*,[14] written in 1815 when he was eighteen, is an early masterpiece of the Romantic art. While the voice presents the narrative, the piano furnishes not an accompaniment but a counterpart; in the literal representation of the horse's hoofbeats, the piano gives not only unity but momentum, not only harmonic but emotional clarification. Rather than using a strophic form in which each stanza has the same music, Schubert set each stanza separately in a through-composed setting that depicts each part appropriately and gives to the whole a single dramatic sweep. Beyond that, he characterized the father, son, and

---

[14] This work is available in numerous collections, in English, French, Italian, and other languages and in all voice registers; the original was in g minor.

demon with tessitura, melodic line, key, and mode: the boy's fears mount in progressively higher keys; the father's reassurances are stated in slow, dignified lines, behind which the activity of the piano takes on the quality of a fearful heartbeat; and the elf king's inducements are couched in gentle, light phrases in the major mode that give him an evil sweetness. The final statement is devoid of the piano's activity, which ceases when the horse stops. The cessation of the ride is made symbolic of the death of the child through the musical setting, and thus the ride and the rider—never identified—are made to represent life itself. The result is a musical embodiment of the Romantic concept of man as heroic in a noble stand against unyielding death.

Der Erlkönig was a dramatic song. But the gentle pastoral also had an important place in Romantic song. It was sometimes a simple form, a single strophe to be sung for all stanzas—the true folk form. But more often it was an expansion of the strophic form. Schubert wrote many such songs; one of his most popular was "Der Lindenbaum." Its musical language is essentially lyrical, concentrating on a lovely musical statement that is graceful and simple but that has great elegance of melodic shape.

Der Lindenbaum   Example 69

FRANZ SCHUBERT

Example 69 (continued)

Example 69 (continued)

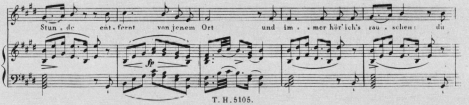

Example 69 (continued)

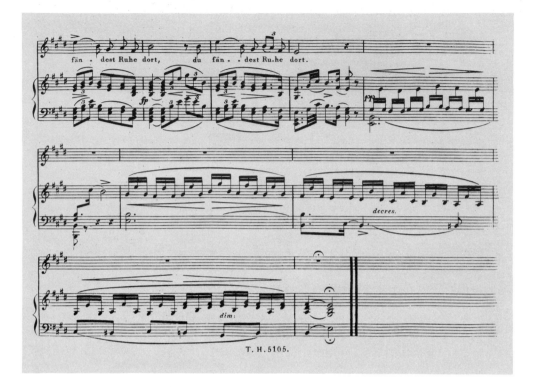

fän . dest Ruhe dort, du fän . dest Ru.he dort.

T. H. 5105.

Am Brunnen vor dem Thore, da steht ein Lindenbaum;
ich träumt' in seinem Schatten so manchen süssen Traum,
Ich schnitt in seine Rinde so manches liebe Wort;
es zog in Freud' und Leide zu ihm mich immer fort.

Ich musst' auch heute wandern vorbei in tiefer Nacht,
da hab' ich noch im Dunkel, die Augen zugemacht.
Und sine Zweige rauschten, als riefen sie mir zu:
komm her zu mir, Geselle, hier find'st du deine Ruh!

Die kalten Winde bliesen mir grad in's Angesicht,
der Hut flog mir vom Kopfe, ich wendete mich nicht.
Nun bin ich manche Stunde entfernt von jenem Ort,
und immer hör' ich's rauschen: du fändest Ruhe dort!

By the well outside the gate stands a linden tree.
Many a sweet dream I dreamt in its shadowy dark,
Many a loving word I carved into its bark;
Drawn in joy and sorrow ever near it to be.

Today I once again passed by it in the deep of night
And, in the darkness there, closed my eyes suddenly;
I heard the branches rustling, as though to call to me—
Come to me, my friend, for here you shall rest tight.

The icy winds were blowing straight ahead into my face;
My hat flew off, and yet I did not turn away.
Though I am many an hour's journey from there today,
I ever hear it rustling—you'd find rest in that place.

TRANS. BY CHRISTIANE COOPER

This song is from the cycle *Die Winterreise*; it is a facsimile from the first edition (1821). The three stanzas are set in a modified stanza form. The second stanza, at the middle of page 21, begins in the minor. The third stanza, at the top of page 24, is vocally the same as the first but has a variant piano counterpart to emphasize the new text. (Courtesy of the Newberry Library.)

From 1790 through the first decades of the nineteenth century, Paris was *Opera* the center of operatic production for all Europe. The newly redefined and expanded opéra comique, not comic but lyric and featuring works by composers both French and Italian, took over the popular theater. The great hit at the end of the century was Cherubini's *Lodoïska* (1791), which was performed two hundred times that year alone.

French and Italian opera in the first third of the nineteenth century was represented by two very successful composers, François-Andrien Boieldieu and Gioachino Rossini, both of whom enjoyed brilliant careers in their own day and continuing performances into the twentieth century. Boieldieu's *La Dame blanche* (The White Lady), based on a story by Sir Walter Scott (1771–1832)—also a literary proponent of the Romantic movement—was one of the most popular operas of all time. Premiered in Paris in 1825, it opened in London in 1826 and New York in 1827; in Paris alone it was performed over one thousand times by 1862 and seven hundred more between 1862 and 1914. The score was lyrical in the best sense—graceful, light, ornate but not forced.

The Italian Gioachino Rossini was as prolific as his French rival. Although his early works tended toward the broader, shorter comic buffa type, the sparkling overtures, such as that to *La Gazza Ladra* (The Thieving Magpie, 1817), are still in the orchestral repertoire. His most important works, *Il Barbiere di Siviglia* (1816) and *Guillaume Tell* (1829), illustrate the change in opera from the early to the fully Romantic concept. The former, based on the same play by Beaumarchais as Mozart's *Le Nozze di Figaro*, was part of the prerevolutionary ferment in France but, like many other humorous works, retained its relevance after the Revolution was over. To this proven text Rossini brought his own theatrical gift of lyric joy and flair, which the poet Leigh Hunt (1784–1859) found magnetic. "Rossini," he wrote, "is the genius of sheer animal spirits." [15] *Guillaume Tell* sums up the international character of Parisian opera. The Italian composer produced a French version of a German Romantic play about a legendary Swiss patriot; the play was *Wilhelm Tell* (1804), a production by Johann Friedrich von Schiller (1759–1805), a poet-dramatist of the *Sturm und Drang*.

It was a German composer who produced the most important theatrical incorporation of the ideals of early Romanticism. Carl Maria von Weber, a pianist and conductor who died of consumption at forty—a romantic figure himself—provided a work that would serve as a rallying point for the coming Romantic generation. This was *Der Freischütz*; it was based on a libretto, by Friedrich Kind, that was taken from one of the collections of folk tales so popular in Germany. Originally produced in Berlin in 1821, it was presented in London in 1824 and was so immediately popular that by the end

---

[15] Quoted in Eric Blom, *The Music Lover's Miscellany*, London: Gollancz, 1935, p. 312.

Der Freischütz, Overture

CARL MARIA VON WEBER

Example 70

Opening page of the first British piano transcription (1826). (Photo by R. E. Kalmbach.)

of the year it was playing at four theaters in that city, as well as in Edinburgh and Philadelphia; in 1825 it was also running in Dublin and New York. The English production was called *The Demon of the Forest* or *The Seventh Bullet*, and it has also been called *The Sharpshooter* and *The Marksman*.

The opera incorporated a summary of Romantic concerns—the forest milieu, the villain who sold his soul to the devil, the devil as an offstage, nonsinging voice, a young forester who sold his soul for seven magic bullets, and a girl (Agatha) so pure that the devil himself was unable to hurt her. The overture, a fully symphonic work incorporating thematic material from the opera, was a model of the orchestral sonata-allegro form.

Popular Music

If Paris was the biggest and busiest center of opera and of theatrical statements in the new philosophy of man, Vienna was still the biggest and busiest center of music as amusement—and of amusement in general. Opera and Singspiel were popular, but even more popular were the dance halls—the waltz rage was still at its height.

The dances reflected little if any of the new Romanticism. They were couched in the language of the eighteenth century at its more conservative level, and they even maintained formal principles that had been current in

Alexander von Bensa, "The Golden Birne Ballroom in Vienna" (lithograph), c. 1830. (Courtesy of the Museum of the City of Vienna.)

ANONYMOUS

THE RIDICULE. a Cotillion.

The top and bottom Couples chasse into the opposite places and rigadoon, each Gent: and his Partner go back to back in each others places, lead up the middle and moulinet to their places, the side Couples the same.

A. The "Madrid Waltz" was printed in 1815. B. "The Ridicule," a cotillion, is from a collection of dances published in 1812, and the dance steps are printed beneath the music. (Photos by R. E. Kalmbach.)

the seventeenth century, some of which were old even then. The punctus, often a double phrase, was the basis of the form. Many dances may have been venerable tunes in new arrangements, and these may account for the continuing use of the old two-part dance form. The da-capo form was common, as was the rondeau and the series of puncti, most often repeated in a manner reminiscent of the estampie. Most tunes were harmonically and tonally restrained. The quadrilles often had the steps printed with them.

❀ Some Important Romantic Classicists

The generation trained in Classicism but working in the atmosphere of Romanticism worked under ideal conditions. Musical training, still centered in the great texts of two generations earlier, was securely based and the public, no longer bewildered by new musical materials, was ready to accept and understand what composers were doing. The Romantic philosophy prepared people to seek heroes. A continuing segregation of operatic from other careers is clear in this generation, as is the leadership of Vienna —though not always the leadership of native Viennese.

CARL FRIEDRICH ZELTER (1758–1832), a German composer, conductor, and theorist, taught at the Berlin Singakademie. He was an active proponent of both new and old: he was a friend of Goethe and set many of his poems, and he organized the J. S. Bach collection of the Berlin Library, which formed the basis for the nineteenth-century Bach revival. As a teacher, Zelter established the Liedertafel ("song table," 1809), one of the first of the men's singing clubs so popular in Germany throughout the century. In addition to about 100 men's choruses for the Liedertafel, Zelter published five volumes of songs (1796 to 1827) that were important in defining the Romantic Lied.

MARIA LUIGI CHERUBINI (1760–1842), an Italian-born, Italian-trained composer, settled in Paris in 1788. He was a chief proponent of the new style in France throughout the French Revolution and the Napoleonic era and was active through the 1830s, retiring as professor of composition of the Conservatoire at the age of eighty-one. The greatest operatic writer of the 1790s, Cherubini enjoyed great success in productions from 1780 to 1833. In addition to 30 operas, he wrote sacred music and textbooks. He was Directeur du Conservatoire from 1822.

LUDWIG VAN BEETHOVEN (1770–1827), a north German of Belgian heritage, settled in Vienna in 1792 and studied with Joseph Haydn, among others. Famous as a pianist until the turn of the century, he was known for the depth of his inspiration as interpreter and improviser. He was slow to reach his full power as a composer, and, working in a period of transition, he composed from about 1795 to 1815 a series of works that Romantics considered the summit of the art. His works include 138 opus numbers, among which were 9 symphonies, 16 string quartets, 9 piano trios, 32 piano sonatas, 10 sonatas for violin and piano, 5 for cello and piano, 5 piano concertos, a violin concerto, and 9 concert overtures. He also wrote a number of vocal works, including the opera *Fidelio, oder die Ehrliche Liebe* (Fidelio, or Married Love, first produced in Vienna in 1805; New York in 1839), 2 Masses, and about 75 songs, including a song cycle *An die ferne Geliebte* (To the Distant Beloved, 1816). Controversial in his day, Beethoven was to become the hero of the following generation, who dramatized his life and career and made him the standard-bearer of the Romantic movement.

ANTON REICHA (1770–1839), one of the many Eastern composers to enrich European music, was born in Prague, studied with his uncle, who was the director of the court orchestra at Bonn, and worked in Hamburg (1794 to 1799), Paris (1799 to 1802), and Vienna (1802 to 1808); he finally settled in Paris in 1809. A flutist, Reicha introduced wind music to the new style. His 26 *Grandes Quintettes pour instruments à vent*—for flute, oboe, clarinet, horn, and bassoon—provided a foundation not only for the woodwind quintet as a type but also for the French love of woodwinds, which was confirmed in the Romantic tradition. A naturalized French citizen from 1829, Reicha was one of the most honored musicians in France. He was named professor of counterpoint and fugue at the Conservatoire, and the roster of his students points to his strong influence in educating the Romantic generation; they included Berlioz, Liszt, Gounod, and even the young Franck. Reicha was prolific, leaving piano music, symphonies, and miscellaneous chamber works, in addition to 3 operas and the woodwind quintets. His theoretical works included books on piano technique as well as on composition.

FRANÇOIS-ANDRIEN BOIELDIEU (1775–1834), a French composer from Rouen, began his career there at the age of fifteen as assistant organist in the Cathedral. His first opera (*La fille coupable*, The Guilty Girl), on a libretto by his father, was produced in Rouen in 1793. Going to Paris in 1796, Boieldieu achieved fame and success the following year in his first production there. He was a professor of piano at the Conservatoire at the age of twenty-three and had a brilliant career. From 1804 to 1810, he was at the Russian court, where he produced a dozen operas (in French), and in 1810 he was welcomed back to Paris with honors. He was elected to the Institute in 1817 and was made a professor of composition at the Conservatoire in 1820. His 40 operas form the basis of his reputation; two of them, *Le Calife de Bagdad* (The Caliph of Bagdad, 1800; New York, 1827) and *la Dame blanche* (The White Lady, 1825; New York, 1827), achieved legendary fame and made Boieldieu a central figure in early Romantic opera.

CARL MARIA VON WEBER (1786–1826), a German pianist and composer, was the son of a music director of a stage company. The boy traveled with the troupe and developed a knowledge of the theater. Precocious, Weber was energetic and largely self-taught, though he had lessons when he could get them (including studying counterpoint with Michael Haydn in Salzburg). He wrote an opera at the age of thirteen (it was not produced), and at fourteen lithographed his piano variations, opus 2, himself. His first operatic production, at fourteen, launched him on a theatrical career. In 1804 he became the conductor of the Breslau Theatre. He wrote 10 operas, along with a considerable body of orchestral, chamber, and piano music. The operas, including *Der Freischütz* (Berlin, 1821; Philadelphia, 1824; New York, 1825), *Euryanthe* (1824), and *Oberon* (London, 1826; New York, 1828), comprise the basis of his fame. *Der Freischütz*, a legend of the new movement, was his greatest success; it became the popular work of the German Romantics.

GIOACHINO ROSSINI (1792–1868) was an Italian composer whose career centered in opera. He achieved fame early with light works and comic operas, including the famous *Il Barbiere di Siviglia* (Barber of Seville; Rome, 1816; New York, 1819). Rossini produced 36 operas in less than two decades, culminating his creative years with the serious opera *Guillaume Tell* (Paris, 1829; New York, 1831). He retired at the age of thirty-seven and became the *doyen* of European musicians, holding court at his home near Paris. He wrote a few works in retirement, notably the *Stabat Mater* (1832 to 1841), and left, in addition, a large number of undated instrumental works (most of them early), including 6 sonatas for two violins, cello, and double-bass and some piano pieces.

FRANZ PETER SCHUBERT (1797–1828), an Austrian composer whose life was spent in Vienna, was a precocious pianist and violinist. As a choirboy in the court school, he was early drawn to the composition of songs in the new lyric style. Prolific, he composed 144 songs in 1815 alone. He was equally prolific in instrumental music, leaving 8 symphonies and 7 overtures, 22 sonatas and 8 impromptus for piano, 15 string quartets, and many operas and choruses. He never found his niche or completely mastered his great gifts in larger forms, but his songs, along with the best of his instrumental works, have ensured his place in the history of the Romantic movement. He is considered the first master of the Romantic Lied; he left over 600 Lieder, many of them still in the repertoire.

The last Song, if play'd very slow, and sung with Expression, is forcibly Pathetic—at least in my Fancy. Both Words & Music were the Work of an hour in the Height of a Storm. But the Imagination of an Author who composes from his Heart, rather than his Head, is always more heated than he can expect his Readers to be.

FRANCIS HOPKINSON *

A New Republic

The early decades of the United States were consumed in settling and expanding. The 1790s saw the building of the city of Washington, the settling of the Ohio Valley, and the exploration of the Northwest Territory. But the American was characterized as a rough-and-ready pioneer type who could not appreciate beauty.

In 1790, the population of the United States stood at about 3,900,000 whites, about 900,000 slaves, and about 100,000 free blacks. Interaction with the Indians had shrunk to one of open conflict or uneasy truce, as the white man pushed them farther and farther from the lands that had been theirs.

20

* 1788. Quoted in Gilbert Chase, *America's Music*, New York: McGraw-Hill, 1955, p. 103.

A small group still hoped to absorb the Indian population, but the burgeoning view of the white as innately superior to both red and black entered even the liberal view.

Black musicians vanished from fashionable dance halls; Indian tunes were no longer considered suitable for musical treatment; and the Turkish themes fell into disfavor. Progress was the watchword, and, by definition, influence from "lower" elements would lead not forward but backward.

The period from 1790 to 1830 was characterized by concerts and operas, imported from Europe, in a few cities; dances and parlor musicales in cities and the smaller settlements; singing schools as a means of educating young people; and folk practices everywhere, as part of a twofold musical culture in the cities and as a strong, individual expression in the territories and the slave compounds.

FORMAL MUSIC

Theaters entered the cultural scene almost as soon as towns were large enough to support them. At the Park Theatre in New York, the English composer James Hewitt, who came to New York from London in 1792, conducted the orchestra, which in 1798, numbered fourteen (including Hewitt). Washington Irving (1783–1859) wrote about the Park Theatre in 1802.

> The gentlemen of our orchestra are very economic of their favours. . . . Our conversation was here interrupted by the ringing of a bell. Now for the play, said my companion. No, said I, it is only for the musicians. These worthy gentlemen then came crawling out of their holes, and began, with very solemn and important phizzes [faces, a slang form of physiognomy], strumming and tuning their instruments in the usual style of discordance, to the great *entertainment* of the audience. What tune is that? asked my neighbor, covering his ears. . . . The bell rung a second time—and then began the tune in reality. . . . What I heard of the music, I liked very well; (though I was told by one of my neighbors, that the same pieces have been played every night for these three years;) but it was often overpowered by the gentry in the gallery, who vociferated loudly for *Moll in the Wad*, *Tally ho the Grinders*, and several other *airs* more suited to their tastes.[1]

Cincinnati, with about twenty thousand inhabitants, supported two theaters in the 1820s. A young apprentice actor, who "trouped the country in the years when theatres were spreading over the frontier and the first showboats were plying the rivers," wrote of his playing in *Pizarro* (music by Hewitt) in Cincinnati in 1820. He said the stage was about 10 feet wide and 8 feet deep and each member of the cast played more than one role.

[1] Quoted in A. M. Nagler, *A Source Book in Theatrical History*, New York: Dover, 1952, pp. 525–528.

For my own part, I was the Spanish army entire! but my services were not confined to that party. . . . Some may think my situation was no sinecure; but being a novice, all *my* exertions were nothing in comparison with those of the Drakes—particularly Sam, who frequently played two or three parts in one play, and, after being killed in the last scene, was obliged *to fall far enough off the stage to play slow music as the curtain descended!* [2]

Concerts continued, featuring symphonies and concertos by European composers or by new immigrants. A subscription concert in Philadelphia in 1792, typical of the era, had the following program:

Act I

Grand Overture of Haydn, called la Reine de France	
Song	Mrs. Hodgkinson
Quartetto composed by Mr. Gehot	
Concerto Violoncello composed by the celebrated Duport	
Sinfonia	Bach

Act II

Quartetto	Messrs. Reinagle, Gehot, Moller, and Capron
Song	Mrs. Hodgkinson
Sonata Piano Forte	Mr. Moller
Double Concerto, Clarinet and Bassoon	Messrs. Wolf and Youngblut
Overture	Reinagle [3]

The Haydn was Franz Joseph, and the "grande overture" doubtless was the first movement of his Symphony in B♭ Major, written for the Paris concerts on 1786 and called *La Reine*. The Bach was Johann Christian, and the symphony could have been any of his. Duport was either of two celebrated French cellists—Jean-Pierre (1741–1818), who was spending the Revolutionary years in Berlin, or his brother Jean-Louis (1749–1819), who was a professor at the Paris Conservatoire. Reinagle was Alexander Reinagle, who had come to the new world in 1786. John Christopher Moller was a harpsichordist, pianist, violist, and player of the glass harmonica. Jean Gehot (1756–1820) was a Belgian composer who had been in London in the 1770s and had just arrived in the United States. Thus the quartet was composed of an international group of gifted and enterprising men; any of them could

[2] Sol Smith, quoted in Walter Havighurst, *Land of the Long Horizons*, New York: Coward-McCann, 1960, p. 242.

[3] Quoted in John Tasker Howard, *The Music of George Washington's Time*, Washington, D.C.: United States George Washington Bicentennial Commission, 1931, p. 6.

have written the quartet of Act II (only Capron left no works in that form) or the songs sung by Mrs. Hodgkinson. These men formed the nucleus of the concert; it would be interesting to know if others joined them in playing the orchestral pieces.

Among his other works, Gehot composed a divertimento titled *Overture, in 12 Movements, expressive of a voyage from England to America.* Typically, such a divertimento presented a string of movements, which were usually short, loosely joined, and related to an action or a central theme. After the Revolution, the battle piece became the most popular of such works in the new republic, as well as in Europe. In the fourteenth century, the battle piece had been popular as a love dialogue, a battle of the sexes; but in the sixteenth century, more literal battle sounds were introduced into the polyphonic chanson, and in the French harpsichord school, the battle appeared as a pièce de clavecin.

Hewitt composed a piano divertimento, the *Battle of Trenton,* which he called a sonata. The work combined several popular elements—the divertimento form, the pianoforte, the patriotic subject, and the battle piece. It mixed the tunes of "Washington's March at the Battle of Trenton," one of the most popular tunes of the century, and "Yankee Doodle"; and it contained representations of trumpet calls and battle sounds and charming movements of independent musical value. Published in 1797, the year of Washington's retirement, the *Battle of Trenton* had entree to both concert hall and parlor; it became part of formal as well as informal music activities.

MUSIC IN THE PARLOR

The parlor musicale, that international bulwark of nineteenth-century music, was flourishing in the United States. Songs and airs, piano sonatas and occasional pieces, violin or flute solos, and dances—all used the piano. In 1810 a commentator wrote, "Almost every house included between Delaware and the Schuykill has its piano or harpsichord, its violin, its flute or its clarinet. Almost every young lady and gentleman, from the children of the Judge, the banker, and the general, down to those of the constable, the huckster and the drummer, can make a noise upon some instrument or other." [4] The period from 1790 to 1830 produced a huge number of pieces, songs, and dances, stylish publications often printed on flamboyantly colored paper or suffused with perfume.

The most popular dance was the *cotillion,* the French word for "petticoat," which showed when the ladies danced. Its nature changed in the second decade of the nineteenth century. Before that, the dance, as its name

[4] Quoted in Arthur Loesser, *Men, Women and Pianos,* New York: Simon and Schuster, 1954, p. 456f.

William Sidney Mount, "Rustic Dance after a Sleigh Ride" c. 1830. (Courtesy of the Museum of Fine Arts, Boston, the Karolik Collection.)

implies, had been French and very lively; based on the minuet, it was performed by four couples in a square. In the nineteenth century, the cotillion expanded in both length and variety, incorporating waltzes and games, reels (chains) and promenades—"Oh, longest and freshest of all dances!" wrote a German observer. "You are half play and half dance!" [5] The *quadrille* was a cotillion of six set figures, less enticing now than the imaginative and expanding cotillion, for which, at the end of the nineteenth century, a Paris master could advertise "a hundred new steps." [6]

An idea of the musical evenings in America can be gained from the accounts of the many European visitors who toured the new country and then wrote books about it. Typical was the book *Travels through North America 1825–1826* by Grand Duke Bernhard-Karl of Saxe-Weimar Eisenach, Germany; he detailed the musical evenings at the socialistic community New Harmony, Indiana.

> In the evening Mr. Owen [the founder of New Harmony] conducted me to a concert in the nondescript building. Most of the members of the society were present. The orchestra was not numerous, it consisted at first only of

[5] Gustav Freytag, quoted in Curt Sachs, *World History of the Dance*, New York: Norton, 1963, p. 423.
[6] Cellarius, quoted in *ibid.*, p. 423.

one violin, one violoncello, one clarionet and two flutes. Nevertheless the concert was surprisingly good, especially as the musicians have not been together a year. The clarionet player performed particularly well, and afterwards let us hear him on the bugle. Several good male and female vocalists then took a part; they sang among other things a trio accompanied by the clarionet only. Declamation was interspersed among the musical performances, Lord Byron's stanzas to his wife after their separation were extremely well recited. Between the two parts of the concert the music played a march, each gentleman gave a lady his arm, and a promenade took place, resembling a Polonaise with pretty figures sometimes in two couples, sometimes in four; two ladies in the middle, the gentlemen separated from the ladies, then again all together. The concert closed with a lively cotillion.[7]

The dance prevailed even at town meetings. The Grand Duke attended one: "In the evening there was a general meeting in the large hall; it opened with music. . . . After the lecture the band played a march, each gentleman took a lady, and marched with her around the room. Lastly, a cotillion was danced."[8]

SINGING SCHOOLS AND TUNE BOOKS

Musical theater, concert, musicale, public dance, and church service, the five formal types of performance at the beginning of the nineteenth century, were distinct yet also overlapped. The operatic and symphonic music of the theater and concert hall, for example, turned up in the parlor musicale in piano arrangements; so did dances. Dance parties, on the other hand, often included poetic recitations and musical solos. In addition, the audiences and participants were widely overlapping; the same folk who attended the theater also went to dances and to church and had pianos in their parlors. Most people were conversant with some music of all five types. An even broader common denominator was the singing school education, shared in that period not only by audiences of formal and parlor performances but by frontiersmen as well.

The years at the turn of the century were the peak years of the fuging tune, with tunes like those of Daniel Read (Example 66) continuing in popularity. The New England school was giving way to the new rural, particularly the southeastern, centers. Camp meetings arose in the rural areas, where regular preaching could not be maintained. A diarist described the four-syllable system taught at the meetings: "Only four notes were in use— faw, sol, law, mi; and the scale ran faw, sol, law, faw, sol, law, mi, faw. The table for 'mi' had to be recited as glibly as the catechism."[9] From 1802, teaching was aided by the use of different shapes for the four syllables—a circle

[7] Quoted in Havighurst, *op. cit.*, p. 238.
[8] *Ibid.*, p. 237.
[9] The Rev. E. Wentworth, in Chase, *op. cit.*, p. 185.

for *sol*, a square for *la*, a triangle for *fa*, and a diamond for *mi*. Using these shapes gave support to the four-syllable system, even though the seven-syllable Italian system, called the "doe rae me," was proposed as a replacement. *The Solfeggio Americano* introduced the Italian seven-syllable system, but it took a half decade and more for the switch to be made. *Fasola* was the system of the singing school at its height.

On the whole, the forty years from 1790 to 1830 comprised a transitional period of individuality, multiple practice, and changing attitudes. About one thousand tune books were published after 1810 (compared with about three hundred in the fifty years preceding), incorporating a great American Protestant tradition of hymnody. The most popular book was probably Little and Smith's *The Easy Instructor*, which had thirty-three editions in shape-note notation from 1802 to 1831 (Example 66).

FOLK MUSIC

By the 1820s, two distinct groups had developed in American society—city people and frontiersmen. Both were practical types. In 1825, President John Quincy Adams attempted, in his annual message, to balance the material with the cultural; he urged a system of highways, canals, and railroads to nurture the former and the establishment of a National University for the nourishment of the arts and sciences through teaching, exploring, and research. It was indicative of the national temper that the people granted the first and rejected the second, leaving the young country as the only nation in the European tradition without official recognition of its cultural elements.

The white attitude toward the red man had changed. Eastern Indians were moving west, often dispossessed. Many were learning white man's ways, but more were rejecting them. The love of music pervaded Indian life, but the Indians were becoming insular, less and less respected by the whites, who, more convinced of their own superiority, now found Indian ways sinister, inexplicable, and frightening. A typical reaction is that of a visitor of 1836, for whom two Indians performed some dances.

> We had the fearful pleasure of seeing various savage dances performed by the Indian agent and his brother, with the accompaniments of complete costume, barbaric music, and whooping. The most intelligible to us was the Discovery Dance, a highly descriptive pantomime. . . . There was a dreadful truth about the whole, and it made our blood run cold.[10]

Informal music thrived at campfire, log cabin, and slave compound. A few folk tunes came into print—"The Old Oaken Bucket" (1817), "The

[10] Harriet Martineau, quoted in Havighurst, *op. cit.*, p. 271.

Minstrel Boy" (1813 in Dublin, but soon popular in the United States), "Home! Sweet Home!" (1821). In addition, a great many reels and hornpipes were published, such as "The Irish Washerwoman" (London, 1794) and, the most popular in the United States, the fiddle tune "Turkey in the Straw"; the latter song was also published as "Zip Coon, a Favorite Comic Song" (about 1830), probably the first Negro tune popular through a published edition.

The blacks were singing the spiritual songs of the white missionaries, decorating them with their own vocal techniques, and they were singing their own songs as well. The whites, who had their own tradition of decorative vocal techniques, heard the music of the slaves and free Negroes. But no music of this tradition is known to have survived, and to the scholar, the first three decades of the nineteenth century can seem like lost years. The power of the music can be judged only by the traditions that emerged, suddenly full and strong, at the end of them.

❊ *Some American Composers of the Romantic-Classicist Generation*

The influx of European musicians and the training of American composers in the European style firmly established the European tradition in the United States in the first third of the nineteenth century. The singing-school style no longer held the central position in the musical art, and eventually it would become a twentieth-century enclave of small country sects in the South and Southeast. The introduction of European techniques into sacred song and the establishment of a system of music education were the primary accomplishments of American composers in the early decades of the nineteenth century.

ALEXANDER REINAGLE (1756–1809) was an English-born, Scottish-educated son of Austrian parents. He knew both Johann Christian Bach, in London, and Carl Philipp Emanuel Bach (briefly), in Hamburg. Reinagle emigrated to the New World in 1786, after a substantial tour of Europe, and settled in Philadelphia, where he was respected and extremely busy. He directed plays and light operas, supervised the construction of the New Theatre (1793 to 1794), and com-

posed and conducted concerts. His works include several operas, keyboard-violin sonatas, piano sonatas, and occasional music.

JAMES HEWITT (1770–1827), a British organist and violinist, emigrated to New York in 1792 and became a central figure in the cultural life in that city; there he produced concerts, directed operas, and introduced American subjects into both opera and program music for piano. Between 1794 and 1800, he produced 1 grand opera (*Tammany*, 1794) and 7 ballad operas. He managed the City Concerts from 1794, having produced a Haydn oratorio in 1793, and conducted the Old American Opera Company Orchestra. His most popular works were piano sonatas, particularly patriotic works such as *The 4th of July: A Grand Military Sonata* and *The Battle of Trenton*. He also composed chamber music and miscellaneous works. From 1798 he was active as a publisher.

LOWELL MASON (1792–1872), the son of a prominent Massachusetts politician and the grandson of a singing-school master, was trained in a singing school and then privately by the local organist. He became a bank clerk but continued his music studies with a German immigrant composer who taught him the new European style. In 1827 he accepted the position of music director of a Boston church, and soon became the most influential musician and music educator of nineteenth-century America. As a musician, Mason tempered the singing-school tunes with European style and disseminated his own and other hymns, songs, and anthems in numerous collections. Of these the most successful were the *Handel and Haydn Society's Collection of Church Music* (seventeen editions from 1722), *Lyra Sacra* (1832), and *Carmina Sacra* (twelve editions from 1841). Mason virtually founded the profession of music education and wrote both school texts in music (such as *The Juvenile Psalmist*, 1829) and methods courses. In the latter, he emulated the educational philosophy of Johann Heinrich Pestalozzi (1746–1827); his great methods text was the *Manual of the Boston Academy of Music, for Instruction in the Elements of Vocal Music, on the System of Pestalozzi* (1834).

I would like to sing like a nightingale, and die of it.

ROBERT SCHUMANN *

The Romantic Generation

Composers in the first two decades of the nineteenth century had worked within the new Romantic ideal, but they had not been born to it. By the 1830s, a new generation was ready to take the reins, not only in music or art, but in the life of Europe. This generation was raised within the Romantic concept and thus was in itself Romantic, not for a conscious artistic application, but in a suffusing, pervading atmosphere.

Romanticism was a youth movement, a protest movement, whose central concern was the redefinition of man; its chief spokesman was the poet. The ideal poet was young, the captive of overpowering forces of genius

* 1840. Quoted in André Boucourechliev (Arthur Boyars, trans.), *Schumann*, New York: Grove Press, Inc., 1959, p. 94.

and emotion, and conceived of as living always beyond his energies, even on the brink of madness.

Music occupied a place within the Romantic philosophy unique in the history of art. It was considered a kind of wordless poetry, dealing directly with the subjective and penetrating to the heart of man without dependence on the intellect. The role of music was to stimulate the imagination and to reach the highest, that is, nonverbal, faculties of man, thus ennobling him. "I am profoundly excited by music," wrote the poet Edgar Allan Poe (1809–1849). "Music is the perfection of the soul, or idea, of poetry. The *vagueness* of exultation aroused by a sweet air (which should be strictly indefinite and never too strongly suggestive) is precisely what we should aim at in poetry." [1]

It was in Germany that the extreme Romantic views were maintained. The English were perhaps too gentlemanly, the French too insouciant, and the Americans too busy to become thoroughgoing Romantics. Nevertheless, the assumption of the superiority of the nineteenth-century European way of life and the faith in "progress"—essential Romantic views—penetrated everywhere.

CENTERS OF MUSICAL ROMANTICISM

The first generation of composers born to Romanticism were an international group whose activities centered in Paris and in several German cities, particularly Leipzig.

Paris

Paris had long been a center of style and a focus of public recognition—a performer had not reached the summit unless he had captured the Paris public. In the 1840s, the city was a beehive of personalities and varying kinds of music by composers and performers of an astonishing number of nationalities. As the decade opened, the city's population, approaching the one million mark, included an estimated fifty thousand amateur pianists. Paris also had fourteen music magazines and supported about two dozen critical writers. The national music school, the Conservatoire, maintained professorships in many fields, giving chairs to writers of both symphonic music and opera (grande and comique) and to teachers not only of piano and voice but of woodwinds and brasses. The new Romantic ballets were the rage. In 1844 the production of *La Sylphide* transformed the art of ballet; a critic wrote that it "marked a new era in choreography. . . . It was given over to gnomes, undines, salamanders, elves, Nixes, Wilis, Peris—to all that strange and mysterious folk who lend themselves so marvelously to the fantasies of

[1] Quoted in Jacques Barzun, *Pleasures of Music*, New York: The Viking Press, Inc., 1960, p. 569.

the *Maître de ballet*." [2] The music is forgotten, but Taglione, in a long tutu and on point for the first time, is still remembered.

Music was at the center of Parisian thought—more than the other arts and more than any other recreation. Hector Berlioz, the critic for the *Gazette Musicale*, summed it up in 1838 with his mettlesome prose: "Never, it seems to me, has Paris been so occupied with music. . . . It rains piano albums, an avalanche of romances, a torrent of 'varied airs,' a cataclysm of fantasies, a waterspout of concertos, cavatinas, comic scenes, of *duos comiques*, of classical sonatas, and romantic rondos." [3] Four years earlier the *Gazette* had remarked that "France has ears only" [4] and had pointed out that in addition to the production of several operas a week, there was a constant stream of "Evening Musicales, Serious Musicales, Musical Performances." [5] The first could be held in a salon and the last perhaps in one of the studios maintained by the instrument makers, notably, of course, the piano manufacturers (chief of which was the house of Pleyel).

The musical life of Paris in the 1840s centered in the piano. Although the semiannual concerts of the Conservatoire orchestra invariably featured a Beethoven symphony (more likely, two Beethoven symphonies), the daily fare was the piano-based musicale. Frédéric Chopin was the darling of Paris salons in the 1830s and 1840s. His playing was much esteemed, he was in demand as a teacher, and he was highly admired as a composer. His use of the entire range of the keyboard, newly expanded from four to six-and-a-half octaves, must have seemed spectacular. In addition, he was much respected for his innovations in the use of dances from his native Poland and in his devising Romantic types—the ballade, the scherzo, and the prelude. He romanticized the keyboard study, or *etude*, and brought the nocturne to an early flowering.

A typical program still contained a variety of mediums. Chopin's last Paris performance, on February 16, 1848, was representative. He played at the Salle Pleyel, sharing the program with two singers, a violinist, and a cellist. The program ran as follows:

Act I

Trio: Mozart, played by Chopin, Alard, and Franchomme
Arias: Mlle Antonia Molina di Mondi
Nocturne and Barcarolle: Chopin
Aria: Mlle Antonia Molina di Mondi
Etude and Berceuse: Chopin

---

[2] Théophile Gautier, quoted in Clive Barnes, "On Their Toes," *New York Times*, Feb. 12, 1967, p. 6.
[3] Quoted in Arnold Perris, "Paris Commentary," unpublished paper delivered at the Midwest Chapter of the American Musicological Society, November, 1968.
[4] *Ibid.*
[5] *Ibid.*

Act II

Scherzo, Adagio, and Finale of Chopin's Sonata in g minor for cello and piano, played by Franchomme and Chopin

New Aria from *Robert le Diable*, by Meyerbeer, sung by Gustave-Hippolyte Roger

Preludes, Mazurkas, and Waltz in D♭ major (Opus 64): Chopin [6]

Chopin performed his own works as soloist in three of the eight groups. The tribute to Mozart was not unusual, nor was the inclusion of contemporary arias. Delphin Alard (1815–1888), the violinist, and Auguste Franchomme (1808–1884), the cellist, were both professors at the Conservatoire; Franchomme was a friend of Chopin's and collaborated with him on the composer's few works for cello.

Chopin's last appearances were in the British Isles. The critic of the Edinburgh *Courant* summed up Chopin's style as a pianist on October 7, 1848: "Of his execution we need say nothing further than that it is the most finished we have ever heard. He has neither the ponderosity nor the digital power of a Mendelssohn, a Thalberg, or Liszt; consequently his execution would appear less effective in a large room; but as a chamber pianist he stands unrivalled." [7]

The Hungarian Franz Liszt was the great piano virtuoso of the day—he set out to do for the piano what Paganini had done for the violin. Liszt gave the first solo piano recital with his profile to his audience—previously, keyboard soloists had faced their audiences. He introduced Hungarian elements and systematically developed technical aspects of the piano, composing works that still challenge ambitious pianists. His etudes were as much technical as musical, and his special contribution to pianistic types was the virtuoso paraphrase, a highly embellished variation of a popular work, often operatic. Such a work is an idiomatic *tour de force*, often of transcendent difficulty and aimed at astonishing the public—a public of amateurs who could appreciate the accomplishment.

The salon and studio appearances of Chopin and Liszt have come to represent Paris of the 1840s, but in fact the spectrum was much broader and the internationality even richer. The Russian Mikhail Glinka was in Paris in 1844 and achieved considerable popularity; the Italian Rossini continued there, of course, and his successors in the Italian opera were still the reigning favorites. Verdi visited Paris in 1848, and the young Offenbach was playing cello at the Opéra Comique (he was made conductor there in 1847).

Also in Paris in the mid-1840s was Louis Moreau Gottschalk, an American and one of the finest pianists of his generation. He had arrived in 1842, at the age of thirteen, and made his piano debut three years later, including

[6] Quoted in Herbert Weinstock, "Chopin at 38," in Leroy Ostransky (ed.), Perspectives on Music, Englewood Cliffs, N.J.: Prentice-Hall, 1963, p. 218.
[7] *Ibid.*, p. 226.

some of his own music on his program. Gottschalk's background was a summary of cosmopolitan influences. His father was the son of a Jewish-English banking family; his mother, the daughter of titled French and Creole heritage. Louis Moreau was born in New Orleans, which was already a center of black music, and he had heard a good many Negro and Creole tunes. One of his pieces, *Bamboula* (opus 2), enjoyed a craze in Paris. Chopin was particularly impressed with Gottschalk, embracing him at his debut and saying that one day he would become the "king of pianists." [8]

Gottschalk enjoyed equal success in Spain, writing to his father in 1851, "The King requested the *Bananier,* one of my own compositions, on a Creole air that you in New Orleans must have heard often." [9] Works such as these, written when Gottschalk was about sixteen, added a dimension to the European musical scene that was more appreciated in France and Spain than elsewhere.

Though many Parisians were happy with a patchwork of many kinds of music, Hector Berlioz was offended by it—he called himself "three-quarters German."

> It is dreadful that in order to hold the crowds the entrepreneurs insist on including popular dance tunes—and place them next to those works of art which ennoble the human spirit. . . . To appreciate a work like the [Beethoven] Symphony in c minor it would be necessary after the first moment—that sublime stroke of despair, most vehement, most poetic, an effect in art like the Othello of Shakespeare—it would be necessary to descend in style to that of a shop-girl.[10]

The attitude of the full Romantic is seen here—the distaste at the juxtaposition of a Beethoven symphony and a popular dance, the need to rank the genius and the shopgirl at opposite poles, and, implicit in the word "descent," the low ranking of popular music. It is interesting that the music hierarchy was so unyielding that the reputation of such an original and powerful creative talent as Chopin was seriously impugned by those who could not grant a full encomium to a composer who did not choose to write symphonies.

If Paris represented the interaction of a variety of musical attitudes, the *Leipzig* cities of Germany represented a triumph of the Romantic view at its most extreme. Perhaps the consummate Romantic was Robert Schumann, whose years spanned the peak of the era's fervor and whose interests—and even personal life—epitomized its concept of the artist.

Schumann was described as melancholy in his youth, and he swung from extreme, even suicidal, despair to an equally extreme joy. His long love for Clara Wieck, a gifted prodigy, caught the hearts of the era. "Today I

[8] Quoted in Jeanne Behrend, *Piano Music of Louis-Moreau Gottschalk,* Bryn Mawr, Pa.: Presser, 1956, p. ii.

[9] *Ibid.,* p. iii.

[10] Quoted in Perris, *op. cit.*

enter my twenty-ninth year," he wrote to Clara in 1839, a year before they were married, "the greater part of my life is doubtless behind me. I shall not live to be very old, I know that with certainty. . . . My great sufferings have torn me to shreds." [11] But later that year he wrote in a creative ecstasy, "Ah, Clara, what divine happiness there is in writing for the voice!" [12]

Such extremes were part of his nature, his professional life, and his music—and these overlapped so that the aspects of the man are difficult to separate. He characterized himself variously as the soulful Eusebius, the love-sick Master Raro, and the tempestuous Florestan; these were all aspects of his personality, and they entered his music at both the conscious and unconscious levels.

From 1834, Felix Mendelssohn held the directorship of the Gewandhaus orchestra, which already had a noble heritage from the days of Telemann and Hiller. These two gentlemen had brought Leipzig to a position of leadership, and Schumann's residence in the city contributed further to its musical nimbus. Mendelssohn was a good foil for Schumann. He was an artist active in drawing and writing as well as in singing, playing, conducting, and composing; he was an aristocrat who never yielded to the extreme emotions of Romanticism, though he furnished many delightful piano pieces for the amateurs, whose musical appetites seemed unquenchable. Mendelssohn's esteem was important to Schumann. "I have spent some hours confiding in Mendelssohn," Schumann said. "He is the most eminent man, . . . a diamond fallen from the sky, the most cultured artistic nature of our time. . . . It is his opinion which counts the most with me." [13]

The Leipzig scene in the 1840s centered in the work of Mendelssohn and Schumann, but the shadow of Johann Sebastian Bach was also much in evidence. Mendelssohn produced the performances that spearheaded a Bach revival, beginning with the *St. Matthew Passion* in 1829. For Schumann, Bach was "that genius who purifies and gives strength." [14]

Interactions with the Paris group were significant. Berlioz and Schumann were the two critics, and they well represented their two spheres. Berlioz, the Frenchman, wrote with wit; Schumann, the German, wrote with passion. The Romantic in Schumann threatened to eclipse the critic. "The best kind of criticism," he said, "is the one that produces an impression comparable to that of the original" [15]—a subjective criticism that describes or parallels the feelings of the listener rather than discussing aspects of the music from a technical view. As early as 1831, Schumann had recognized Chopin in a famous review, but he incorporated and gave more space to

---

[11] Quoted in André Boucourechliev (Arthur Boyars, trans.), *Schumann*, New York: Grove Press, Inc., 1959, p. 93.

[12] *Ibid.*, p. 94.

[13] *Ibid.*, p. 134.

[14] *Ibid.*, p. 42.

[15] *Ibid.*, p. 55.

his own double character than to Chopin, who supposedly was the subject of the article.

> Eusebius appeared the other day, opening the door very quietly. You know the ironic smile on this pale face with which he seeks to arouse curiosity. I was sitting at the piano with Florestan. Florestan is, as you know, one of those rare musicians who can anticipate, far in advance, anything that the future may hold of the new and the extraordinary. With the words "Hats off, gentlemen, a genius," Eusebius put down a piece of music whose title we could not see.[16]

Chopin visited Schumann in Leipzig in 1836; Berlioz came in 1843. Schumann's admiration for Chopin was confirmed by the young pianist's visit, but Berlioz, whose music Schumann had introduced to German audiences, remained a figure for whom Schumann felt a deep ambivalence. Berlioz "conducted admirably," wrote Schumann. "Much in his music is insufferable, but much also is extremely intelligent and even full of genius." [17]

Liszt was closer to both Robert and Clara Schumann than were the others; he played Schumann's works and, in 1841, gave a recital jointly with Clara. She noted of the thirty-one-year-old virtuoso (she was twenty-two), "He is good, over-bearing, amiable, arrogant, noble, and generous, often hard with others. . . . I am very near to detesting him as a composer, but as a virtuoso he has sent me into a transport of admiration." [18]

Schumann had tremendous advantages as a composer. His piano music was played by Clara, who remained popular as a virtuoso, and by Liszt, who was even more in demand. Mendelssohn sang Schumann's early songs in their first performances (1840), with Clara at the piano, and also introduced Schumann's symphonies at the Gewandhaus. Liszt became the director at Weimar in 1847 and continued to support Schumann's music.

INSTRUMENTAL MUSIC

Orchestral Music

The music of the Paris and Leipzig groups had in common a whole musical esthetic. The productions of the early years had included the piano concertos of Chopin and the *Symphonie fantastique* of Berlioz. Berlioz subtitled his symphony *Episode in the Life of an Artist* and furnished the listener with a detailed program, beginning with a general statement about the work.

> A young musician of morbid sensibility and ardent imagination poisons himself with opium in a fit of amorous despair. The narcotic dose, too weak

[16] *Ibid.*, p. 179.
[17] *Ibid.*, p.135.
[18] *Ibid.*, p. 136.

to result in death, plunges him into a heavy sleep accompanied by the strangest visions, during which his sensations, sentiments, and recollections are translated in his sick brain into musical thoughts and images. The beloved woman herself has become for him a melody, like a fixed idea which he finds and hears everywhere.[19]

The subject—with his "morbid sensibility," "despair," and "visions" of a "sick brain"—comprised an incorporation of Romanticism at its height. The work was performed in Paris in 1830, and by the time of its second performance, two years later, all Paris knew that the "beloved woman" was the English actress Harriet Smithson, who was living there and with whom Berlioz was in love (though they had never met). The injection of the personal life of the artist into his art made the Romanticism of the work complete. The poet Heinrich Heine (1797–1856) attended the second performance; he wrote that he thought it a "bizarre nightpiece—the best part of it is a Witches' Sabbath."

> My neighbor in the next seat, a talkative young man, showed me the composer, who stood at the far end of the hall, in a corner of the orchestra, playing the timpani—for the drum is his instrument. "Do you see," said my neighbor, "a plump Englishwoman in one of the forward boxes? That is Miss Smithson. For three years M. Berlioz has been madly in love with her, and it is to this passion that we owe the symphony we shall hear today." And indeed there sat, in a forward box, the famous actress from Covent Garden. Berlioz looked unswervingly in her direction, and whenever her glance met his, he beat upon his drum like a man in a fury.[20]

The five movements of the *Symphonie fantastique* were given suggestive titles.

    I: Dreams, Passions
   II: A Ball
  III: Scene in the Fields
   IV: March to the Scaffold
    V: Walpurgis Night's Dream

The movements were described in the program, though not in detail. The single melodic element of the "beloved woman," the *idée fixe* ("fixed idea"), was used musically as a unifying device and justified in the program through constant thoughts of the beloved. The artist imagines that he murders his beloved, whom he sees at the ball, and that he is consequently sent to the gallows. The finale is the witches' Sabbath, a legendary event that took place on the eve of the Feast of St. Walpurgis, an eighth-century abbess (a holiday comparable to Halloween); the witches' Sabbath was an abiding fascination of the Romantics.

[19] Quoted in Nicolas Slonimsky, "Berlioz," *Baker's Biographical Dictionary of Musicians*, 5th ed., New York: Schirmer, 1958, p. 138.
[20] Quoted in Barzun, *op. cit.*, pp. 308–309.

Liszt went further and developed a musical parallel of a poem or story —a *symphonic poem* or *tone poem*. The most famous of these was *Les Préludes,* which was begun in 1848 and first performed in 1854 at Weimar. It was the parallel of a Romantic poem of the same name, by the Frenchman Alfonse-Marie de Lamartine (1790–1869), which depicts the alternate suffering and rebirth of the self (the latter through the forces of nature). The poem made an excellent schema for musical deployment in what amounted to almost a series of variations on one or two musical motives. Liszt called the thematic technique "transformation" rather than development, because the theme itself appeared in different guises rather than in the unstable series of partial changes characteristic of development.

Symphonies and concertos were being written on the German front as well, with works by Mendelssohn and Schumann preeminent. But the very Beethoven worship that made the symphony a holy form (Wagner called Beethoven "our sacred genius") [21] made the quest for a work to be worthy of that master's inheritance almost unattainable. The composers who followed him found their fulfillment in writing for the piano.

Chopin was one of the original harmonists of the century. He introduced a highly expanded chromatic logic, and he couched harmonies in idiomatically pianistic figurations; these were tremendously innovative and revealed a new technique essential to Romantic piano music. During the careers of Chopin and Schumann, the modern piano came into being. The overstringing, the pedal refinements, and, from the United States, the cast-iron frame gave the instrument strength and dynamic brilliance; and for these advantages the Romantics were willing to sacrifice the subtlety and finesse of the gentler instrument they had inherited. Chopin, Schumann, and Mendelssohn wrote pieces for wide distribution and enjoyment, as well as more difficult works for more advanced pianists.

The Piano

Chopin was famous for his introduction of the Polish idiom, particularly the mazurka, with its characteristic rhythm. His Mazurka opus 17, no. 4, which was published in 1834, is representative. It has a simple three-section form, preceded and followed by a tonally enigmatic four-measure phrase (xABAx). It is otherwise tonally unified, with the key of *a* minor unchallenged in the first and third sections and changed only in mode in the second. The language is homophonic, giving different roles to the two hands and working idiomatically with the piano, which was still generally treated in the Classical, symphony-related manner. The left hand, in Chopin's fully developed style, expanded its scope in harmonic figures, while the right hand developed the ornate melodic language. And the harmonic language was itself increasingly chromatic; it is interesting to find so many altered tones in a section whose essential harmonic action is limited to tonic and dominant. It was this kind of skill and scope that led Schumann to say

[21] Quoted in *ibid.,* p. 275.

of Chopin, "Chopin did not make his appearance accompanied by an orchestral army. . . . He possesses only a small cohort, but to him belongs every soul to the last hero." [22]

Schumann's *Träumerei* (Dreaming) was one of the *Kinderscenen: Leichte Stücke für das Pianoforte* (Children's Scenes: Easy Pieces for the Pianoforte), thirteen pieces published as opus 15 in 1839. Like Chopin's Mazurka, it is a short work that the amateur could play, and it became one of the most widely played—and loved—of all Romantic piano pieces. It is a simple piece, homophonic and clearly sectional ($AABA^1$). Its subtlety and variation comes from a harmonic grace, in which progression is constant, gentle, and imaginative, with full exploitation of the potential of F major and its closely related keys. Particularly effective is the reaching of the principle theme to different harmonic and melodic high points—to the simple subdominant chord under f^2 and the dominant of a minor under a^2 in the initial statement, to the dominant ninths of g minor under eb^2 and of d minor under bb^2 in the middle section, and finally to the dominant ninth of c major under a^2. The melody is wide-ranging yet rhythmically predictable, allowing agogic freedom for expressive purposes.

Many other popular piano works were composed by that first generation and were widely circulated. The Mendelssohn *Sechs Lieder ohne Worte* (Six Songs without Words, opus 62), of 1844, dedicated to Frau Clara Schumann, were published in France as *Six Romances*; in England, with the German title and the subtitle *The Fifth Book of Original Melodies*. Even more popular was a piano transcription of a Liszt song, "O Lieb" (O Love), of 1847, which appeared in 1850 as "Liebestraum" (Dream of Love).

Longer works for piano, in addition to concertos, included sonatas, suites, virtuoso paraphrases and variations, and program pieces with and without specific parallels in literary works. Liszt wrote paraphrases, variations on the Paganini *a* minor Caprice, and such works as the *Etudes d' exécution transcendante* (Transcendental Etudes), which were beyond the capacity of any but the few exceptionally skilled pianists.

More significant to the Romantic movement were the program pieces represented by the Chopin ballades and the longer works of Schumann. The first of Chopin's ballades, opus 23 (1836), which was inspired by the poem "Konrad Wallrod," by the Polish poet Adam Mickiewicz, is in *g* minor. The ballade presents a sonata-like design and is couched in a Romantic musical fabric that easily exploits the dramatic aspects of that design. It is difficult and demands high technical and musical skills. Schumann called it Chopin's "most spirited, most daring work." [23]

Schumann's *Carnaval* (1835) is a series of short pieces describing a carnival or, more precisely, depicting the characters attending it. As usual,

[22] Quoted in James Huneker, *Chopin: The Mazurkas*, New York: Schirmer, 1915, p. v.
[23] Quoted in Ernest Hutcheson, *The Literature of the Piano*, New York: Knopf, 1948, p. 205.

Example 72

Träumerei

ROBERT SCHUMANN

Our photograph is a facsimile of a mid-nineteenth-century edition of *Kinderscenen* (Scenes of Childhood), which was originally published in 1838. (Courtesy of the University of Michigan Library. Photo by R. E. Kalmbach.)

Schumann's personal life entered his musical language, so though the characters from the Commedia dell' Arte—Pierrot, Columbine, Harlequin—are included, so are Eusebius, Florestan (with reference to one of Schumann's earlier works), Clara, Paganini, and Chopin (in a nocturne-like melody for which Schumann specified the quirky fingering Chopin was noted for). The finale presents Schumann's partly imaginary club, the Davidsbundler, in a "March Against the Philistines" (musical, of course). The individual movements range from easy to difficult; most are simple in form, many in the two-section Baroque dance form. The fabric, like Chopin's, is varied, knowledgeably handled, and often homophonic.

In addition, the piano remained the chief purveyor of popular music, both song and dance, as well as the indispensable—and, in Germany, the ennobled—counterpart of the voice in serious song.

VOCAL MUSIC

Although most composers of the generation composed songs, Schumann was the standard-bearer for the Lied. In 1840, the year of his marriage, he wrote more than 130 Lieder, making this his "year of song." He set poems by virtually all the early Romantic composers, from Goethe to Heinrich Heine, from the nature-loving Joseph Baron von Eichendorff (1788–1857) to the sentimental Adalbert von Chamisso (1781–1838). Schumann had the advantages of being a child of the Romantic movement, having more thoroughly Romantic lyrics to set, and being a pianist. In Schumann's Lieder the piano counterparts used the full scope of the Romantic style; in their solid, often powerful harmonic elements, they often symbolized a masculine component, in contrast to the feminine, flowing vocal line. The masculine-feminine symbolisms of the Romantic were fulfilled especially in the Lied with soprano voice. As the balancing element, the piano counterpart of the Schumann Lieder often completed the song alone in an extended coda.

Serious Song

The solo song recital had not yet developed. Combining songs, detached arias (from both grand and light opera), dances, chamber music, and piano solos comprised the usual music program, in spite of the solo recitals of Liszt and a few others before the mid-century mark. A London concert of 1837, called a "piano evening," produced by the pianist Ignaz Moscheles (1794–1840), was typical:

Part I

Grande Sonata brillante (C major in four movements) Pianoforte, Mr. Moscheles	Weber
Cantata, "Mad Bess" Miss Birch	Purcell

Three Preludes and Fugues (C♯ major, C♯ minor, and D major Pianoforte, Mr. Moscheles	[J.] S. Bach
German Song, "Das erste Veilchen" (The first Violet) Miss Masson	Mendelssohn
Sonate dramatique (d minor [Op. 31 #2], in three movements) Pianoforte, Mr. Moscheles	Beethoven

Part II

A selection from the Suites and Lessons (including the celebrated Cat's Fugue), as originally written for the harpsichord, and, by desire, performed on that instrument by Mr. Moscheles	D. Scarlatti
"The Harmonious Blacksmith," with Handel's Variations. Mr. Moscheles	Handel
Duet, "Così fan tutte" Miss Birch and Miss Masson	Mozart
Les Adieux, l'Absence, et le Retour, sonate caractéristique [Op. 81a] Pianoforte, Mr. Moscheles	Beethoven
Glee, "Go, feeble tyrant" Miss Birch, Miss Masson, Messrs. Vaughan and Bradbury	Jackson
A selection of new manuscript studies Pianoforte, Mr. Moscheles	Moscheles [24]

Opera

The state of theater music had not changed much in Europe or America. The operatic successes were those of Meyerbeer, especially *Les Huguenots* (1836); Vincenzo Bellini (1801–1835), whose *Norma* (Milan, 1832; London, 1833; Dublin, Philadelphia, and New York, 1841) was his most successful work; and Gaetano Donizetti (1797–1848), whose sixty stage works included *Lucia di Lammermoor* (Naples, 1835; London, 1838; New Orleans, 1841; New York, 1843), on a novel by Sir Walter Scott. The works of these men maintained the supremacy of the vocal art; they used Romantic subjects and often up-to-date harmonic and rhythmic ideas but centered in the Classical, often coloratura vocal line. In Italy the singer was still the musical hero or, more likely, heroine, able to command public attention and esteem as no other figure in the arts (and few in any other profession) could. A correspondent for *The Pictorial Times* sent the following report back to London in 1843:

[24] Quoted in Eric Blom (ed.), *The Music Lover's Miscellany*, London: Gollanz, 1935, pp. 121–122.

The last appearance of Cerito in Milan was marked by an enthusiasm, fortunately—we may perhaps say—unknown in this country. She was called upon the stage fifty-two times, and 1,494 bouquets and 836 garlands were thrown to her. Among the bouquets was one of such gigantic proportions that it required two porters to carry it to the theatre. It is expected by the Taglioni-ites that the approaching reception of their favorites will be still more pompous, nearly all the hot-houses and flower gardens of Lombardy having been bought up for the occasion.[25]

Popular Music

Popular music was generally static from 1830 to 1850. The custom of printing songs and detached airs in two lines (bass and treble), in the manner of a song with continuo but without figures, persisted from the end of the eighteenth century. The salon or parlor song might well be a Mendelssohn or Schubert, or even a Schumann Lied, or one of the folk songs (or folk-like songs) of the popular Scottish and Irish traditions.

The popular music that was more distinct from serious music was that of the bands, which began to gain momentum in the 1840s. The acceptance of the cornet (not to be confused with the earlier cornett or cornetto), a soprano brass instrument with pistons, signaled the beginning of a century of popularity for the solo cornet. In 1833 the Prussian band introduced cornets, and within five years the band had been redefined. Development of other brass instruments soon followed, and the brass band was somewhat determined by 1840. Comparing the Prussian band of 1838 with the English Cavalry Band (Fourth Light Dragoons) of 1842 reflects both similarities and differences.

Prussian (1838)	English (1842)
1 small cornet (high B♭)	3 B♭ cornets
2 soprano cornets (E♭)	5 trumpets
4 B♭ cornets	2 horns
2 tenor horns	1 keyed bugle
8 trumpets	1 ophicleide
1 euphonium	3 trombones
3 bombardons (twelve-keyed ophicleides)	—
	15
21	

The mouth organ, or harmonica, entered the European scene (from the Orient) by way of Vienna in 1829. This small, free-reed instrument, with reeds alternately placed for pressure (exhaling) and suction (inhaling), proved a fine portable instrument—a hip-pocket folk instrument more versatile than the Jew's harp. It was capable of being easily learned yet was susceptible to skillful handling. The larger keyboard type, called the harmonium,

[25] Quoted in *ibid.*, p. 51.

made its appearance in 1840; it had a pedal mechanism that activated a bellows to supply pressure (no suction). The harmonium was to be the only rival to the piano as a parlor instrument.

Vienna was still the leader in popular music and in entertainment fads as well—the Viennese took their pleasures seriously. A newspaper of 1832 described a fireworks display (newspaper critics reviewed fireworks as they did musical and dramatic productions) in which a scene from *Faust* was represented. "Faust was viewed [at supper], drinking one cup after another, to the sound of diabolical music and of thunder-claps. The black, terrible shapes of dancing demons, surrounded by red flames obtained with chemical powders, produced a most fearsome effect." [26]

The dance hall still reigned supreme. A visitor in Vienna from 1833 to 1837 wrote of the many "dance palaces," such as the Tivoli, the Odeon, and the Apollo.

> Austrian sensuality is neither vulgar nor sinful; it is that of mankind before the fall. . . . Under illuminated trees and in open arcades people are seated at innumerable tables eating and drinking, chattering, laughing, and listening. In their midst is the orchestra, from which come the new waltzes, the bugbear of our learned musicians, the new waltzes that stir the blood like the bite of a tarantula. In the middle of the garden on the orchestra platform there stands the modern hero of Austria, *Le Napoléon Autrichien*, the musical director, Johann Strauss. The Strauss waltzes are to the Viennese what the Napoleonic victories were to the French, and if only the Viennese possessed cannon, they would erect a Vendome column to him.[27]

Strauss went on tour later in 1837 with his orchestra of fourteen, taking the Viennese waltz to the rest of Europe and then to England. The waltz was a salient factor in the entertainments accompanying the coronation of Queen Victoria in 1838.

The dance craze continued. It was at its height in Vienna, but Paris was not immune. The French especially loved the Polish dances popularized by Chopin. Many dance texts appeared in these years, and many of them make explicit the relationship between the dance as an art and as a socially and sexually symbolic activity. *La Polka enseignée sans Maître* (The Polka Taught without a Teacher, 1845), a do-it-yourself text, said, "Tell me how you do the polka, and I will tell you how you love." [28]

In America the urban concerts and the parlor musicales paralleled those in Europe, except that the upright piano challenged the typically European square piano and the waltz challenged the cotillion. The more truly American music was comprised of the songbook literature, on the one hand, and

[26] Quoted in Marcel Brion (Jean Stewart, trans.), *Daily Life in the Vienna of Mozart and Schubert*, London: Weidenfeld and Nicholson, 1961, p. 124.
[27] Heinrich Laube, quoted in *ibid.*, p. 193.
[28] Quoted in Curt Sachs, *World History of the Dance*, New York: Norton, 1963, p. 189.

country music and popular song, on the other. *The Sacred Harp* (1844), by
B. F. White and E. J. King, was a remarkable example of the fasola tradition; with revisions in 1850, 1859, 1869, 1911, and 1936, it is still in use.

The railroads were the greatest enthusiasm of the Americans. Tracks
were being laid and the trains sent out; the West was being opened, and
folk songs of the railroad and of lonesome cowboys began to appear. Tunes,
brought from Europe or written by hand and handed down from father to
son, went west in song books. James Gray, who settled in Iowa in 1820, had
such a book; its fiddle tunes, such as "The Devil among the Tailors" and
"Pleasure of the Town," are representative.

Pleasure of the Town and The Devil among the Tailors   **Example 73**

JAMES GRAY

These tunes are from a manuscript book (c. 1820) by James Gray. Gray was an
immigrant to Iowa from England. (Courtesy of Mrs. Edith Gray Pierce.)

The songs, barn dances, and house raisings of the pioneers, along with the plantation entertainments and dockside dances of the Negroes, furnished a sturdy and many-faceted tradition, but unfortunately, few documents remain.

❊ Some Composers of the Romantic Generation

Brought up and educated in a time of remarkable unity, the composers of the Romantic generation were precocious and energetic, and their relative unanimity of training and goal gave them a rare esprit de corps. Their years of exhilarating interaction covered the two decades before the middle of the nineteenth century.

GIACOMO (JACOB) MEYERBEER (1791–1864), the son of a wealthy banker in Berlin, studied as a boy (with Clementi and Zelter) to be a pianist. In 1817, he was sent to Italy, where he began writing operas, but it was in Paris that he achieved his great success as a composer. This was accomplished with his grand opera *Robert le Diable* (Robert the Devil), which was produced in Paris in 1831. In 1832 it was playing in three London theaters and one in Dublin, and it played in New York in 1834. *Les Huguenots* (1836) followed, and his other works maintained his success. These included *Le Prophète* (1849) and *L'Africaine* (posthumously produced in 1865). He produced light operas as well, along with a considerable amount of sacred and instrumental music.

HECTOR BERLIOZ (1803–1869), born in the French Alps, went to Paris in 1821 to study medicine; there he switched to music and won the Prix de Rome in 1830. From 1834 to 1859 he was a critic for the *Gazette musicale*, and in 1839 he was made the librarian of the Conservatoire. He traveled widely, conducting his works on the Continent and the British Isles, and he knew many of the important musicians of his time. Berlioz wrote books as well as music, including an important *Grand Traité d'instrumentation et orchestration modernes* (Grand Treatise of Modern Instrumentation and Orchestration, 1844). He composed 12 orchestral works, including *Symphonie fantastique* (1830), *Harold en Italie* (1834), and *le Carnaval romain* (Roman Carnival, 1844); 5 theater works, including *Benvenuto Cellini* (1838) and *l'Enfance du Christ* (The Childhood of Christ, 1854); about 40 songs; and several important choral works, including 8 *Scènes de Faust* (1829) and the *Requiem* (1837).

JOHANN STRAUSS (1804–1849), a Viennese conductor and composer, organized his own (fourteen-man) orchestra in 1826 and began a career of international reputation by touring frequently. From 1834 he was bandmaster of the Viennese Militia, and from 1845 he was in charge of the court ballroom music. In 1838 he increased his orchestra to twenty-eight and made a successful trip to Paris and then to London for the festivities in connection with the coronation of Queen Victoria. Strauss composed 253 works, chiefly dances and marches and including 152 waltzes, on which his fame rests.

MIKHAIL IVANOVICH GLINKA (1804–1857), a Russian amateur who was educated in St. Petersburg by Irish and German musicians, worked in the government service until 1828 and studied in Italy (1830–1832) and Germany (1833). In 1834, he returned to Russia, where he fostered Russian nationalism by writing national operas— *A Life for the Czar* (1836) and *Russlan and Ludmilla* (1842). In 1848, he composed *Kamarinskaya*, an "orchestral fantasy," which was one of the first tone poems. He also wrote many other works, including a string quartet (1830), a trio for piano, clarinet, and bassoon (1827), 40 piano pieces, about 90 songs and duets, a cantata on the accession of Nicolas I (1825), and a few sacred works.

FELIX MENDELSSOHN-BARTHOLDY (1809–1847), known as *Mendelssohn*, was the son of a wealthy banker in Hamburg; he had many advantages in teachers (Zelter) and prominent friends (Goethe) and the money to hire his own orchestra to try out his youthful efforts. At fifteen, he had composed several symphonies and an opera; at seventeen, he wrote the overture to *Midsummer Night's Dream*; and at twenty, he was a famous pianist and composer. From 1829 to 1833 he traveled extensively, and in 1835 he moved to Leipzig to be director of the Gewandhaus concerts; he founded the Leipzig Conservatory in 1843. Particularly popular in the British Isles, he wrote the oratoria *Elijah* for the Birmingham Festival of 1846 and conducted the first performance there. Several of his eight volumes of *Songs without Words* were also written for the English—the first volume (1832) was titled *Melodies for the Pianoforte*. Mendelssohn was a prolific composer, leaving a tremendous number of many kinds of published works and a considerable number in manuscript. He wrote many piano works, including some with orchestra, 5 symphonies, several concertos for piano and one for violin, program overtures, large choral works, over 80 songs, many anthems (Mendelssohn was a Lutheran) and men's choruses, and chamber music.

FRÉDÉRIC CHOPIN (1810–1849), a Polish-born son of a French father teaching in Warsaw, settled in Paris, giving his first concert there in 1831. He became a favorite personality of the Paris *haut monde* and made his living as a teacher; the Rothschild daughters studied with him and assured his financial success. Chopin's works were almost exclusively for the piano; his style was personal, was established early (his *f* minor piano concerto was written in 1829), and was much admired by French, German, and English contemporaries. In addition to 2 concertos and 3 sonatas for piano, he published thirteen volumes of mazurkas, nine of nocturnes, two of etudes, six of waltzes, four of scherzos, six of polonaises, two of preludes, three of impromptus, three of fantasie, and four of ballades. He wrote a few songs and a few works for cello, including a sonata and a set of variations on an air from Meyerbeer's popular opera *Robert le Diable*. His last performances were in the British Isles in 1848.

ROBERT SCHUMANN (1810–1856), a German composer and writer, studied law at Leipzig, settling there as a journalist and critic. He founded the *Neue Zeitschrift fur Musik* (New Music Magazine) in 1834, and, along with composing, it became the chief focus of his life. As a youth he had studied piano, but an injury to his hand forced him to give up hopes of a virtuoso career. His output centered in his 30 piano pieces and over 240 songs, but he also composed 4 symphonies, 1 concerto each for piano, cello, and violin, a substantial amount of chamber music, and large vocal works.

FRANZ LISZT (1811–1886), the son of a musician of Prince Esterházy, was recognized as a prodigy and given excellent training at an early age. Of Hungarian descent, he was brought up in Vienna and studied with Carl Czerny (1791–1857), a famous student of Beethoven. Liszt's first tour (1824) brought him fame in Paris and London, and for twenty years he reigned as the supreme pianist in an age when the piano was the ultimate instrument. In 1849 he moved to Weimar as conductor, and in the 1860s he moved to Rome. There he took minor orders and (known as the Abbé Liszt) turned to the composition of church music. His creative output mirrors the phases of his professional life: piano works dominated his youthful efforts; orchestral composition, the middle years; and sacred music, the last phase. He left about 400 works, including sonatas, 20 Hungarian rhapsodies (some of which were later orchestrated), occasional pieces, 2 symphonies, 12 symphonic poems, organ works, and songs. He made an astounding number (900) of piano paraphrases and transcriptions in addition to his own works.

LOUIS MOREAU GOTTSCHALK (1829–1869) was born in New Orleans of mixed Jewish-English and French-Creole parentage. He showed his gifts early and at thirteen was sent to Paris, where he made a successful debut three years later and included his own compositions in his programs. He was famous for his Negro tunes but even more so for his Romantic works such as *The Dying Poet* and *The Last Hope*. A hugely successful virtuoso, he toured Europe, the United States, Cuba, and South America, where he died of yellow fever at the height of his phenomenal success.

HENRY RUSSELL (1812–1900), an English singer and composer, visited both Italy and France, managing to study briefly with Rossini and to make the acquaintance of Meyerbeer. He also traveled to Canada and the United States, where he was organist of a Rochester (New York) church from 1833 to 1841. During this time, he collaborated with such lyricists as Gen. George F. Morris, a New York journalist, in composing the first of his many songs and ballads. Some of these had simple lyrics, others had dramatic and more complex ones. Russell returned to England in 1841 and had a long career, leaving about 1,000 songs in addition to a textbook on singing.

Melody, unexhausted, nay inexhaustible, is pre-eminently the source of musical beauty. Harmony, with its countless ways of transforming, inverting, and intensifying, offers the material for constantly new developments; while rhythm, the main artery of the musical organism, is the regulator of both.

EDUARD HANSLICK *

The Later Romantics

23

Although the Romantics turned back to the tales and romances of the Medieval era, they had more in common with Renaissance thinkers in their central concern with man and in their self-consciousness. Like Renaissance men, the Romantics named their own epoch and then dubbed their predecessors as grotesque or jejune. And like Renaissance ideals, Romantic ideals stretched forward to influence several generations and to spark inventiveness and exploration—of man, the heavens, and the earth.

The middle of the nineteenth century represents the fulfillment of the Romantic ideal. It was the time of Darwin, Mendel, and Marx, of the

* 1854. Gustav Cohen (trans.), *The Beautiful in Music*, New York: Liberal Arts, 1957, p. 47.

forging of the economy in the United States, of the establishment of a balance of power in Europe. Man was ennobled but also ranked—men could be creators, but most men were lesser souls able only to worship genius from afar or, lesser still, incapable of penetrating its depth. *Genius* was a power that held a soul in its grasp and would not let it go; it was *daemonic* (not *demonic*), a word still defined as referring to "the involuntary element in the activity of creative genius," [1] perhaps a pre-Freudian concept of the unconscious. To the Baroque and Classical mind, genius had meant character, taste, or presiding spirit; to the Romantic, as the poet James Russell Lowell (1819–1891) put it, "Talent is that which is in a man's power; genius is that in whose power a man is." [2]

It was a century of inventions, and the appearance of so many marvels was the essence of progress to most of the people. The idea of progress was given impetus through the idea of evolution, which was being worked into a systematic theory by the English scientist Charles Darwin (1809–1882). The concept was not new, nor was Darwin the only scientist working on a theory of it; what was new was a theory about the *means* of evolution, the concept of how new types of life can be originated through the survival of the fittest, how the preservation of successful characteristics creates new species. Darwin's *Origin of Species by Means of Natural Selection* was published in 1858—it was to have ramifications beyond the biological sphere of which it spoke.

Darwin's writings led to ideas about man and art as evolving from lower forms. Man was the latest and highest form of life—a view complimentary, highly satisfying, and quite consonant with nineteenth-century man's desire to rank whatever he found. And man was seen as verging on perfection.

In the latter part of the nineteenth century, the ideas of the arts, in their highest forms, as being noble, the products of genius, and capable of reaching to the deepest part of man's being were carried on. Matthew Arnold wrote that art must possess "high seriousness," [3] a dictum, accepted by all camps, that was part of the separation between serious art and amusement. Nowhere was the difference clearer than in the art of music.

THE PHILOSOPHY OF MUSIC

"Music opens the entrance of an unknown world to men," [4] E. T. A. Hoffmann had said, and his concept was basic to music criticism through the nineteenth century. Critics sought to capture the effect rather than analyze

[1] *Webster's New International Dictionary of the English Language,* 2d ed., Springfield, Mass.: Merriam, 1944.

[2] *Ibid.*

[3] *Time,* Dec. 27, 1968, p. 47.

[4] Quoted in Max Graf, *Composer and Critic,* New York: Norton, 1946, p. 192.

the technique. The respected critic James Huneker (1860–1921) wrote of the Chopin mazurkas,

> Within the tremulous spaces of this miniature dance is enacted the play of the human soul, a soul that voices the revolt and sorrow of a dying race, of a dying poet. . . . Like hardy, simple wild flowers they are mostly for the open air, . . . but even in the open, and under the moon, the note of self-torture, of sophisticated sadness is not absent. . . . The Pole suffers in song the joy of his sorrow.[5]

Huneker's analysis of the *a Minor Mazurka* (op. 17 #4) begins by stating that the piece is known to some as the "little Jew." The remainder of his critique reads as follows:

> [It is] rather doleful and there is a triplet of interrogation (the poor little Polish Jew of the story always asks, "What was that?") standing sentinel at the fourth bar, but it is also in the last phrase. But what of that? For me the *a* minor Mazurka is despairing, and with its serpentine chromatics and apparently suspended close—on the chord of the sixth—creates an impression of morbid irresolution modulating into a desperate gayety.[6]

Probably the most influential writer on music in the second half of the century was the Prague-born, Viennese critic Eduard Hanslick (1825–1904). A well-educated man, he summed up the views on music at the middle of the century in a famous monograph, *Vom Musikalisch-Schönen* (*On the Beautiful in Music*). The monograph was published in 1854 and enjoyed a long life of growing influence; it had nine editions in German and, toward the end of the century, translations into French, Italian, English (1891), and Russian.

Hanslick's summary of musical materials is illuminating. First was the distinction between noise and music and a lengthy denial that natural sounds, such as bird calls and the howling of the winds, were musical. These anti-nature remarks were directed against the arch-Romantic writers, chiefly the poets of the previous generation, whose nature worship had led them to eulogize not only the music of the earth, such as the song of the nightingale, but also the unheard music of the heart. Schumann had written in 1831 that "the veiled enjoyment of music one does not hear has something magical in it." [7] More representatively, the poets Shelley, Keats, and Byron had incorporated an essential musical metaphor into their poems. Keats spoke of that magic:

> Heard melodies are sweet, but those unheard
> Are sweeter; therefore, ye soft pipes, play on;

---

[5] James Huneker (ed.), *Chopin: The Mazurkas*, New York: Schirmer, 1915, p. iii.
[6] *Ibid.*
[7] In André Boucourechliev (Arthur Boyars, trans.), *Schumann*, New York: Grove Press, Inc., 1959, p. 179.

Not to the sensual ear, but, more endear'd,
Pipe to the spirit ditties of no tone. . . .[8]

The question of natural versus artificial music had little relevance in
the composer's workroom. More likely to involve him was the question of
the true subject matter of music, which for many writers and even for some
composers had become the literary or visual idea. Eduard Krüger (1807–
1885), a German musicographer, claimed that there was common subject
matter for all the arts. Literature tells the story, painting depicts the appearance of the actor or actors at one instant in time, and music portrays
the motion rather than the appearance of the action.

[8] "Ode on a Grecian Urn," 1819.

Anders Zorn, "Barn Night during Midsummer's Celebration,"
1897. (Courtesy of the Na-
tionalmuseum, Stockholm.)

All plastic figures . . . exhibit . . . the state of things at a given moment. . . . [Music] supplies to those plastic and quiescent forms the motive force, the active principle, the inner waves of motion; and whereas in the former instance we knew the true but inert subject to be anger, love, etc., we here know the true and active subject to be loving, rushing, heaving, storming, fuming. . . . The painter represents Orestes, pursued by the Furies: his outward appearance. . . . The composer does not exhibit fleeing Orestes in fixed lines but from a point of view from which the painter cannot portray him: he puts into his music the tremor and shuddering of his soul, his inmost feelings.[9]

Hanslick answered that music cannot depict a young Greek but can present only such musical elements as "chords of a diminished seventh, themes in minor keys, a rolling bass, etc.—musical forms, in brief, which might signify a woman just as well as a young man, one pursued by Myrmidons instead of Furies" [10] or, in short, any subject of similar type. "Music consists of successions and forms of sound, and these alone constitute the subject." [11] No composer would have argued with Hanslick in the matter of the ability of music to depict a young Greek. But given the aid of a program, which the listener could have in hand at the performance and which would describe the events taking place, many composers would have rebutted that to parallel a literary or visual subject was a true function of the musical art, that even the poet could not portray more truly the fear of Orestes. (The composer was often called a tone poet for this reason.) Yet virtually all composers, who were, after all, craftsmen as well as poets, agreed that with or without a program, a work of music had to be complete in itself. The program might spark a composer's creative fire or give him ideas about form, but it could not replace form.

Literary parallels added resonances to the musical work and gave additional dimensions of meaning to the Romantic. Schumann's *Phantasie,* a three-movement piano work published in 1839, was, the composer wrote to his Clara, "three poems which I shall call 'Ruins, Triumphal Arches, Starry Brightnesses.' [But] it is nothing but a long cry of love for you." [12] The work appeared with a dedication to Liszt (who had suggested its composition as a monument to Beethoven) and an inscription from the poet Friedrich von Schlegel (1772–1829).

> Through the numberless sounds
> Which fill the world's gay dream,
> One song, barely heard,
> Calls to the secret listener.[13]

---

[9] Quoted in Eduard Hanslick (Gustav Cohen, trans.), *The Beautiful in Music,* New York: Liberal Arts, 1957, p. 119f.

[10] *Ibid.,* p. 120.

[11] *Ibid.,* p. 119.

[12] Boucourechliev, *op. cit.,* p. 73.

[13] *Ibid.,* p. 74.

But he wrote to Clara, "Are you not the song mentioned in the quotation? Yes, and you know it." [14] Here are circles within circles.

The concept of evolution was already strong in Hanslick's generation, though the term itself did not appear. It was easy to see musical evidence of evolution; in the natural order of events, the major-minor tonal-harmonic system had been conceived and had developed, from the definition of materials in the seventeenth century, through the invention of forms in the eighteenth, to a transcendence of both in the nineteenth. Similarly, the symphonic form had grown steadily since its beginnings. At the middle of the century, when Hanslick was writing, music could well have seemed to be in the process of continuing evolution to ever higher states. If historians ignored everything before the tonal-harmonic system, disregarded everything but the West European art-music tradition, and assumed that the great forms of the days of Beethoven were the only important forms, they could embrace the concept of evolution.

It was the coincidence of time and general philosophy that enabled the nineteenth-century musicographer to maintain this narrow channel of thought. For in the nineteenth century, the materials of an entire musical system were at a point of culmination that demanded works of grandeur. It was not the task of the Romantic composer to define or justify his materials, for this had already been done by men of the previous generation. Nor was it his task to question his materials and to begin the restive probe for new principles and new techniques, for this would be the task of the generation to come. The task of the Romantic composer was to live at the apex of his musical esthetic and to fulfill its potential.

The Romantics were right in viewing the composer as a hero, for they could see nothing but their own music's life arc. The art of music had emerged from a "primitive" state after 1600; Corelli was the first composer to write music worthy of the name; Bach was the first great master (in England, this would have been Handel); and a steady evolution was clear from that early point through the transcendent climax of Beethoven. (Haydn and Mozart were the chief rungs on the ladder.) In 1850 all this was clear; Beethoven was the musical master and worship of him grew to ever more effulgent expression. The evolutionary view of the place of this master was often couched in a metaphor of a flowing stream that grows in size, depth, and power as it progresses. A short version of this metaphor appeared in one of the commemorative publications of 1870, which was the centennial year of Beethoven's birth.

> Haydn appears to us like a sparkling stream, in which the blue sky, the light cloud, the flower, the trembling leaf, and many other delightful objects of nature, are reflected with delicious clearness. Mozart resembles a majestic river, swollen by tributary streams, and gliding on to mingle its waters with those of the ocean; while Beethoven seems like a mountain tor-

[14] *Ibid.*

rent, breaking over rocks and down precipices, and often rising towards heaven in foam, and smoke, and mist.[15]

The English novelist E. M. Forster (1879–1968) wrote in 1910 that "It will be generally admitted that Beethoven's Fifth Symphony is the most sublime noise that has ever penetrated the ear of man." [16] That composer and that work were to continue to embody the Romantic ideal. Its opening subject, so essentially Classical in its texture of short repeated notes followed by one long note and akin more to the opening figure of the Renaissance chanson than to the long legato thematic ideal of the Romantic esthetic, was seen as being symbolic of destiny knocking at the door.[17] Furthermore, because the Morse code uses three dots and a dash for the letter V and because Winston Churchill often held up two fingers in the form of a V to signify victory, the symphony served as a battle challenge for the British and Americans during World War II. For over a century the Beethoven Fifth Symphony (in c minor, Op. 67) was probably the most frequently performed work of the serious orchestral repertoire and thus, given the prevailing ranking system, was considered to be the greatest work in the history of music.

THEORY

Composers agreed on the basic elements of music—melody, harmony, and rhythm. Hanslick defined them, in evolutionary terms, as follows:

> The systematic succession of measurable tones which we call "melody" . . . is the "initial force," the lifeblood, the primitive cell of the musical organism.
> Harmony, like melody, is an achievement of man, only belonging to a much later period. . . . All the intervals which our present system of harmony puts into requisition had to be discovered one by one. . . . Neither the race that most cultivated art in ancient times [the Greeks] nor the most erudite composers of the early part of the Middle Ages were able to do what our shepherdesses of the most out-of-the-way mountains can do at the present day—to sing in thirds. [Hanslick was unaware of the practice of gymel.] It must not be supposed, however, that the introduction of harmony was an additional source of light to music, for it was through harmony that the art first emerged from utter darkness. . . .
> Nature is destitute both of melody and harmony; but there is a third factor regulating the two former, which existed prior to man and is consequently not of his creation. This factor is rhythm . . . in music there is no independent rhythm; it occurs only in connection with melody and harmony expressed in rhythmical order.[18]

[15] James Pech, *The Beethoven Centennial*, New York: Hurd & Houghton, 1870, p. 30f.
[16] Quoted in Eric Blom (ed.), *The Music Lover's Miscellany*, London: Gollancz, 1935, p. 123.
[17] Robert Louis Stevenson, quoted in *ibid.*, p. 419.
[18] Hanslick, *op. cit.*, pp. 105–106.

Hanslick did not mention any other element of music in his discussion. He ranked these three and assigned to each of them an assumed evolution into the modern, West European type.

A work of music (considering only the high ranking symphonic form) was a creation of a serious nature by a man of genius. Its chief element was *theme*, and its predominant characteristic means was development.

> The principal theme [is] the true topic or subject of the entire composition. . . . The theme, not unlike the chief hero in a novel, is brought by the composer into the most varied states and surrounding conditions, and is made to pass through ever-changing phases and moods—everything, no matter what contrasts it may present, is conceived and formed in relation to the theme. . . .
>
> Thus the theme or the themes are the real subject of a piece of music. . . . German theorists and executants prize the musical working-out far more than the inherent merits of the theme. But whatever is not contained in the theme (be it overtly or in disguise) is incapable of organic growth, and if the present time is barren of orchestral works of the Beethoven type, it is, perhaps, due not so much to an imperfect knowledge of the working-out, as to the want of symphonic power and fertility of the themes.[19]

Musically, the thematic concept of musical form suited the needs of all camps, whether or not they believed in the validity of nonmusical subject matter. Musical form became the deployment of themes. The highest ranking form, the sonata allegro, was defined as follows: the *exposition* contained two themes, contrasting in character and key (ideally as masculine and feminine entities); the *development*, as described by Hanslick, leads one or both of the themes through chains of reason or adventure; and the *recapitulation* provides the return and the rounding of the tonal form by returning to the tonic level. The overture to Glinka's *Russlan und Ludmilla* (1842) is a beautiful incorporation of the Romantic concept of the sonata allegro. Its two protagonists inspire the two themes, the forthright, masculine one and the supple, feminine one. In addition, the work points to both past and future—to the past by a rhythmically Classical subject (long, short, short, long) serving as an additional element throughout and to the future by a whole-tone scale, twice descending in steady half notes in stentorian trombones in the coda (measures 357 to 360, 365 to 368).

The education of the musician was codified. In most conservatories in Europe and America, students were given two years of harmony and then one year of species counterpoint—figured bass was still the bulwark of the first, and Fux's species of the second. The composer was still learning a craft, and he was still put through an apprenticeship, though this was now in a school rather than a cathedral or court. Harmony, counterpoint, ear training, and instrumental technique (most often of the piano) were the cornerstones of the craft. Ear training consisted of learning to recognize in-

---

[19] *Ibid.*, pp. 124–125.

tervals, chord structures, and chord progressions, all within the tonal system.

For the layman, the picture had changed radically. The public was reading books, written specifically for them, that told about music and set up guides for listening. The art of composition was defined, even by some composers, as the wringing out of music almost without human will—a concept that led to the popular idea that composition was a matter of inspiration rather than craft. The daemonic character of art, precisely the Romantic contribution, was involuntary, and the mistrust of the head in favor of the heart reinforced this view. Even Richard Wagner, in his "Centenary Essay" on Beethoven, said that the master had been "truly daemonic" and that his music "speaks the highest wisdom in a language that cannot be understood by his reason." [20] A later Romantic put it out of the range of words altogether: "The gift of self-expression is, in its most perfect sense, one that can be exercised only by artists in moments of supreme ecstasy. It cannot be described; it can only be felt." [21] Thus the span of the Romantic esthetic was a long one. A century earlier, in 1794, William Billings had foreshadowed the Romantic view of composition:

> Musical composition is a sort of something, which is much better felt than described, (at least by me) for if I was to attempt it, I should not know where to begin or where to leave off; although I am not confined to rules prescribed by others, yet I come as near as I possibly can to a set of rules which I have carved out for myself; but when fancy gets upon the wing, she seems to despise all form, and scorns to be confined or limited by any formal prescriptions whatever. [22]

PERFORMANCE

The role of the performer within the Romantic ideal was distinctly different from his role in any other. Essentially, the difference lay in his assessment of responsibility toward the composer and toward the music. To the composer, he owed literal adherence to the score, a rigid concept that had not been of great moment before the nineteenth century. The ripieno players had been bound by their written parts, but no soloist had considered himself to be so until the Romantic era. And conversely, the performer owed the music its balance of sound; this had not been his province in the eighteenth century when the balance between players had been written into the music by the composer. Wagner wrote that "the greatest merit of the virtuoso

[20] Quoted in Graf, op. cit., p. 204.
[21] Fritz Kreisler, quoted in Edward F. Murphy, "Subject: Music," New York Times Magazine, Sept. 27, 1964, p. 56.
[22] Hans Nathan (ed.), The Continental Harmony, Cambridge, Mass.: The Belknap Press, Harvard University Press, 1961, p. xxxi.

consists in imbuing himself completely with the musical perception of the score, without introducing modifications of his own." [23] And yet, without the addition of imagination, the performance would be "without soul." [24]

The piano, the Romantic solo instrument above all others, had little variety of tessitura, for each string sounded its own comfortable pitch. Therefore the keyboard represented a neutral rank of pitches within which the performer could create a seemingly infinite variety of balances. In this, the orchestra, the only medium to outrank the piano, imitated it by having the several registers sounded by instruments of appropriate ranges, each devoted to its own most natural register. Thus the orchestra presented a variety of colors within a consistently neutral tessitura. Good orchestration was defined to a large degree as that which preserved the neutrality.

The ideal of quality was the singing tone and the seamless voice. Singers strove for a total range of full, rich quality, with no change in quality from one register to the other. Violinists sought a rich singing tone as well, seamless not only in register but also in legato. String players sought a new legato technique, in which disconnected tones were exceptional—they even sought the skill of being able to change the direction of the bow imperceptibly. In addition, violinists made the vibrato a constant rather than a decorative aspect of tone and sought intensity as part of the basic quality.

The pianist used the damper pedal to create resonances that would give the illusion of sustained legato phrases. Perhaps the voluptuous piano tone, because of its obvious impossibility in an instrument whose strings are activated by percussion and whose tones can be sustained only in a constant decrescendo, was the triumphant achievement of the Romantic era.

Equal to the pianist was the singer, who has always achieved a unique embodiment of the ideals of his time. The Lied had been the Romantic vocal form of the first half of the nineteenth century, while opera had retained much of its Classical heritage. The vocal ideal was still Classical in quality but was changing rapidly, and in the second half of the century, the two types reversed their roles—opera would be the late Romantic vocal form, while the Lied carried on the tradition established by Schubert and Schumann. The vocal ideal was of the large voice, handled with power rather than delicacy. Like the violinist, the singer accepted the vibrato as part of the constantly rich tone quality. To the Classicist, it was the end of the art of singing, summed up by Rossini's lament that singers no longer sang. "They all yell," [25] he accused. But to the Romantic, it was the apex of the evolution of the art of the voice.

In order to savor the richness of melodic ligament and harmonic fullness, performers favored slower tempos than they had previously; they liked their own music to be leisurely, and they turned back to their predecessors

[23] Quoted in Frederick Dorian, *The History of Music in Performance*, New York: Norton, 1942, p. 283.

[24] *Ibid*.

[25] Harold Schonberg, *New York Times*, Dec. 1, 1968, p. D19.

and reinterpreted them accordingly. Orchestral and choral works were performed by increasingly large contingents, with the result that the music slowed down as the number of performers increased—the clarity of the small group was exchanged for the power of the large. By Beethoven's centennial (1870), the slower tempos were so thoroughly accepted that when Beethoven's own metronome markings were discovered, they were disbelieved. In 1872 a scholar, discussing them, wrote that "the metronome markings of some symphony movements, in particular, strikes us as too rapid; . . . a mistake can be assumed." [26] Carl Czerny (1791–1857), Beethoven's student, adjusted the tempos in his edition of the Beethoven piano sonatas, slowing them by a few degrees. It was suggested that Beethoven had erred "because of impatience." [27]

In addition to the slower tempo, a Romantic *rubato*—one of the beat itself—was considered essential. Czerny wrote, "in almost every line there are certain notes and passages where a little ritardando or accelerando is necessary, to beautify the reading and to augment the interest." [28] Such a concept was not practical within complex rhythmic organization. Only two, three, or four beats to the measure were allowable—Hanslick would find the five-beat measure of the Scherzo of Tchaikovsky's *Pathétique* Symphony "disagreeable" and "intolerably worrisome" [29]—and these were kept simple.

In summary, the Romantic performer's goal was a strong body of sound enriched with vibrato and capable of an intense legato phrasing throughout a seamless range. The glories of sound were to be savored through dynamic and metrical flexibility, which would at the same time serve the purposes of interpretation. The orchestral and pianistic ideal, which also was of a large, grand sound and of neutrality of tessitura, allowed the performer to elicit a dynamic scheme that could support or contrast the natural dynamics of the music, producing a tension—an added dimension—unknown to the earlier ideal.

The singer, the pianist, and the conductor would vie for top place in the second half of the century; their ideals were the same, and each emulated the others to some extent. The conductor sought for the orchestra the unity of the piano—in tessitura but also in ensemble and concept. He symbolized this oneness, giving the audience a visual focus, so that the sound of the entire orchestra seemed to channel itself through the single dynamic figure who shaped it. The pianist sought the force and dramatic power of the orchestra—in virtuoso paraphrases and transcriptions or in the four-hand versions of important orchestral works. And both the conductor and the pianist emulated the singer, with his direct lyricism, immediacy, and power of interpretation; the singer, in turn, sought the tonal power, the strength, and the seamless range of the others.

---

[26] Quoted in Dorian, *op. cit.*, p. 200.
[27] *Ibid.*, p. 201.
[28] *Ibid.*, p. 205.
[29] Quoted in Henry Pleasants III (ed.), *Vienna's Golden Years of Music—1850–1900*, New York: Simon and Schuster, 1950, p. 302.

The Romantically conceived pipe organ also emulated the orchestral ideal. Organ builders developed orchestral reeds among an ever-increasing number of stops that imitated instrumental qualities. The symphonic blend was desired, and the contrasts of quality and space, cherished in the Baroque, gave way to the new ideal; the organs were enclosed in swell boxes to allow for superimposed dynamics. Composers wrote "symphonies" for organ, the Baroque instruments were rebuilt as Romantic instruments, and the Baroque ideal was relegated to an evolutionary phase.

NATIONAL ATTITUDES

Germany was the center of the Romantic movement and retained leadership in Romantic philosophy and esthetics. She was well aware of her position and felt both the responsibility and security that such a position inevitably produced. France, in a sense, was the least Romantic country in Europe, although her music was fully contemporary in the essential concept of materials. What was different was the continuing love of the French for small forms and for color (harmonic and instrumental) and their unwillingness to rank quite so thoroughly or rigidly as their German contemporaries. The national conservatory system guaranteed recognition of a variety of music types and musical instruments, and France pioneered in the production of instruction books for the general literate public. In 1830 the first such book appeared in Paris. The work of a Belgian musician and critic, François-Joseph Fétis (1784–1871), it was titled *La Musique mise à la portée de tout le monde* (Music Put at Everyone's Door) and had many editions in French, English, Italian, German, Spanish, and Russian. It was designed to give readers the knowledge to follow musical events, "furnished so that it costs no more trouble to acquire it than one would take to keep abreast of current politics by reading a newspaper." [30]

Fétis's history deals with three major epochs—ancient times, the Middle Ages (to 1600), and "modern music." The concepts of evolution (called an "uninterrupted succession" [31]) and of West European supremacy are strong, both implicitly—only the West European tradition is discussed—and explicitly—"All peoples do not use the same scale.—It is not proved that that of the European is perfect, but it is the best." [32]

Many of the discussions in the book are nationalistic. The Germans hold the highest place in the symphony; the Italians are the greatest singers and teachers of singing; the German violinists are "distinguished by the facility of their left hand"; [33] the French have an excellent bowing technique;

[30] François-Joseph Fétis, *La Musique mise à la portée de tout le monde*, 2d ed., Paris: Duverger, 1837, p. iii.
[31] *Ibid.*, p. 72.
[32] *Ibid.*, p. 435.
[33] *Ibid.*, p. 209.

the English have good cellists and brass players, though German wind players are better at playing softly, whereas the French are too loud. Yet the concept of the materials of music were truly international; melody and harmony, regulated by rhythm and put into symmetrical form, are the basic elements.

At the middle of the nineteenth century, the British, Americans, and Russians were still importers of music, and their native musicians were expected to complete their education in German (or possibly, though not often, in French) centers. The second half of the century would see the expansion of attempts to build national styles within a German concept of what music should be and within the Romantic musical esthetic.

The piano is
A good old beast—
Peaceful and meek, without complaint,
    It suffers much
    Abuse and such
In patient self-restraint.

WILHELM BUSCH *

Philosophy and Theory

The musical problem in the second half of the nineteenth century was the problem of all movements that have just attained a zenith. The generation that attains a zenith lives with the excitement of discovery and experiment; the next generation sees this attainment in retrospect and must carry on without suspense, burdened with having inherited the answer and thus being in a sense disenfranchised from discovery. Musicographers after 1850 were faced with devastating questions: If Beethoven represents perfection, who can follow him? If the accepted tonal-harmonic system is to be the language of music forever, what steps are now possible in carrying forward the art of music? What will be the music of the future? There was no single answer, and the unanimity of Romanticism gave way to divisiveness.

22

* C. 1875. Translation by Christiane Cooper.

MUSICAL FACTIONALISM

Several kinds of factions existed in European music after the middle of the nineteenth century. First, within Germany, was the philosophical division between the proponents of "absolute music" and those who espoused the concept of the "total art work." The members of the first camp, with Hanslick as their verbal and Brahms as their musical spokesman, followed the tradition of J. S. Bach, Mozart, Beethoven, and Schumann. They sought the man who could follow Beethoven at the summit of the musical art, that is, as a symphonist, and they found him in Brahms. The members of the second camp, with Wagner as both verbal and musical spokesman, followed the tradition of Gluck, Mozart, Beethoven, and Weber and sought a German art. As bitter as their mutual opposition was, however, both German camps also opposed the Italian ideal. The Italians followed the tradition of Puccini, Bellini, and Rossini. Verdi was their hero, and they sought new dramatic depths in grand opera.

The largest group was the one that recognized Brahms as its preeminent member. It included not only many Germans but also a substantial number of men of other nationalities who had come to Germany to study— Dvořák from Bohemia, Grieg from Norway, Tchaikovsky from Russia, Elgar from England, and, later, MacDowell from the United States. Only France did not send her musicians to Germany.

Brahms

The Brahms tradition included virtually everything but musical theater— Brahms wrote symphonic music and a substantial amount of piano and chamber music and carried on the Lieder tradition. His piano works included two concertos and a number of difficult concert pieces, but he also composed smaller pieces—intermezzi, ballades, and rhapsodies. These represent a large, continuing literature of piano works incorporating a later Romantic style. They evidenced a greater complexity than the earlier piano music for the amateur, reflecting his increased skill in coping with the complexities of development yet offering him the expressive possibility of the short piano piece, with its formal simplicity and stylistic directness. The piano was a standard instrument in chamber groups, with the notable exceptions of the string quartet and the woodwind quintet, and was used automatically in support of virtually any soloist.

The symphony was still at the top in the hierarchy of musical types, still the most complex and intellectual of forms, and still the focus of considerable attention. Many felt that successors to Beethoven had to prove themselves in this form, even though the tone poem, generally a one-movement program symphony or overture, was a more perfectly Romantic concept.

Intermezzo in E major, opus 116, no. 6

Example 74

JOHANNES BRAHMS

Example 74 (continued)

A facsimile from the first edition, by Simrock, 1892. (Courtesy of the University of Michigan Library. Photo by R. E. Kalmbach.)

After a post-Beethoven generation of less heroic works by Mendelssohn and Schumann and a decade or so of little symphonic production, in the mid-1860s the symphonies of the later Romantics began to appear. The four Brahms symphonies, dating from 1875 to 1885—the heart of the late Romantic years—formed the basis of the late symphonic literature.

But more innovations were taking place in the tone poems and in the ballet suites that were becoming popular at orchestra concerts. The symphonic poems flourished more broadly than the symphony, with a substantial number of works, including opera, overtures, dances, and marches, contributing to orchestral programs.

Subjects of tone poems were Medieval legends or Romantic poems or stories, often based on Medieval legends. At least thirty composers dealt with *Faust*; Mussorgsky's *Night on Bald Mountain* (1867) and Saint-Saëns' *Danse macabre* (1875) represented the supernatural; and Liszt's *Mazeppa* (1851), on a work by Victor Hugo, and Grieg's *Peer Gynt* (1875) represented the historical and heroic. The Tchaikovsky *Romeo and Juliet* (1870), a program overture, is perhaps an archetype; it utilizes an expansive sonata allegro form in which the two themes can symbolize the two lovers and their families, and the development can symbolize the strife that leads to a tragic denouement.

A larger and larger number of works were being written on nationalistic subjects. These included some of the most long-lived of the tone poems, such as a series of six titled *Ma vlast* (My Country), by the Bohemian Bedřich Smetana (1824–1884); the most famous of this series is *The Moldau*. Nationalistic works were at first patriotic but soon became exotic, with the Spanish idiom the most popular. One such work was *España* (1882), an "orchestral rhapsody" by Chabrier. Works of this type were written not by Spaniards but by composers who were attracted to the Spanish idiom.

Verdi

Although Verdi and Wagner had much in common and their work was unanimously grounded in the Romantic ideal, their musical fabrics and forms were quite different—radically different, to nineteenth-century observers. These observers saw the composers, not as two men trying to bring the new Romantic vocal ideal to the serious ("high") musical theater, but as antithetical figures in inimical stance. Each was very much a nationalist and each had his ardent adherents.

Verdi, as an Italian, was thoroughly committed to the concept of grand opera. Living in Milan most of his creative life, he was connected with La Scala; however, several of his important works were presented elsewhere, for he moved freely throughout Europe, except in "Wagner country." *La Traviata* (The Castaway, 1853) was premiered at Venice; *Il Trovatore* (The Troubadour, 1853) and *Un Ballo in Maschera* (A Masked Ball, 1859) at Rome; *La Forza del Destino* (The Force of Destiny, 1862) at St. Petersburg; *Don Carlos* (1867) at Paris; and *Aïda* (1871) at Cairo.

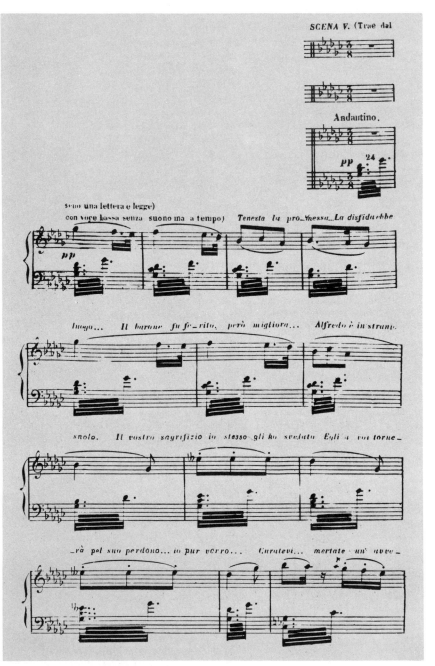

Example 75 (continued)

Example 75 (continued)

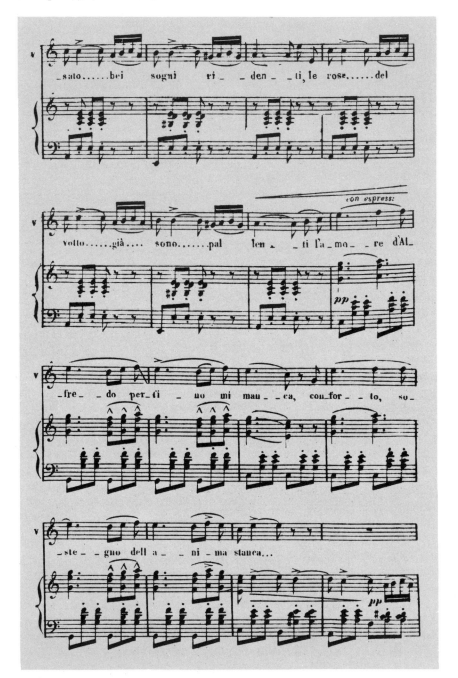

Example 75 (continued)

Example 75 (continued)

Example 75 (continued)

Example 75 (continued)

Violetta reads the letter:

You kept your promise . . .
the duel was fought . . . the baron was wounded, but he
is mending. Alfredo has gone abroad.
I myself revealed to him your great sacrifice.
He will return to you to beg your forgiveness; I will
see to it that you are cured and that your future will
be better. . . . Georgio Germont.

Recitativo:

He's too late! I waited and I waited but he never came
to me! Why did I remain silent? But the doctor kept
urging me to hope. Ah! with such an illness all hope
is dead.

Aria:

Farewell to all the pleasant dreams of the past, like a
rose after a short time, I am already growing pale.
Everything is denied me—comfort, solace for my weary
soul, even Alfredo's love.
He smiled upon La Traviata with desire once, I forgive
him and welcome you, O God.
Everything is ended. Joy and sorrow are soon finished;
the grave holds a deadly grip on everything.
My grave will have no tears or flowers.
No cross with my name will cover these bones.
He smiled upon La Traviata with desire once,
I forgive him and welcome you, O God.
Everything is ended.

TRANS. BY JON RINKA

The facsimile is of an early piano score (1871). The scene is Violetta's death.
(Courtesy of the University of Michigan Library. Photo by R. E. Kalmbach.)

Aïda (1871) is often considered Verdi's masterpiece, but many people
prefer the dramatically genuine *La Traviata* of his earlier years and the almost philosophical works on Shakespearean subjects of his later years—

Otello (1887) and *Falstaff* (1893). *La Traviata* was an adaptation of *La Dame aux Camelias*, a Romantic novel and play by the French Negro writer Alexandre Dumas, fils (son, 1824–1895). The libretto was conceived as a series of scenes from different points in the story. The situations led naturally to various types of music, including solos, duets, and choruses. Verdi made use of *set pieces*. There are two parties depicted in the opera, which he turned into scenes of revelry—a chorus for the revelers, solo arias, duet arias, and quartets or quintets, all connected by dances, interludes, or recitativos, as the plot line suggested. The individual pieces of music were conceived as independent and were often performed in concerts of the day.

Verdi's innovations, within the traditional operatic structure, were based on an expansion from the reflection of a general mood to the depiction of specific responses, of character as well as emotion, and to the interaction between character and plot. Yet his set pieces were, above all, vocal—lyrical and theatrical—splendid vehicles for the Romantic vocal technique.

Beginning in the 1850s, the Verdi operas were widely performed in Europe and America, usually as soon as possible after their premiere. *La Traviata*, for example, which was, as Verdi wrote, a "fiasco" at its premiere, was soon restaged with greater success. Within three years it was playing in London, New York, and Paris, where it was performed at both the Opéra and the Opéra Comique. In addition, in 1864, a French version called *Violetta* was produced, with equal success, at the Théâtre Lyrique.

It is important for the historian to note the changes that occurred in the forty years between *Traviata* and *Falstaff*—the changes in both the composer and the world into which he projected his work. The expectations of the public of 1893 were very different from those of the public of 1853. It is a tribute to Verdi that he was able to forge a new consummation within the tradition of music and also to leave it on the brink of the future. In this sense, Verdi is in the company of such men as Dufay, Monteverdi, and Haydn—life-long modernists, a rare breed.

The German answer to the problems of late Romanticism was very different from that of the Italians. Italians had always loved the human voice, so it was perhaps inevitable that Italian grand opera would center on a new glorification of that instrument. The Germans, on the other hand, had entered the nineteenth century as proponents of the Romantic philosophy, which was equally committed to the high rank of instruments.

Wagner

Wagner, like Verdi, achieved his first successes in the 1850s and, as a true German Romantic, spent a large portion of his youth in philosophical and literary pursuits. Of his books on these subjects, the most widely known was *Das Kunstwerk der Zukunft* (The Artwork of the Future, 1850). It proclaimed the *Gesamtkunstwerk* (variously translated as the "collective," "all-inclusive," or "universal" artwork) as the summit of man's attainment.

The Gesamtkunstwerk was to mirror the entire artistic attainment of man and be based on the twofold literary achievement of the Teutonic myth set into an artistic entity, thus embodying the two categories of creators—

the *folk* and the *artist*. Since the artwork would include both music and the visual arts, it would be a theatrical production, but, rejecting the terms *theater* and *opera* as representative of lesser enterprises, Wagner selected the term *music drama* to designate it.

Wagner's musical esthetic was Romantic, grounded in the threefold concept of melody, harmony, and rhythm, but he saw these elements related to one another in a new way. The traditional view saw melody and tonal harmony as the defining elements, regulated and given size by the primordial element of rhythm. For Wagner, however, melody and rhythm were finite elements that were set into the infinite primordial element of harmony.

> If *rhythm* and *melody* are the shores at which the tonal art meets with and makes fruitful the two continents of the arts primevally related to it, then time itself is the primeval fluid element, and the immeasurable expanse of this fluid is the sea of harmony. . . .
>
> Harmony grows from the bottom up as a true column of related tonal materials, fitted together and arranged in strata laid one above another. The ceaseless changing of such columns, constantly rising up anew, each one adjoining another, constitutes the possibility of absolute harmonic movement on a horizontal plane. . . . Harmony knows only the beauty of the changing play of the colors of its columns, not the charm of their orderly arrangement as perceived in time—for this is the work of rhythm. . . . The realm of harmony, then, knows no beginning or end.[1]

The thematic element was conceived as an aural symbol of a dramatic element, which was typically short and suggestive rather than lyrical in nature. It might appear in the vocal parts but was more likely to be woven into the dominating orchestral fabric. The element was called a *Leitmotiv* (plural, *Leitmotive*; a "leading motif"), for it directed the attention of the listener to the symbol of the composer's focus.

During Wagner's lifetime, his musical influence expanded at a slower pace than the controversy over his goals. His later works, which incorporated his goals, were performed outside Germany only at the end of his life or after his death (in 1883). His great work was *Der Ring des Nibelungen* (The Ring of the Nibelung), a cycle of four operas which he called a "Festival Play for Three Days, with a Preliminary Evening."

> *Das Rheingold* (The Rhine Gold) was finished in 1854 and performed in Munich in 1869 (London, 1882; New York, 1889).
> *Die Walküre* (The Valkyrie) was finished in 1856 and performed in Munich in 1870 (New York, 1877; London, 1882).
> *Siegfried* was finished in 1869 and performed in Bayreuth in 1876 as part of the complete cycle (Vienna, 1878; London, 1882; New York, 1887).
> *Gotterdämerung* (Twilight of the Gods) was finished in 1874 and performed in Bayreuth in 1876 as part of the complete cycle (London, 1882; New York, 1888).

[1] Quoted in Oliver Strunk (ed.), *Source Readings in Music History*, New York: Norton, 1950, pp. 885, 887.

This was the Gesamtkunstwerk, for which Wagner served as the creator-artist—poet (playwright), composer, designer, producer, and conductor. He was even the designer of the *Festspielhaus* (Festival Performance Hall), which, by having the orchestra out of sight, contributed both to scenic realism and to the mystery and infinity of the harmony.

In these examples of music drama, Wagner achieved the effects he had sought. The "immeasurable expanse" was the orchestra, whereas the voices presented the finite, the specific melody, and the singers sang the poetry in a style that was neither recitativo nor aria. Music drama had no set pieces but maintained the continuing dialogue heightened in music. Its continuity plus the fact that it was not thematic led to its being called "endless melody," a suitable parallel to "infinite harmony." Rhythm, however, was finite and specific and performance had to be exact. The natural tendency of musicians to blur the distinction between the dotted eighth plus sixteenth ♩. ♪ and the similar triplet ♩ ♪, for example, was not allowed at Bayreuth. Wagner had a huge dotted eighth and sixteenth painted on the wall of the orchestral anteroom as a constant reminder of the need for rhythmic precision.

Performances of the entire *Ring* were rare outside of Bayreuth, because the score was expensive and the piano version had no great appeal to either pianists or singers (for neither of which group it had been conceived). Thus the *Ring* had less influence than Wagner's shorter works. But the music Wagner developed from the Medieval epic *Tristan und Isolde* (Munich, 1865; London, 1882; New York, 1886) was of great significance to the succeeding generation. The plot of the opera, which Wagner called a "tragic music drama," concerned the passionate and hopeless love of a knight and the princess who is supposed to marry the knight's overlord. However, the Munich public, to whom an adulterous affair of Wagner's was no secret, was offended by the opera. The premiere was announced in the Munich *Volksbote:* "On Friday next Adultery with Drums and Trumpets, complete with the entire Music of the Future, is to appear at the Court and National Theatre." [2]

The prelude of *Tristan und Isolde* introduced the Leitmotive of confession of love, desire, the glance, the love philtre, the magic casket, and love death in an orchestral piece of traditional form (an arch *ABA*) but extraordinary fabric. [3] The fabric incorporates the composer's musical esthetic; harmony is the essential element, and melody and rhythm are conceived as structures related at times to one another but not related to a single tonal center. The fabric was highly chromatic, so traditionalists had no vocabulary except the Leitmotive with which to discuss it. Tonal analysis was useless except for negative terms—"no clear key," "no resolution." To Hanslick the "Vorspiel" of *Tristan und Isolde* was "chromatic whining." [4]

---

[2] Eric Blom (ed.), *The Music Lover's Miscellany*, London: Gollancz, 1935, p. 230.
[3] For a perceptive analysis of this work, see William J. Mitchell, *The Music Forum*, New York: Columbia, 1968, vol. I., pp. 162–203.
[4] Max Graf, *Composer and Critic*, New York: Norton, 1946, p. 134.

Tristan und Isolde, Einleitung (Prelude)   Example 76

RICHARD WAGNER

The first page of a piano score printed c. 1880. (Courtesy of the University of Michigan Library. Photo by R. E. Kalmbach.)

SONG

German Lied carried through the second half of the nineteenth century, with the heritage of Schubert and Schumann continuing in Brahms and Hugo Wolf (1860–1903), a songwriter and critic. Brahms left about thirty volumes of songs; Wolf left the *Spanisches Liederbuch* (Spanish Song Book, 1890), on translations by Goethe and others, the *Italienisches Liederbuch* (Italian Song Book, two volumes, 1890 and 1896), and the *Goethe Lieder* (fifty-one settings of Goethe's poems, 1889). Altogether Wolf left about 300 songs, including three on poems by Michelangelo.

But the Romantic song, far from remaining a German art, was now international. In France, the leading songwriter was Gabriel Fauré; he wrote sixty detached songs (1868 to 1900) and five cycles (1891 to 1922). In Russia, the leading songwriters were Mussorgsky, Tchaikovsky, and Alexandre Borodin (1833–1887), whose songs and opera, *Prince Igor* (1890), were very popular. In Norway, Halfdan Kjerulf (1815–1868) composed over one hundred songs and about thirty men's choruses. His songs, which are of high quality, were among the earliest of the Romantic school; they were sung by Henrietta Sontag (1805–1854) and Jenny Lind (1820–1887), who made them extremely popular. Edvard Grieg left twenty-five sets of songs, on both Norwegian and German poems. The immensely popular "Jeg elsker dig" (I Love You, often in German as "Ich liebe dich," 1865) was on a poem by Hans Christian Andersen (1805–1875).

Slavic song flourished as well. The Czech Bedřich Smetana wrote in both German and Czech—German songs in his youth and a Czech cycle, *Vecerni pisně*, in 1880. Antonin Dvořák wrote about seventy-five songs between 1865 and 1894, including the cycle *Pisně milostné* (Love Songs, 1888) and a group of *Zigeunermelodien* (Gypsy Songs, 1880), published in German translations. The latter group became extremely popular, particularly its fourth song, "Als die alte Mutter," in many English editions as "Songs My Mother Taught Me." Dvořák's *Biblické pisně* (Biblical Songs) were published in New York in 1894.

The British were more prolific with lighter than with serious songs. Their most popular song was Arthur Sullivan's "The Lost Chord" (1877), a sentimental ballad composed for voice, piano, and harmonium.

OPERETTA

The centers for grand opera were Milan and Bayreuth; the centers for operetta were Paris, Vienna, London, and New York. The great musical figures were Jacques Offenbach, Johann Strauss (the Younger), and Arthur

Sullivan. Both Offenbach and Strauss were skillful orchestral writers as well as melodists. Offenbach had a flair for theatrical humor and Strauss caught the Viennese love of luxury, lavish settings, and waltzes. Many of his waltzes were extremely popular, and their orchestrations were often masterly. Overtures and incidental pieces from the operettas were often found on orchestral programs. But the English operetta—the work of Sullivan in particular— were a craze throughout Europe.

Arthur Sullivan, after early service as a choirboy in the Royal Chapel, was trained in Europe (at Leipzig) and, like Offenbach and Strauss, was thoroughly skilled. In 1875, Sullivan produced the first of his collaborations with the poet-satirist William Schwenk Gilbert. Their fourth production, *H.M.S. Pinafore, or The Lass that loved a Sailor* (1878), created a sensation. The international success of *Pinafore* was immediate; by 1879 it was playing not only in London but also in twenty-one theaters in the United States. Gilbert and Sullivan's ninth operetta, *The Mikado, or The Town of Titipu* (1885), may well be the single greatest hit in the musical theater. It was produced almost at once in French, German, and Russian translations and became a craze from Russia to Australia. It has been constantly on the boards since its premiere and consistently popular.

Both *Pinafore* and *The Mikado* represented brilliant versifying and stunning satire. The productions were colorful and exuberant, the texts whimsical and often hilarious, the plots often zany and sometimes parodies of grand opera labyrinths, and the music full of melodic grace and rhythmic zest. Gilbert was a master of verbal rhythms, and the operettas are characterized by a rhythmic life that the text often demands and always supports. In their works, Gilbert and Sullivan brought the *patter song,* a long complex poem sung very rapidly, to perfection. The total was a mixture of spoken dialogue, often humorous, which carried the plot along; lyrical ballads; duets or other solo ensembles; choruses of men, women, or both; patter songs; and dances. These elements would define the operetta and musical comedy for the next three-quarters of a century.

POPULAR MUSIC

The popular music of the second half of the nineteenth century, as always, centered in song and dance. And as the Romantic ideal dictated, the piano was featured in both and provided the chief popular means for the study of higher forms.

The most representative publication was the voice-piano collection, perhaps with a short introductory section offering pedagogical suggestions. A typical volume was *les Maîtres de la musique* (Masters of Music)—seventy-one items for solo, duet, and choir, collected and arranged by Leopold Dauphin (evidently a Paris teacher of music) and published in 1886. The book includes an introduction on the history of music, "Advice to the young student of singing," and "Advice to the young piano student." The vocalist was to avoid high and low registers and to "seek above all to produce beautiful sounds in the middle." [5] The pianist was told to "apply yourself to making your instrument *sing*." [6] Both were "to try to portray all the emotion, all the poetry that is awakened within you by the sentiments expressed in the musical idea you are interpreting." [7] The music spans the two centuries from Lully to Bizet, with short biographies and small line portraits of fifty composers, and the book concludes with notes on living composers (by country) and a short dictionary of musical terms.

All the arrangements were for voice (or voices) and piano. For such works as a Chopin nocturne and a Wagner march, words were added and the piano part simplified. Grétry and Offenbach are representative of the composers in *Les Maîtres de la Musique*. A duet from Grétry's *Richard Coeur-de-Lion* (1784) and the air "Vendredi" (Friday) from Offenbach's *Robinson Crusoé* (1867) were included. They represent the detached air, which is by far the most common type of piece in the collections.

[5] Leopold Dauphin, *les Maîtres de la musique*, Paris: Colin et Cie, 1886, p. 9.
[6] *Ibid.*, p. 12.
[7] *Ibid.*

Some Later Romantic Composers

The two generations of composers born in the Romantic era and writing at the end of the century were different from their predecessors. The Romantic concept included living to the hilt, and many of the earlier generation died young. The younger generation lived much longer, in several cases maintaining their creative energies into their sixties or beyond. It was chiefly on the periphery—in Russia and America, where Romanticism flowered later—that the creative life seemed to burn itself out in youth.

JACQUES OFFENBACH (1819–1880), a German Jew whose father was a cantor, went to Paris as a boy (1833) to study cello. He played in the orchestra of the Opéra Comique from 1834 and became its director in 1847. He wrote some instrumental works, produced a one-act opera in 1853, and from 1855 devoted himself to musical theater as an innovative entrepreneur and popular composer. Naturalized a French citizen in 1860, he remained in Paris most of his life but traveled to the United States and Germany. His greatest successes included *Orphée aux Enfers* (Orpheus in the Underworld; Paris, 1858; New York, 1861; London, 1865), *La belle Hélène* (The Beautiful Helen; Paris, 1864; London, 1866; New York, 1868), and *la Vie parisienne* (Paris Life, 1866); the last-named opera was his greatest hit. *Contes d'Hoffmann* (Tales of Hoffmann), based on three stories by E. T. A. Hoffmann, was posthumously produced in Paris in 1881, New York in 1882, and London in 1907; it was his only grand opera. An aria from Offenbach's *Geneviève de Brabant* (1868) was adopted, with new words, as "The Marines' Hymn" in 1919.

ANTON BRUCKNER (1824–1896), an Austrian organist and composer, was one of the last court musicians in the history of Europe, assuming the post of organist of the imperial court in

Vienna in 1867. In 1868 he was made professor of organ, harmony, and counterpoint at the Vienna Conservatory; in 1875 he was awarded a lectureship at the University; and in 1891 he was given an honorary doctor's degree. Bruckner left 122 opus numbers, of which his 9 numbered and 2 unnumbered symphonies comprise the most significant part; he also left many Masses, Psalms, and cantatas.

JOHANN STRAUSS II (1825–1899) followed his father's career, organizing his own fifteen-man orchestra at the age of nineteen and becoming extremely popular very early as both conductor and performer. Upon his father's death in 1849, Strauss united the two orchestras and began one of the most successful international touring careers of the century, adding Poland, Russia, and the United States to his circuit. Of his 500 dances, the most famous were the waltzes of the late 1860s—"Geschichten aus dem Wiener Wald" (Tales from the Vienna Woods, 1868), "Wein, Weib, Gesang" (Wine, Woman, and Song, 1869), and, probably the single most popular song of the half-century, "An die chonen blauen Donau" (The Blue Danube, Op. 314, 1867). After a tour to the United States in 1872, he began a career in operetta, with success equal to that of his other activities. His operetta *Die Fledermaus* (The Bat; Vienna and New York, 1874; London, 1876) was one of the most popular in history and is now in the serious operatic repertoire. *Der Zigeunerbaron* (The Gypsy Baron; Vienna, 1885; New York, 1886) was revived in London in 1935.

JOHANNES BRAHMS (1833–1897), the son of a double-bass player in a theater orchestra, was brought up in Hamburg. He was recognized early and in his teens won the backing of Liszt and Schumann. He visited Vienna as director of the Singakademie from 1863 to 1864 and again to conduct orchestral concerts from 1871 to 1874; he settled permanently in Vienna in 1877.

Brahms's fame centered in his works for piano, his 4 symphonies (1876 to 1885), his concertos (2 for piano, 1854 and 1878–1881, and 1 for violin, 1878), a double concerto (for violin and cello, 1887), thirty volumes of Lieder, and a large amount of chamber music, choral pieces, and orchestral works. In addition to the 2 concertos, his piano music included seven volumes of pieces (intermezzi, ballads, rhapsodies), six sets of variations, a volume of waltzes, 3 sonatas (all before 1854), and four volumes of Hungarian dances for four hands.

CAMILLE SAINT-SAËNS (1835–1921), a French pianist, organist, composer, and poet, entered the Paris musical scene early and stayed late, touring, teaching, composing, and influencing French musical life. In 1915, at the age of eighty, he toured the United States as far west as San Francisco. He made thirteen trips to London between 1871 and 1913, six to Spain between 1880 and 1906 and three to South America between 1899 and 1916. In 1896 Saint-Saëns celebrated the fiftieth anniversary of his debut by composing and premiering his fifth piano concerto. His 169 opus numbers cover a wide variety of types—12 operas, 3 symphonies, 9 tone poems (including the famous *Danse macabre*, 1875), 5 piano concertos, 3 for violin, 2 for cello, a considerable amount of chamber music, over 100 songs, 4 oratorios, and music for the piano. He also edited works by Lully and Rameau.

RICHARD WAGNER (1813–1883), a German composer and dramatist, began by composing instrumental music (2 piano sonatas, 1 symphony) before finding his way to a career of theatrical works. His early productions, *Rienzi* (Dresden, 1842), *Der Fliegende Hollander* (Dresden, 1843), and *Tannhäuser* (Dresden, 1845), were not immediately successful. *Lohengrin*, produced by Liszt at Weimar in 1850, was the turning point. From that time, Wagner was a powerful force in European music—either deified or vilified but never ignored. His operas, which he called music dramas, became the center of a cult in Germany and, following an average twenty-year lag, were also performed abroad. In 1872, he built his own theater in Bayreuth, but *Tristan und Isolde* was produced in Munich in 1865 (London, 1882; New York, 1886). Wagner's later works were *Die Meistersinger von Nürnberg* (Munich, 1868; London, 1882; New York, 1886) and *Der Ring des Nibelungen* (The Ring of the Nibelung), "A Festival Play for Three Days, with a Preliminary Evening." The entire cycle was first performed at Bayreuth on August 13, 14, 16, and 17, 1876 (New York, 1900). His last music drama was *Parsifal* (Bayreuth, 1882; New York, 1903; Paris and London, 1914). In addition to his own librettos, Wagner also wrote critical and philosophical books.

GIUSEPPI VERDI (1813–1901) studied in Milan, where his first opera was produced in 1839 and his first success (*Nabucco*, 1842) was achieved. From 1843, when he produced an opera with political implications, which contributed to the Italian movement for unification and freedom, he was a favorite of his countrymen. His first hit was *Hernani* (on a story by Victor Hugo), which premiered in Venice in 1844 and was sung in fifteen theaters by 1845 (London, 1845; New York and Boston, 1847). From 1851, when *Rigoletto* (also on a story by Hugo) was produced, Verdi wrote a series of works that became the foundation of the grand opera repertoire throughout Europe and America—*Il Trovatore* (1853), *La Traviata* (1853), *Un Ballo in Maschera* (A Masked Ball, 1859), *La Forza del Destino* (The Force of Destiny, 1862), and *Aïda* (1871, produced in Cairo in honor of the opening of the Suez Canal). In all, he composed 26 operas. Verdi's last years were also creative—*Otello* (1887) and *Falstaff* (1893) were both on Shakespearean subjects, and at the end of the century, he was writing large choral works. Verdi's output was almost exclusively vocal, both theatrical and sacred. His choral-orchestral *Requiem* (1874) was considered one of the great works of the century.

PETER ILYITCH TCHAIKOVSKY (1840–1893), a Russian composer, came to his professional music career after he was trained in the law and had served briefly as a government clerk. In 1865 he was graduated from the music institute of St. Petersburg (now Leningrad), and in 1866 he began teaching harmony at the Moscow Conservatory. He composed prolifically and entered the Central European music scene, contributing significantly to the major forms—6 symphonies (1874 to 1893), 3 ballets (from which he also made orchestral suites), popular concertos for violin (premiered in Vienna in 1881) and piano (premiered in Boston in 1875), 3 string quartets, several volumes of piano works, and considerable vocal music, including sacred and secular choral music, and about 100 songs. Many of his works, including the last three symphonies, the fantasy overture *Romeo and Juliet* (1869, revised 1879) and the ballets *Swan Lake* (Moscow, 1877) and *The Nutcracker* (St. Petersburg, 1892), became extremely popular. Like many other Romantics, Tchaikovsky became known by short early works, particularly the "Chant sans paroles" (Song without Words), from the *Trois Morceaux* (Three Pieces) for piano (1868), and the song "Nur wer die Sehnsucht kennt" (None but the Lonely Heart, to Goethe's lyric), from the *Six Romances* of 1869.

CÉSAR FRANCK (1822–1890), a Belgian-born organist, composer, and teacher whose father was a bank clerk, went to Paris in 1835 to study with Anton Reicha at the Conservatoire. He remained in Paris and became a naturalized French citizen in 1873. As a student, Franck won first prizes in piano (1838), fugue (1840), and organ (1841). Later, he taught piano and was the organist at a succession of churches until, in 1858, he was selected as *Maître de Chapelle* for the new Sainte-Clotilde, a post he held for the remaining thirty-two years of his life. In 1872 he was made professor of organ at the Conservatoire. He composed slowly and sought his way carefully, leaving a small body of works that climaxed in the *Variations symphoniques* for piano and orchestra (1885), the *Sonata for Violin and Piano* (1886), and the *Symphony in d minor* (1889). His fame rests on these, plus his 71 organ works, including the *Pièce heroïque, Cantabile, Pastorale*, and the 3 *Chorales* (long virtuoso works), and 2 concert piano sets, the *Prélude, choral et fugue* (1884) and the *Prélude, aria et final* (1887).

ANTONIN DVOŘÁK (1841–1904), born near Prague, made his way slowly, studying at the Prague Organ School and playing viola in the theater orchestra. He left that position in 1873 to take the post of organist at the St. Adalbert Church. Meanwhile he was gaining skill as a composer and in 1875 won an Austrian national stipend for his Symphony in E♯ major (his third). His fame spread, helped by both Brahms and Liszt. A professorship in composition at the Prague Conservatory secured his living, and his reputation as a teacher began. Maintaining Prague as his home base, he traveled to England for performances of his large choral works (such as the *Stabat Mater*, in 1884) and to the United States, where he directed the new National Conservatory in New York from 1892 to 1895. Dvořák wrote 9 symphonies (of which 7 were published), including the famed Symphony in e minor, *From the New World* (written and premiered in New York, 1893); 8 operas (all in Czech); a number of choral works; 8 orchestral overtures and tone poems; about 25 chamber works (including 13 string quartets); and four volumes of Slavonic dances for four hands (each later orchestrated). In addition, he wrote piano music, including the famous "Humoreske" (1894), and about 75 songs.

EMMANUEL CHABRIER (1841–1894) was a French lawyer who worked for the government until 1879, at which time he became an assistant to the conductor Charles Lamoureux (1834–1899). Chabrier was known particularly for his four volumes of piano music, his orchestral works, and his 4 operas (only 3 performed); his most successful works were the orchestral rhapsody *España* (1882) and the opera *le Roi malgré lui* (The Reluctant King, 1887), both of which remained in the repertoire.

ARTHUR SULLIVAN (1842–1900) was a choirboy in the Royal Chapel at London and then studied at the Royal Academy from 1856 to 1858 and at the Leipzig Conservatory from 1858 to 1861. His first success was the cantata *Kenilworth* (on a subject by Sir Walter Scott), which was performed at the Birmingham Festival in 1864. Sullivan soon turned to the theater and wrote the comic opera *Cox and Box* (privately produced in 1867). He found his foil in William S. Gilbert (1836–1911), a satiric poet, with whom he wrote 13 operettas that were perhaps the most widely performed works in the history of the theater. In addition to the operettas, Sullivan composed serious stage works, including the grand opera *Ivanhoe* (1891), and many songs and hymns. He composed a tune for the hymn "Onward, Christian Soldiers" (1871). The chorus "Come, Friends," from *The Pirates of Penzance* (1879), was reissued in New York in 1917, with new words by Theodora Morse, as "Hail! Hail! The Gang's All Here."

MODEST MUSSORGSKY (1839–1881) was a Russian army officer and, later, a government civilian employee. An amateur musician in the best sense, he composed continually and was a good pianist. He left 62 songs; about 20 piano works, including *Pictures at an Exhibition* (1874); a few works for orchestra; and a group of theater works, notably the opera *Boris Godunov*, on a poem Aleksander Sergeevich Pushkin (1799–1837). *Boris Godunov* was originally composed in 1869 but was rewritten in 1874, shortened for publication in the same year, and revised and reorchestrated by Rimsky-Korsakov in 1896; this version was also "retouched" for publication in 1928. However, it is the 1896 revision that is generally performed. (The original versions were published and performed in Leningrad in 1928, in London and Paris, 1935.)

EDVARD HAGERUP GRIEG (1843–1907), a Norwegian pianist and composer, studied at the Leipzig Conservatory from 1858 to 1862, where he learned the heritage of Schumann and Mendelssohn. In addition, he met Liszt in Italy and widened his knowledge of the German traditions. Grieg was extremely successful throughout Europe as a pianist, composer, and conductor and was honored internationally. He published several volumes of songs, in Norwegian and German; about fifteen volumes of piano works, including ten called *Lyric Pieces* (1867–1901); two sets of dances for four hands (later orchestrated); orchestral suites; and dramatic music. Of the latter, the music for *Peer Gynt* (1876), a play by Henrik Ibsen (1828–1906), was very popular, but even more so was the *Concerto for Piano*, composed in 1868, performed in Copenhagen in 1869, and published in Leipzig in 1873. Although Grieg centered his career in Germany, he was held in the greatest esteem in France, where he was made a corresponding (foreign) member of the National Institute.

NIKOLAI RIMSKY-KORSAKOV (1844–1908), a Russian naval officer, retired in 1873 to devote himself to teaching and composing. He taught composition and orchestration at the St. Petersburg Conservatory from 1873 to 1905.

His 15 operas included *Mozart-Salieri* (1897), on a play by Aleksander Pushkin, and *Zolotoy Pietushok* (The Golden Cockerel, in French *le Coq d'or*, posthumously produced in 1909). His symphonic works were also successful; *Scheherazade* (1888) was made into a ballet in 1909 by Sergei Diaghilev.

GABRIEL FAURÉ (1845–1924), a French organist, composer, and teacher, was professor of composition at the Conservatoire and its director from 1905 to 1920. He was respected as a composer and revered as a teacher. His works included about 60 solo songs and 50 piano pieces, for which he is chiefly remembered, but he also wrote 2 operas, 10 chamber works, and several choral works, some with orchestra.

EDWARD ELGAR (1857–1934), an English musician whose principal instrument was the violin, was largely self-taught as a composer and gained major standing in that profession only in his forties, after a long period of growth. Although some of his earlier short works—for example, the *Salut d'Amour* (1889)—were popular, his success was assured by two works a decade later—the orchestral *Variations on an Original Theme*, known as the *Enigma Variations* (1899), and his second oratorio, *The Dream of Gerontius* (1900), which was a setting of a poem by John Henry Cardinal Newman (1801–1890). Elgar's works included 10 oratorios; several orchestral suites, overtures, and marches (the famous "Pomp and Circumstance #3," 1901); concertos (violin, cello); chamber music; organ works; and songs for solo voice and choir.

Germany and Italy have since been transported to America, and, musically, we live in a new earth and a new heaven.

THE REV. E. WENTWORTH *

An Expanding Nation

24

Nowhere were the schisms within serious music and the differentiations of serious and popular styles more evident than in the United States. German groups founded orchestras, while others provided operatic performances. By 1900, orchestras were established in New York (Philharmonic, 1842; New York Symphony, 1878), Boston (1881), Chicago (1891), Cincinnati (1895), and Philadelphia (1900). Opera was established in New York, Brooklyn, Boston, New Orleans, Philadelphia, St. Louis, Chicago, Boston, and San Francisco, among other centers. And popular music was flourishing everywhere.

There was little difference between European and American programs,

* C. 1880. Quoted in Gilbert Chase, *America's Music*, New York: McGraw-Hill, 1955, p. 185.

but Americans were generally somewhat behind the Europeans in hearing new works. A premiere in America—like that of the Tchaikovsky piano concerto in Boston in 1875—was a rarity, as was the appearance of a work by an American-born composer. Composition and concert performance were provinces of immigrants or of Americans trained abroad.

In grand opera, America was caught in a new "war of the tongues," basically a battle between the German and Italian traditions with the French somewhere between. When the Metropolitan Opera opened in New York in 1883, its first performance was Gounod's *Faust*. As a French opera based on a German drama and performed in Italian, it provided a satisfactory compromise of international interests. But the "war" continued. In the 1880s the Metropolitan was a Wagnerian bastion, whereas the Chicago Opera remained under Italian control and the American Opera Company (New York) tried opera in English, a solution that seems to have pleased nobody. This new language conflict produced strange turnabouts. In 1889 Wagner's *Lohengrin* was produced in Italian in Chicago and Verdi's *Un Ballo in Maschera* was done in German at the Metropolitan in New York.

The importance of opera as the symbol of European breeding and culture gave it as much a social as a musical nature. In fact, the elegance of the Met's audiences led to the naming of the row of boxes "The Diamond Horseshoe." However, light operas and operettas were more popular than opera, and even more popular were band concerts, minstrel shows, and circuses.

But the United States had unique problems. In the first third of the nineteenth century the issue of slavery had grown increasingly, and during the middle third of the century, it became the main focus of attention, culminating in the Civil War (1861–1865). The last third of the century was a time of completing the process of conquering the West and of subjugating the Indians. The postwar period saw many men, white and black, North and South, head West to enter into a way of life that soon became the subject of a vast international literature and the basis of the Continental view of the Western Hemisphere. Americans thought of themselves as independent. It is not surprising that most of them did not find their musical taste fulfilled in either the symphony concert or grand opera. Their music centered in the piano and in gala performances, in folk songs, dances, and the popular musical theater.

THE PIANO

The piano was the one European vehicle of serious music that America embraced wholeheartedly at virtually all levels. The prim young ladies of Eastern cities, the cowboys who frequented saloons on Saturday nights, and the circuit-riding preacher who heard hymns accompanied by the church piano or an upright in his camp wagon all knew the sound of the piano. In 1851, *Harper's Magazine* published "Mems for Musical Misses," a set of instructions for playing the piano, instructions that were not only Romantic but also particularly American.

> Sit in a simple, graceful, unconstrained posture. Aim more at pleasing than at astonishing. Be above the vulgar folly of pretending that you cannot play for dancing; for it proves only that if not disobliging, you are stupid. Although you must be strictly accurate as to time, it should sometimes be relaxed to favor the expression of Irish and Scotch airs. Never bore people with ugly music merely because it is the work of some famous composer, and do not let the pieces you perform before people not professedly scientific be too long.[1]

In the 1860s, the piano concert took on importance in American life, and American piano manufacture was second to none. In 1876, at the centennial celebration in Philadelphia, there was an exhibition of pianos manufactured in both the United States and Europe. An observer wrote that

[1] Quoted in Arthur Loesser, *Men, Women and Pianos*, New York: Simon and Schuster, 1954, p. 509.

The American piano design by Steinway and Sons won the grand prize at the Paris Exposition of 1867. Placing the lowest strings at an angle over the lower-middle–range strings created a brilliant sound that the exposition report called "extraordinary" and that elicited a letter of admiration from Hector Berlioz. (Courtesy of the University of Michigan Library. Photo by R. E. Kalmbach.)

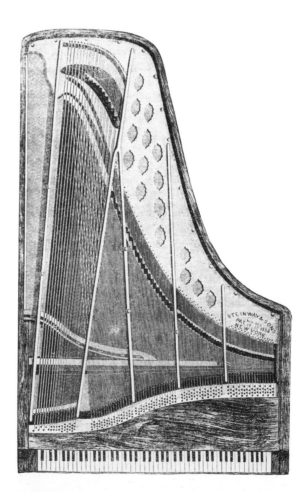

"while a most courteous and hospitable demeanor was evinced by the judges toward European exhibitors, there was no use trying to conceal the fact that the first-class American pianos exhibited excelled the best instruments of European makers in every respect." [2] Manufacture of concert instruments continued to center in New York, but the parlor pianos—the square and upright instruments—were made farther west, in Chicago, Grand Rapids, and Rockford; they were sold by traveling piano agents who were as much a part of the American scene as the iceman and the scissors grinder.

At the end of the century two developments gave added impetus to the piano. In 1897 the Aeolian Piano Company patented the first mechanical piano, called the *pianola*, which used punched paper rolls turned by a foot pedal. And in that same year the first *Rag Time Instructor*, by Ben R. Harney, was published, in response to the public rage for the new ragtime music. By the beginning of the twentieth century, there were more pianos and harmoniums in the United States than bathtubs. [3]

THE GALA PERFORMANCE

The British festival had been imported to the United States, at least to the centers with a large British population. Boston's Handel and Haydn Society was probably the most directly British, but before the end of the nineteenth century, other cities had established choruses that produced Handel's *Messiah* every year or in alternate years, spaced by a variety of other works. The Bethlehem Choral Union (Pennsylvania), founded in 1882, inaugurated the (Johann Sebastian) Bach Festival based on the Mass in *B* Minor. Other festivals, such as the Cincinnati May Music Festival, founded in 1871, were more versatile.

But the most prevalent galas and the performances of traditional music heard by the largest numbers were the band concerts of the last third of the century. Bands had been popular since prerevolutionary days, but after 1860 (sparked to an extent by the Civil War bands) the band became the center of national concert life. The Irish-born cornet player Patrick Gilmore (1829–1892) settled in Massachusetts after a Canadian tour with a British band. He founded his own band in 1859 and gave his first festival in New Orleans in 1864 while he was in the Army. For this festival, he combined the forces of 500 army musicians with 5,000 singers recruited from New Orleans schools. For the grand finale, "Hail, Columbia," he used three dozen cannons. From that beginning, Gilmore progressed to larger and larger groups, twice doubling

---

[2] Daniel Spillane, quoted in Rita Benton, "The Early Piano in the U.S.," Unity Sherrington and Guy Oldham (eds.), *Music, Libraries and Instruments*, London: Hinrichsen Edition, 1961, p. 189.

[3] Gerald Carson, "The Piano in the Parlor," *American Heritage*, vol. XVII, no. 1, p. 58, December, 1965.

the contingents, once for a National Peace Jubilee (1869) and again for a World Peace Jubilee (1872), both in Boston. For the 1872 jubilee, he used a band of 2,000 and a chorus of 20,000, which he termed "colossal," [4] plus cannons, anvils, and bells. After this event, he moved to New York, and that city became his base for organizing and touring with Gilmore's Full Military Band, which enjoyed great and continuing popularity in the United States and Canada. In 1878, he toured Europe as well.

Gilmore's programs included a variety of music of four main types—band transcriptions of serious orchestral works, popular pieces, solo works done by guest artists (most often cornet or voice, but sometimes others as well), and works written for the band. A program of 1877 is representative.

Part First

1. Overture, "Stabat Mater" Gilmore's Band	Rossini
2. Piccolo Solo, "Canary Polka" Signor De Carlo	De Carlo
3. Andante, Fifth Symphony Gilmore's Band	Beethoven
4. Cornet Solo, "Fantasie Original" Mr. M. Arbuckle	Hartmann
5. Piano Solo, "Paraphrase on Themes from Rigoletto" Master Hermann Rietzel	Liszt
6. Song, "Goodbye, Sweetheart" Mr. W. H. Stanley	Hatton

Part Second

7. Grand Opera Fantasie Including the gems of *Le Prophète, L'Africaine, L'Etoile du Nord, Les Huguenots* and other Operas. Gilmore's Band	Meyerbeer
8. Scene from *Il Trovatore* Miss Lillian B. Norton [Nordica]	Verdi
9. Saxophone Solo—Variations on "Casta Diva" [from *Norma*] Mr. E. A. Lefebre	Bellini
10. Overture, "Jubel" Gilmore's Band	Weber [5]

[4] Nicolas Slonimsky, "Gilmore," *Baker's Biographical Dictionary of Musicians*, 5th ed., New York: Schirmer, 1958; Richard Franko Goldman, "Band Music in America," in Paul Henry Lang (ed.), *One Hundred Years of Music in America*, New York: Schirmer, 1961, pp. 128–139.
[5] *Ibid.*, pp. 131–132.

If the Gilmore Band represented the "big league" of band concerts, then the smaller town bands represented a thriving "little league," fed by a growing number of products of the public schools' new music education programs. The typical town park had a bandstand where concerts were given on summer evenings, political speeches were made during campaigns, and entertainments were mounted at such traditional celebrations as the annual Fourth of July picnic.

City performances could take on a Continental sophistication, sometimes literally, by importing a famous conductor. Jacques Offenbach, whose operettas were doing brisk business in New York and elsewhere, came to the United States in 1876 for the celebration of the national centennial. He did not conduct his own operettas during his visit but appeared as guest conductor in concerts similar to those of Gilmore's Band. He wittily documented his visit in a diary and in letters to his family, which he combined into a volume of *Notes d'un musicien en voyage* (Notes of a Traveling Musician), published in 1877. Offenbach was pleased with Gilmore's Hall, where he performed, and described it in detail.

> Imagine an immense covered garden, filled with a thicket of tropical plants, where stands a platform for an orchestra of a hundred or a hundred and twenty musicians. All round are grass, flowers, flower beds, through which the public can circulate freely. Immediately opposite the entrance door a large waterfall amuses people during the intervals. It imitates Niagara during entr'actes. The corners of the garden are occupied by little chalets, each having room for seven or eight people, which very cleverly take the places of boxes in a theatre. A large gallery with ordinary loges and seats that rise by tiers enables those who like to look and listen from an elevated place to satisfy their taste. The general impression of the garden recalls somewhat the *Jardin d'Hiver* [Winter Garden] which once had so great a vogue in the Champs-Elysées. The hall can contain eight or nine thousand people. I should add that it is brilliantly lighted. Coloured window panes make rainbows, a most picturesque effect.
>
> Delighted with my concert hall, I asked Mr. Grau, the director, some details about the orchestra I was to conduct. He answered, "We have hired the hundred and ten musicians you asked for, and I can assure you they are the best in New York." I soon saw that he had not deceived me. . . . I am very pleased to state, the orchestra was a superior one. For each of my works two rehearsals were always sufficient to assure a brilliant execution.[6]

However, another American orchestra, raised quickly in an unnamed town between Philadelphia and Chicago, Offenbach described bitingly as "small, but execrable. . . . Out of twenty-five musicians there were eight who were pretty good, six quite mediocre, and all the rest absolutely bad." [7]

[6] Lander MacClintock (trans. and ed.), *Orpheus in America*, London: Hamish Hamilton, 1958, pp. 29ff.
[7] *Ibid.*, p. 105f.

In another letter, the composer talked of the performances he had attended, including *Henry V* (at Booth's Theater), a French comedy, a popular American work called *The Mighty Dollar*, and a revival of Meyerbeer's opera *Star of the North* (Paris, 1854; New York, 1856). He regretted that a grand opera was not on the boards while he was in New York and mentioned the Lyceum Theater, where Dumas's *Camille* had just completed a successful run. The theater interested him. "Dramas with orchestra and chorus have been played there also. It was at the Lyceum Theatre that for the first time the orchestra was placed out of sight of the public, a scheme which Wagner is trying again at this very moment at Bayreuth." [8]

THE MINSTREL SHOW

The theater that most intrigued Offenbach was the music hall in which the San Francisco Minstrels, the only resident minstrel company in New York, were holding forth.

The Americans, who had little enthusiasm for intellectuality, had huge enthusiasm for the music hall entertainment or, as it was sometimes called, the variety show. The British music hall and the French vaudeville traditions provided skits, acrobats, songs, dances, and other acts. These joined important national elements to create the minstrel show.

The minstrel show was an American entertainment. Its essential characteristics were blackface makeup, the dialect associated with the Negro, and the banjo, bones, and tambourine, all instruments of the African heritage. But the background of the shows was mixed. The use of blackface was an imitation of the slave entertainments, of which little is known except through the minstrel shows. The dialect was patterned on the pidgin English used in the play *Robinson Crusoe and Harlequin Friday* (London, 1786). And the Negro "type" was based on the Irish buffoon. In the British play *The Triumphs of Love* (1795), which was brought to the United States and popularized here, an Irish comic role was switched, as written, to blackface. [9] The use of banjo, bones, and tambourine had not been comic at first. In 1799, there was a revival in Boston of the old play *Oroonoko* (1695), by the British playwright Thomas Southerne (1660–1746). The play listed an "African prince" in its cast of characters, and for the revival, a new song, "The Gay Negro Boy," was interpolated and performed in blackface to a banjo. In addition, the blackface comic performances of Thomas D. ("Daddy") Rice in his "plantation songs and dances" popularized the shuffle and paralleled the new craze for "Ethiopian" music, which was probably the direct antecedent of the minstrel show. In 1843, the violinist-director-composer

[8] *Ibid.*, p. 39.
[9] See Sterling A. Brown, "The Negro in the American Theatre," Phyllis Hartnoll (ed.), *The Oxford Companion to the Theatre*, 2d ed., Fair Lawn, N.J.: Oxford University Press, 1957, pp. 565–572.

Daniel Emmett (1815–1904) produced an "Ethiopian concert," with what he advertised as "the novel, grotesque, original and surpassingly melodious Ethiopian Band, entitled the Virginia Minstrels." [10] The group, which was four in number, played the fiddle, banjo, bones, and tambourine while dressed in tattered costumes and in blackface. They sat with the violin and banjo in the middle and the percussions on the side, and they introduced comic dialogue, acted out ballads, and danced in a parody of what they called plantation style.

Within a decade the minstrel show was the most popular entertainment in the United States. Large cities had permanent companies, whereas outlying areas had to be content with companies on tour. The towns along the waterways, chiefly the Ohio and Mississippi Rivers, could count on the yearly showboat, which docked in town and called the people with trumpets and drums. These boats provided, in addition to minstrel shows, a circus, regular concerts, plays, and variety shows, and they generally housed a small museum as well.

It was in the formality and balance of structure that the minstrel show was strongly linked, particularly in its spatial and antiphonal elements, to the African heritage. In its full form, it had two sections, the *first part* and the *olio*, sometimes followed by a one-act play or *afterpiece*. The show began with a grand entrance of the entire assembly, dressed elegantly in swallow-

[10] Quoted in Gilbert Chase, *America's Music*, New York: McGraw-Hill, 1955, p. 259.

The showboat Cotton Blossom, docked at Cincinnati. (Courtesy of the Ohio Historical Society.)

tail coats. They were all in blackface but the middle man, called the inter-locutor, who was in whiteface. After the opening chorus, during which the group formed a semicircle, the dignified interlocutor intoned, "Gentlemen, be seated!" and the show was under way. The first part contained a string of dialogue, generally quick one- or two-liners in which the interlocutor served as straight man for the two end men, one of whom played the bones and the other the tambourine—they were Mr. Bones and Mr. Tambo.

INTERLOCUTOR: Mr. Tambo, why in the world did you name your little girl Onyx?
END MAN: Because she was Onyx-pected.[11]

Interspersed with the comic sallies, in which the interlocutor was no match for the irrepressible end men, were solos by members of the company—mostly sentimental plantation ballads of the type already being sung in countless American parlors.

The olio was a short variety show that included quartet singing, soft shoe and clog (tap) dancing, acrobatic acts, and skits (often parodies of popular plays or Italian operas) in which men took the women's parts. The olio was concluded by a parody, a sketch (the comic dialogue "Reuben, Reuben, I've Been Thinking," of 1871, was one) or plantation festival (Emmett's "Dixie's Land" was one), and a grand finale, with a dance for the whole company called the *general ruckus* or *walk-around*.

If an afterpiece was to be presented, a few numbers would be played by the instrumentalists during the change of scene. The afterpiece was gen-erally a one-act musical comedy; Arthur Sullivan's *Cox and Box* was one that became very popular.

E. P. Christy (1815–1854) was the most famous of the early minstrel entrepreneurs. His Christy's Minstrels played in New York from 1846 to 1857; and in 1853, he started Philadelphia's first resident minstrel company —a company that was to remain in existence for three-quarters of a century.

In his shows, Christy used the songs of Stephen Collins Foster (1826–1864), who knew something of Negro music from his childhood attendance, with a servant, at Negro church services and from listening to work songs of the black stevedores at the Pittsburgh levee. Foster's brother wrote, "In 1845, a club of young men, friends of his, met twice a week at our house to prac-tice songs in harmony under his leadership" (an American glee club). And, "at that time, Negro melodies were very popular." [12] At twenty-one, Foster saw his "Susanna," taken west in the gold rush of 1849, become the most popular tune in the country. In 1852, he wrote to Christy that he wanted to establish himself as "the best Ethiopian song-writer." Foster's "Old Folks at Home" (1851) became the most popular of all plantation melodies, with

---

[11] Quoted in Walter Monfried, "Minstrel Show," *The Milwaukee Journal*, Feb. 8, 1963.
[12] Quoted in Chase, *op. cit.*, p. 289.

several others, such as "Camptown Races" (1849) and "My Old Kentucky Home" (1852), not far behind.

But by 1870 the minstrel show was facing the greatest competition it could have—girls. On the legitimate stage, girls, dressed daringly in tights, danced the cancan and the ballet. And in *The Black Crook*, a musical extravaganza that opened in 1866 at Niblo's Garden (rebuilt for the production), they were shown flying through the air on guy wires. This musical was based on a Romantic story, of an alchemist who sells his soul to the devil, combined with a French ballet. It was so popular that it ran for a year and a half and was on the road for over forty years afterward.

Then in 1869 came the British Blondes, a troupe of variety artistes specializing in *burlesque* ("parody"). A critic wrote, "It is impossible to give an idea of this sustained burlesque. It resembles an Irish stew as one minute they are dancing a cancan and the next singing a psalm tune. It is a bewilderment of limbs, belladonna and grease paint." [13] The public was faced with a moral question. Another critic summed up the dilemma and the American attitude. "The propriety of visiting the Blondes is a question which each individual must decide for himself. The number of individuals who have decided this question, by the way, is something astonishing." [14]

The variety show also was expanding to compete with the minstrel show. Formerly, the variety show had been a beer-hall entertainment for men only, with a few songs and dances to a honky-tonk saloon piano and a few girls to perform and act as hostesses. But by the end of the century, this entertainment developed in three separate directions.

First was the parody minstrel show, which used girls instead of men. In 1869 Mme. Rentz's Female Minstrels appeared and soon the producer began to present a new edition every year. The first part and the walk-around became girl shows and the comedy-centered olio continued as variety acts, with an occasional "added attraction." This was to become the modern burlesque.

The second direction of the saloon show was the variety show as we know it—vaudeville. In the 1870s, saloon entertainment had been growing not only in scope but also in the degree of obscenity in its dialogue. Then in 1881, one of the beer-hall managers opened a "clean" show, with eight acts of comedy, song, dance, and acrobatics and a female impersonator—in other words, an olio. The success of this venture was immediate. A special theater was built to house this and by 1890, vaudeville was firmly established on the American scene. Each show had an average of fifteen acts, including jugglers, knife throwers, contortionists, ventriloquists, animal acts, and musical specialists such as accordionists and performers on the musical glasses.

The third direction of the saloon show was the dance hall, in which

[13] Quoted in Bernard Sobel, A *Pictorial History of Burlesque*, New York: Bonanza Books, 1956, p. 19f.
[14] *Ibid.*, p. 20.

the entertainment was exclusively musical and included both instrumental (band or orchestra) and vocal numbers—to be both listened and danced to. Ballroom dance groups were as old as the ballroom, and in Europe small orchestras like that of Johann Strauss provided music for the private balls given by the nobility and the wealthy. In the new world, the wealthy continued to hire private orchestras, but the vast majority of people went out to dance. At the end of the century, the club, particularly the nightclub, satisfied the public's desire to hear popular music and to dance.

The increasing popularity of the rival forms doubtless contributed to the decline of the minstrel show. But it had probably been doomed as soon as it lost its original simplicity and directness. These qualities were possible only when the concept was fresh and the ensemble small. From Emmett's handful to a dozen men a decade later, and about twenty in Christy's company, expansion was swift. Troupes toured the country, and some were even sent to England. In addition, the Civil War ended the white man's monopoly of the shows. Black minstrel companies, playing in blackface (and whiteface) like their white rivals, soon started competing with the white companies. Moreover, independent dance teams and comics, Irish tenors, and other dissonant elements entered the shows. In 1879, Haverly's Minstrels, a Negro company, played Niblo's Garden. The playbill read:

> Splendid Achievement. The Success Unequalled in the Annals of Colored Minstrelsy. Haverly's genuine colored Minstrels: 100 performers, 20 end men, 3 middle men, 40 female jubilee singers, 20 [instrumental] musicians, 17 vocalists. . . . Gigantic First Part. Cotton field pastimes, canebrake frolics, flatboat varieties, plantation revels, levee comicalities, camp meeting refrains; the best ever seen, and at once gorgeous and immense.[15]

The Negro minstrels of the last third of the century contributed some lustrous names and enduring music to the theater. Billy Kersands, who called himself "King Rastus," was a notable comedian, and James A. Bland (1854–1911), a freeborn Negro from Flushing, New York, was a star of Callender's Georgia Minstrels and the only postwar rival to Stephen Foster. Bland's songs included "In the Evening by the Moonlight," "Oh Dem Golden Slippers" (1879) and "Carry Me Back to Old Virginny" (1878), which became the official state song of the commonwealth of Virginia.

But even the melodic gifts of James Bland could not save the minstrel show. It was no longer possible to think of plantation serenades as they had been thought of fifty years before—and even in the early years, serious Negro musicians had found the minstrels galling. As early as 1836, Thomas J. Bowers, a renowned American tenor, wrote of the offense to his race, saying that in his own concert work he was "striving to give the lie to 'Negro serenaders' and to show to the world that colored men and women could sing

[15] Monfried, *op. cit.*, p. 1.

classical music as well as the members of the other race by whom they have been so terribly vilified." [16] Elizabeth Taylor Greenfield (called "the black swan"), who was compared to Jenny Lind, also resented the minstrel stereotype. She left the United States, giving her farewell concert in New York to an enthusiastic crowd of four thousand, and attained a successful career in Europe.

MUSIC OF THE NEGRO

The minstrel show was not an authentic Negro concept, though its best features were founded in the African heritage. True Negro music was found elsewhere.

Many black musicans continued in the tradition of dance music, which went back a century to the time when Sy Gilliat was the best fiddler in the colonies and the official state fiddler of Virginia. In 1839, a traveler attending a dance in Virginia wrote that "the orchestra was filled by Negro musicians; the bands being almost always formed by coloured people." [17] The jazz musician George Morrison (born in 1891) said in a biographical interview:

> My father was a musician. In fact, as far back as you can trace the Morrison family, the men were all fiddlers—in those days instead of violinists they called them fiddlers. There was Uncle Jack and Uncle Alfred and my father, Clark Morrison. He was the king fiddler of the State of Missouri. He played those old time fiddling tunes like "Arkansas Traveler," "Devil's Dream," and "The Fisher's Hornpipe," for square dances [quadrilles]. The only thing they knew in those days was square dancing. They didn't play any concert music or anything. They couldn't read a note—never knew what a note looked like—played everything by ear. But they had the natural talent that God blessed them with.[18]

Morrison's father and uncles were of the generation after the Negro musicians, who doubtless knew music notation, described by the 1839 visitor to Virginia. At the end of the century, large ballrooms were more scarce, and the education of Negro musicians much more haphazard.

The music, both vocal and instrumental, practiced by the slaves had centered in work songs, Sunday dancing, and religious observances, which included both song and dance. The work songs of oarsmen and stevedores were described by several visitors to the docks, where blacks often had to

[16] Quoted in John P. Davis, *The American Negro Reference Book*, Englewood Cliffs, N.J.: Prentice-Hall, 1966, p. 751.

[17] *Ibid.*, p. 750.

[18] Quoted in Gunther Schuller, *Early Jazz: Its Roots and Musical Development*, Fair Lawn, N.J.: Oxford University Press, 1968, p. 359. The use of the term "king fiddler," which is reminiscent of the Medieval "king of the minstrels," is interesting.

wait for the arrival of boats and amused themselves while waiting. In 1876, a description of such entertainment was published in the Cincinnati *Commercial*, under the title "Levee Life: Haunts and Pastimes of the Roustabouts, Their Original Songs and Peculiar Dances." The author wrote of the "wild banjo thrumming" in the clear air.

> You may hear old Kentucky slave songs chanted nightly on the steamboats, in that wild, half-melancholy key peculiar to the natural music of the African race; and you may see the old slave dances nightly performed to the air of some ancient Virginia-reel in the dance-houses of Sausage Row. [In the dance house] a well-dressed, neatly-built mulatto picked the banjo, and a somewhat lighter colored musician led the music with a fiddle, which he played remarkably well and with great spirit. A short, stout negress, illy dressed, with a rather good-natured face and a bed shawl tied about her head, played the bass viol, and that with no inexperienced hand.
>
> The musicians struck up that weird, wild, lively air, known perhaps to many of our readers as the "Devil's Dream." . . . The dancers danced a double quadrille, at first, silently and rapidly; but warming with the wild spirit of the music, leaped and shouted, swinging each other off the floor, and keeping time with a precision which shook the building in time to the music. The women, we noticed, almost invariably embraced the men about the neck in swinging, the man clasping them about the waist. Sometimes the men advancing leaped and crossed legs with a double shuffle, and with almost sightless rapidity.[19]

As the music became wilder, "men patted juba and shouted, the Negro women danced with the most fantastic grace. . . . The white female dancers seemed heavy, cumbersome, ungainly by contrast." [20] And in conclusion, the author stated that "even the curious spectators involuntarily kept time with their feet; it was the very drunkenness of music, the intoxication of the dance." [21]

In European terms, the combination of fiddle, bass, and banjo was Baroque; in African terms, it was a combination of elements, of quality, rhythm, and pitches, indivisible from the instruments that produced them and creating a musical fabric indivisible from the tune or function of the occasion. It was the totality of the Negroes' musical experience that Europeans could not comprehend, for by the second half of the nineteenth century, serious music had become so "civilized" in Europe that it was extrapolated from the stuff of everyday life.

The accompaniment of instrumental music by vocal interjections was also an African characteristic, but the shuffling step was akin to the European Renaissance basse danse, in which the feet seldom left the floor. The leaping was the chief characteristic of the volta, a popular sixteenth-century Southern

[19] Lafcadio Hearn, quoted in Chase, *op. cit.*, p. 436f.
[20] *Ibid.*, p. 437.
[21] *Ibid.*

European dance. And the wild turning, when the ladies held the men around the neck while being held at the waist, could be a description of the East European polka, about which a French dancing book of 1845 had said "to dance the *polka* men and women must have hearts that beat high and strong." [22]

The Sunday dance at the plantation, called the cakewalk, was a larger, more formal social occasion but had fewer set patterns than the quadrille. One such event was described in later life by a son of freed slave parents in Tennessee.

> The cakewalk was originally a plantation dance, just a happy movement they did to the banjo music because they couldn't stand still. It was generally on Sundays, when there was little work, that the slaves both young and old would dress up in hand-me-down finery to do a high-kicking, prancing walk-around. They did a take-off on the high manners of the white folks in the "big house," but their masters, who gathered around to watch the fun, missed the point. It's supposed to be that the custom of a prize started with the master giving a cake to the couple that did the proudest movement.[23]

The slaves' religious services, if they did not include dancing, were often followed by a song and dance session called a "shout," a term of Biblical association.

> The true "shout" takes place on Sundays, or on "praise" nights through the week. Very likely more than half the population of a plantation is gathered together. The benches are pushed back to the wall when the formal meeting is over, and old and young, men and women, all stand up in the middle of the floor, and when the "sperichil" is struck up begin first walking and by and by shuffling around, one after another, in a ring. The foot is hardly taken from the floor. Sometimes they dance silently, sometimes the song itself is also sung by the dancers. Song and dance are alike extremely energetic, and often when the shout lasts into the middle of the night, the monotonous thud, thud of the feet prevents sleep within a half mile of the praise-house.[24]

The spiritual song was the first authentic Negro music to be appreciated, written down, and studied. In 1861, "O! Let My People Go" was published (now it is known, to a tune published in 1872, as "Go Down, Moses"). "Roll, Jordan, Roll" followed in 1862. The first important collection, called *Slave Songs of the United States*, was published in 1867. By William Francis Allen, Charles Pickford Ware, and Lucy McKim Garrison, this book was a landmark in American musicology. Each spiritual was notated at its source and preceded by a commentary on the performance.

---

[22] Quoted in Curt Sachs, *World History of the Dance*, New York: Norton, 1963, p. 434.
[23] Quoted in Chase, *op. cit.*, p. 439.
[24] *Ibid.*, p. 256.

I'm Troubled in Mind

ANONYMOUS

Example 77

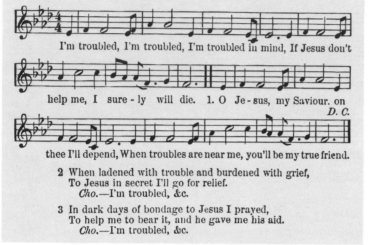

No. 53. I'm Troubled in Mind.

[The person who furnished this song (Mrs. Brown of Nashville, formerly a slave), stated that she first heard it from her old father when she was a child. After he had been whipped he always went and sat upon a certain log near his cabin, and with the tears streaming down his cheeks, sang this song with so much pathos that few could listen without weeping from sympathy: and even his cruel oppressors were not wholly unmoved.]

I'm troubled, I'm troubled, I'm troubled in mind, If Jesus don't help me, I sure-ly will die.   1. O Je-sus, my Saviour. on *D. C.*

thee I'll depend, When troubles are near me, you'll be my true friend.

2 When ladened with trouble and burdened with grief,
   To Jesus in secret I'll go for relief.
   Cho.—I'm troubled, &c.

3 In dark days of bondage to Jesus I prayed,
   To help me to bear it, and he gave me his aid.
   Cho.—I'm troubled, &c.

A spiritual from *The Story of the Jubilee Singers with Their Music.* The form is of a burden and verses. (Photo by R. E. Kalmbach.)

A portrait of the Jubilee Singers, which is the frontispiece of *The Story of the Jubilee Singers with Their Music,* 1883. (Photo by R. E. Kalmbach.)

Roll, Jordan, Roll   Example 78

ANONYMOUS

A spiritual from *The Story of the Jubilee Singers with Their Music*. The form is
of a burden and verses. The flat seventh, the cambiata figure, and decorations such
as *tirata* are clear. (Photo by R. E. Kalmbach.)

But the first significant contribution to the popular dissemination of
the Negro spiritual was the tours of eleven young Negro singers. From 1871,
they toured, in support of Fisk University in Nashville, as the Fisk Jubilee
Singers. Changing personnel over the years, the group traveled in the United
States first and later in Europe and Great Britain, remaining popular for

many decades. Their collections, which were very important in the popularization of the spiritual, included *Jubilee Songs*, published in New York in 1872, and *The Story of the Jubilee Singers*, published in London in 1875. The former book contained "Swing Low, Sweet Chariot," and the latter included "Deep River."

But performance was highly embellished, and the notation, which was traditional, could not represent the pitches or rhythms. In 1899, an article in *Popular Science Monthly* attempted to present the spiritual "Mary and Marthy" with the notation of the actual performance, including the embellishments the Negroes called "trimmings." The author pointed out that

Mary and Marthy   Example 79
ANONYMOUS

The facsimile is from an article on African music in America. The author attempted to notate the music exactly as it was performed, though she mentioned that it was never twice the same and that some pitches were not available in Western notation. (Jeanette R. Murphy, "The Survival of African Music in America," *Popular Science Monthly*, vol. 60, September, 1889, p. 665.)

there were problems in notating spirituals because the Negroes needed to "break every law of musical phrasing and notation." [25] But the notation was closer to the actual sound, and it is revealing.

This spiritual, like many, is based on the opening minor third, with major seconds on either end of a passing or decorative nature and a final tone a major second lower still. Other tones occur in a much freer, more spontaneous way and doubtless are the center of the aspect that was "never twice the same."

Much of the style of the spirituals was African. But slave songs and dances had also been influenced by the singing school music, which the Negroes learned and evidently loved. The slaves took their religious instruction seriously, particularly in the second quarter of the century, and they attended camp meetings as well. In 1843, a visitor in Virginia noted that the Negroes were singing at work and wrote that "all their tunes are psalm tunes." [26] In many cases, the spirituals could be easily harmonized in the traditional manner, and they were so presented by the Jubilee Singers in their publications.

THE AMERICAN INDIAN

As the United States pushed the Indians aside to make room for the white man, the attitude toward the Indians was that they were to be elevated from savagery to civilization. The Indians were expected to reach joyously to the white man's culture, because, in the nineteenth-century view, its superiority was self-evident. Thus the music of the Indians was little studied; serious books dealt only with occasional, specific aspects of it. But this type of study was practically useless, because music was inseparable from the fabric of Indian life—song was used in virtually all activities. Like Negro and troubadour music, Indian music was rhythmic and melodic, centering in the minor third and major seconds. It used percussion that was important and often independent and was associated with the dance.

Indian music confounded the white scientists who studied it. The drums often beat a pulse different from that of the song they accompanied. For example, a drum might be beaten in hemiola relation to the beat of a song—quarter-note drumming against a basic dotted quarter. Moreover, the voices frequently sang syllables rather than a verbal text. An observer late in the century wrote, in *A Study of Omaha Music* (1893), that many songs rearranged, fragmented, or modified the words "to make them more melodious."

[25] Jeannette R. Murphy, "African Music in the United States," *Popular Science Monthly*, September, 1899, p. 665.
[26] Quoted in Chase, *op. cit.*, p. 236.

> A majority of the songs, however, are furnished almost wholly with syllables which are not parts or even fragments of words but sounds that lend themselves easily to singing and are without definite meaning; yet when a composer has once set syllables to his song, they are never changed or transposed but preserved with as much accuracy as we would observe in maintaining the integrity of a poem.[27]

Not only did the Omaha sing syllables, but they felt that a song with a text was a combination of two arts. The author continued, "Words clearly enunciated in singing break the melody to the Indian ear and mar the music. They say of us that we talk a great deal as we sing." [28]

The first extensive study of Indian music was written in Germany as a doctoral thesis in musicology at the University of Leipzig. *Über die Musik der Nordamerikanischen Wilden* (On the Music of the North American Savages, 1882), by a New Yorker, Theodore Baker (1851–1934), was based on the author's sojourn, during the summer of 1880, in western New York and in an Indian school in Pennsylvania. There he notated the music of the Seneca and the Iroquois. Baker's treatise included musical examples of interest to composers and analyses of value to musicologists, but the book was not translated and thus was not available to the general public.

However, interaction between the Indian and the white man was lessening, and influences that might have bent Indian music toward the white man's had not entered Indian life. The distance between European and Indian practice was too great, and after the turn of the century, when Negro music was winning a wider public, Indian music became more and more obscure. It would finally be of interest only to scholars.

POPULAR MUSIC

At the midpoint of the nineteenth century, the parlor was still the locale of most spontaneous music-making in the Eastern cities. It was there that people danced to piano arrangements of favorite waltzes and galops, and it was there that thousands of boys and girls dutifully practiced. In the small towns and the expanding West, it was the barns and meeting houses that still reverberated with the reels and quadrilles of the square dance.

However, many cultural enclaves also existed in the New World. One could find mountaineers singing and fiddling English folk songs in the Appalachians, Norwegians dancing to the Hardanger fiddle in Wisconsin, guests swirling a polka at a Czech wedding in Chicago, and a cantor intoning an ancient chant at a Bar Mitzvah in New York. Many second-generation Americans were bimusical as well as bilingual, and even when immigrants permitted their children to speak only English, they maintained their musical tradition.

[27] Natalie Curtis Burlin, *ibid.*, p. 413.
[28] *Ibid.*

Thus, the chief characteristic of American popular music was its variety of type and derivation. The most popular parlor song of the third quarter of the century was "Listen to the Mocking Bird" (1855), by Richard Milburn, a Philadelphia Negro barber; the song had been published as a "sentimental Ethiopian ballad." Civil War tunes remained popular after the war —Emmett's "Dixie" (1859) and the folk tune "The Yellow Rose of Texas" in the South and Henry Clay Work's "Marching through Georgia" in the North. The folk tunes "Polly-Wolly Doodle" and "Shoo, Fly, Don't Bother Me" were sung with equal gusto by both sides. By 1875, Viennese waltzes and marching songs were also at their apex. Of the former, "The Blue Danube," by Johann Strauss the Younger, was tremendously popular; of the latter, the "Triumphal March" from *Aïda*, which had been published in a four-hand version in 1872, was most often played.

Mildred S. Hill, "Good-Morning to All." This song, which is the original of the universally known "Happy Birthday to You," is from *Song Stories for the Kindergarten,* published in 1892. The book was one of many contributions of American educators, at the end of the nineteenth century, to an enlightened music study for children. (Photo by R. E. Kalmbach.)

In the 1880s, a more unified American style became apparent. Such genial favorites as "While Strolling through the Park" reflected the leisure-time activities of a busy nation. And then, in the Gay Nineties, sentiment became sentimentality. The waltz song still had its simple moments, with such tunes as "A Bicycle Built for Two," but from 1893, when the ballad "After the Ball," by Charles K. Harris (1865–1930), became the hit song of the decade, the sentimental song (still in waltz time) became a craze. "The Little Lost Child" (1894), by Marks and Stern, sung to the accompaniment of photographic illustrations projected from slides, became a favorite vaudeville number. Songs in this genre, including those with titles such as "The Picture That Is Turned toward the Wall" and "My Mother Was a Lady" were called *tearjerkers*.

Even farther from good taste was a rash of Irish and Negro takeoffs that were popular at the end of the century. Such songs, along with tear-jerkers and sentimental piano pieces such as "Narcissus" (1891), by Ethelbert Nevin (1862–1901), comprised the last excesses of popular Romanticism. Only such works as the marches of John Philip Sousa (1854–1932) remained strong and energetic.

Melodically full of clichés and rhythmically effete, the decadent music types could not long survive in a robust cultural environment. A stronger style was beginning to be felt. The cakewalk and the clog dance of the American Negro included fresh rhythmic and melodic elements that could enliven popular music yet were conceived within a base of key tonality (used not as restriction, but frame) that made them easily understood and hence immediately acceptable. The cakewalk often included the shuffle, while the clog dance was also called a *rag*. The rhythm of the clog was called ragtime, which by the middle of the Gay Nineties had moved from the minstrel show to the center of popular style. Ragtime music was made a national craze by Scott Joplin's piano performances at the Chicago World's Fair of 1893.

The remarkable development at the turn of the century was the split into conservative and modernist camps within popular music. By 1900, the two main popular song styles (not counting theatrical types), the lachrymose waltz and the ragtime tune, were well defined.

It was with the sentimentality of the waltz song and the rising energy of the rag, the turkey trot, and the one-step that the twentieth century began. A young lady playing the piano for her friends in 1910, though expected to perform the music of Beethoven, Chopin, Mendelssohn, and perhaps even the more modern Brahms and to balance it with waltzes and sentimental pieces, would find the new rags indispensable. A pianist of that time wrote of Joplin, "Yes, he was big in my girlhood, and his 'Maple Leaf Rag' was one of my repertoire that I was *always* asked to play." [29]

[29] Marie Borroff Scott, letter of March 28, 1969.

RELIGIOUS MUSIC

No discussion of popular music in the second half of the nineteenth century can ignore the popular anthologies of religious music; they included some of the best sellers of the century. Early collections were in the tradition of the New England singing-school heritage. But Lowell Mason had yielded completely to the European tradition. Although he was perhaps the last of the self-taught New Englanders, he sent his sons to Europe to study, and he himself went to Zurich, later in his life, to study educational methods. He then turned his attention to the public schools and became an important influence in the growth of music education.

Lowell Mason's many collections of sacred songs culminated in the thirteen editions of the *Carmina Sacra* (1841 to 1860), which sold over a half-million copies. His works were followed by other collections in the same style. The hymns in these compendiums, written in four parts with the tune in the soprano, became popular in the home as well as in church. They were parallel to the popular songs of the day, becoming poetically sentimental and musically derivative by the end of the century.

American oratorios and cantatas were performed from time to time, and the influence of their composers was large. Prominent among these composers was John Knowles Paine (1839–1906), a German-trained organist, singer, conductor, and composer; he was awarded the first professorship of music in America—at Harvard College in 1875. Horatio Parker (1863–1919), another oratorio composer, became Paine's opposite number at Yale in 1894. Thus, the composition of church and sacred concert music was in the hands of proponents of European tradition.

The place of religious music, and of music in general, in the national life was reflected in the music at the national centennial. This was celebrated in an exposition in Philadelphia, from May to November, 1876, with attendance of well over nine million. The exposition was concerned almost entirely with mechanical and commercial exhibits, and the only musical exhibits were pianos, harmoniums, and the centennial carillon (of thirteen bells). But band concerts, including children's concerts, were frequent, and a short daily piano recital was offered by the Weber Piano Company.

The huge opening ceremonies went to the heart of the nation. An immense platform had been erected to hold the band, orchestra, and choir, and a pipe organ had been built. The ceremonies began with the band playing thirteen national anthems, beginning with that of the United States and ending with that of Russia. Next came a newly commissioned "Inaugural March" by Richard Wagner. Then, after an invocation, a new hymn by John Greenleaf Whittier (1807–1892), with music by John Knowles Paine, was performed by the choir, organ, and orchestra. A cantata on the past century, by the poet-composer Sidney Lanier, was then presented, preceding the opening speeches. Finally, President Grant declared the exposition officially open. The climax of the occasion occurred as the flag of the United States was unfurled—"the Hallelujah Chorus was rendered with orchestral and organ accompaniment, and a salute of 100 guns was fired from George's Hill, together with the ringing of chimes from different parts of the grounds." [30]

[30] Frank F. Norton (ed.), *Historical Register of the Centennial Exposition, 1876,* New York: Frank Leslie, 1877, p. 78.

Part Six

THE NEW MUSIC

The fugue form is as dead as the sonata form; and the sonata form is as dead as Beethoven himself.

GEORGE BERNARD SHAW *

Traditionalists

and Iconoclasts

25

The two decades before World War I comprised a period of merriment almost innocent in its disregard for consequences—as though the haut monde knew that the elegant days would not come again. In England, the Victorian period gave way to the Edwardian; in France, the period was called *la belle époque* (the lovely time); and in Austria, the elegant gaiety of the Viennese operetta epitomized the era. The proud citizens of Western Europe were convinced they had forged the highest form of civilization man had yet attained and that they would progress to undreamed-of heights.

Yet even as these Europeans spoke proudly, doubters were at work. Darwin had given scientific approval to self-assured superiority, but Sigmund Freud (1856–1939) was providing scientific basis for doubt. The Romantic

* *London Music in 1888–89*, London: Constable, 1937, p. 69.

assumption that the European was innately superior by evolution was challenged by the Freudian theory that each man lives through a complete evolution in himself, born a savage and always in conflict with the savage instincts with which he lives in a truce that can always be broken.

Like other aspects of life, artistic endeavor was suffused with dissatisfaction with old ideas and methods, which artists saw as comfortable but no longer creative. In such an age it was natural to search for new methods and for the search to be multifaceted. Idealistic movements, most of them centering in the visual arts, proliferated. For musicians, several were important.

> *Impressionism* was the first of the modern movements to embody new techniques rather than new subjects. In painting, the techniques concerned light—attempts to depict light as it is actually diffused and perceived, in order to give the impression rather than the precise shape of the subject. A French movement, Impressionism was espoused by such painters as Paul Cézanne (1839–1906) and Claude Monet (1840–1926). Later, during the Postimpressionist period, shadow was treated the same way.
>
> *Symbolism* was a poetic movement from 1880 to 1900 in France and Belgium by which supraverbal meanings and emotions were presented obliquely through symbols, suggestions, and evocations. The symbolists emulated the mystical power of music through rhythm and sound. The chief poets of the movement were Paul Verlaine (1844–1896), Stéphane Mallarmé (1842–1898), and Maurice Maeterlinck (1862–1949).
>
> *Pointillism* is a painting term denoting the atomization of objects. Paintings done in this technique depict objects by small, systematically positioned "flicks" of color, which the viewer organizes into images. The motivating figure of pointillism, a French technique, was Georges Seurat (1859–1891). His most famous work was *Un dimanche d'été à la Grande Jatte* (A Summer Sunday at the Grande Jatte [Park], 1886), which is now at the Chicago Art Institute.

DIVIDED MUSICAL TRADITIONS

In music, the work of the generation before World War I was based on the three elements—melody, harmony, and rhythm—already clear in the work of the later Romantics. But intellectual interaction with the various *isms,* along with a continuation of interest in folk idioms and new instrumental color, led to the first intimations of the coming of new music. In addition, popular music was developing rapidly, especially in the United States, where ragtime, the blues, and jazz would soon become important to the whole spectrum of song, dance, and theater. A growing number of observers felt that the cherished traditional forms had been used up.

In 1890, Brahms and Verdi were still active elder statesmen of music; they made Vienna and Milan magnetic centers of musical opinion. But if Vienna and Milan were centers for two traditions, Bayreuth was the shrine of a third—Wagner had created not so much a camp as a cult, and the

Festspielhaus near Munich drew his followers, in increasing numbers after his death, not just as listeners but as pilgrims. A critic who had worked for the Wagner cause in Vienna at the end of the nineteenth century wrote: "The spirit of Richard Wagner was still alive in the Vienna opera house. . . . We took an oath to continue fighting for Wagner, for his work, and for his ideas. It was a sacred oath and we kept it." [1]

The opposing camp, the central tradition of German Romanticism, was less fanatical but had a broader influence. The Leipzig Conservatory, founded by Mendelssohn in 1843, was thoroughly permeated with Schumann's presence and, through Moscheles (who taught there from 1846 to 1870), with the memory of Beethoven. The school had done its work well, and former Leipzig students were teaching in important positions throughout Europe and America. Thus the next generation was educated in the Schumann-Brahms tradition in virtually all conservatories and schools.

Four musical developments represent European music at the end of the nineteenth century: the expansion of the German tradition; the continuation of the Italian tradition; a new nationalism, seen in the rise of peripheral nations within the European musical art; and a new prominence of French leadership.

The German Tradition

The German tradition was deeply shaken, divided between conservatives (Brahmsians) and radicals (Wagnerites). German works of music expanded literally—larger orchestras and longer forms. The symphony became longer and longer, and composers strove for grand philosophical import.

Brahms had his successors in Anton Bruckner and Gustav Mahler; they carried the symphonic tradition forward. But Wagner had no successors in the musical drama; Wagnerian works were still being established and Wagner's ideas would be transferred to other forms.

The dominating figure of the German tradition was Richard Strauss, a compromise who proved acceptable in some degree to all factions in and out of Germany. He wrote large works for orchestra, which was still the most prestigious musical medium; he composed tone poems on German subjects, which suited the Wagnerites; he programed his music in detail, which pleased the arch-Romantics; he was a master of orchestral color, which pleased the French; and he wrote songs and operas, which pleased the Italians. Strauss was staunchly German and Romantic. His tone poems were about Romantic figures of the past (*Don Juan, Don Quixote, Till Eulenspiegel*) or based on German Romantic literary works (*Also sprach Zarathustra*, Thus Spoke Zoroaster), and on personal Romantic programs (*Domestic Symphony; Ein Heldenleben*, Hero's Life). His orchestra was huge and his details of subject matter were influenced by Freudian ideas. He infused the Wagnerian Leitmotif into the tone poem and was proud of his ability to suggest literal action. "I can express in music the moving of a pencil from one place to

[1] Max Graf, *Composer and Critic: Two Hundred Years of Musical Criticism*, New York: Norton, 1946, p. 18.

another," [2] he said. In addition, he was a new type of personality, not a wild-looking, impractical genius, but a well-groomed businessman of the arts.

The Italian tradition, spared the clashes of the German scene, was at its height. Giacomo Puccini was the last composer of the full Italian tradition. In a sense, he was the luckiest composer of his time. Not only had Verdi left Romantic opera at the crest, but singers were at the climax of Romantic vocal techniques. Thus, Puccini was in the center of a generation of resplendent artists during the Golden Age of singing.

Puccini worked for more realistic vocal inflection, for a vocal line closer to that of natural speech—not in the manner of recitativo but in the shape of the whole, recitativo and aria alike. His orchestra was larger than Verdi's, and it was characteristic of Puccini's style to maintain a stable vocal phrase, even a rhythmic declamation of a single tone, while the orchestra rang changes on it. The New York production of Puccini's *Madama Butterfly* in 1907 was doubtless one of the great nights in the history of opera. The composer, at the crest of his career, was present, and the singers were Geraldine Farrar (1882–1967), Enrico Caruso (1873–1921), Antonio Scotti (1866–1936), and Louise Homer (1871–1947), four of the fabled stars of the Golden Age.

In the years before World War I, the center of the operatic world was still La Scala in Milan. And Italian opera, with a repertoire that was established and to a large extent sacrosanct, was dominated by the producers, conductors, and singers. The Golden Age of La Scala came with the impressario Giulio Gatti-Casazza (1868–1940), a naval engineer turned theater director. When, in 1898, Gatti-Casazza was appointed director of La Scala, he hired Arturo Toscanini (1867–1957) as chief conductor and Caruso as the star; and when, in 1908, he was made director of the Metropolitan Opera in New York, he brought the two men with him. New York became a world center of the Italian grand opera tradition.

Enrico Caruso could well symbolize the Golden Age of singing; he created the standard of a huge voice, at its best in a dramatic aria. And his career symbolized the era. Although he had a magnificent voice schooled in a sure Italian tradition, he capitulated to American glamour and the prestige of the Metropolitan Opera and led a frenetic life of opulence within a basically conservative musical discipline.

Love for native soil, comfort with native customs and tastes, and pride in native accomplishments have always motivated men in one way or another. In politics, the Romantic form of these feelings was called patriotism; in the arts, it was called nationalism or, when exploring different cultures, exoticism.

Folk tunes or national songs were used in a number of basic ways. Composers were interpolating tunes into concert music and were using

[2] Quoted in Arnold Schoenberg, *Style and Idea*, New York: Philosophical Library, 1950, p. 209.

foreign idioms as exotic flavors to create a special atmosphere in an opera or a tone poem. Popular dances, from the early pavane and volta to the more modern polka, schottische, fandango, and maxixe, were expressions of the consistent fad of the exotic. Verdi's *Aida* and Bizet's *Carmen* both owed part of their success to their exotic elements. Many characteristic national dances, from Chopin's soulful mazurkas to Brahms's Hungarian dances, were presented as exotic enjoyment as well as expressions of pride for the nationals.

The most important use for national idioms was made by composers of peripheral nationality. They were seeking significant expression of their own musical inheritance. In some cases, they substituted a folk tune for a theme in a Romantic form, but later, they tried to incorporate a national essence, particularly the fabric of rhythm, melodic materials, medium, and color of the national art.

Musicians still felt they had to go to one of the large European centers to finish their education and make a reputation, but most went home again to join the effort to build a national art. The first nation to attain a unique style in the new terms was Russia. Her national literature, given a foundation by Pushkin, Feodor Dostoevsky (1821–1881), and Leo Tolstoy (1828–1910), had made her a powerful literary force. In music, Glinka had fostered the use of national elements, and the theater under Stanislavsky and the ballet under Marius Petipa were in the vanguard of European art. Tchaikovsky was perhaps the most skillful Russian composer of the last third of the nineteenth century—he was certainly the most skilled of the Russians in the German techniques. But the group of musical nationalists that included Modest Mussorgsky, Alexandre Borodin, and Nicolai Rimsky-Korsakov were more consciously Russian. By 1867 the effort to achieve a national movement in the field of music was clear enough for a Russian writer to speak of a *kutchka*, a "mighty handful of Russian musicians" [3] who would create a national musical art. By the end of the century, the St. Petersburg Conservatory, under Rimsky-Korsakov, was one of the best schools in Europe.

Another growing school was in Helsinki, Finland. Jean Sibelius (1865–1957), who was given his early training there, came to represent the intensely patriotic and musically conservative elements in European music. His tone poem *Finlandia* (1899) became one of the most popular works in the first half of the twentieth century.

British attempts at nationalization started more slowly. Sullivan's operettas were popular throughout the world, but the oratorio remained at the forefront of British interest and the festivals offered opportunities for hearing new works. Edward Elgar produced a setting of the mystical poem "The Dream of Gerontius," by John Henry Cardinal Newman, which was premiered at the Birmingham Festival in 1900 and presented in Chicago in 1903. The oratorios of Samuel Coleridge-Taylor, including *Kubla Khan* (1906), *A Tale of Old Japan* (1911), and the famous trilogy *The Song of*

[3] Quoted in Nicolas Slonimsky, *Baker's Biographical Dictionary of Musicians*, 5th ed., New York: Schirmer, 1958, p. 1140.

Hiawatha (1900), were more far-reaching; they represent the search for exotic subjects and materials. Coleridge-Taylor also wrote orchestral works on African tunes, a concert overture called *Toussant l'Ouverture*, a rhapsodic dance (*Bamboula*), and more typical works such as an orchestral suite called *Scenes from an Everyday Romance*.

But it was Spain's musical tradition that was the most thoroughly exploited by Europeans and Americans. Perhaps the most representative Spanish figure of the generation was Isaac Albeniz (1860–1909), a Catalonian Spaniard. Precocious and restless, he toured as a child prodigy at the age of seven and, by the time he was fifteen, had spent two years on his own in Puerto Rico and the United States, where he played to support himself. He then studied in Brussels and Leipzig and went to Budapest to see Liszt. Settling in Paris in 1893, he continued his international connections, staging works in Brussels, Madrid, Barcelona, and London, as well as Paris. In 1899 he presented a nationalistic work, *Catalonia* (a rhapsody for piano and orchestra), but his fame rested on his works for piano solo. Of these, the most famous were the dozen pieces called *Iberia*; they transcended the narrow concept of national elements as flavor or even fabric to achieve new structural and pianistic techniques.

Portuguese and Latin American centers had been importing international early nineteenth-century operatic traditions. Native composers were sent to Naples or Paris to study and, if they returned, continued to propound a conservative mainstream art. Daniel Alomias Robles (1871–1942), a Peruvian of Indian and European heritage, exceptionally, was self-taught; his importance lay chiefly in his collection of over 1,200 Indian tunes from Peru, Bolivia, and Ecuador. Alberto Nepomuceno (1860–1920), on the other hand, studied in Rome, Berlin, and Paris. He brought unusual breadth to his directorship of the Instituto Nacional de Musica (1902–1916), produced the Portuguese opera *O Garatuja* in Rio de Janeiro (1904), and introduced Brazilian music to European audiences at the Brussels Exposition of 1910.

French Leadership

Paris in the generation before World War I was a city of artistic pronouncements, protests, and experiments. By 1890, poets and painters had propounded experimental theories and the new medium of the moving picture was causing a sensation in the two- and three-minute films of George Méliès (c. 1860–1938). All the senses were bombarded by the experimenters. The use of electric lighting to change hues was described in 1900 as "an orgy of color"—"Wonderful luminous streams of light" changed color with the rhythm of the dance. And in 1902, an olfactory musical presentation was advertised as "the first experimental perfume concert." [4]

Of course, music also had its old guard, who accepted the German musical ideal and the Romantic assumption that the German principles were

[4] Quoted in Walter Sorell, *The Dance through the Ages*, New York: Grosset & Dunlap, 1967, p. 153; and Curt Sachs, *The Commonwealth of Art*, New York: Norton, 1946, p. 232.

immutable and subject only to a crowning phase of evolution. But an avant-garde musical coterie was already producing intimations of the new music. Early interests—in exotic color and in nationalism—caused the French to look both outward and inward with equal intensity.

The first international exposition, in Paris in 1867, was a powerful outward look. Although it was devoted to science, the arts, and industry, music was also of great importance, and the exposition included exhibits of instruments and performances of an amazing number of cultural groups. The second international exposition, in Paris in 1889, comprised a crescendo of all elements—scientific, artistic, and industrial. The musical exotica were more skillfully presented, with the instrumental color and scale materials of a Javanese *gamelan* coming under special discussion.

The French love of color grew by exposure to other cultures. At first, the inward examination was a recognition of the validity of French style. Claude Achille Debussy, a Prix de Rome winner at the age of twenty-two, had been drawn to the works of Mussorgsky and had also been much interested in the gamelan at the exposition of 1889.

The French love of color also grew by interaction with the other arts. In vogue at the time were Impressionist paintings and symbolist poetry. The opposition to a highly programed style led naturally to a movement for subjective rather than objective music—equally a Romantic concept but the obverse. Debussy's orchestral *Prélude à "l'Après-midi d'un faune"* (Prelude on "The Afternoon of a Faun," 1894) caused a furor at home and abroad, but an English critic understood the composer's aims.

> He has invariably chosen delicate, intangible subjects and flights of fancy which gain preeminently an added and prolonged eloquence in music. To those who would attempt to define the unknowable, and who would limit the arts to precise expression or imitation of what they call realities, Debussy's choice of poets, his association of ideas to music, even his Nature studies and impressions, must seem antagonistic and incomprehensible. He is averse to binding music down to the exact reproduction of set programmes, but has rather chosen to amplify and expand evanescent, shadowy thoughts—to distil their essence and then capture and protract it in sound. . . .
>
> All through the piece the composer preserves this feeling of elusiveness, of mirage: he attains it by the use of delicate unusual harmonies and by the silvery, web-like tracery of the phrases. The frequent use of the scale of whole tones and the unresolved dissonances produce a distinct charm of their own. The chords are of exceeding richness and present a depth of glowing color. The interspersed solos for violin, oboe, clarinet, cor anglais, resemble dainty broidery, and portray intimately the ramifications of doubt and longing in the faun's mind.[5]

Debussy also worked out his ideals in a series of works for the piano, rethinking the piano as an idiomatic instrument. Layers of sound, pedal

[5] Quoted in Norman Demuth, *An Anthology of Musical Criticism*, London: Eyre & Spottiswoode (Publishers), Ltd., 1947, pp. 319–320.

The first page of Claude Debussy's *Iberia* (1910). The scoring is for an expanded symphony orchestra—3 flutes, 1 piccolo, 2 oboes, 1 English horn, 3 clarinets, 3 bassoons, 1 contrabassoon, 4 horns, 3 trumpets, 3 trombones, 1 tuba, timpani, tambourine, castanets, snare drum, cymbals, 2 harps, and strings. (Courtesy of Elkan-Vogel, Inc., for Durand, Fils, and Cie.)

574

effects, characteristic rhythms used decoratively, carefully specified dynamics, and the use of rubato in relation to harmonic (rather than melodic) elements—all were incorporated. From the sybaritic "L'Isle joyeuse" (Isle of Joy) to the brooding "Cathédral engloutie" (Sunken Cathedral), his pieces caused controversy because of their unorthodox goals and means. The latter piece was in his first book of *Préludes* for piano (1910), which also included such obviously impressionistic titles as "Des pas sur la neige" (Steps in the Snow) and "Ce qu'a vu le vent de l'Ouest" (What the West Wind Saw).

It is clear that what Debussy was creating was new fabric for Romantic works. His intention differed from that of Strauss. The Teutonic ideal was to create a subjective parallel of a concrete program; the French ideal was to create a lucid presentation of the inexpressible. Yet both were using rich chords unaffiliated with key center, both were fully concerned with the full Romantic symphony orchestra, and both were seeking a future for that medium. Contemporaries called Strauss's tone poem *Also sprach Zarathustra* a work of "cosmic magnificence" and said that Strauss was "the first complete *realist* in music"; [6] whereas *Prélude à "l'Après-midi d'un faune"* was described as "music of the most inveterate subtlety, of the most aerial refinement," [7] and Debussy was considered a musical *Impressionist*.

THE DANCE

The traditional classical ballet of the nineteenth century—formal choreography applied to highly Romantic music—still comprised a vital art in French artistic life. But in the dance, the modernist philosophies sparked by the cancan, the maxixe, and the cakewalk, on one hand, and a new respect for the "primitive," on the other, were at work with particular vigor. The American dancer Isadora Duncan (1878–1927) proposed a new esthetic of the dance—a love of motion, the rhythms of life, and the relationships of space, motivated but not programed by music; her teachers, she said, had been "wind and wave and the winged flight of bird and bee." [8]

Emile Jaques-Dalcroze (1865–1950), a popular composer, developed a synthesis of musical and nonmusical ideas in a system of motion that he considered a physical counterpart of vocal sol-fa exercises; he called this system *body solfege* or *eurythmics*. It sought transcendence—a total, multifaceted penetration of the meaning of personality and art—and Jaques-Dalcroze presented it in a series of lectures titled *l'Education par le rythme* (Education through Rhythm, 1907). He founded his own school, with enormous success, near Dresden in 1910, and within two years, branches were opened in France, Germany, England, Russia, and the United States.

---

[6] Ernest Newman, quoted in Graf, *op. cit.*, pp. 293, 294.
[7] Lawrence Gilman, quoted in Graf, *op. cit.*, p. 320.
[8] Quoted in Sorell, *op. cit.*, p. 178.

Although the Jaques-Dalcroze system was neither a dance method nor a philosophy (or was perhaps both), it was studied seriously by dancers, musicians, and thinking men in general. It was not a method for learning playwriting or theatrical production, but the writers George Bernard Shaw (1856–1950) and Paul Claudel (1868–1955) went to the school, as did the theatrical set designer Adolph Appia (1862–1928) and the entrepreneur Max Reinhardt (1873–1943). What eurythmics was was a system of educating the body, and its initial impact was felt in the world of the dance. Before 1910, Jaques-Dalcroze–inspired dance concerts were on tour. The presence of these dancers in Paris in the first decade of the twentieth century coincided with the establishment there of the Ballets Russes (Russian Ballet). Under the direction of Serge Diaghilev (1872–1929), the company arrived in Paris (1909) with a production of Rimsky-Korsakov's *Scheherazade*. Diaghilev was not himself a musician or dancer but an entrepreneur who could bring the right people together in the right atmosphere of creative excitement. He was not committed to any one element of the ballet but thought of the theater as "created by the very closest fusion of three elements—dancing, painting,

The program cover of the Ballets Russes, Paris, 1909. (Courtesy of Photo Lauros.)

and music." [9] Diaghilev worked with Debussy, Maurice Ravel (1875–1937), Manuel de Falla (1876–1946), and even Richard Strauss. But above all, he worked closely with a young Russian student of Rimsky-Korsakov, Igor Stravinsky. Son of a Russian opera singer, Stravinsky was sensitive to the theatrical, yet he had come to music late and thus had the objectivity of initial distance. Infused with Rimsky-Korsakov's love for the exotic and young enough to be influenced by the new Freudian concept of the "primitive," Stravinsky proved a catalyst of such value to the Russian company that, although he composed only eight works for the Ballets Russes, his name is linked to Diaghilev's more firmly than any other musician's.

The culmination of the early years of the Ballets Russes in Paris was the premiere of *Le Sacre du Printemps* (The Rite of Spring) in 1913. It was conceived by Diaghilev, composed by Stravinsky, and the choreography was by Waslaw Nijinsky (1890–1950), who studied at the Jaques-Dalcroze school in 1912; Nijinsky also starred in the ballet. The American writer Gertrude Stein (1874–1946), a member of the modernist group in Paris, attended the premiere and described it.

> The performance began. No sooner had it commenced than the excitement began. The scene now so well known with its brilliantly coloured background now not at all extraordinary, outraged the Paris audience. No sooner did the music begin and the dancing than they began to hiss. The defenders began to applaud. We could hear nothing, as a matter of fact I never did hear any of the music of the Sacre du Printemps because it was the only time I ever saw it and one literally could not, throughout the whole performance, hear the sound of music. The dancing was very fine and that we could see although our attention was constantly distracted by a man in the box next to us flourishing his cane, and finally in a violent altercation with an enthusiast in the box next to him, his cane came down and smashed the opera hat the other had just put on in defiance. It was all incredibly fierce.[10]

Subtitled "Scenes from Pagan Russia," the ballet strove to exploit current interest in the so-called barbaric, which in large part consisted of aggressive sound, irregular rhythm, and compulsively repeated melodic thrusts. Its primitivism was opulent and unconfined, an orchestration of the Romantic concept of the savage. Nonetheless, *Le Sacre du Printemps* rearranged the triangle of melody, harmony, and rhythm with a post-Freudian rhythmic primacy; melody and harmony added abrasion to vigorous passages and color to quieter ones. To an audience taught to listen for themes, which were supposed to proceed in a clear, form-defining order, the effect was startling. It would be another generation before the music of this ballet would be evaluated calmly. In 1913 the score's compulsive qualities linked it in the public mind to the dark subconscious, the newly discovered, frightening inner world of psychoanalysis.

[9] *Ibid.*, p. 161.
[10] Quoted in Eric Blom, *The Music Lover's Miscellany*, London: Gollancz, 1935, p. 52.

MUSICOLOGY

The French investigation of non-European music was generally artistic and intuitive. Its results were used for the benefit of the modernists who were searching for new effects of instrumental and harmonic color. Debussy had looked to the East, and even in such "nature studies" as *La Mer*, he used techniques derived from Oriental practice. Others had followed in the same spirit. In 1910 a gamelan concert, using violin, flute, celeste, and glockenspiel, was presented in Paris—a very different emulation from the Turkish dances of Telemann and Rameau.

But the French had also looked back to Rameau. Following the German publication of the complete works of J. S. Bach (issued 1851–1899), Handel (issued 1858–1903), Beethoven (issued 1862–1888), Mozart (issued 1876–1886), and Schubert (issued 1888–1897), the French began their publishing with the works of Rameau (issued 1895–1924), and Saint-Saëns was editor-in-chief.

Historical publications were one phase of the developing profession of musicology, bringing different disciplines to bear on music in a scientific way. Preparing music for publication was not new, but collecting and preparing music from the past required historical as well as editorial techniques, and new types of studies were required. Interest in Medieval and Renaissance music was growing, but the farther back in time the scholars looked, the greater were the problems of presenting music in a modern version. By the end of the nineteenth century, several disciplines were serving the new studies.

acoustics, the study of sounds, was perhaps the earliest science to become involved with musical research. Attempts to define precise pitch ratios and mathematically to form scales began in pre-Christian times. The study of temperaments and exotic systems and the measurement of loudness were carried out in the nineteenth century, as were new types of studies of musical instruments. Classification of instruments by means of their tone activation (chordophones, aerophones, idiophones, and membranophones) was introduced. With these categories, all instruments—not just European—could be discussed and studied. In 1866 Philipp Reis, a German musician, reproduced musical sound electromagnetically, and in 1878 Edison registered the patent for the phonograph.

historical musicology was devoted to the huge job of discovering and understanding the forms and techniques of the music of the past. Historical musicologists were often paleographers, theorists, and editors as well. A great deal of the knowledge they discovered was presented to other scholars in journals and at meetings of musicological societies.

paleography is the study of old forms of writing for the purposes of deciphering and translating documents of the past, ascertaining their date and place of origin, and clarifying their original function. In music, documents related to music theory and instruction, the social roles of musicians, the manufacture of instruments, and so on, needed to be collected. And in addition, the obsolete notations had to be deciphered and translated into modern approximations. Music had always taken little interest in the past, so its entire early history awaited unearthing. In general, the deciphering of notation proceeded backward in time, each generation forming a bridge to the one behind. By 1910, late sixteenth-century notation was understood, and the works of some earlier Renaissance composers (notably Josquin) had been discovered. Medieval notations were still in varying degrees of obscurity, but many significant discoveries had been made.

editing is the preparation of music for publication. Two kinds of publication developed—those used for study and those used for performance. Musicological texts were predominantly of the former type; they concentrated on making a translation visually as close as possible to the original notation (using whole notes for breves, for example). The works of some composers were published in their entirety, and the newly deciphered Medieval and Renaissance manuscripts were brought out in series. Texts for performing were seldom prepared by scholars; concert music was edited by virtuosos, who provided personal (generally Romantic) interpretations, and folk music was harmonized by composers.

comparative musicology (now called *ethnomusicology*), the study of music other than West European art music, had the immediate job of collecting music. At the end of the nineteenth century, many composers were working to notate the folk music of their own people, and there was a proliferation of both scholarly and popular collections. In addition, the study of exotic music, which began with a few studies of Oriental music in the eighteenth and early nineteenth centuries, continued by means of exhibits and concerts, chiefly at the many international expositions. The notation of the Negro spiritual "Mary and Marthy" (Example 79) is representative of early attempts to transcribe folk materials accurately.

In the United States, many studies of Indian, Negro, Appalachian, Western, and other musical types were made as part of museum anthropological programs. These tended to stress the importance of the social setting and cultural significance of the music. In 1892, phonograph recordings of songs of the Zuni and Passamaquoddy Indians demonstrated the value of the new mechanism to the discipline of musicology.

lexicography, the compilation of special dictionaries and encyclopedias, entered musicology very early. Important volumes were published in the eighteenth century, and their number and scope increased with expanding musicological research.

music bibliography is the compilation and evaluation of music texts, reference works, and studies. As musicologists produced more books, the music collection and music library came into prominence. In 1902, a chief librarian was assigned to the music division of the Library of Congress for the first time. The national collection, with its archive of American folk song, was and still is the largest music library in the United States. Most European capitals also have national libraries, some of which are modern continuations of royal libraries, and they contain the accumulation of four or more centuries. During the early years of the twentieth century, a few of the great university libraries instituted special music divisions, often built on excellent private collections.

By the end of the nineteenth century, musicology had begun to be acknowledged as a profession, and a few chairs in musicology were created in European universities. The field also became a fashionable interest for amateurs, many of whom produced important works.[11] Harvard was the first American university to grant a Ph.D. for work in music. The organist-composer Louis Adolphe Coerne (1870–1922), who had studied in Munich, earned that degree in 1905. Musicologically, the United States was a German colony, and the long reach of the Romantic hierarchical view of music is clearly shown in Coerne's dissertation, *The Evolution of Modern Orchestration*. His thesis was that each orchestral instrument had progressed to its current state of perfection through evolution, by means of a Darwinian process of selection and survival of the fittest. Modern instruments had "once for all instituted a rational and permanent foundation for obtaining solidity of tone." The strings were at the top of the hierarchy, because "the construction of stringed instruments suggests a more advanced stage of intellectuality. . . . By a judicious selection of the superior and a suppression of the inferior types of viols were the violas and violoncellos evolved; and the theorbo and chitarrone were permanently supplanted by the double-bass." [12] Coerne's book was published in 1908, and his teaching career expanded its influence.

THE UNITED STATES

The United States entered the twentieth century without a unified national heritage of music. Theodore Baker's study, written in German, of the Indian music in New York and Pennsylvania was a reference for the few musicians who felt that using North American Indian themes would lead to an American style. Edward MacDowell, who had studied and taught in Germany through his formative years (1876–1888), was familiar with the Baker dissertation and used its materials in his *Indian Suite;* he based each of the five movements on one or two tunes. An alternative suggestion for developing a national style was made by Antonín Dvořák; he proposed that Negro music be used as a basis. But MacDowell could accept neither the Indian nor the Negro heritage as a background for an American nationalism. "I do not believe in 'lifting' a Navajo theme and furbishing it into some kind of musical composition and calling it American music." [13] And of Dvořák's suggestion to use Negro music, he commented,

---

[11] Even Sherlock Holmes was given a musicological hobby, the Motets of Lassus. See Sir Arthur Conan Doyle, "His Last Bow," *The Complete Sherlock Holmes*, New York: Garden City, 1922, p. 1093.

[12] Quoted in Leroy Ostransky, *Perspectives on Music*, Englewood Cliffs, N.J.: Prentice-Hall, 1963, pp. 42, 44, 50.

[13] Quoted in Gilbert Chase, *America's Music*, New York: McGraw-Hill, 1955, p. 363.

> We have here in America been offered a pattern for an "American" national musical costume by the Bohemian Dvořák—though what the Negro melodies have to do with Americanism in art still remains a mystery. . . . [America needs] absolute freedom from the restraint that an almost unlimited deference to European thought and prejudice has imposed upon us. Masquerading in the so-called nationalism of Negro clothes cut in Bohemia will not help us.[14]

The key word is "masquerade," for the Indian and Negro traditions were more foreign to MacDowell (and to virtually all other "serious" composers) than were Dvořák's *Slavonic Dances*.

There was no hope for Americanism in Indian music, for the Indian heritage had been rejected out of hand. But the Negro, even in the midst of prejudice, was exerting strong musical pulls on the popular art, and that art, being strongly American (and ignored as beneath the dignity of the European tradition), was ready to receive it.

Coleridge-Taylor, in his four trips to the United States, encouraged the American Negro to see himself as capable of providing the seeds for the creation of an American musical style. Henry T. Burleigh (1866–1949), a Negro composer and renowned baritone who had influenced and been influenced by Dvořák during that composer's visit to the United States, created highly successful piano accompaniments for many Negro spirituals. Burleigh helped to popularize these songs and introduced them to the concert stage, where they became staple features as a final group in Lieder recitals.

Ragtime and the Blues

Music by blacks was proceeding in both serious and folk traditions, but in the long run, the folk tradition was more important. In the early years of the twentieth century, it centered in the development of ragtime and the blues, notably the works of Scott Joplin and W. C. Handy (1873–1958), whose heritage was both African and American.

Handy spoke of the musical techniques he saw, heard, and used as a child, when he listened to the fiddler known as Uncle Whit Walker, who "stomped" as he played:

> Uncle Whit could stomp the left heel and the right forefoot and alternate this with the right heel and the left forefoot, making four beats to the bar. That was real stomping. . . . We Handy's Hill kids made rhythm by scraping a twenty-penny nail across the teeth of the jawbone of a horse that had died in the woods near by. . . . We sang through fine tooth combs, . . . and made rhythmic sounds rattling our teeth.[15]

The body and mirliton (comb) techniques were directly African, as was the strong rhythmic motivation.

[14] *Ibid.*, p. 355.
[15] *Ibid.*, p. 459.

Joplin and Handy were dance musicians. In the first decades of the twentieth century there was a dance craze in America that could be compared with that in Vienna when the waltz made that city "dancing mad." The maxixe, turkey trot, one-step, two-step, shimmy, Charleston, conga, rhumba, tango, and fox-trot, the later jitterbugging and big apple, and even the twist and the frug—all were part of the dance madness that began with the cakewalk and ragtime.

In the years before World War I, the dance bands in the new tradition were called *ragtime bands*. But in a time when the highest ranking medium was the symphony orchestra of the late Romantic tone poem, the small dance combo seemed a low, even primitive group. It was small; the instruments were diverse, including drums, banjo, and saxophone, as well as the orchestral trumpet, cornet, trombone, string bass, and piano; and instead of working toward homogeneity, the band was working toward individuality of line (apposition rather than blend).

Ragtime bands were playing in many cities, but New Orleans was the largest center. Brass bands had been popular in the second half of the nineteenth century, when European towns maintained them for civic parades and most American parks had bandstands for summer concerts, and in New Orleans the tradition was still strong. Gilmore's first Jubilee had been held there, and at the end of the Civil War a large number of military instruments had flooded the New Orleans secondhand shops, so horns were cheap. Schools and orphanages had bands, and white, Creole, and black clubs maintained them as well. "All we had in a band, as a rule, was bass horn, trombone, trumpet, an alto horn and maybe a baritone horn, bass, and snare drum—just seven pieces, but, talking about noise, you never heard a sixty-piece band make as much noise as we did." [16]

In New Orleans and other cities, bands were used in funeral processions. A ragtime musician who grew up at the turn of the century wrote,

> Joe Blow would die, and maybe he belonged to some society, so they would get the money together and have a band for his funeral. . . . They sure played ragtime on the way back from the graveyard. There were dozens of fine musicians who played ragtime in the parades and at the funerals. . . . We called the music ragtime, whether it was a piano or a band playing. We never heard the word jazz until many years later.[17]

A bandsman who had played in New Orleans toward the end of the century told of playing in "parades and advertising wagons and, excuse me the expression, honky tonks." [18] Parades and wagons draw crowds, and the New Orleans bands had an almost Elizabethan color and energy, with

[16] Jelly Roll Morton, quoted in Chase, *op. cit.*, p. 476.
[17] Eubie Blake, quoted in Leonard Feather, *The New Edition of the Encyclopedia of Jazz*, New York: Bonanza Books, 1962, p. 22.
[18] "Bunk" Johnson, quoted in Chase, *op. cit.*, p. 471.

buskers and children and frank acceptance of bawdiness. (Many ragtime players began their careers in New Orleans bawdy houses.)

Ragtime was a dance term (from the minstrel and variety show clogs) and was instrumental. But the vocal art of the Negro was also actively developing. The voice contrasted with instruments not only in medium but also in its soulful, introverted style, which balanced the kinetic, extroverted style of ragtime. The folk ballad and the slow tune had ancient traditions; what was new was that ballad singers—and women ballad singers at that—toured with bands to spell the dances with solo song. Basing their music on the long sorrow of their people's heritage, they sang ballads of rejection and loneliness, which they called *blues*. Ma Rainey (1886–1939) and her student Bessie Smith (1894–1937), who toured in their teens and were famous before World War I, brought the blues to an early height. They sang simple songs, often a three-line poetic stanza, made up of an opening, its repetition, and a final, contrasting line called the *response*—the trouvères' ballade form.

The classic blues consisted of three short puncti of nine or ten beats each extended by seven or six beats of rest to bring the total to sixteen, or four bars. The total of the three puncti was the twelve-bar blues. Separation of phrases by breaks of 1½ measures gave the singer a spot to improvise or to think of the next phrase while one of the instrumentalists interjected a solo, also called a break. The first published blues song was Handy's "Memphis Blues" in 1912; the more famous "St. Louis Blues" followed in 1914. Both titles cite cities in which the tradition of the blues was strong.

Vocal decoration was intense. By providing key and meter, the European art provided the musicians with a sturdy basis on which to superimpose African techniques. Complex rhythms pulling against a metric frame produced syncopations and tense off-accents, and variable intonations produced the "blue" notes. Long melismas often used fragmented words and syllables chosen for sound.

The technique of singing sounds, called *scat singing*, enabled the singer to dispense with the acting-out of a ballad text and to take part in a combo as one of the instruments. Instruments reciprocated with the solo techniques of talking a tune, of shaping it with inflections and rhythms associated with speech. In the trumpeter's use of the mute, vocal emulation could be uncanny.

In 1917, a new spirit that had been growing in the ragtime movement culminated in the development of a style called *jazz*, which was characterized by a faster beat and an expanded melodic improvisation. The word *jass* was Creole for "speeding up," but it was also a "four-letter word" common in the New Orleans brothels. As late as 1970, the ragtime pianist Eubie Blake (born 1883) declined to use it in a lecture, replying to a questioner, "It's a bad word, you know; I never say it in front of ladies." [19] The first jazz

---

[19] Rutgers University, June, 1970.

"The Jelly Roll Blues"   Example 80
FERDINAND (JELLY ROLL) MORTON

The twelve-bar blues form was put into a series of double statements akin to both
the Renaissance dance form and the popular waltzes of a century before. The
cover illustrates Jelly Roll Morton's conviction that both the African and the
Spanish heritage were present in ragtime music. (Courtesy of Melrose Music
Corp.)

group comprised five white New Orleans musicians (piano, drums, cornet,
clarinet, and trombone) and was led by Nick La Rocca (1889–1961), the
cornetist. By 1919 the group, touring abroad, was advertised as "The Original
Dixieland Jazz Band, the Creators of Jazz," a claim widely disputed but
restated by La Rocca as late as 1959.

The year 1917 witnessed not only the organization of the first jazz band
but also the introduction of jazz recordings. Thus the change from easy
ragtime to the high-powered jazz style that would dominate and symbolize
the Roaring Twenties was the first musical style to be documented from its
beginning. Also in 1917 the New Orleans honky-tonks were closed, bringing
the heyday of New Orleans to an abrupt close. However, the country was
eager for the new style, and the large number of jazz musicians who left
New Orleans established jazz colonies in northern cities. Ferdinand Joseph
La Menthe (1885–1941), the Creole pianist who took the name Jelly Roll

The Jelly Roll Blues. 3-2

The Jelly Roll Blues. 3-3

Morton, was playing stomp tunes and rags in New Orleans sporting houses; Louis Armstrong (born 1900), who had been a busker in New Orleans at the age of seven, was studying cornet at the Waif's Home and playing parades and picnic gigs; and "Duke" Ellington (born 1899), the son of a Washington, D.C., Navy blueprint maker, was in high school, studying piano and listening to the ragtime pianists who came to his city. The ragtime lessons of these boys would come to fruition in the jazz decade.

The United States before World War I was as frenetic as Europe. It was a time of excesses and of direct confrontation of the iconoclasts with the American puritan ethic of work and sobriety.

French artists held New York exhibits, and George Méliès opened cinematography shows in New York (1904), Santa Barbara, and Santa Monica. American film makers turned to American subjects, and in 1915 excess

Mainstream
Popular Music

reached the screen in D. W. Griffith's *The Birth of a Nation*. In 1916, that movie's sequel, *The Fall of a Nation*, used a synchronized music score written by Victor Herbert.

American music of the first decade of the century included a large variety of types, and each was supported by enough of a public to assure its continuation. Three works that premiered in New York in 1907 represented the nostalgic, the comfortable present, and the avant-garde, respectively— Lehar's *Merry Widow*, which ran for 242 performances, Puccini's *Madama Butterfly*, and Strauss's *Salome*. Victor Herbert was operetta's man of the hour, and vaudeville was flourishing with George M. Cohan (1878–1942). Cohan serenaded his two great loves, show business and America, with "Give My Regards to Broadway" (1904) and "You're a Grand Old Flag" (1906). Perhaps Harry Von Tilzer (1872–1946) was the most prolific composer of the decade, writing several types of popular song—the tearjerker ("A Bird in a Gilded Cage"), the drinking song ("Down Where the Wurzburger Flows"), and the minstrel show song ("I'd Leave My Happy Home for You"). And the world of Tin Pan Alley, a term originating in Von Tilzer's office in about 1908, saw the rise of a new concept in extravaganza—Florenz Ziegfeld's Follies, which were to become a symbol of Broadway glamour in the twenties. Finally, Irving Berlin's (born 1888) huge hit "Alexander's Ragtime Band" (1911) added still another category, ragtime tunes, to the Broadway scene.

Parlor songs were flourishing as well and included sentimental songs, popular settings of Negro spirituals, a few Western folk songs, and some folklike songs such as "Casey Jones" (1909). The late Romantic concert song was represented by the works of Carrie Jacobs Bond (1862–1946), for which she was poet as well as composer—"I Love You Truly" (1901) and "Perfect Day" (1910). And the guitar and banjo were also important; the *Comprehensive Method for the Guitar* (1874), by Justin Holland, was still a best seller.

Perhaps the most creative proponents of the old style were Negro composers, such as Burleigh, for whom the Romantic ideal was still fresh, who took Dvořák's advice to heart, and who could succeed because the Negro idiom was no "masquerade" for them. These composers were not ragtime musicians but men educated in music theory by German-trained conservatory professors. Their aim was to bring certain idioms of the Negro art into the mainstream of music by utilizing tunes within the Romantic forms and organizing them through Romantic techniques. One of the prominent men in this group was R. Nathaniel Dett, whose orchestral works, piano pieces, songs, and choral numbers were both popular in general appeal and highly respected by serious musicians.

Representative of Dett's works is "Listen to the Lambs" (1914), which he styled as "A Religious Characteristic in the Form of an Anthem." It is for an eight-part chorus of mixed voices without instruments and is based on a spiritual. The fabric of the anthem is alternation between partial and full choir, between spare and thick chordal deployments, and between chromatic and diatonic usage. The contrasts are heightened not only by immediate juxtaposition but also by exaggeration in each direction. It uses both African and European elements to produce a fabric that the nearly exhausted European tradition alone could not provide. Such works were prophetic. What was intimated in their juxtapositions had already been proclaimed by a group of iconoclasts, and these radicals, who represented a small but noisy minority in the first quarter of the century, would find a larger scope and less strident voice in the second.

❋ *Some Composers in the Beginning of the Twentieth Century*

The separation of composers by the increasing stratification of musical types was most evident in the first decades of the twentieth century. No esthetic consensus was possible and none can be found in the work of a generation that was divided between trying to extend the Romantic past and searching for new techniques and a new esthetic. In the long transition, this generation was dominated by the conservatives.

GIACOMO PUCCINI (1858–1924), an Italian trained in Lucca and Milan, was an opera composer. He was successful in Italy with *Le Villi* (1884) and internationally with *Manon Lescaut* (Turin, 1893; London and Philadelphia, 1894; New York, 1898), *La Bohème* (Turin, 1896; London and Los Angeles, 1897; New York, 1898; Paris, 1900), *Tosca* (Rome and London, 1900; New York, 1901; Paris, 1903), and, above all, *Madama Butterfly* (Milan, 1904; London, 1905; New York, 1907). After seeing *The Girl of the Golden West*, a play by David Belasco, Puccini had an Italian libretto made; his opera, titled *La Fanciulla del West*, opened in New York in 1910 (London and Rome, 1911). Although Puccini's fame rests on these and other operas, he also wrote a choral Mass, an orchestral work called *Capriccio Sinfonico*, and some chamber music.

VICTOR HERBERT (1859–1924), an Irish cellist, studied in Germany and joined a Viennese waltz ensemble in 1880. He married a Viennese opera singer and they emigrated to New York, where he joined the Metropolitan Opera orchestra and began a remarkable career in the popular theater. Although he composed instrumental works (such as cello concertos), his 48 operas were the basis of his fame. They include *Babes in Toyland* (1903), *Mlle. Modiste* (1905), *The Red Mill* (1906), *Naughty Marietta* (1910), *Sweethearts* (1913), and *Princess Pat* (1915). Herbert was one of the founders of ASCAP and, from 1898 to 1904, was conductor of the Pittsburgh Symphony Orchestra.

GUSTAV MAHLER (1860–1911), a Bohemian conductor and composer, studied with Bruckner in Vienna, serving as conductor at the opera from 1897 to 1907. He was a great symphonist; all his works were characterized by largeness of size and concept, and of his 10 symphonies, 5 include voices. *Das Lied von der Erde* (Song of the Earth; Munich, 1911; London, 1913; Philadelphia, 1916), a song cycle on a German translation of eighth- and ninth-century Chinese poems, for tenor and contralto with orchestra, is considered his greatest work, but the early song cycles with orchestra, though shorter, were equally renowned.

EDWARD MACDOWELL (1861–1908), an American pianist and composer, was the son of a well-to-do businessman in New York City. He was sent to Europe to study when he was fifteen and stayed there twelve years, returning briefly at twenty-three to marry. He settled in Boston in 1888, where he performed and composed. In 1896 he was appointed to the new chair in music at Columbia University, where he remained until 1904. His works included 2 piano concertos, 4 sonatas, and several volumes of piano music. His orchestral suites and tone poems included *Lancelot and Elaine*, *The Saracens*, and *Hamlet and Ophelia*, as well as the *Indian Suite*. He wrote many characteristic piano pieces; "To a Wild Rose," from *Woodland Sketches*, was probably the most popular of his works. He also wrote about 40 songs, most of them on sentimental Romantic lyrics.

CLAUDE ACHILLE DEBUSSY (1862–1918), a student at the Paris Conservatoire from 1874, won the Prix de Rome in 1884. In 1894, he produced the *Prélude à "l'Après-Midi d'un Faune"* (Prelude to "The Afternoon of a Faun," a poem by Mallarmé), which pulled Debussy to the forefront of critical controversy. He was equally famous for his large output of piano works and for his tone poems. The former included 2 "Arabesques" (1888), *Suite Bergamasque* (1890), *Images* (1905 and 1907), *Children's Corner* (1908), *Préludes*, and *Etudes*. The latter include *La Mer*, 3 symphonic sketches (1905), and *Nocturnes*, 3 orchestral pieces—"Nuages" (Clouds), "Fêtes" (Festivals), and "Sirènes" (Sirens), the last with women's voices. In 1912 his ballet *Jeux* was produced at the Ballets Russes. But he also wrote 60 songs, a substantial amount of chamber music, and an opera, *Pelléas et Mélisande* (to a libretto by Maeterlinck, 1902), that used a thoroughly French fabric with Wagner's ideal of infinite harmony.

RICHARD STRAUSS (1864–1949) was a Bavarian composer and conductor known as a follower of Wagner but had both songs and tone poems (most of them early) to his credit as well as operas. Strauss wrote on Medieval, Romantic, and personal subjects, including *Till Eulenspiegels lustige Streiche* (Till Eulenspiegel's Merry Pranks, 1895), *Don Juan* (1888), *Death and Transfiguration* (1889), *The Domestic Symphony* (1903), and the autobiographical *Ein Heldenleben* (A Hero's Life, 1899). The first of the post-Freudian opera composers, he shocked Europe and America with *Salome* (on Oscar Wilde's play, 1905) and *Elektra* (1909), charmed them with *Der Rosenkavalier* (The Knight of the Rose; Dresden, 1911; London and New York, 1913), and educated them in new chamber-orchestra techniques in *Ariadne auf Naxos* (1912).

SAMUEL COLERIDGE-TAYLOR (1875–1912), a London-born son of a Negro doctor, was known as a violinist when still a boy, won a composition scholarship at the Royal Academy in 1893, and by the time he was twenty-three was a violin teacher there. In 1898 his orchestral *Ballade* was performed at the Gloucester Festival, and from 1904 he was the conductor of the London Handel Society. Coleridge-Taylor's success was based on his 8 oratorios, but he also wrote 2 operas, 2 operettas, 12 orchestral works, songs, 1 choral rhapsody (*Sea Drift*, on a Whitman text), anthems, songs with orchestra, and piano works. His most famous work was a trilogy of oratorios on Longfellow's *Song of Hiawatha*—*Hiawatha's Wedding Feast* (1898), *The Death of Minnehaha* (1899), and *Hiawatha's Departure* (1900). The trilogy was performed in Washington, D. C., in 1904, with the composer conducting. He used Negro tunes in several works—*African Suite*, *Symphonic Variations on an African Air*, and others. In 1905 he published *Twenty-Four Negro Melodies* for piano.

SCOTT JOPLIN (1868–1917), an American Negro pianist and composer, was an important artist of the ragtime style. Starred at the Chicago World's Fair of 1893, he was a huge success. His rags included *Easy Winner* (1901), *Original Rag*, *Shadow Rag Wall Street*, and, his most famous, *Maple Leaf Rag* (1899). His ragtime operas, *A Guest of Honor* (St. Louis, 1903) and *Treemonisha* (New York, 1911), though little known to the general public, exerted strong influence on jazz composers. Joplin also wrote 6 piano studies of considerable difficulty, called *The School of Ragtime* (1908).

RALPH VAUGHAN WILLIAMS (1872–1958), an English composer educated in Germany and France, collected folk songs and worked with Renaissance music as a young man; he devoted his career to developing an English idiom based on both forms. A versatile and vigorous composer, Williams produced 9 symphonies, choral works, 7 operas, several ballets, and masques, a long list of chamber works, and numerous songs and settings of folk tunes. *On Wenlock Edge*, for voice, string quartet, and piano (1909), *Three Norfolk Rhapsodies* (1906 and 1907), *Fantasia on a Theme by Tallis*, for string orchestra (1910), and the ballad opera *Hugh The Drover* (completed in 1914 and produced in 1924) were popular examples of the national style.

MAURICE RAVEL (1875–1937), a French composer, was known for his piano music and his orchestral style. He turned to the Medieval-Renaissance and to the Spanish idiom for materials, becoming popular through his piano work on old modal and dance styles, the *Pavane pour une Infante défunte* (1899). His work, in addition to a substantial number of piano and chamber works, included ballets, a lyric fantasy *L'Enfant et les sortilèges* (The Child and the Charms, on a libretto by Colette, 1925), and many songs. In addition, he orchestrated Mussorgsky's *Pictures at an Exhibition* (1922). The famed *Bolero* was written for a dance recital in 1928.

R. NATHANIEL DETT (1882–1943), a Quebec-born Negro composer and director, came to the United States, received a degree from the Oberlin Conservatory in 1908, and continued his studies at Columbia, Harvard, Eastman, and Howard. Thoroughly trained in the Romantic tradition, Dett was active in church music, choir settings of spirituals, and piano music. His early successes were the *Magnolia Suite* (1911) and *In the Bottoms Suite* (1913), both for piano. The latter contained the "Juba Dance," which became extremely popular. He was respected in many quarters and led an active career in the United States and abroad.

IGOR STRAVINSKY (born 1882), a Russian-born composer who studied with Rimsky-Korsakov, entered the Paris scene in 1910 and wrote for the Ballets Russes. He became a naturalized French citizen in 1934 but later (1945) became a citizen of the United States. His early ballets made him famous; they included *l'Oiseau de feu* (Fire Bird, 1910), *Petrouchka* (1911), and *Le Sacre du printemps* (The Rite of Spring, 1913). In the 1920s he turned to smaller ensembles and to seventeenth- and eighteenth-century style with such works as the ballet *Apollon Musagète* (Apollo, Chief of the Muses, 1927) and the opera *The Rake's Progress* (Venice, 1951). Stravinsky also used the ragtime and jazz idioms very early in their development, contributing to both the post-Freudian and the new religious oratorio with *Oedipus Rex* (1927) and the *Symphony of Psalms* (1930), respectively. At the end of a long creative career, he turned to serial techniques with such works as *Septet* (1953) and the ballet *Agon* (1957).

I was born to a world that explained itself
largely in dogmatic terms and I have lived,
through several changes of management, to
a world that rationalizes itself almost entirely in psychoanalytic terms.

IGOR STRAVINSKY *

Between Two Wars

Even before World War I was over, iconoclasts had begun to propound
the antiwar and antiestablishment ideas that were to thrive and become increasingly pervasive in the next generation. They were not opposed merely
to the war—they sought to expose the entire system that had made the war
possible and, in the end, inevitable. Artists were among the earliest to seek
change; they started movements calling for an enlargement of perception
that would prod the viewer and the listener to see and hear in new ways. In
the twenties and thirties, the arts leaned in two directions—the expansion
of *materials*, independent of subject matter and the pursuit of an extreme or
superrealism in a context defined in Freudian terms, that is, surrealism.

26

* 1963. Quoted in Elliott Schwartz and Barney Childs (eds.), *Contemporary Composers
on Contemporary Music*, New York: Holt, 1967, p. 52.

As before, Paris was a chief center of ferment, and manifestos issued from the French capital with amazing frequency. The period between the wars saw the establishment of an even greater number of "isms" than the period before. Of particular importance to music were the following:

> *Dadaism* was a postwar protest movement, nihilistic yet playful (*dada* is French nursery talk for a "hobbyhorse"). It used non-art, non-sense, and intermedia absurdities with boundless zest and imagination. The Dadaists had no technique but the irreverent, the unexpected, and the unfettered; they used irrational juxtapositions and chance factors. Their sometimes elaborate staging of multimedia nonperformances kept them in the public eye.
>
> *Surrealism,* a French movement founded in 1924, was an offshoot of Freudian ideas seeking to involve the unconscious life through incongruous, dreamlike juxtaposition. The Spanish painter Salvador Dali (born 1904) was probably its most famous exponent. The movement was related to a general interest in fantasy, both abstract, as depicted by Paul Klee (1879–1940), and representational, as depicted by Marc Chagall (born 1887). Works depicting juxtapositions of the two sought to transcend perception and, particularly, time.
>
> *Imagism* was a literary, particularly poetic movement that sought to do away with symbolism and to replace it with a series of separate, literal images that would produce effects through clarity and juxtaposition; it was presented most often in free verse.
>
> *Existentialism* was a philosophical and literary movement. In philosophy it proclaimed an identity between external and internal reality, and in literature it perceived experience as separate moments having no purpose or connection.

Music reflected the new ideas. Traditionalists were seeking change, mild or radical, *within* the Romantic ideal; iconoclasts were attempting to root out the assumptions of the Romantic traditions, with varying types and degrees of acknowledgment to the heritage of the past. However, although the iconoclasts had begun their work before the end of the nineteenth century, they had only limited influence on the main stream until the period between the wars.

SEEDS OF CHANGE

At the beginning of the twentieth century, composers had been concerned with revising certain facets of their techniques rather than founding an esthetic basically different from the established approach. Debussy had experimented with harmonic entities that were conceived as harmonic colors separated from tonal function. But more radical composers had also been at work. They carried the experiments farther, using structures built on fourths instead of thirds, experimenting with microtonal (quarter-step, sixth-step, or even smaller) intervals, or basing their compositions on the belief that the traditional (triadic) relationships of pitch levels were irrelevant. The composers following the latter route tried to do away with regulating pitch relationships altogether, generally in connection with experiments in timbre. Anton Webern's *Fünf Sätze für Streichquartett* (Five Movements for String Quartet, 1909), for example, had sought new sounds rather than new chords or new progressions, sonorities rather than harmonies. It was an investigation into the totality of the string quartet as four idiomatic instruments, exploiting natural but previously unexplored effects of the orchestral strings. The work necessitated playing with the wood of the bow, bowing at the bridge,

Fünf Sätze für Streichquartett   Example 81

ANTON WEBERN

This is the beginning of the fourth movement, which concludes in four more measures. (Courtesy of the Theodore Presser Company.)

hitting the side of the instrument with the bow, and using the high tessitura of the instrument in harmonic tones, tones without vibrato, and so on.

Arnold Schoenberg had worked to include the human voice in the redefinition of sonority. He proposed a style of singing (or nonsinging) that was in essence dramatic; it was a heightened speech that added inflection and projection rather than pitch and melody to the text, resulting in a musically filtered recitation rather than a song. Schoenberg incorporated his ideas into a song cycle, which he called *Three Times Seven Poems from Albert Giraud's Pierrot Lunaire* (moonstruck Pierrot); it was composed to a German translation by Otto Hartleben and was first performed in 1912. The poems dated from 1884 and were pre-Freudian symbolist evocations using the Romantic Pierrot, who "paints his face in a style sublime with a single fantastic moonbeam" and sees the moon as a "gleaming scimitar" that decapitates him.[1] The voice, combined with violin, viola, cello, flute, piccolo, clarinet, bass clarinet, and piano in varying (but never total) combinations, was used as part of a complete concept of evocative sound that strongly paralleled that of the poems. Schoenberg called for the use of the *Sprechstimme* ("speaking voice") and furnished a notation that specified shape and rhythm but not the pitches of the vocal line. He instructed the reciter, in part:

> The melody indicated for the speaking voice by notes (apart from a few specially indicated exceptions) is not meant to be sung. The rhythm [but not the intonation] must be kept absolutely strict, . . . whereas the sung note preserves the pitch, the spoken gives it at first, but abandons it either by rising or by falling immediately after.[2]

The musicians of the avant-garde were trying to get people to use their ears in new ways. The emphasis was shifting away from the work of art, with unity and variety supplied by a creative master, toward the *perception* of the work of art, involving revelation to the perceiver.

The one agreement in all the arts was the need for expanded perception. "Surprise Me!"[3] Diaghilev said in giving instruction to his artists, and D. W. Griffith, an early artist of the motion picture, summed it up, "The task I'm trying to achieve is above all to make you see."[4] Artists in fields other than music found it easier to cast off the traditional views about music, because they had not served a musical apprenticeship within those views. In 1913, an Italian painter in Paris issued a manifesto titled *The Art of Noises*. He suggested a classification of sounds by type rather than pitch.

[1] Arnold Schoenberg, *Pierrot Lunaire*, Los Angeles, Calif.: Belmont Music Publishers, 1912, pp. 29–30. (Trans. by Louise E. Cuyler.)
[2] Quoted in Frederick Dorian, *The History of Music in Performance*, New York: Norton, 1942, pp. 333–334.
[3] Quoted in Walter Sorell, *The Dance through the Ages*, New York: Grosset & Dunlap, 1967, p. 171.
[4] Quoted in Daniel S. Davis, "On Film," *New York Times Magazine*, Sept. 13, 1964, p. 60.

ARNOLD SCHOENBERG

From *Pierrot Lunaire*, opus 21 (1914). (Courtesy of Belmont Music Publishers.)

Group 1: Booms, Thunder claps, Explosions, Crashes, Splashes, [and] Roars.

Group 2: Whistles, Hisses, [and] Snorts.

Group 3: Whispers, Murmurs, Mutterings, Bustling noises, [and] Gurgles.

Group 4: Screams, Screeches, Rustlings, Buzzes, Cracklings, [and] Sounds by friction.

Group 5: Noises obtained by percussion or metals, wood, stone, and terracotta.

Group 6: Voices of animals, men; Shouts, Shrieks, Groans, Howls, Laughs, Wheezes, [and] Sobs.[5]

The Dadaists carried the musical parallels into their programs of combined art forms; they saw juxtaposition as a means of educating in perception. Henri Bergson (1859–1941), a philosopher, wrote that "diverse images, borrowed from very different orders of things, may, by the convergence of their action, direct the consciousness to the precise point at which intuition can be grasped." [6] Kurt Schwitters (1887–1948), a German Dadaist, conceived a new art form, which he named *Merz.* (The name came from a syllable he had chosen at random from a newspaper headline to paste onto one of his early canvasses.) Schwitters's technique consisted of making up a long list of random objects and then creating a work of art from them. In his article "Merz" (1921), he included such a list and described his procedure.

> Now begin to wed your materials to one another. For example, you marry the oilcloth table cover to the Home Owner's Loan Association, you bring the lamp cleaner into a relationship with the marriage between Anna Blume and A-natural, concert pitch. . . .
> And now begins the fire of musical saturation. Organs backstage sing and say: "Futt, futt." The sewing machine rattles along in the lead. A man in the wings says "Bah." Another suddenly enters and says: "I am stupid." . . . Between them a clergyman kneels upside down and cries out and prays in a loud voice: "Oh mercy seethe and swarm disintegration of amazement Hallelujah boy, boy marry drop of water." A water pipe drips uninhibited monotony.[7]

A critic of Merz coined the word *Gesamtkunstmerz* [8] in a genial comparison with Wagner's ideal of the collective work of art, but the difference between Wagner and Schwitters was crucial. Wagner's work existed by itself, complete as Wagner produced it, whereas Schwitters's Merz was intended to be completed and invested with meaning by the perceiver.

Traditionalists still defined music as a combination of theme, harmony, and measured rhythm. A leading music appreciation text of 1896 stated that the "three elements on which music rests [are] Melody, Harmony, and Rhythm. The life-blood of music is Melody. . . . The fundamental principle of Form is repetition of melodies, which are to music what ideas are to poetry." [9] But modernist composers were sure that the old esthetic was

---

[5] Quoted in Elliott Schwartz and Barney Childs (eds.), *Contemporary Composers on Contemporary Music,* New York: Holt, 1967, p. 255.

[6] Quoted in Roger Shattuck, *The Banquet Years,* Garden City, N.Y.: Anchor Books, Doubleday & Company, Inc., 1955, p. 342.

[7] Quoted in William S. Rubin, *Dada, Surrealism, and Their Heritage,* New York: Museum of Modern Art, 1968, p. 57f.

[8] Rubin, in *ibid.,* p. 59.

[9] Henry Edward Krehbiel, quoted in Leroy Ostransky, *Perspectives on Music,* Englewood Cliffs, N.J.: Prentice-Hall, 1963, pp. 33–34.

used up; the assumptions of Romanticism had lost so much of their tension that they had become flaccid metaphors. "If Man is the tonic and God the dominant," Samuel Butler had written, "the Devil is certainly the subdominant and Woman the relative minor." [10] Schumann had said, "I would not like being understood by everyone," [11] but that was exactly the fate to which the Romantics had been subjected. Sifted, analyzed, and codified, they had been robbed of their essential mystery.

Theorists and teachers, convinced of their authority and of the essential, permanent craft of which they were custodians, found the modernists mischievous, recalcitrant, anarchistic. In 1898, a theorist-teacher threw up his hands at increasing chromaticism, "From continually shifting key, music may get to such a persistently enharmonic condition as to be never at any moment in less than two keys at once, and hence *in no key at all!*" [12] Theorists were further frustrated by the failure of musical facts to conform to the evolutionary concept. They saw Baroque monody as primitive two-part harmony leading, through the three-part structure of the trio sonata, to the ultimate four-part ideal. (The Medieval-Renaissance developments were unknown or discounted.) But attempting to view Haydn and Mozart, for example, as links in this harmonic evolution led to frustration for men such as Coerne.

> In [Baroque] three-part writing, not only the violoncellos and basses progressed simultaneously in unison or octaves, but also the viola, if present, reënforced the bass in slavish delineation. It is obvious that this practice was the result either of sophism or of indifference and ignorance. And the fact that as late as the eighteenth century no less a composer than Haydn or even Mozart should have continued frequently to employ three-part writing for the strings is certainly a paradox and tends to prove how circuitous the process of evolution is.[13]

Performers were in a predicament. Trained specifically in the virtuoso style of the late Romantic ideal, they could either remain with the Romantic literature, join one of the modernist camps, or turn to the past in a revival of pre-Romantic performing techniques. Most performers chose the first alternative, which led to a separation between the arts of composition and performance.

The public was confused, but an audience was growing that appreciated a variety of musical experiences. A perceptive man could enjoy grand opera on a Wednesday and a popular musical on Saturday, play in a recorder club on Monday, sing Gregorian chant in his church choir on Sunday, and then come home and listen to a jazz record.

[10] Quoted in Eric Blom, *The Music Lover's Miscellany*, London: Gollancz, 1935, p. 611.

[11] Quoted in Paul Henry Lang, *Music in Western Civilization*, New York: Norton, 1941, p. 809.

[12] William Foster Apthorp, quoted in Jacques Barzun, *Pleasures of Music*, New York: The Viking Press, Inc., 1951, p. 607.

[13] Quoted in Ostransky, *op. cit.*, p. 55.

A PERIOD OF TRANSITION

Composers between the wars were involved in a confusion of musical vocabulary and techniques. As in other transitional periods, the cutting edge comprised the rejection of those elements of the past that were no longer fruitful, a maintenance of those elements still viable, and the infusion of new elements from outside the musical art that reflected current cultural interests.

The primary element to be rejected was the harmonic system—the whole Romantic triangle of theme and harmony regulated by meter. But different composers found different approaches to rejection.

Rejection

The French dealt with modalism, neo-Classicism, extended tonality, and primitivism, as well as post-Romanticism and Impressionism. They formed groups—Les Six, The Arceuil Group, La Jeune France. Les Six, which embraced a conscious, systematic eclecticism, had among its members Francis Poulenc and Darius Milhaud. Poulenc was influenced by Stravinsky and also very strongly by Cocteau. Speaking of music hall tunes, Cocteau told Poulenc that to write a good tune, "You must make it well, but rotten." [14] Poulenc was much involved with painters and theater artists—his *Mouvements perpetuels* for piano were performed at "painting and music concerts." Yet he called Mozart's *Jupiter* Symphony "the summit of music" and advised examination of the score "to relish the interlacings." [15] As late as 1952, he advised a student to "listen to all music without prejudice, and study it deeply." [16] The Arceuil Group moved toward simplicity, and La Jeune France, in a reaction against abstractionism, felt that "the mission of the musical art is humane and religious"—a concept that would be potent in the new music.

The Germans developed the new theories of pitch relations that were to dominate musical thought. Paul Hindemith's theory of consonance and dissonance (*The Craft of Musical Composition*, 1937) expanded the traditional concept of structure. In the symbolistic theory of chord relationships proposed in the preface to his song cycle *Das Marienleben*, he assigned literary meaning to each tone and then activated chordal progression by a logic of verbal allusion.

But the most famous and long-lived Germanic theory of pitch relation was that of Arnold Schoenberg. In 1908, Schoenberg gave up the use of key signatures, and from 1924 he wrote in the technique for which he is known.

[14] Quoted in an anonymous review of *Francis Poulenc: Correspondance, 1915–1963, Times Literary Supplement*, Jan. 18, 1968, p. 84.
[15] *Ibid.*
[16] Letter to Edith Borroff, Feb. 16, 1952.

He proposed that the twelve tones of the equal-tempered scale should be used with equal favor and instituted a system of pitch organization in which the twelve pitches could be assured equal favor by being used in a consistent order. An arbitrary listing of the twelve tones, called a *Reihe* ("row") or *series*, formed a structural basis; used either in order, in inversion, in retrograde, in retrograde inversion, or in any of these forms transposed, the series assured the use of each pitch as often as every other. Schoenberg drew adherents, students, and disciples mostly from the younger generation, and the twelve-tone technique was ramified in their works into as many means as there were exponents. Webern and Berg became serialists, and analytical systems arose to explain the workings of serial structure. In addition to serialism, Schoenberg and his followers were associated with *expressionism* and, in spite of Schoenberg's objection, with *atonality*.

Other composers were dealing with other techniques, and those who were neither French nor German were more likely to combine techniques. Stravinsky himself conducted a one-man exploration of new means within the old triangle. The many names of techniques attest to the inventiveness of the generation—nonserial atonality, panchromaticism, pointillism, pandiatonicism, bichordalism, bitonality, polytonality, pantonality.

A strong return to folk traditions provided materials for some composers who were counterreacting to serial techniques. Americans turned to the folk music of the frontier—of the barn dance, hoe-down, and lonely open spaces. Aaron Copland was the chief proponent of this new folk tradition, and his greatest successes in it were his ballets *Billy The Kid* (1938) and *Rodeo* (1942). Originally written for theater orchestras, they were later reorchestrated for symphonic performance.

The chamber orchestra helped clarify the musical elements of the new style. Many modernist composers were turning to smaller groups that could use the voice, often a solo, as a member. In these groups, the new techniques could be sharply etched and clearly perceived.

In addition to the modernist experiments with small groups, the traditional mediums were still popular. The symphony orchestra continued to enjoy top prestige, though with an ever-shrinking body of new works. But from the 1930s to the 1970s, orchestra conductors have witnessed a gradual decline in support for this Romantic medium. Composers have been working with new mediums, since fewer and fewer of them are able to find life in orchestral forms, and to conductors it has seemed that the whole art of composition is in decline.

Maintenance—

Traditional Mediums

The ideal orchestra had been defined at various stages of its life, most recently in the last quarter of the nineteenth century. The New York Philharmonic and the Bayreuth Festspielhaus orchestras represented the Romantic goals of valid generality and Wagnerian particularity.

In 1961, over 1,150 orchestras were listed for the United States (35 in Canada) by the American Symphony Orchestra League, and about 800 of

New York Philharmonic
in 1896

69 strings
 18 first violins
 17 second violins
 13 violas
 14 cellos
  7 double basses
3 flutes
3 oboes
3 clarinets
3 bassoons
4 horns
3 cornets
4 trombones
1 tuba
1 timpanist with 3 timpani
1 percussionist with bass drum, snare drum, and triangle
1 harp
——
96

Bayreuth Festspielhaus Orchestra
in 1876

64 strings
 16 first violins
 16 second violins
 12 violas
 12 cellos
  8 double basses
3 flutes
3 oboes
1 English horn
3 clarinets
1 basset horn
3 bassoons
8 horns
3 trumpets
3 trombones
1 bass trumpet
2 tenor tubas
2 bass tubas
1 contrabass trombone
1 contrabass tuba
2 pairs of timpani
1 cymbals
1 bass drum
6 harps
——
109

Seating plan of the New York Philharmonic Orchestra, 1896. (Courtesy of Charles Scribner's Sons.)

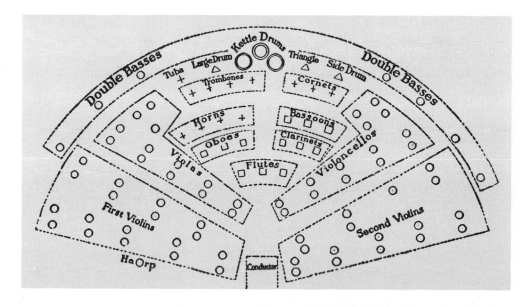

these were classified as "community" orchestras, which were replacing town bands in popularity. Only in the high school and on the football field did the band maintain sovereignty.

Grand opera was less fortunate. The Chicago Civic Opera flourished through the twenties only to perish in 1932 in the Depression. But others, such as the San Francisco Opera, survived. European opera was state supported and tended to continue in traditional practice. In 1934 John Christie founded a Festival Theatre for opera at his estate at Glyndebourne, England, and in 1954, after the death of his wife (the singer Audrey Mildmay), gave the property to the Glyndebourne Arts Trust Ltd.

But modernists were presenting new operas. Alban Berg's twelve-tone and, in part, serial opera *Wozzeck* was performed in Berlin in 1925 and Philadelphia in 1931. Schoenberg's short work *Die Glückliche Hand* (The Lucky Hand, composed in 1913), which used pantomime and color play as well as dramatic action and singing, was performed in Vienna in 1924 and Philadelphia in 1930.

In the United States in the 1930s, the Works Progress Administration subsidized musical, dramatic, and operatic projects, emphasizing the training of young professionals. Movies brought scenes of opera or orchestra to millions—a *Tosca* scene in *Here's to Romance* (1935), Jeannette MacDonald and Nelson Eddy in Herbert's *Naughty Marietta* (1935), and Deanna Durbin singing with a symphony orchestra conducted by Leopold Stokowski in *One Hundred Men and a Girl* (1937). But in the years between the wars, music prospered most in the popular theater.

The inventions of instruments comprised a significant infusion of the cultural concerns of the time, giving to the art of music an array of new timbres and instrumental techniques.

Infusion— New Instrumental Sounds

The modernists of the twenties and thirties were emphasizing percussion instruments, because these instruments could produce incisive rhythmic effects and because their sounds tended to the mysteries of exoticism and unplumbed resonance. In 1926, Edgard Varèse completed *Ionisation,* a work for about forty percussion instruments played by thirteen players. The instruments included several kinds of drums, cymbals, and less usual but not unprecedented instruments such as the anvil and whip; however, it also introduced the maracas and guiro (Brazilian gourd scraper), two sirens, and the piano played with the forearm.

Other men were inventing new mechanisms, especially electric and electronic instruments. The early ones were electrophonic and electromagnetic, made possible by the invention of the rotating electromagnetic generator in 1897. The telharmonium (1906) was an electromechanical instrument whose tone was created by these generators. The choralcelo was an instrument of variable units—hard wood, soft wood, aluminum bars, glass, and piano strings, plus a bass of buggy springs—all used as natural sounding bodies. These were activated by magnets tuned to their frequencies and placed near but not on them, causing the bodies to vibrate instantaneously upon electrical stimulation of their individual magnets via a keyboard. In addition, it was possible to alter the spectrum of partials to create timbres as yet unheard. The sounding of wood bars and piano strings without initial percussion, particularly the sustaining of these tones, was also a new effect. This instrument was featured in concerts from 1919 to 1923.

In 1927 the first public demonstrations of the theremin, invented by a Russian astronomer, were given in Europe. In 1930 the inventor presented his instruments in Carnegie Hall, and two years later produced an "electrical symphony orchestra" concert. The instrument's tone was generated by two supersonic oscillators, one of fixed and one of variable frequency. It produced resultant or different tones, one pitch at a time, which the performer could change by means of a projecting metal rod that controlled the variable frequency. The ondes martenot (1928), whose tone was generated by one fixed and one variable radio frequency oscillator, was similar.

Electrophonic organs, whose tone is generated by electronic circuits, have been manufactured since about 1930. The aim has been to duplicate the sounds of the pipe organ and compete with that instrument through smaller size and lower cost. Many of these organs have been made in Europe and America.

Harry Partch (born 1901) was building an array of instruments, which could produce not only new sounds but new scales. These included an adapted cello (with brads for thirty-seven notes to the octave, 1928), a huge kithara (about 6 feet tall, with seventy-two strings tuned variously, 1938 to 1943), and adapted guitars (1935 to 1953, one with six strings tuned in unison). Partch favored a scale of forty-three tones to the octave, which he derived from American and Oriental speech patterns.

By World War II, a great variety of new sounds had entered the musical potential through the experiments of modernists and traditionalists alike. Some of the most important sounds of the period were created in the popular art, which was thriving.

ROARING TWENTIES
AND DEPRESSION THIRTIES

With the emergence of jazz on the national scene, the advent of prohibition, and the rise of the speakeasy, the postwar generation, with energy and free-wheeling insouciance, created the Roaring Twenties. It was characterized by its music as strongly as any short period in history: high society frequented the Diamond Horseshoe of the Metropolitan Opera, the flapper did the Charleston at the dance hall, and everyone listened to the new jazz artists, idealized the stars of the Ziegfeld Follies, and went to the movies on Saturday nights.

The 1930s began with a crash—the stockmarket crash of October, 1929. Everyone was suddenly plunged into a long, deep poverty that would be a crucial factor in shaping the next generation. The Great Depression was worldwide, and the reversal of man's progress completed his disenchantment with the Romantic view of European civilization.

The Roaring Twenties was a decade of theater, and New York City was its world capital. The peak year was 1927, when 268 productions opened in legitimate theaters in the small Manhattan district called "Broadway," and vaudeville and burlesque shows made the number even higher. There was tremendous variety—Max Reinhardt brought his German company to New York and produced *Everyman* and there were new productions of Shaw's *The Doctor's Dilemma*, with Alfred Lunt and Lynn Fontanne, Sullivan's *The Mikado*, and Shakespeare's *Midsummer Night's Dream*.

Musical Theater

Musical theater was also flourishing. Over fifty new musical shows were introduced in 1927 alone, and the songwriters made up an energetic and gifted group. But in the 1930s the number dwindled, and the costs of production kept it down to around a dozen a year after 1933. The trend toward genuine dramatic content was clear in Jerome Kern's *Show Boat* (1927), and social commentary became strong in Gershwin's *Of Thee I Sing* (1932), the first musical to get a Pulitzer Prize. Other shows commented on the Depression and dispensed with the Romantic operetta world. Some went so far as using an unpleasant protagonist in an unpleasant story (e.g., *Pal Joey*, by Richard Rodgers, 1940) or introducing dreams in a psychoanalytical context (Kurt Weill's *Lady in the Dark*, 1941). Such a musical production was not a show; and it was less a musical comedy (the name in the early 1930s) than a musical play.

Negro shows were infused with new life by the jazz idiom, which was tremendously popular in New York. *Shuffle Along* (1921), which starred its composers, Noble Sissle and Eubie Blake, was the first of an increasingly rich vein of Negro shows, which comprised a new style more than a new form. Lew Leslie's *Blackbirds* (annually from 1927 to 1930) introduced such stars as Josephine Baker, Bill Robinson, and Ethel Waters. The musical play turned to the Negro when DuBose Heyward made a libretto from his play *Porgy* and Gershwin composed an opera, *Porgy and Bess* (1935), upon it. Because both its subject and musical tradition were outside the operatic hierarchy, Gershwin's work was too distant from tradition to be honored as an opera and was produced as a musical show instead. It was only in 1955, during a European tour, that the work was given its due; it received a "tumultuous reception" in Moscow.[17]

An important Negro-jazz type of music before and during World War II was the modernized version of a standard work. In 1939 two versions of

[17] Arnold Shaw, "Popular Music from Minstrel Songs to Rock 'n' Roll," in Paul Henry Lang (ed.), *One Hundred Years of Music in America*, New York: Schirmer, 1961, p. 168.

Sullivan's *The Mikado* were produced—*The Swing Mikado* and *The Hot Mikado*. The latter, which starred Bill Robinson, was the hit of the New York World's Fair. In 1943 Bizet's *Carmen* was transformed, in a lavish production by Billy Rose, into *Carmen Jones* and was a great hit.

A few original musicals for Negro stars also were composed. Vernon Duke's *Cabin in The Sky* (1940), with Ethel Waters and Rex Ingram, and *Carib Song* (1945), by Baldwin Bergersen and starring Catherine Dunham, were notable.

On the whole, musicals reflected times and trends and served to synthesize rather than innovate. The Romantic operetta yielded to the *revue*, which dominated the 1920s. Often a topical and unified variety show, the revue drew talent from vaudeville and burlesque. New shows frequently were produced annually, and the most successful, such as the Ziegfeld Follies and the George White Scandals, appeared year after year. Lavish, constantly changing, they featured individual and team acts put together into a set of contrasting types—singers, solo and chorus-like dancers, comedians (solo and team), and specialty acts including everything from magicians to dog acts. The revue was basically the minstrel show's second part (olio) and generally ended with a walk-around—a parade of girls with rich costumes, in the tradition of the spectacular. Ziegfeld specialized in a grand finale during which girls would slowly descend a staircase wearing sequined and feather costumes that featured huge hats.

Virtually all the acts used music, and show songs of the 1920s were the hit songs of the period. But revues were generally assembled quickly. The musical score comprised tunes that were often from several composers, and songs were expanded into dance numbers by specialists. The total was thus a composite of musical skills as well as of tunes.

The revue, in turn, yielded to the musical comedy and the musical play, in which dramatic action was seriously developed and the musical numbers worked in as the drama suggested. The chorus line gave way to ballet, and the role of the star changed. The star of a revue had had only to sing; the star of the musical play had to sing, act, and, hopefully, dance.

Radio

Radio's heyday was from 1930 to 1945. It was the perfect medium for the Depression, serving as an inexpensive entertainment and a cohesive force, uniting the nation in the prewar and war years. The first part of the minstrel show, a mixture of song and comic dialogue, became the basic format for radio shows. Bob Hope's weekly program was representative. A half-hour long, it included an opening monologue, comic dialogue, musical numbers, a guest spot, and an afterpiece. The latter was a tune, Robin and Rainger's "Thanks for the Memory" (from a 1938 movie). New words were written for it each week, and it became Hope's theme song. The show's format was lively, varied, and versatile, and it lasted through World War II.

In addition to the longer format, producers developed a number of short show types, notably soap operas and children's adventure serials, to serve daytime audiences. Generally, these shows lasted fifteen minutes and were aired five days a week; they inaugurated a new way of using sound that would be crucial to the new music.

A *theme song*, always the same and generally a recording, served as an identifying introduction. *Musical interludes* were used to connect sections of dialogue and to announce changes of scene by setting the mood—they were provided by an organist-composer, who used a separate microphone. And, to provide aural illusion, *sound effects* were used. These consisted of recordings of characteristic noises (crickets, rain, thunder); props, such as a door in a frame for opening, closing, and squeaking; door and telephone bells; and special-effects devices, such as suspended wood blocks, which could be lifted and dropped rhythmically to suggest marching feet, or a piece of cellophane, which, when slowly crinkled, simulated the sound of frying eggs. The sound-effects men worked from a central position, surrounded by their props, mechanisms, two or more record turntables, and their own microphones. The shows also used *background music* with certain passages of dialogue to enhance the emotion of a particular scene.

Collaboration between the organist-composer and the sound-effects man was vital. The sound effects could pick up rhythmic features from the music, and "the organ could pick up the pitch of a ringing telephone," [18] for example, and give it a musical background that would suggest the emotional implication of the telephone call.

[18] Letter from Marie Baldwin (musician on the "Jack Armstrong" show), June 1, 1969.

A broadcast in progress, 1936. A group of actors is at one microphone, and sound-effects men, using a device to simulate the sound of hoofbeats, are at another. The musicians' microphone, not in the picture, is probably to the right of the sound mike. In the background, the sound engineer is controlling the mix of sounds to create the whole. A large cast would necessitate the use of another mike for actors, and still another mike would be required for the sound men if the script required an unusual number of effects or if recorded sounds were used. (Courtesy of the CBS Radio Network.)

The musical interludes or connecting passages were measured in seconds, generally lasting from five to ten seconds depending on the psychic distance to be bridged. The interlude could be discrete, that is, parenthetical to the script, beginning and ending with autonomous musical elements, or it could rise into prominence from behind the action or fade into the next scene, melting into night sounds, footsteps, or other noises. The length of time for each piece of background music could be even shorter; often it consisted of only a single chord to suggest a sudden realization or to underline an implied action. The shortest was a single accented chord called the *stinger*, which the organist achieved by opening the volume pedal and then playing the chord while closing it quickly. The organist "improvised from the script, working from short melodic, rhythmic, and harmonic units jotted down in musical shorthand." [19]

The broadcast was controlled by the director with gestures very much like those of an orchestra conductor. He created the tempo for all participants, cuing their entries and indicating fades and other interrelations. The *mix* of the sounds of the five or more microphones—two for the actors and announcer, one for the organist, and two for the sound-effects men—was the province of the sound engineer, who created layers of sound by regulating the various elements into foregrounds and backgrounds.

A new reciprocity between music and sound was being developed. It was in the collaboration of the musician, the sound-effects man, and the engineer that early experiments in the new music, which derived specifically from musical and mechanical radio techniques, would take place.

Movies

Movies had sounds similar to those of radio programs, but fewer of them required artificially produced sound effects. The technical process of producing sound in films was the creation of a *sound track*, a band of sound that runs parallel to the picture on the edge of the film strip. Two problems to be dealt with in making a sound track were synchrony and mix. Mix involved essentially the same problems as it did in radio and was handled in essentially the same way. *Synchrony* involved the precise matching of all sound—musical and vocal—with the visual images.

In early sound pictures, independently activated recordings were used, and inevitably there were difficulties in synchrony. But soon the sound equipment was synchronized electrically with the cameras, and a sound track was made by transforming the sound frequencies into light waves running sideways on the film-strip margin. The major disadvantage of the technique was that only frequencies of from 50 to 8,000 vibrations per second could register, whereas human beings can perceive sounds of from about 30 to 12,000 vibrations per second. However, this disadvantage was outweighed by the possibility of achieving exact sound-image synchrony, an innovation that was crucial to the future development of the cinema.

[19] *Ibid.*

Movie composers had to think in both theatrical and musical time. A *bit*, a short piece of stage business, might be as small as a glance and call for a single orchestral sforzando in imitation of the organ's characteristic stinger; an *action sequence,* such as a chase, might consume six minutes and require a complete musical entity in itself. But as the glance might be part of the chase, the chase was also part of the larger rhythm of the entire film, which lasted perhaps ninety minutes. Composers could use the sound track for timing music, cutting the track to synchronize the score precisely with the action. With twenty-four frames per second, time could be measured precisely in inches of track.

The musical score was sometimes written before, sometimes after the filming. In either case, the technique of preparing the sound track involved the *playback* of the music so as to work out exact correspondences. The composer might work out rhythms while the previously filmed images were projected on a screen, or the director might synchronize action while the previously composed music was played in the playback. The final sound track was recorded by a studio orchestra with the conductor facing a large screen (behind the orchestra) on which he saw the action projected and wearing earphones through which he heard the sounds of the action as recorded at the time of filming.

Jazz

The Roaring Twenties were the Golden Age of jazz. Dancing was still essential, and new dances—the shimmy, Charleston, black bottom, rumba—were being continually introduced. A dance critic said that "the twentieth century has rediscovered the body; not since antiquity has it been so loved, felt, and honored"; the generation of the twenties wanted "to exchange stereotyped movement for something genuinely of the soul." [20] Although musicians served as disseminators of jazz techniques, even more important were phonograph records, which made new techniques and sounds available in all areas and at low cost. The years 1926 to 1929 were the great years of jazz recording.

The materials and performance style were those of ragtime, and the bands were small, generally six to ten men. The leader was also a performer, and his personal style, as much as his instrument, characterized his group. King Oliver (1885–1938), a cornet player who left New Orleans for Chicago in 1918, recorded in 1923 with six side men; these included Louis "Satchmo" Armstrong, another New Orleans musician. In 1924 Armstrong moved to the Roseland Ballroom in New York, where he built his own legend as trumpeter, singer (particularly, *scat* singer), and bandleader. In 1926 Jelly Roll Morton was recording in Chicago with a group he called the Red Hot Peppers; the group was representative in that all but one member had been active in New Orleans ragtime.

Jazz was essentially a semiimprovised variation on a preexisting tune. The tunes were based on sixteen-beat rhythmic units, four bars long; each

[20] Curt Sachs, *World History of the Dance,* New York: Norton, 1963, p. 447.

Ferdinand "Jelly Roll" Morton with The Red Hot Peppers, about 1927. (Courtesy of the New Orleans Jazz Museum.)

unit held one phrase of song plus additional open beats as connectives. The structure was tonal and based on an agreed slow-motion harmonic progression, often of the lower and upper dominants and tonic chords.

Two song types flourished. Blues songs were short and were composed of three phrases (twelve bars), most often extended by repetition to thirty-six or forty-eight bars. Basic jazz was longer and was composed of four double phrases with eight bars in each, resulting in an *AABA* thirty-two–bar form, in which *B*, called a *release* or *bridge*, was contrasting material.

Jazz groups assigned the phrases in succession to specific members, using an odd number of soloists to assure an isorhythmic complexity. (Four soloists rotating the phrases in a twelve-bar blues or three soloists alternating on a thirty-two–bar number would never solo twice on the same phrase.) Punctus construction in jazz was basic. The variable elements were the melodic embellishment and the instrumental timbre, whereas the beat, the length of the phrase, and the harmonic progression remained fixed in order to provide the frame for the melodic and rhythmic embellishment of the soloists.

The early blues singers were women—Ma Rainey, Bessie Smith (the "Empress of Blues"), and Ella Fitzgerald (the "First Lady of Song"). They were virtuoso artists of the blues and were important figures in a long and many-faceted heritage. The songs themselves went back to the nineteenth

607

Field Holler   **Example 83**

ANONYMOUS

The descending pattern is characteristic not only of hollers and the blues but also of American Indian music. The notes marked (x) are *blue notes*. (Courtesy of Oak Publications.)

century, to the beginnings of slavery, but Negro field workers in the twentieth century still sang work songs and hollers. (The heritage was old but was constantly being reborn.) The lyric was central to blues, and a blues man, like a Medieval minstrel, was actually singing his poem.

Son House's *Depot Blues* (recorded in 1942), which was a twelve-bar blues with guitar, was representative. The falling line of the phrases, the talking style, the poetic *AAa* form, and the banjo-like guitar style were all from the Afro-American heritage. Static harmonic elements—*on E* rather than *in E*—combined with variable elements is more generally non-European, or at least non-Romantic. Like other examples of jazz and the blues, this piece has more in common with Medieval music than music of any other Western period. Its variable intonations resembled the chromatic semitone but were more extensive. A *blue note* (marked *x* in the example) could occur on the scale seventh, third, fifth, and sixth.

Basic jazz was more complex, because the jazz group contained more elements. Actually, the group was composed of soloists, who alternated in improvising variations on the song phrases, and a rhythm section, using combinations of piano, banjo, guitar, and drums (generally two or three). As notated, the song line was *straight*; embellished, it was called *hot*.

Jazz techniques were those of performance; Jelly Roll Morton said that jazz was a style, not a composition. Repeated harmonic patterns, called *riffs*, and extended virtuoso breaks pulled the music forward, set up frames for soloists, and helped shape the performance but did not contribute to the form per se.

Antiphony and interaction were basic to the music, as was its strong rhythmic impulse. Most striking and highly motivating was the equal strength of four beats in the usual duple measure with percussion emphasis on the second and fourth; they were called the *back beats*.

The relationship between voice and instruments was lively and in-

Depot Blues

Example 84

SON HOUSE

The guitar is notated at pitch, and notes marked (x) are blue notes. The work is recorded on Folkways FA 2467. (Courtesy of Oak Publications.)

imitable. Scat singing was a technique in which the voice used instrumental attacks and became an embellishment of the instrument. And conversely, instruments used vocal imitations—laughing (clarinet), crying (trombone), sliding, growling, and *wa-wa* and other muting techniques. The basic instrumental style of jazz with its incorporation of vocal elements is a chief characteristic of the art.

To the jazz purist, the *jam session*, a spontaneous improvisation by professionals after work, was the truest form of jazz. All other types of performance were lesser, with the completely orchestrated arrangement at the opposite pole. The popular theater could, and often did, provide tunes for jazz, but a theater performance, which had to be carefully synchronized and rehearsed, lacked the essential freedom, even when emulating jazz.

Louis Armstrong, the king of jazz trumpet players between the wars, wrote many pieces, such as "Big Butter and Egg Man" and the scat song "Skid-Dat-De-Dat." But he also played many show tunes. His solo on the first eight measures of "I Can't Give You Anything but Love, Baby," a tune for the show *Blackbirds* (1928), by Jimmy McHugh, is typical of Armstrong's imaginative transformation of line and rhythm.

In spite of the use of jazz techniques in the musical theater and of show tunes in the jazz traditions, jazz and popular music were not joined. Their differences of technique, place and purpose of performance, and type of audience led to a mutual disdain. Jazz men looked on the traditionally schooled musicians as squares; pop musicians called the jazz men illiterate; and both were dismissed by "serious" musicians.

A few popular musicians were trying to give jazz validity in concerts as symphonic jazz. In a strange amalgam of orchestral music, theater music, and jazz, the bandleader Paul Whiteman (1890–1967) sponsored George Gershwin's *Rhapsody in Blue* (1924), for solo piano and jazz orchestra, at a concert in Aeolian Hall in New York.

American critics were nonplussed by the confusion of styles represented by such a work, and the American public was biased by its association of jazz with dance and its prejudice toward Negroes. Europeans had a very dif-

Improvisation   Example 85

LOUIS ARMSTRONG

This improvisation is from Jimmy McHugh's "I Can't Give You Anything but Love, Baby" (1928). (Courtesy of Mills Music, Inc. and André Hodeir.)

ferent reaction, seeing jazz either as an authentic folk art to be honored and classified as another transitional technique or as a low musical form beneath the whole hierarchy of musical types. The latter view kept jazz out of music schools but at the same time added to its glamor in the minds of the public. No less a figure than the French minister of national education said, "Jazz is the only accomplishment of collective imagination since the end of the art of conversation." [21]

Europeans studied jazz with appreciative seriousness. In France, Stravinsky had utilized ragtime elements in the theatrical chamber work *l'Histoire du soldat* (The Soldier's Tale, 1918) and in *Piano Rag Music* (1920), and Darius Milhaud utilized jazz sounds in the ballet *la Création du monde* (The Creation of the World, 1923). In Germany, experiments in new sounds were entering both "serious" and popular music, and jazz was added as one more technique. The most popular new opera of the period was *Jonny spielt auf* (Johnny Gets Hot), by Ernst Křenek (born 1900). It was first performed in Leipzig in 1927 with a Negro hero; later (1929) it was produced at the Metropolitan in New York in blackface. Eventually this work was produced in eighteen translations throughout the world.

More important, Europeans were following the jazz movement by means of imported phonograph records, so touring jazz groups found themselves public figures. In France and England, jazz was considered worthy of a large critical literature, and the jazz public on the Continent was well informed on many details of both general and individual styles. The French were the most ardent followers of the movement, and French record companies began very early to issue their own records, both of French editions of American performances and performance by their own practitioners.

Swing and the Big Bands

In the 1930s, the radio and movies were bringing popular music into the daily lives of people throughout the United States. Like all arts when they are diffused and popularized, jazz took on some aspects of the older tradition. Men with traditional training were attracted in increasing numbers to careers in popular music, and they created a slower, larger, and simpler style, which they called *swing*. Jazz had been an elite art, practiced and savored by a few connoisseurs, but for an exciting decade, swing was the musical passion of a whole nation. The years from 1935 to 1945 comprised the peak years of the "era of the big bands."

Perhaps the greatest big bands were those of Benny Goodman (born 1909) and William "Count" Basie (born 1904). Goodman, a clarinetist from Chicago, was a radio musician in New York who formed his own band in 1934. His success came the following year, overnight, during an engagement at the Palomar Ballroom in Los Angeles, and in that same year he made his first record, "The King Porter Stomp." Count Basie also started his career on radio but in Kansas City. He took over the Bennie Moten Band

21 Quoted in André Francis, *Jazz*, Paris: Solfèges, 1958, p. 188.

after Moten's death in 1935 and moved the band to New York in 1936. By 1937, the band was recording under Basie's name.

Many bands reached stardom in the decade after 1935. Artie Shaw's (born 1910) fifteen-piece band became popular in 1937 and Glenn Miller (1904–1944) formed his first band in 1937 and was popular by 1939.

The Goodman and Basie bands were representative of them all. Instead of the sharply etched sound of the small jazz combos, the bands used doublings and created a fuller, smoother effect. Most had fourteen to sixteen members, though some had twenty or more. The big bands used a slower beat in a four-beat bar, without back beats, and strove for an intense energy that was compelling and danceable. The thirties were a decade of dancing, with bobby-soxers doing the big apple and the jitterbug in theater aisles.

Benny Goodman's Band in 1937	Count Basie's Band in 1940
3 trumpets	4 trumpets
2 trombones	3 trombones
4 saxophones	4 saxophones
1 clarinet (Goodman)	4 rhythm instruments
4 rhythm instruments (piano, drums, guitar, bass)	(piano [Basie], drums, guitar, bass)
14	15

The swing sound was also ideal for Hollywood musicals and for singing, and the hit songs of the decade were movie songs. As early as 1929, the movies had begun to pull songwriters westward. "In Tin Pan Alley and on Broadway," an observer reminisced, "1929 is remembered as the year of the California gold rush." [22] Over fifty musicals a year were produced from 1934 to 1944; bands were heard in all of them and featured in many. Louis Armstrong was in *Pennies from Heaven*, Duke Ellington was in *The Hit Parade of 1937*, and Benny Goodman was in *The Big Broadcast of 1937*. The Hollywood musical at its height used such stars as Fred Astaire and Ginger Rogers and such innovative directors as Busby Berkeley, whose production numbers explored the camera's ability to see in a new way.

Some singing artists were Nat "King" Cole (1917–1969), who formed his own trio of piano, guitar, and bass; Ella Fitzgerald (born 1918), who sang with Chick Webb (1907–1939); Sara Vaughan (born 1924), who sang with Earl Hines (born 1905) and Billy Eckstine (born 1914); Peggy Lee (born 1920), who sang with Goodman; and Frank Sinatra (born 1917), who sang with Harry James. Their styles ranged from the rich instrumental style of Sara Vaughan and the smooth elegance of Nat "King" Cole to the jazz-based improvisation of Peggy Lee.

[22] Jack Burton, *The Blue Book of Hollywood Musicals*, Watkins Glen, N.Y.: Century House, 1953, p. 11.

The last big craze before World War II was boogie-woogie. It was based on a revival of the "Honky Tonk Train Blues" (1929) beat of Meade Lux Lewis (born 1905), which had a fast, eight-to-the-bar ostinato pattern exploiting the flat seventh. Boogie-woogie was a good foil for the swing sound; together they entered the forties.

❀ Some Composers Active between the Wars

The two generations of composers active between the world wars sought to find their way into a new art. Their greatness was not that of the creators who ride the crest of a movement handed them by others, but of the experimenters who move slowly and without consensus toward a goal felt but not yet defined.

ARNOLD SCHOENBERG (1874–1951), a Viennese cellist and composer, was precocious and self taught. His early employment was in the popular theater—playing, arranging, and, in 1901 and 1902, directing. In 1904, Schoenberg produced his first experimental works and organized a union to foster modern music. His increasingly radical compositions made him a highly controversial figure. From 1910 he taught in Vienna and Berlin, and in the years just before World War I, he toured widely, conducting his own works. After the war, he became more active as a teacher, and from 1925 to 1933 he taught in Berlin. In 1933, fired by the Nazis because of his Jewish heritage, he emigrated to the United States, where he became a naturalized citizen in 1941. His compositions were extensive and included a dozen volumes of songs, works for both symphony and chamber orchestra, four dramatic works, including *Moses und Aron*, to his own libretto, a number of choral works, and a substantial amount of chamber music. His theory text, *Harmonielehre* (1911), was published in a shorter English version as *Theory of Harmony* (1947).

CHARLES IVES (1874–1954), a Connecticut-born musical experimenter, worked in the business world. His musical life was that of a maverick, for he composed works with freely synchronized groups, spatial concepts, microtones, optional parts, and interpolations of patriotic tunes. Recognition was slow and, on a national scope, confined to his late years. His third symphony (1911) brought him a Pulitzer Prize in 1947. Many of his works, such as the *Concord Sonata* (1919), for piano, and a volume of 114 songs (1922), Ives published himself. His output included choruses, orchestral works, a large amount of chamber music, and 5 symphonies.

BÉLA BARTÓK (1881–1945), a Hungarian who studied in Budapest, collected Slavic, Magyar, North African, and other folk music and espoused advanced techniques in composition. An excellent pianist, he became professor of piano at the Hungarian National Academy in 1907 and a few years later director of music at the national cultural museum. Bartók was a prolific composer and was versatile in style. His opera, *Bluebeard's Castle* (1911), and his ballet, *The Miraculous Mandarin* (1919), were controversial; his 6 string quartets (1907–1931), however, were to become important works of the modernist movement. He wrote piano works that were equally important, particularly the six volumes of 153 didactic piano pieces, arranged in progressive difficulty, called the *Mikrokosmos*. His longer works include 3 piano concertos, 2 concertos for violin and 1 for viola, and several works for large chamber groups (such as the *Music for String Instruments, Percussion and Celesta,* 1937), and the *Concerto for Orchestra* (1945). In addition, he harmonized about 75 folk songs and dances and carried on research on folk music. Bartók went to New York in 1940 to participate in a conference on folk music and remained in the United States.

ANTON WEBERN (1883–1945), an Austrian who studied musicology, wrote his Ph.D. dissertation on Heinrich Isaac's *Choralis Constantinus,* of which he edited parts I and II. In 1904 Webern met Schoenberg; he studied with him until 1910. From 1908 Webern was an orchestra conductor in Austria and abroad, directing the orchestra of the Vienna Radio until its demise in 1934. His output was varied; it included 5 orchestral works (including 1 short symphony, 1928), 9 chamber works (of which 3 were for string quartet), 5 choral works, and 1 work for piano (*Variations,* 1936). The bulk of his works were for voice; he wrote about 4 dozen songs, with piano or varying instrumental components. In addition, Webern left a substantial amount of unpublished music, which was eventually placed in the Moldenhauer Archives in Spokane, Washington.

ALBAN BERG (1885–1935), a Viennese composer, also studied with Schoenberg, from 1904 to 1910. Berg was active in promoting the new techniques of composition; he was a member of Schoenberg's union and also of the Austrian chapter of the International Society for Contemporary Music. He wrote a substantial amount of chamber music, a piano sonata, a few songs, "Der Wien" (a solo aria for soprano and orchestra), a chamber concerto for piano, violin, and thirteen wind instruments (1925), and a violin concerto (1935), which is a standard of the modern repertoire. Berg's masterpiece, the opera *Woz-*

zeck, was written after World War I and produced in Berlin in 1925, creating a furor of disfavor. Its first successful performance, which led to the purchase of the original score for the Library of Congress, was in Philadelphia in 1931 under Leopold Stokowski.

EDGARD VARÈSE (1883–1965), a Paris-born composer, studied at the Schola Cantorum and worked as a choirmaster in Paris and Berlin. At the age of thirty he emigrated to the United States and settled in New York, but he was at home in both France and the United States. He was amazingly varied in his interests. He was active in the American Dada group and, during World War I, founded the New Symphony Orchestra for the performance of contemporary music. He also founded the Composer's Guild (1921) and the Pan American Society (1926) and worked with both electrophonic and electronic instruments. A modernist all his life, Varèse left a legacy of works now considered classics of the new music. In addition to chamber and symphony orchestra pieces, he wrote *Ionisation; Equatorial* (1934), for solo bass voice, brass, organ, percussion, and theremin; *Density 21.5* (1935) for unaccompanied flute; *Deserts* (1954), for winds, percussion, and tape tracks; and a *Poème eléctronique* (for the Brussels World's Fair of 1958), which was presented over 425 loudspeakers.

JELLY ROLL MORTON (Ferdinand Joseph La Menthe, 1885–1941), a composer, pianist, bandleader, and singer of early jazz, was born in Louisiana. A Creole, he started his musical career in 1892 in New Orleans as a guitarist but switched to piano in 1895. Morton was an early composer of the blues and gained prominence with the "New Orleans Blues" (1902) and "The Jelly Roll Blues" (1905). The latter song was published in 1915, perhaps the first jazz orchestration to be so honored. Morton left New Orleans in 1907 and worked in many cities, but he remained faithful to the New Orleans tradition all his life. He was one of the first jazz recording stars (with his band, Morton's Red Hot Peppers) and, later in his life (1938), cut a series of records for the Library of Congress.

DARIUS MILHAUD (born 1892), a French composer and teacher, traveled in both South and North America as a young man, adding Latin and jazz idioms to his technique. By his sixty-fifth birthday he had composed over 350 works in an amazing number of types and styles and at seventy-five he was professor at both Mills College (California) and the Paris Conservatoire. In addition to more than a dozen symphonies, Milhaud has written several operas, piano suites, a substantial number of songs and chamber works, piano pieces, and ballets.

WALTER PISTON (born 1894), a pianist and saxophonist from Rockland, Maine, studied in Boston from 1904 and, after graduation from Harvard, in Paris. He then joined the faculty of Harvard University, and has had a distinguished roster of students. His works include 4 symphonies, 3 string quartets, the ballet *The Incredible Flutist* (1938), which is his most popular work, a substantial amount of orchestral and chamber music, and a small amount of vocal music. In addition, he wrote texts on *Harmony* (1941) and *Counterpoint* (1947) that were influential within traditionalist schools.

PAUL HINDEMITH (1895–1963), a German composer and one of the literate proponents of modern musical theories, was a violinist and violist in a string quartet and concertmaster of the Frankfurt Opera from 1915 to 1923; his early works and his work with the Musical Youth Movement date from those years. From 1927 he was a professor of composition in Berlin, but the Nazis blackballed him and he left Germany in 1935. In Turkey and the United States he was welcomed as one of the foremost composers of his day. He conducted in many countries and taught in Zurich, Switzerland, at Yale University in Connecticut, at Harvard University in Massachusetts, and Aspen, Colorado. Hindemith was a polyphonist of great skill. His works include the *Ludus Tonalis* (Tonal Games, 1943), a volume for piano including 12 fugues and using a variety of learned techniques; the opera *Mathis der Maler* (Mathias the Painter, 1934, made into a symphonic suite in 1939), on the life of a Renaissance painter; a host of orchestral and chamber works; and a substantial number of vocal pieces, including the song cycle *Das Marienleben* (1924, revised in 1948) and several volumes of folk-song harmonizations. His books include *The Craft of Composition* (1941) and *A Composer's World* (1952).

ROGER SESSIONS (born 1896), a Brooklyn-born composer, studied with Horatio Parker at Yale. One of the most influential teachers of the transitional period, Sessions has taught at Smith College, the Cleveland Institute of Music, the University of California (Berkeley), and Princeton University. His works include 8 symphonies, 2 operas, several string quartets, piano music, choral works, and organ chorale-preludes. He has been awarded two Guggenheim Fellowships (1926, 1927), a Fellowship of the American Academy in Rome (1928–1931), and a Carnegie Fellowship (1931–1932).

GEORGE GERSHWIN (1898–1937), an American pianist and composer, was born in Brooklyn. He studied piano and theory intermittently, turned early to the popular music and made his mark at the age of nineteen with "Swanee." Gershwin devoted himself to the popular theater, writing for the George White Scandals (1920–1924) and sixteen musical comedies, including *Lady Be Good* (1924), *Girl Crazy* (1930), and *Of Thee I Sing* (1931), which won a Pulitzer Prize. From 1924 he composed symphonic works in the popular idiom. Of these, *Rhapsody in*

Blue (1924), for piano and jazz orchestra, was his most popular work. Gershwin also wrote 3 *Preludes for Piano* (1936), but his masterpiece is generally considered to have been the opera *Porgy and Bess* (1935).

FRANCIS POULENC (1899–1963), a French composer and pianist, belonged to the group called Les Six. He was known early for his smaller works such as the *Mouvements perpetuels* for piano (1918) and *Le Bestiare* (1919), a song cycle for flute, clarinet, bassoon, and string quartet. His prolific output included religious choral works (*Mass*, 1937; *Stabat Mater*, 1951), several volumes of piano works, several volumes of songs (1919 to 1942), concertos (including 1 for organ, strings, and timpani, 1941), and many stage works, from the early ballet *Les Biches* (The Does, 1924) to the later opera *Les Dialogues des Carmelites* (1957).

DUKE ELLINGTON (Edward Kennedy Ellington, born 1899), was born in Washington, D. C., and was educated there and in New York. From his first song, the "Soda Fountain Rag" (1916), he was active as a performer and composer in the jazz tradition, making about 1,200 recordings and composing over 350 songs in the next forty years, and from 1928, he was at Harlem's Cotton Club with his own band. In the 1930s, many of his finest works were written, including "Mood Indigo" (1930), "Sophisticated Lady" (1933), and "In a Sentimental Mood" (1935). His recording career was aided by the stability of his band, which had few changes in personnel during the decade. His peak year for recording (56 numbers) was 1940, and from 1943 to 1950, he gave annual jazz concerts at Carnegie Hall. For his concerts, Ellington wrote extended works —*Black, Brown, and Beige, The Deep South Suite*, and others. In the 1950s Ellington's band toured America and Europe and played at the Newport Festival (1956); Ellington wrote the score for the film *Anatomy of a Murder* in 1959. In the 1960s, he ex-

panded further, to works of symphonic proportion and chamber music, for his continuing international tours. In June, 1967, his music for the *The Jaywalker* was performed in England's Coventry Cathedral, and in 1969 he was honored at the White House by an evening recognizing his achievements and celebrating his seventieth birthday.

DIMITRI TIOMKIN (born 1899), a Russian-born son of a physician, studied at the St. Petersburg Conservatory and played piano in a movie theater. He learned ragtime from a Negro student and began to compose in the modern popular style. He left Russia in 1919 and went to Berlin, Paris, and finally, in 1925, to New York, where he met Gershwin. Tiomkin married a ballerina, began to compose ballet scores, and in Hollywood, where his wife was a choreographer, began writing for films. He wrote over 60 scores before winning his first oscar, for *High Noon* (1952). His films include *The Sundowners, Friendly Persuasion*, and *The High and the Mighty*.

AARON COPLAND (born 1900), a Brooklyn-born pianist and composer, was educated in New York and Paris. Upon returning to the United States, he entered the fields of teaching and concert organization in support of young composers and new works. He has lectured widely, at Harvard in 1934, 1944, and 1951–1952 and at Tanglewood for several summers. Many techniques are represented in such works as the piano *Variations* (1930); a turning to Latin-American materials is seen in *El salon Mexico* (1936); and the influence of American frontier folk music is seen in a series of ballets, culminating in *Appalachian Spring* (1944), for which he won a Pulitzer Prize. For the voice, Copland published two volumes of songs in 1950, one on poems by Emily Dickinson; a substantial amount of chamber music; 3 symphonies; and a work for speaker and orchestra (*Lincoln Portrait*, 1942). Between 1939 and 1950 he wrote film scores for six movies, including *The Heiress* (1950), which won an Academy Award. His book *What to Listen For in Music* (1938) attained considerable popularity.

WILLIAM WALTON (born 1902), a British composer, was trained as a choirboy at Oxford, where he later attended the university. His highly rhythmic *Portsmouth Point Overture* (1926) established him as a national figure; it followed his insouciant experimental accompaniments for six players to Edith Sitwell's *Façade* (1923). His many important works include the oratorio *Belshazzar's Feast* (1931), 2 concertos for violin, and 1 each for viola and cello, the opera *Troilus and Cressida* 1954), and several film scores, notably those for Lawrence Olivier's productions of Shakespeare's *Henry* V (1944) and *Hamlet* (1947). Walton was knighted in 1951.

LUIGI DALLAPICCOLA (born 1904), an Italian composer and teacher, studied in Trieste, Austria, and, finally, Florence. From 1931 he was a professor at the Cherubini Conservatory in Florence. Always interested in expanding harmonic language, he adopted twelve-tone serial techniques, using them in a highly personal way from 1939—he is known for his ability to write serially for the voice. Dallapiccola became a frequent guest lecturer in London, at Tanglewood, and at the University of Michigan. His works include operas, a ballet, orchestral works, violin and orchestra pieces, and a substantial number of songs with instruments.

WILLIAM SCHUMAN (born 1910), a New York–born composer, studied in New York (at the Juilliard School of Music) and Salzburg and taught at Sarah Lawrence College (from 1935). A series of performances from 1939 to 1941 brought him into national prominence, and the Guggenheim Awards of 1939 and 1940 gave him time to pursue his craft. In 1945 he was appointed president of the Juilliard School, gave up his professorship at Sarah Lawrence, and devoted himself to administration at Juilliard and, from 1962 to 1969, at Lincoln Center. In 1969 he retired to return to creative work. His works include 9 symphonies, 4 string quartets, a number of choral works, and theater music.

The electronic medium is also adding an unbelievable variety of new timbres to our musical store, but most important of all, it has freed music from the tempered system, which has prevented music from keeping pace with the other arts and with science. . . . Composers and physicists are at last working together and music is again linked with science as it was in the Middle Ages.

EDGARD VARÈSE *

A New Sound

27

Twentieth-century laymen, educated by nineteenth-century Romantics, had been taught to perceive melody as primary and to think of it as founded in a pervading harmonic scheme within a key. Such men would be not only confused by nonmelodic, nonharmonic music, but frustrated by it. The frustration would be immediate in the denial of the very elements they had been taught to depend on and would be compounded by the futility of deepening their efforts to understand it.

The problems were inevitable. First, men trained in the Romantic tradition perceived the new music as illiterate, or even as no music at all. Second, early writers on the new music were largely limited to a vocabulary

---

* 1962. Quoted in Elliott Schwartz and Barney Childs (eds.), *Contemporary Composers on Contemporary Music*, New York: Holt, 1967, p. 208.

of negatives—"no melody," "no key center," "no regular meter"—which could confound the old but was incapable of defining the new. Third, the gap between the traditionalists and the proponents of the new music increased with growing rapidity as teachers, having little positive to teach of the new, persisted in teaching the old. And fourth, most performers, trained in the old ideal, were neither willing nor able to change their techniques, so the old music was retained in the concert hall.

All four problems needed to be resolved. The definition of music had to be widened; musicians had to work toward a positive rather than a negative vocabulary; the gap between varying views had to be bridged; and performers had to learn new techniques and begin to learn new works. Slowly the reeducation began as part of a new philosophy of man and art, an agony of rejection and reappraisal that characterized the quarter century after World War II.

Maurits Escher, "Three Worlds," a lithograph. The work shows an interest in visual "zones of intensity," which are comparable to the zones of intensity desired in music by Varèse. (Courtesy of the Escher Foundation.)

A NEW HUMANISM

After two world wars, men could no longer accept the sanguine nine-teenth-century expectation of the imminent perfection of man—of West European man, to be more exact. Uneasiness was compounded by the projec-tions of scientists with regard to machines and their relationship to man, particularly their potential for controlling him. The uneasy feeling that man, far from approaching perfection, was being mechanized and debased added to the dissatisfactions with the hierarchical views of the traditionalists and helped foment a new movement toward a total equality among men.

Like Romantic humanism, the new movement was proclaimed with par-ticular zest by a radical younger generation, who demanded new social defini-tions. But unlike Romantic humanism, with its heroic figures and worship of the self, the new movement focused on the nonhero or even the antihero, and it looked outward, not only from self but from the modern West European culture. The young took to wearing non-European clothes and non-European beards; they broke away from the old values and proclaimed themselves through a new art of folk singing.

Like the Medieval troubadours, the young poet-musicians wrote texts that were studied as seriously as was their music. And like their predecessors, they were poets, composers, singers, and guitarists, pulling into song the fourfold discipline of their art. The popular poet-musicians took on the musical goals of the older, mainstream avant-garde, seeking to expand per-ception, renew the self, and change the world. By the late 1960s rock and mainstream experimental composers were making similar statements. Richie Havens (born 1941), a popular poet-musician, summed up the renewed be-lief in music as a healing art by defining an esthetic that is both simple and penetrating: "Music allows a person to look at the person inside of him. It expands the space around you and lets you dance into that space." [1] And John Cage, an iconoclast of the mainstream avant-garde, said the same thing: "Art is about becoming open to our environment; art is a way of changing oneself." [2] The two musical traditions had met in their ideals if not in the concert hall.

Musique Concrète

Within the Parisian movements, manifestos, and countermanifestos, two groups, the Zodiaque and the twelve-tone serialists, comprised the two chief musical factions in the years after the war; they were joined later by the Domain Musical. The groups had grown out of mainstream music traditions. The Zodiaque proclaimed themselves against systems, prejudices, habits, and

---

[1] Quoted in Daniel Chapman, "High Flyin' Bard," *Look* Magazine, Nov. 26, 1968, p. 20ff.
[2] On "Camera Three," CBS-NBC, May 31, 1969.

fashions, and the serialists were becoming more devoted to system. They continued to diverge.

During the 1940s, Pierre Schaeffer (born 1910), a French radio sound engineer, was producing experimental recordings, using radio sound-effects records that he organized through manipulation and assembly. The first *Concert des bruits* ("concert of noises") was broadcast in 1948 and included such works as the *Etude aux chemins de fer* (Railroad Study). In 1950, Schaeffer proposed the name *musique concrète* for the new sounds, and in 1951 the *Groupe de Recherches de Musique Concrète* (Research Group for Concrete Music), including as members Olivier Messiaen and Pierre Boulez, was organized. The group shortened its name in 1957 to the *Groupe de Recherches Musicales* (Group for Musical Research). In 1959 a member spoke of its goals: "The practically infinite richness of natural sounds, made available by recording, is further multiplied by the possibilities of transformation. Thus is born, spontaneously, a surrealist or expressionist esthetic that fits in wonderfully well with the needs of radio, cinema, or theatre." [3]

The associations of musique concrète with the popular mediums of radio and the movies and with the surrealist esthetic of revelation through juxtaposition were natural ones. Broadcasting studios had already perfected the techniques of producing sounds—natural, recorded, and simulated—and combining them imaginatively. They even maintained sound-effects libraries, and the new techniques involved the selection, manipulation, and assembly of these sounds.

The experiments in musique concrète were paralleled in the United States in the work of popular musicians. Les Paul (born 1916), a jazz and popular guitarist in the mid-1940s, combined as many as twelve separate layers of sound to produce a composite in both the guitar and the vocal. Paul "recorded directly on disc," and said that he developed the technique of

> using two recording lathes and using the process of playing the second part along with the already recorded first part and recording the two parts. This process was repeated over and over until the necessary number of parts were completed. . . .
>
> "How High The Moon" was recorded in a basement apartment in Jackson Heights, New York, and was almost a heart-breaking experience. About the time we had eight or nine parts recorded a plane would fly over from nearby La Guardia Airport, or the phone would ring, or some other disturbance would occur, thus making us go back and start the whole thing over again. We lost track of the number of attempts made before the thing was finished. . . . There were at least twelve voices. The same holds for guitar parts—rhythm, bass, lead, harmony, etc., again about twelve parts. [4]

Perhaps Paul's most imaginative pressing was the "Walkin' and Whistlin' Blues," a composite of footsteps, guitars, and whistling.

---

[3] From the annotations on the record "disques BAM" LD 070.
[4] Letter to Edith Borroff, June, 1969.

The techniques of musique concrète depend on the unprejudiced ear— "a sort of sonorous eye, sensitive to the forms and colors of sounds," [5] Schaeffer called it. By 1952, composers of musique concrète were recording sounds themselves rather than depending on the studio library. A member of the Groupe wrote a description of procedure that virtually defined the techniques of the new style.

> The composition of concrete music begins after the choice of raw materials, after the analysis, and after the manipulations; but these steps determine the composition. The composer must first choose sounds as raw materials for his work. They may be anything from a trumpet note to the sound of a brick being smashed by a hammer, but, whatever they be, they must have elements of the type which the composer wishes to manipulate. After recording, analysis will reveal the elements and their characteristics. . . .
>
> The composer will then set about manipulating them in order to form the units which he has in mind for his composition. After recording the results of his manipulations, the composer is in possession of a repertoire of sounds, constructed and molded by himself. These, not the original noises which served as raw material, are the sounds which will make his composition.
>
> He must now make a schema representing the order of sounds, the rhythm, the polyphony, and so on. The execution of the schema will be carried out by two processes: montage—specifically the cutting and pasting of recorded fragments—and mixage—the superimposition of recorded sounds which are re-recorded on a single tape.[6]

The selection and initial recording of the sounds comprised the precomposition lineup of raw materials, whereas the assembly was the actual composition. Both procedures were clearly analogous to procedures of traditional composition.

But the defining techniques most idiomatic to musique concrète were those of manipulation, which had no analogy in traditional music except in certain aspects of development. Early examples of musique concrète, like the early assemblages of Les Paul, were accomplished with disk recordings, which were versatile but physically clumsy. Two or three turntables could be used at once to combine and juxtapose sounds, speeds of 78, 33⅓, and 16 rpm were available, and it was also possible to play records backward. By recording at one speed, using another for the playback, and re-recording at the new speed, the composer could enter new realms of sound. Such pleasures as hearing bird calls in slow motion and at low pitch, the result of playing them at a slower speed, or the piano tone reversed to present a crescendo followed by a percussive hammer stroke reflected an exhilaration with sound that could only inaugurate a search for aural beauty—a search that had been deflected in the panics of a painful transition.

In 1951, the practitioners of musique concrète turned from the disk

[5] Quoted in Roger Maren, "Concrete Music," a booklet with Folkways Records, FX 6160.
[6] *Ibid.*

recording machine to the magnetic tape recorder. The advantages of the new device were superior sound reproduction, portability, and ease of manipulation of the resulting tape—it could be assembled as pieces of any length spliced together in any order. In addition, by moving at a constant speed, the tape equated distance with time; musical time units could be measured in inches, so that synchrony could be much more accurate and detailed and the techniques of movie sound tracks could be utilized to advantage.

Synthesized Sound

Early in the twentieth century the need for a new type of sound production was being expressed by a growing number of composers. By the beginning of World War II, composers were searching for total creation of sound by technological means. In 1939, Varèse said, "Personally, for my conceptions, I need an entirely new medium of expression: a sound-*producing* machine (not a sound-*reproducing* machine)." [7]

At the same time that early experiments in musique concrète were taking place in Paris, the Germans were hearing experimental demonstrations of synthesized sound. The French experiments were founded in radio techniques, the German in clinical phonetics. In Germany after World War II the Bell Telephone Laboratory demonstrated the *vocorder*, a synthesizer of speech sounds that had been demonstrated at the New York World's Fair of 1938–1939. By 1951, experiments in the synthesizing of music were well underway, and by 1952, laboratories at Eindhoven (Holland) and Cologne were functioning.

In 1953, the first works of synthesized music were heard, and a year later, Henk Badings's (born 1907) radio opera *Orestes*, which used synthesized sounds along with traditional music, was produced. It won the Prix Italia and had over 200 performances by 1961. In 1958, Varèse, working in his long-dreamed-of new "sound-*producing* machine" at Eindhoven, composed a *Poème Electronique*, which was performed at the Brussels World's Fair over 425 loudspeakers. In 1961 an electronic studio was opened in Moscow.

In the United States, university studios were underway early in New York and California, with concerts at Columbia University, and the Museum of Modern Art in New York in 1952 and at Radio Station KPFA in Berkeley, California, in 1954. In 1959, with $250,000 in Rockefeller foundation funds, the Columbia-Princeton Electronic Music Center was established under the directorship of Vladimir Ussachevsky (born 1913) and Otto Luening (born 1900). In 1962 a survey indicated that fourteen electronic music studios were functioning in Europe and seven in the United States. By 1966 there were thirty-three studios in the United States.

The basic equipment of the synthesizer is the oscillator and generator. The oscillator produces a sinusoidal tone or *sine wave*, a single frequency oscillation; this sound, like that of a tuning fork, is without partials. But

---

[7] Quoted in Elliott Schwartz and Barney Childs (eds.), *Contemporary Composers on Contemporary Music*, New York: Holt, 1967, p. 197f.

because the perception of tone is strongly linked to the perception of partials, sine waves are in a sense reluctant sounds, tending to quiet, other-worldly effects. An amplifier is needed to produce musically viable sine waves.

The generator produces tones with partials; these tones are named for the visual wave forms seen on the oscilloscope, which turns sound waves into visual wave forms. *Square waves* include the fundamental plus odd-numbered partials; *sawtooth waves* include the fundamental plus all partials. (The term *generator* is often used for any tone producer.) Because of their strong partials, the square-wave and sawtooth-wave tones are piercing and reedy.

A fourth type of synthetic sound is a random distribution of all audible frequencies, called *white noise*, by analogy with light waves. This is a steady sound with the effect of rushing air, such as that heard on a television channel after it has signed off.

An important adjunct to the tone generator is the filter, which can exclude a band of frequencies or, conversely, can exclude everything but a band—the size and location of the bands are under the control of the machine operator. Filtering is especially important in connection with white noise, which, because it contains all frequencies, has no discernible pitch. Without filtering white noise can be varied only in dynamic level. Filtering is sometimes called *tone shaping* or *coloring*, and the filtered bands of sound are called *colored noise*.

Like all musical mediums, synthesizers produce idiomatic effects. The easiest to obtain is the *glissando*; it is created simply by turning the generator's frequency control knob. Early music using synthesized sound abounded in glissandi. *Resultant tones* are more difficult and involve an additional piece of equipment—the ring modulator. This is a circuit with two input terminals, one for each of two tones, which modify each other and produce a resultant tone. Other special effects may come from jarring a circuit box or, as in Badings's ballet *Cain and Abel* (1956), by tapping the diaphragm of a microphone.

A single gesture or event of synthesized sound had to be regulated as to *wave form* (tone quality), *amplitude* (loudness), and *frequency* (pitch). But it also had to be shaped in time, to have an *attack* (beginning) and *decay* (ending), to make it a psychological entity. This dynamic character, called an *envelope*, must be superimposed on the products of the generator, as though to humanize them, which requires the use of special equipment called *gates* or *gating circuits*.

As in musique concrète, the assembly of suitable raw materials is preliminary to the manipulation, synchrony, and mix that constitute the actual composition. In the early phases of their art, the two schools of concrète and synthesized sound saw themselves as using very different techniques. But in 1956, Karlheinz Stockhausen, who had worked in both Paris and Cologne, produced the *Gesang der Jünglinge* (Song of the Youths), which made use of both sound sources. The French school was represented by the concrète recording of a boy's voice, in both speech and song, and the German school was represented by synthesized sounds. The phonetic elements provided a mutual interest and means of unification. Stockhausen also introduced spatial elements as part of his design. "This work is the first to use the direction of the sounds and their movement in space as aspects of the form," he wrote. "The score calls for five groups of loud-speakers to be set up surrounding the audience." [8]

Electronic Music

The basic element of electronic music is a taped unit of sound, called an *event*, which Varèse had termed the objet sonore ("sonorous object"). Whether this be made from natural sounds, recorded musical excerpts, white noise, pitch-defined wave forms, or a mixture of any or all of these, it comprises the materials the composer begins with.

Handling the materials first involves *manipulation*, several types of which are idiomatic to tape recorders. Using one recorder for playback and another to record, the composer can re-record part or all of an event at a different speed, raising or lowering the pitch and diminishing or enlarging its movement through time. He can also run a tape backward and re-record the material in cancrizans, or crab, motion, with the speed and pitch at the same or at a new level. By a technique known as *feedback*, a short part of the playback can be returned to the input, to be re-recorded again and again in a series of reverberating echoes, growing or fading in power according to the control of an amplifier. Such expanding reverberation, or *reverb*, is a basic characteristic of electronic music.

Simpler techniques in manipulating the event involve a sudden holding or pulling of the playback tape, to make it slow down or even stop or speed up. The result is often a slide, quick or slow; the variable speed unit on a tape recorder can accomplish many of the same effects. Another simple idiomatic technique is a new kind of ostinato. This is created by splicing the end of a piece of tape to its beginning so that when it is played, it sounds over and over again, forming a repetition stopped only by stopping the machine. An ostinato so formed is called a *loop*, because its physical form is a loop of tape. Loops are simple to make and easy to work with; they can be as short as the distances on the equipment permit or as long as desired (the nonplaying end controlled by someone at some distance from the tape deck). A loop can be presented at different speeds, which retains its character but varies its effect. In addition, any playback tape can be fed into a filter, gating circuit, or ring modulator to modulate or change the sounds by electronic means. And, the sounds can also be put through an echo chamber or given an artificial vibrato.

The use of three tape recorders offers further possibilities. Duplicate playbacks create a canon in the Medieval sense of any independent use of the same material by two or more parts. A time sequence of the same level

[8] From the annotations on the record "Deutsche Grammophon Gesellschaft," 138 811 SLPM.

(a canon at the unison in tonal music) is only one kind of tape canon. A proportional canon can be created by beginning the two tapes together and running them at different speeds. Or one tape can be played forward, the other backward to produce a cancrizans canon. Because events are conceived neither metrically nor as having mandatory pitch, the canonic distances are not limited to multiples of metric units but can explore more subtle relationships. Two playbacks may be of different materials—two loops of different lengths may be superimposed to create an isorhythmic structure, or one series of events may serve as a background or counterpoint to another.

The electronic composition is an assembly of tapes, each spliced together in a succession of events and worked into a final composite through temporal synchrony and dynamic mix. Edgard Varèse, as early as 1936, had envisioned the effect of such composition.

> When new instruments will allow me to write music as I conceive it, the movement of sound-masses, of shifting planes, will be clearly perceived in my work, taking the place of the linear counterpoint. . . . Such an acoustical arrangement would permit the delimitation of what I call "zones of intensities." These zones would be differentiated by various timbres or colors and different loudnesses. Through such a physical process these zones would appear of different colors and of different magnitude, in different perspectives for our perception. The role of color or timbre would be completely changed from being incidental, anecdotal, sensual or picturesque; it would become an agent of delineation, like the different colors on a map.
> In the moving masses you would be conscious of their transmutations when they pass over different layers, when they penetrate certain opacities. . . . An entirely new magic of sound! [9]

The combining of tapes was conceived as a spatial polyphony in which independent materials were superimposed, controlled in a dynamic mix that created levels—Varèse's zones or planes—of foreground and background. These were independently created and, ideally, independently sounded in the concert hall as well. A four-track tape could be performed through four loudspeakers placed so that the audience could perceive interactions from a position *within* the music. Henk Badings's *Genese*, a three-movement, wholly synthesized work composed in 1958, was spatially conceived. Badings wrote, "The original composition was realized in four sound tracks. When these are played through loudspeakers, one in each of the four corners of a hall, the sound flows spatially around the listener." [10] Badings's *Evolutions,* a ballet suite of six movements (Overture, Air, Ragtime, Intermezzo, Waltz, and Finale) was greeted in Vienna in 1958 as a "desecration of the sacred halls" of the State Opera House, but after that a reviewer wrote, "This fantastic-sounding and fantastically-danced vision of the future received, to the surprise of all, tempestuous applause from the conservative Viennese opera

[9] Quoted in Schwartz and Childs, *op. cit.*, p. 197ff.
[10] From the annotations on Epic Records, BC 1118.

audience, and was undoubtedly the most important event of this season at the Vienna State Opera." [11] The other-worldly character of synthetic sounds had already been recognized in the art of the motion picture. In 1956 the MGM film *Forbidden Planet*, by Louis and Bebe Barron, used a score made entirely of electronic (synthesized) music.

During the second half of the 1950s, the Cologne, Milan, and New York studios, among others, were producing a series of works in which synthesized and concrète sources were exploited, often in connection with vocal technique. Stockhausen's compositions both led and reflected the growing confidence in the new techniques. His *Studie I* (1953) had used sine-wave tones, and his *Studie II* (1954) had used complex wave forms; the *Gesang der Jünglinge* had combined sources and exploited the spatial elements of multisource performance. John Cage's *Aria with Fontana Mix* combined voice with electronic sounds, the singer performing live.

Early examples of electronic tapes combined with traditional instruments were produced in the United States and in Holland. In 1953 a New York composer known as Moondog (born 1917), a percussionist in the jazz-popular tradition who had composed a string quartet, collaborated with Tony Schwartz, a sound engineer who recorded the night noises of New York docks. Together they produced a *Piece for String Quartet and Harbor Sounds,* a haunting evocation of the city at night.

In 1959, the Swedish composer Karl-Birger Blomdahl (1916–1968) completed *Aniara*, a futuristic opera whose action takes place in a space ship in the year 2038. The machine-goddess speaks on tapes that combine noises, manipulated voices, and synthesized sound. In the opera's orchestral portions, traditional instruments emulate certain electronic idioms; and this emulation projects the work into the spirit of the new music, in which reciprocal influence would be assumed.

During the years of the development of the techniques of electronic music, the traditionalists and iconoclasts were continuing their experiments, carrying them as far as the materials were capable of being carried. In the years just after World War II, traditionally based music went in two directions, seemingly opposed and very different in technique and effect yet both related to modern aspects of mathematics.

Super Serialism and Chance Music

One direction was extreme control, in which serialism took over rhythmic and dynamic structures as well as pitch materials. Olivier Messiaen (born 1908), who was teaching serialism in Paris after the war, serialized durations, dynamics, and pitches in a piano work, the *Mode de valeurs et d'intensities* (Mode of Time Values and Intensities, 1949). Messiaen's student, Pierre Boulez, carried the expanded serialism through his *Polyphonie X* (1952), for seventeen instruments, to his climactic *le Marteau sans maître* (The Hammer without a Master, 1954), one of the most influential

---

[11] *Ibid.*

works of the decade. The latter work is a setting of three surrealistic poems by René Char, using an alto voice, alto flute, vibraphone, xylophone, guitar, viola, and percussion (bongos, maracas, tambourines, claves, bells, tam-tam, triangle, gong, and both large and small cymbals). The three songs are interspersed within a group of instrumental movements of a variable number of participants. One critic greeted it as "a new development . . . whose aim is the effective control of fluctuating masses, colors, densities, and intensities of sound." [12] The instrumentation was a considerable departure from traditional concepts, and another critic spoke of its "aura of inspired unpredictability" and its "chirping, knocking, porcelain-like sounds." [13]

In Germany in the same year, Karlheinz Stockhausen composed his *Klavierstücke III* (Piano Pieces #3), in which the piano is subjected to the same kind of controls. The rhythmic difficulties are similar to those in Boulez's work, and the dynamic specifications require a precise attack and are particularly demanding in single sonorities incorporating variables of pitch, duration, and dynamic.

The short third piece of the *Klavierstücke* illustrates the style and the effect. The chord at measure 7 shows the precision of control in combined elements demanded of the pianist, whereas the rhythm of measure 11 demonstrates the detail of the structure of durations that creates the same "aura of inspired unpredictability" noted in Boulez. The control of three dynamic levels and three variable durations in one sonority is difficult for the pianist, but the synchrony is easier and errors are much less costly. Like the Boulez, it is pointillistic in part and concerned with densities.

These works were seemingly completely opposite to improvised works, yet they had a strange affinity to the latter type, which was characteristic of certain of the iconoclasts. The most influential iconoclast, particularly in Europe, was John Cage, an American, who pulled away one seemingly necessary musical component after another in a series of experiments of scope, imagination, and enthusiasm. In 1954, sound itself was pulled away, in Cage's piano work *4′ 33″*; it consisted of four minutes and thirty-three seconds of silent contemplation of the open piano by the soloist, a work that puzzled and angered a British audience but delighted the irrepressible Italians.

Cage worked toward what he named *indeterminacy*, using random sounds, giving performers basic choices of procedure, and retaining for himself only the specifications of overall length, locale, personnel, and instruments. He also contributed to the development of the "prepared piano" (in the 1930s), used the electronic studio in Milan, and experimented with new sounds on other instruments. His performances often depended on visual effects as well as (sometimes more than) audible ones, and many of them were basically theatrical occasions in which appearance and physical

[12] Eric Salzman, *Twentieth Century Music*, Englewood Cliffs, N.J.: Prentice-Hall, 1967, p. 180.
[13] H. H. Stuckenschmidt, *Twentieth-Century Music*, New York: McGraw-Hill, 1968, p. 214.

Klavierstücke no. 2, III

KARLHEINZ STOCKHAUSEN

Example 86

This is the beginning of the third piece, which concludes in three more measures. (Courtesy of the Theodore Presser Company, for Universal Editions.)

motion were essential elements rather than decorations or by-products of music-making.

The theatrical tendency was joined to "chance" techniques from both East and West, including Chinese coin-throwing and elements of the Theater of the Absurd. *Theatre Piece 1960*, done in New York's Circle in the Square Theater, was a polyphony of events, musical and theatrical, in a loose synchrony.

The piece was based on a scheme of simultaneous incoherent actions and "happenings." The performers shot at balloons filled with paint; one of them had a shave while the March from *Tannhäuser* issued from a loudspeaker and the contralto sang Lucienne Boyer's twenties hit *Parlez-moi d'amour*.

Cage's role was restricted to standing in a corner of the little arena and counting very slowly from one to twenty-three. The whole affair was cheerful rather than outrageous, rather like a circus taken over by the clowns.[14]

Cage's extreme view is summed up in his statement, "My purpose is to eliminate purpose." [15] The esthetic might be summed up as "anything goes," but it is more than that—it is a statement, basically surrealist, that juxtaposition reveals more than its instigator can imagine and that nothing of man is to be denied to art.

Other composers used variables in connection with other, less extreme goals. In 1958 Boulez wrote an article, called *Alea*, on the use of chance factors, in which he spoke of "absorbing" chance, of structuring possibilities and giving alternatives rather than open choice to the performer. His third *Piano Sonata* (1957) had exemplified his concept of aleatory music. The work is a composite of five movements, which, in turn, are composites of short units that contain variable elements; the pianist plays the *Sonata* by deciding the order of the movements, and, within the movements, the order of the units.

Another mathematical technique was added by Iannis Xenakis, a Greek mathematician and architect working in Paris. He used the new theories of probability in composition and coined the term *stochastic* (from the Greek *stochastikos*, able to hit the mark, shrewd, sagacious). His *Metastasis* ("a changing"), performed in 1955, set forth his idea of stochastic music. A critic wrote of it:

> The piece is written for 63 instruments (mainly strings) and lasts seven minutes. It is built primarily from the string glissando. The notation consists of straight lines with defined pitches at their upper and lower limits. The glissandi are played simultaneously and produce a "statistical" effect, a kind of cloud of sound in which no individual note can be distinguished. Xenakis makes a comparison with the sound of the chirping of thousands of cicadas, where no individual note can be heard but whose overall impression is unambiguous and wholly characteristic: we immediately recognise it as the sound of cicadas. The drumming of heavy rain on a roof is similarly a "statistical" sound, not a species of polyphony. . . . His music, which he calls "stochastic," gives little inkling of the complicated probability-calculus techniques that it employs. The listener's impression is of a "global acoustical event," which is as Xenakis wishes. It is immaterial in his view whether a particular note is played or not, since the ear cannot in any case perceive it as a discrete entity.[16]

Another critic described *Metastasis* as "sliding, shifting masses and densities whose definition is derived by a 'satistical' probability method." [17]

[14] *Ibid.*, p. 223.
[15] Quoted in David Hamilton, "A Synoptic View of the New Music," *High Fidelity*, September, 1968, p. 56.
[16] Stuckenschmidt, *op. cit.*, p. 208f.
[17] Salzman, *op. cit.*, p. 182.

As the 1960s began, a reaction against extreme positions was being felt—Boulez had condemned both extremes of control and noncontrol as "refusals to choose" [18]—and the days of iconoclasm were numbered. "How can you make a revolution," asked a young composer, "when the revolution before last has already said that anything goes?" [19]

A NEW NOTATION

Notation in general reflects the central interests of the composers who use it, and nineteenth-century notation dealt centrally with pitch and metric time relationships. Boulez, in *le Marteau sans maître*, was less interested in pitch than in "fluctuating masses, colors, densities, and intensities of sound," [20] less interested in meter than in fluctuations in natural, theatrical, or existential time. Thus the traditional notation, aside from being overgrown with difficulties, forced the performers to focus on the very things the composer wanted *not* to dominate the total effect.

From the early years of the century, a vocabulary of new effects, instrumental and vocal, had been building, and these new directives called for new symbols. By 1960, even conservative scores were likely to require an introductory explanation of symbols, with still other directives appearing in the music. The modernists were combining the new sounds in new constructions that used aleatory elements. Composers needed a means of specifying those factors of performance they were most interested in controlling, a means that at the same time freed the performer in those particular aspects in which the composer had little interest. A string section might be formed into a cluster by dividing the section, with slightly different notation, to spell out the "cloud of sound" in a statistical effect—perhaps using signs for quarter tones. Or the composer could outline the extent of the cluster and allow each player to select his own pitch within it, without reference to any notatable pitch. Such a specified limitation was given the mathematical term *parameter*; composers who wished to control the parameters found that a *graphic notation* was easier for the performers to read and more directly attuned to the essential stuff of the music.

In 1964, the *Ferienkurse*, the international summer music festival at Darmstadt, held a special congress on notation, and a number of papers were read by various composers, performers, and scholars, surveying the needs of the new notation. In 1966, a book on the new notation was brought out, compiled by Erhard Karkoschka. By then the existence of a new art was enough accepted for Karkoschka to name his book *Das Schriftbild der neuen Musik* (The Graphic Notation of the New Music). It was not the first use

[18] Stuckenschmidt, *op. cit.*, p. 219.
[19] Charles Wuorinen, quoted in Hamilton, *op. cit.*, p. 48.
[20] Salzman, *op. cit.*, p. 180.

of the term *new music* in the twentieth century—and far from the first use
in the history of the Western art—but the book still serves as a symbol that
a new day had come for music.

THE NEW MUSIC

As early as the 1950s, a new appreciation was beginning to emerge.
This appreciation was evidenced in a turning of the chroniclers of the avant-
garde from antitraditional diatribes to genuine pleasure in the new sounds.
"The composer's chief concern," wrote one, "is with the harmonious fashion-
ing and arrangement of delectable sonorities." [21] And the Xenakis statistical
sound was described as "interlacing glissandi of an extraordinary shimmer;
these are gigantic and multicolored spider-webs, designed to break into delicate and intensely poetic sonorities." [22]

A sense of beauty, after a generation or more of its seeming irrelevance,
brought a widening audience to concerts of new works, and a cycle of expanding acceptance was underway. The younger composers called their art
the *new music*. New techniques for traditional instruments, perhaps the
earliest facet of the new music to be explored, were vital to the excitement
in new sounds. Many composers in the late 1960s were still developing new
wind-instrument techniques, such as double stops for clarinet or bassoon or
mouthpiece techniques for brass instruments. Strings, by using statistical
techniques, were emulating synthesized sound.

Electronic music provided a lively aspect of the vocabulary of the new
music. Tapes became more commonly found in orchestral works, as one
source of sound among many. Electronic compositions mixed not only concrète and synthesized sounds, but also parts of previously composed works
and sounds of traditional instruments, including the voice. The techniques of
synchrony by montage and of mix were adapted for use in live performance.
And sounds of electronic music, both concrète and synthesized, were taken
into the instrumental idiom.

Serialism was bent to new purposes. Its central concern with exact
pitches and metered duration was largely beside the point in forming "delectable sonorities," but the equality of tones could be useful in statistical
techniques. Earle Brown (born 1926), an American composer, summed up
the redefinition of twelve-tone serialism.

> I could never accept the idea that, in twelve-tone counterpoint, one
> avoided consonances; [I] liked the idea of "the liberation of dissonance"
> but did not agree that it should mean the enslavement of consonance.

[21] Henri Pousseur, quoted in the annotations on Time Records, 58002.
[22] "Disques BAM," *op. cit.*

. . . A row was an efficient means of distributing the twelve available tones in a context, [and I] thought of "coherence" as contextual rather than hieratical.[23]

"The twelve available tones" relates to those instruments (the vibraphone, piano, etc.) that are tuned to twelve equal semitones per octave. Instruments capable of producing other pitches were considered as having other tones available as well, in both slides or changing pitches and sustained tones. Quarter steps and random microtones were basic to the new concept—for string players and singers they are as ready as other tones, and wind players can use the embouchure to change intonation. The use of microtones was less the addition of smaller intervals than an enlargement of the concept of materials without reference to intervals.

Music of other cultures was reconsidered as contributing to the available sounds. Pitch systems, instruments, and techniques all provided potential materials. Characteristically, proponents of the new music were interested in exact techniques and accurately assessed materials used objectively rather than in exotic "flavor" or "color" used subjectively. More important, the esthetic of music was opened to the philosophies of other cultures. The idea of the essential superiority of Western Europe was dismissed as part of the Romantic harness and was replaced by interest in all music and by genuine potential respect for all esthetics.

Music of the past was used in the same way; Medieval sounds, for example, were sought along with their spatial deployments. The popular art was reconsidered as well. The traditions of the people, folk song and jazz, were acknowledged as strong creative arts in their own right, different rather than lesser. The ideal of speaking not just to fellow professionals but to nonmusicians regained respect. Music and ideas, music and the other arts, music and the new humanism were paired in fruitful combinations.

Early works in the new music used a variety of techniques. Stockhausen's *Kontakte* (1959, 1960) was first an electronic piece and, in a second version, an interaction between tapes and live performers (two pianists and a percussionist). Brown's *Available Forms I* (1961), for five string, six woodwind, three brass, and two percussion players (vibraphone, xylophone, marimba, chimes, and timpani) is a musical mobile, with six loose pages of four or five events each, ordered by the conductor with a call board. Luciano Berio's *Circles* (1960), for solo soprano and percussionists, to texts by e. e. cummings, is performed live, whereas his *Visages* (1961) uses a vocal performer and taped electronic sounds. Stockhausen's *Momente* (1962) uses chorus and percussion (including keyboard).

In the early years of the new music, a group of works by Polish composers created a culmination. In 1958, Witold Lutoslawski wrote *Funeral Music*, the first of several Polish works for strings only. A four-movement

[23] Time Records, *op. cit.*

work dedicated to Bartók's memory, *Funeral Music* is serial, featuring semitones and tritones. Krzysztof Penderecki followed with three works for orchestral strings—*Tren: Ofiarom Hiroszimy* (Threnody: To the Victims of Hiroshima, 1961), for fifty-two players, *Polymorphia* (1961), for forty-eight players, and *Canon* (1963), for fifty-two string players and tape. In these works, Penderecki explored special string effects, both instrumental and statistical, scoring for each instrument separately. Related in style were other orchestral works, such as *Atmosphères* (1961), by György Ligeti, which extended the technique to the whole orchestra.

The effects of *Atmosphères* were new but were painstakingly scored on eighty-seven staves in old notation. The Penderecki *Threnody* achieved very much the same effects with the new notation; the beginning of the piece not only can be written on ten lines but achieved the same statistical effects through simpler means. Penderecki used the new notation. The symbols and abbreviations, explained in the preface to the work, are as follows.

	raised by ¼ tone
	raised by ¾ tone
	lowered by ¼ tone
	lowered by ¾ tone
▲	highest note of instrument (no definite pitch)
↑	play between bridge and tailpiece
	arpeggio on four strings behind the bridge
	play on tailpiece (arco)
	play on bridge
	percussion effect—strike the upper sounding board of the violin with the nut or the fingertips
⊓ ⋁	several irregular changes of bow direction in succession
∿	molto vibrato
∿	very slow vibrato with a ¼-tone frequency difference produced by sliding the finger
	very rapid nonrhythmical tremolo
ord.	ordinario
s. p.	sul ponticello
s. t.	sul tasto
c. l.	col legno
l. batt.	legno battuto

In an *ABA* form with simple overall design and subtle detail, *Threnody* is an essay in new techniques. The fabric is statistical, the form is tightly controlled, and the total effect is powerful.

Threnody: To the Victims of Hiroshima   Example 87

KRZYSZTOF PENDERECKI

Ofiarom Hiroszimy

TREN

KRZYSZTOF PENDERECKI
1859 - 1961

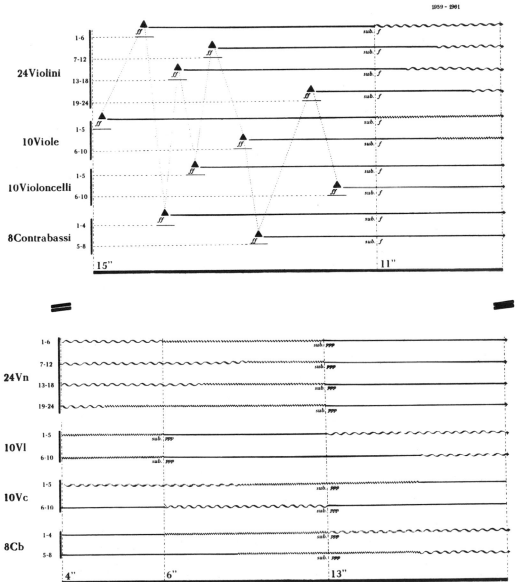

635

Example 87 (continued)

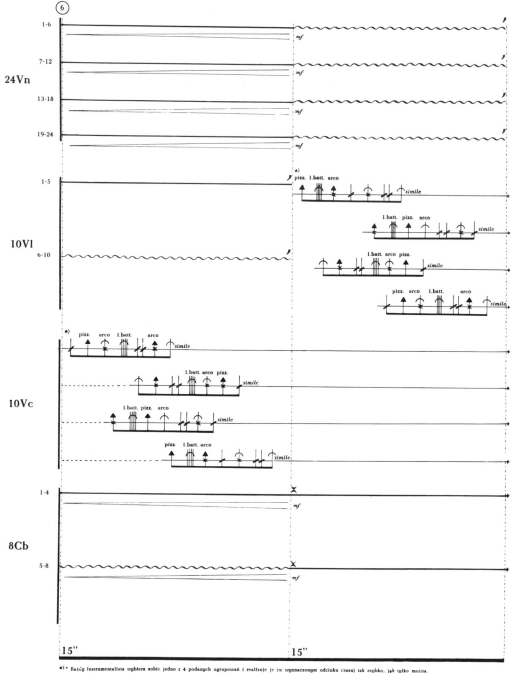

*) * Każdy instrumentalista wybiera sobie jedno z 4 podanych ugrupowań i realizuje je (w wyznaczonym odcinku czasu) tak szybko, jak tylko można.

Jeder Instrumentalist wählt eine der angegebenen 4 Gruppierungen und spielt sie (im bestimmten Zeitabschnitt) so schnell wie möglich.

Each instrumentalist chooses one of the 4 given groups and executes it (within a fixed space of time) as rapidly as possible.

Chaque exécutant choisit un des 4 groupements donnés et l'exécute (dans le segment de temps indiqué) aussi vite que possible.

Example 87 (continued)

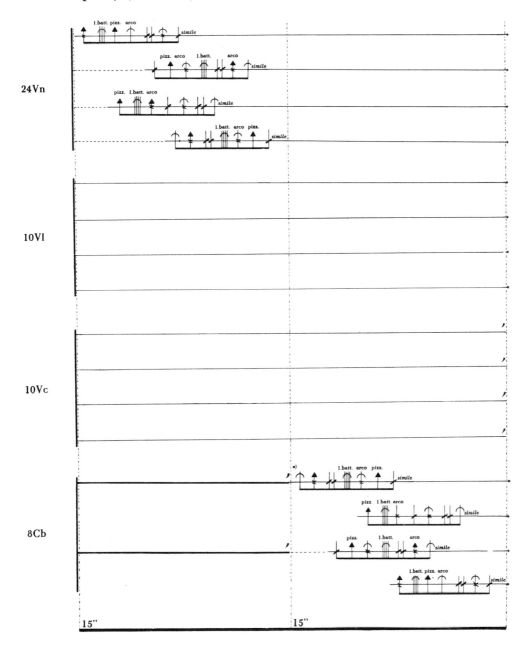

Example 87 (continued)

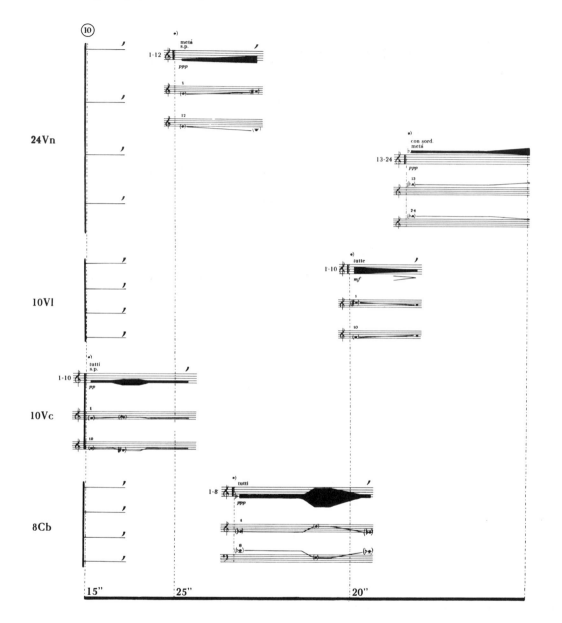

Example 87 (continued)

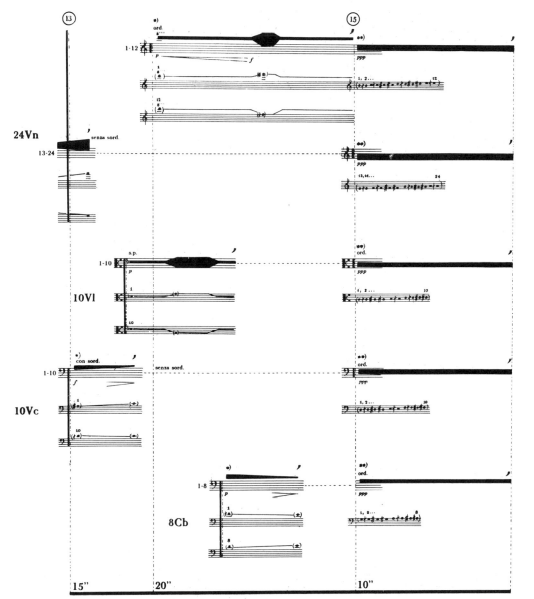

*) * patrz uwaga na s. 6 / vgl. Anmerkung auf Seite 6 / cp. note on page 6 / voir note page 6

**) ** Każdy instrumentalista wykonuje przeznaczony dla niego dźwięk, co w rezultacie daje równoczesne brzmienie całej skali ćwierćtonowej między podanym dolnym a górnym dźwiękiem.
Jeder Instrumentalist spielt den seinem Instrument zugeordneten Ton, so daß gleichzeitig die ganze Vierteltonskala zwischen den angegebenen unteren und oberen Grenztönen erklingt.
Each instrumentalist plays the tone allocated to his instrument, so that the whole quarter-tone scale between the indicated lowest and highest tone sounds simultaneously.
Chaque exécutant joue uniquement le son dévolu à son instrument de façon à ce qu'on entende en même temps toute l'échelle des quarts de ton comprise entre les hauteurs extrêmes indiquées.

Example 87 (continued)

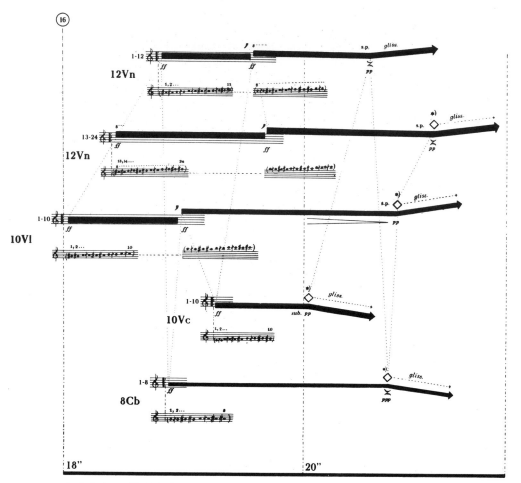

*) • flżoleky kwartowe / Flageolettöne / flageolet tones / harmoniques

Example 87 (continued)

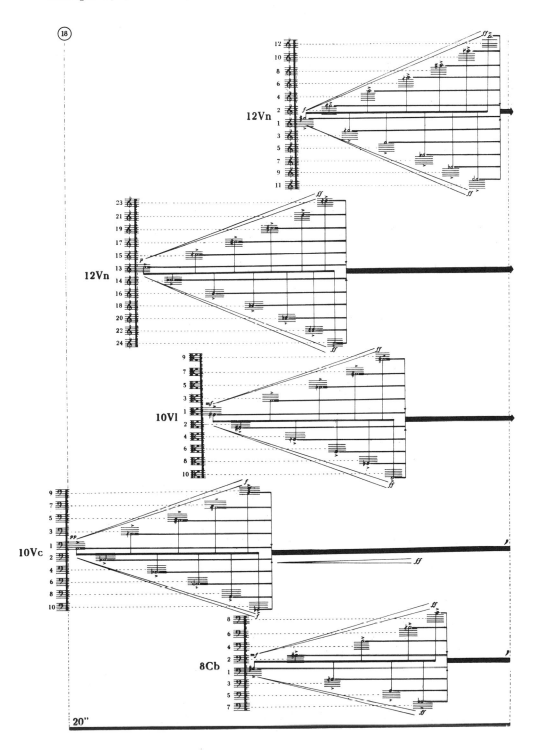

Example 87 (continued)

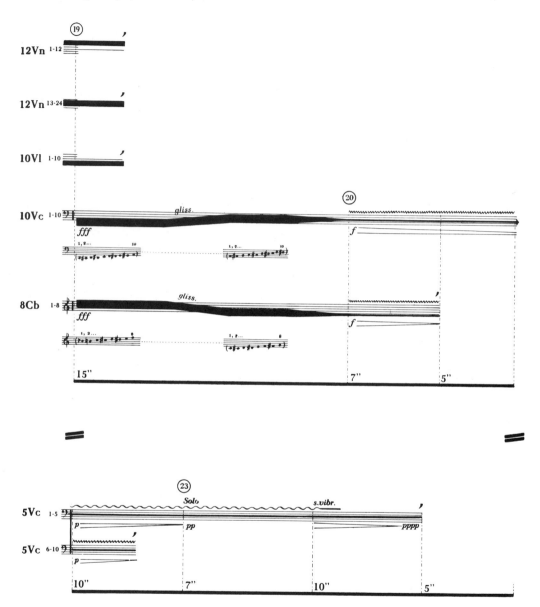

Example 87 (continued)

Example 87 (continued)

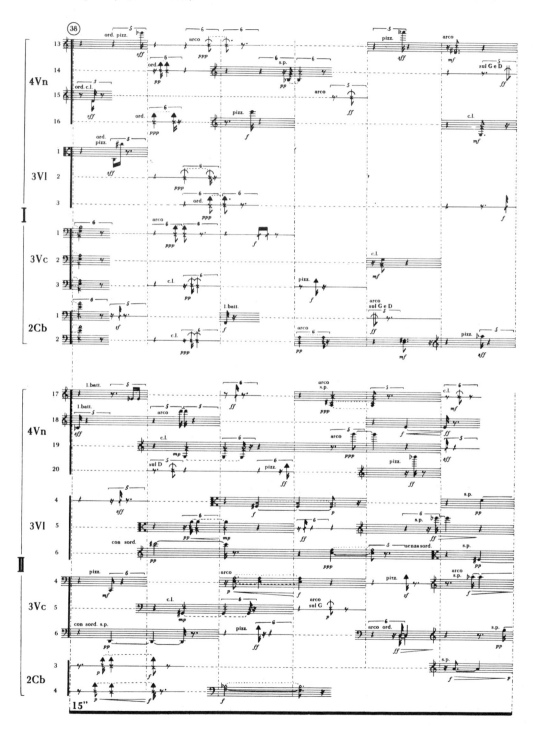

Example 87 (continued)

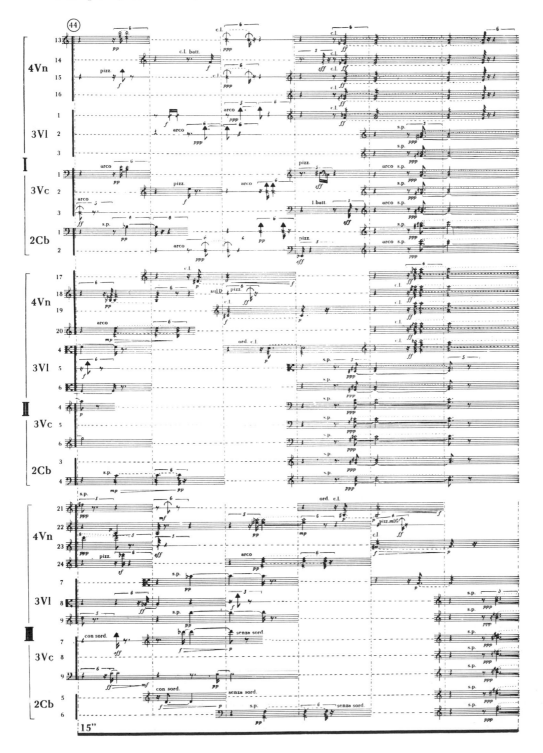

Example 87 (continued)

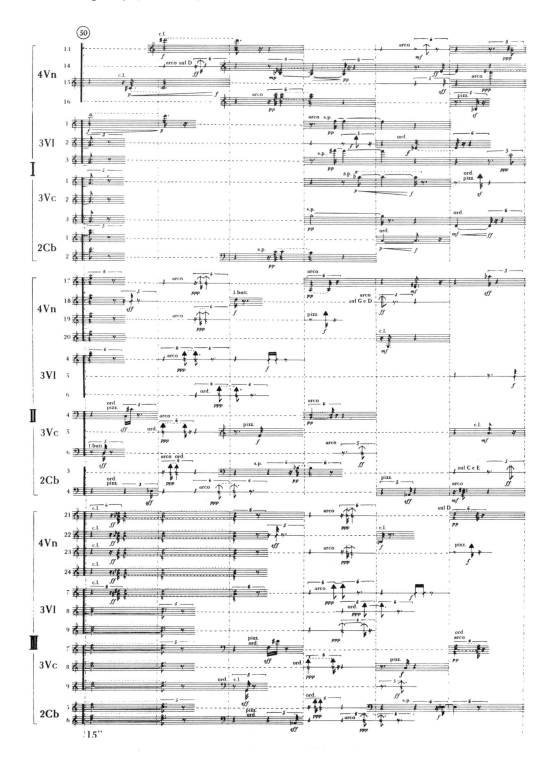

Example 87 (continued)

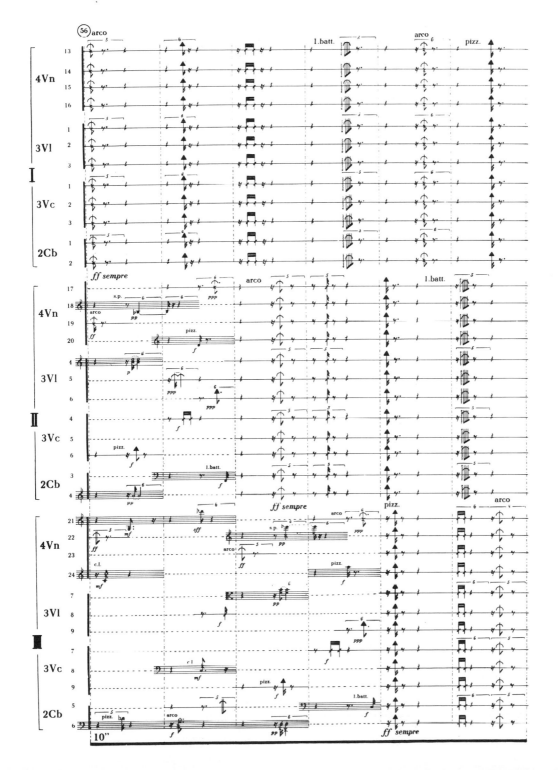

Example 87 (continued)

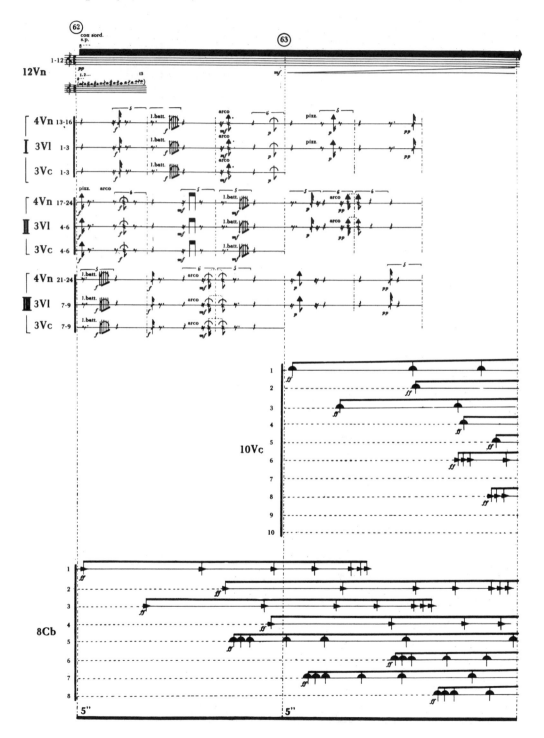

Example 87 (continued)

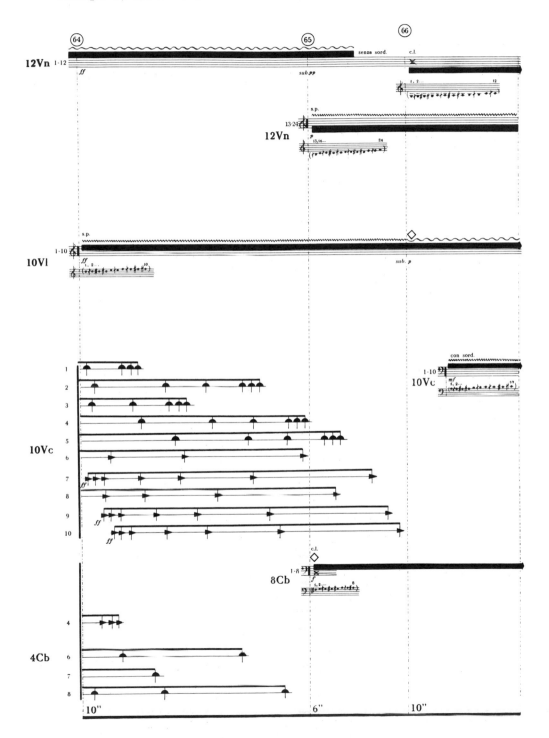

Example 87 (continued)

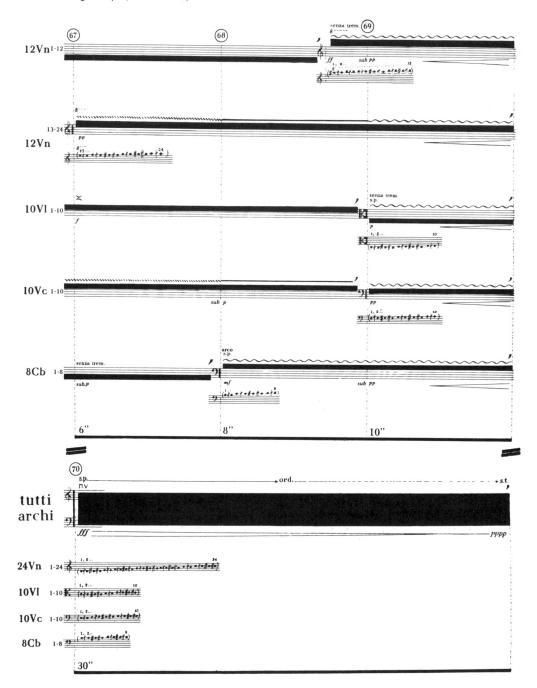

One of the first works in the new notation, *Threnody* (1961) demonstrated the versatility and economy of indicating the parameters of statistical sounds by that notation. (Courtesy of Agencja Autorska, Warsaw.)

In the mid 1960s, a group of choral works thrust the new music into its first broad public dissemination and performance. The vocal sounds of the new music had revealed the potential for expression, and once the new techniques were solidified, composers found a particular fruition in choral works. Lutoslawski's *Trois poèmes d'Henri Michaux* (Three Poems of Henri Michaux), a work with separate choral and orchestral scores requiring two

Witold Lutoslawski, *Trois poèmes d'Henri Michaux* (1963), page 29 of the vocal score. The three poems, all of which are presented by chorus and orchestra, are staged separately according to a chart conceived by Lutoslawski. For each poem, the orchestra is led by a different conductor, who uses a separate, loosely synchronized score. Page 29 contains events 42 to 46 of the second poem. The sopranos (S) and altos (A) are divided and present overlapping glissando wheels to the text, "The hoop falls that has rolled so long." Event 42 comprises approximately ten seconds of this statistical sound. Tenors (T) and basses (B) enter together at event 43. The orchestral activity is shown below in abbreviated form. (Courtesy of Polish Music Publishers, Krakow.)

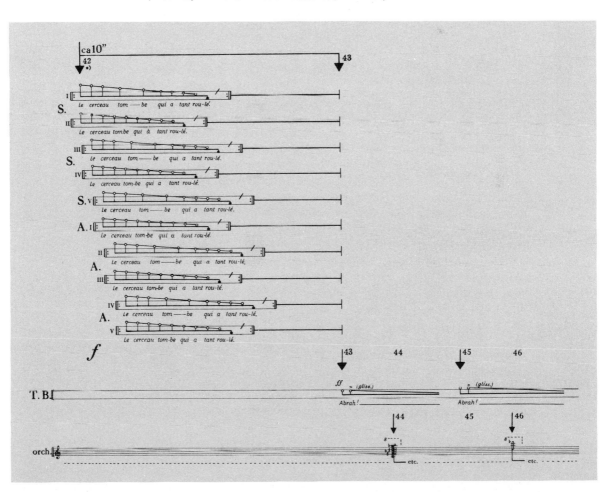

conductors, was an immediate success at the Zagreb *Biennial* of 1963, and it was soon performed in several centers. The choral cycle *Still Are New Worlds* (1963), by Ross Lee Finney (born 1906), an American composer, increased the elements in Lutoslawski's work to include a speaker and electronic sounds. In a newspaper review, I described Finney's work as follows:

> A complex work based on texts that range from Kepler and Donne to Akenside and Camus, it concerns man and space, finite and infinite, the circle and the stretching to break out of the circle. It is an idiomatic work, not in the old sense of producing sounds comfortable for the instruments and voices, but by drawing from them new sounds which are so right that they do not so much surprise us as educate us to an increased sense of what they are meant to do.[24]

The most immediately successful choral work of the mid-1960s was Penderecki's *Passio et Mors Domini Nostri Jesu Christi secundum Lucam* (Passion and Death of Our Lord Jesus Christ According to Saint Luke), composed for the seven hundredth anniversary of Munster Cathedral, where it was premiered in 1966. Like Finney's work, it uses a composite text, centering in St. Luke's account of the Crucifixion but also including Psalm verses, a brief passage from the Gospel of St. John, quotations from the Roman *Breviary*, and the sequence *Stabat Mater* (incorporating the composer's 1962 setting of the text for three choirs unaccompanied). The textual arc of the *Passion* is incorporated in a spatial fabric of performing elements —the work uses soprano, baritone, and bass soloists; a speaker; three mixed choruses; a boys' choir; and an orchestra. An expanded Baroque medium defines the language of the score: the speaker, as the Evangelist, serves as testo or historicus; the baritone serves as Christ; the soprano and bass, as more than one character; and the choir, as the crowd or turbo. In addition, the musical motto $B\flat–A–C–B\natural$ (B–A–C–H) is used both to symbolize the Cross, the single focus of the work, and to pay obeisance to Johann Sebastian Bach.

But the language of Penderecki's *Passion* transcends the idiom of any one era. The *Stabat Mater*, dating originally from the time of the founding of the Munster Cathedral, serves to bracket the centuries being commemorated in the work. Much in the *Passion* is Medieval, but the essential thrust is the meaning of the ancient texts in 1966. A New York critic said that Penderecki's *Passion* "achieves a dark, timeless mysteriousness." [25] In a review, I also mentioned the *Passion's* symbolism, when discussing the *Stabat Mater*, which uses three choirs.

> Its concern with vocal and spatial deployments of simple elements, its pervading mysticism, and its embellishment of the word "Christ" with a symbolic nimbus of sound and the word "Gloria" with a triune sonority [a fully resonant major triad] mark the work as close to the Medieval in spirit and techniques.[26]

[24] Edith Borroff, *Ann Arbor News*, Nov. 3, 1966, p. 39.
[25] Robert Jacobson, in the *Saturday Review*, March 22, 1969, p. 79.
[26] Edith Borroff, *Ann Arbor News*, Oct. 20, 1968, p. 3.

Other critics have sensed the primary importance of new techniques and new sounds in the work, and still others have recognized its value as a catalyst and spokesman for the new music. Within three years of its premiere, the work had been performed in sixteen metropolitan centers around the world— an unprecedented response even for a small piece easy to produce and a triumph for so difficult a work.

In short, Penderecki's *Passion* served to present the new music as a full participant in the present rather than as a parenthetical experiment. It is, above all, a *communication,* and as the first widely accepted work of its type, it serves as a symbolic stepping of the young composers from the theory to the reality of the new music.

❀ *Some Composers Active after World War II*

The two generations of composers active after World War II represent an amazing range of geographic and musical backgrounds but have an increasingly unified musical technique. The trends away from negation of the old and toward affirmation of the new, as well as toward synthesis of type and method, are clear in the younger generation.

JOHN CAGE (born 1912) is a California-born pianist and composer who studied briefly with Schoenberg and Varèse. He devoted himself to experimentation, writing for prepared piano and mounting a vast array of innovative music ranging from random noise to total silence. In addition, Cage contributed a significant number of works to the mainstream avant-garde. Among his more influential works were the ballet *Bacchanal* (1938), for prepared piano, the synthesized *Williams Mix* (1952), a piano concerto (1958), *Aria with Fontana Mix* (1958), *Theatre Piece 1960,* and *Atlas Eclipticalis* (1961), an orchestral work. A thirty-year retrospective catalogue of his works was published in 1962.

WITOLD LUTOSLAWSKI (born 1913), a Polish composer who studied at the Warsaw Conservatory, has contributed to orchestral, piano, and choral literature and worked with Polish folk songs. His early works include a symphony (1947), a *Silesian Triptych* for soprano and orchestra (1951), *5 Dance Preludes,* and for piano, a sonata (1934), *12 Folk Melodies* (1945), and *Variations on a Theme of Paganini* (two pianos, 1941). He turned to the new music and became one of the important figures of the Polish school. His later works include *Jeux vénétiens* (Venetian Games, 1961) and the highly influential *Trois poèmes d'Henri Michaux* (1963) for choir and orchestra.

BENJAMIN BRITTEN (born 1913), a British composer and pianist, was trained in London but was in North America from 1939 to 1942. He is most famous for his vocal works: about a dozen operas, including *Peter Grimes* (1945), *The Rape of Lucretia* (1946), and *A Midsummer Night's Dream* (1960); several large choral works, including *A Ceremony of Carols* (1942), for boys' choir and harp, and the *War Requiem* (1962); and several volumes of songs. His instrumental works include the early orchestral *Young Person's Guide to the Orchestra* and three concertos—for piano (1938), violin (1950), and cello (1964). After 1960, he spent more and more time organizing and working as director-conductor of the Aldeburgh Festival.

MILTON BABBITT (born 1916), an American composer born in Philadelphia and associated with Princeton University both as student and teacher (from 1938). An experimentalist, he has worked in serialism since 1948, more recently in total serialism (*Composition for Twelve Instruments*) and electronic music (*Ensembles for Synthesizer*; *Correspondences* for strings and tape, 1968). He has also contributed substantially to the experimentalist literature for traditional mediums (string quartets, songs, piano music). He is one of the most articulate proponents of experimentation.

ALBERTO GINASTERA (born 1916) is an Argentinian composer educated in Buenos Aires. After spending time in the United States, he returned to Buenos Aires as a professor at the National Conservatory, with guest lectureships in Europe and the United States. His works include orchestral and chamber music, but his fame resides in his vocal works since 1960—the *Cantata para America Magica*, for soprano and fifty-three percussion instruments, and the operas *Don Rodrigo* (1964) and *Bomarzo* (1968).

JOHN LEWIS (born 1920), a pianist, arranger, and composer, was born in Illinois but raised in Albuquerque. There he studied piano from childhood and majored in anthropology at the University of New Mexico. After the war, he played in Dizzy Gillespie's band and studied at the Manhattan School of Music, where he received two degrees and later taught piano and theory. He worked in Paris, toured (here and abroad) as Ella Fitzgerald's accompanist, and worked as pianist and arranger in the nine-piece Miles Davis group. From 1952 he was associated with the Modern Jazz Quartet. In addition, Lewis has written film scores for French and American movies, has issued solo record albums, and has served as musical director at jazz festivals in Lenox, Massachusetts, and Monterey, California.

IANNIS XENAKIS (born 1922), a Greek composer, worked in France as an assistant to the architect Le Corbusier, then turned to music. His *Metastasis* (A Changing, 1955), for sixty-three instruments, drew attention to his theories. Other important works include the *Concret PH* (1958), which uses electronic techniques and was composed for the Brussels Fair, and *Terrektorh* (1969), for orchestra. He has also written articles and books, including *La crise de la musique serielle* (The Crisis of Serial Music, 1958) and *Musiques formelles* (1963).

GYÖRGY LIGETI (born 1923), a Hungarian composer, was a serialist in his early works but became an ardent proponent of the new music after leaving Hungary in 1956. He worked at the Cologne electronic studio (1957–1958) and taught in the International Courses for New Music at Darmstadt (from 1959). Since 1962 he has lived in Vienna. *Volumina* (1962), for organ, and *Aventures* (1965), for three singers with flute, horn, cello, string bass, piano, harpsichord, and percussion, are summaries of the stunning sounds of the new style. Ligeti has also composed for orchestra—*Apparitions* (1959) and *Atmosphères* (1961). His choral works include *Requiem* (1965), for double chorus, soprano and mezzo-soprano soloists, and orchestra, and *Lux Æterna* (1967), for choir and orchestra. His *Poème symphonique* (1965), for 100 metronomes without other instruments, was premiered in Buffalo, New York.

LUIGI NONO (born 1924), an Italian composer, studied with Schoenberg disciples and created a scandal in 1950 with the modernity of his *Variazioni Canoniche* (Canonic Variations). He built a reputation for revolutionary vocal works, through such compositions as the *Epitaffio per F. Garcia Lorca* (1954), and *Il Canto Sospeso* (1956), for chorus, soloists, and orchestra; the latter was written for texts taken from letters from World War II resistance fighters. His opera *Intolleranza* (1960), a protest against cruelty and repression, has been widely played.

HENRY MANCINI (born 1924), a composer most noted for his film scores, was born in Cleveland and educated in Pittsburgh and New York. He played flute and piano in dance bands and joined Tex Beneke's band in 1946. He joined Universal Pictures in 1951 and was nominated for an Oscar for his first film score, *The Glenn Miller Story*. Mancini has worked in both movies and TV, for which his theme song for *Peter Gunn* was an immediate hit. In 1961 he won an Academy Award for the score of *Breakfast at Tiffany's* (the theme plus the song "Moon River") and again in 1962 for *Days of Wine and Roses*. Other nominations were for *Charade* (1963) and *The Pink Panther* (1964).

PIERRE BOULEZ (born 1925), a French composer and conductor, studied with Messiaen at the Conservatoire, graduating in 1945. From 1948 he conducted a theater orchestra and in that year he finished his second piano sonata. His output has not been prolific, but a number of chamber works (including those with voice) from 1948 to 1965 made his works significant in experimental music. His early works, such as the *Livre* (Book; 1949), for string quartet, and the *Sonatine* (1950), for flute and piano, tended toward traditional combinations. Later works searched out new groupings and new sounds. They include *Polyphonie X* (1952), for seventeen instruments; *le Marteau sans maître* (The Hammer without a Master, 1954), for soprano and instruments; the third *Piano Sonata* (1957); *Pli selon pli* (1960), for soprano and instruments, on poems of Mallarmé; and *Eclats* (1965). *Pli selon pli* was called "onomatopoetic serial music" at its second Paris hearing (1969). From 1965 Boulez turned again to conducting and writing; an English volume, *Notes on an Apprenticeship*, was published in 1968. In 1969, Boulez was appointed music director of the New York Philharmonic; he will begin in that post in 1971.

LUCIANO BERIO (born 1925), an Italian composer, studied in Milan and the United States. He was the director of the Milan experimental group from 1953 to 1960 and editor of an avant-garde magazine. His works helped to explore the new sounds; they were chamber works for the most part— *Chamber Music* (1952), for voice, clarinet, cello, and harp, on poems by James Joyce; *Serenata* (1957), for flute and fourteen instruments; *Différences* (1959), for five instruments and tape tracks; *Circles* (1960), for voice, percussions, and harp; and *Visages* (1961), for voice and tapes. His larger works include *Allelujah I* (1956), for orchestra; *Mutazion* (electronic, 1957); *Allelujah II*, for five small groups, and *Sinfonia* (1968). From 1950, Berio has spent much of his time in the United States, where he has taught at Indiana University and at the Juilliard School of Music.

HANS WERNER HENZE (born 1926), a German composer, settled in Naples, Italy, in 1956. His early years were prolific, and at forty he had amassed a body of works including 6 full-length operas, several short and radio operas, 12 ballets, 5 symphonies, a violin concerto, a piano concerto, and a substantial number of large choral works and Lieder. The operas, the most successful of modern German productions, include *König Hirsch* (King Stag, 1956), *Elegy for Young Lovers* (1961), *Der junge Lord* (1965), and *Die Bassariden* (The Bassarids, 1966). The vocal works include the *Fünf neapolitanische Lieder* (Five Neapolitan Songs, 1956), *Novæ de infinito laudes* (1963), the *Musen Siziliens* (Sicilian Muses, 1966) and *Moralitaten* (Fables, 1967). His film scores include *Young Torless* (1968).

KARLHEINZ STOCKHAUSEN (born 1928), a German composer, studied in both Germany and France, with Messiaen, Milhaud, and Schaeffer. He worked at the electronic studio at Cologne, becoming its director in 1963. Prolific and continually inventive, Stockhausen has provided a large literature of important works of wide scope. Among them are the *Kontra-Punkte* (1952); the electronic *Studie II* (1954, known for having a published score); the *Gesang der Jünglinge* (Song of the Youths, 1956); *Zeitmasse* (1956), for five woodwinds; *Telemusik* (1966), which uses folk materials; and *Prozession* (1967), for tam-tam, viola elektronium, piano, filters, and potentiometers. His larger, spatially deployed works include *Carré* (1956), for four choruses and four instrumental groups; *Gruppen* (1957), for three orchestras; *Kontakte* (1959–1960); *Originale* (1961), a Cage-inspired happening during which *Kontakte* was played and the pianist brewed tea and changed clothes at the piano; and *Momente* (1962), for four choirs, soprano soloist, and thirteen instruments.

THEA MUSGRAVE (born 1928), a Scottish composer, studied at the University of Edinburgh and then for four years in Paris with Nadia Boulanger. Musgrave's work has paralleled development of the new music and includes a wide variety of types: *Scottish Dance Suite* (1959) and *Sinfonia* (1963), for orchestra; operas, including *The Abbot of Drimock* (1955) and *The Decision* (1965); choruses, including *The Phoenix and the Turtle* (for chorus and orchestra, 1962); chamber works, including *Music for Horn and Piano* (1967), *Soliloquy for Guitar and Tape* (1969), and *Elegy for Viola and Cello* (1970); and songs and 2 piano sonatas. In 1969, Musgrave produced *Memento Vitæ*, a collage for orchestra, using modifications of themes by Beethoven and personifying the antitheses of the old and new styles.

BURT BACHARACH (born 1928), a Kansas City–born pianist and composer, was trained in Montreal, New York, and California (with Milhaud). He turned to the popular field, working on television and in the movies and was nominated four times for Academy Awards, for "What's New, Pussycat," "Alfie," "The Look of Love and "Raindrops Are Fallin' on My Head," the last of which won an Oscar in 1970. His vocal pieces have been successful as well, notably those for the singer Dionne Warwick. In 1968 he composed his first musical show, *Promises, Promises*.

HENRI POUSSEUR (born 1929), a Belgian composer who studied with Boulez, worked at the Cologne and Milan electronic studios and then founded a studio in Brussels. He was a serialist as well as an electronic music experimenter. His *Quintet* of 1955 was written in memory of Webern. Other works include *Seismogrammes* (1963), an electronic piece; *Symphonies* (1955), for fifteen soloists; *Mobile* for two pianos 1958; *Madrigal I, II, and III* (1962); and an opera, *Votre Faust* (your Faust).

CRISTOBAL HALFFTER (born 1930), a Spanish composer trained in the French modern school, from 1962 has been a professor of composition at the Madrid Conservatory. He tends to large, spatial compositions—*Antifona* (1952); *Formantes* (1961), for two pianos; *Espejos*, for three percussion groups with tape tracks; and *Yes, Speak Out, Yes*, for antiphonal choruses, orchestra, soloists, and tape tracks. The latter work was composed for the United Nations celebration of Human Rights Day, December 10, 1968.

KRZYSZTOF PENDERECKI (born 1933), a Polish composer trained in Cracow, achieved recognition with his *Psalms of David* (1958), for choir and percussion. He continued to define elements of the new music—idiomatic techniques in *Strophen* (1959), for soprano, narrator, and instruments; spatial techniques in *Dimensions of Time and Silence* (1960); statistical sounds in *Threnody: To the Victims of Hiroshima* (1960); orchestral writing in *De Natura Sonores*; and vocal writing in the *Stabat Mater* (1962), for three choirs without instruments. His large works were among the first classics of the new music—*The Passion according to St. Luke* (1966), in which the *Stabat Mater* was included; a *Dies Iræ* (called the *Auschwitz Oratorio*, 1967); *Utrenja*, for soloists, choirs, and orchestra (1970); and the opera *The Devils of Loudon* (1969), based on a book by Aldous Huxley.

PETER MAXWELL DAVIES (born 1934), a British composer, studied in Manchester, Rome, and, after three years of high school teaching (1959–1962) that brought considerable attention to his methods, in the United States. He has turned strongly to Medieval and Renaissance techniques, with such instrumental works as the *Alma Redemptoris Mater* (1957), for wind sextet; *Ricercar and Doubles* (1959), an octet; *Fantasia on Innomine of John Taverner* (I in 1962, II in 1964); and *Shakespeare Music* (1963), dances for eleven instruments. His vocal music includes two cycles of carols and instrumental interludes, for choir, soloists, and orchestra, and the *Leopardi Fragments* (1961), for two solo voices and instruments, on which much of his early recognition rested.

RICHARD RODNEY BENNETT (born 1936), a British composer who studied in London and Paris (with Boulez from 1957 to 1959), has worked in a variety of musical idioms. Two early string quartets (1952 and 1953) owed much to Bartók, but with *Calendar* (1960) and *Nocturnes* (1962), he found a personal style. He turned increasingly to the theater, composing for the ballet (in which he has used the rock idiom), opera, radio, movies, and television. He wrote the opera *The Mines of Sulphur* (1965) and the score for the film *Far from the Madding Crowd* (1967).

PAUL MC CARTNEY (born 1942) is a British rock artist and composer whose career is synonymous with The Beatles. The fame and influence of the group was a sudden aftermath of the release of the song "I Want to Hold Your Hand" (1964) and continued through *Revolver* and *Sergeant Pepper's Lonely Hearts Club Band* (1967). The group has also made movies, notably *A Hard Day's Night* (1966) and the animated *Yellow Submarine* (1968).

For centuries we have dealt with intervals of pitch; but what about similar intervals, or proportions, of rhythm, volume, timbre and other musical elements? We talk about an octave, which means the higher note has twice the vibrations of the lower, but what about an octave of volume, one level being double the other? Or a fourth of rhythm, or a major seventh of timbre?

KARLHEINZ STOCKHAUSEN *

Philosophy and Theory

28

Primary to the new music was a differentiation between structure and form, or between structuring musical events and marshalling events into a whole composition. The old concentration on form had led to the teaching of musical forms without reference to fabric. But in the new esthetic, fabric was basic.

Composers spoke of *sonority* rather than chords, implying the total vertical sound rather than a mathematical relationship of pitches. The reversal is implicit in the term. A *chord* was *spelled*, that is a $V{^6_5}$ of F was spelled $E–G–B\flat–C$ or, as any deployment of the V_7, $C–E–G–B\flat$ that has E on the bottom. If a Romantic had been asked, "Is it loud or soft? high or

* *Time*, Sept. 8, 1967, p. 78.

low? wide or narrow? serene or tempestuous?" he would have replied that those details were immaterial to the concept of V of F. In the new music, the *sonority* was *qualified*, that is, the specifications of medium, register, range, dynamics, electronic filtering or echoing, and its general effect as sound, were specified. If the composer had been asked, "What pitch is on the bottom?" he might have replied that the exact pitch was immaterial to the concept of the sonority. The composer of new music is less concerned with consonance and dissonance than with resonance.

Composers also spoke of melodic *gesture* rather than theme, implying a discrete and kinetically conceived horizontal element. As one unit of gesture might or might not be of significance in a choreography, so the musical gesture might or might not be of significance in a musical structure. It might well be secondary or even decorative. And composers spoke of an *event* rather than a phrase, choosing to emphasize the short unit as a totality in itself rather than to use the metaphor of connectedness.

Thus two out of the three essential elements of Romantic music were shorn of their functional power. Both harmony and theme were so redefined as to require new words to replace them. Rhythm remained, but only to denote that forward motion through time that all music shares.

TIME

Composers in the twentieth century were concerned with the flow of time rather than its regulation. The designation of time factors in music was increasingly drawn from theatrical concepts, where timing is vital but meter is irrelevant. The idea that time should be divided into measures was reversed—time should be defined by the events that create it. Artists had redefined space in the same way; a painter wrote that "it is no longer a question of an object in space. It is the object which will become space." [1] Varèse spoke of musical form as "the result of process," which he said was analogous to crystallization, similar to a growth into time.[2]

The rhythms—of speech, motion, and natural and mechanical noises—were all examined. Proportional and isorhythmic structures, exotic rhythmic structures (particularly from India and Africa), and random rhythms (statistically random, or indeterminate) were all considered viable. Regular pulse and meter were not excluded; they were now a matter of choice and could, in fact, achieve a considerable thrust by contrast with other kinds of rhythm.

But the new music pointed to the artificiality of regularity. Composers studied *life rhythm*—a woman might be sweeping in a regular duple rhythm

---

[1] André Masson, quoted in Francis Routh, *Contemporary Music*, London: English Universities Press Ltd., 1968, p. 203.
[2] *Ibid.*, p. 201.

(meter), a man might walk by in a separate steady pulse (another meter), the dog might rush in an irregular crescendo to the window and bark at the man in a series of related but unmeasured sforzandos, and the woman might talk (in speech rhythms) to a child playing in random rhythms in the yard. The combining of such patterns, each with its own integrity, must be synchronized rather than regulated, put into a coherence of independent life. Such a concept calls for exact relationships in *clock time*. *Synchrony* specified beginnings—unanimous, staggered (quick or relaxed), or canonic—durations, and, overall, a dynamic scheme which is itself essentially rhythmic.

The accumulation, ringing forth, and culmination of a single sonority, seeming to bloom in slow motion with natural spontaneity, in reality has a rhythmic life that must be structured and designated. Such a sonority might combine several instruments and require precise synchrony. Several internal rhythms might be part of the event, in which throbbing resonance, though combining tone colors and spatial factors, is nonetheless essentially rhythmic in its organic life.

The ordering of events, like the events themselves, could be conceived in clock time or in meter, in either case drawing on life rhythms, with such elements as interruptions, pressures, separations, relaxations, and steady progressions. The separateness of the event allowed for a leisurely appreciation of its beauty, and the sonorous, resonating event, completing its arc, might be sustained at pleasure. Pierre Boulez, asked why he had held a sonority so long when conducting his *Eclats* in 1967, replied, "I don't need to be in a hurry to get to the next sound." [3]

[3] "Camera Three," National Educational Television, Nov. 6, 1967.

A geodesic dome, designed by Buckminster Fuller. The clarity of the structural unit as an additive cell was clear in the 1960s in architecture as well as in music. (Courtesy of the Quebec Government Office.)

SOUND

Basic to the new music was the idea of sound, particularly its quality as timbre or tone color. If elements were to retain individuality of rhythm, they must also be heard as separate color-tonal entities.

A Romantic term for total sound was texture, used in a special sense no longer heard; in this sense, texture had been considered irrelevant to music. Edward MacDowell, speculating on the futility of introducing exotic sounds into Western music, stated that texture is separate from music.

> If we could eliminate from our minds all thoughts of music and bring ourselves to listen only to the *texture* of sounds, we could better understand the Chinese ideal of musical art. . . . It is the Chinese conception of music that *the texture of a sound is to be valued*; the long, trembling tone-tint of a bronze gong, or the high, thin streams of sound from the pipes, are enjoyed for their ear-filling qualities, . . . sound without music.[4]

The sound sources of the new music were multiple—concrète and synthesized sounds, the voice, traditional instruments used in both traditional and radical techniques, new and exotic instruments, and "lesser" instruments newly promoted to a position of central importance. Concrète and synthesized sounds were subjected to a variety of electronic manipulations, in which temporal, dynamic, and wave-length factors were interdependent. Individual sounds were prized as effective or beautiful both by themselves and in context. Traditional instruments, in the view of some composers, were no longer useful. Boulez said that "the instruments have come to the end of their possibilities."[5] But others saw them as still capable of effective color-tonal enlargement; they reexamined all the physical components of the instruments and all their natural sounds, creating a new array of techniques and effects.

Also vital was the concept of *tessitura*. Instead of using the central instrumental range, music could demand notes at the edge of possibility, adding the stress of technique to the quality of the sound. The importance of tessitura to the new music had been announced in the opening notes of Stravinsky's *le Sacre du printemps* in 1913, when the new voice of the bassoon, in the high register previously avoided, presented a sound that must have astounded its first listeners.

Differentiation of sonorous elements, accomplished through enlargement of the concepts of sound and rhythm, was often further clarified through distance and the direction of the source of sound in performance. The exact

Architectural Space

[4] Edward MacDowell, "Music of the Chinese" (1912), in W. J. Baltzell (ed.), *Critical and Historical Essays*, New York: Da Capo Press, 1969, p. 60.

[5] National Educational Television, *op. cit.*

placement of performers became important; percussion units were divided and space between players increased, as the desire for unanimity was replaced by the desire for individuality. Scores often had stage charts, including both the instruments and their placement. Electronic compositions were also centered in the placement of sound sources; specification of the number of speakers and their location was vital to the total work. Relationships of tone color, register, and deployment in space were all significant, and the separation of participating elements created a fluid interaction.

A more vital type of space in the composition of music (as opposed to its performance) is that realm of musical space that uses a vocabulary drawn by metaphor from physical space. Traditionally, musical space has been chiefly concerned with *high* and *low*. The idea of *register* had ceased to exercise a primary influence in matters of pitch deployments and had entered the area of color, particularly in regard to tessitura. *Musical Space*

Still drawing its metaphor from physical space, the new techniques were concerned with a polyphony of planes or layers, conceived as foreground, background, and middle ground. The new concept is basically one of distance, of depth rather than height. The visual analogies of distance prove extremely creative. The differentiations of foreground and background relate specifically to size, color, and speed. Perception of elements in a landscape, for example, show the foreground objects larger than those in the background, so that a man may seem larger than a distant barn. The foreground object is clearer in color and also in outline, and the color tends to greater liveliness. And, if the landscape is viewed from a moving train, the foreground object moves with greater speed, so that planes can be readily perceived through the varying speed of the objects occupying them.

The composer uses dynamic strength, tone color, and rhythm to project the shifting planes of sound. The feedback echo recedes or approaches in space, in the aural counterpart of the visual perception in size. Principal elements are given to more vivid tone colors and assume the foreground; duller, less provocative sounds form the background. And layers of sound maintain integrity by moving at independent rates and manners; they can be diaphanous or opaque, dense or clear.

COMPOSITION

The structure and form of works of music in general are basically concerned with repetition, verbal phrase or punctus structure, variation, departure, and return—all of which appear in one way or another throughout the world. The Romantic concept of organic form had been exceptional in its ideal of an almost literary continuity, and its esthetic closeness to the verbal arts was conscious and purposeful. In spinning out the musical tale, the

Romantic composer had accomplished a remarkable synthesis of elements. One can think of humming a symphony or at least following it in a succession of themes. But the new ideal of time, sound, and space is not thematically conceived or appropriate for humming. In the new music, the musical event itself may be a collage, a complex yet indivisible fabric perceived as a totality of temporal, sonorous, and spatial elements.

The analogies of the new music are visual and theatrical rather than literary, and the technical vocabulary is that of the sciences—cybernetic, mathematical, and kinesthetic. The composer thinks of his methods as similar to those of the painter, sculptor, or choreographer rather than to those of the author. Time in art, for example, has been reexamined; poets have tried to overcome the limitations of verbal succession; surrealists have painted sequences or led the viewer through chains of meanings that expand "the object which will become space" into the object that will become time.

Composers now speak of *composition* much as an artist might, as an aggregate of elements, a composite—which is actually what the word means. The musical composite is a putting together of events through spatial and temporal polyphony to create an esthetic whole. This composite may be created by synchronizing tape lengths, by ordering live performance, or by coordinating a mixture. Or the assemblage may include slides, action, and other theatrical elements, each conceived as one aspect of the total polyphony. It is then a *mixed-media* work.

Succession of events is crucial to a composite form, and simple succession is, in fact, the basic structural principle. However, like the punctus structure, which it most resembles, it contains many possibilities of interior reference and overall shape.

The relationship of new music to the word and to vocal techniques is fascinating. Each musical era has afforded a special and highly significant role to the human voice, redefining it, reshaping its techniques, and calling for a new sound. New music is no exception, and the voice contributed a large share to its early successes. The whole concept of voice and of the text has been reevaluated, as part of the total reassessment of sound. First a word was a sound. Then it was a designation out of context and might contain other designations, as the word *terror* contains both *tear* and *roar*. Finally, a word could enter into context and interaction with other words and other sounds.

An interesting paradox of the new vocal techniques is the great interest in words and the simultaneous desire to transcend them. The literary focus of traditional Romanticism had led to the assumption that thought is basically verbal and that all valid entities of thought can be expressed in words, an idea rejected by twentieth-century modernists. Of all artists, the musician, through vocal music, is able to transcend the limitation of words. Through fragmentation, overlapping, statistical techniques, and the qualities of total sonority, composers of the new music evoke worlds of meaning that words in themselves cannot attain.

In general, the style of the new music steered a course between the extremes of the superserialists and the total aleatorists. Its parallels with Medieval practices are many—love of tone color; spatial, additive, and sectional structures; technical elements such as hocket and isorhythms. But these elements, though Medieval in Western tradition, are found in many nonwestern cultures. The fabric of the new music is closer to the universal than were the harmonic structures of the Classical and Romantic eras.

Sound is central to the new music and central to the enthusiasm of its proponents, both professional and lay. But although the hi-fi set has given the layman an appreciation of the beauties of new sounds, it has also created problems for the acceptance of the new style. First, spatial aspects of performance cannot be represented effectively on records, even stereophonic records. The size of the hall, the distances between speakers, choruses, or instrumental groups, and even the presence of an audience create an added temporal and sonorous nimbus that can be sensed only when one is at a performance. Further, the visual aspects of performance are missing from records. The listener to a recording of traditional music can envisage the stage, the physical appearance of the instruments, and of the stance and gestures of the performers. But the new techniques and new instruments leave the visualization unfulfilled for those listeners who have never been to a concert of similar works. All new styles have been slow in establishing themselves in the fabric of public life; it is interesting to speculate on the effect of recordings on the dissemination and acceptance of the new music.

New music in 1970 was still concerning itself with structural techniques rather than forms, using the simple forms that have proved readily adaptable to new styles of music in many places and times. But each era has developed types that represent its particularity in a vivid and almost defining sense and serve in retrospect to summarize its esthetic; such forms have yet to be developed in the new music.

THE COMPOSER

Many characteristics of the new music are based implicitly on a new attitude toward composers. Respect for the esthetics of other cultures and the seeking of new methods in other arts, in the sciences, and in the natural and random materials of life itself destroy the image of the artist as a man in the toils of daemonic inspiration. It may be that the Romantic composer had been able to distrust the intellect and play down the role of craft simply because the grammar of music had become second nature and functioned subconsciously; it was not in the grammatical aspects of music that the modernity of the Romantic movement lay.

Even after World War II, the Romantic vision of the musician persisted, but more strongly for the performer than for the composer. The

Many artists and an increasing number of literary figures believed that not everything can be expressed objectively in words. (Courtesy of Paul Peter Porges.)

"Describe your dream fully."

pianist, the singer, and, above all, the orchestra conductor continued to maintain the Romantic stance of a genius separated from other men. The attention of the public was drawn to these figures, and the new generation of composers seemed less glamorous.

Composers of the new music, like the new artists, found themselves less often in Paris attics than in American university studios. They were likely to look less like starving geniuses than professors or businessmen, and they were likely to concentrate more on their craft than on their image. They turned to other cultures, examining all the music they could find, and they looked with new respect on popular music, particularly jazz and rock.

The young composers had turned away from the heroes of their predecessors and recognized new ones. They admired the American iconoclast Charles Ives and turned to other composers lost in obscurity, becoming more historians than were their counterparts in other eras. Among their new idols, perhaps the most honored were Varèse, Schoenberg, and Webern. Composers had a new list of revered classics: Berg's *Wozzeck*, Varèse's *Ionisation*, the entire output of Webern, and Schoenberg's *Pierrot Lunaire* and *Moses und Aron*. Also included were later works such as Boulez's *le Marteau sans maître*, Stockhausen's *Gesang der Jünglinge*, Berio's *Circles*, Penderecki's *Stabat Mater*, and Lutoslawski's *Trois poèmes d'Henri Michaux*.

The new role of the composer was that of an equal member of society, concentrating on his craft and on his influence on the next generation—through teaching as well as composing. His renunciation of the Romantic image had been foreseen by the Dada artist Jean Arp (1887–1966), who had spoken of the need "to cure human beings of the raging madness of genius and return them modestly to their rightful place in nature." [6]

[6] Quoted in Harold Rosenberg, "Arp: Pro-Art Dada," *The New Yorker*, June 21, 1969, p. 92.

665

The event (for this is the proper word for *Immobiles*) is one of a succession of sonic tableaux, involving, in this performance, strings, winds, voices, pitched percussion, non-pitched percussion, movement, strobe lights, black lights, police lights, visual "projections of symbolism," suggestion, mystery, magic, life, flux, creation.

CHARLES WHITTENBERG *

The United States

During the years the new style was developing, traditional types of concert music were being maintained, but with increasing difficulty. Symphony orchestras had a larger repertoire of both older and newer works, including the works of Classical composers such as Carl Ditters von Dittersdorf and such Romantic figures as Hector Berlioz and Anton Bruckner. Members of the older generation composed new orchestral works, of which the following are representative:

29

* Program note for the first performance by the Electric Circus (1968) at Madison Square Garden, New York. The production was titled *Immobiles for Tape and or Diverse Instruments*, by Mel Powell.

1959: Hindemith, *Pittsburgh Symphony*
1960: Schuman, *Symphony No. 7* and Messiaen tone poem *Chronochromie*
1961: Piston, *Symphony No. 7*
1963: Poulenc, *Sept Répons de Ténèbre* (Seven Responses for Holy Week), premiered posthumously in New York
1964: Copland, symphonic suite *Music for a Great City* (the city was New York but the premiere was in London)
1965: Stravinsky, *Variations for Orchestra*

But the number of symphonies, in the old sense, was on the wane.

Works for chorus and orchestra were more fortunate, for choral techniques were important in forming the new style. Britten's *War Requiem* (1952), Stravinsky's *Canticum Sacrum* (1956), and Poulenc's *Gloria* (1961) were transitional works. In the mid-sixties, a few of the choral works of the new music began to appear in orchestral concerts. Composers of new music were also interested in the concerto; such works as Thea Musgrave's *Clarinet Concerto* (1968) and the *Violin Concerto* of Paul Cooper (born 1926) explored new instrumental relationships, redefining rather than rejecting the orchestra and exploiting new techniques of tonal and spatial interaction.

Second only to symphonic music in the strength of its tradition was the music of the Christian churches. Although many churches had erected modern buildings and commissioned modern stained glass windows, few had been willing to introduce parallel innovations in music. Several Protestant groups were revising hymnals with the help of musicologists, but they were re-creating the older hymns, setting aside the revisions of the nineteenth century and returning to the verbal (rather than the metrical) rhythms and, in some cases, to the pretonal harmony of the originals.

The Second Vatican Council (1962–1965) of the Roman Catholic Church made recommendations on music that may prove to be more important than those of the Council of Trent (1545–1563). Vatican II was concerned with *aggiornamento*—updating church practice and reconstituting the basic services, particularly the Mass. The decision to use the vernacular had far-reaching musical results, because translations changed the essential

Adulation of Beethoven was inherited by the post–World War II generation in a somewhat insouciant form. In this *Peanuts* cartoon, Schroeder is playing Beethoven's Sonata opus 10 no. 2. (© 1959 United Feature Syndicate.)

rhythms of the texts and thus required new musical settings. Many churches accepted the guitar, and a simple, direct folk Mass developed quickly in university chapels and city churches. The more elaborate jazz Mass, with a larger variety of instruments, was less common; its earliest examples were Anglican rather than Roman.

The nature of Jewish services makes them much less subject to experimentation and revision than are Christian services. Orthodox synagogues maintain a heritage measured in millenniums; Conservative and Reform temples have experimented with new sacred compositions, including some by Israeli composers, but much less so than either Protestant or Catholic churches. The greater impact of Hebrew music has been in folk song, carried to the United States by visitors—Israeli musicians performing in America and Americans returning from trips to Israel.

Like symphony orchestras, opera companies also turned to the past, producing such works as Rossini's *Siege of Corinth* (1820; revived at Milan in 1969) and Cavalli's *L'Ormindo* (1644; revived at Glyndebourne, England, in 1967 and New York in 1968). Turning to the transitional and the new was easiest in the state-supported houses of Europe, notably Germany, where Henze's operas were produced, but a few appeared in the United States. New operas included:

1959: Poulenc, *La voix humaine* (The Human Voice; Paris); Britten, *Noye's Fludde* (Aldenburgh, England).
1960: Nono, *Intolleranza* (Venice).
1967: Ginastera, *Bomarzo* (Washington, D. C.; 1968, New York).
1969: Penderecki, *The Devils of Loudon* (Hamburg, Germany, and Santa Fe, New Mexico).

Ballet was already enjoying a rebirth. The evocative sounds and kinesthetic nature of recent music had captured the imagination of choreographers, and new dancing techniques were already developed. Traditional ballet and modern dance were equally popular; in 1958 there had been 75 dance companies in the United States, by 1970 there were over 450. Jazz, special instruments, and electronic and other new musical techniques were welcomed for their sonorous and rhythmic suggestiveness, as were spatial elements.

A synthesis of elements from the popular theater had joined the dance traditions as well. As early as the forties, experiments were introducing parallels between music and the dance. In 1947, Gian-Carlo Menotti (born 1911) wrote the popular opera *The Medium*, in which an important role, that of a mute, was played by a dancer. Originally a New York Ballet Society experiment, *The Medium* played on Broadway but was shunned by opera companies. In 1948, Baldwin Bergersen (born 1914) composed, to a book by the playwright-director William Archibald, an experimental lyric drama, *Far Harbour*; it also was produced by the Ballet Society. *Far Harbour* used three levels of movement—*action, motion,* and *dance* (comparable to the three vocal levels of *speech, recitativo,* and *song*)—to a score that synthesized popular and traditional operatic styles. The work suffered from the problems of other experiments: its operatic techniques were foreign to popular singers, and its popular techniques were foreign to opera singers. At that time the difficulties of production were insuperable. But within twenty years, a solid start had been made on synthesis, and dance had come into its own.

The piano was still an instrument of the home and the concert hall, still a culture symbol but a declining one. For the young, it was being replaced not only by the dance but also by the guitar, an instrument eclipsed by the Romantic legato ideal but reborn in popular music even before the turn of the century. The piano's usefulness in the teaching of music theory, at least in any study based on twelve equal semitones per octave, was still great. However, except for clusters, it was unable to produce statistical effects, and without tampering, its tone quality was limited. The new music found the piano most useful in percussion groups, in which the expanded techniques of the prepared piano were freely used.

A NEW MANDATE

A threefold mandate to musicians and their educators was clarified—to acknowledge the changing styles in the history of music as equally valid, to recognize the music of other cultures with an open mind, and to develop a new pedagogy so that music of all kinds might be studied. Substantial beginnings in all three areas have been made by a few composers, performers, and schools.

The United States was assuming a position of musical leadership in the sixties, and American universities were shaping the future more and more surely. Not only did the universities sponsor performances of new music, but they also took on lively programs of exchange with guest com-

Artist's rendition of the opera house in Sydney, Australia. (Courtesy of Australian News & Information Bureau.)

posers—popular as well as classical—from home and abroad. This, in turn, drew gifted faculty and students, making the American university community a vital, creative energy. Such men as Ross Lee Finney, Chou Wen-Chung (born 1923), Ulysses Kay (born 1917), Paul Cooper, George Crumb (born 1929), Charles Wuorinen (born 1938), Alan Stout (born 1933), and Salvatore Martirano (born 1927) are representative of the several hundred American composers of virtually all styles who were enriching the musical art at American universities in 1970. The trend in universities toward sustaining composers in residence and a theory faculty including active composers has made these institutions chief supporters of new music. The need for a new concept of the performing group was answered by such innovations as the Columbia University Group for Contemporary Music (founded in 1962), which performed over 100 twentieth-century works in its first four years, and the Monday Evening Concerts in Los Angeles.

High schools were also a focus of change. Beginning in 1959, the Ford Foundation began placing young composers in school communities, and by 1967 forty-four school systems were in the program. In cities throughout the nation the artists of the Young Composer Project were composing new music for school choirs and bands; they sought to involve both schools and communities in the excitement of working with and hearing music of their own time. (A significant number of YCP composers are now teaching in the universities.)

A few older composers have written for bands as well. Although the town band is a thing of the past, about 20,000 high school bands were functioning in 1960 and 30,000 in 1970. However they were sustained by a literature based on the ideals of nineteenth-century bands and were becoming increasingly distant from the mainstream. A few composers recognized the need of the school band for a modern literature and turned to that medium. Such works as William Schuman's "Chester" (1956) and Aaron Copland's "Emblem" (1963), both of which used tunes from the American singing-school tradition, began to provide an interaction with the mainstream. Other composers writing for bands included Vaclav Nelhybel (born 1919). His works, for both chamber and large groups, have provided solid fare for bands; they include *Trittico* (1963), for concert band, *Symphonic Requiem* (1965), for bass-baritone solo and band, and *Sine Nomine*, for soloists, chorus, and orchestra (Dijon, 1968; Chicago, 1970).

POPULAR MUSIC

The postwar years began with a many-faceted popular tradition—of swing, boogie-woogie, and musical theater, and vestiges of hot jazz and the blues. Western and gospel music also became popular. Many of the postwar figures were familiar—from the thirties or even the twenties. Duke Ellington was still the most popular musician; touring Europe after the war (1948 and 1950), he won a series of popularity polls. Blues singer Huddie Ledbetter (1888–1949), known as Leadbelly, enjoyed a comeback and recorded "Goodnight, Irene"; he toured in France the last year of his life. Louis Armstrong toured in both Europe (1948–1949) and Japan (1954). And popular singers carried on in the big-band tradition; Tony Martin, Teresa Brewer, Johnny Mathis, and Tony Bennett joined Nat "King" Cole and the other singers of swing, even after the big bands were on the decline. Singing groups such as the Ames Brothers climbed in popularity.

The first notable new style of the postwar years emerged in the music of Miles Davis (born 1926), a trumpeter. He worked with a group of five, six, or nine but rejected the big-band sound and sought a lighter style called *cool jazz*. By 1948, Davis was popular in the United States, and in 1949, he was touring in France.

Jazzmen were seeking new sounds and were examining historic and exotic practices. Bongo drums and Latin rhythms were popular, as were the flute, violin, vibraphone (vibes), xylophone, and French horn. A few individual experiments pointed to a broader reference. The New Friends of Rhythm, a sextet of string quartet, guitar, and harp, recorded paraphrases of classics such as Mozart's overture to the *Marriage of Figaro* and a variation, with a stunning tritonal passage, on Paganini's *24th Caprice*. Moondog produced *Tell It Again*, a setting of nursery tunes for soprano, baritone, flute, and percussion; it had isorhythmic structures, a polyphony of elements in an African technique, *tabla* rhythms deriving from India, and a fast beat in units of fives and sevens as well as threes and fours.

The 1960s saw the fruition of much of the preceding experimentation. John Lewis's Modern Jazz Quartet—piano, vibes, bass, and drums—was one of the most innovative groups of the decade. Such numbers as "Under the Jazzblue Tree" clearly showed the African-Indian influence. It had long sustained chords—each on a drone bass and so long that it created a separate static element—few changes, ornate melodic traceries in unison between piano and vibes, and an overall sense of fabric rather than melody or form. Lewis also composed *The Comedy*, a work for the Modern Jazz Quartet plus four ballet dancers. The work, which Lewis called a "jazz entertainment," was first produced in Paris in 1960. It was received with acclaim and was presented on tours throughout Europe and America.

Jazz critics, from 1950, became increasingly serious about their subject, ignoring "popular" music but supporting jazz by covering the jazz festivals at Newport, Rhode Island (from 1954), Monterey, California (from 1958), and other cities in the United States and abroad. In 1959, 70,000 people attended a three-day jazz festival in Chicago, indicating that interest in jazz was widespread. Ten years later attendance had more than doubled.

A culmination of the pure, hot-jazz style came in the mid-1940s, in the improvisations of Charlie Parker (1920–1955), called Yardbird, a master of the alto sax. A critic summed up many concurring opinions.

In bringing the art of improvisation to a new peak of maturity, Parker had an inestimable influence on jazz musicians regardless of what instrument they played. From the mid-40's on, it was almost impossible for any new jazzman anywhere in the world to escape reflecting to some degree, consciously or unconsciously, a Parker influence; his work set a new standard on every level—harmonic, tonal, rhythmic and melodic.[1]

The sweep of Parker's improvisation can only be suggested, in notation, which cannot illustrate spontaneity. Instrumental skill of consummate virtuosity must be assumed, leaving the artist free for rhythmic subtlety and expansiveness and for melodic shape and embellishment, the hallmarks of great jazz playing.

After World War II, the social channels of music shifted. The postwar generation had been brought up with the movies, the radio, and records.

[1] Leonard Feather, *The New Edition of the Encyclopedia of Jazz*, New York: Bonanza Books, 1962, p. 376.

Improvisation   **Example 88**

CHARLIE PARKER

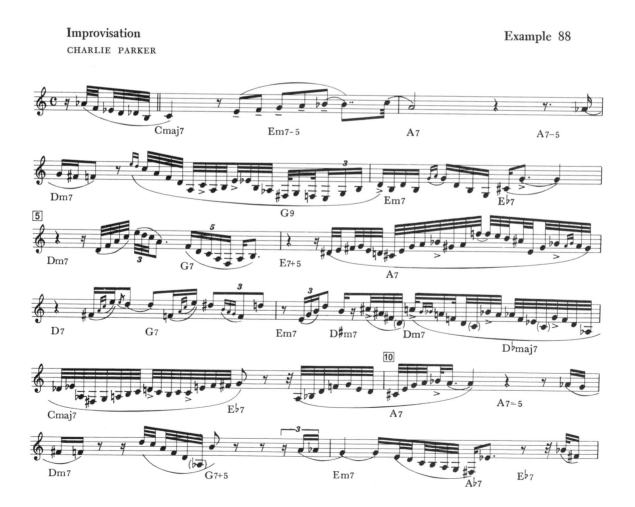

Example 88 (continued)

The alto saxophone line incorporates a simple form (*aaba*) with variations, so measures 1, 9, and 25 each begin the same element. (Courtesy of Librairie Larousse.)

The movies were well established and were on a cycle of continuation, but the record industry was still in its defining years, and the invention of the long-playing (LP) record was to inject it with new power. It provided sustained music for dancing and spelled the decline of the ballroom as the center of popular music.

Radio had suffered a traumatic blow after the war by the sudden rise of television, but it changed its format and began to provide talk shows and, more important, record shows. These were largely improvised, informal, and discursive, lasting from one to several hours, often early in the morning or late at night when formal entertainment was not available. They were dependent to a large degree on the personality of the man who ran the show, the *disc jockey*. From the late forties, the record show took the position of leadership in the presentation of popular music away from the ballroom. The days of the touring bands were over, and musical reputations were subsequently made or broken with records. The disc jockeys, with their power to feature or ignore new releases, had become the kingpins of the record industry and crucial figures in the dissemination of new styles. They were responsible in part for such phenomenal hits as Irving Berlin's "White Christmas"; over 40 million records and 5 million copies of sheet music of this song were sold by 1962, probably the greatest sale in the history of the music industry.

In the mid-1950s, there began a trend toward a synthesis of the various styles—a hybrid of hillbilly, western, blues, gospel, and jazz called *rock and roll*, or *rock 'n' roll*. And on the crest of this trend rode the western-hillbilly guitarist-singer Elvis Presley (born 1935). In such hits as "Hound Dog," Presley established the basic fabric. It was driven by beat and was kinetic, loud, and metered in four, with heavy triplets that threw much of the rhythmic drive to the eighth note. It had decoratively treated basic triads and heightened blues intonation. The form was generally the twelve-bar blues. Two characteristics were mildly antitraditional but significant, because they would be expanded in the 1960s. One was the rhythmic concept of layers of activity—the basic fast beat of triplets (eighth notes) for the instruments, the slower vocal beat (quarter notes), and a visual beat that Presley maintained in pelvic body-English, bringing the visual elements back into the art. The other antitraditional characteristic was a harmonic pattern including a regressive progression from upper to lower dominant, a reversal of the centripetal defining progression of key tonality. The usual harmonic scheme was I-IV-I-V-IV-I, still tonal but weak in its emphasis on the subdominant, as well as in the V-IV progression.

Rock 'n' roll was a teen-age fad, but soon a new dance craze, beginning with the twist (1960), reached the whole range of the nightclub and dancing set. As the rhythmic layers of early rock paralleled African concepts, so did the twist and its successors; they were single-position dances done individually with a repeated motion rather than a series of contrasting steps. The dance craze led to a new type of dance hall, the discothèque, a flamboyantly

Rock

decorated room, often lined with mirrors and enlivened by kaleidoscopic light shows. These rock records were played at high volume and customers became intoxicated on sound, light, and motion. Rock groups began to be prominent, and the combo of three or four became standard.

In 1964, the most influential phenomenon of the defining years of rock burst on the public, this time from an even more unexpected source. The Beatles, a four-man group from Liverpool, England, captured America and Europe with the song "I Want to Hold Your Hand." The effect of the Beatles was summarized by Ellen Sander, a critic, in 1968 when she said they had succeeded in "innovating, experimenting, and consummating the musical concepts of pop," becoming not only a sociological phenomenon but a musically sophisticated group of real power. "But if their importance lies in their growth, perfection, and influence, their appeal still lies in their vitality, the utter joy they communicate, their consistent, esthetic effervescence. They asserted that seriousness of artistic intention and lightheartedness of content are not incompatible elements in the conception of an art form." [2]

The Beatles not only were concerned with the jazz-rock elements from the popular traditions, but also were active in experimenting with the triangulations of the new music and, in a more personal contribution, with the traditions of India. Their album *Sergeant Pepper's Lonely Hearts Club Band* (1967), including works by Paul McCartney and George Harrison, was admired on all sides and was regarded as a classic of the genre. Sander continued:

> Without a doubt, the masterwork of the [rock] movement is *Sergeant Pepper's Lonely Hearts Club Band*. Of first importance was the conceptualization of the album, its identity as a complete work. The first and twelfth cuts (title song and reprise) circumscribe a concert of ten songs, each of which is a phase, or movement in musical development. In and of themselves the songs are brilliant, from the mischievous *Lovely Rita Meter Maid* to the more imposing *Within You Without You*, which wanders from Eastern to Western resolutions, surrounding a free-form lyric about an ultimate mystic revelation. One cut melts imperceptibly into the next, forming a perfect sequence.
>
> A celebration of the absurd pervades each of the twelve cuts in the concert. . . . The scoring and production of the album are exquisite. The arrangements are effected in layer upon layer of sound, each imposing a particular effect on the body of the song. The textures, movements, subtleties, and separations were achieved over several months of recording, overdubbing, and mixing. The album has been justifiably described as a visual, sensual, intellectual, and emotional as well as musical experience. [3]

Sander makes it clear that the technique of accumulation, both in musical space and in time, was operative in rock as well as in the new music. The

[2] Ellen Sander, "Pop in Perspective: A Profile," *The Saturday Review*, Oct. 26, 1968, p. 80.
[3] *Ibid.*, p. 8of.

use of electric guitars, overdubbing, and mixing also link rock to the new music.

Incorporating social commentary as well as creative synthesis, such Beatles' works as Harrison's "Within You Without You" and McCartney's "Lucy in the Sky with Diamonds" (to words by John Lennon) are total works of poetry and music; an important text is set in a musical fabric designed for and with the poem. Harrison's "Within You Without You" is in the sitar-violin-tabla style of India, which is appropriate to its mystical text; it is in free verse but carefully incorporates internal rhymes and repetitions. The Lennon-McCartney "Lucy in the Sky with Diamonds" contains greater internal contrast; it has a harmonic quarter-note $\frac{3}{4}$ beat, ligamented inner voices, and a hauntingly Romantic style, followed by a hard rock eighth-note $\frac{4}{4}$ beat, *fortissimo*, made of a repeated two-measure unit. The piece ends with a slow fade-out. Form is sectional, from a simple *ABA* da capo aria to complex verse sections with first, second, and third endings; most of the songs have codas. One contains a statistical crescendo of both volume and pitch that speaks of McCartney's awareness of new-music techniques.

After the Beatlemania had abated slightly, it was evident that the Beatles were the pacesetters for an amazing number of rock groups. There were about 2,000 professional groups in 1968 and an estimated 300,000 amateur groups in 1970.[4] The professionals related music to the new humanism and the young generation's hope of changing the world and moved toward the new music, toward the past, and toward pure jazz. Many members of the leading groups were literate and perceptive. They became troubadours, writing songs about their world, and several volumes of their lyrics have been published as poetry.

The strength of the rock groups lay in their commitment to musical reality, their commitment to the human condition, and their confidence of a binding relationship between the two. In practical terms, they were musical eclectics, and they were moving closer to Bach, Webern, and Stockhausen.

By 1968, rock groups were combining instruments with electronically manipulated tapes. The Mothers of Invention were described as "a ten-man electronic chamber orchestra that specializes in satirical rock and jazz."[5] The Chrome Circus, another group, produced a rock score for Robert Joffrey's ballet *Astarte* in 1967, and rock elements also entered jazz as part of the new wave. Charles Lloyd, a tenor sax artist, appearing in San Francisco, spoke in the same vein. "Music is like breathing. When one *is* and when one breathes and says to the world, 'I'm here,' there's something quite cosmic about it. We're all here. All in harmony. Only the chords are different. I play about the unity of everything. The love, the totality—like bringing everyone together in a joyous dance. I play love vibrations."[6] Again the human element

---

[4] "Start Up a Combo," *Better Homes and Gardens*, May, 1970, p. L-6.
[5] Douglass Watt, "Popular Records," *The New Yorker*, June 14, 1969, p. 92.
[6] *Time*, Feb. 3, 1967, p. 38.

was incorporated in a musical eclecticism. A review of Lloyd's concert said that "communication is his prime concern, and he achieves it by drawing freely on a wide variety of styles—from calypso to hootchy-kootchy, from Bartók to Indian ragas." [7]

The basic concepts of rock had been instrumental, using voices traditionally or in an instrumentally informed technique. A strong counterpart in the vocal area was a blend of urban blues and hard rock called *soul*. The whole concept of soul was black, the great soul artists were black, and its center was Motown Records in Detroit. Aretha Franklin said in 1968, "I sing to people; I sing about what matters," and she added, "Dig me if you dare!" [8] Another soul singer wrote, " 'Soul' is black dignity and pride. 'Soul' is a depth of emotion and feeling born out of hurt, struggle and trouble. 'Soul' is having lived the black life in White America." [9] Soul, with its hard rock beat and increased loudness and in its passionate communication and direct vocal decoration, was close to pure blues.

The end of the 1960s saw such separate genres as rock, new wave jazz, cool jazz, country western, gospel, and soul. Although separate social contexts tended to keep these types individual, the pull toward synthesis was becoming stronger. The Memphis Birthday Blues Festival in 1969 included a variety of types whose tendency toward synthesis was epitomized by a group called The Insect Trust, which was billed as "the world's first country-jazz-folk-blues-rock-swing band."

[7] *Ibid.*
[8] Quoted in J Marks, *Rock and Other Four Letter Words*, New York: Bantam, 1968.
[9] Glenda J. Fears, letter to Edith Borroff, April, 1968.

Bob Dylan in California. (At the left is Pete Seeger.) (Courtesy of Jim Marshall.)

When Irving Berlin wrote the hit song "There's No Business Like Show Business" for the show *Annie Get Your Gun* in 1946, he was speaking of that part of the theater involved in the production of Broadway shows. By that year, the musical had turned to American subjects (*Annie* was the Western heroine Annie Oakley), and both verbal and musical idioms had been Americanized. The musical show continued to be popular in the postwar generation; it turned toward a more open musical view, spurred by other forms of musical theater such as the ballets of Aaron Copland, experimental productions, the new jazz and, later, rock styles, and the new international folk-song repertoire, along with a few formal traditions of the past.

Show Business

The postwar musical tended toward here-and-now American themes and faraway-but-relevant subjects. Irving Berlin's *Call Me Madam*, which parodied the Truman administration, exemplified the former type, and Richard Rodgers's *The King and I*, based on a journal of a governess at the court of Siam in the mid-nineteenth century, exemplified the latter. A typical musical was based on an American literary source, informal and with a colorful milieu, and contained a variety of songs and dances conceived in a variety of styles suggested by the action. An excellent example of such a musical was Frank Loesser's *Guys and Dolls* (1950), an adaptation of Damon Runyon's stories of the New York underworld. The musical scope of the score is evidenced in the separate traditions incorporated in the various numbers—a dance tune, a ballad, a burlesque tune, a spiritual, a Gilbert and Sullivan specialty character humor, a straight popular tune, a Salvation Army band tune, and an Irish folk ballad.

Later in the fifties the same general types prevailed. Examples of the two were Meredith Willson's *The Music Man* (1957), to his own story and book, and Frederick Loewe's *My Fair Lady* (1956), an adaptation by Alan Jay Lerner of George Bernard Shaw's *Pygmalion* (1912). Both these shows included beat-infused talk songs using *Sprechstimme* notation and percussive rhythmic delivery. *The Music Man* opened with a train scene, in which the men's chorus created the train through rhythm and the use of long *S* sounds suggesting steam. The show also included a barbershop quartet, a hoedown, a fast "gossip" song that combined with the traditional "Goodnight, Ladies," a talk song, and a rousing march, "Seventy-six Trombones," that was a transformation of the gentle waltz ballad "Goodnight, My Someone."

The two types continued as representative, though not exclusive. The faraway-but-relevant show, particularly off Broadway, went farther away from tradition and culminated in a show that might be classified as "social fantasy." In 1968 composer Galt MacDermot turned to both the literary and musical essence of rock to produce, in New York, *Hair: The American Tribal Love-Rock Musical*. Within a year it was playing in several other cities as well, in both Europe and America. Musically, it might be described as super rock. From its opening electronic moments to its finale, the score is purposefully eclectic, with American Indian war whoops, jazz (both classical and modern), country and western, soul, and the music of India. Here, too, eclecticism is associated with the new humanism, symbolically uniting people through their music. A setting for Shakespeare's "What a Piece of Work Is Man" is a conscious link to an earlier humanism.

The here-and-now American theme was represented by Burt Bacharach's *Promises, Promises* (1968), with lyrics by Hal David, on Neil Simon's adaptation of the 1960 movie *The Apartment*. Although one critic felt it seemed "more like a comedy with incidental songs than a musical," [10] the music gives reality to the city, particularly in its kinetic score. The score was stylized and innovative for the Broadway musical in its introduction of prose rhythms, shifting meters, and fast beats (counting eighth-notes).

Each score—for *Hair* and for *Promises, Promises*—represented one heritage of the American musical past, and each was reaching out to expand its concept. *Hair* reached toward Frank Zappa's group, The Mothers of Invention and *Promises, Promises* reached for Stravinsky's *le Sacre du printemps*, but both nevertheless show the beginnings of a synthesis, hardly defined, that may presage a new life for the musical in America.

Meanwhile, the daily bread of show business had switched to television, which had absorbed elements of theater, vaudeville, and radio. In 1946, the United States had had about 7,500 television sets, but in 1948 there were 16,500, and a decade later 50 million. The great early shows were vaudeville shows, olios that included many kinds of acts. From 1948, the Ed Sullivan show presented visual as well as aural acts—acrobats, magicians, dog acts, and, above all, dancers—that the radio program could not have. The Rowan and Martin Laugh-In (from 1967) resembled a minstrel show even more, with the same snappy one-liners, the same stage business, and stereotyped characters whose predictable reactions appear from week to week.

The solo song or other musical act is basic to the variety show, but only a variety show such as Ed Sullivan's could juxtapose the many styles popular in the United States after the war. An opera singer might be followed by a rock group (it was on Sullivan's show in 1964 that The Beatles were first seen in the United States); a specialty act might be followed by the Vienna choirboys; a Scottish pipe and drum tattoo might be on the same program with folk dancers from Russia. Thus, rock, jazz, popular, folk, exotic, and serious music might be separate musical elements in a total mosaic.

Television drama required the same musical support the movie drama required. Henry Mancini's theme for *Peter Gunn* was to become popular as a recording. Some scores were handled with care and effectiveness; the scores for the *Perry Mason* series, for example, used Fred Steiner's theme in a series of variations ranging in mood from suspense to tumult. Stanley Wilson's score for the TV movie *Fear No Evil* (1969) used both instruments and electronic sounds, opening with a menacing overlay of vocal whispers in a statistical technique.

Television could produce original opera or ballet as well. The National Broadcasting Company commissioned Stravinsky's *Noah and the Flood*

10 Henry Hewes, *Saturday Review*, Dec. 21, 1968, p. 13.

(1952) and produced Gian-Carlo Menotti's *Amahl and the Night Visitors* (1951), probably the most widely performed original TV musical theater piece. Ballet—dance in general—was again given the dimension of camera angles and other film techniques that the movies had given the musical in the 1930s, but TV added innovations such as film overlays, dubbing, and light shows, which are most effective in a musical context of expanded sound.

The movie musical continued to be an offshoot of Broadway, but background scores for dramatic films were expanding their scope, as were other kinds of music. In 1948, the movie *The Quiet One* had a score, by Ulysses Kay, that eloquently and hauntingly commented on the black experience. In the 1950 score to the film *Asphalt Jungle*, Miklos Rozsa used jazz to create tension; he demonstrated the untapped versatility of jazz by producing moments of genuine malevolence. In 1955, the score of *The Man with the Golden Arm* incorporated jazz more essentially; and in 1956, the science fiction movie *Forbidden Planet* used a score composed entirely from synthesized sound. In 1958, cool jazz trumpeter Miles Davis furnished a score for the French film *Ascenseur pour l'échafaud* (Elevator for the Scaffold); and in 1960, the French film *les Liasons dangereuses* used a score by the hot jazz–bop pianist-composer Thelonious Monk (born 1920). In the 1960s, further style extensions were represented by Ravi Shankar's score for *Charly* (1968).

In addition, the movies furnished new popular songs, most often as single records derived from the theme of a dramatic score. Noteworthy examples range from David Raskin's "Laura" (1944) to Dimitri Tiomkin's "High Noon" (1952) and Henry Mancini's "Days of Wine and Roses" (1962).

Perhaps the most prophetic synthesis of musical elements in the late 1960s was effected by *2001: A Space Odyssey* (1967), in which an eclectic score combined sacred and secular, popular and symphonic, old and new by including Gregorian chant, the Johann Strauss orchestral waltz *The Beautiful Blue Danube* and the György Ligeti *Atmosphères*. The intense musical clarity of the Strauss and the equally intense spatial revelations of the Ligeti, with its shifting layers redefining distance in a new realm of musical imagination, combined in a multidimensional commentary on the new paths of man as he entered the space age.

AT THE END OF THE SIXTIES

The arts were very much in the Space Age, and the cumulative aims of artists were to retain their individuality, to savor contrasts and exploit them, and to rejoice in open movement from one element to another. Architects were seeking new relations between the indoor and outdoor elements in their work; artists, dancers, playwrights, and composers were seeking new interactions, new means to combine materials with independence and fluidity.

Independence and *fluidity* were salient words—gentle in the mellow and strident in the young—in the total cultural goals of the late 1960s. In general, dissatisfaction with the scientific philosophy was growing. Like rock, new music had entered the lists for the new humanism. Benjamin Britten's *War Requiem* (1952), Luigi Dallapiccola's *Canti di liberazioni* (1960), Krzysztof Penderecki's *Threnody: To the Victims of Hiroshima* (1961)— all were protest works against war. Karlheinz Stockhausen's *Hymnen* (1967), was called "an expression of global brotherhood in sound" and the reviewer spoke of its "*Leitmotif* of an all-encompassing 'family of man' or a 'harmony of the world.'" [11] And in 1968, on the twentieth anniversary of the Declaration of the Rights of Man, the United Nations presented a Human Rights Day concert. Featured was a work commissioned for the occasion— the oratorio, *Yes, Speak Out, Yes*, by Cristobal Halffter—a new music work of grandeur that was composed to a text by Norman Corwin, which he drew from the Declaration itself. The Minnesota Symphony and the Augsburg College Choir, with two conductors (Stanislaw Skrowaczewski and Halffter), were spatially deployed, and the work also used electronic tapes.

The diversity of musical production in 1969 was splendid. About thirty-five music festivals in that year presented jazz, opera, folk, rock, popular, chamber music, and traditional orchestral and solo concerts—all enthusiastically attended. A few highlights of the year's musical adventures follow.

In Europe, a number of festivals took note of the Berlioz centennial, reviving his opera *les Troyens* and featuring several of his other works.

At a folk-music festival in Gatlinburg, Tennessee, ballads dating back to the sixteenth century were sung, alone and with traditional accompanying instruments, including guitar, zither, and banjo. The slides, flat tone, and decoration would have been at home in a Medieval puy or a nineteenth-century slave compound.

In New York City, the oratorio *The Light in the Wilderness*, by jazzman Dave Brubeck, incorporated both rock (and raga) and jazz elements.

On concert tour, the violinist Tossy Spivakovsky was programing both the *24th Caprice* of Paganini and the J. S. Bach Sonata in g minor for unaccompanied violin. For the latter, he was using a specially made (though historically inaccurate) bow in a search for a true Baroque style.

In Vienna, the state opera celebrated its hundredth birthday with a gala performance of Mozart's *Don Giovanni*.

In Los Angeles, 30,000 people jammed a single performance at a rock festival and 60,000 more rioted outside when they found they would not be admitted.

In Michigan, a concert featured Medieval songs, unaccompanied and in the mixed tone colors of minstrelsy.

In Zagreb, Yugoslavia, at an international festival of new music, the United States was represented by *Available Forms II*, by Earle Brown.

In California, American students presented a gamelan concert with authentic Javanese instruments as part of a university program in ethnomusicology.

---

11 Wolf-Eberhard von Lewinski, "Where Do We Go From Here?" *The Musical Quarterly*, vol. 60, no. 2, p. 196, April, 1969.

At the Billy Graham crusade in Madison Square Garden, a chorus of 2,000 sang nineteenth-century hymns, and guest soloists presented a variety of traditional, folk, and popular religious songs.

In a college chapel in Wisconsin, an English Mass celebrated by a Dominican chaplain included improvised prayers from the congregation of mixed lay and religious communicants. Folk song, with guitar, provided the musical embellishment.

At Bayreuth, Wagner as usual.

At the White House, a birthday party was held in honor of Duke Ellington. A jazz concert was given, and the President honored his guest with a Freedom Medal.

On television, Vladimir Horowitz presented a piano recital in the virtuoso tradition, closing the program with his electrifying transcription of the "Habañera" from Bizet's *Carmen*.

The scope of performance in both time and place was part of the new concept of music. Composers of the main traditions agreed with the definition Varèse had advocated in 1962:

> I should like you to consider what I believe is the best definition of music, because it is all-inclusive: "the corporealization of the intelligence that is in sound." . . . If you think about it you will realize that, unlike most dictionary definitions, which make use of such subjective terms as beauty, feelings, etc., it covers all music, Eastern or Western, past or present, including the music of our new electronic medium.[12]

The rock musician, jazz player, and university composer would subscribe to the essential definition. More important, a synthesis of these traditions was already in motion. The rock musician might lecture at a university, and the university professor might become a sideman at a jazz performance on Saturday night. Such American professors of music as Mel Powell (born 1923) and Kenneth Gaburo (born 1926) were jazz musicians composing works that bridged the final gap. Powell's "Immobiles for Tape and or Diverse Instruments" (1968) was first performed by the Electric Circus; Gaburo's "Exit Music II: Fat Millie's Lament" (1965) combines both concrete and synthesized sounds in a rock-bound work.

It may be that the future of music will reflect the future of man and that the musical visionaries of the sixties have correctly assumed a tie between musical and humanistic forces. It is certain that composers of the new music are at the point of joining with past composers, who, in other centuries, found artistic exhilaration in their new art and felt a freedom from the past, as though for the first time. "Composers are now able, as never before," said Varèse in 1962, "to satisfy the dictates of that inner ear of the imagination." [13]

[12] Quoted in Elliott Schwartz and Barney Childs (eds.), *Contemporary Composers on Contemporary Music*, New York: Holt, 1967, p. 207.

[13] *Ibid.*, p. 208.

Part Seven

HISTORY AND MUSIC

And let us, ciphers to this great accompt,
On your imaginary forces work. . . .
Piece out our imperfections with your thoughts:
Into a thousand parts divide one man
And make imaginary puissance.
Think, when we talk of horses, that you see them
Printing their proud hoofs i' the receiving earth.
For 'tis your thoughts that now must deck our kings,
Carry them here and there, jumping o'er times,
Turning the accomplishment of many years
Into an hourglass.

WILLIAM SHAKESPEARE *

The Practicality of History

30

Unlike the music of most of the world, Western music has undergone many changes, producing not one but a series of esthetics—musical ideals have changed virtually from generation to generation. But within this chain, historians agree on six eras that represent musical ideals consistent enough for valid style generalizations. The ideals are equally splendid, and each one culminated in distinctive mediums, techniques, and forms. Each began with transition and formation, proceeded to clear definition and fulfillment, and then became too secure, taken for granted, and, eventually, tired, giving way to another transition.

Composers do not choose the time in which they work; they respond to the condition of their art as they reach maturity. If a musical language

* 1599. Prologue to *Henry V*.

is unformed, they seek to define it; if a form is defined, they seek to fulfill it; if a concept has been used up, they reject it. The relationship of this cycle to individual personalities is one of the most fascinating studies in music.

If the cycle determines *what* composers set out to do, their individuality determines *how* they do it. Yet individuality of men and works is formed from common heritage and common vocabulary. This is true even of the dissenters in music, for one must acknowledge an idea in order to deny it. Thus even an exceptional genius must be appreciated in the context of his time. Assessment of Machaut's Mass, for example is heightened by seeing it not simply as a four-part harmonic work but as a four-part harmonic work composed in the time of a three-part polyphonic norm.

Most composers work in sympathy with their times, and the creative cycle calls for different kinds of genius. When a new musical language is being worked out, a formative genius is needed. Confusion is virtually inevitable at such times, because composers have rejected basic concepts of the immediate past but have not yet determined new concepts to replace them. Many composers must experiment, with small successes and failures, before a new style can be forged. The inventive geniuses who guide new ideas through their initial stages are generally, and, in this concept, inevitably, little known, but they are fascinating in historical perspective.

In contrast, consensus illuminates the great periods of musical culmination. During these periods, composers are in basic agreement concerning the essentials of musical language and the forms it should have. It is such a time that can produce a Josquin or a Mozart.

And finally, when forms are fulfilled and in danger of losing their excitement, a third type of genius is needed to discover a final expansion. Composers of this type, who lead a musical language to further (generally emotional) meanings, can also seem like transitional figures. Dufay, Monteverdi, and Beethoven are examples of such men.

Thus each of the six historical periods can be seen as a cycle of formation, culmination, and transcendence, broken at the last by decline and esthetic confusion (chaos to the ears of the conservative) that led to a new period of formation. And such a view is useful. But, in addition to the basic cycles, Western music contained many overlapping rhythms, developments, and counterpulls. These formed complex interactions, even though individually each tended to simplicity.

TIME

The forward impetus of sound in time is essential to all music. Music is created by combining living sounds (palpable vibration) and binding sounds (including measured silence) in temporal relation through rhythmic organization.

Pulse and Meter

Like the spoken word, music can proceed in either free (prose) or metered (poetic) rhythmic language, tending toward the latter in any formal or symbolic use. Prose rhythm in music has two main functions—presenting in music prose texts with the rhythm of language and elaborating musical ideas in parabolic variation. In Western music, the prose texts of the early churches (both Jewish and Christian) were performed in prose rhythms. Later the recitativo, *fioratura*, *cadenza*, and unmeasured prelude (the latter three of the Baroque) represent nonverbal prose rhythms in Western music, which is not rich in such practice. Conversely, dance, processional music, and work songs represent strong, regular rhythmic motion in virtually all cultures and times.

For centuries the basic unit of musical momentum in Western music has been called the *pulse*, though it has not always been steady or regular. Even where music with prose rhythm has flourished, the fact that music for work, dance, and processions flourished beside it made a concept of a relatively steady, measured pulse basic. But attitudes in the West toward the musical pulse have differed widely through the eras of music history.

Within the Medieval ideal solo performance was not common, except in the declamation of a poetic tale to the harp or the private intonation of a love lyric. Minstrels seldom performed alone; pipe-and-tabor soloists most often played for dancers; choirs sang plainchant. Pulse was conceived as a regulator, a means of coordination. It was directly regulating in popular music but subject to complex and touchy coordinations in polyphony, particularly and spectacularly in the sophisticated proportions of the mannerists of the Ars nova. The proportional system separated the coordinating tactus from the rhythmic actuality of the musical lines; they proceeded independently, each with its own impulse and related to the tactus but not necessarily duplicating it.

In the Renaissance, the pulse continued to serve as a regulator, but the growth of the harmonic element simplified the problems of synchrony by forcing composers to sacrifice rhythmic intricacies for vertical clarity. The Medieval division of the pulse had been mainly triple; the Renaissance division was generally duple. Later, the pulse aided dramatic expression in the madrigal, in which accents could emphasize words or underline feelings. At the end of the Renaissance, the solo madrigal and the new monody encouraged a free beat to foster rhetorical expression.

Even more, the pulse became a factor in harmonic motion, and, increasingly, in the definition of tonal center. The Baroque era found excitement in the unity of pulse and rhythm, and the pulse itself varied in tempo. The measure bar entered notation as a definitive element, accenting the pulse in regular twos, threes, or fours. Baroque composers were excited by metrical ideas, often creating music whose chief subject was the beat itself or working over a single rhythmic activation of a tone. The relentless, driving beat of Bach and Vivaldi, so taxing for the performer, is the essence of the Baroque spirit and the key to the Baroque style. And yet movements of impelling metricality were often preceded by free recitativo or prelude, which emphasized the contrast between the two rhythmic concepts. In virtuoso solo movements, including arias, the regular beat was typically suspended toward the end; this was done to allow the performer to demonstrate his skill in improvising a cadenza by developing a fioratura or embellishing a subject while the accompanying instruments held at a fermata.

The Classical era saw the relaxation of this intense concentration on the metrical pulse. The Classicist turned to experimentation of design *within* the meter. Rather than directly pulsive music, he wrote movements in which many subjects brought variety of line, texture, and key within a single meter and tempo. Classical expressiveness gave rise to use of the rubato—the bending of the pulse in a solo melody over a steady beat and meter.

It was but a short step from contrasting designs to contrasting moods. The Romantic composer saw pulse itself as fluctuating. He introduced contrasting tempos, with attendant ritard, accelerando, and allargando markings, within a single movement (actually a contradiction in terms). Romantic rubato, unlike its Classical predecessor, stretched the beat itself, pulling and compressing the pulse for purposes of sentiment, and a steady beat was rare except in very fast movements. Both free beat and extreme tempos required a simple rhythmic structure, because rhythmic niceties cannot be perceived within an extensive rubato.

Late Romantic composers became increasingly aware of the need for rhythmic experiment and review of the theories of pulse and meter, and a renewed interest in the rhythmic element of music became both desirable and practicable. The first half of the twentieth century witnessed an array of rhythmic infusions. Interest in "primitive" art fostered the use of asymmetrical meters such as $\frac{5}{4}$, $\frac{7}{8}$, $\frac{11}{8}$, or an $\frac{8}{8}$ comprised of a regular $3 + 3 + 2$, all of which had been used for millennia in other cultures. The forthright Baroque pulse was introduced in ragtime and jazz and in music emulating the sounds of exotic cultures. Or a compulsive beat might be created by retaining a common note value (generally the eighth note) while making frequent changes in its organization as meter.

In addition to experimenting with these innovations, which were heard and enjoyed by the listener, composers turned more and more to rhythmic structures not perceived as metrical but related to theatrical and clock time. The techniques used in such structures were not reflected by standard notation, which often bristled with changes of meter signature and complex rhythms of an antimetrical nature; such metric notation enabled performers to synchronize their parts but had no meaning to the listener. The metrical intricacies of the twentieth century proceeded increasingly in a complexity of notation irrelevant to the musical ideas, which were often antimetrical.

By the middle of the twentieth century, rhythmic practice in the West enjoyed the broadest scope of effect since Medieval days. Popular music, in the forms of jazz, swing, the blues, and rock, returned to a concept of the beat as motivating and central to musical perception. Concert music using conventional mediums turned to metrical irregularities, exotic techniques, and antimetrical rhythms, as well as to the steady rhythms of folk and popular music. Experimentalists freely explored all these but began to concentrate on techniques of clock and theatrical time. Composers began to indicate overall rather than exact rhythmic content, either using noteheads without rhythmic specifications or spacing generally on the page to suggest temporal interactions and to achieve spontaneous and statistical effects. Association of musical rhythms with linear measurement (as inches of tape or frames of film) gave composers techniques for dealing with psychological time rather than with meter; electronic composition used such techniques directly, and instrumental and vocal music also became increasingly concerned with them. By 1970, the combining of electronic elements with vocal and instrumental performances was natural and practical in both concert and popular music. Either sphere might use the rhythm of a barn dance, of a tape loop, of an Indian *tala*, of contrasting layers of musical activity at independent speeds and of varying types, or of overlapping free performance of wheels by a number of orchestral or choral musicians. The differences are being developed and exploited, not to judge or select among them, but to provide variable effects within a rhythmic spectrum; this is surely one of the chief excitements of the new music.

Tempo

The study of speed in music is complex and fascinating, but it has generally been oversimplified in the West during the three and a half centuries of metric rhythm. Recently, however, many problems of time have become immensely stimulating to scientists, philosophers, authors, and artists. The modern Western concepts of linear time—even of past, present, and future —are being examined and questioned.

For the practical musician and his audience, time, particularly the perception of speed or tempo, is basic. Perception of speed is directly produced by the expenditure of energy in relation to time. Fast music is that in which many notes occur in a given period of time; slow music is that in which few notes appear in a comparable interval or, in harmonic music, when more or fewer chord changes occur. Also, perception of speed is modified to a certain extent by energy factors—disjunct melodic subjects, loud sounds, and incisive, staccato attacks require greater energy than quiet melodics, soft sounds, and legato playing. Thus a clear, highly energized performance is perceived as faster than a placid or muddled one. Acoustical factors also modify the perception of speed; musicians know that they must perform faster in outdoor concerts than they would in a hall in order to create the same effect. And finally, our physiology modifies perception of tempo. Basically, we perceive a musical pulse as slow or fast in relation to our own heartbeat. Thus, although a group of listeners will agree unanimously on the speed of an extreme tempo, in the middle range (close to the rate of the human pulse), considerable disagreement is likely. One listener may feel a tempo is generally fast while another feels that it drags. This inner speedometer presents an inexperienced performer with a special problem—having rehearsed a movement at a precise tempo, he may arrive at the moment of performance in a state of excitement that has caused his heart to beat faster and may unconsciously increase the tempo of his performance proportionately. With the aid of adrenalin and technical proficiency, a soloist may turn this to brilliant account, but the performer who has no technical reserves or the chamber musician coordinating with others may come to grief through his altered perceptions.

Aside from the general problems of the perception of speed, the historian deals with questions of changing taste in tempo, for the several eras have had different opinions on the subject. In general, when melodic line, instrumental color, and high surface texture have been prized, a quick tempo has proved desirable. Thus, styles such as the Gothic, Baroque, and, almost as strongly, the early Renaissance and Classical require brisk tempos for their ideals to be fulfilled.

Medieval music, with its strong linear emphasis, needed to move forward smartly if the perception of separate lines was to be maintained, for individuality of line is lost in sustained sound. For the twentieth-century performer, the problem of tempo in Medieval music is basically the confusion caused by modern notation. The driving Medieval beat, triply divided, was transcribed as three whole notes, three half notes, or three quarter notes. Since the count is *one*, the use of three eighth notes (as in all the examples in this book), with a steady ♩. from 60 per minute in a slow piece (as in Giraut's alba, Example 2) to 88 or even 92 per minute in a fast piece (as in the rota "Sumer is icumen in," Example 24), is musically more suggestive in modern terms. Performers must translate dotted whole notes or dotted half notes of other versions to the musical value of the dotted quarter. It is imperative to assess the value that represents the single beat.

The same problem holds for late Renaissance polyphony, though the basic division of the beat was then duple and the precise value is more difficult to assess. The late Renaissance madrigal, either harmonic or solo, was less interested in linear independence than in vertical and interpretive unity. Discontinuation of the more difficult rhythmic proportions and the stating of purely chordal passages in long notes give evidence of a twofold concept— that the traditional faster tempo prevailed for the imitative style and a slower tempo was available for the newer material of expressive or dramatic character. Although in modern notation the main beat is harder to assess, the performer has two aids. First, using simple proportional shifts, such as the hemiola, requires a tempo quick enough to force the listener to hear the shifts as a change of the beat itself, rather than of groupings of beats. Second, suspensions prepared as a syncope were basic to the harmonic language, and a slow tempo deprives them of their essential rhythmic off-accent. A tempo that maintains the shifts and syncopations is true to the Renaissance concept.

Baroque music, centering in contrast, featured juxtapositions of slow and fast movements and included unmeasured preludes and cadenzas along with free recitativo, in which pulse stopped, time seemed suspended, and a parenthetical phrase or section completed itself before the piece was resumed. In opera, music was often associated with a text or a dance, so tempo was seldom independently musical. This was true in the dance suite as well, for rhythmic character was its essential element.

The Baroque love of the beat also implied love of an exactly right tempo, and the excitement of a perfect beat or speed was primary to Baroque music. The few measurements that came from writers of the seventeenth and eighteenth centuries indicate that tempos were lively, and interestingly, Johann Sebastian Bach was reputed to prefer fast tempos. Quantz (1752) gave a norm of $\quarternote = 80$ for an allegro assai in $\frac{4}{4}$ and $\quarternote = 40$ for an adagio in the same signature (twice as fast in alla breve); because both were likely to deal in sixteenth-note figurations, these tempos are quick. The performer must maintain the beat as primary and motivating. Contrasts between movements are essential, and internal details secondary. As in the Renaissance style, the Baroque syncopation is basic and needs to sound as an off-accent.

The Classical interest in shifting textures within a continuing tempo inaugurated a relaxation of speed and a gradually changing emphasis toward the slower tempo and expressive rubato that would characterize the Romantic era. In this sense, the Classical period was transitional, with the beat still lively but not directly propulsive. Baroque music had thrived on the intoxication of the beat; Classical music lived in the exhilaration of changing textures and subjects within a continuing meter, a delight in musical design and meaning that implies a steady, rhythmic flow. Continuing thrust had to be maintained if contrasts were to be fully realized and the changing textures perceived and savored.

The Romantic esthetic was less directly musical; the attention of the listener was more often directed to his own responses as the nineteenth-century ideal developed. This presupposed a ruminative technique of listening that was supported by a basically harmonic-thematic fabric. This method of listening was further encouraged by an increasing dynamic level and the long-limned themes that stretched in a leisurely arch of a single idea. The increasing size of the orchestra, for example, which acoustically required more time to make individual chords sound, led automatically to slower tempos in orchestral music. By the second half of the century, music was perceptibly slower, and even the meager literature of older music left in the repertoire had been given Romantic tempos—in many cases cut to half or less than their original speeds. Where note values had shifted, the slowdown was more often to one-quarter of the original speeds. For example the Renaissance breve ($\diamond$) equaled the modern whole note in the notation but the modern quarter note in performance. The expansive Romantic tempo was burdened neither with the need for a steady beat nor with the desire for the juxtaposition of contrasting subjects. The interpretive and meditative aspects of music were further enhanced by the extensive and then standard use of a tempo rubato in all but very fast and highly characteristic pieces.

Early in the twentieth century, the general interest in concepts of time brought a return to a preference for faster tempos. A renewed interest in older music led to research and editing, the republication of texts from other centuries, and increased attention to authenticity of style in the performance of older music. Composers began to infuse their music with Baroque and Classical idioms, most notably subjects and textures, which necessitated tempo change as well. In addition, a rising interest in clock time and un-measured time led to experimentation with the most basic concepts of musi-cal time. A number of new alternatives, many based on either theatrical or technical machine coordinations, have led to perceptual methods of time organization that have become an essential concern of the new music. From compulsive Baroque or rock beats that return to the primacy of tempo to an almost disembodied hovering of time with the illusion of having no tempo at all, the new music is returning to a view of time as a direct, pri-mary, and compelling element of the musical fabric.

SOUND

Sound is the very essence of music, and its effect is created largely by color and texture. Color is the *timbre* or quality of sound; texture is both *surface texture*, the quality of attack or connectedness, and *structural texture*, the complex of simultaneous activity that makes the fabric complicated or simple, thick or thin, busy or serene.   *Timbre*

Interest in the means of producing musical sounds has been universal. In Western theory, a distinction is made between mechanical means (instru-ments) and natural means (human voice, hand clapping, etc.); this distinc-tion too is universal, though by no means always drawn in the same terms. Both vocal and instrumental sounds embrace color and texture; they are linked in ideals of technique that have changed from era to era, with each period characterized by its musical fabric as vividly as each culture by its language.

Men of the Medieval era delighted in the colorful trappings of the tournament and the brilliant displays of the parade; high contrasts in musi-cal colors and textures served their ideal exactly. They loved bells, reed in-struments, jingling percussions, plucked and bowed strings, and the natural nasal voice—all sounds that carry well out of doors or in great halls and that maintain individuality easily.

The late Medieval period was perhaps the richest in instruments in the history of Western music. It is difficult to select representative instruments of this era, but there was tremendous scope and variety. The Medieval pipe organ incorporated the ideal of high, nasal sounds. The famed Winchester organ was described by a monk in the tenth century:

Twice six bellows above are ranged in a row, and fourteen lie below. These, by alternate blasts, supply an immense quantity of wind, and are worked by seventy strong men, labouring with their arms, covered with perspiration, each inciting his companions to drive the wind up with all his strength, that the full-bosomed box may speak with its four hundred pipes which the hand of the organist governs. . . . The music is heard throughout the town, and the flying fame thereof is gone out over the whole country.[1]

The organ had a five-octave range, of eight notes to the octave (the hexachord plus the two notes of the chromatic semitone)—forty pitches sounded by ten *ranks*, or sets, of pipes. The ranks were 8', 4', 4', 2⅔', 2⅔', 2', 2', 1⅓', 1⅓', 1'.[2] They all sounded, for there were no stops—the effect must indeed have been astounding.

Historians still have much to do in identifying instruments of this period; difficulties are both pictorial and literary. The naqqara, for example, was a small kettledrum of metal or wood with a laced head that was used in pairs in North Africa and the Near East. Introduced to Europe in the thirteenth century, it took an Anglicized name, nakers, and was popular through the fifteenth century, appearing in minstrelsy (page 45) and martial music. Certain pictures appear to show snares but may not; no definitive research has yet been done on the use of snares before the fifteenth century, but they were common in Africa and the East much earlier. On the other hand, literary references to the echiquier, a keyboard instrument, exist from the fourteenth century to the sixteenth, the most tantalizing perhaps in an early fifteenth-century letter to the duke of Burgundy. The letter describes the instrument as "resembling the organ but sounded by strings." [3] References are complicated by the use of the same term for *keyboard*, *chessboard*, and *abacus*. At any rate, no description or picture of an echiquier has yet been found.

Instrumentally, the Renaissance was a period of transition between the nasal ideal of the Medieval era and the sweet, manipulable ideal of the Baroque. The popular instruments of the Renaissance were those that sounded best indoors—lutes, recorders, viols, Krummhorns, positive organs (movable tabletop instruments), and small harpsichords, notably virginals (table instruments). All received impetus through the architecture of the time and through the Renaissance sound ideal of blend and harmony in the

---

[1] Wolston (or Wulston) the Deacon, quoted in E. J. Hopkins and E. F. Rimbault, *The Organ*, 3d ed., London: Robert Cocks & Co., 1877.

[2] Because they were not separable, the different ranks of pipes were not given separate names. They can be identified only by the length (in feet) of the pipe sounding on activation of the c key (8' at actual pitch, 4' an octave higher, 2⅔' a twelfth higher, etc.). The Winchester organ thus had pipes sounding the fundamental, plus the second, third, fourth, sixth, and eighth partials.

[3] Sibyl Marcuse, "echiquier," *Musical Instruments: A Comprehensive Dictionary*, Garden City, N.Y.: Doubleday, 1964.

The mechanism of the pipe organ; the console is at the bottom. From Dom Bedos de Celles, *Art du facteur d'orgues*, 1766–1778. (Courtesy of the University of Michigan Library. Photo by R. E. Kalmbach.)

modern sense. The lute already had an unbroken tradition measured in millenniums and had been used in Medieval music to present one line in minstrelsy, but its sudden emergence at the beginning of the sixteenth century as a harmonic instrument made it the first popular household instrument in the West. A tablature notation was evolved for it just when the art of printing was being developed, and the availability of lute books gave further impetus to a cult of amateurs who could play only one instrument. To musicologists, lute tablature has special importance; in representing exact finger positions, it indicates precise pitches and clarifies the practice of musica ficta, the alteration of pitches in polyphonic music with particular reference to the creation of leading tones in cadential formulas. Interestingly, the *intabulation* (writing in tablature) of a polyphonic chanson by two lutenists most often produced two versions of the chromatic details.

In addition to indoor instruments, outdoor instruments, with an increasing specialization of function, continued to thrive. The cornett, a wooden instrument that was bound in leather, had a mouthpiece of wood or ivory, and was played with fingerholes, joined the shawms, sackbuts (early trombones), and drums as instruments of the courtyard and the larger chapels. Cornetts were very popular; a theorist of the early seventeenth century said their sound was "similar to the brilliance of a ray of sunshine appearing in the shadow or darkness, when it is heard among the voices in cathedral or chapel." [4] Cornetts and sackbuts were used in the chapel to

[4] Marin Mersenne, quoted in Roger E. Chapman (ed.), *The Books on Instruments*, The Hague: M. Nijhoff, 1957, prop. XXII, p. 345.

double the voices in what was called *a cappella* style. The pipe and tabor, the bagpipe, and the kazoo (a mirliton) were popular folk instruments in the sixteenth century. Fifes (crossblown pipes) and snare drums were used in the infantry, as shawms, trumpets, and kettledrums were used for cavalry.

The Baroque era was a brilliant instrumental period; the love of variety and juxtaposition was again dominant and at a time when mechanical and technical advances were inspiring instrument makers and performers alike. Important Baroque instruments are easier to identify—the treble violin, recorder, and flute; the balancing viola da gamba and bassoon; the accompanying theorbo, harpsichord, and organ; and the newly devised or focused orchestral oboe, horn, and clarinet.

The great instrument of the Baroque was the pipe organ. It incorporated virtually the whole ideal—tonal and spatial contrast and the potential for rivalry and balance. Organs with fifty or more stops were not uncommon; they posed musical and mechanical problems in deployment of several thousand pipes from 2 inches to 16 feet in length. The tonal variety and interplay available to Baroque organists can be seen clearly by examining the list of stops of the instruments played by François Couperin and Johann Sebastian Bach.

Each stop is listed by name and by the length (in feet) of the pipe sounding on activation of the *c* key (see footnote 2) or by the number of ranks or sets of pipes if the stop is a mixture, that is, if it is made of more than one rank of pipes (III indicates a mixture of three ranks). The name of the stop indicates its sound or its structural type.

Organ Specifications

Stops on the organ of Saint-Gervais in Paris, built by Langhedul, 1601—the organ of François Couperin.[5]

GREAT ORGAN

Montre 16' (Open diapason)
Montre 8'
Bourdon 8'
Flûte ouverte 4' (Nachthorn)
Flûte bouchée 4' (Stopped flute)
Doublette 2' (Stopped diapason)
Flageolet 1'
Fourniture III
Cymbale III
Grosse tierce 3⅕'
Nazard 2⅔'
Cornet V
Trompette 8'
Clairon 4'
Voix humaine 8'

CHOIR ORGAN

Bourdon 8'
Prestant 4' (Open diapason)
Doublette 2' (Stopped diapason)
Flageolet 1'
Fourniture III
Cymbale III
Cromorne 8'

PEDAL ORGAN

Flûte 8'

---

[5] Poul-Gerhard Andersen, *Organ Building and Design*, London: G. Allen, 1969, p. 142.

Stops on the large organ of the Thomaskirche, Leipzig, as they were in 1723—the organ of J. S. Bach.[6]

GREAT ORGAN

Principal 16' (Open diapason)
Principal 8'
Quintadena 16'
Octava 4'
Quinta 3'
Super octava 2'
Spiel-Pfeiffe 8'
Sesquialtera II (Mixture)
Mixtur 6' (VII–X ranks)
Tremulant
Vogelgesang (Bird song)
Cimbelstern (Rotating star with small bells)

CHOIR ORGAN

Principal 8' (Open diapason)
Quintadena 8'
Lieblich Gedackt 8' (Stopped diapason)
Klein Gedakt 4'
Traversa 4' (Flute)
Violin 2'
Rauschquinte II
Mixtur IV
Spitzflöte 4'
Schallflöte 1'
Krumbhorn 16'
Trommet 8'

ECHO ORGAN

Grossgedackt 8' (Stopped diapason)
Principal 4' (Open diapason)
Nachthorn 4'
Nasat 3'
Gemshorn 2'
Cimbel II
Sesquialtera (Mixture)
Regal 8'
Geigendregal 4'

PEDAL ORGAN

Sub-bass 16'
Posaunenbass 16'
Trommetenbass 8'
Schallmeyenbass 4'
Cornett 3'

The violin was also an instrument of the Baroque. At the beginning of the seventeenth century, it was associated with the theater (particularly with the dance). And toward the middle of the century, a theorist still held this association: "The violins are suited principally for dances, balls, ballets, mascarades, serenades, morning concerts, banquets, and other joyful passtimes, having been judged more appropriate for these recreational practices than any other kind of instrument."[7] But within a hundred years the violin was a virtuoso concert instrument. In 1738 a survey in the *Mercure de France* said the violin was the "most common" of instruments.

> Its sounds are more lively, and affect the spirit more strongly than all other instruments, of which some have called it the King. . . . This instrument has been ennobled in our day; it is no longer shameful for honest men to cultivate it, and they would afford a sort of glory and esteem to those who excel in it, among whom one can count Lords of the highest Rank.[8]

[6] William Leslie Sumner, *The Organ*, New York: Philosophical Library, 1953, p. 361f.
[7] François Lesure, "Pièrre Trichet, Traité des instruments," in *Annales musicologiques*, 1956, vol. IV, p. 228.
[8] *Mercure de France*, June, 1738, p. 1113.

The violin emulated the soprano voice. But all Baroque instruments, including the voice, shared an ideal of balance, sweetness of tone, clarity, and fleetness that enabled them to balance each other in many contrasts and combinations. The Baroque technique served the ideal of clarity by centering in high surface texture, a direct musical texture in which each note had a separate impetus. The short bow was designed to produce individual bow strokes for the violin, and wind instruments were designed for individual tonguings, because such techniques supported the ideal of clarity. Girolamo Fantini's *Trumpet Method* (1638) contained seventy pages of tonguing patterns with no slurred notes at all.

The Classical era gave surface texture a primary place in performance. The standard came to be individual attacks mixed with couplet slurs and, as the nineteenth century approached, longer phrases of legato playing. Development of the ideal orchestral sound was a chief concern of the eighteenth-century instrumental art. Horns and oboes had entered in the seventeenth century, but the clarinet, though developed in about 1700, entered much later. The clarinet was an enlarged chalumeau, a single reed instrument associated with rustic music; it was altered so that it would overblow directly from the fundamental to the third partial (a twelfth). Early clarinets had a fundamental f and overblew to c^2, but b^1 was missing, so early music for the instrument omitted that tone. For example, the two Vivaldi concertos for two clarinets and two oboes skipped b^1 in the clarinet runs but not in those for the oboes; otherwise, the runs are played in unison.

The Classical orchestral sound was a transition between the lively contrasts of the Baroque rivalries and the string-dominated blend of the Romantic ideal. A group of two oboes, two horns, and a small string choir maintained a balance between texture and blend that proved immensely successful. For the strings, the longer bow, developed about 1780 by François Tourte (c. 1750–1835), answered the need for an increased amount of tone and legato.

Instruments were sorted and examined in the divertimento and other chamber forms; only a few survived. The Baroque ideal had welcomed gamba and cello, recorder and flute, clavichord, harpsichord, and, at the end, piano; but the Romantic ideal preferred to select a few instruments and dispense with the rest. The new ideal of legato was joined to that of a full tone without differences of tessitura (except in the clarinet and the viola), and instrument makers worked for mechanical devices that would allow smoother, fuller melodic playing.

The violin family replaced the viols, and the violin was so modified that the modern instrument is as far from the seventeenth-century violin as a piano is from a clavichord. Increase in the length of the fingerboard, for example, caused greater string tension and hence contributed to a more penetrating tone. Loudness and smoothness replaced sweetness and clarity as the ideal of the string player; the Romantic instrument was as suited to the ideal of its time as the Baroque violin had been.

If the Baroque violin had emulated the voice, reciprocity occurred in the Golden Age of grand opera, at the end of the nineteenth century. And pianists, in spite of the impossibility of a hammer action's sustaining a soaring sound, also emulated the voice; the piano had the advantage of having no problems of tessitura. Piano makers increased the tone of the instrument by overstringing, using a steel frame for more tension and brilliance, and adding pedal mechanisms to increase the sustaining potential. Pianists spoke of a "singing tone," and a piano book of 1886 told the student, "Apply yourselves to making your instrument *sing,* thus giving nuance to the sounds, and to trying to make it speak all the emotion, all the poetry that the sentiments expressed in the musical ideas that you interpret awaken in you." [9]

The rich instrumental sound of the late nineteenth century centered in the orchestra, the voice, and the piano. These instruments made up a musical aristocracy, but toward the end of the century, the very unanimity of the tonal ideal began to make musicians restless. Higher color was attainable only by introducing instruments from outside the aristocracy—the saxophone, harp, celesta, and, in the United States, the banjo and other instruments associated with ragtime music.

The new sounds of the twentieth century branched out even farther from the traditional aristocracy. The new music sought out, from the past, from other cultures, and from popular music, instruments—notably percussion instruments—that were considered vulgar. In addition, new effects were found in the traditional instruments. And finally, new instruments were invented. The whole gamut of tone, "the great raw realm of sound," [10] now respectable as musical material, could be introduced and dealt with in the art of music composition.

Though not a musical instrument, the computer could also be utilized. Most frequently it was programed for traditional theoretical structures, but it could also be programed to work out complex equations of total serialism. Musicologists were using computers more than composers, to amass memory banks of thematic and textual materials; they hoped to identify and put in order the music of earlier days when composers used themes more than once and borrowed from others as well as from themselves and when scribes were careless about attributions.

By 1970, composers and theory students were learning, as a matter of course, the technological languages of the synthesizer and of tape manipulation, whether or not they intended to specialize in electronic composition. Never has the composer needed to master so many mediums of tone production, for in the Medieval era, the one period of equal richness, the management of qualities of sound and their deployment in performance was the province of the producer. It is worthy of note that today, in an age of increasing specialization, the composer, with less need to be a fine performer,

[9] Louis Dauphin, *Maîtres de la Musique,* Paris: Colin, 1886, p. 12.
[10] Louise Cuyler, unpublished lecture, Ann Arbor, Mich., 1957.

has taken to himself an increased responsibility for the details of performance. His concern reflects the importance of the qualities of living sound to the current art of music. That a composer should find timbre essential is hardly surprising; what is astonishing is that, in the art music of the West, it could have been secondary for a long time.

Ideas of tempo and timbre are important aspects of a recurring swing that comprises one of the most fascinating phenomena in the history of Western music. This is the swing between the ideals of one location and multiple locations of sound in performance. Every culture and every esthetic recognizes and uses both small and large ensembles, private and public music. Yet in the fulfillment of each esthetic, one type tends to dominate the other and the periods of the small versus the large groups emerge clearly. Many Medieval terms are designations of such deployment. *Antiphonal* and *responsorial*, for example, referred to the placement of performers, but the interactions of spatially opposed sound sources were vital to the music composed for such groups. The alternation of refrain-verse-refrain in the virelai, rondeau, and popular dances of the era were spatially inspired.

Size and Space

Conversely, the consort of the central Renaissance maintained the ideal of spatial unity that was essential to the Renaissance concern with the vertical element in music—the harmony of pitch relationships that replaced the harmony of contrasting sounds. The polyphonic chanson, Mass, and motet were based on structural techniques of continuation and succession rather than alternation; the cantus firmus, for example, was linear, not circular.

The end of the Renaissance witnessed an increase in size and an expansion of spatial elements in music; these would provide a strong motivation for the forms of the Baroque. Opposition of forces was the basis of the stile concertato, and multiple sources of sound, in sanctuary or hall, provided the foundation for both fabric and form. The quick ricochet of subjects in Corelli's sonatas and the alternation of ritornello-solo-ritornello in Vivaldi's concerto structures exemplify a keen enjoyment of space. And surviving annotations make it clear that spatial elements of these works were exploited in performance—part books were often marked to indicate the placement of players.

The Classical divertimento and such chamber forms as the string quartet and the woodwind quintet returned to the unity of the consort; they introduced a century and a half of music whose ideal, even in the symphony, was of the illusion of one source of sound. The piano incorporated this ideal with particular force, and the total unity of solo performance was enriched by the Romantic view of the virtuoso bending the mighty instrument to his will. The drama of will was also symbolized by the orchestra conductor. He wrested psychological unanimity from a large group of performers through his personality and dominance and provided a visual and psychological focus for the audience, as though he were the funnel through which all the energies of the orchestra were transmitted.

At the end of the nineteenth century, virtually all concert performances were as unified as possible. The singer stood in the bend of the piano and a quartet stood or sat as close together as they could. Even the early revivals of Baroque music were unified; Bach organ works appeared in sumptuous orchestrations, for example, or were brought to the concert stage as virtuoso piano transcriptions. The pipe organ was redesigned to emulate the orchestra; organists wrote large works which they called "symphonies."

A rediscovery of architectural space, which seems to be related to the return to smaller performing groups, has sparked excitement in the twentieth century. Popular music, particularly rock, separated performers both musically and personally; composers of electronic music began to specify the placement of speakers in relation to the audience; and new scores for traditional groups often included stage charts to ensure the correct arrangement of sound sources in the hall. Frequently, the orchestra was divided into sections placed far apart, perhaps with groups at the sides and back of the hall, in the balcony, or even farther away in a spot from which the sound could be carried into the hall through the vents of the heating system.

As in other aspects of the new music, creative reexamination of the sounds of the past has injected a new dimension into current experiments. Performance of a Baroque concerto with its original number and placement of performers both whets a new recognition of the Baroque style and opens new directions to the composer.

The relation of size and space to musical experimentation is fascinating and affects tempo, timbre, and length of the musical form. It is evident that a composer's experiments with a new kind of music must be with short pieces performed by a few musicians. Because a new kind of music has no defining techniques, it cannot have a sizable form; because it has no public recognition, it has no large social context. A general rule is that the more radical the experiment, the greater the need for smallness. Experimentation in music is also associated with precision of line, with improvisation and embellishment; and smallness facilitates this as well.

The advantage of clarity is attained by smallness, by the individuation of line characteristic of an instrumental solo, and by the use of one performer to a part. The jazz combo incorporates some of these elements—clarity of line, individuation of timbre, and freedom to improvise and embellish. Medieval improvisations may have been as rich, but we cannot know how they sounded because literary references only hint at Medieval practice. However, we have an immediate knowledge of jazz, for it is documented, at least in part, by sound recordings. A middle path is represented by Baroque improvisation, for which a few documents exist in texts or annotated music.

The opposite of the small, experimental group is the large, culminative one; it offers magnificence and social splendor instead of delineation and innovation. The large ensemble implies public enthusiasm and support, a large number of readily available performers familiar with the style, and an almost sanctified agreement of esthetic purpose. Most huge performances are of works hallowed by time, such as the Handel commemoratives, which have been presented in England since the end of the eighteenth century, and the Mozart *Requiem,* which was presented with a huge chorus and orchestra at the funeral Mass of Napoleon. The revolutionary hymns composed for public rallies in France in the 1790s, like the oratorio for the opening of the Centennial Exposition in Philadelphia in 1876, have been quickly swallowed by time. But the great works that survive are the oratorios from the end of the Baroque, which represent a fulfillment of a musical language and its esthetic, a culmination of a style that had its start in small, experimental works perhaps a century earlier.

The two types are opposed in appeal. The intoxication with clarity in the small, experimental group and the thrill of losing oneself in the cosmic symbolism of the great, culminative performance are equally compelling. But it is the burden of cosmic symbolism to be blind to anything outside itself; it is the advantage of an experimental era to be open to many kinds of truth and to seek a variety of experience. Today, we are fortunate to be able to enjoy a spectrum of musical experiences beyond any the West has yet known.

EMBELLISHMENT AND IMPROVISATION

All structures, from buildings to clothing, distinguish between structural and decorative elements. Their functions are distinct, but the assignment of each physical part to one or the other is not always so clear. A pin is functional and a jewel is decorative, but a jeweled pin is both. Basically, decoration is capable of esthetic independence, although specific decoration must be suited to the object to which it is applied.

In music, decorative elements are part of fabric and style. A basic problem in the performance of music (of any style) is to distinguish that which is structural from that which is decorative. Nothing determines tempo and phrasing so thoroughly, and nothing is more essential to musical fabric. Although not all fabrics can serve every formal type, a wide scope is possible. A fugue by Handel and a fugue by Hindemith share significant structural similarities, as do sonata movements by Mozart and Brahms, yet the styles vary widely and we could not confuse Handel with Hindemith or Mozart with Brahms.

Musical form is created by the composer and is made clear by the performer; but the musical fabric—the quality of sound, the precise tempo and rhythmic life—are directly under the performer's control and most surely reflect his individuality. The first Prelude of Johann Sebastian Bach's *Das wohltemperirte Clavier,* for example, is structurally a series of chords exploring C major and related tones; it is a harmonic conception, and its tempo is the speed of the chord progression. What melodic material the Prelude contains is decorative, and the chief element of decoration is the figuration of the chords, a straightforward figuration without nonchord tones, in imitation of lute technique. A similar structural concept is found in the first Chopin Etude, opus 28, also in C major. This is also a harmonic structure, a series of chords presented in a figuration, but here the unsteady rhythmic flow, with pauses on the third beats (emphasized by their higher pitches), and the fuller left hand, create a Romantic fabric. Appoggiaturas and passing tones add to the tension. And the greater number of notes, the pianistic idiom, and the element of the virtuoso lend the Prelude a surging, almost tumultuous quality. In many other simple songs the situation is reversed—melody is structural and the harmonic element is supportive or even nonexistent.

Monophonic melody was based on frame and figure. The frame in troubadour music, plainsong, and folk music in the Medieval and Renaissance periods was often a fifth plus a minor seventh, as in the opening punctus of Giraut's alba (Example 2), with decorative tones acknowledged as broderie. And further embellishment, garibles, could be added in performance.

In organum, the frame consisted of the points where new tones entered in the tenor, with the duplum and triplum conceived as freely parabolic from point to point. Doubtless much organum was improvised, because improvisation was a valued skill throughout the Medieval era; it remained part of the puy and continued in popular music as both a delight in variation and an intellectual fascination. Leonardo da Vinci said that "variation mirrors time, in which nothing is twice the same; . . . music dies while it is born." [11]

The addition of a primary harmonic element tended to change the definition of embellishment to harmonic terms. The new definition included both decorative and passing chords of small structural function, particularly, melodic elements, often called nonchord or nonharmonic elements, pulling against the harmony. In Renaissance polyphony, the use of passing tones, surrounding notes, and cambiatas made separate lines more graceful, and the suspension injected off-accents into a regular rhythmic progression. But decorating tunes in doubles and divisions continued as a strong heritage. Early textbooks in the sixteenth century concentrated on variation as a skill of performer and composer alike, and charts of suggested divisions were vital to such books.

Baroque decoration tended to extremes, with fiorature and cadenzas added to such an extent that the original melody was often obscured. Singers "improved" their solos until the arias were mere frames for improvisation and at times the composer's skill was secondary. Virtuoso violinists did the same to the solo sonata and concerto.

Composers of the Baroque used contrasts to enliven the musical fabric, employing echo and ricochet (both imply a concern with space used decora-

---

[11] Quoted in Emanuel Winternitz, "Leonardo's References to Music," unpublished paper read to the American Musicological Society, 1963.

A Table of Divisions

SILVESTRO GANASSI

Example 89

Ganassi's divisions are from his book *Opera intitulata fontegara* (1535). Each short pattern in the first column at the left is followed by a series of divisions numbered 1 to 10. The double proportion sign (a circle over a broken circle) indicates that the rhythm may be read as either perfect (triple) or imperfect (duple). (Courtesy of the Library of Congress.)

Improvised cadenza

CARLO BROSCHI (FARINELLI)

Example 90

Example 90 (continued)

This phrase is part of the aria "Quell 'usignolo" from the opera *Merope* (c. 1734), by Geminiano Giacomelli. (Courtesy of the Theodore Presser Company, for Universal Editions.)

Solo Sonata opus 12 no. 5   **Example 91**
ARCANGELO CORELLI

The facsimile is the opening adagio of the sonata, as printed in England in 1711. The bottom two staves comprise the original as Corelli notated it; the upper staff presents suggested divisions for the soloist. (Photo by R. E. Kalmbach.)

tively). In the concerto grosso and the large choral forms, dynamic and spatial effects were both decorative and functional. Contrasts in tone quality also achieved this twofold purpose; in such works as the Telemann double concerto for recorder and flute, the contrasting qualities enhance the fabric and, through a brisk repartee, also motivate subject and form.

Keyboard performers, having control of the whole musical fabric, were able to develop the art of improvisation to particular heights, and the virtuoso was expected to improvise whole pieces. The tradition was particularly strong with German organists, who were required to improvise on chorale tunes in both simple and fugal style. Also, harpsichordists and pianists, from Chambonnières to Beethoven, were famous for their improvising.

But improvisation declined with the close of the Baroque era. The Classical era saw the start of a return to control by the composer, and by the beginning of the nineteenth century, the performer was no longer able to change the music at will or whim. Embellishment of melody was more and more often indicated in notation, both by writing out the melodic details of slow movements and by adding ornament signs. The eighteenth century saw the apex of the use of ornament signs—before, performers more often had free rein, and afterward, composers more often chose an exact notation.

The cadenza came under the control of the composer as well. Beethoven improvised cadenzas, but he also wrote down cadenzas to his own concertos, which were printed separately as appendixes. A few Romantic virtuosos, notably Liszt, maintained the tradition of using their own cadenzas but generally composed them beforehand.

The Romantic ideal gave the performer unprecedented freedom in tempo rubato and dynamic nuance; both these decorative elements were necessary to the Romantic sound. Legato, which had been occasional and decorative, became a standard part of the Romantic fabric. Tone became the primary concern of the performer, who strove for the perfect, full, seamless quality that bound notes together in a glory of sensuous effect. Conversely, the performer gave up all control of pitch elements, so a singer could hold a high note at will, even to the point of rhythmic distortion, but would not have dreamed of adding a single note to the written page.

Thus the nineteenth century witnessed the apex of pitch control by the composer and the authority of the printed page. It comprised the only esthetic in Western history (and in the entire world) in which written musical pitches were taken as immutable and a piece of music was held to exist independent of its performance. Variation was no longer the performer's art but was under the aegis of the composer.

Within the complexity of decoration and the roles of composer and performer, the changing musical esthetic of the twentieth century comes into focus with particular clarity. As early as the first decade of the century, Debussy's piano pieces and Webern's movements for strings made use of new instrumental effects, in which the performer was more actively re-creating the music rather than reproducing it. By the end of World War I, techniques had appeared that reversed the concept of the set and the variable. Sprechstimme, for example, indicated that dynamic and rhythmic detail were essential to the structure of the voice part but that pitch was secondary and approximate.

The performer was pulled in two directions—toward nonentity, as the superserialists and then the electronic composers sought total control over the performer and finally dispensed with him altogether, and toward spontaneity and even total improvisation, as the proponents of instrumental mobiles and theatrical happenings threw musical components onto the stage and listened entranced to the resulting sounds. Form was computed and mathematical on the one side, unplanned and irrational on the other, the composer either completely unyielding or attempting to disappear altogether into the moment.

The middle course between these extremes was most creatively maintained in the popular art, where the fresh and vigorous interaction of elements created the composer-performer of jazz. The movement away from the literal page was enriched by the long Afro-American tradition of techniques

The table of embellishments from Jean-Henry d'Anglebert, *Pièces de clavecin* (1689). For two of d'Anglebert's pièces, see Example 51. (Photo by R. E. Kalmbach.)

Directions on how to play a trill, from Leopold Mozart, *Versuch einer grundlichen Violinschule* (Treatise on the Fundamental Principles of Violin Playing). The facsimile is from the second edition, 1770. (Courtesy of the University of Michigan Library. Photo by R. E. Kalmbach.)

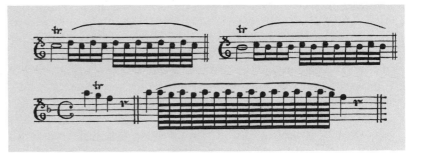

that were closer to the universal concepts of living music than the over-refined extremes of West European art.

A critic paying posthumous tribute to Coleman Hawkins (1905–1969), a tenor saxophonist, summed up the essence of the jazz esthetic, as embodied in Hawkins's "musical adventurousness" and "unstemmable creativity." For Hawkins, creativity was always spontaneous.

> He spent most of his life *improvising*, which means that he altruistically gave part of himself away night after night, month after month, year after year. A sculptor can touch his work, a painter can stare at his finished canvas, but improvisation—except in the rare instances when it is recorded—is borne away the second it is uttered.[12]

This is virtually the statement of Leonardo da Vinci four-and-a-half centuries before.

WESTERN THEORIES OF MUSIC

Western music, in maintaining a succession of ideals, has propounded a succession of theories as well. Each esthetic built on the last and reached to the next, forming a chain through time. But three radical breaks have occurred in the chain. One was at the start of the second millennium, toward the end of the era of monophony—when polyphony cut Western music off from the rest of the world. The second break occurred at the beginning of the seventeenth century—when monody was introduced and key tonality became a regulator of fabric and form in music. The third break occurred relatively recently—when key tonality was no longer able to provide motivation for new links in the chain and sciences and technologies provided them.

The first period was hexachordal. The simple hexachord, which had gaps between its statements at different registers, was expanded by Guido

---

[12] "The Talk of the Town," *The New Yorker*, May 31, 1969, p. 27.

707

d'Arezzo at the end of the first millennium into a system of overlapping hexachords. Then, through additional musica ficta and transpositions, the hexachord systems achieved a thoroughly chromatic expansion at the end of the sixteenth century. However, the essential unity of the hexachord systems was still recognized in 1597; Morley began his explanation of pitch organizations in his text *The Plaine and Easie Introduction to Practicall Musicke* by stating, "There be in music but six notes."

The second period was based on a system of twelve tones, first defined as overlapping and uncomfortably unstable major and minor tones. It was then stabilized through equal temperament in a key-tonal harmonic definition of fabric and form and finally was dispersed in decentralizing but still harmonic concepts of panchromaticism.

The third period is just beginning. The new music is still young, still virtually an upbeat in a new esthetic, but a few of its characteristics seem fairly certain and it is possible to recognize significant and defining elements. In the new esthetic, sound is multifaceted and pitch is part of quality. After centuries of concern with consonance and dissonance, composers are more interested in resonance, in total sound, in sounds. Interestingly, this concern is closer to universal than traditional theories. It is perhaps ironic that the refusal to limit music to a few precise pitch relationships, a refusal characteristic of electronic music theory, is close to the view of pitch of eighteenth-century West African marimba bands; there each instrument and each piece of music worked out its unique pitch relationships and was centrally concerned with layered fabric and spontaneous variation.

The two major periods that form separate theoretical chains, plus the still unfulfilled theory of new music, can be charted simply. The table on page 709 is suggestive rather than definitive and should open rather than close discussion.

IDIOMS

In all human activities, conventions dictate basic form and a large part of style. Their use is convenient but goes far beyond convenience. Convention serves convenience by eliminating the need to work out new means for each repetition of a basic experience; conversely, it serves uniqueness by enabling exception to stand out clearly and attract attention easily.

A short typical unit of speech is called an *idiom*. Verbal idioms are essential to the fabric of language and thus indirectly to meaning, both literal and suggestive. Everyone uses verbal idioms—combining, varying, or avoiding them—to set a mood and stake out individuality. And the past is characterized by idioms, in a complex of matter and manner of which they are the very essence.

Musical idioms are just as essential to fabric and bear the same relation to meaning and to the characterization of the past. The single chord

	Hexachordal Period		**Twelve-tone Period**			
	MEDIEVAL	RENAISSANCE	BAROQUE	CLASSICAL	ROMANTIC	THE NEW MUSIC
Pitch Materials	Simple hexachord with chromatic semitone	Overlapping hexachords — Modality — Expanded system of hexachords	*Tone Key* — Major-minor system — Equal temperament		Expanding Chromaticism	Multiple concepts of materials—historical, exotic, electronic, popular — Antitonality
Rhythmic Organization	*Proportions* — Basic triple — Mannerism	Basic duple and hemiola — Simplification	*Meter* — Exploited beat	Assumed continuing meter	Fragmentation — Disintegration	Clock or theatrical time — Steady beat in popular style
Linear Unit	Punctus		Subject		Theme	Gesture
Vertical Unit	*Accumulation of Intervals* — Through linear interaction	Often independently conceived	*Chord* — Motivated in bass	Invertibility	Motivated variously — Nonmotivated	Sonority — Event
Construction Principles	Accumulation of linear elements		Polar texture of treble-bass	Contrasting subjects, keys, textures	Architectural form thematically based	Accumulation of vertical units (gestures, events) — Superimposition
Ideal of Sound	Vocal—emulation of the reeds		Instrumental— emulation of the voice			Multifaceted, often disembodied; when visually related, often kinesthetic
Ideal of Combined Sounds	Simultaneous and successive contrasts — Independent lines — Spatial deployments	Blend—the consort	Split choirs — Combined consorts — Spatial deployments	Contrast within a blend— the orchestra — Unity of source	Big, full, connected sound	Complex of sounds — Independence by overlapping elements — Spatial deployments
Relation to Text	Illumination		Interpretation			Transcendence

or subject may characterize and be assigned time, place, and function as clearly as a word or phrase in language.

A. Solo soprano and basso continuo

B. Undesignated

C. Orchestral strings

D. Piano

E. Voices

The five musical excerpts, A to E, clearly demonstrate the essential nature of idiom. The medium is first, with each (including the undesignated) segment indicating an essential, characterizing element of a norm. Further, in A the use of voice and basso continuo is Baroque in general whereas the 3-5-1 of the solo is an idiom of French recitativo in particular, and the 5̷ is a figure used in French continuo practice. In B the use of tenor register in notation is Medieval, but the double leading-tone cadence with the 7-6-8 top voice is a Landini formula of the Ars nova (see Cadence Chart, page 720). In C, the successive diminished-seventh chords in orchestral string tremolo is a Romantic cliché. In D, the punctiliously designated piano notation is late Romantic, whereas the use of the twelve notes of the piano octave within the measure suggests panchromatic or serial technique. And in E, the imitative entrance of separate lines points to Renaissance polyphony, whereas the characteristic rhythmic formula points specifically to the opening of a Renaissance polyphonic chanson.

In music, idiom is the basic concern of the listener, because it is the basic element of fabric and style. Its importance to the musical experience can be shown in several ways. It is primary in performance and, as a necessity within any musical language, in composition as well. Music is difficult to listen to when its idioms are unfamiliar—it is quite literally a foreign language. As with words, music for casual entertainment or as a background for other experiences must remain close to the idiomatic, whereas music to be enjoyed on a more intense level can vary and depart more often from idiom.

Recognition and evaluation of particular works in relation to period, national, or individual style is based on familiarity with its idioms. Structural aspects of music become evident more easily through a study of idiom. Even the elementary skill of recognizing repeated musical ideas is immensely helped by idioms; they are indispensable, even in subconscious identification.

HISTORY AND THE MUSICAL EXPERIENCE

Music is intangible and has some elements of dreams. The reality of music is the living sound. The printed score is a symbol that can represent the reality in differing kinds and degrees to people of differing experience. It is not in itself living music and cannot in itself suggest the quality of sound. The musician can forget how much meaning is left out of notation. Much of the communication of music writing lies in unstated assumptions, which are known to the performer by tradition. He does not play exactly what is written; indeed, the subtle nuances of phrasing, dynamics, rubato, tone quality, and resonance cannot be notated at all in our system and must be supplied by the performer. He relies primarily on technique (control of his instrument), interpretive traditions (sense of style), and taste.

The historian plays a decisive role in the second of these, interpretive traditions. The performer generally learns the traditions of his teacher's generation and often must turn to others to learn the traditions of the past and those on the cutting edge of the future. Knowledge of past traditions is particularly important, because notation, by omitting so much of quality and style, has left older music vulnerable to basic misunderstandings. Traditions of other cultures are becoming important as well, and the problems of notation of other cultures are multiplied for us. Today's listeners and performers are seeking familiarity with virtually all the eras of Western music and with other esthetics as well.

But study in depth is a life's work; a musicologist can spend an entire creative career studying one esthetic, the music of one era or of one country.

How can a performer work within so vast a scope? He must rely on generality. Generality is in bad repute because of its obvious dangers of oversimplification and omission. It is a particular danger to the historian. For the performer, however, generality and rules of thumb, approached with common sense, afford a means of intelligent approach to unfamiliar music and, in their very broadness, are a protection against overdirection and pedantic specification.

In spite of the enormous variety of musical practice in any one era, a summary of general musical goals can be a practical help. Such a summary is given on page 713; it is definite enough to be useful but avoids the confinement of specific directives. The listener can use it as a basis for understanding an individual work as an embodiment of or departure from the general ideal of its era, and the performer can use the summary as a basis for translating written notes into living music. By immersing himself in the style of an era, the performer can go beyond knowledge to instinct, beyond conviction to subtlety.

How can a listener or performer best use such a summary? First, he should recognize that the statements outline the central concerns of the eras. These concerns were embodied in the language and idioms of the music of a certain time, in whose terms a composer had to communicate whether or not he personally subscribed to the ideal they incorporated. The greatest percentage of music in any era strongly represents its central concerns. The performer should attempt to enter the spirit of the age whose musical product he is exploring, wholeheartedly approaching the music in its contemporary terms before concluding that it is exceptional. (In the latter case, this procedure will be his greatest aid in understanding *how* it is exceptional.)

Second, the reader should be careful not to read more into the statements than they contain. To say that the crescendo is not a Baroque means is *not* to say that strict dynamic monotone was practiced. Such concepts as crescendo, rubato, and ritard must be defined as *changes heard by the listener as shifts from one plane to another*. But the natural shaping of phrases involved considerable variation *not heard* as new levels of dynamics or tempo. Such negative approaches are basically dangerous, for ideals are not negative. The Baroque lack of crescendo is a reversal of a positive concern with sectional architectural forms in which blocks of sound contrasted excitingly with one another over a constant, motivating beat. Even though the crescendo was inconsistent with such forms, its avoidance cannot produce a Baroque style.

Third, the reader should recognize that musical exceptions were products of their own times just as much as were the works that fit comfortably into the generality. Every era has had its nonconformists, but such men have always been dependent on the realization of their era's generality, for they had to acknowledge a standard in order to deny it, and if their denial was to be effective, it had to be couched in the idiom of their own time.

Fourth, the reader should seek to feel the truth rather than to duplicate the fastidious accuracy of a style; he should look for the spirit rather than the letter of the esthetic. The revival of old instruments is a salient development of the twentieth century, but lively performance on familiar modern

General Ideals of Western Music

The assumptions of the *Medieval Era* were that music is melodic and created as separate lines written successively; that music is primarily vocal; that both harmony and rhythm are proportional; that the beat in polyphonic music serves to coordinate performance; that form derives essentially from patterns of text; that the separate lines should be presented in individual tone colors; that the resulting consonances are interesting in themselves and should be further explored; and that the job of the performer is to present his part as a vital element in a proportioned structure.

The assumptions of the *Renaissance* were that music is conceived as an accumulation of separate lines into patterns both horizontal and vertical; that music can enhance the meaning of words; that the steady beat serves as a cohesive force; that sounds should be gentle and well blended; that harmony has implications in defining form and that these functions should be further explored; that instruments can present musical statements even though they cannot produce words; and that the job of the performer is to present melodic lines with a lively sense of shape and with independence, dexterity, and taste.

The assumptions of the *Baroque Era* were that pulse is essential; that music "rides" the beat; that melodic interest is based on the figure and is secondary to the rhythmic impulse; that music—even vocal music—is instrumentally conceived; that form is architectural, built on both spatial and musical contrasts; that key tonality is an exciting new concept with formal implications that should be further explored; and that the job of the performer is to present with clarity what the composer has written.

The assumptions of *Classicism* were that music is capable of many shapes and textures; that these shapes and textures (both surface and structural) can, through contrast within a continuity of pulse and meter, create musical designs that are exciting and moving in themselves; that harmony and key are vital; that confrontation of different musical ideas can be dramatic and that such confrontation should be further explored; and that the job of the performer is to communicate contrasting textures and shapes, thus re-creating the musical reality.

The assumptions of *Romanticism* were that melody is primary to both language and form in music; that pulse is fluid and varies for the sake of expression; that a rich, full tone quality is desirable to interpretation; that harmony is functional and based on a triadic system from which it is expanding through chromaticism; that other cultures utilize sounds and effects that are sometimes interesting in themselves and that should be further explored; and that the job of the performer is not merely to present the music but to evoke the emotional meaning behind the music.

The assumptions of the *new music* are that sounds are endlessly various and exciting and that any of them may be used in musical composition; that form results from a composite of elements in layers of time and space; that music is not separate from the other arts or from the human condition; that the universal elements of music should be explored for possible synthesis; and that the performer, when part of a work of music, should again accept a share of the composer's joys, risks, and victories.

instruments is preferable to flaccid and hesitant performances on authentic old ones. And the use of one old instrument in a group of modern ones, or vice versa, can disconcert the players and destroy balance.

Balance is doubtless of primary importance in a search for authenticity of ideal. The modern violin cannot balance a harpsichord, for example, and insistence on the one authentic instrument may be less important than maintenance of the basic polarity of sound and energetic forward thrust essential to the Baroque ideal. In presenting a work for violin and continuo with violin and piano, the pianist can achieve polar balance through dynamic control; he can perform the linear bass at the same dynamic level as the violin solo while subduing the right hand in dynamics and activity. This is essentially a different technique for the pianist, who generally balances the left hand with the right, and it carries further implications of left-hand autonomy and importance. The left hand can emulate the style of the violin, for example, but the right hand must not, and the pianist should turn pages with the right hand, leaving the left to play the bass line. Such a balance is true to the spirit of the Baroque solo sonata and is much more preferable than combining a modern violin with a harpsichord (often without a cello) or than postponing playing the music until authentic instruments are available.

Hearing good performances on authentic instruments with singers knowledgeable in early techniques is exciting and highly desirable (for the historian, it is essential). But it is not practical to limit performance to authentic instruments. Carried to the extreme, such a policy would necessitate a pianist's using separate instruments for each item on a program—not only a harpsichord for J. S. Bach, but a square piano, a Stein, a Broadwood, and a Pleyel to play C. P. E. Bach, Mozart, Beethoven, and Chopin.

And finally, to use the summary effectively, the reader should apply large amounts of good will and common sense to all specific problems. Only the former can lead through the generalities of an era to its cutting edge of modernity, in order to reveal the contemporary sense of exploration and excitement implicit in music of the past. And only the latter can mediate between nineteenth-century performing traditions and the ever-sharpening demands of twentieth-century composers and audiences.

The twentieth-century ideal includes an active enjoyment of music of many times and places that is seemingly unique in the history of music; perhaps this scope will prove to be the most important element of its theory. Certainly the implications of this aspect of the new esthetic, both in the new humanism of world politics and in the whole spectrum of education, are immense.

For the listener the new esthetic can present a vast storehouse of pleasure, an expanding universe of musical experiences. He can accept them on the primary level of kaleidoscopic, sensually breathtaking joy or on other levels as well, through the heightened responses that history can make available to him. He can listen as he will, engaging his listening skills as he wishes, for he is in the best sense an *amateur*.

And the professional musician—composer, performer, teacher, scholar— is also a listener, hopefully always an amateur listening to music for pleasure. But in his professional capacity, a musician must forego the freedom of kaleidoscopic joy and maintain a professional stance.

With so vast an amount of knowledge to cope with, the professional balance is difficult to define. Like a Medieval mean, it is found somewhere between the freewheeling "anything goes" and the punctilious "nothing is accurate enough," between the blissful fearlessness of ignorance and the paralysis of pedantry. Above all else, history can chart the mean, revealing many paths and many answers.

Abbreviations

Med	Medieval era
Ren	Renaissance era
Bar	Baroque era
Cla	Classicism
Rom	Romanticism
20th	New music or the period after the Romantic ideal leading to the new music
Folk	Folk or universal music
lit.	literally

Glossary

The glossary is designed to aid aural recognition and analysis of styles. Specification of period is intended as a guide to the most characteristic use of idioms, not to indicate all uses. A figuration or technique may have been used throughout the history of music but be associated as a conscious style factor in only one or two eras; in such a case, only the one or two eras are specified for that idiom. The ideal of a style, rather than its exceptional practice, is always intended.

accelerando (Rom), lit., "speeding up"—a quickening of the beat to create excitement. Before Romanticism, such effects were written in by the composer as faster note values.

acciaccatura (Bar, Cla, Rom), lit., "crushing"—a decorative technique. In the Baroque harpsichord technique, acciaccatura consisted of a quickly released (and unresolved) abrasive second added for accent. These dissonances were notated, but a related effect, also an acciaccatura, achieved by a quick arpeggiation of a chord with added passing notes was indicated by a slash across the stem between the two chord notes to be connected with passing tones. (*See also* appoggiatura.)

Alberti bass (Cla), a keyboard figuration named for Domenico Alberti (1710–c.1740), a composer—the breaking of accompanying chords into an arpeggiated figure for rhythmic flow. Characteristically, Alberti bass was used in the left hand, one figuration constantly repeated with harmonic changes where necessary and in the service of one melody. The most frequently cited example is the Mozart Piano Sonata no. 15 in C major (K.545).

answer (Bar; *see* subject).

appoggiatura (Bar, Cla), lit., "leaning"—a long dissonant tone played deeply on an accent and resolved by step in a consonant tone. The appoggiatura was notated as a small note added to a line that was temporally complete without it. It took most or even all the time value of the following note, to which it belonged and to which it resolved. (The exact value of the appoggiatura was not related to the value of the small note as printed.) The special form of notation alerted the performer to the special nature of the note. In the Baroque era, an appoggiatura was often assumed by tradition in certain contexts, notably in a descent by leap to the supertonic or to the tonic from the mediant at a cadence. It was automatically added by the performer, without being indicated in the notation.

In Romanticism, the appoggiatura was written out in the main context of the notation, and the added small note in notation was turned over to the *grace note*, a short note preceding the accent and unstressed. Although a slash mark through the small note was initially used to distinguish a grace note from an appoggiatura, so many Romantic editions of Classical works turned appoggiature into grace notes that any grace note in the Classical style must be doubted by the performer. Grace notes were occasionally found in Classical fast movements but not in slow ones, where they should be assumed to be appoggiature. The Romantic grace note was sometimes called an acciaccatura because it used a slash in notation.

basso ostinato (*see* ostinato).

Bebung in German; **balancement** in French (Bar, Cla)—the characteristic vibrato of the clavichord.

bichordal structures (20th)—chords made by combining two other recognizable, generally simple chords. Combinations can include elements within a single key (G–B–D, A–C♯–E) in a technique related to *pandiatonicism;* bitonal materials (C–E–G, A♭–C–E♭), in a technique related to *polytonality;* or triads with roots a tritone apart (E♭–G–B♭, A–C♯–E), creating sounds similar to those of the *whole-tone scale.*

bimodality (Late Bar, Cla, Rom)—the intermixing of elements of the major and minor modes within a single key.

bitonality (20th)—the simultaneous use of materials of two keys, through either linear or chordal techniques. When bitonality is expanded to include three or more keys, the result is called *polytonality.*

breaking (Bar, Cla, 20th)—alternation in a single line between registers. In the Baroque and Classical periods, breaking was related to harmonic clarity; in the new music, it is related to serial or pointillistic techniques.

broderie (Med)—a trouvère term for melodic embellishments, chiefly the use of turning figures.

cadence, lit., "a falling"—the final element of a phrase, section, movement, or work that provides a conclusion appropriate in its degree of finality to its structural placement and esthetic intent. Cadences in Western music have tended to become formalized and hence have maintained formulas that are vital to the understanding of period styles.

In Western monophonic music (including folk, troubadour, and sacred song), the basic cadential formula consisted of a descent to the last tone (finalis) from the tone above it (superfinalis). But even in monophonic music, the open cadence (ouvert), generally higher or rising, was distinguished from the final or closed cadence (clos), generally lower or falling.

Polyphonic cadences were based on the accommodation of added voices to the descending tenor. A chart of cadences to 1600 appears on page 720.

Final harmonic cadences in the periods of key tonality were based on progression to dominant and resolution to tonic. The leading tone was crucial to the dominant as a demand for tonic. It was established through placement of a chord containing the subdominant directly before it.

Expectation of the ensuing tonic was necessary in the cadence of key tonality. The tonic could thus be granted or withheld, the latter by either a delay or a surprise substitution of some other chord for the expected tonic (a deceptive cadence). The *open, incomplete,* or *half cadence,* comparable to the ouvert as an internal, nonfinal punctuation, comprised a pause on the dominant.

In Romanticism, the cadence progression directly from the lower dominant to the tonic was used occasionally. This subdominant cadence was called *plagal,* as distinguished from the more usual upper dominant, or *authentic* cadence. In addition, the use of the third or fifth of the tonic triad, in the chief melodic upper line, entered as a variant; such a melodic feature classified the cadence as *imperfect.*

In the new music, chords seldom delineate cadences, which are more often attained through dynamics, musical shape, and the logic of musical events. (*See also* fadc.)

cadenza (Bar, Cla, Rom)—an ornamental fioratura. In the Baroque era, a cadenza was often a single phrase, improvised by a soloist on the two notes prior to the final chord of a cadence. Also, it was any interpolated improvised fioratura during which the pulse of the music stopped. In Classicism, a cadenza was a free section, most often extended, that was improvised by the soloist between the I_6
                                                                                                                                                    $_4$
V_7 of the final cadence of a concerto movement. The cadenza in the Romantic period was the same as that in the Classical, but it was less often improvised and more often composed, frequently by the composer of the concerto, though still occasionally by the soloist.

cambiata (Med, Ren, Folk), lit., "changing." In the Renaissance, cambiata was a free tone used as a changing or escape note decorating a fourth by a passing note that was generally a major second below the top note of the fourth. It can be traced from earlier (and virtually universal) usage as a *cambiata figure* or fourth, made up of a second plus a third, in diatonic terms (in some contexts the third was not considered a leap).

chromatic semitone (Med, Ren)—the variable tone B (hard or soft, ♮ or ♭ in modern terms) connecting the registers of the natural hexachord. This was a free or variable tone whose intonation was decided by the performer, with the help of tradition, rules, and occasional specification by the composer. With a signature

Common Cadences before 1600 (1 = Final, in Tenor)

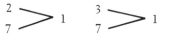

1100   1) *Occursus*

2) *Contrary-motion cadences*

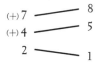

1200   3) *Gothic cadence*

1300   4) *7–6–8 (Landini) convention*

    TWO PARTS   THREE PARTS

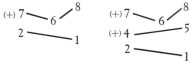

1400   5) *5–5 Crossover cadences*

                  WITH SUSPENDED
   LANDINI   LEADING TONE

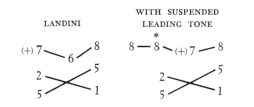

1500   6) *5–1 Cadence with suspended leading tone*

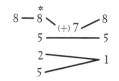

7) *Two-part Renaissance cadence*

1600   8) *Late Renaissance full cadence*

       SIMPLE   WITH CAMBIATA

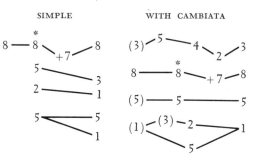

(+)   sometimes raised to form leading tone
+   raised to form leading tone
*   suspension

of one flat, the location of the chromatic semitone was transposed along with the gamut, the chromatic semitone then being E (E♭).

     circle sequence (Bar)—a sequence progressing by fifths around the circle of fifths in triads or seventh chords. The circle sequence was characterized by a slow, even, majestic harmonic motion and by one diminished fifth, without which the sequence would go too far afield tonally to be practical. It was used in modulations as a device to leave the tone or key.

     coloratura (Bar, Cla, Rom)—decorative florid passage-work. In the late Renaissance, the term was used for lute and keyboard division figures, but in the Baroque and Classical eras, it referred increasingly to vocal fioratura, less often improvised. In Romanticism coloratura referred to fioratura composed for the high sporano voice, which still sang florid passage-work, and to that voice itself. (*See also* fioratura, cadenza, division.)

 consort (Ren)—a group of instruments of the same kind—viols, recorders, or others—in different ranges, conceived as a single musical quality. They played as soloists, one instrument to a part. A later idea, of a mixed blend, was the *broken consort*; it was a consort with one contrasting voice, generally the top one and generally solo. An early Baroque idea was the *mixed consort*, a variable makeup of high (loud) or low (soft) instruments to form a choir.

 Corelli clash (Bar)—a dominant-to-tonic cadential progression containing straightforward successive seconds in two upper parts over a dominant bass tone. The top line proceeds from supertonic to tonic with an added tonic anticipation (figured 5 4 over the dominant bass tone) while the second line holds the tonic tone over the dominant as a suspension that then resolves to the leading tone (figured 4 3). In the Baroque style, the resolution preceded the anticipation (figured $\frac{5}{4} - {}^4$), but in some cases the two proceeded together (figured $\frac{5}{4}$ $\frac{4}{3}$). The latter was named the Corelli clash, after Arcangelo Corelli, who was said to relish the sound of it.

 couplet slurs (Cla)—two-note groups played legato as one unit within a generally detached language.

 crescendo (Cla, Rom, 20th)—a gradual steady increase of sound through a rise in dynamic level. The change must be from one level to another rather than be part of the natural rises of phrasing and expression within one level. The crescendo was exceptional at the end of the Baroque, a special effect in the Classical, and a standard device in the Romantic era and the new music.

 division (Med, Ren, Bar)—dividing a long note into shorter notes, with implications of decoration, most often in the form of variation. Division was a primary technique in the sixteenth and seventeenth centuries and was chiefly associated with improvised division on a known tune or over a ground. (*See also* fioratura, garribles.)

 dodecaphonic (20th), lit., "of twelve sounds"—refers to the view that the twelve tones of equal temperament are equal. (*See also* panchromatic.)

 dotted figure (Bar, Cla, Folk)—a virtually universal characteristic of certain dance rhythms. In the Baroque, the dotted figure, in a slow, majestic tempo, became characteristic of the French overture. In Classicism, it became one of the two-note figures used widely to achieve textural contrast. (*See also* Lombardy rhythm, couplet slur.) In the Renaissance and Romantic eras, the national character of dance rhythms was exploited in folk-derived dances, which achieved particular popularity.

 double leading tone (Med)—the use of a leading tone to both the octave and the fifth at a cadence. (*See* Cadence chart, page 720.)

 drone (Med, Folk)—the continuous sounding of a pitch, often with its octave and/or fifth, underlying a melodic element. The many bagpipes in the world attest to the universality of the drone, and the appearance of bagpipes in illustrations indicate that Medieval and Renaissance popular tunes were frequently heard with drones.

 dry upbeat (Cla)—an eighth-note upbeat detached from the ensuing downbeat. The reverse, an upbeat together with the ensuing downbeat as a couplet slur in a context of detached notes, was much less common but equally Classical.

One example is the opening of the slow movement of the Mozart Symphony #40 in g minor (K. 550).

event (20th)—a general term for a musical unit. An event is roughly comparable to a phrase or subject in the older styles but includes all elements. Certain forms in the new music are considered a succession of events.

fade (20th)—a gradual change from or to silence, superimposed on a musical fabric in lieu of either beginning or close of a movement or section. The most common fade is a *fadeout*, often over a wheel, to close a piece, but in electronically controlled music, the *fadein* or *fadeup* can be used as well.

familiar style (Ren)—polyphonic music in which all parts were based on the same rhythm. The term was used in apposition to *imitative style*, in both the composition of whole works (or sections of works) and the setting of one or two words, for textual emphasis or musical contrast, in an imitative work.

fauxbourdon (Med, Ren)—the technique, related to the older *discant*, of adding at sight a part above a written tenor line. The fauxbourdon was characterized by successive thirds (major and minor) after an initial fifth and ending on a fifth. In conjunction with a written part characterized by successive sixths above the tenor after an initial octave and ending on an octave, it produced a characteristic sound of successive 1-3-6 structures. By the middle Renaissance and in later styles, phrases using the characteristic 1-3-6 sounds of fauxbourdon but with all voices notated were available as inherited vocabulary.

feminine cadence (Cla)—a tonal cadence achieving final resolution on the strong beat while some or all of the upper parts (occasionally all parts) delay resolution, with appoggiature or a continuing dominant sonority producing a similar demand for resolution. The term is taken from the poetic term *feminine ending*, which refers to a line that ends on an unstressed syllable, particularly one in the midst of many that end on strong syllables. This concept can be applied to Medieval monophonic punctus structure.

fioratura (Bar), lit., "flowered"—a highly ornate melodic line, often improvised, in a virtuoso solo. (*See also* coloratura, cadenza, division.)

garibles (Med)—a trouvère term indicating improvised embellishments. They were added to a tune in performance.

gesture (20th)—a short linear figure, sometimes of two tones but often longer, recognizable as a melodic unit within a larger context. In pointillistic technique, a two-note gesture may comprise an event or phrase.

glissando (Rom, 20th), lit., "sliding"—a stepwise, generally quick, rise or fall between two tones. On instruments such as a violin, cello, or trombone, the glissando is defined by the two notes on either end, with no tones defined between them, and is properly termed a *portamento*. On such instruments as the harp and piano, the glissando is similarly defined by two tones, the tones between being defined but unstressed. In Romantic piano virtuoso techniques, the glissando could be played in octaves or on the black keys. It is notated ⁓⁓⁓ .

After the Romantic period, the glissando became an idiom of electronic and new music, where it is used as a structural element, particularly in statistical sounds. (*See also* passages, tirata, portamento.)

ground (late Ren, Bar)—a bass ostinato. It was used, particularly by players of the viol, as a basis for improvised variations or divisions.

hemiola (Med, Ren), lit., "one-and-a-half"—a proportional shift comparable to that from a quarter note to a dotted quarter-note beat, with a sound often comparable to a free mixture of $\frac{3}{4}$ and $\frac{3}{2}$ ($\downarrow.+\downarrow$) measures or $\frac{3}{4}$ and $\frac{3}{8}$ ($\downarrow+\downarrow.$). In the Medieval era, this was one of the simpler proportional shifts; in the Renaissance, it was the most important of the remaining proportional shifts. In Baroque music in $\frac{3}{4}$, the $\frac{3}{2}$ measure was used as a cadential preparation. And in Romanticism, the $\frac{3}{2}$ pattern was used in a $\frac{3}{4}$ meter as a rhythmic crosshatch, often involving syncopation. It was associated with late nineteenth-century music and was idiomatic to Brahms.

hocket (Med), lit., "hiccup"—the rhythmic breaking of a melodic line through the alternation of short notes and short rests. Hocketing often involved two singers alternating in a rapid exchange of notes and rests in off-rhythm.

imitation (Med, Ren)—entering a musical line with an idea recognizably derived from a previous entrance. Such lines *may* continue imitatively but generally do not. Pieces with more systematic imitation are usually given other names (i.e., caccia, canon, rota). The *imitative point* (Ren) was a punctus or point comprising successive imitative entrances of a number of voices and their achievement of a cadence. The imitative point became the standard phrase unit of the imitative or learned style. (*See also* familiar style.)

In the Baroque period, the use of polyphonic textures was called *learned* or *worked*, and this technique achieved its height in the working of a subject in fugue.

isorhythm (Med, Folk)—a repeated rhythmic pattern, used independently of pitch materials. In the Medieval era, isorhythms were basic to improvised percussion parts that were added as independent elements to other music. In late Medieval composition, a rhythmic figure (talea) could be maintained in interaction with a melodic line (color).

Landini cadence (Med)—a cadence in which an upper voice interposes a decorative "escape" or free tone between a leading tone and its progression to the final. In its most characteristic form, the upper voice outlines a 7–6–8 pattern (the 6 being the free tone) over a 2–1 tenor, counting the tenor final as 1 and its octave as 8. (*See* the cadence chart, page 720.)

layer or *plane* (20th)—the concept of independent musical elements conceived as relating in spatial distance as foreground and background rather than as high pitches and low pitches in musical range. (*See also* overlap.)

legato (Rom)—an intense linear connecting of one note to another. In the Baroque and Classical eras, legato was part of the decorative technique, reserved for embellishments (trills, tirate, etc.), couplet slurs, appoggiature, and other two- or three-note groups. But in the Romantic era, the legato melodic performance became standard; by the end of the nineteenth century, it was considered a desirable aspect of virtually all melody.

linear bitonality (20th)—the simultaneous appearance of two melodic lines, each with a clear reference to a key center, thus presenting the materials of two keys at once separated as two linear elements. If the technique is expanded to include three or more independent linear references, the result is called *linear polytonality*.

Lombardy rhythm (Cla, Folk)—a couplet slur, notated as a reverse dotted figure, generally a sixteenth plus dotted eighth, and accented on the sixteenth. Originally, it was associated with the dance patterns of Lombardy and was so used in the Renaissance and Baroque. The same pattern was also associated with Scotland and Ireland and was called the *Scottish snap*. In addition, the rhythm was characteristic of other nationalities, including the Slavic ones. In Classicism, the Lombardy rhythm became part of the general rather than the dance vocabulary and, along with a variant form in which 2 thirty-second notes replaced the initial sixteenth, became a characteristic idiom of the period.

loop (20th)—a repeated element in electronically manipulated music, created by a loop of tape engaged at the input that sounds over and over again. A loop can be any length manageable for the player, and it can be subjected to techniques of manipulation, most often change of speed or running in reverse. (*See also* ostinato.)

melisma (Med), lit., "melody"—a punctus or part of a punctus of plainsong in which several or many notes are used on one syllable. One melisma in an otherwise syllabic setting could emphasize a word by length and shape; or a generally melismatic punctus (such as an Alleluia) might suggest a heightened mood.

microtones (Ren, 20th)—notes in addition to the twelve tones. They are derived through quarter tones or other intervals of less than a half step and are used systematically. In the eras of key tonality, unmeasured microtones appeared in decorative idioms such as vibrato and portamento.

modulation (Bar, Cla, Rom)—change from one key center to another. The term may mean the recognition of the new tonal level, which the music may simply assume in an abrupt switch. Or, where the music is led through a transition so that the listener hears a turning from the old and then a focus on the new key center, the term may mean the process of transition itself.

mordent, in French, *pincé* (Bar)—an ornament added by the sign $\mathcal{N}$. It indicates that after the written note has been played or sung on the accent, the lower auxiliary and a return to the written note were to be added, at the general speed of the piece. At the end of the Baroque, the mordent was taken into full notation. (*See also* Schneller.)

motive (Rom)—a short figure of a combined rhythmic motto and melodic shape (not always of exact melodic intervals). It was used structurally and often associated with a nonmusical element for the purpose of programmatic reference. (*See also* theme, subject.)

murky bass (Cla, Rom)—the breaking of a piano bass line into octave tremolo. In Romanticism, the technique was less likely to be confined to the left hand, and the term became less useful.

mutation (20th), lit., "change" or "modification"—a term used by serial composers to denote modifications and fragmentations of the tone row. The term was borrowed from the Medieval technique of changing from one hexachord to another.

ostinato (Ren, Bar, 20th)—a figure or phrase used in successive repetitions. The *basso ostinato* served as a basis for variations at the end of Renaissance and through the Baroque (*see* ground). Repeated short figures, in any register, have been called *wheels* in the new music. In electronically composed music, they are made with loops of tape (*see* loop).

overlap (20th)—a technique of beginning and ending separate elements independently so that they overlap each other and create layers of sound. The technique generally involves both temporal and dynamic independence.

panchromatic (20th)—the integration and esthetic equality of all tones within the chromatic scope of materials. Although the expanded gamut of the

Renaissance was panchromatic (based on twenty tones within an octave), the term *panchromaticism* refers to posttonal techniques based on the twelve tones of equal temperament. Panchromatic music can be either free or serialized; it is theoretically in apposition to key tonality, which is based on the inequality of selected pitch materials. An equality of the twelve tones of the equally tempered scale is also called *dodecaphonic*.

pandiatonic (20th)—the integration and esthetic equality of all tones within one diatonic scope of materials. Pandiatonicism is theoretically in apposition to key tonality, which is based on the esthetic inequality of selected pitch materials. Although Guido's gamut was pandiatonic, the term is used for posttonal integrations. (*See also* quartal structures.)

passages (Med, Ren, Bar)—decorative elements, whether notated or improvised, of the nature of passage-work or busywork. In the Medieval era, passages were passing notes and runs; in the Renaissance, they were formulas associated with divisions; in the Baroque, they were increasingly repetitive, the creative embellishment yielding to the more general terms *fioratura* and *coloratura*.

plane (*see* layer).

point (*see* punctus).

pointillism (20th)—a technique of creating the appearance of an object by painting separate dots of various colors, which are integrated by the viewer. In music, the term refers to the technique of building a musical fabric either by passing a linear element from player to player or by using short gestures, so that single tones or gestures stand out as separate elements in the fabric.

polytonality (20th)—the simultaneous use of the materials of more than two keys. (*See also* bitonality, bichordalism, pandiatonicism.)

portamento (Rom)—the gradual sliding from one pitch to another as a decorative or expressive addition to a melodic line. Portamento is distinguished from the tirata and the keyboard glissando in that it does not define separate pitches. It is thus characteristic only of instruments that can avoid specific pitches, notably the voice, the trombone, and the bowed strings. The *portamento attack* (also ROM) begins at an indefinite pitch and arrives at the notated tone through portamento, either upward or downward but most often upward. (*See also* Schmaltz.)

proportional shift (Med, Ren)—a shift from one rhythmic basic unit to another by changing the proportion to the tactus, or regulating beat. The most common was probably the switch from duple to triple units—from two to three notes per tactus or per half tactus, from 4 eighth notes to 6 eighth notes as two triplet groups. This is roughly equivalent in $\frac{2}{4}$ metric rhythm to a change from 2 quarter notes to 3 quarter notes as a single large triplet. Introduction of triplets in an ornate melodic phrase remained common through Classical and into Romantic style. (*See also* hemiola, another common shift.)

punctus (Med, Ren, Folk), in English, *point*—a melodic phrase conceived as a structural unit. A simple correlation between punctus and poetic line—one punctus for each line—is basic to folk music and to popular song in all eras. The single punctus of vocal music and the double punctus of the estampie were basic to Medieval structure. In the Renaissance, the concept of the point expanded to include both the imitative and familiar styles. Single points were composed as organ versets or short keyboard pieces. In the Baroque, the point continued to be basic in matters of instrumentation and in antiphonal aspects of performance.

Through the latter, it was of significance in Baroque structure. (*See also* familiar style, imitative point.)

quartal structures (20th)—chords built in fourths and resulting in a sound characterized by combined major seconds, perfect intervals, and minor sevenths such as $C–F–B\flat$ $(–E\flat–A\flat)$ or $C–D–F–G$ $(–B\flat–C)$. Such structures are vital to pandiatonic techniques. Their obvious kinship to the cambiata figure and to pentatonic scales has given them greater interest to composers interested in folk or universal materials.

quarter tones (*see* microtones).

ritard (Rom)—a slowing of the beat beyond the tolerance in rubato for its tempo, generally in preparation for the final cadence of a section or movement. Before Romanticism, such preparation was written into the music through proportional shifts or a change of harmonic motion, so a ritard in addition was unnecessary and would comprise a double slowing down.

rocket (Cla)—an upward tirata played by orchestral violins with a crescendo. Also called the *Mannheim rocket* because it entered the orchestral vocabulary by being used in the court orchestra at Mannheim.

rubato (Cla, Rom), lit., "robbed"—the free stretching or contracting of the beat within a metric rhythm for purposes of expression. In Classicism, as in jazz in the twentieth century, rubato was an attribute of the melodic line without reference to the accompanying lines, which remained steady. In Romanticism, the technique suffused the entire fabric and applied to all lines at once.

Schmaltz (Rom), lit., "grease"—an idiomatic melodic decoration, generally constant and characterized by use of rubato, vibrato, portamento, and portamento attacks. The name derisively refers to violin technique, where such a style of performance gives the impression of a greased fingerboard. (*See also* portamento, vibrato, rubato.)

Schneller (Cla, Rom)—an ornament. In late Classicism, it was indicated by small added notes and was played with the main tone on the accent, followed by the upper neighbor and a return to the main tone. The Schneller was first mentioned by Carl Philip Emanuel Bach. It was always a German idiom, not used in the French and Italian styles and appearing in British usage only by importation. The Schneller was a quick ornament, in contrast to the slower mordent, to which it was a mirror image. In Romanticism, the Schneller took the symbol of the short trill ($\sim$), by then obsolete. After about 1830, the accentuation was reversed, so the last tone received the accent, the first two preceding the beat. (*See also* mordent.)

Scottish snap (*see* Lombardy rhythm).

sequence (Bar, Cla, Rom)—the repetition of a musical phrase at a different pitch level while maintaining pitch and rhythmic relationships. In the Baroque, the step and circle sequences were means of modulation, in the Classical and Romantic eras, they were associated with phrase extension and development.

serialism (20th)—the use of a series or order for a musical variable as a basis of structure. Early serialists dealt with an order of the twelve notes of equal temperament, the *tone row*; it was a twelve-note melodic series with each note used once (hence the term *twelve-tone music*). The row is used as a constant order of notes; it may also be used in retrograde (in reverse), retrograde inversion, transposition, and mutation. In the 1950s, serializations of durations, registers, dynamic levels, and (in orchestral works) instruments were added, leading to a statistical fabric of independent and interacting elements sometimes called *total serialism*.

Sprechstimme (20th), lit., "speaking voice"—a declamatory vocal technique in which register, melodic shape, and rhythm, but not exact pitch, are specified.

statistical structure (20th)—a structural type in ensemble works of the new music. Its basic technique is the staggering of several versions of the same general event, with each performer providing a slight deviation from the others. The deviations are generally in both pitch and time.

stretto (Bar)—in imitative and particularly in fugal style, the foreshortening of imitative accumulation by repeating entries closer than expected. The result is an intense overlapping of statements of the subject.

subito piano (Cla, Rom), lit., "suddenly soft"—an expressive device of sudden contrasting softness, generally following a crescendo and creating a reverse accent.

subject (Bar, Cla)—a musical unit of a few notes of characteristic rhythm, frequently of characteristic melodic shape as well. In the Baroque, the subject was the basic melodic element, essentially concerned with beat, meter, and tone. It was treated in a variety of ways, but chiefly by repetition and contrast. The most complex treatment was in a fugue, in which a subject in a dialogue was given to a specific number of lines (called voices whether vocal or instrumental). A statement of a fugal subject was followed by its answer at the distance of a fourth or a fifth but within the tone, reversing the roles of tonic and dominant notes in the *head*, or opening figure (G–C is answered by C–G and vice versa), to retain a single tone or key for both. Thus the answer is *at* the dominant level rather than *in* the dominant key, and the relationship between subject and answer in the fugue is special and tonal. Sometimes literal transposition *at* the dominant suffices, but just as frequently a modification is required by the tonal relationship. The subject and answer in fugal writing were also called the *dux* (leader) and *comes* (follower, companion).

In Classicism, subjects proliferated in contrasting pairs or groups, expanding the textural aspects of music. Subjects were treated in *development*, generally by maintaining some aspects and changing others.

In Romanticism, subject in general gave way to theme and was reserved for fugal techniques.

surface texture—the smoothness or roughness of the musical fabric, related to materials but defined by articulation and type of attack. A *high surface texture* (Bar, Cla) was achieved through a semi-staccato, standard style of performance, with legato avoided or reserved for special and decorative effects. High surface texture was associated with subject, and in the Classical period the contrasts of texture in themselves attained structural importance.

suspension—a demanding dissonant tone that delays a desired consonance, to which it resolves by a step downward. Its character depends on clear harmonic progression, for the suspension does not enter the musical fabric as a dissonance but as a member of a chord, a consonant and thus undetected tone. At a point of harmonic progression, that tone remains when the others change to form a new chord, becoming dissonant in the new context. Thus in performance the singer and linear instrumentalist increase the dynamic level of a tone as it becomes a suspension, while the pianist must stress the preparatory consonance in order to assure the tone's duration through its change to dissonance and demand for resolution. Although the suspension has been used in all chord fabrics, it was an essential idiom in the late Medieval, the Renaissance, and the Baroque, when it served in standard cadence formulas. (*See* the cadence chart, page 720.)

terraced dynamics (Rom)—a term used by Romantic performing groups to describe an imitation of Baroque and Classical dynamic contrasts. These contrasts were originally achieved by varying the number of players in successive phrases, but in Romantic interpretations, they were effected by varying the dynamic levels in individual parts.

theme (Rom)—a melodic unit conceived as a structural element, customarily made of related, balancing, or extending phrases and comprising a linear entity. The theme was most often performed as a legato, lyrical line. (The Baroque-Classical subject was replaced by theme and motive.) In earlier periods, *theme* was a literary term, and its association with verbal and programmatic aspects during the Romantic period remained strong. (*See also* motive, subject.)

tirata (Bar, Cla)—a run connecting two notes of a leap. It was sometimes notated   or   , a notation later used for the glissando, instead of being written out. When written out, it generally was stated in whatever note values would come out even. Nevertheless, whether written or abbreviated, the notes of the *tirata* presented a connecting span of sound without reference to the specific pitches or durations of the notes of the run. (*See also* rocket.)

tone row (20th)—an arbitrary order of succession of the twelve notes of equal temperament, without reference to rhythm, register, or medium. Tone row was conceived as a basis for the deployment of pitches in composition.

tremolo—a regular undulation of tone through variation of attack or pressure without change of pitch. The *orchestral tremolo* is a technique of the string instruments by which rapid bowing on a single tone sustains the sound, even at a high dynamic level. It was used as early as 1607 (in Monteverdi's *Orfeo*) but is characteristic of Classical and Romantic orchestral sound, in Classicism as part of textural contrast and in Romanticism to achieve dynamic brilliance. The *organ tremolo*, an undulation of tone through systematic variation of air pressure became standard in Romanticism (*see* Schmaltz). In the Romantic period, the pianist achieved an effect similar to the *string tremolo* through rapid alternation of notes an octave apart. In the left hand the technique was called a *murky bass*. (*See also* vibrato.)

trill (Bar, Cla)—a decoration, most often indicated by an added sign, comprising an alternation between the written note and a dissonant tone one step above the written note. Conceived as a series of falling appoggiature, the trill stressed the dissonant tone. It took on the character, particularly the speed and dynamic quality, of the movement and was often described as varying its speed within the tempo of the movement. A final turn was often added, but the turn was indicated in the notation and was added only when indicated. This was common in Classicism, and, within that style, more common in slow movements. In the Baroque, the trill was often a matter of tradition, automatically used in certain melodic contexts—notably on the supertonic preceding the tonic in a cadence—without indication in the notation.

In Romanticism (c.1830), the trill became uniformly fast and its relationship to the appoggiatura was lost. Thus it began on the written note and stressed it. A final turn was generally added whether or not it was indicated in the notation.

triplets—three-note rhythmic divisions in place of two.

tutti, lit., "all"—a term used in scores and parts in the Baroque to indicate that the full component of performers was involved. (It was contrasted to a *solo* marking.)

vibrato (Cla, Rom)—a decorative aspect of tone effected by a slight undulation of pitch above and below the main tone that was sufficient to enliven the quality but not to change the perception of pitch level. In the Baroque and Classical styles, the vibrato was related to the trill and was reserved for special effects. In Romanticism, it became a standard aspect of tone production. (*See also* tremolo.)

walking bass (Bar, 20th)—a steady bass part in continuous eighth or quarter notes.

wheel (*see* ostinato).

whole-tone scale (Rom, 20th)—the use of six whole steps within an octave. In late Romanticism (beginning with Glinka's overture to *Russlan und Ludmilla,* 1842), whole-tone melodic and chordal elements were featured as exotic elements. They served to weaken key tonality in a general expansion from diatonic materials.

Index

Italic page numbers refer to either illustrations or musical examples. The letter *b* following page numbers refers to a composer's biography.

"A the syghes," *137*
Abbot of Drimock (Musgrave), 656
Académie de Musique, 288, 292, 369
Académie de Musique Orchestra, 378–379
Academy of Sciences, 372
Acis et Galatée (Lully), 290–*291*
Acoustics, Baroque era, 311
  defined, 578
Adagio, Baroque era, 273–274, 314–315, 327
  Romantic era, 460
Adam de la Halle (1240–1288), 30, 38, 48*b*, 107, 115
Adam of St. Victor (c. 1110–1177), 68*b*
Adams, John, 415
Adventure serial, 603
Africaine, L' (Meyerbeer), 503
African music, improvisation, 13
  instruments, 247–248, 430–436
  song, 428, 437–439
  structure, 436–439
  vocal technique, 429, 437
African Suite (Coleridge-Taylor), 588
"After the Ball" (Harris), 562
Afterpiece, 549–550
Agnes de Navarre-Champagne, Comtesse de Foix (14th century), 48*b*
Agnus Dei, Medieval era, 51–52, 63
  Protestant music, 215
  Renaissance era, 151–152, 178–179, 207–212
Agon (Stravinsky), 589
Agréments (*see* Embellishment)
Aïda (Verdi), 523, 539, 561, 571
"Air de Marlbourouck," 445
Airs de Différent Auteurs, 232
Akenside, Mark (1721–1770), 652
Alard, Delphin (1815–1888), 489–490
Alba, 21, 22, 26, 78
Albeniz, Isaac (1860–1909), 572
Alberti bass, 718
Albinoni, Tomaso (1671–1750), 259
Alceste (Gluck), 406

Alceste (Lully), 290
Alea (Boulez), 630
Aleatory music, 630, 664
"Alexander's Ragtime Band" (Berlin), 586
"Alfie" (Bacharach), 656
Alfonso X, el Sabio, 15, 23, 36–37
Alfred (Arne), 323
"Alkmoonok," 447
Alla breve, 200
Alleluia, 51–52, 58–59, 85–87
Alleluia, Pascha Nostrum, 58–59
Alleluia, plainsong and organum, *85*
Allelujah I (Berio), 655
Allelujah II (Berio), 655
Allen, William Francis, 555
"Alma redemptoris mater" (Davies), 657
"Alma redemptoris mater" (Hermannus), 68
Alsloot, Denis van, 303
Also sprach Zarathustra (R. Strauss), 569, 575
Alternation, Baroque era, 278, 281
Alto horn, 582
Alto sax, 671, 673
Alumnaxkaki, 251
Amadis (Lully), 290
Amahl and the Night Visitors (Menotti), 680
"Amarilli" (Caccini), 237
Amati, Nicolo (1596–1684), 261
Ambira, 434
Ambitus, 58
Ambrosian chant, 50
America (colonial), composers, 441
  concerts, 416–417
  dance, 356–357, 417, 445–446
  popular song, 356–357, 425–427, 445
  singing schools, 417–421, 445, 483–484
  slave music, 427–428
America (pre-Colombian), improvisation, 13
  instruments, 249–253
American Opera Company, 543
American Singing Book, The (Read), 441
American Symphony Orchestra League, 600
Ames Brothers, 671
Amiens, Guillaume d', 32–33

"Amor con fede" (Landini), *123–125*
"Amor con l'arco tesso," 138, *139–140*
Amphion Anglicus (Blow), 318
Amplifier, new music, 624
Amplitude, new music, 624
Anatomy of a Murder, 616
Andersen, Hans Christian (1805–1875), 535
Aniara (Blomdahl), 627
Anonymous IV, 89
Anthem, 419, 422
Anthony and Cleopatra (Shakespeare), 407
Antifona (Halffter), 656
Antiphon, 53, 54, 68
Antiphony, Aztec music, 251
  jazz, 608
Anvil, 600
Apartment, The, 679
Apollon Musagète (Stravinsky), 589
Appalachian Spring (Copland), 616
Apparitions (Ligeti), 654
Appia, Adolph (1862–1928), 576
Appoggiatura, Baroque era, 314–315
  Classical era, 363, 374, 382, 401
  Medieval era, 120
  Romantic era, 702
  (*See also* Embellishment)
Aquilano, Seraphino, 138
Aquinas, St. Thomas (d. 1274), 60, 68*b*, 89
Arcadelt, Jacob (c. 1510–1560), 203–204*b*
Arceuil Group, The, 597
Archibald, William, 668
Archlute, 231
Arezzo, Guido of (c. 990–1050), 56, 73–78, 707–708
Aria, Baroque era, 266–267, 270–271
  improvisation, 702
Aria da capo, 266–267, 280
Aria with Fontana Mix (Cage), 627, 653
Ariadne auf Naxos (R. Strauss), 588
Ariadne Musica (Fischer), 334–336, 345
Arianna (Monteverdi), 239, 286
Arien (Krieger), 302, 319
Aristotle (384–322 B.C.), 7–8
Armstrong, Louis (b. 1900), 584, 606, 610, 612, 671

Arne, Michael (1741–1786), 348b
Arne, Thomas Augustine (1710–1778), 323, 347–348b, 356, 375–376, 410–411, 427
Arithmetic divisions (see Mode)
Arnold, Matthew (1822–1888), 507
Arp, Jean (1887–1966), 665
Arpeggiation, 292
Ars antiqua, 114–115
Ars cantus mensurabilis (Franco of Cologne), 89
Ars nova, Avignon school, 125–126
    composers, 142–144
    composition, 117–122, 127–129
    Italy, 121–125
    meter, 687
    proportions, 114–115
    rhythm, 114–115
Art de Toucher le Clavecin, L' (F. Couperin), 317
Art of Noises, The, 593
Art of Playing upon the Violin, The (Geminiani), 417
Ascenseur pour l'echafaud, 680
Asphalt Jungle, 680
Assyrian musicians, 4
Astaire, Fred, 612
Astarte (Joffrey), 676
Atlas Eclipticalis (Cage), 653
Atmosphères (Ligeti), 634, 654, 680
Atonality, new music, 598
Attack, Classical era, 362–363
    new music, 624
Atterbury, Luffman (d. 1796), 375, 377
Aubade, 26
Augustine, St. (354–430), 56
Authentic cadence, defined, 307
    (See also Cadence)
Autoharp, 447
Available Forms I (Brown), 633, 681
Aventures (Ligeti), 654
Avignon school, 125–126
    composers, 142–144
Ayacachtl, 251

Babbitt, Milton (b. 1916), 653–654b
Babes in Toyland (Herbert), 587
Bacchanal (Cage), 653
Bach, Carl Philipp Emanuel (1714–1788), 366, 372, 379b, 380–382, 412, 448, 485
Bach, Johann Christian (1735–1782), 382, 411, 412b, 417, 480, 485
Bach, Johann Sebastian (1685–1750), 324, 326, 335–339, 345b, 347, 379–380, 412–413, 476, 492, 511, 520, 578, 652, 676, 681, 687, 695–696, 714
Bacharach, Burt (b. 1928), 656b, 679

Background music, 604
Badings, Henk (b. 1907), 623–624, 626
Bagpipe, ancient, 5, 9
    Medieval, 45–46
    Renaissance, 196
Baker, Josephine, 602
Baker, Theodore (1851–1934), 560, 580
Bakwesi song, 438–439
"Balaam/Balaam," 97–98
Balbulus, the Stammerer (see Notker Balbulus)
Balet Comique de la Royne (Baltazarini), 243, 288
Ballad, Africa, 437–438
    Avignon school, 126
    Baroque era, 323
    Medieval era, 27–29, 34, 107
    Renaissance era, 186, 193–194
    Romantic era, 489, 496
Ballade (Coleridge-Taylor), 588
Ballata, Ars nova, 123–125
    Medieval era, 38
    (See also Virelai)
Ballet, Baroque era, 288
    Classical era, 408
    modern, 668
    Romantic era, 488–489, 539
    television, 679–680
Ballet suite, Romantic era, 523
Ballets Russes, 576–577
Ballo in Maschera, Un (Verdi), 523, 539, 543
Baltazarini (c. 1540–1585), 243b
Bamboula (Coleridge-Taylor), 572
Bamboula (Gottschalk), 491
Bananier (Gottschalk), 491
Banchetto Musicale (Schein), 245
Bands, colonial America, 425
    ragtime, 582
    Romantic era, 500, 543, 545–546
    twentieth century, 611–612, 670
Banister, John, 296
Banjo, African music, 434–436
    jazz, 608
    minstrel show, 548
    Negro music, 554–555
    ragtime, 582
Bannister, Christopher, 330
"Barbara Ellen," 357
Barbershop quartet, 219–220, 550
Barbiere di Siviglia (Rossini), 471, 477
Bard, 8
Baritone horn, 582
Barn dance, 445, 503, 598
Baroque era, aria da capo, 266–267
    basso continuo, 262–265, 296, 302, 308–310, 328–329, 341
    beat, 312, 713

cantata, 267–270
    composers, 271, 284–286, 315–320, 333–339, 342–348
    composition, 308
    defined, 258
    embellishment, 264, 273, 276, 292, 313–315, 702
    Germany, 300–304
    improvisation, 300, 702
    instruments, 263, 265, 267, 270, 272–284, 288, 291, 302, 327–344, 695–697
    opera, 259–261, 265, 270–272, 284–286m, 288–292m, 303–304, 322–323
    oratorio, 270, 284–286, 326
    performance, 271–272, 289, 296, 312–315
    song, 323–326
    structure, 266–267, 270–281, 284
    theory, 304–312, 329, 713
    vocal techniques, 259–261, 265–272, 284–285, 697
Bartók, Béla (1881–1945), 613–614b, 634, 657, 677
Bartolomaeus Anglicus, 69
Basie, William "Count," 611–612
Bass horn, 582
Bassariden, Die (Henze), 655
Basse dance, 224
Basso continuo, Baroque era, 262–263, 265–266, 272, 296, 302, 308–310, 328–329, 341
    Classical era, 362, 365, 382
    Renaissance era, 236, 238
    Romantic era, 500
Bassoon, Baroque era, 261, 263, 279, 291, 322, 341–342, 695
    Classical era, 371, 377–378, 385
    colonial America, 425
    new music, 632
Basuku song, 439
Battle of Trenton (Hewitt), 481, 485
"Bear Went Over the Mountain, The," 445
Beat, African music, 429, 439
    Baroque era, 312, 713
    jazz, 607–608
    Medieval era, 713
    rock, 674
    Romantic era, 454
    (See also Meter; Tempo)
Beater, 430, 433
Beatles, 657, 675–676, 679
Beatriz, Comtesse de Dia (fl. 1160), 48b
"Beatus vir" (Isaac), 182–184
Beautiful Blue Danube, The (J. Strauss II), 538, 561, 680
Beethoven, Ludwig van (1770–1827), 434, 454–461, 464, 476b, 489,

Beethoven, Ludwig van (*cont.*)
    495, 499, 504, 510–512, 516,
    520, 546, 562, 569, 578, 667,
    686, 705
Beggar's Opera, The (Pepusch),
    323
Bei prati, fresci riui (Scarlatti), 267,
    268–269
Bel canto, Baroque era, 259–261
Belasco, David, 587
Belle Hélène, La (Offenbach), 537
Bellerman, Constantin, 321
Bellini, Vincenzo (1801–1835), 499,
    520, 546
Bells, African music, 432, 434
    Medieval era, 35, 46–47, 692
    pre-Colombian era, 249
Belshazzar's Feast (Walton), 617
Benedictus, 51–52, 179, 215
Beneke, Tex, 655
Benevoli, Orazio, 213
Bennett, Richard Rodney (b. 1936),
    657*b*
Bennett, Tony, 671
Bensa, Alexander von, 473
Benvenuto Cellini (Berlioz), 503
Berg, Alban (1885–1935), 598, 600,
    614*b*, 665
"Bergerette savoyene" (Josquin), 186,
    187–189
Bergersen, Baldwin (b. 1914), 603,
    668
Berio, Luciano (b. 1925), 633, 655*b*,
    665
Berkeley, Busby, 612
Berlin, Irving (b. 1888), 586, 674,
    678
Berlioz, Hector (1803–1869), 61,
    476, 489, 491, 493–494, 503*b*,
    544, 666, 681
Bernart de Ventadorn (fl. 1150–
    1180), 35, 47–48*b*
Berneville, Gillebert de (fl. 1255–
    1280), 28–29
Bernhard, Christoph, 215
Bernhard-Karl of Saxe-Weimar Eisen-
    ach, Grand Duke, 482–483
Bestiare, Le (Poulenc), 616
Bettera, Bartolommeo (c. 1600),
    265
Biber, Heinrich (1644–1704), 319*b*
Biblické pisne (Dvořák), 535
Biches, Les (Poulenc), 616
Bichordalism, new music, 598
"Bicycle Built for Two, A," 562
Big apple, 582
Big Broadcast of 1937, The, 612
"Big Butter and Egg Man" (Arm-
    strong), 610
Billings, William (1746–1800), 418–
    422, 426, 441*b*, 514
Billy the Kid (Copland), 598

Binchois, Gilles (c. 1400–1460),
    130–132, 143*b*, 149
"Bird in a Gilded Cage, A" (Tilzer),
    586
Birth of a Nation, The (Griffith),
    586
Birth of Venus, The (Lully), 290
Birthday Blues Festival, 677
Bitonality, new music, 598
Bizet, Georges (1838–1875), 571,
    602, 682
Black bottom, 606
Black, Brown, and Beige (Ellington),
    616
Black Crook, The, 551
Blackbirds (Leslie), 602
Blackbirds (McHugh), 610
Blainville, Charles-Henri (1711–
    1777), 373
Blake, Eubie (b. 1883), 583, 602
Bland, James A. (1854–1911), 552
"Blasted Herb, The," 425
Blomdahl, Karl-Birger (1916–1968),
    627
Blondel de Nesle (c. 1150–c. 1200),
    48*b*
Blow, John (1649–1708), 318*b*
"Blue Danube, The" (J. Strauss II),
    538, 561, 680
Bluebeard's Castle (Bartók), 613
Blues, 583, 607–609, 670–671,
    677
Blumen-Strauss (Fischer), 333–334
Boccherini, Luigi (1743–1805), 384,
    413*b*, 425
Boesset, Antoine (1586–1643), 246*b*
Boethius (c. 475–c. 525), 71
Bohème, La (Puccini), 587
Boieldieu, François-Andrien (1775–
    1834), 471, 476–477*b*
Boismortier, Joseph Bodin de (c.
    1689–1755), 347*b*
Bolero (Ravel), 589
Bologna, Jacopo da (c. 1300–c.
    1365), 142*b*
Bomarzo (Ginastera), 654, 668
Bonanni, Filippo, 357, 436
Bonaventure, St. (1221–1274), 60
Bond, Carrie Jacobs (1862–1946),
    586
Bones, 548–550
Bono, Pietro, 138
Boogie-woogie, 613, 670
Book of Ayres (Pilkington), 246
Book of Common Prayer, 214, 354
Boris Godunov (Mussorgsky), 540
Bornelh, Giraut de, 21–23, 48*b*
Borodin, Alexandre (1833–1887),
    535, 571
Borroff, Marie, 3
Boston Symphony, 542
Boulanger, Nadia, 656

Boulez, Pierre (b. 1925), 621, 627–
    628, 630–631, 655*b*, 656–657,
    660–661
Bow, violin, 313, 369, 634, 696–697
Bowers, Thomas J., 552
Boyce, William (1710–1779), 369,
    379*b*, 411, 425
Brahms, Johannes (1833–1897),
    520–523, 535, 538*b*, 562, 568–
    569, 571, 701
Brandenburg Concertos (J. S. Bach),
    343, 345
Bransle, 224
Breakfast at Tiffany's (Mancini), 655
Breaking, 281, 284, 401
Breve, 200
Brewer, Teresa, 671
Brigs, London, 447
"Brimbledon Fair," 194, *195*
British Blondes, 551
"British Grenadiers, The," 425
Britten, Benjamin (b. 1913), 653*b*,
    667–668, 681
Broadsheets, 193
Broderie, Medieval era, 25, 46
Brossard, Sebastian de, 294, 306, 309
Brown, Earle (b. 1926), 632–633,
    681
Brubeck, Dave, 681
Bruckner, Anton (1824–1896), 537–
    538*b*, 569, 587, 666
Brulé, Gace (c. 1179–1212), 48*b*
Bruno, Count of Egisheim (d. 1054),
    68*b*
"Bull dance of the Mandan Indians,"
    353
Bull roarers, 432
Buona Figliuola, La (Piccini), 405
Burden, 40, 110–111
Burgundian school, 129–133
Burleigh, Henry T. (1866–1949),
    581, 586
Burlesque, 551, 602–603
Busch, Wilhelm, 519
Buskers, 195–196
Butler, Samuel, 596
Buxtehude, Diedrich (1637–1707),
    301, 319*b*
Byrd, William (c. 1540–1623), 241*b*,
    297
Byron, Lord George Gordon (1788–
    1824), 508

Cabezón, Antonio de (1510–1566),
    243*b*
Cabin in the Sky (Duke), 603
Caccia, 121
Caccini, Francesca (1588–c. 1640),
    245
Caccini, Giulio (c. 1548–1618), 236–
    238, 245*b*
Cadence, Ars nova, 120, 131, 133

Cadence (*cont.*)
  Baroque era, 275–276, 291, 307–308, 310, 314, 687–688, 702
  Classical era, 382, 386
  Renaissance era, 207, 209, 232
  Romantic era, 705
Cage, John (b. 1912), 620, 627–628, 630, 653b, 656
Cain and Abel (Badings), 624
Cakewalk, 555, 562, 575, 582
Caldara, Antonio (1670–1736), 344–345b
Calendar (Bennett), 657
Calife de Bagdad, Le (Boieldieu), 477
Call Me Madam (Berlin), 678
Calypso, 677
Calzabigi, Ranieri di (1714–1795), 406
Cambiata, African music, 437
  ancient, 13
  Aztec music, 251
  Renaissance era, 178, 200, 207, 702
Cambrensis, Giraldus, 17
Camerata Fiorentina, 238
Camille (Dumas), 548
Camp meetings, 483, 559
"Camptown Races" (Foster), 550–551
Cancan, 551, 575
Cancrizans, 625–626
Canon (Penderecki), 634
Canon, Medieval era, 51
  new music, 625–626
Cantabile (Franck), 540
Cantata, Baroque era, 265–270, 284–285, 301–302, 326
  Romantic era, 563
  Scarlatti, 267–270
Cantata para America Magica (Ginastera), 654
Canti di liberazioni (Dallapiccola), 681
"Canticle of the Creatures" (St. Francis), 38
"Canticle of the Sun" (St. Francis), 38
Canticum Sacrum (Stravinsky), 667
Cantigas de Santa Maria (Alfonso X), 36–37
Cantiones sacrae (Hassler), 244
Cantiones sacrae (Schütz), 318
Cantique spirituel, 215–216
Cantus firmus, Baroque era, 328
  Medieval era, 2, 83–85, 87, 96, 106
  Renaissance era, 150–152, 201, 209, 221, 699
Canzo, 21, 28, 33
Canzona, Baroque era, 265
  defined, 222
  Medieval era, 19
  Renaissance era, 185

Canzonetta, 185, 264
Capriccio Sinfonico (Puccini), 587
Caprice (Paganini), 671, 681
Carib Song (Bergersen), 603
Carissimi, Giacomo (1605–1674), 151, 270, 284–285b, 316
Carmen (Bizet), 571, 603, 682
Carmen Jones (Rose), 603
Carmina Sacra (Mason), 486, 563
Carnaval (Schumann), 496
Carnaval romain, le (Berlioz), 503
Carole, choral dance, 38–40
  Medieval era, 19, 21, 25, 110–112
Carrousels, 288
"Carry Me Back to Old Virginny" (Bland), 552
Caruso, Enrico (1873–1921), 570
Cascia, Giovanni de (active c. 1340–1350), 142b
Caserta, Antonellus de (active c. 1375–1400), 142–143b
"Casey Jones," 586
Cassatio in G (L. Mozart), 370
Castiglione, Baldassare, 205
Castor and Pollus (Rameau), 402
Castrato, Baroque era, 260–261, 299
  Classical era, 374, 405–406
Catalonia (Albeniz), 572
Catch clubs, 265
Catch songs, Baroque era, 296, 323–324
  Classical era, 375
  colonial America, 421
  Renaissance era, 219
"Catch That Catch Can," 219
Cathédral engloutie (Debussy), 575
Cathedral Music (Boyce), 379, 411
Cathedrals, Baroque era, 296, 323–324
  Classical era, 375
  colonial America, 421
  Medieval era, 84, 87–88
Catone Vticense (Albinoni), 259
Caurroy, Eustache du (1549–1609), 243b
Cavalli, Pier Francesco (1602–1676), 284b, 668
Cavazzoni, Girolamo, 243
Cavazzoni da Bologna, Marc' Antonio (c. 1490–1560), 242–243b
Cello, Classical era, 371, 384
  new music, 601, 656
"Centenary Essay" (Wagner), 514
Cercamon, 20, 47
Ceremony of Carols, A (Britten), 653
Certon, Pierre (c. 1510–1572), 191–192, 204b
Cesti, Marc Antonio (1623–1669), 271, 285b
Chabrier, Emmanuel (1841–1894), 540b

Chaconne, 294
Chalumeau eunuque, 196
Chamber Music (Berio), 655
Chamber music, Baroque era, 295, 327, 344
Chambonnières, Jacques Champion de (1602–1672), 292, 315b, 705
Chamisso, Adalbert von (1781–1838), 498
Champagne, Thibaut IV de (1201–1253), 48b
Chance music, 629–630
Chanson, Ars nova, 136
  Avignon school, 126
  Medieval era, 26, 28, 107–110, 116
  Renaissance era, 185–189, 191–192, 201, 216–220
Chanson de geste, 46
Chansonnier Cordiforme, 136, 139
Chant, ancient, 9
Char, René, 628
Charade, 655
Charleston, 582, 606
Charpentier, Marc-Antoine (c. 1636–1704), 316b
Cherubini, Maria Luigi (1760–1842), 461, 471, 476b
Cherubini Conservatory, 617
"Chester" (Billings), 418–420, 420, 426
"Chester," 670
Chi soffre speri (Mazzachi), 271
Chicago Civic Opera, 543, 600
Chicago Symphony Orchestra, 542
Chicahuatl, 250, 252
Children's Corner (Debussy), 588
Chitarrone, 262
Choice Collection of Lessons for the Harpsichord or Spinet (Purcell), 318
Choir, Baroque era, 294
  colonial America, 418–419
  Medieval era, 66
  Renaissance era, 201–202
Chopin, Frédéric (1810–1849), 489–493, 495–496, 498, 501, 504b, 537, 562, 571, 702
Choralcelo, 600–601
Chorale prelude, 224
Choralis Constantinus (Isaac), 180–181, 203, 614
Chorus, Baroque era, 270–271, 302, 326
  modern, 667
Chou Wen-Chung (b. 1923), 670
Christie, John, 600
Christmas Oratorio (Shütz), 302
Christofori, Bartolommeo (1655–1731), 366
Christy, E. P. (1815–1854), 550
Christy's Minstrels, 550, 552
Chromatic scale (*see* Scale)

Chromatic semitone, Ars nova, 120, 128, 130
  Medieval, 72–73, 77, 82, 90, 107, 177
  Renaissance, 217–218, 232, 495, 533
  Romantic era, 713
Chrome Circus, 676
Chronochromie (Messiäen), 667
Chronometer, 311
Ciconia, Johannes (c. 1335–1412), 143*b*
Cincinnati May Music Festival, 545
Cincinnati Symphony, 542
Circles (Berio), 633, 655, 665
Circus, 404, 543, 549
Cithara, 66
Citole, 35, 45–46
Clapper, 4, 6
Clarinet, Baroque era, 279, 695
  Classical era, 369, 382, 697
  colonial America, 425, 447
  jazz, 584
  new music, 573, 632
Clarinet concerto (Musgrave), 667
Clarino trumpet, 261, 279
Classical era, composers, 369, 379–380, 382–384, 411–413
  composition, 362–363
  improvisation, 403, 705
  instrumental forms, 362, 365–371, 382–491, 697
  meter, 688
  Mozart, 442–444
  notation, 705
  opera, 443–444
  orchestra, 376, 378–379
  performance, 374–379, 445
  style, 362–367
  texture, 362, 401, 697, 713
  theory, 371–373, 713
Claude le Jeune, 241*b*
Claudel, Paul (1868–1955), 576
Clavecin, 288
Clavichord, Baroque era, 329, 332–333
  Classical era, 365–367, 447–448
  fretted, 332
  mechanics, 367
  Romantic era, 455
Clog dance, 562
Cocoloctl, 251
Coerne, Louis Adolphe (1870–1922), 580, 596
Coffey, Charles, 323, 355, 409
Cohan, George M. (1878–1942), 586
Coincy, Gautier de (1178–1236), 37, 48
Cole, Nat "King" (1917–1969), 612, 671

Coleridge-Taylor, Samuel (1875–1912), 571–572, 581, 588*b*
Colman, George, 425
Colored noise, new music, 624
Columbia-Princeton Electronic Music Center, 623
Columbian Harmonist, The (Read), 441
Comb-and-paper, 196, 581
Combo, rock, 675
Comédie Italienne, 347, 405
Commedia dell'Arte, 498
Commemoratio Brevis, 56
Compline, divine office, 54
Composer's Guild, 614
Composer's World, A (Hindemith), 615
Composers, Ars nova, 142–144
  Baroque era, 271, 284–286, 315–320, 333–339, 342–348
  Classical era, 369, 379–380, 382–384, 411–413
  colonial America, 441
  Medieval era, 14–15, 37, 47–48, 67–68
  Renaissance era, 202–204, 236, 239–246
  Romantic era, 475–477, 485–486, 503–505, 537–541
  twentieth century, 587–589, 606, 613–617, 653–657, 664–665
Composition, Ars nova, 117–122, 127–129
  Baroque era, 308
  Classical era, 362–363
  history of, 685–686
  Medieval era, 43, 54–64, 85–87, 90–93, 95–103, 108–110
  new music, 622, 626, 658–664
  Renaissance era, 150–153, 177–180, 182, 191, 193–196
  Romantic era, 514
  (*See also* Technique; Theory)
Composition for Twelve Instruments (Babbitt), 654
Comprehensive Method for the Guitar (Holland), 586
Computer, new music, 698
Concert des amateurs, 380
Concert des bruits (Schaeffer), 621
Concert series, Classical era, 385
  colonial America, 355–356
  Romantic era, 462
Concert spirituel, 326, 342, 346, 363–364, 370, 380–381
Concertino, Baroque era, 341, 343–344
  Classical era, 367–368
Concertmaster, Romantic era, 462

Concerto, Baroque era, 341–344
  Classical era, 367–369, 443
Concerto ecclesiastico, Renaissance era, 224
Concerto for Violin, Two Trumpets, Two Horns, Two Flutes, Two Oboes, Two Bassoons, and Concerto Grosso (Telemann), 344
Concerto in C for Two Oboes, Two Clarinets, and Concerto Grosso (Vivaldi), 282–283
Concerto in D (Telemann), 344
Concerto in d minor (Vivaldi), 341
Concerto in e minor for Flute, Recorder, and Concerto Grosso (Telemann), 344
Concerto in F major (Vivaldi), 341
Concerto in G Major (Beethoven), 459
Concerto in the Italian Taste (Bach), 336
Concerto per due violini e leuto (Vivaldi), 341
Concerto Grosso (Telemann), 344
Concerto grosso, Baroque era, 265, 272, 278–284, 296, 341–344
  classical era, 367
  defined, 278
Concerto ripieno, Baroque era, 278, 341–342, 344
Concerts, Classical era, 445
  colonial America, 416–417
  Romantic era, 479–480
Concerts royaux (F. Couperin), 317
Concord Sonata (Ives), 613
Concret PH (Xenakis), 654
Concussion sticks, 432
Conductor, Classical era, 369
  Romantic era, 462–463, 516
  twentieth century, 598
Conductus, Medieval era, 94–95, 99, 103, 107, 127
Conflictus, 19
Confucius (551–478 B.C.), 8, 11, 13
Conga, 447, 582
Conservatoire, Paris, 488–489, 503, 615
Consort, Baroque era, 228–229, 263, 265, 278, 296
  broken, 228–229
  Renaissance era, 201–202, 220–221, 224, 226–229, 239
Contes d'Hoffmann (Offenbach), 537
Continental Harmony, The (Billings), 441
Contrafactum, colonial America, 425–426
  hymns, 215, 216
  Medieval era, 50
Contrast, Baroque era, 263, 266, 278
  Classical era, 385–387

Contratenor altus, 138
Contratenor bassus, Medieval era, 138
  Renaissance era, 148, 177, 198
Cooper, Paul (b. 1926), 61, 667, 670
Coperario, John (c. 1575–1626),
  317b
Copland, Aaron (b. 1900), 598, 616–
  617b, 667, 670, 678
Coq d'or, le (Rimsky-Korsakov), 541
Cordier, Baude (active c. 1400–
  1420), 126, 143b
Corelli, Arcangelo (1653–1713), 274–
  279, 286b, 296, 328, 343, 345,
  460, 511, 699, 704
Coriolanus (Beethoven), 464
Cornetto, Renaissance era, 227–228,
  272, 303, 342, 582, 584, 694
Coronation Anthem (Lawes), 317
Correspondences (Babbitt), 654
Corwin, Norman, 681
Così fan tutti (Mozart), 444, 499
Cotillion, 481–483, 501
Cotton, John, 85–86
Cotton Club, 616
Council of Trent, 60, 206
Countermelody, Medieval era, 83,
  85–86
Counterpoint (Piston), 615
Counterpoint, Baroque era, 329
  Medieval era, 86
  Romantic era, 513
Countertenor, Renaissance era, 152,
  178
Country music, 502
Country western music, 677
Couperin, François (1668–1733),
  294, 317b, 695
Couperin, Louis (1626–1661), 317b
Couplet slur, Classical era, 401
Courante, 224
Courier-whips, 371
Cox and Box (Sullivan), 540, 550
Craft of Musical Composition, The
  (Hindemith), 597, 615
Crang, John, 329
Creation, The (Haydn), 411, 461
Création du Monde, la (Milhaud),
  611
Credo, 51–52, 62, 151–152, 215
Crisis of Serial Music, The (Xenakis),
  654
"Critique," 325
Croesus (Keiser), 304
Cruce, Petrus de, 113, 127
Crüger, Johann (1598–1662), 318–
  319b
Crumb, George (b. 1929), 670
Crwth, 5, 45, 66
cummings, e. e., 633
"Cunctipotens Genitor Deus" (Tuo-
  tilo), 68

Cunning-Man, The (Rousseau), 402
Cupid and Death (Locke), 318
Cut time, 200
Cymbal, ancient, 4
  Medieval era, 46–47, 79
Czerny, Carl (1791–1857), 504, 516

Dafne (Schütz), 318
D'Alembert, Jean le Rond (1717–
  1783), 372–373
Dallapiccola, Luigi (b. 1904), 617b,
  681
Dame aux Camelias, La (Dumas),
  524
Dame Blanche, La (Boieldieu), 471,
  477
Damett, Thomas (died c. 1430),
  143b
Damper action, harpsichord, 330
  piano, 367, 515
Dance hall, Romantic era, 501, 551–
  552
Dance Preludes (Lutoslawski), 653
Dance song, ancient, 10
  Ars nova, 141–142
  Baroque, 274, 291, 297, 328
  Classical era, 382–383, 444–447
  colonial America, 356–357, 417,
    445–446
  Medieval era, 15, 23–25, 28, 34,
    37–41, 106–107
  Negro, 554–555
  Renaissance era, 223–226
  Romantic era, 473–475, 481–483,
    501, 551, 560–562, 575–577
  twentieth century, 548, 570–571,
    575–577, 582, 598, 606, 608,
    668, 674–675
Dance suite, Baroque era, 288
"Dancing on Christmas Eve," 142
D'Anglebert, Jean-Baptiste-Henry
  (1661–1747), 316b
D'Anglebert, Jean-Henry (1628–
  1691), 292–293, 316b, 706
Danse macabre (Saint-Saëns), 523,
  538
Dauphin, Leopold, 536
D'Aurenga, Raimbaut, 21, 23–25
David, Hal, 679
Davies, Peter Maxwell (b. 1934),
  657b
Davis, Miles (b. 1926), 654, 671, 680
"Days of Wine and Roses" (Man-
  cini), 655, 680
De Institutione Musica (Boethius),
  71
"De moi dolereus vos chant" (Gille-
  bert), 29
De Natura Sonores (Penderecki), 656
"De plus en plus" (Binchois), 130,
  131–132

De Profundis (Delalande), 295
De Profundis (Gluck), 412
De Vaqueiras, Raimbaut, 24–25
"Death and the Lady," 194–196
Death and Transfiguration (R.
  Strauss), 588
Death of Minnehaha, The (Cole-
  ridge-Taylor), 588
Debussy, Claude Achille (1862–
  1918), 573–575, 577–578, 588b,
  591, 705
Decay, new music, 624
Decision, The (Musgrave), 656
Delalande, Michel-Richard (1656–
  1726), 294, 316b
Density (Varèse), 614
"Deo gratias Anglia," 129
Depot Blues (House), 608, 609
"Der Freischütz" (Weber), 472
"Der Lindenbaum" (Schubert), 467–
  470
Des Prez, Josquin (see Josquin des
  Prez)
Deschamps, Eustache, 115
Dett, R. Nathaniel (1882–1932),
  586, 589b
Deutsche Messe und Ordnung Got-
  tesdienst (Luther), 213
Development, 385
"Devil among the Tailors, The"
  (Gray), 502
Devil to Pay, The (Coffey), 323, 355,
  409
Devils of Loudon, The (Penderecki),
  657, 668
Devin du Village, Le (Rousseau),
  402, 409
Diaghilev, Serge (1872–1929), 576–
  577, 593
Dialogues des Carmelites, Les (Pou-
  lenc), 616
Diane et Actéon (Boismortier), 347
Diatonic scale (see Scale)
Dickinson, Emily, 616
Dido and Aeneas (Purcell), 298–299,
  318
"Dido's Lament" (Purcell), 299
"Dies Irae," 56, 60–61, 68
Différences (Berio), 655
Dikubila, 431
Dimensions of Time and Silence
  (Penderecki), 656
Dindo, 431
Dindo moana, 431
Disc jockey, 674
Discant, Ars nova, 128, 133 ·
  Medieval era, 111
Dissonance, Baroque era, 309, 311,
  315
  Renaissance era, 199

Dissonance (*cont.*)
  Romantic era, 597
Dittersdorf, Karl Ditters von (1739–1799), 382, 384–385, 412*b*, 461, 666
Divertimento, Classical era, 368–371, 382–384
Divertimento a nove stromenti (J. Haydn), 382–383
Divertimento in D Major (M. Haydn), 382
Divertimento in F (L. Mozart), 370–371
Divertissements (Mouret), 347
Divine Office, 53–54
Division of the octave, Baroque era, 265, 280, 703
  Renaissance era, 222
"Dixie" (Emmett), 561
"Dixie's Land" (Emmett), 550, 561
Doctor's Dilemma, The (Shaw), 602
Domestic Symphony (R. Strauss), 569, 588
Dominican rite, 60
Don Carlos (Verdi), 523
Don Giovanni (Mozart), 443, 681
Don Juan (R. Strauss), 569, 588
Don Quixote (Cervantes), 219
Don Rodrigo (Ginastera), 654
Donizetti, Gaetano (1797–1848), 499
Donne, John (1573–1631), 304, 652
Dostoevsky, Feodor (1821–1881), 571
Double punctus, Ars nova, 117
  Baroque era, 294, 334
  Renaissance era, 222, 239
  (*See also* Punctus structure)
Double stopping, Baroque era, 281
  Romantic era, 459
Doubling, Baroque concerto, 342
Dowland, John (1562–1626), 232–233, 246*b*
"Down Where the Wurzburger Flows" (Tilzer), 586
Dramma per musica, 238–239
  (*See also* Opera)
Dream of Gerontius, The (Elgar), 541, 571
Dreigroschen Oper (Weill), 323
"Drink to Me Only with Thine Eyes," 445
Drinking song, ancient, 7
  Renaissance, 231
Drone bass, 671
Drums, African, 428, 430–432, 437
  American Indian, 251, 559
  ancient, 7, 10
  jazz, 584, 608, 671
  Medieval era, 35, 45, 47, 79
  pre-Colombian, 249

ragtime, 582
  Renaissance era, 694
Drury Lane Theatre, 408
Dryden, John (1631–1690), 298
Dufay, Guillaume (c. 1400–1474), 130–131, 133, 143–144*b*, 147–150, 221, 524, 686
Duke, Vernon, 603
Dulcimer, 433
Dumanoir II, Guillaume, 44
Duncan, Isadora (1878–1927), 575
Dunham, Catherine, 603
Dunstable, John (c. 1370–1453), 128–129, 143*b*, 149
Duplum, Medieval era, 83, 85–86, 702
Duport, Jean-Louis (1749–1819), 480
Duport, Jean-Pierre (1741–1818), 480
Durbin, Deanna, 600
Dvořák, Antonin (1841–1904), 520, 535, 540*b*, 580–581, 586
Dying Poet, The (Gottschalk), 505
Dylan, Bob, 677

"E dame jolie," 30
Eagle Dance, 352
Easy Instructor, The (Little and Smith), 446, 484
Easy Winner (Joplin), 588
Echiquier, 694
Echo, Baroque era, 702
Eckstine, Billy (b. 1914), 612
Eclats (Boulez), 655, 660
Eclogue, 19
Eddy, Nelson, 600
Eichendorff, Joseph Baron von (1788–1857), 498
Ein Heldenleben (R. Strauss), 569
Eisteddfod, 42
Electric Circus, 682
Electromagnetic instruments, 600–601
Electronic composition, 689
Electronic music, 625–627, 632–633, 659, 661–662, 668, 681, 700, 706, 708
Electronic techniques, 676, 678
Elegy for Viola and Cello (Musgrave), 656
Elegy for Young Lovers (Henze), 655
Elektra (R. Strauss), 588
Elémens de musique (d'Alembert), 372
Elgar, Edward (1857–1934), 520, 541*b*, 571
Elijah (Mendelssohn), 504
Ellington, Duke (b. 1899), 585, 612, 616*b*, 670, 682
Embellishment, African music, 429, 439
  Ars nova, 120–121

Baroque era, 264, 267, 273, 276, 292, 313–315
  Classical era, 364, 374, 401, 704
  history of, 701–707
  jazz, 607–609
  Medieval era, 15, 23, 25, 46, 57–58, 115, 702
  Negro music, 558–559
  Romantic era, 465
"Emblem" (Copland), 670
Emmett, Daniel (1815–1904), 549–550, 552, 561
Emperor Concerto (Beethoven), 459
Enfant et les sortilèges, L' (Ravel), 589
Enharmonic system, 198, 306
Enigma Variations (Elgar), 541
Ensembles for Synthesizer (Babbitt), 654
Envelope, new music, 624
Enzo Re (c. 1225–1272), 38
Ephrata Hymn Collection, 354
Epitaffio per F. Garcia Lorca (Nono), 654
Equatorial (Varèse), 614
Erlkonig, Der (Schubert), 466–467
"Erste Veilchen, Das" (Mendelssohn), 499
Escher, Maurits, 619
España (Chabrier), 523, 540
Espejos (Halffter), 656
Essercizi per gravicembalo (Scarlatti), 331, 346
"Essercizo in *a* minor" (Scarlatti), *331*
Estampie, 40–41, 44, 106–107
Esterháza Orchestra, 378
Estro Harmonico, L' (Vivaldi), 343
Estro poetico-armonico (Marcello), 345
Ethiopian band, 549
Ethnomusicology, 579, 581
Etude (Chopin), 702
Etude (Debussy), 588
Etude, Romantic era, 489–490, 588, 702
Etudes aux chemins de fer (Schaeffer), 621
Eunuch flute, 196
Euryanthe (Weber), 477
Eurythmics, 575–576
Evelyn, John, 287
Event, new music, 625–626, 659–660, 663
Evolution of Modern Orchestration, The (Coerne), 580
Evolutions (Bading), 626
"Exaudi Deus" (Isaac), *180–181*
"Exit Music II: Fat Millie's Lament" (Gaburo), 682
Exsulta Satis, 57–58

Facade (Walton), 617
Factionalism, Romantic era, 520–524
Faidit, Guacelme (fl. 1185–1215), 48*b*
Fall of a Nation, The, 586
Falla, Manuel de (1876–1946), 577
Falstaff (Verdi), 524, 539
Fanciulla del West, La (Puccini), 587
Fancy, 224
Fandango, 571
Fantasia, Baroque era, 296, 301
    Renaissance era, 221–222, 224
Fantasia on a Theme by Tallis (Williams), 589
Fantasia on Innomine of John Taverner (Davies), 657
Fantíni, Girolamo, 697
Fanueil Hall, 356
Far Harbour (Bergersen), 668
Far from the Madding Crowd (Bennett), 657
Farinelli, Carol Broschi, 703
Farrar, Geraldine (1882–1967), 570
Fasola, Romantic era, 483–484, 502
Fauré, Gabriel, 535, 541*b*
Faust (Berlioz), 501, 503
Faust (Goethe), 466
Faust (Gounod), 543
Fauxbourdon, Ars nova, 133
Favart, Charles-Simon (1710–1792), 404–405, 409–410
Fear No Evil, 679
Feedback, new music, 625
Ferienkurse, 631
Festa, Costanzo (c. 1495–1545), 241–242*b*
Festspielhaus, 533, 569
Festspielhaus Orchestra, 598–599
Fétis, François-Joseph (1784–1871), 517
Fiddle, Medieval, 21, 35, 45–46
    Negro music, 553–554
    ragtime, 581
    United States, 549–550
Fidelio (Beethoven), 476
Field holler, 608
Fife, Aztec, 251
    colonial America, 447
    Renaissance, 695
Fife-and-drum, Ars nova, 135
    colonial America, 426
Fifteen Mysteries of the Virgin Mary (Biber), 319
Fifth Symphony, in c minor, opus 67 (Beethoven), 512
Figured bass, 291, 308–310, 513
Fille coupable, La (Boieldieu), 477
Filter, new music, 624–625
Finlandia (Sibelius), 571
Finney, Ross Lee (b. 1905), 652, 670

Fioratura, Baroque era, 687–688, 702
Fiori Musicali (Frescobaldi), 245
Fischer, Johann Casper Ferdinand (d. 1746), 333–334, 336, 345*b*
Fisk Jubilee Singers, 555, 558
Fitzgerald, Ella (b. 1918), 607, 612, 654
Fledermaus, Die (Strauss II), 538
Fliegende Hollander, Der (Wagner), 538
Flora, or Hob in the Well, 355
Florentia, Giovanni de (active c. 1340–1350), 142*b*
"Flow My Teares" (Dowland), 232, 233–235
Flute, African, 248, 432, 437
    ancient, 5–7, 10
    Baroque era, 261, 279, 291, 322, 327, 341, 343–344, 695
    Classical era, 377–378, 385, 387
    colonial America, 417, 447
    jazz, 671
    Medieval era, 46, 66
    Renaissance, 228
    Toltec, 249
Folk Melodies (Lutoslawski), 653
Folk song, ancient, 9
    colonial America, 357
    early United States, 484–485
    Israeli, 668
    pre-Colombian, 254
    Renaissance, 193–196
    twentieth-century, 598, 620, 678
    (*See also* Popular song)
Fontaine, Pierre (c. 1380–1450), 143*b*
Fontainebleau Orchestra, Château de, 378
Fontanne, Lynn, 602
Fontenelle (1657–1757), 311
"For He's a Jolly Good Fellow," 445
Forbidden Planet, 627, 680
Formantes (Halffter), 656
Formes fixes, Medieval era, 26–33, 117
Forster, E. M. (1879–1968), 512
Forza del Destino, La (Verdi), 539
Foster, Stephen Collins (1826–1864), 550–552
Foundling Hospital Orchestra, 378
Four-hand music, Romantic era, 463, 464, 465, 516
Fox-trot, 582
Fragmentation, new music, 663
Franchomme, Auguste (1808–1884), 489–490
Francis of Assisi, St., 68
Franck, César (1822–1890), 476, 539–540*b*
Franco of Cologne, 89–90, 92, 96–97

Franco-Flemish school, 150, 185–186, 202–203
Franconian motet, 96–97
Frankfurt Opera, 615
Franklin, Aretha, 677
Freischütz, Der (Weber), 471, *472*, 473, 477
Frequency, new music, 624
Frescobaldi, Girolamo (1583–1643), 245*b*, 319
Fricassée, 186
Friction drum, 249
Friendly Persuasion, 616
Froberger, Johann Jacob (1616–1667), 303, 319*b*
Frottola, 138, 185–186
Frug, 582
Frye, Walter (d. 1450), 143*b*
Fuenllana, Miguel de, 245*b*
"Fugen oder wie es de Italiener nennen, canzoni alla francese," 224
Fuging tune, 419, 422, 445–446, 583
Fugit nox (Boismortier), 347
Fugue, Baroque, 265, 274, 276, 301, 308, 326–328, 334, 336–339
    Renaissance, 224
Funeral Anthem (Billings), 422
Funeral Music (Lutoslawski), 633–634
Fünf neapolitanische Lieder (Henze), 655
Fünf Sätze für Streichquartett (Webern), 592
Fünffstimmigte blasende Musik (Pezel), 319
Fux, Johann Joseph (1660–1741), 328–329, 344, 381, 513

Gabinetto Armonico (Bonanni), 357, 436
Gabrieli, Andrea (c. 1510–1586), 228, 230, 243*b*
Gabrieli, Giovanni (1557–1612), 243–244*b*, 272, 284, 318
Gaburo, Kenneth (b. 1926), 682
Gace Brulé (c. 1179–1212), 48
Galliard, 224
Gallican chant, 50
Gallican rite, 127
Gallus, Jacobus (1550–1591), 240*b*
Galop, 560
Gamelan, 681
Gamut, African music, 1
    Guidonian system, 75–76
    Medieval era, 89
    Renaissance era, 178, 218
Ganassi, Silvestro, 703
Garibles, 15, 46, 115, 702
Garrick, David (1717–1779), 408, 410
Garrison, Lucy McKin, 555

Gating circuits, new music, 624–625
Gatti-Casazza, Giulio (1868–1940), 570
Gaultier, Denys (1603–1672), 245
Gaultier, Ennemond (c. 1575–1651), 244–245b
Gautier de Coincy (1178–1236), 37, 48b
Gavotte, 224, 417
"Gay Negro Boy, The," 548
Gazette Musicale, 489, 503
Gazza Ladra, La (Rossini), 471
"Gebet an Pierrot" (Schoenberg), 594
Gehot, Jean (1756–1820), 480–481
Geistliche Gesänge (Schütz), 318
Geistreiches Gesang-Buch (Bernhardt), 215
Geminiani, Francesco (1687–1762), 342–343, 417
Generator, new music, 623–624
Genese (Badings), 626
Geneviève de Brabant (Offenbach), 537
Geoffrey de Vinsauf, 113
George White Scandals, 603, 615
Georgia Minstrels, 552
Gershwin, George (1898–1937), 602, 610, 615–616b
Gesang der Jünglinge (Stockhausen), 624, 627, 656, 665
Gesture, new music, 659
Gesualdo di Venosa, Carlo (1560–1613), 218, 242b
Gewandhaus Orchestra, 492–493, 504
Geystliche, Gesangk-Buchleyn (Walther), 241
Gibbons, Orlando (1583–1625), 244b
Gigue, 303, 328
Gilbert, William Schwenk, 536
Gillebert de Berneville (fl. 1255–1280), 28–29
Gillespie, Dizzy, 654
Gilliat, Sy, 440, 447, 553
Gilmore, Patrick (1829–1892), 545–547
Gilmore Band, 546–547
Ginastera, Alberto (b. 1916), 654b, 668
Giraut de Bornelh (fl. 1165–1200), 21–23, 48b
Giraut Riquier (d. 1294), 48b, 78
Girl Crazy (Gershwin), 615
"Girl I Left Behind Me, The," 425
Girl of the Golden West, The (Puccini), 587
"Give My Regards to Broadway" (Cohan), 586
Glarean, Heinrich (1488–1563), 198
Glass harmonica, 424, 441
Glassy-chord, 424

Glee, 219, 375–376, 499, 550
Glenn Miller Story, The, 655
Glig, 35
Gligcraeft, 35
Gligman, 35
Glinka, Mikhail Ivanovich (1804–1857), 490, 503–504b, 513, 571
Glissando, new music, 624, 630, 651
Gloria (Poulenc), 667
Gloria, 51–52, 62, 133, 151–153, 215
Gluck, Christoph Willibald (1714–1787), 405–407, 412b, 520
Glückliche Hand, Die (Schoenberg), 600
Glyndebourne Arts Trust Ltd., 600
Go Yuy, 9, 13
"God Save America," 426
"God Save the King," 426
Goethe, Johann Wolfgang von (1749–1832), 407–409b, 466, 476, 504, 535, 539
Goethe Lieder (Wolf), 535
Goldsmith, Oliver (1728–1774), 450
Goliards, 26, 33, 40
"Good-Morning to All" (Hill), 561
Goodman, Benny (b. 1909), 611–612
"Goodnight Irene" (Ledbetter), 671
Gospel music, 674, 677
Gossec, François-Joseph (1734–1829), 369, 380b
Gotterdämerung (Wagner), 532
Gottschalk, Louis Moreau (1829–1869), 490–491, 505b
Götz von Berlichingen (Goethe), 407, 409
Goudimel, Claude (c. 1505–1572), 241b
Gounod, Charles François (1818–1893), 476, 543
Goûts Réunis, Les (F. Couperin), 317
Grace (see Embellishment)
Gradual, 51–52, 59
Gradus ad Parnassum (Fux), 381
Graffito, 80
Grand motet, 294–295
(See also Motet)
Grand traité d'instrumentation (Berlioz), 503
Gray, James, 502
Greek scales, 198
Greenfield, Elizabeth Taylor, 553
Grenon, Nicolas (c. 1375–c. 1450), 143b
Grétry, André-Modeste (1741–1813), 384, 405, 412–413b, 537
Grieg, Edvard Hagerup (1843–1907), 520, 523, 535, 541b
Griffith, D. W., 586, 593
Group for Contemporary Music, 670

Groupe de Recherches Musicales, 621
Gruppen (Stockhausen), 656
Guacelme Faidit (fl. 1185–1215), 48b
Gualdo, John, 416–417
Guarnieri, Giuseppi (1683–1745), 261
Guédron, Pierre (c. 1570–c. 1620), 246b
Guest of Honor, A (Joplin), 589
Guglielmo, Ebreo (c. 1440–c. 1500), 223
Guido d'Arezzo (c. 990–1050), 56, 73–78, 707–708
Guidonian system, 73–76, 83, 106, 128, 130, 177, 197–198, 218, 304, 312, 418
Guignon, Jean-Pierre, 44
Guilds, 35, 67
Guillaume D'Amiens, 32–33
Guillaume de Machaut (c. 1305–1377), 48b, 115–119, 122, 142, 686
Guillaume Tell (Rossini), 471, 477
Guitar, adapted, 601
    ancient, 4
    Baroque, 279, 288, 322
    Classical era, 368
    colonial America, 417
    jazz, 608, 671
    modern, 656, 668–669, 674–676
    Romantic era, 455
Guys and Dolls (Loesser), 678
Gymel, 108, 111, 128

"Habañera" (Bizet), 682
"Haec Dies," 92, 93
"Hail, Columbia," 545
"Hail! Hail! The Gang's All Here," 540
Hair: The American Tribal Love-Rock Musical (MacDermot), 678–679
Halffter, Cristobal (b. 1930), 656b, 681
Halle, Adam de la (1240–1288), 30, 38, 48b, 107, 115
Hamlet (Shakespeare), 617
Hamlet and Ophelia (MacDowell), 588
Handel, George Frideric (1685–1759), 326, 343, 345–346b, 355, 410, 499, 511, 545, 578, 701
Handel and Haydn Society, 545
Handel and Haydn Society's Collection of Church Music (Mason), 486
Handy, W. C. (1873–1958), 581–583
Hanslick, Eduard (1825–1904), 506, 508–513, 516, 520, 533

"Happy Birthday to You" (Hill), 561
Hard Day's Night, A, 657
"Hare, Hare/Balaam!/BALAAM,"
　99, 100–102, 106
Harmonie Universelle (Mersenne),
　305
Harmonielehre (Schoenberg), 613
"Harmonious Blacksmith, The"
　(Handel), 499
Harmonium, Romantic era, 500–501,
　545
Harmony (Piston), 615
Harmony, African music, 427–428
　Bach, 701
　Baroque era, 265, 275, 309–311
　Cambrensis on, 17
　Chopin on, 702
　Classical era, 373
　Medieval era, 45, 713
　Rameau on, 373
　Renaissance era, 200, 687
　Romantic era, 495, 512, 532–533
　universal concept, 11–13
Harney, Ben R., 545
Harold en Italie (Berlioz), 503
Harp, African music, 433
　ancient, 5, 8, 17
　Medieval, 20, 35, 66
Harpsichord, Baroque era, 265, 302–
　303, 329–331, 695
　Classical era, 362–365, 367, 377–
　　378
　colonial America, 417
　improvisation, 705
　mechanics, 329–330
　Renaissance era, 198, 236, 694
　technique, 329–331
Harris, Charles K. (1864–1930), 562
Harrison, George, 675–676
Hartleben, Otto, 593
Hasse, Johann Adolph (1699–1783),
　377
Hassler, Hans Leo (1564–1612),
　244b
Hässler, Johann Wilhelm (1747–
　1822), 413b, 448–450
Hautboy, 425
　(*See also* Oboe)
Havens, Richie (b. 1941), 620
Haverly's Minstrels, 552
Hawkins, Coleman (1905–1969),
　707
Haydn, (Franz) Joseph (1732–1809),
　370, 381–382, 384–385, 388,
　402, 411b, 443–444, 447, 454,
　460, 476, 511, 524
Haydn, (Johann) Michael (1737–
　1806), 382, 411–412b, 461, 477
"Hearts of Oak," 425
Heine, Heinrich (1797–1856), 494–
　498

Heiress, The (Copland). 617
Heldenleben, Ein (R. Strauss), 588
Helmershausen, Roger of, 49
Hemiola, African music, 429
　Baroque era, 278, 311
　Medieval era, 112
　Renaissance era, 236
Henze, Hans Werner (b. 1926),
　655b, 668
Herbert, Victor (1859–1924), 586,
　587b, 600
Here's to Romance, 600
Hermannus Contractus (1013–1054),
　68b
Hernani (Verdi), 539
Hertel, Johann Wilhelm (1727–
　1789), 371, 380b, 382
Heterophony, African music, 436–
　437
Hewitt, James (1770–1827), 479,
　481, 485b
Hexachord system, 71–78, 197, 216,
　707–709
Heyward, DuBose, 602
Hiawatha (Coleridge-Taylor), 572
Hiawatha's Departure (Coleridge-
　Taylor), 588
High and the Mighty, The (Tiom-
　kin), 616
High Noon, 616, 680
Hill, Mildred S., 561
Hiller, Johann Adam (1728–1804),
　407, 409–410, 412b, 492
Hindemith, Paul (1895–1963), 597,
　615b, 667, 701
Hines, Earl (b. 1905), 612
Histoire du Soldat (Stravinsky), 611
History, musical periods, 685–686,
　711–712
Hit Parade of 1937, The, 612
Hocket, African music, 429
　Ars nova, 121–122
　Classical era, 374
　new music, 664
　Renaissance era, 182
Hoe-down, 598
Hoffmann, Ernst Theodor Amadeus
　(1776–1822), 453–454, 507,
　537
Holland, Justin, 586
"Home! Sweet Home!" 485
Homer, Louise (1871–1947), 570
"Homme armé, L'," 136
"Honky Tonk Train Blues" (Lewis),
　613
Hootchy-kootchy, 677
Hope, Bob, 603
Hopkinson, Francis (1737–1791),
　426–427, 441b, 445, 478
Horn, African, 432
　Baroque, 291, 341, 344, 695

Classical era, 369, 371, 377–378,
　382, 385, 697
　colonial America, 425
　jazz, 671
　Medieval, 15
　new music, 656
Hornpipe, 194–195, 485
Horowitz, Vladimir, 682
Hot Mikado, The, 603
Hothby, John (c. 1418–1487), 197
"Hound Dog," 674
House, Son, 608–609
"How High the Moon" (Paul), 621
Huchbald (840–930), 56
Huehuetl, 252
Hugenots, Les (Meyerbeer), 499, 503
Hugo, Victor, 523, 539
"Humoresque" (Dvořák), 540
Huneker, James (1860–1921), 508
Hungarian dances (Brahms), 571
Hunt, Leigh (1784–1859), 471
Hunt Symphony (L. Mozart), 370
Hurdy-gurdy, 322
Hymn, ancient, 5–7, 10, 53
　Baroque, 300
　colonial America, 419
　Medieval, 53, 61–62
　Renaissance, 221, 223
Hymnen (Stockhausen), 681
Hymni Totius Anni (Victoria), 240

"I Can't Give You Anything but
　Love, Baby" (McHugh), 610
"I Love You Truly" (Bond), 586
"I Want to Hold Your Hand" (Mc-
　Cartney), 657, 675
Iberia (Albeniz), 572
Iberia (Debussy), 574
Ibsen, Henrik (1828–1906), 541
"Ich liebe dich" (Grieg), 535
"I'd Leave My Happy Home for
　You" (Tilzer), 586
"I'm a Poor Wayfaring Stranger,"
　357
"I'm Troubled in Mind," 556
Images (Debussy), 588
Imitative point, Baroque era, 264,
　274, 276
　colonial America, 422
　Renaissance, 212
*Immobiles for Tapes and/or Diverse
　Instruments* (Powell), 666, 682
Improvisation (Armstrong), 610
Improvisation (Parker), 672–673
Improvisation, African music, 429,
　434, 436
　Ars nova, 115, 125
　Baroque era, 300, 702
　Classical era, 403, 705
　harpsichord, 705
　history of, 702–707

Improvisation (*cont.*)
jazz, 609, 672–673
Medieval era, 42, 65, 83, 104, 106, 702
organ, 705
piano, 705
popular song, 415
Renaissance era, 222
universal elements, 13–14, 44
"Improvised cadenza" (Broschi), 703–704
"In a Sentimental Mood" (Ellington), 616
"In' gesach," 34
In the Bottoms Suite (Dett), 589
"In the Evening by the Moonlight" (Bland), 552
"Inaugural March" (Wagner), 563
Incoronazione de Popea, L' (Monteverdi), 246
Incredible Flutist, The (Piston), 615
Indes galantes, Les (Rameau), 401–402
Indeterminacy, new music, 628
Indian Suite (MacDowell), 580, 588
Ingram, Rex, 603
Innomines, 297–298
Insect Trust, 677
Instruments, African, 247–248, 430–436
ancient, 3–10
Baroque, 261–263, 265, 267, 272–286, 288, 291, 302, 305, 327–344, 695–697
Classical era, 362, 365–371, 382–401, 697
Indian, *51*, 350–353, 357, 559–560
Medieval, 15, 21, 35, 44–46, 66, 79, 104, 110, 138, 141, 692–694
new music, 600–601, 632
pre-Colombian, 249–252
Renaissance, 196, 201–202, 220–225, 227–229, 242–245, 694–695
Romantic era, 697–698
traditions, 7
universality, 11–12
Interludes, new music, 604–605
Intermezzo in E major (Brahms), 521–522
Intolleranza (Nono), 654–655, 668
Intraden 2 4 (Pezel), 319
Introit, 50, 52
Inventions (Bach), 336, 345
Ionisation (Varèse), 600, 614, 665
Iphigénie en Aulide (Gluck), 406
Isaac, Heinrich (c. 1450–1517), 134, 180–186, 189–190, 203*b*, 216, 614
"Isbruck, ich muss dich lassen" (Isaac), 186, 189–190, 215, 216

"Isle Joyeuse, L'" (Debussy), 575
Isorhythmic motet, 95–96, 99, 115–116
Isorhythmic structure, African music, 429
Ars nova, 128
Medieval era, 79
new music, 626, 659, 664
universal elements, 13
Italienisches Liederbuch (Wolf), 535
Ite, missa est, 51–52
Ivanhoe (Sullivan), 540
Ives, Charles (1874–1954), 613*b*, 665

Jackson, William (1815–1954), 499
Jacopo da Bologna (c. 1300–c. 1365), 142*b*
Jacopone da Todi (c. 1230–1306), 60, 68*b*
Jagd, Die (Hiller), 410, 412
Jam session, 609
James, Harry, 612
Janequin, Clément (c. 1480–1560), 203*b*
Jaques-Dalcroze, Emile (1865–1950), 575–577
Jaywalker, The (Ellington), 616
Jazz, 585–587, 606–611, 670–673, 706–707
"Je n'ose être content" (Certon), 186, *191–192*
"Je puis trop bien" (Machaut), *117–119*
"Jeg elsker dig" (Grieg), 535
"Jelly Roll Blues, The" (Morton), *584–585*, 614
Jelyotte, Pierre, 370
Jenkins, John (1592–1678), 317*b*
Jephte (Carissimi), 284
Jerome, St. (c. 340–430), 55–56
Jerome of Moravia, 57
Jeu de Robin et Marion, Le (de la Halle), 31–32
Jeune France, La, 597
Jew's harp, 356–357, 433, 500
Jig, 417, 446–447
Jitterbugging, 582
Joffrey, Robert, 676
John the Deacon, 61
Joliot, Louis, 350
Jongleurs, 20, *21*, 25, 42
(*See also* Minstrelsy)
Jonny spielt auf (Křenek), 611
Joplin, Scott (1868–1917), 562, 581–582, 588–589*b*
Josquin des Prez (c. 1445–1521), 134, 150–153, 177–179, 186–188, 202–203*b*, 207–209, 579, 686
Journal du Printemps (Fischer), 345
Joyce, James, 655

"Juba Dance" (Dett), 589
Jubilee Singers, 559
Jubilee Songs, 558
Jubilus, 58, 65, 78, 90
Juilliard School of Music, 617
Junge Lord, Der (Henze), 655
Jupiter Symphony (Mozart), 597
Juvenile Psalmist, The (Mason), 486

"Kalenda maya" (Raimbaut), 23, *24*, 25–26
Kamarinskaya (Glinka), 504
Karkoschka, Erhard, 631
Kay, Ulysses (b. 1917), 670, 680
Kazoo, 196, 695
Keats, John (1795–1821), 508
"Kedron," *420*, *421*
Keiser, Reinhard (1674–1739), 304, 320*b*, 409
Kenilworth (Sullivan), 540
Kepler, Johann (1571–1630), 652
Kern, Jerome, 602
Kersands, Billy ("King Rastus"), 552
Kettledrums, 10, 201–202, 693–695
Key, Baroque era, 263, 265, 267, 275, 280, 292, 301, 308
(*See also* Tone)
Kind, Friedrich, 471
Kinderscenen: Leichte Stücke für das Pianoforte (Schumann), 496
King, E. J., 502
King and I, The (Rodgers), 678
"King Porter Stomp, The," 611
Kircher, Athanasius (1602–1680), 304–305
Kirchgassner, Marianne, 424
Kithara, 4, 10, 601
Kjerulf, Halfdan (1815–1868), 535
Klavierstücke no. 2, III (Stockhausen), 628, 629
Klee, Paul (1879–1940), 591
Klinger, Friedrich Maximilian von (1752–1831), 408
Köchel, Ludwig von (1800–1877), 413
König Hirsch (Henze), 655
"Konrad Wallrod" (Mickiewicz), 496
Kontakte (Stockhausen), 633, 656
Kontra-Punkte (Stockhausen), 656
Křenek, Ernst (b. 1900), 611
Krieger, Adam (1634–1666), 302, 319*b*
Krüger, Eduard (1807–1885), 509
Krummhorn, 200, 201, 228, 694
Kubla Khan (Coleridge-Taylor), 571
Kunstwerk der Zukunft, Das (Wagner), 524
Kyrie, 50–52, 63–64, 127, 133, 151–152, 179, 215

Lady Be Good (Gershwin), 615
Lady in the Dark (Weill), 602
Lamartine, Alfonse-Marie de (1790–1869), 495
Lament, Baroque era, 299
Laments d'Arianna (Monteverdi), 266
Lancelot and Elaine (MacDowell), 588
Landa, Bishop Diego de, 247
Landini, Francesco (c. 1325–1397), 122–125, 130, 142*b*
Langue d'oc, 26, 38
Langue d'öil, 26
Langton, Stephen (d. 1228), 60
Lanier, Sidney (1842–1881), 564
Lantins, Hugo de (active c. 1420), 143*b*
Lassus, Roland de (1531–1594), 42, 213, 240*b*, 243
Last Hope, The (Gottschalk), 505
"Lauda Sion" (Aquinas), 68
Lauds, divine office, 53–54
Laugh-In, 679
"Laura" (Raskin), 680
"Laura Gentile" (Negri), *225*
Lawes, Henry (1596–1662), 298, 317*b*
Lawrence of Cordoba, 138
Lay, 15, 19, 21, 26
Le Jeune, Claude (c. 1528–1600), 241*b*
Leading tone, Ars nova, 120
Baroque era, 276, 310
Renaissance era, 198, 694
Learned style, Baroque era, 301, 333
colonial America, 422
Leclair, Jean-Marie (1697–1764), 328, 346*b*
Ledbetter, Huddie "Leadbelly" (1888–1949), 671
Lee, Peggy (b. 1920), 612
Legrenzi, Giovanni (1626–1690), 273, 286*b*
Leipzig Orchestra, 378
Leitmotif, 532–533, 569
Lennon, John, 676
Leonardo da Vinci (1452–1519), 134, 141, 148, 702, 707
Leoninus (active c. 1160–1180), 89–92
Leopardi Fragments (Davies), 657
Lerner, Alan Jay, 678
Leslie, Lew, 602
Lesson, divine office, 53
Letz, 21, 223
Lewis, John (b. 1920), 654*b*, 671
Lewis, Meade Lux (b. 1905), 613
Ley (*see* Lay)
Liasons dangereuses, les, 680
Liber Usualis, 50, 53, 63–64, 68, 78

"Liberty Song" (Boyce), 425
Lied, 185, 465–470, 498–499, 515, 520, 535
(*See also* Popular song)
Lied von der Erde, Das (Mahler), 587
Liederbuch, 185
Liedertafel, 476
Life for the Czar, A (Glinka), 503
Ligeti, György (b. 1923), 634, 654*b*, 680
Light in the Wilderness, The (Brubeck), 681
Lincoln Portrait (Copland), 616
Lind, Jenny (1820–1887), 535, 553
Lindenbaum, Der (Schubert), 467–470
Lingita, 431
"Listen to the Lambs" (Dett), 586
"Listen to the Mocking Bird" (Milburn), 561
Liszt, Franz (1811–1886), 61, 476, 490, 493, 495–496, 498, 504–505*b*, 510, 523, 538, 546, 572, 705
Litaniæ Lauretanæ (Fischer), 345
"Little Lost Child, The" (Marks and Stern), 562
Livre (Boulez), 655
Lloyd, Charles, 676–677
Lobkowitz, Prince, 412
Locke, Matthew (c. 1630–1677), 317–318*b*
Lodoïska (Cherubini), 471
Loeillet, Jean-Baptiste (1680–1730), 343
Loesser, Frank, 678
Loewe, Frederick (1796–1869), 678
Lohengrin (Wagner), 538, 543
"Look of Love, The" (Bacharach), 656
Loop, new music, 625
"Lord Rendal," 196, 357
"Lost Chord, The" (Sullivan), 535
Loulié, Etienne (c. 1650–1702), 311
Love song, 6, 20–21, 116, *251*
Lovely Rita Meter Maid, 675
Low music, 201, 228
Lowell, James Russell (1819–1891), 507
Lucia di Lammermoor (Donizetti), 499
"Lucy in the Sky with Diamonds" (McCartney), 676
Ludus, Tonalis (Hindemith), 615
Luening, Otto (b. 1900), 623
Lully, Jean-Baptiste (1632–1687), 291, 295–296, 316*b*, 343, 406, 422, 537–538
Lunt, Alfred, 602
Lur, 6

Lute, archlute, 231
Baroque era, 265, 279, 302, 341
chitarrone, 262
Medieval era, 46, 138
Renaissance, 201, 202, 220–222, 231, 236
South American, 253
theorbo, 231
Lute song, Baroque, 302, 357
Renaissance, 231–236, 245–246
Luther, Martin (1483–1546), 213–214, 241
Luthier, 261
Lutoslawski, Witold (b. 1913), 633, 651–652, 653*b*, 665
Lux AEterna (Ligeti), 654
Luzzaschi, Luzzasco (1545–1607), 242*b*
Lyceum Theatre, 548
Lyra Britannica (Boyce), 379
Lyra Sacra (Mason), 486
Lyre, 66, 433
Lyric Pieces (Grieg), 541

Ma vlast (Smetana), 523
MacDermot, Galt, 678
MacDonald, Jeanette, 600
MacDowell, Edward (1861–1908), 520, 580–581, 587–588*b*, 661
Machaut, Guillaume de (c. 1305–1377), 48*b*, 115–119, 122, 142, 686
Machines, in opera, 258–259, 270–271, 287, 299, 326, 403, 405
Madama Butterfly (Puccini), 570, 586–587
Maddalena (Rossi and Monteverdi), 285
"Madrid Waltz," *474*
Madrigal, Baroque era, 284–285
composers, 143
Medieval era, 121, 142, 216–220, 231, 245–246, 687
Madrigal I, II, and III (Pousseur), 656
Madrigali Spirituali (Marenzio), 242
Maeterlinck, Maurice (1862–1949), 568, 688
Magic Flute, The (Mozart), 444
Magnolia Suite (Dett), 589
Magnus Liber Organi, 89–90
Mahler, Gustav (1860–1911), 569, 587*b*
Maîtres de la musique, les (Dauphin), 536
Malimba, 433
Mallarmé, Stéphane (1842–1898), 568, 588, 655
Man with the Golden Arm, The, 680
Mancini, Henry (b. 1924), 655*b*, 679–680

Mandolin, 279
Manipulation, new music, 625
Mannerism, Ars nova, 121
  Avignon school, 125
Mannheim Orchestra, 378
Manon Lescaut (Puccini), 587
Manual of the Boston Academy of Music (Mason), 486
"Maple Leaf Rag" (Joplin), 562, 588
Marcabru (active 1129–1150), 20, 47*b*
Marcello, Alessandro (1684–1750), 342, 345*b*
Marcello, Benedetto (1685–1739), 345*b*
"March against the Philistines" (Schumann), 498
Marches, 562
"Marching through Georgia" (Work), 561
Marenzio, Luca (1553–1599), 242*b*
Marian antiphons, 68
Marie de France (fl. 1181–1216), 48*b*
Marienleben, Das (Hindemith), 597, 615
Marimba, 249, 251, 433–434, 436
Marini, Biagio (c. 1595–1665), 272–273, 286*b*
Marquette, Jacques, 350
Marriage of Figaro (Mozart), 443, 471, 671
Marteau sans maître, le (Boulez), 627–628, 631, 655, 665
Martin, Tony, 671
Martirano, Salvatore (b. 1927), 670
"Mary and Marthy," 558, 579
Mason, Lowell (1792–1872), 485–486*b*, 563
Masque, Baroque era, 298, 323
Masque for the Entertainment of the King: Venus and Adonis (Blow), 318
Masquerades, Baroque era, 300
  Classical era, 444
Mass, Ars nova, 133
  composers, 239–240
  Easter, 58–59
  history, 51–52
  modern, 668
  order of, 50–51
  ordinary, 62–63
  performance, 52
  polyphonic, 150–179
  Renaissance era, 207–213
  (*See also* Missa)
Mass in D (Stamitz), 380
Mathis, Johnny, 671
Mathis der Maler (Hindemith), 615
Matins, divine office, 53

Mattheson, Johann (1681–1764), 328–329, 342, 381
Maxixe, 571, 575, 582
May dance (Raimbaut), 24, 78
Mazeppa (Liszt), 523
Mazurka, 495, 571
Mazurka (Chopin), 495, 508
Mazzochi, Domenico (1592–1665), 266, 271, 284*b*
Mbanakum, 433
Mbila, 433
McCartney, Paul (b. 1942), 657*b*, 676
McHugh, Jimmy, 610
Medici, Lorenzo de, 203
Medieval music, characteristics, 79–80
  composers, 14–15, 37, 47–48, 67–68
  embellishment, 15, 23, 25, 46, 57–58, 115, 702
  harmony, 713
  improvisation, 42, 65, 83, 104, 106, 702
  instruments, 15, 21, 35, 44–46, 66, 79, 104, 110, 138, 141, 692–694
  performance, 14–15
  philosophy, 69–71
  popular song, 135–140
  rhythm, 713
  theory, 713
Medium, The (Menotti), 668
Meistersinger, 35
Meistersinger von Nürnberg, Die (Wagner), 35, 539
Méliès, George (c. 1860–1938), 572, 585
Melisma, Medieval era, 25, 57–58, 65, 86–87, 90–92, 121–122
  new music, 583
Melodies for the Pianoforte (Mendelssohn), 504
Melothesia (Locke), 318
Memento Vitæ (Musgrave), 656
"Memphis Blues" (Handy), 583
Mendel, Gregor Johann (1822–1884), 506
Mendelssohn-Bartholdy, Felix (1809–1847), 490, 492–493, 495, 500, 504*b*, 520, 541, 562, 569
Menotti, Gian-Carlo (b. 1911), 668, 680
Mer, La (Debussy), 578, 588
Merry Cobbler, The (Coffey), 323
Merry Widow (Lehar), 586
Mersenne, Marin (1588–1648), 304–306
Merz, 595
"Meschëans d'Amors," 28, 29
Messe des vivants (Gossec), 380

Messiaen, Oliver (b. 1908), 621, 627, 655, 667
Messiah (Handel), 326, 346, 355, 545
Metastasis (Xenakis), 630, 654
Meter, Baroque era, 266, 275–276, 278, 290, 304, 311, 336
  Classical era, 688
  colonial America, 419, 422
  history of, 686–689
  Renaissance era, 232, 236
  twentieth century, 659–660, 674
Metronome, 441, 516
Metropolitan Opera, 543, 570
Meyerbeer, Giacomo (1791–1864), 490, 499, 503*b*, 504–505, 546, 548
Michelangelo Buonarroti (1475–1564), 134, 148, 535
Mickiewicz, Adam, 496
Micrologus (Guido d'Arezzo), 73
Microtone, new music, 591, 633–634
Midsummer Night's Dream, A (Britten), 653
Midsummer Night's Dream (Mendelssohn), 504
Midsummer Night's Dream (Shakespeare), 602
"Mighty Fortress Is Our God, A" (Luther), 214
Mikado, The (Sullivan), 536, 602
Mikrokosmos (Bartók), 613
Milano, Francesco da (1497–1543), 243*b*
Milburn, Richard, 561
Mildmay, Audrey, 600
Milhaud, Darius (b. 1892), 597, 611, 615*b*, 655–656
Military Divertimento (L. Mozart), 370
Miller, Glenn (1904–1944), 612
Milton, John (1608–1674), 298, 304
Mime, Classical era, 402
  Medieval era, 45
Mimus, 19
Mines of Sulphur, The (Bennett), 657
Minnesinger, 33–35
Minnesota Symphony, 681
"Minstrel Boy, The," 485
Minstrel show, 404, 543, 548–553, 603
Minstrelsy, 5, 18–26, 35–36, 42–44, 47–48, 687, 694
Minuet, 291, 417, 445–446, 461
Miracle plays, 67
Miraculous Mandarin, The (Bartók), 613
Mirliton, 430–431, 433, 581
Miserere (Scarlatti), 346
Missa cuiusvis toni (Ockeghem), 151

Missa Gloria Tibi Trinitas (Taverner), 298
Missa in Dominicalis (Victoria), 207, 212
Missa in H-moll (J. S. Bach), 345
"Missa Hercules Dux Férrarie" (Josquin), 151
Missa L'homme armé (Josquin), 152–153, 153–177, 177–179, 207, 208–209
Missa Martyribus (Isaac), 179
Missa Mi-Mi (Ockeghem), 151
Missa Pange lingua (Josquin), 150
Missa Prolationum (Ockeghem), 151
Missa Se le face ay pale (Dufay), 150
Missa sine nomine, 151
Mix, new music, 605, 624, 626, 632
Mlle. Modiste (Herbert), 587
Mme. Rentz's Female Minstrels, 551
Mobile (Pousseur), 656
Modalism, new music, 597
Mode, ancient, 8
  arithmetic divisions, 77–78
  Classical era, 373
  hexachord system, 76–78
  harmonic divisions, 77–78
  Renaissance era, 198–199
Mode de valeurs et d'intensities (Messiaen), 627
Modern Jazz Quartet, 654, 671
Modulation, Baroque era, 274, 308, 310–311
  Classical era, 385–386
Moldau, The (Smetana), 523
Moller, John Christopher, 480
Momente (Stockhausen), 633, 656
Monastery, sacred song, 66–67
Mondonville, Jean-Joseph Cassanéa de (1711–1772), 342, 348b, 364, 402
Monet, Claude (1840–1926), 568
Moniot D'Arras (13th century), 48b
Monk, Thelonious (b. 1920), 680
Monody, Baroque era, 258, 266, 288–289
  drama per musica, 238–239
  Renaissance era, 206, 229–237
Monophony, hexachord system, 71–74
  Medieval era, 15, 25, 35–36, 78–80
  (*See also* Plainchant)
Monterey Festival, 671
Monteverdi, Claudio (1567–1643), 239, 246b, 266, 271, 284–286, 363, 524, 686
"Mood Indigo" (Ellington), 616
Moondog (b. 1917), 627, 671
Morales, Christobal de (c. 1500–1553), 239–240b
Moralitaten (Henze), 655

Morley, Thomas (1557–c. 1603), 73, 199, 242b, 708
"Moro lasso" (Gesualdo), 218
Morris, George F., 505
Morrison, George, 553
Morton, Jelly Roll (1885–1941), 584–585, 606, 607, 614–615b
Morton, Thomas, 349
Moscheles, Ignaz (1794–1840), 498–499, 569
Moses und Aron (Schoenberg), 613, 665
Moten, Bennie, 611–612
Motet, Ars nova, 127–128
  composers, 239–240, 284–285
  declamatory, 128
  Franconian, 96–97
  grand motet, 294–295
  Medieval, 88, 106–107, 115, 142
  performance, 104
  Petronian, 127
  Renaissance, 180–184, 210–214
Mothers of Invention, 676–679
Moulinié, Antoine, 315–316b
Moulinié, Etienne, 315–316b
Mount, William Sidney, 482
Mouret, Jean-Joseph (1682–1738), 346–347b
Mouth organ, 500
Mouvements perpetuels (Poulenc), 597, 616
Movies, music in, 605–606, 612, 680
Mozart, Leopold (1719–1787), 365, 370, 372, 380b, 413, 707
Mozart, Nannerl, 365
Mozart, Wolfgang Amadeus (1756–1791), 365, 370, 381, 384–401, 410, 412, 413b, 424, 442–444, 447, 454–455, 460–461, 489–490, 499, 511, 520, 578, 597, 671, 681, 686, 701, 714
Mozart-Salieri (Rimsky-Korsakov), 541
Musæ Sionæ (Praetorius), 244
Musen Siziliens (Henze), 655
Musgrave, Thea (b. 1928), 656b, 667
Music drama, 532–533, 539
Music for a Great City (Copland), 667
Music for Horn and Piano (Musgrave), 656
Music for String Instruments, Percussion and Celesta (Bartók), 614
Music hall, 404
Music in Miniature (Billings), 441
Music Man, The (Willson), 678
Musica politico-practica (Pezel), 319
Musica Transalpina, 217
Musical bow, Africa, 433–436, 435

Musical glasses, 423–424, 551
Musical Youth Movement, 615
Musicalischer Parnassus (Fischer), 334–335
Musicals, 602–603
Musicology, 578–580, 698
Musique concrète 620–623, 632, 661
Musique mise à la portée de tout le monde, La (Fétis), 517
Mussorgsky, Modest (1839–1881), 523, 535, 540–541b, 571, 573, 589
Musurgia Universalis (Kircher), 305
My Fair Lady (Loewe), 678
"My Mother Was a Lady," 562
"My Old Kentucky Home" (Foster), 551
Mystery plays, 67

Nabucco (Verdi), 539
Nakers, 694
Naqqara, 693
"Narcissus" (Nevin), 562
National Conservatory (France), 380
National Peace Jubilee, 546
Nationalism, music and, 523, 570–572
Naughty Marietta (Herbert), 587, 600
Navarre-Champagne, Agnes de, 48b
Nchabagome, 428
Ndamutsu, 428
Ndembo, 431
Negri, Cesare, 224
Negro music, nineteenth century, 550, 553–559, 562
  twentieth century, 602–603
  (*See also* Slave music)
Neidhart von Reuenthal, 34, 36
Nelhybel, Vaclav (b. 1919), 670
Nepomuceno, Alberto (1860–1920), 572
Neu-eroffnete Orchestre, Das (Mattheson), 328
Neue Zeitschrift fur Musik, 504
Nevin, Ethelbert (1862–1901), 562
New England Psalm Singer (Billings), 418–421, 441
New England School, 418–419, 483
New Friends of Rhythm, 671
"New Orleans Blues" (Morton), 614
New World Symphony (Dvořák), 540
New York Philharmonic, 542, 598–599
Newman, John Henry Cardinal, 541, 571
Newport Festival, 616, 671
Nezahualcoyotl, 250
Ngundu, 431
Nibelungen songs, 18

Niblo's Garden, 551–552
Night on Bald Mountain (Mussorgsky), 523
Nijinsky, Waslaw (1890–1950), 577
Nivers, Guillaume-Gabriel (1632–1714), 306–308
Nkoko, 431
Nkole-nkole, 431
Noah and the Flood (Stravinsky), 679
Nocturnes (Bennett), 657
Nocturnes (Debussy), 588
None, divine office, 54
"None but the Lonely Heart" (Tchaikovsky), 539
Nono, Luigi (b. 1924), 654*b*, 668
Nonserial atonality, 598
Norma (Bellini), 499
North, Roger (c. 1651–1734), 295–296, 299
Notation, African music, 438–439
    American Indian, 358
    ancient, 7, 53
    Ars nova, 114
    Avignon school, 126
    Baroque era, 271, 292–294, 300, 314, 328, 687
    Classical era, 705
    colonial America, 446
    Medieval era, 20, 23, 28–29, 33, 36, 46, 72–73, 79, 83, 89–90, 114
    Negro music, 558–559
    Renaissance era, 153, 199–200, 221, 223, 227, 691, 694
    twentieth century, 631–632, 634
Notes d'un musicien en voyage (Offenbach), 547
Notes on an Apprenticeship (Boulez), 655
Notes on Virginia (Jefferson), 435
Notker Balbulus (c. 840–912), 54, 59, 65, 67–68*b*
Notre Dame polyphony, 87–103
Notre Dame school, 127
"Nova, Nova," 39
Novæ de infinito laudes (Henze), 655
"Nove Geniture," 94
Noverre, Jean-Georges (1727–1810), 408
Noyes' Fludde (Britten), 668
Ntumpani, 431
Nuove Musiche, Le (Caccini), 236, 237, 245
Nur wie die Sehnsucht kennt (Goethe), 466
Nutcracker, The (Tchaikovsky), 539

"O Bread of Life," 216
O Garatuja (Nepomuceno), 572

"O! Let My People Go," 555
"O Lieb" (Liszt), 496
"O Maria virgo Davitica/O Maria Maris stella/VERITATEM," 96, 97–98
"O Rosa Bella," 128
"O Welt ich muss dich lassen" (Isaac), *215*
Oberon (Weber), 477
Oboe, Baroque era, 261, 279, 282–283, 291, 341–342, 344, 695
    Classical era, 371, 377–378, 385, 387, 697
    colonial America, 426, 447
    twentieth century, 573
Obras de musica (Cabezón), 243
Obrecht, Jacob (c. 1452–1505), 202*b*
Ockeghem, Johannes (c. 1430–1495), 151, 202*b*
Ode to Music (Hopkinson), 441
Odhecaton (Petrucci), 187
Odington, Walter, 108, 122
Odo of Cluny (d. 982), 56
Oedipus Rex (Stravinsky), 589
Of Thee I Sing (Gershwin), 602, 615
Offenbach, Jacques (1819–1880), 490, 535–536, 537*b*, 547
Offertory, 51–52, 57–58
"Oh Dem Golden Slippers" (Bland), 552
Oiseau de feu, l' (Stravinsky), 589
"Old Folks at Home" (Foster), 550
"Old Oaken Bucket, The," 484
Olio, 549–551, 679
Oliver, King (1885–1938), 606
Olivier, Lawrence, 617
Ollivier, Michel, 370
On the Music of the North American Savages (Baker), 560, 580
On Wenlock Edge (Williams), 589
Ondes martenot, 601
150 Pseumes (Le Jeune), 241
One Hundred Men and a Girl (Stokowski), 600
One-step, 582
Onion flute, 196
Opera, Baroque era, 259–261, 265, 270–272, 284–286, 288–292, 303–304, 322–323
    Classical era, 401–411, 443–444
    comic, 402, 404–405
    Mozart, 443–444
    Piccini, 405
    Romantic era, 471–473, 499–500, 515, 523–524
    Singspiel, 407–410
    Verdi, 523, 531
    United States, 543

    twentieth century, 570, 600, 602, 627–628
    (*See also* Dramma per musica)
Opera, Paris, 408
Opera Comique, 347, 405, 413, 490
Opera intitulata Fontegara (Ganassi), 703
Opera theater of the Florentin, orchestra, 378
Operetta, 403–404, 535–536
Opus Musicum (Gallus), 240
Opus numbers, origin, 286
Oratorio, Baroque, 270, 284–286, 326
    Romantic era, 461
    twentieth century, 571
    United States, 563
"Orbis factor," *64*
Orchestra, Classical era, 369, 376, 378–379
    Mannheim style, 363–364
    Romantic era, 461–463, 493–495, 515
    twentieth century, 598–600, 667
Orestes (Badings), 623
Orfeo (Monteverdi), 246, 271
Orfeo (Rossi), 284, 289
Orfeo ed Euridice (Gluck), 406, 412
Organ, Bach, 336–339
    Baroque era, 263, 265, 297, 300–301, 333, 340, 695–696
    electrophonic, 601
    mechanics, 33, *340*
    Medieval era, 692–693
    Renaissance era, 198, 220–221, 229
    Romantic era, 517
    specifications, 695–696
Organum, 81–93, 104, 702
Orgelbüchlein (J. S. Bach), 336, 339
Original Rag (Joplin), 588
Originale (Stockhausen), 656
Orione (J. C. Bach), 412
Ormindo, L' (Cavalli), 668
Oroonoko (Southerne), 548
Orphée (Gluck), 406
Orphée aux Enfers (Offenbach), 537
Orphenica Lyra (Fuenllana), 244
Orpheus Britannicus (Purcell), 318
Oscillator, new music, 623
Ospitale della Pièta, 279
Ostinato, new music, 625
Otello (Verdi), 524, 539
Ouvertures (Telemann), 344
Overture, in 12 Movements (Gehot), 481
Oxyrhynchos papyrus, 52

Pachacuti (1438–1475), 249
Pachelbel, Johann (1653–1706), 301, 319–320*b*
Paganini, Niccolò (1782–1840), 459, 490–496, 498, 671, 681

Paine, John Knowles (1839–1906), 563
Pal Joey (Rodgers), 602
Palestrina, Giovanni Pierluigi di (1526–1594), 151, 213, 240*b*, 329
Pamela (Richardson), 405
Pammelia, 219
Panchromaticism, 598, 708
Pandiatonicism, 598
"Pange Lingua," 68
Panpipes, 251–252, 432
Pantonality, 598
Parameter, new music, 631
Paride ed Elena (Gluck), 406
Park, Mungo, 415
Parker, Charles "Yardbird" (1920–1955), 671–673
Parker, Horatio (1863–1919), 563
"Parlez-moi d'amour" (Boyer), 629
Parlor music, 481–483, 501
"Parody Parodised, The," 425
Parsifal (Wagner), 539
Part book, 699
Part song, Baroque era, 323
  colonial America, 419
  Medieval era, 107–110
Partch, Harry (b. 1901), 601
Partials, Baroque era, 306
  Classical era, 373
  new music, 624
"Pascha nostrum" (Leoninus), 90, 91–92
Passion according to St. John (Schütz), 302
Passion according to St. Luke (Penderecki), 652, 656–657
Pastoral song, 289–290
Pastorale (Franck), 540
Pathétique Symphony (Tchaikovsky), 516
Patriotic song, 425–426, 445
Patter song, 536
Paul, Les (b. 1916), 621–622
Pavane, 224, 571
"Pavane" and "Galliard" (Byrd), 297
Pavane pour une Infante défunte (Ravel), 589
Peer Gynt (Grieg), 523, 541
Peirol of Auvergne (1160–1225), 48*b*
Pelléas et Mélisande (Debussy), 588
Penderecki, Krzysztof (b. 1933), 634, 652, 656–657*b*, 665, 668, 681
Pennies from Heaven, 612
Pepusch, John, 323
"Perfect Day" (Bond), 586
Performance, ancient, 4
  Ars nova, 129–130, 135
  Baroque era, 263, 271–272, 289, 296, 312–313
  Beethoven on, 455

Classical era, 374–379, 445
  dramma per musica, 238–239
  Medieval era, 14–15, 23, 25, 43–47, 52, 65–67, 79, 82, 94–95, 103–104, 112
  new music, 662, 664
  Renaissance era, 195–196, 219–220, 226–229, 236
  Romantic era, 460, 489, 514–517, 545–548
  United States theater, 479–480
  universal elements, 11
Pergolesi, Giovanni Battista (1710–1736), 323, 347*b*, 402
Perotinus (active c. 1180–1200), 89, 92–93
Perry Mason, 679
Perusio, Matheus de (active c. 1380–1410), 143*b*
Pes, *109–110*
Pestalozzi, Johann Heinrich (1746–1827), 486
Peter Grimes (Britten), 653
Peter Gunn, 655, 679
Petipa, Marius, 571
Petrarch, Francisco, 38, 115, 121, 130
Petrouchka (Stravinsky), 589
Petrucci, Ottaviano dei (1466–1539), 185, 187, 203
Petrus de Cruce, 113
Pczcl, Johann Christoph (1639–1694), 319*b*
Phantasie (Schumann), 510
Philadelphia Symphony, 542
Philidor, André Danican (c. 1643–1730), 316*b*, 405
Philidor, Anne-Hyacinthe Danican (d. 1728), 316
Philidor, François André Danican (1726–1795), 316*b*
Philosophy, Medieval era, 69–71
  new music, 620
  Romantic era, 507–512, 520–534
  Wagner, 532–533
  (*See also* Technique; Theory)
Phoenix and the Turtle, The (Musgrave), 656
Phrygian cadence, Baroque era, 275–276
Phythagoras (c. 582–c. 500 B.C.), 7
Piano, Classical era, 366–367, 382, 387, 447–450
  colonial America, 417, 424, 447
  early United States, 501
  jazz, 584, 608, 671
  mechanics, 367
  ragtime, 582
  Romantic era, 454–460, 463–467, 495–499, 515, 520, 543–545, 698
  square, 367, 382, 545

twentieth century, 573, 575, 600, 656, 669
  upright, 545
Piano Rag Music (Stravinsky), 611
Piano Sonata (Boulez), 630, 655
Pianoforte, 265–267, 366
Pianola, 545
Pibrochs, 107
Piccini, Louis (1766–1827), 412*b*
Piccini, Niccolò (1728–1800), 405–407, 412*b*
"Picture That Is Turned toward the Wall, The," 562
Pictures at an Exhibition (Mussorgsky), 540, 589
Piece for String Quartet and Harbor Songs (Moondog-Schwartz), 627
Pièce heroïque (Franck), 540
Pièces de clavecin (d'Angelbert), 292, 316, 706
Pièces de clavecin (Fischer), 334
Pièces de clavecin (Rameau), 346
Pièces de clavecin (Schobert), 365
Pièces de clavecin en concerts (Rameau), 364–365
Pièces de clavecin en sonates (Mondonville), 364
Pierre de la Croix, 113
Pierre de la Rue (c. 1460–1518), 203*b*
Pierrot Lunaire (Schoenberg), 593–594, 665
Pilkington, Francis (c. 1565–1638), 246*b*
Pinafore (Sullivan), 536
Pink Panther, The, 655
Pipe, 21, 45
Pipe-and-tabor, 43, 687, 695
Písně milostné (Dvořák), 535
Piston, Walter (b. 1894), 615*b*, 667
Pitch, African music, 439
  ancient, 7, 9, 13
  Baroque era, 306–307, 311
  Renaissance era, 197
  Romantic era, 705
  twentieth century, 592, 597–598, 631–632, 658–659
  universal element, 11–14
Pittsburgh Symphony (Hindemith), 667
Pittsburgh Symphony Orchestra, 587
Plainchant, 49–50, 52–68, 253
Plaine and Easie Introduction to Practicall Musicke, A (Morley), 73, 199, 708
Plainsong, 14, 179, 702
Plaint, 26
Planctus, 19
Planh, 21
Play of Daniel, 42
Playback, new music, 606, 626

"Pleasure of the Town" (Gray), 502
Plectrum, 329–330, 367, 433
Pli selon pli (Boulez), 655
Plica, 91
Pluriarc, 434–437
    (*See also* Musical bow)
Poe, Edgar Allan (1809–1849), 488
Poème eléctronique (Varèse), 614, 623
Poème symphonique (Ligeti), 654
Poetry, Medieval era, 35, 38, 115–119, 121
    Renaissance era, 231–236
Pointillism, 568, 598
Polka, 501, 554, 560, 571
"Polly-Wolly Doodle," 561
Polymorphia (Penderecki), 634
Polyphonie X (Boulez), 627, 655
Polyphony, African music, 436–437
    chanson, 107–112
    dance, 106–107
    Mass, 150–179
    motet, 95–103
    Notre Dame school, 87–103
    organum, 81–87, 90–93
    performance, 103–104
    popular, 105–112, 185–193
Polytonality, 598
"Pomp and Circumstances" (Elgar), 541
Popular song, African, 437–439
    Baroque era, 323–326
    Classical era, 374–376, 410, 445
    colonial America, 356–357, 425–427, 445
    Medieval era, 135–140
    Protestant, 214–215
    Renaissance era, 185–193, 245–246
    scat, 583
    United States, 502, 561–562, 583, 585–587, 607–609, 670–671, 677
    (*See also* Song)
Porges, Paul Peter, 665
Porgy and Bess (Gershwin), 602, 616
Portamento, 439
Portsmouth Point Overture (Walton), 617
Positive organ, 103, 223
Poulenc, Francis (1899–1963), 597, 616b, 667–668
Pouplinière, Le Riche de la (1693–1762), 364
Pouplinière Orchestra, La, 278, 280
Pousseur, Henri (b. 1929), 656b
Powell, Mel (b. 1923), 682
Power, Leonel (d. 1445), 143b
Praetorius, Michael (1571–1621), 244b, 435

Praxis Pietatis Melica (Crüger), 319
Prelude, Baroque, 265, 294, 300, 687, 690
    Renaissance, 221
    Romantic, 489
    unmeasured, 292–294
Prélude, aria et final (Franck), 540
Prélude, choral et fugue (Franck), 540
Prélude a "l'Après-midi d'un faune" (Debussy), 573, 575, 588
Prélude and Courante (d'Anglebert), 292, 293
"Prelude and Fugue in C Major" (Bach), 337–339
Préludes (Debussy), 575, 588
Préludes, Les (Liszt), 495
Preludes for Piano (Gershwin), 616
"Prendes i garde" (D'Amiens), 32–33
Prepared piano, 628
Presley, Elvis (b. 1935), 674
Prince Igor (Borodin), 535
Princess de Navarre, La (Rameau), 402
Princess Pat (Herbert), 587
Procession in Brussels (Alsloot), 303
Processional music, 88, 94–95, 300, 303
Promises, Promises (Bacharach), 656, 679
Prophète, Le (Meyerbeer), 503
Proportions, Ars nova, 114–115, 117, 119–120, 130
    Avignon school, 126
    Baroque era, 304
    Medieval era, 112, 138
    Renaissance era, 199–200, 232
    universal element, 11
    (*See also* Tactus; Meter)
Protestant music, 206, 213–216, 241
Prussian Sonatas (C. P. E. Bach), 379
Psalm Singer's Amusement (Billings), 441
Psalms, colonial America, 354, 422
    Protestant, 214–215
Psalms of David (Penderecki), 656
Psyche (Lully), 290
Puccini, Giacomo (1858–1924), 520, 570, 586, 587b
Punctus structure, American Indian, 350–352
    Ars nova, 127
    Baroque era, 264, 272–273, 275–276, 278, 323
    Classical era, 375
    colonial America, 419, 422
    jazz, 607
    Medieval era, 40–41, 46, 61–62, 85, 89, 92, 108–110, 122

Renaissance era, 186, 194–195, 221, 223–225
    Romantic era, 475
Purcell, Henry (c. 1659–1695), 298–299, 318b, 326, 343, 498
Pushkin, Aleksander Sergeevich, 540–541, 571
Puy, 42, 99, 125
Puzzle, The (Hilton), 324
Pygmalion (Shaw), 678

Quadrille, 445, 475, 482, 560
"Quam pulcra es" (Dunstable), 128
Quantz, Johann Joachim, 313–315, 361, 372
Quiet One, The, 680
Quinta Estampie Réal, La, 40–41
Quintet (Pousseur), 656
Quintet in A Major (Boccherini), 425
Quodlibet, 186

Racine, Jean (1639–1699), 406
Radio, music on, 603–605, 621, 674
Rag Time Instructor (Harney), 545
Raga, 11, 677
Ragtime, 562, 581–585, 606, 611
Raimbaut d'Aurenga, 21, 23–26
Raimbaut de Vaqueiras (c. 1155–1205), 23–26, 38, 48b, 78
"Raindrops Are Fallin' on My Head" (Bacharach), 656
Rainey, Ma (1886–1939), 583, 607
Rake's Progress, The (Stravinsky), 589
"Rambling Sailor, The," 194, 196
Rameau, Jean-Philippe (1683–1764), 323, 346b, 364, 372–373, 401, 423, 538, 578
Rape of Lucretia, The (Britten), 653
Raskin, David, 680
Rattles, 249, 357, 432, 436
Raüber, Die (Schiller), 407, 409
Ravel, Maurice (1875–1937), 577, 589b
Read, Daniel (1757–1836), 441b, 445–446, 483
Recapitulation, Classical era, 386
    Romantic era, 513
Recitativo, Baroque era, 266–271, 289–290, 687
    Renaissance era, 238–239
Record player, 578, 606, 611, 674
Recorder, Baroque era, 302, 343–344, 695
    Medieval era, 46–47, 110
    Renaissance era, 196, 201–202, 228–229, 694
Recordings, 664
Red Hot Peppers, 606–607, 615
Red Mill, The (Herbert), 587
Reel, 417, 446, 482, 485, 560

Refrain, 23, 27–28, 38–40, 117
Register, new music, 659
Reicha, Anton (1770–1839), 455, 476b
Reinagle, Alexander (1756–1809), 480, 485b
Reinhardt, Max (1873–1943), 576, 602
Reis, Philipp, 578
"Reis glorios," 22
Renaissance era, chanson and madrigal, 185–189, 191–192, 201
   composers, 202–204, 236, 239–246
   dance, 223–226
   dramma per musica, 238–239
   instruments, 196, 201–202, 220–225, 227–229, 242–245, 694–695
   meter, 232, 236
   monody, 229–237
   performance, 195–196, 200–202, 219–220, 226–229, 236
   popular song, 185–196
   Protestant music, 213–216, 241
   style, 152–179
   technique, 195
   theory, 197–200, 713
Repetition, Baroque era, 293
   Classical era, 385–386
   Medieval era, 25
Requiem (Berlioz), 503
Requiem (Ligeti), 654
Requiem (Verdi), 539
Resonance, new music, 708
Responsorium, divine office, 53
Reuenthal, Neidhart von, 34, 36
Reusner, Esaias (1636–1679), 319b
Revolver (McCartney), 657
Revue, 603
Rhapsody in Blue (Gershwin), 610, 615–616
Rheingold, Das (Wagner), 532
Rhétorique des Dieux (Gaultier), 245
Rhumba, 582
Rhythm, African music, 427–429
   Ars nova, 114–115
   Baroque era, 273–274, 336
   Broadway show, 678
   Classical era, 401
   colonial America, 422
   Medieval era, 23, 58–59, 78–79, 138, 713
   new music, 659–660, 674
   Renaissance, 178, 186, 199, 232–236
   Romantic era, 512, 532–533
   universal element, 12–13
   (See also Beat; Meter; Proportion)
Rice, Thomas D., 548
Ricercar, 221–222, 224
Ricercar and Doubles (Davies), 657

Richard Coeur-de-Lion (Grétry), 413, 537
Richard the Lion-Hearted (1157–1199), 48b
"Ridicule, The," 475
Rienzi (Wagner), 538
Riff, 608
Rigoletto (Verdi), 539
Rimsky-Korsakov, Nikolai (1844–1908), 541b, 571, 576–577, 589
Ring des Nibelungen, Der (Wagner), 532–533, 539
Rinka, Jon, 119, 125, 132, 192, 291, 531
Ripieno, Baroque era, 278, 280, 341
   Classical era, 385
Ripresa, 38
Riquier, Giraut, 48b, 78
Ritard, Baroque era, 311
Rite of Spring, The (Stravinsky), 577
Ritornello, Baroque era, 267, 270, 280–284, 291
   Classical era, 443
   Medieval era, 443
   Romantic era, 459
Robert le Diable (Meyerbeer), 490, 503–504
Robert the Pious, King (d. 1031), 60
Robertsbridge Codex, 41
"Robins m'aime" (Adam de la Halle), 31–32
Robinson, Bill, 602–603
Robinson Crusoé (Offenbach), 537
Robinson Crusoe and Harlequin Friday, 548
Robles, Daniel Alomias (1871–1942), 572
Rock music, 674–678, 700
Rodeo (Copland), 598
Rodgers, Richard, 602, 678
Roger, Gustave-Hippolyte, 490
Roger of Helmershausen, 49
Rogers, Ginger, 612
Roi malgré lui, le (Chabrier), 540
"Roll, Jordan, Roll," 555, 557
Roman rite, 60–64
Romantic era, ballet, 488–489
   Brahms, 520–523
   composers, 475–477, 485–486, 503–505, 537–541
   concerto, 459–460
   dance form, 473–475, 481–483, 501, 551, 560–562, 575–577
   defined, 487–488
   factionalism, 520–524
   Germany, 491–493, 517–518
   instruments, 697–698
   lied, 465–470, 498–499
   meter, 688
   opera, 471–473, 499–500, 515, 523–536

orchestra, 461–463, 493–495
   Paris, 488–491
   performance, 460, 489, 514–517, 545–548
   philosophy, 507–512
   piano, 454–459, 463–465, 495–498
   popular music, 473–475, 500–503, 536–538
   symphony, 460–463
   technique, 459–461, 495–496, 515
   theory, 512–514, 713
   Verdi, 523–524
   Wagner, 524, 532–534
Romanus, S. Picard, 262
Romaunt of the Rose, 105
Romeo and Juliet (Tchaikovsky), 523, 539
Rondeau, Avignon school, 126
   Classical era, 387–388
   Medieval era, 27, 30–33, 39, 107–108
Rore, Cipriano de (1516–1565), 242b
Rose, Billy, 603
Rosenkavalier, Der (R. Strauss), 588
Rossi, Luigi (1597–1653), 271, 284b
Rossi, Salomone (c. 1565–1628), 285–286b
Rossini, Gioachino (1792–1868), 270, 471, 477b, 490, 505, 520, 546, 668
Rota, 108, 109–110
Round, 421
Royal Fireworks (Handel), 343
Rozsa, Miklos, 680
Rubato, Classical era, 688
   Romantic era, 516
"Rule, Britannia," 323
Rules How to Compose (Coperario), 317
Rumba, 606
Runyon, Damon, 678
Russell, Henry (1812–1900), 505b
Russlan and Ludmilla (Glinka), 503, 513

Sacbuts, 248, 694
Sachs, Hans (1494–1576), 35, 147
Sacre du Printemps, Le (Stravinsky), 589, 661, 679
Sacred Harp, The (White and King), 502
St. Cecilia Society, 416
St. Francis, 38
St. Gall, monastery of, 54–56, 67–68
Saint-Georges, Joseph Boulogne, Chevalier de (c. 1739–1799), 440
"St. Louis Blues" (Handy), 583
St. Martial of Limoges, 87, 89
St. Matthew Passion (J. S. Bach), 492
St. Petersburg Conservatory, 571

Saint-Saëns, Camille (1835–1921), 61, 523, 538b, 578
Salieri, Antonio (1750–1825), 413b
Salimbene, 14–16
Salle Pleyel, 489
"Sally in Our Alley," 356
Salome (R. Strauss), 586, 588
Salomon, Johann Peter (1745–1815), 460
Salon Mexico, El (Copland), 616
Saltarello, 224
Salut d'Amour (Elgar), 541
Salve Regina (Scarlatti), 346
Salzburg Orchestra, 378
San Francisco Minstrels, 548
San Francisco Opera, 600
Sanctus, 51–52, 62–63, 151–152, 177, 179, 210–212, 215
Sander, Ellen, 675
"Sankarabhana," 11
Sansa, 433–434, 435, 436
Santiago de Compostela, 85, 87, 89
Sarabande, 291
Saracens, The (MacDowell), 588
Sarum chant, 50
Sarum rite, 127
Sauveur, Joseph (1653–1716), 311
Sawtooth waves, new music, 624
Saxophone, 582
Scale, ancient, 7–9
    chromatic, 7, 13–14
    diatonic, 7, 13–14, 198, 232, 306
    enharmonic, 7, 10, 13–14
    Greek, 198
    pentatonic, 13
    universal element, 13–14
    whole-tone, 513, 573
Scarlatti, Alessandro (1660–1725), 267–270, 285b, 323
Scarlatti, Domenico (1685–1757), 331, 345, 346b, 499
Scat song, 606, 610
Scenes from an Everyday Romance (Coleridge-Taylor), 572
Schaeffer, Pierre (b. 1910), 621–622, 655
Schedel, Hartmann, 142
Scheherazade (Rimsky-Korsakov), 541, 576
Scheidt, Samuel (1587–1654), 245b
Schein, Johann Hermann (1586–1630), 245b
Scherzi, 264
Scherzi musicali (Monteverdi), 273
Schiller, Johann Friedrich von (1759–1805), 407, 471
Schlegel, Friedrich von (1772–1829), 510
Schlick, Arnold, 223
Schmid the Younger, Bernhard (b. 1548), 224

Schobert, Johann (c. 1735–1767), 365, 380b, 382
Schoenberg, Arnold (1874–1951), 591, 593, 597–598, 600, 613b, 653–654, 665
Schola Cantorum, 614
School of Ragtime, The (Joplin), 589
Schottische, 571
Schriftbild der neuen Musik, Das (Karkoschka), 631
Schroeder, Friedrich Ludwig (1744–1816), 408
Schubert, Franz Peter (1797–1828), 413, 461, 466–470, 477b, 500, 515, 535, 578
Schuman, William (b. 1910), 617b, 670
Schumann, Clara Wieck, 491–493, 496, 498, 511
Schumann, Robert (1810–1856), 487, 491–493, 495–498, 500, 504b, 508, 510, 515, 520, 523, 535, 538, 541, 569, 596, 667
Schütz, Heinrich (1585–1672), 302, 318b
Schwartz, Tony, 627
Schwitters, Kurt (1887–1948), 595
Scop, 35
Scott, Sir Walter, 471, 499, 540
Scotti, Antonio (1866–1936), 570
Scottish Dance Suite (Musgrave), 656
Scrapers, 432, 600
Sea Drift (Coleridge-Taylor), 588
Seasons, The (Haydn), 411, 461
Seasons, The (Lully), 290
Seasons, The (Vivaldi), 286
Sechs leichte Sonaten (Hassler), 448
Seeger, Pete, 677
Seismogrammes (Pousseur), 656
Senfl, Ludwig (1488–1543), 203b
Sept Répos de Ténèbre (Poulenc), 667
Septet (Stravinsky), 589
Sequence, Baroque, 280–281, 310
    Medieval, 59–61, 68
    Renaissance, 206
Serena, 21, 26
Serenade, 26
Serenata (Berio), 655
Sergeant Pepper's Lonely Hearts Club Band (McCartney), 657, 675
Serialism, 598, 620–621, 627–629, 632, 664, 698, 706
Sermisy, Claudin de (c. 1490–1562), 203b
Serrana, 21
Serranilla, 21
Serva Padrona, La (Pergolesi), 347, 402
Sessions, Roger (b. 1896), 615b

Set piece, colonial America, 422–423
    Romantic era, 524, 533
Sext, divine office, 54
Sforzando, Baroque era, 276
    new music, 660
Shadow Rag Wall Street (Joplin), 588
Shaker, 432
Shakespeare, William (1564–1616), 685
Shakespeare Music (Davies), 657
Shankar, Ravi, 680
Shape note, 483–484
Shaw, Artie, 612
Shaw, George Bernard, 567, 576, 602
Shawm, 695
"Sherburne," 445, 446
Shimmy, 582, 606
Shinbone, 5
"Shoo, Fly, Don't Bother Me," 561
Shout, 555
Show Boat (Kern), 602
Show business, music in, 678–680
Shuffle, 562
Shuffle Along (Sissle and Blake), 602
Sibelius, Jean (1865–1957), 571
Siege of Corinth (Rossini), 668
Siegfried (Wagner), 532
Signature, Ars nova, 120
    Baroque era, 335
Silesian Tryptych (Lutoslawski), 653
Simon, Neil, 679
Sinatra, Frank (b. 1917), 612
Sine Nomine (Nelhybel), 670
Sine waves, new music, 623–624, 627
Sinfonia (Musgrave), 656
Sinfonia a 8 (Stamitz), 369
Singakademie, 538
Singing Master's Assistant, The (Billings), 418, 421, 441
Singing school, colonial America, 417–421, 445, 483–484
Singing tone, Romantic era, 454–455, 465, 515, 537
Singspiel, 303–304, 407–410
Sirens, 600
Sirventes, 21
Sissle, Noble, 602
Sistrum, 5, 9, 47
Sitwell, Edith, 617
Six, Les, 597
Six Romances (Tchaikovsky), 539
Six Songs without Words (Mendelssohn), 496
"Skid-Dat-De-Dat" (Armstrong), 610
Skrowaczewski, Stanislaw, 681
Slave music, 427–428, 581
Slave Songs of the United States (Allen, Ware, and Garrison), 555
Slavonic Dances (Dvořàk), 581
Slur, Baroque era, 314–315
    Classical era, 374, 697

Smetana, Bedřich (1824–1884), 523, 535

Smith, Bessie (1894–1937), 583, 607

Smithson, Harriet, 494

Snare, 45, 582, 694–695

Soap opera, music in, 603

Society for the Preservation and Encouragement of Barbershop Quartet Singing in America, 220

"Soda Fountain Rag" (Ellington), 616

Solfeggio Americano, The, 484

Soliloquy for Guitar and Tape (Musgrave), 656

Solo Sonata (Corelli), 704

Sonata, Baroque era, 272–278, 286
  Classical era, 364–365
  defined, 265
  Romantic era, 459, 513
  trio sonata, 272–278, 286, 295, 327–328

Sonata brillante (Weber), 498

Sonata da camera, 273–274

Sonata da chiesa, 273–277, 279

Sonata for Violin and Piano (Franck), 540

Sonata in C Major (Hassler), *448–450*

Sonata in g Minor for violin (J. S. Bach), 681

Sonata Pathétique, opus 13 (Beethoven), *455–458*

Sonata per il violino per Sonar con due corde (Marini), 273

Sonata Pian'e Forte (Gabrieli), 227–228, 272

Sonate dramatique (Beethoven), 499

Sonates Pour Le Clavecin (Mozart), 365

Sonatine (Boulez), 655

Song, ancient, 5, 7, 9–10
  Baroque era, 323–326
  blues, 607–609
  Classical era, 374–377, 444–447
  colonial America, 445
  Indian, 350, 356, 417
  laude spirituali, 38
  Medieval era, 15, 17–68
  patter, 536
  plainchant, 49–68
  pre-Colombian, 251–252
  Renaissance, 236–237
  Romantic era, 465–470, 498–499, 535, 538–539
  (*See also* Popular song)

Space, historic view, 699–701
  new music, 661–662
  Renaissance era, 699

Spanisches Liederbuch (Wolf), 535

Spectacle, Classical era, 404

"Spem in alium" (Tallis), 213

Spinet, 329–330, 366, 447

Spiritual song, 214–216, 302, 326, 485, 555–559

Spivakovsky, Tossy, 681

Spohr, Ludwig (1784–1859), 463

Sprechstimme, 593, 678, 706

Squarcialupi Codex, 123

Square dance, 560

Square piano, 367

Square waves, new music, 624

"Stabat Mater," 56, 60, 68

Stabat Mater (Dvořák), 540

Stabat Mater (Penderecki), 656, 665

Stabat Mater (Pergolesi), 347

Stabat Mater (Poulenc), 616

Stabat Mater (Rossini), 477

Stabat Mater (Scarlatti), 346

Stage charts, new music, 662

Stamitz, Johann (1717–1757), 363, 369, 379–380b

Stamitz, Karl (1746–1801), 380b

"Stammering Lover, The" (Arne), 375, 376

Stanza form, African music, 437
  Ars nova, 121
  colonial America, 419, 422
  Machaut, 117
  Medieval era, 20–23, 25, 38–40

Star of the North (Meyerbeer), 548

Static bass, 309–310

Statistical sound, new music, 630–632, 651

Steffani, Agostino (1654–1728), 285b

Steiner, Fred, 679

Steinway and Sons, 544

Stile concertato, 262, 265, 326, 344, 361

Stile expressivo, 236

Stile nuovo, 236, 239, 301, 304, 354

Stile recitativo, 236

Still Are New Worlds (Finney), 651–652

Stimmtausch, 108

Stinger, 605–606

Stochastic, 630

Stockhausen, Karlheinz (b. 1928), 624–625, 627–629, 633, 655–656b, 658, 665, 676, 681

Stokowski, Leopold (b. 1882), 600, 614

Stollen, 34

Stonehenge, choral dance, 40

Stop, harpsichord, 330
  organ, 695–696

Storace, Stephen (1763–1796), 384

Story of the Jubilee Singers, The, 558

Stout, Alan (b. 1933), 670

Stradella, Alessandro (1645–1681), 285b

Stradivari, Antonio (1644–1737), 261, 275

Stradivarius violin, 460

Strambotto, 185

Strauss, Johann (1804–1849), 501, 503b, 552, 680

Strauss II, Johann (1825–1899), 535, 538b, 561

Strauss, Richard (1864–1949), 569–570, 586, 588b

Stravinsky, Igor (b. 1882), 577, 589b, 590, 597–598, 611, 661, 667, 679

String bass, 582, 671

String quartet, Classical era, 384–385
  colonial America, 424
  jazz, 671
  new music, 592–593
  Mozart, 442–443
  Romantic era, 520

String quintet, 442

Strophen (Penderecki), 656

Strophic form, 466–467

Structure, African music, 436–439
  American Indian music, 559–560
  Baroque era, 266–267, 270–281, 285
  blues, 583
  colonial America, 419
  hexachord system, 71–72
  jazz, 606–607
  Medieval era, 25–26, 549–550
  new music, 658–659
  Renaissance era, 152
  Romantic era, 460–462, 533
  spirituals, 559
  (*See also* Technique; Theory)

Studie I (Stockhausen), 627

Studie II (Stockhausen), 656

Study of Omaha Music, A, 559–560

Sturm und Drang (Klinger), 408–409

Sturm und Drang movement, 409, 424, 471

Style, free, 327–328
  learned, 327
  worked, 327–328

Su le sponde del Tebro (Scarlatti), 270

Subject, 308, 313, 385–388, 401

Suffolk Harmony, The (Billings), 441

Suite Bergamasque (Debussy), 588

Suite in F (Telemann), 344

Suites de symphonies (Mouret), 347

Sullivan, Arthur (1842–1900), 525–536, 540b, 550, 602–603

Sullivan, Ed, 679

"Sumer is acumen in," 108, 109–110

Sundowners, The, 616

Surrealism, 590–591

"Susanna" (Foster), 550

Swan Lake (Tchaikovsky), 539

"Swanee" (Gershwin), 615

Sweelinck, Jan Pieterszoon (1562–1621), 244b
Sweethearts (Herbert), 587
Swing, 611–613, 670
"Swing Low, Sweet Chariot," 558
Swing Mikado, The, 603
Symbolism, 568
Symphoniæ sacræ (Schütz), 318
Symphonic Requiem (Nelhybel), 670
Symphonic Variations on an African Air (Coleridge-Taylor), 588
Symphonie fantastique (Berlioz), 493–494, 503
Symphonies (Pousseur), 656
Symphonies pour les soupers du Roi (Delalande), 316
Symphony, Classical era, 369
  Mannheim style, 363–364
  Romantic era, 460–463, 520, 523, 568–569
Symphony (*instrument*), 45
Symphony No. 7 (Piston), 667
Symphony No. 7 (Schumann), 667
Symphony in Bb major (Mozart), 386–401
Symphony of Psalms (Stravinsky), 589
Synchrony, new music, 605, 623–624, 626, 632, 660
Syncopations, 276
Syncope, 311
Syntagma Musicum (Praetorius), 244, 436
Synthesized music, 623–625, 698

Tablatura Nova (Scheidt), 245
"Table of Divisions" (Ganassi), 703
Tactus, 120, 199, 312
Tafelmusik (Telemann), 344
Taglione, Marie, 489, 500
Tala, 689
Tale of Old Japan, A (Coleridge-Taylor), 571
"Tales from the Vienna Woods" (Strauss II), 538
Tallis, Thomas (c. 1510–1585), 212, 241b
Tambourine, Medieval, 35, 47, 79, 382–383, 548
Tammany (Hewitt), 485
Tangent (*clavichord*), 329, 332–333, 367
Tango, 582
Tannhauser (Wagner), 538
Tape recorder, new music, 623, 625–626, 632–633, 677
Tasso, Torquato (1544–1595), 229
Taverner, John (c. 1495–1545), 298
"Taxed Tea, The," 425
Tchaikovsky, Peter Ilyitch (1840–1893), 516, 520, 523, 535, 539b, 571

Technique, Ars nova, 117–120, 128–131, 133
  Avignon school, 126
  band music, 612
  Baroque era, 280–281, 284, 291
  Classical era, 366, 382–388
  Colonial America, 419
  dramma per musica, 238–239
  Guidonian system, 106
  harpsichord, 329–331
  jazz, 606–610
  Medieval, 103, 105–107, 111–112, 136–138, 141–142
  Renaissance era, 195, 218–219, 232, 236
  Romantic era, 459–461, 495–496, 515
  twentieth century, 591–601, 604–606, 623–629, 658–664, 674–677, 698
  (*See also* Composition; Philosophy; Theory)
Telemann, Georg Philipp (1681–1767), 343–344, 347b, 379, 412, 492, 578, 705
Telemusik (Stockhausen), 656
Television, music on, 679–680
Telharmonium, 600
Tell It Again (Moondog), 671
"Tell Me Then the Reason Why" (Atterbury), 377
Temple of Minerva, The (Hopkinson), 441
Tempo, Baroque era, 266, 273–276, 278–280, 312–315
  Medieval era, 23, 56–57, 78–79, 111–112
  Renaissance era, 207
  Romantic era, 515–516
  twentieth century, 692
  (*See also* Beat; Meter; Proportion)
Tenorista, 138
Tenso, 21
Teponaztl, 251
Tepuzquiquiztl, 251
Terce, divine office, 53–54
Terminorum Musicae Diffinitorum (Tinctoris), 75
Terpsichore (Praetorius), 244
Terrektorh (Xenakis), 654
Tessitura, Medieval era, 58, 83
  new music, 593, 661–662
  Renaissance era, 198
  Romantic era, 515
Tetzilacatl, 251
Teufel ist Los! Der (Weisse), 409
Texture, African music, 428
  Baroque era, 313, 327
  Classical era, 362, 401, 697, 713
  defined, 692
  Medieval era, 14
  new music, 661

Thalberg, Sigismund (1812–1871), 490
"Thanks for the Memory" (Robin and Rainger), 603
The 4th of July: A Grand Military Sonata (Hewitt), 485
Theater, Baroque era, 258–259, 288–292, 298–300
  Negro, 602–603
  Renaissance era, 229–230
  United States, 602–603
Théâtre de la Foire, 405
Theatre Piece 1960 (Cage), 629, 653
Theme, Classical era, 401
  Romantic era, 513
Theorbo, 231, 236, 262–263, 333, 342, 695
Theory, ancient, 7–10
  Baroque era, 304–312, 329, 713
  Classical era, 371–373, 713
  Medieval era, 108, 110, 713
  new music, 658–665
  Renaissance era, 197–200, 713
  Romantic era, 512–514, 713
  (*See also* Philosophy; Technique)
Theory of Harmony (Schoenberg), 613
Theremin, 601
"There's No Business Like Show Business" (Berlin), 678
Thibaut IV de Champagne (1201–1253), 48b
Thomas a Celano (c. 1200–1256), 61, 68b
Three Norfolk Rhapsodies (Williams), 589
Threepenny Opera (Weill), 323
Threnody: To the Victims of Hiroshima (Penderecki), 634, 635–650, 656, 681
Thumb piano, 433
Tibia, 5
Till Eulenspiegel (R. Strauss), 569, 588
Tilzer, Harry von (1872–1946), 586
Time, Baroque era, 311
  defined, 686–692
  new music, 625–626, 659–660
  universal element, 11–12
Timpani, 371, 385, 377–378
Tin Pan Alley, 586, 612
Tinctoris, Johannes, 75, 78, 149
Tiomkin, Dmitri (b. 1899), 616b, 680
Tirata, 374
Tischler, Hans, 98, 102
Titelouse, Jehan (1563–1633), 244b
Titon et l'Aurore (Mondonville), 348
Tlapanhuehuetl, 252
Tlaipztalli, 251

"Toast to Washington," *426*, 427
Todi, Jacopone da, 68*b*
Toccata, 222–223, 265, 301
Tone, African music, 428
    Baroque era, 266, 275, 281, 306–308, 311, 334–336
    Classical era, 373, 383, 385, 387–388
    (*See also* Key; Mode)
Tone poem, 495, 523, 569, 571
Tonguing, Baroque era, 313–314
Tordion, 224
Torelli, Giuseppi (c. 1650–1708), 279, 286*b*
Tornada, 25
Tosca (Puccini), 587
Tosi, Pier Francesco, 257
Tourte, François (c. 1750–1835), 697
Toussant l'Ouverture (Coleridge-Taylor), 572
Toy Symphony, 370
Traité de la Composition de Musique (Nivers), 306
Traité d'harmonie (Rameau), 372
Transcendental Etudes (Liszt), 496
Träumerei (Schumann), 496, 497
Travels through North America, 1825–1826 (Bernhard-Karl), 482
Traviata, La (Verdi), 523–524, 524–530, 539
Treemonisha (Joplin), 589
Tremolo, African music, 439
    Classical era, 401
Triangle, 47
Trill, Baroque era, 315
    Classical era, 374, 401
    (*See also* Embellishment)
Trimmings, Negro music, 559
Trio sonata, Baroque era, 272–273, 286, 295, 327–328
Trio Sonata (Corelli), 276–277
Trio Sonata in C Major (Corelli), 275, 276–277
Triomphe de l'Amour, Le (Lully), 290
Triplum, 89, 702
Tristan und Isolde (Wagner), 533, 534, 539
Trittico (Nelhybel), 670
Triumphs of Love, The, 548
"Triumphs of Oriana, The," 219
Troilus and Cressida (Walton), 617
Trois poèmes d'Henri Michaux (Lutoslawski), 651, 665
Tromba marina, 322
Tromboncino, Bartolomeo (c. 1470–c. 1535), 203*b*
Trombone, Baroque era, 302–303, 342
    jazz, 584
    ragtime, 582
    Renaissance era, 227

Trope, "Orbis factor," 64
    plainchant Mass, 59
    Tuotilo, 68
Troubadours, 20–26, 35–38, 47–48, 676
    (*See also* Minstrelsy)
Trouvères, 26–33, 99, 107, 115–116
    (*See also* Minstrelsy)
Trovatore, Il (Verdi), 523, 539
Troyens, les (Berlioz), 681
Trumpet, African music, 432
    American Indian, 249, 251
    ancient, 6–7
    Baroque era, 291, 342, 344
    clarino, 261
    Classical era, 371, 385, 377–378
    coiled bark, 357
    jazz, 671
    Medieval era, 35, 45
    ragtime, 582
    Renaissance era, 695
Trumpet Method (Fantini), 697
Tschaikovsky (*see* Tchaikovsky)
Tune book, 483–484
Tuotilo (d. 915), 68*b*
"Turkey in the Straw," 485
Turkey trot, 582
Turkish dance, 382–383, 444
Twelve-tone technique, 598, 600, 620–621, 632–633, 708–709
Twenty-four violins (English), 296
Twist, 582, 674
Two for One (Colman), 425
2001: A Space Odyssey, 680
Two-step, 582

Uber die Musik der Nordamerikanischen Wilden (Baker), 560, 580
"Under the Jazzblue Tree" (Lewis), 671
Universal elements, 11–14, 133
"Ut queant laxis," 61, 73–74

"Va loin," 9, 14
Van Eyck, Jan (c. 1370–1441), 129
Vanhall, Johann, 384–385
Vaqueiras, Raimbaut de (c. 1155–1205), 38, 48*b*
Varèse, Edgard (1883–1965), 600, 614*b*, 618, 623, 625–626, 653, 659, 665, 682
Variations (Copland), 616
Variations (Webern), 614
Variations for Orchestra (Stravinsky), 667
Variations on a Theme of Paganini (Lutoslawski), 654
Variations symphoniques (Franck), 540
Variazioni Canoniche (Nono), 654
Variety show, 551

Vaudeville, 404, 551, 585, 602–603, 679
Vaughan, Sara (b. 1924), 612
Vecerni pisně (Smetana), 535
"Veni Sancte Spiritus," 60, 68
Venosa, Carlo Gesualdo di (1560–1613), 242*b*
Venus and Adonis (Blow), 318
Ventadorn, Bernart de, 35, 47–48*b*
Verdi, Giuseppi (1813–1901), 490, 520, 523–531, 539*b*, 543, 546, 568, 570–571
Verlaine, Paul (1844–1896), 568
Vernacular, Medieval era, 19–20, 26, 38
    Renaissance era, 213–215
Vers, 26
Versuch einer grundlichen Violinschule (L. Mozart), 380, 707
Versuch über die wahre Art das Clavier zu spielen (C. P. E. Bach), 379
Vesperae seu psalmi pro toto anno (Fischer), 345
Vespers, divine office, 54
Vibraphone, 633, 671
"Vicar of Bray, The," 356
Vicentino, Nicola (1511–1572), 198, 217
"Victimae Paschali Laudes" (Wipo), 60, 68
Victoria, Tomás Luis de (c. 1549–1611), 207–212, 240*b*
Vidal, Peire (fl. 1175–1215), 48*b*
Vie parisienne, la (Offenbach), 537
Vielle, Baroque era, 322
    Medieval era, 45, 46–47, 104
Vienna State Opera, 626–627
Vihuela, 253
Villancico, 185
Villanella, 186
Villi, Le (Puccini), 587
Vingt-Quatre Violons du Roy, Les, 288, 291
Viola, Baroque era, 342, 344
    Classical era, 371, 377–378, 382, 384
    Medieval era, 66, 110, 138
    new music, 656
Viola da gamba, Baroque era, 263, 272, 695
    Renaissance era, 231
Violin, Baroque era, 261–262, 279, 281, 284, 322, 327–328, 341–342, 344, 695–697
    Classical era, 362, 364–365, 371, 377–378, 382, 384
    colonial America, 356–357, 424, 446
    Corelli, 274–275
    jazz, 671
    Renaissance era, 227

Violin (*cont.*)
   Romantic era, 459, 515
   twentieth century, 573
Violin Concerto (Cooper), 667
Violincello, Classical era, 377
Viols, Baroque era, 265, 281, 296–
   297, 302
   Renaissance era, 201, 220, 224,
   228–229, 694
Virelai, 27, 29–30, 38–39, 107, 126
Virginal, 296–298, 329, 694
"Virgine Bella," 130
Virginia Minstrels, 549
Visages (Berio), 633, 655
Vitry, Philippe de (c. 1291–1361),
   114–116, 120, 142
Vittoria (*see* Victoria)
Vivaldi, Antonio (c. 1676–1741),
   279–284, 286*b*, 328, 336, 341–
   343, 687, 697, 699
Vocal Grove, The (Arne), 376
Vocal techniques, African music, 429,
   437
   ancient, 10
   Baroque era, 259–261, 265–272,
   284–285, 697
   Caruso, 570
   castrato, 260–261, 299, 374, 405–
   406
   Classical era, 374–376, 444
   colonial America, 419
   Medieval era, 35–36, 47, 82–84,
   139–140, 692
   new music, 663
   Renaissance era, 207, 213, 218,
   226
   Romantic era, 499, 515, 537
Vocavit Iesus, 86–87
Vocorder, new music, 623
Vogelweide, Walther von der (d.
   1230), 34
Voix humaine, La (Poulenc), 668
Volumina (Ligeti), 654
Vom Musikalisch-Schönen (Han-
   slick), 508
Votre Faust (Pousseur), 656

Wagner, Richard (1813–1883), 35,
   495, 514, 520, 523, 537, 538–
   539*b*, 543, 548, 563, 568–569,
   588, 595
Walk-around, 550–551
Walker, Uncle Whit, 581
"Walkin' and Whistlin'" (Paul), 621
Walküre, Die (Wagner), 532
Walther, Johannes (1496–1570),
   241*b*, 306

Walther von der Vogelweide (d.
   1230), 34
Walton, William (b. 1902), 617*b*
Waltz, 444–445, 473–475, 482, 501,
   560
War Requiem (Britten), 653, 667,
   681
War songs, 425, 445, 481
Ware, Charles Pickford, 555
Warwick, Dionne, 656
Warwick, Thomas, 226
"Washington's March at the Battle
   of Trenton," 445, 481
Water Music (Handel), 343, 346
Waters, Ethel, 602–603
Wave form, new music, 624
"We Won't Go Home Until Morn-
   ing," 445
Webb, Chick (1907–1939), 612
Weber, Carl Maria von (1786–1826),
   471–472, 477*b*, 498, 520, 546
Webern, Anton (1883–1945), 592,
   598, 614*b*, 656, 665, 676, 705
Weill, Kurt (1900–1950), 323, 602
Weisse, Christian Felix (1726–1804),
   409
Welsh music, 5, 36, 42
Wentworth, E., 542
"What a Piece of Work Is Man"
   (MacDermot), 679
What to Listen For in Music (Cop-
   land), 617
"What's New Pussycat" (Bacharach),
   656
"When Jesus Wept" (Billings), 418,
   421
"While Strolling through the Park,"
   562
Whip, 600
Whistles, 432
White, B. F., 502
White, Thomas, 298
"White Christmas" (Berlin), 674
White noise, new music, 624
Whiteman, Paul (1890–1967), 610
Whittenberg, Charles, 666
Whole-tone scale, 513, 573
Wieck, Clara, 491–493, 496, 498,
   511
Wien, Der (Berg), 614
Wilhelm Tell (Schiller), 471
Willaert, Adrien (c. 1480–1562),
   242*b*
William IX, Count of Poitou (1072–
   1127), 47*b*
William Tell (Rossini), 270
Williams Mix (Cage), 653

Williams, Ralph Vaughn (1872–
   1958), 589*b*
Willson, Meredith (b. 1902), 678
Wilson, Stanley, 679
"Wine, Woman, and Song" (Strauss
   II), 538
Winterreise, Die, 470
Wipo (c. 1000–1048), 60, 68*b*
"Within You Without You" (Harri-
   son), 674–675
Wohltemperirte Clavier, Das (Bach),
   336–339, 345, 701
Wolf, Hugo (1860–1903), 535
Wood, William, 350
Woodland Sketches (MacDowell),
   588
Work, Henry Clay (1832–1884), 561
Works Progress Administration, 600
World Peace Jubilee, 546
Wozzeck (Berg), 600, 614, 665
Wuorinen, Charles (b. 1938), 670
Wurtemberg Sonatas (C. P. E. Bach),
   379

Xenakis, Iannis (b. 1922), 630, 632,
   654*b*
Xylophone, 671

"Yankee Doodle," 416, 425, 481
"Yellow Rose of Texas, The," 561
Yes, Speak Out, Yes (Halffter), 656,
   681
Yobhel, 5
Yodel, 429, 439
Young Composer Project, 670
*Young Person's Guide to the Or-
   chestra* (Britten), 653
"You're a Grand Old Flag" (Cohan),
   586

Zampiere, Domenico, 262
Zarlino, Gioseffo (1517–1590), 199
Zeitmasse (Stockhausen), 656
Zelter, Carl Friedrich (1758–1832),
   466, 476*b*, 503–504
Ziegfeld, Florenz (1867–1932), 586,
   603
Ziegfeld Follies, 601, 603
Zigeunerbaron, Der (Strauss II), 538
Zigeunermelodien (Dvořák), 535
"Zip Coon," 485
Zither, 4, 433
Zolotoy Pietushok (Rimsky-Korsakov),
   541
Zorn, Anders, 509
Zumpe, Johann, 366